T0265359

A Practical Guide to SysML
The Systems Modeling Language

A Practical Guide to SysML
The Systems Modeling Language

Third edition

Sanford Friedenthal

Alan Moore

Rick Steiner

AMSTERDAM • BOSTON • HEIDELBERG • LONDON
NEW YORK • OXFORD • PARIS • SAN DIEGO
SAN FRANCISCO • SINGAPORE • SYDNEY • TOKYO

Morgan Kaufmann is an imprint of Elsevier

Acquiring Editor: Steve Elliot
Editorial Project Manager: Kaitlin Herbert
Project Manager: Priya Kumaraguruparan
Cover Designer: Mark Rogers

Morgan Kaufmann is an imprint of Elsevier
225 Wyman Street, Waltham, MA, 02451, USA

Copyright © 2015, 2012, 2009 Elsevier Inc. All rights reserved.

No part of this publication may be reproduced or transmitted in any form or by any means, electronic or
mechanical, including photocopying, recording, or any information storage and retrieval system, without
permission in writing from the publisher. Details on how to seek permission, further information about the
Publisher's permissions policies and our arrangements with organizations such as the Copyright Clearance
Center and the Copyright Licensing Agency, can be found at our website: www.elsevier.com/permissions.

This book and the individual contributions contained in it are protected under copyright by the Publisher (other
than as may be noted herein).

Notices

Knowledge and best practice in this field are constantly changing. As new research and experience broaden our
understanding, changes in research methods or professional practices, may become necessary. Practitioners and
researchers must always rely on their own experience and knowledge in evaluating and using any information
or methods described herein. In using such information or methods they should be mindful of their own safety
and the safety of others, including parties for whom they have a professional responsibility. To the fullest extent
of the law, neither the Publisher nor the authors, contributors, or editors, assume any liability for any injury and/
or damage to persons or property as a matter of products liability,negligence or otherwise, or from any use or
operation of any methods, products, instructions, or ideas contained in the material herein.

Library of Congress Cataloging-in-Publication Data
Friedenthal, Sanford.
   A practical guide to SysML: the systems modeling language / Sanford Friedenthal, Alan Moore, Rick
Steiner. -- Third edition.
      pages cm
1. Systems engineering. 2. Computer simulation. 3. SysML (Computer science) I. Moore, Alan, 1961-II. Steiner,
Rick. III. Title.
   TA168.F745 2014
   620.001'171--dc23

                              2014027624

British Library Cataloguing-in-Publication Data
A catalogue record for this book is available from the British Library.

ISBN: 978-0-12-800202-5

Printed in the United States of America

For information on all MK publications
visit our website at www.mkp.com

Working together
to grow libraries in
developing countries

www.elsevier.com • www.bookaid.org

Contents

PART I INTRODUCTION

PART III EXAMPLES OF MODEL-BASED SYSTEMS ENGINEERING METHODS

PART IV TRANSITIONING TO MODEL-BASED SYSTEMS ENGINEERING

CHAPTER 18 Integrating SysML into a Systems Development Environment **507**

CHAPTER 19 Deploying SysML in an Organization **543**

Preface

Systems engineering is a multidisciplinary and holistic approach to develop solutions for complex engineering problems. The continuing increase in system complexity demands more rigorous and formalized systems engineering practices. In response to this demand—along with advancements in computer technology—the practice of systems engineering is undergoing a fundamental transition from a document-based approach to a model-based approach. In a model-based approach, the emphasis shifts from producing and controlling documentation about the system to producing and controlling a coherent model of the system. Model-based systems engineering (MBSE) can help to manage complexity, while improving design quality and cycle time, enhancing communication among a diverse development team, and facilitating knowledge capture and design evolution.

A standardized and robust modeling language is considered a critical enabler for MBSE. The Systems Modeling Language (OMG SysML™) is one such general-purpose modeling language that supports the specification, design, analysis, and verification of systems that may include hardware and equipment, software, data, personnel, procedures, and facilities. SysML is a graphical modeling language with a semantic foundation for representing requirements, behavior, structure, and properties of the system and its components. It is intended to model systems from a broad range of industry domains such as aerospace, automotive, health care, and others.

SysML is an extension of the Unified Modeling Language (UML), version 2, which is the de facto standard software modeling language. Requirements were issued by the Object Management Group (OMG) in March 2003 to extend UML to support systems modeling. UML was selected as the basis for SysML because it is a robust language that addresses many of the systems modeling needs, while enabling the systems engineering community to leverage the broad base of experience and tool vendors that support UML. This approach also facilitates the integration of systems and software modeling, which has become increasingly important for today's software-intensive systems.

The development of the language specification was a collaborative effort between members of the OMG, the International Council on Systems Engineering (INCOSE), and the AP233 Working Group of the International Standards Organization (ISO). Following three years of development, the OMG SysML specification was adopted by the OMG in May 2006, and the formal version 1.0 language specification was released in September 2007. Since that time, new versions of the language have been adopted by the OMG. This edition is intended to reflect the SysML 1.4 specification. It is expected that SysML will continue to evolve in its expressiveness, precision, usability, and interoperability through further revisions to the specification based on feedback from end users, tool vendors, and research activities. Information on the latest version of SysML, tool implementations of SysML, and related resources, are available on the official OMG SysML web site at http://www.omgsysml.org/.

BOOK ORGANIZATION

This book provides the foundation for understanding and applying SysML to model systems as part of a model-based systems engineering approach. The book is organized into four parts: Introduction, Language Description, Examples of Model-Based Systems Engineering Methods, and Transitioning to Model-Based Systems Engineering.

Part I, Introduction, contains four chapters that provide an overview of systems engineering, a summary of key MBSE concepts, a chapter on getting started with SysML, and a sample problem to highlight the basic features of SysML. The systems engineering overview and MBSE concepts in Chapters 1 and 2 set the context for SysML, and Chapters 3 and 4 provide an introduction to SysML.

Part II, Language Description, provides the detailed description of the language. Chapter 5 provides an overview of SysML diagrams and some common diagrammatic notations. Chapters 6 through 14 describe key concepts related to model organization, blocks, parametrics, activities, interactions, states, use cases, requirements, and allocations. Chapter 15 describes the SysML specification and language architecture, and extension mechanisms to customize the language. The ordering of the chapters and the concepts are not based on the ordering of activities in the systems engineering process but are based on the dependencies between the language concepts. Each chapter builds the reader's understanding of the language concepts by introducing SysML constructs: their meaning, notation, and examples of how they are used. The example used to demonstrate the language throughout Part II is a security surveillance system. This example should be understandable to most readers and has sufficient complexity to demonstrate the language concepts.

Part III, Examples of Model-Based Systems Engineering Methods, includes two examples to illustrate how SysML can support different MBSE methods. The first example in Chapter 16 is a functional analysis and allocation method to specify and design a water distiller system. The second example in Chapter 17 applies to the design of a security system consisting of a central monitoring station and multiple sites that are monitored. It uses a comprehensive object-oriented systems engineering method (OOSEM) and emphasizes how the language is used to address a range of systems engineering concerns, including black-box versus white-box design, logical versus physical design, and the design of distributed systems. While these two methods are considered representative of how MBSE with SysML can be applied to model systems, SysML is intended to support other MBSE methods as well.

Part IV, Transitioning to Model-Based Systems Engineering, addresses key considerations for transitioning to an MBSE approach with SysML. Chapter 18 describes how to integrate SysML into a systems development environment consisting of multi-disciplinary engineering tools. It describes the different types of models and tools, the type of data that is exchanged, and mechanisms and standards for data exchange. It also includes a discussion on the selection criteria for a SysML modeling tool. Chapter 19 is the last chapter of the book and describes processes and strategies for deploying MBSE with SysML in an organization. Emphasis is placed on leveraging the organization's improvement process to assess, plan, and pilot the MBSE capability prior to deploying the capability to projects, and on other essential elements for a successful implementation of MBSE.

Questions are included at the end of each chapter to test readers' understanding of the material. The answers to the questions can be found on the web site for this book at http://www.elsevierdirect.com/companions/9780123852069/.

The Appendix contains the SysML notation tables. These tables provide a reference guide for SysML notation along with a cross reference to the applicable sections in Part II of the book where the language constructs are described in detail.

USES OF THIS BOOK

This book is a practical guide targeted at a broad spectrum of industry practitioners and students. It can serve as an introduction and reference for practitioners, as well as a text for courses in systems modeling and model-based systems engineering. In addition, because SysML reuses many UML concepts, software engineers familiar with UML can use this information as a basis for understanding systems engineering concepts. Also, many systems engineering concepts come to light when using an expressive language, which enables this book to be used to help teach systems engineering concepts. Finally, this book can serve as a primary reference to prepare for the OMG Certified System Modeling Professional (OCSMP) exam (refer to http://www.omg.org/ocsmp/).

HOW TO READ THIS BOOK

A first-time reader should pay close attention to the introductory chapters, including Getting Started with SysML in Chapter 3 and the application of the basic feature set of SysML to the Automobile Example in Chapter 4. The introductory reader may also choose to do a cursory reading of the overview sections in Part II, and then review the simplified distiller example in Part III. A more advanced reader may choose to read the introductory chapters, do a more comprehensive review of Part II, and then review the residential security example in Part III. Part IV is of general interest to those may be involved in deploying MBSE with SysML in their organization or project.

The following recommendations apply when using this book as a primary reference for a course in SysML and MBSE. An instructor may refer to the course on SysML that was prepared and delivered by the Johns Hopkins University Applied Physics Lab that is available for download at http://www.jhuapl.edu/ott/Technologies//Copyright/SysML.asp. This course provides an introduction to the basic features of SysML so that students can begin to apply the language to their projects. This course consists of eleven modules that use this book as the basis for the course material. The course material for the language concepts is included in the download, but the course material for the tool instruction is not included. A shorter version of this course is also included on the Johns Hopkins site, which has been used as a full-day tutorial to provide an introductory short course on SysML. A second course on the same website summarizes the Object-Oriented Systems Engineering Method (OOSEM) that is the subject of Chapter 17 in Part III of this book. This provides an example of applying a MBSE method to the specification and design of a security system.

Refer to the End-User License Agreement for each course (included with the download instructions on the Johns Hopkins site) for how this material can be used. An instructor can further tailor this material to their needs.

A typical use of the book is to require the students to review Chapters 1 and 2, and then study Chapter 3 on Getting Started with SysML. This chapter includes an introduction to SysML Lite, a simplified MBSE method, and a general SysML modeling tool. The student then studies the automobile example in Chapter 4.

The instructor may then teach the language concepts in more depth, depending on the time allotted to this subject, and require the students to review the chapters in Part II. The instructor may focus on the SysML basic feature set, which is identified by the shaded sections throughout each chapter in Part II. The notation tables in the appendix can be used as a summary reference for the language syntax.

It is helpful for the instructor to present a simple example model of a system, such as the compressor model in Chapter 3, the automobile model in Chapter 4, or the distiller model in Chapter 16, and require student projects of similar complexity. The student projects may be performed by teams or individuals. The projects require the student or teams to incrementally develop their models throughout the course in alignment with the sequence of course modules. If a tool is required, the course should also include introductory tool instruction for the selected tool. Alternatively, if a modeling tool is not required, the students can use the Visio SysML template available for download on the OMG SysML website (http://www.omgsysml.org/).

This book is also intended to be used to prepare for the OMG Certified Systems Modeling Professional (OCSMP) exams to become certified as a model user or model builder. For the first two levels of certification, the emphasis is on the basic SysML feature set. The automobile example in Chapter 4 covers most of the basic feature set of SysML, so this is an excellent place to start. One can also review the shaded paragraphs in each of the chapters in Part II, which cover the basic feature set, as do the shaded rows in the notation tables in the Appendix. The unshaded rows in the Appendix reflect the additional features of the full feature set, which is covered in the third level of OCSMP certification.

CHANGES FROM PREVIOUS EDITION

This edition is intended to update the book content to be current with version 1.4 of the SysML specification, which was recently adopted as of the time of this writing. The SysML specification versions are available from the OMG website at http://www.omg.org/spec/SysML/, and the specific changes to the SysML 1.4 specification can be identified by change bars in the specification document.

In addition to reflecting the SysML 1.4 changes in Part II, this edition includes refinements to the MBSE methods in Chapters 16 and 17 in Part III, and substantive changes to the contents of Chapters 18 and 19 in Part IV. The discussion on the Integrated Systems Development Environment in Chapter 18 was substantially rewritten to address model and tool integration, along with emerging tool integration standards such as OSLC and FMI. A new section that discusses elements of a deployment strategy is added to Chapter 19. In addition to content changes, all of the chapters are updated to improve quality and readability.

Acknowledgments

The authors wish to acknowledge the many individuals and their supporting organizations who participated in the development of SysML and provided valuable insights throughout the language development process. The individuals are too numerous to mention here but are listed in the OMG SysML specification. The authors wish to especially thank the reviewers of this book for their valuable feedback; they include Conrad Bock, Roger Burkhart, Lenny Delligatti, Jeff Estefan, Doug Ferguson, Dr. Kathy Laskey, Dr. Leon McGinnis, Dr. Øystein Haugen, Robert Karban, Dr. Chris Paredis, Dr. Russell Peak, Ed Seidewitz, Bran Selic, and Joe Wolfrom. The authors also wish to thank Yves Bernard, Paul Pearce, Axel Reichwein, John Watson, and Dirk Zimmer for contributing to the review of the third edition. Finally, the authors recognize Joe Wolfrom as the primary author of the Johns Hopkins University Applied Physics Lab course material on SysML and OOSEM referred to above.

SysML is implemented in many different tools. For this book, we selected certain tools for representing the examples but are not endorsing them over other tools. We do wish, however, to acknowledge some vendors for the use of their tools, including Enterprise Architect by Sparx Systems, MagicDraw by No Magic, ParaMagic® for MagicDraw by InterCAX, and the Microsoft Visio SysML template provided by Pavel Hruby.

About the Authors

Sanford Friedenthal is an industry leader in model-based systems engineering (MBSE) and an independent consultant. As a Lockheed Martin Fellow, he led the corporate engineering effort to enable Model-Based Systems Development (MBSD) and other advanced practices across the company. In this capacity, he was responsible for developing and implementing strategies to institutionalize the practice of MBSD across the company and to provide direct model-based systems engineering support to multiple programs.

His experience includes the application of systems engineering throughout the system lifecycle from conceptual design through development and production on a broad range of systems. He has also been a systems engineering department manager responsible for ensuring that systems engineering is implemented on programs. He has been a lead developer of advanced systems engineering processes and methods, including the Object-Oriented Systems Engineering Method (OOSEM). Sandy also was a leader of the industry team that developed SysML from its inception through its adoption by the OMG.

Mr. Friedenthal is well known within the systems engineering community for his role in leading the SysML effort and for his expertise in model-based systems engineering methods. He has been recognized as an International Council on Systems Engineering (INCOSE) Fellow for these contributions. He has given many presentations on these topics to a wide range of professional and academic audiences, both within and outside the US, and he teaches an MBSE course as part of a master's program in systems engineering.

Alan Moore is an Architecture Modeling Specialist at the MathWorks and has extensive experience in the development of real-time and object-oriented methods and their application in a variety of problem domains. Previously at ARTiSAN Software Tools, he was responsible for the development and evolution of Real-time Perspective, ARTiSAN's process for real-time systems development. Alan has been a user and developer of modeling tools throughout his career, from early structured programming tools to UML-based modeling environments.

Mr. Moore has been an active member of the Object Management Group and chaired both the finalization and revision task forces for the UML Profile for Schedulability and Performance and Time, and was a co-chair of the OMG's Real-time Analysis and Design Working Group. Alan also served as the language architect for the SysML Development Team.

Rick Steiner is an independent consultant focusing on pragmatic application of systems modeling techniques. He culminated his twenty-nine-year career at Raytheon as an Engineering Fellow, Raytheon Certified Architect, and INCOSE Expert Systems Engineering Professional (ESEP).

Mr. Steiner has been an advocate, consultant, and instructor of model-driven systems development for over twenty years. He served as chief engineer, architect, or lead system modeler for several large-scale electronics programs, incorporating the practical application of MBSE methods including OOSEM and the generation of Department of Defense Architecture Framework (DoDAF) artifacts from complex system models.

Mr. Steiner has been a key contributor to both the original requirements for SysML and the development of the SysML specification. His main technical contribution to the specification is in the areas of allocations, requirements, and the sample problem. Mr. Steiner also served as co-chair of the SysML Revision Task Force (RTF). He continues to provide frequent tutorials and workshops on SysML and model-driven engineering topics at INCOSE events, NDIA conferences, and other corporate engagements.

INTRODUCTION

Part I contains four chapters that provide an overview of systems engineering, a summary of key model-based systems engineering (MBSE) concepts, a chapter on getting started with SysML, and a sample problem to highlight the basic features of SysML. These chapters provide foundations for MBSE with SysML, and prepare the reader for the details of the language in Part II.

PART

1

INTRODUCTION

SYSTEMS ENGINEERING OVERVIEW

The Object Management Group's OMG SysML™ [1] is a general-purpose graphical modeling language for representing systems that may include combinations of hardware and equipment, software, data, people, facilities, and natural objects. SysML supports the practice of model-based systems engineering (MBSE) that is used to develop system solutions in response to complex and often technologically challenging problems.

This chapter introduces the systems engineering approach independent of modeling concepts to set the context for how SysML is used. It describes the motivation for systems engineering, introduces the systems engineering process, and then describes how this process is applied to a simplified automobile design example. This chapter also summarizes the role of standards, such as SysML, to help codify the practice of systems engineering.

1.1 MOTIVATION FOR SYSTEMS ENGINEERING

Whether it is an advanced military aircraft, a hybrid vehicle, a cell phone, or a distributed information system, today's systems are expected to perform at levels unimagined a generation ago. Competitive pressures demand that these systems leverage technological advances to provide continuously increasing capability at reduced costs and within shorter delivery cycles. The increased capability often drives requirements for increased functionality, interoperability, performance, and reliability, often within smaller and smaller devices.

The interconnectivity among systems also places increased demands on systems. Systems can no longer be treated as stand-alone entities. They behave as part of a larger whole that includes other systems, devices, and humans. This interconnected system of systems (SoS) is not static but changes over time as systems are added or removed and as their uses change. These changes result in evolving requirements on constituent systems that may not have been anticipated when the system was developed. An example would be a mobile device that originally provided e-mail communication but evolved to provide Internet functionality, including access to video, global positioning services, and social media. Systems such as automobiles, airplanes, and financial systems are also continuously subject to changing requirements, particularly as they become more interconnected.

Systems engineering is an approach that has been widely accepted in the aerospace and defense industry to provide system solutions to technologically challenging and mission-critical problems. The solutions often include hardware and equipment, software, data, people, and facilities. The potential value that systems engineering offers for managing complexity and risk and improving productivity and quality has been gaining recognition and acceptance across other industries, such as automotive, telecommunications, and medical equipment, to name a few.

1.2 THE SYSTEMS ENGINEERING PROCESS

A **system** consists of a set of elements that interact with one another, and can be viewed as a whole that interacts with its external environment to achieve an objective. **Systems engineering** is a multidisciplinary approach to develop balanced system solutions in response to diverse stakeholder needs. Systems engineering includes both management and technical processes to achieve this balance and mitigate risks that can affect the success of the project. The systems engineering management process is intended to ensure that development cost, schedule, and technical performance objectives are met. Typical management activities include planning the technical effort, monitoring technical performance, managing risk, and controlling the system technical baseline. The systems engineering technical processes are used to analyze, specify, design, and verify the system to ensure the pieces work together to achieve the objectives of the whole. The practice of systems engineering is not static but evolves to deal with the increasing demands mentioned previously.

A simplified view of the systems engineering technical process is shown in Figure 1.1. The *System Specification and Design* process is used to specify system requirements that will meet the needs of the stakeholders. It then allocates the requirements to the components of the system. The components are designed, implemented, and tested to ensure they satisfy the requirements. The *System Integration and Test* process includes activities to integrate the components into the system and verify that the system satisfies its requirements. These processes are applied iteratively throughout the development of the system, with ongoing feedback from the different processes. In more complex applications, multiple levels of system decomposition begin at an enterprise or system of systems level. In those cases, variants of this process are applied recursively to each intermediate level of the design, down to the level at which the components are procured or built.

The *System Specification and Design* process in Figure 1.1 includes the following activities to provide a balanced system solution that addresses the diverse stakeholders' needs:

- Elicit and analyze stakeholder needs to understand the problem to be solved, the goals the system is intended to support, and the effectiveness measures needed to evaluate how well the system supports these goals and satisfies the stakeholder needs.
- Specify the required system functionality, interfaces, physical and performance characteristics, and other quality characteristics to support the goals and effectiveness measures.

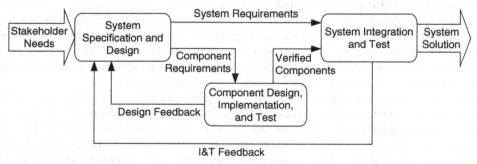

FIGURE 1.1

Simplified systems engineering technical processes.

- Synthesize alternative system solutions by partitioning the system design into components that can satisfy the system requirements.
- Perform analysis to evaluate and select a preferred system solution that satisfies the system requirements and maximizes the effectiveness measures.
- Maintain traceability from the system goals to the system and component requirements and verification results to ensure that requirements and stakeholder needs are addressed.

1.3 TYPICAL APPLICATION OF THE SYSTEMS ENGINEERING PROCESS

The *System Specification and Design* process described in Section 1.2 can be illustrated by applying this process to an automobile design. A multidisciplinary systems engineering team is responsible for executing this process. The participants and roles of a typical systems engineering team are discussed in Section 1.4.

The team must first identify the stakeholders and analyze their needs. Stakeholders include the purchaser of the car and the users of the car, which includes the driver and the passengers. Each of their needs must be addressed. The stakeholder needs depend on the particular market segment, such as a family car, sports car, or utility vehicle. For this example, we assume the automobile is targeted at a typical mid-career individual who uses the car for his or her daily transportation needs.

In addition, a key tenet of systems engineering is the idea of addressing the needs of other stakeholders who may be affected throughout the system's lifecycle. Additional stakeholders include the manufacturers that produce the automobile and those who maintain the automobile. Each of their concerns must be addressed to ensure a balanced lifecycle solution. Less obvious stakeholders are organizations and governments that express their needs via laws, regulations, and standards. Clearly, not each stakeholder's concern is of equal importance to the development of the automobile, and therefore stakeholder concerns must be properly prioritized and weighted. Analysis is performed to understand the needs of each stakeholder and to define effectiveness measures and target values that quantify the value for the stakeholders. The target values for these measures are used to bound the solution space, to evaluate alternative solutions, and to discriminate one solution from another. In this example, the effectiveness measures may relate to the primary goal of addressing the transportation needs, such as the availability of transportation, the time to reach a destination, safety, comfort, environmental impact, and other important measures that may be difficult to quantify, such as aesthetic qualities. The measures will also account for the total cost of transportation. These effectiveness measures can be used to evaluate alternative transportation solutions that include driving an automobile or taking the bus or train. If driving an automobile is the only solution being considered, the effectiveness measures can be more specific, such as the costs associated with purchasing and owning an automobile, measures that do not apply to taking a bus or train.

The system requirements are specified to address the stakeholders' needs and associated effectiveness measures. Many different kinds of requirements must be specified, including functional, interface, performance, physical, and other quality characteristics.

The definition of the system boundary is an important starting point for specifying the requirements. It allows clear interfaces to be established between the system and external systems and users as shown in Figure 1.2. In this example, the driver and passengers (not shown) are external users who interact with the automobile. The gas pump and maintenance equipment (not shown) are other examples of external systems that the vehicle must interact with. In addition, the vehicle interacts with the physical environment, such as the road. All of these external systems, including users and the physical environment, must be identified to clearly demarcate the system boundary and its associated interfaces.

The functional requirements for the automobile are specified by analyzing what the system must do to support its overall goals, such as functional requirements to meet transportation needs. The vehicle must perform functions related to accelerating, braking, and steering, and many additional functions to address driver and passenger needs. The functional analysis identifies the inputs and outputs for each function. As shown in the example in Figure 1.3, the functional requirement to accelerate the automobile include an input from the driver to the system to produce the output forces needed to accelerate the automobile and to estimate the automobile's speed for the driver. The analysis also specifies the sequence of functions, such as starting the vehicle before accelerating the vehicle.

Functional requirements must also be evaluated to determine the level of performance required for each function. As indicated in Figure 1.4, the automobile is required to accelerate from 0 to 60 miles per hour (mph) in fewer than 8 seconds under specified conditions. Similar performance requirements can be specified for stopping distance at various speeds and for the steering response.

Additional requirements are specified to address other concerns of each stakeholder as defined by the system goals and effectiveness measures. Example requirements include specifications for riding comfort in terms of road vibration and noise levels, fuel efficiency, reliability, maintainability, safety

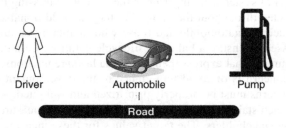

FIGURE 1.2

Defining the system boundary.

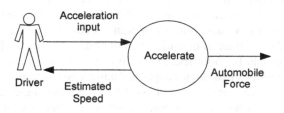

FIGURE 1.3

Specifying the functional requirements.

characteristics, and emissions. Physical characteristics, such as maximum vehicle weight, may be derived from the performance requirements, while maximum vehicle length may be dictated by other concerns, such as standard parking space dimensions. The system requirements must be clearly traceable to stakeholder needs and validated to ensure that the requirements address those needs. The early and ongoing involvement of representative stakeholders in this process is critical to the success of the overall development effort.

System design involves identifying system components and specifying the component requirements so that the system requirements will be met. This may involve first developing a logical system design that is independent of the technology used, and then a physical system design that reflects specific technology selections. (Note: A logical design that is technology independent may include a component called a torque generator; alternative physical designs that are technology dependent may include a combustion engine or an electric motor.) In the example in Figure 1.5, the system's physical components include the *engine, transmission, differential, body, chassis, brakes*, and so on.

As noted in Section 1.2, systems often include multiple levels of system decomposition. As an example, the internal combustion engine can be further broken down into its components, such as the engine block, pistons, connecting rods, crankshaft, and valves, each of which may require further specification.

Design constraints are often imposed on the solution. A common constraint is the reuse of a particular component. For example, a requirement might stipulate the reuse of an engine from the inventory of existing engines. This constraint implies that no additional engine development is to be performed. Although design constraints are typically imposed to save time and money, further analysis may reveal that relaxing the constraint would be less expensive. For example, if the engine is reused, expensive filtering equipment might be needed to satisfy newly imposed pollution regulations, while an engine redesign that incorporates newer technology might be a less expensive alternative. Systems engineers should validate the assumptions that drive the constraints and perform the analysis to understand their impact on the design.

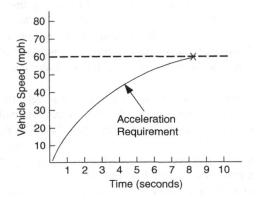

FIGURE 1.4

Automobile performance requirements.

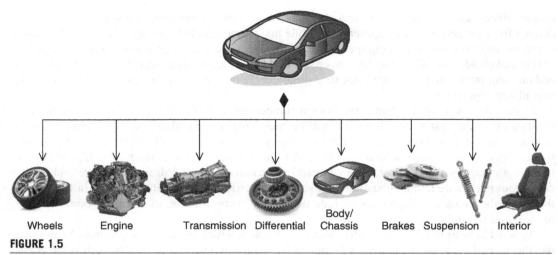

Wheels   Engine   Transmission   Differential   Body/
Chassis   Brakes   Suspension   Interior

FIGURE 1.5

Automobile system decomposition into its components.

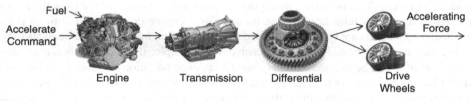

FIGURE 1.6

Interaction among components to achieve the system functional and performance requirements.

The component functional requirements are specified to satisfy the system functional requirements. The power subsystem shown in Figure 1.6 includes the *engine*, *transmission*, and *differential* components. The functions for each of these components is specified to provide the power to accelerate the automobile. Similarly, the steering subsystem includes components that must control the direction of the vehicle, and the braking subsystem includes components that must decelerate the vehicle.

Multiple analyses are performed to determine the components' performance and physical requirements needed to satisfy the system requirements. As an example, an analysis would determine the component requirements for engine horsepower, coefficient of drag of the body, and the weight of each component in order to satisfy the system requirement for vehicle acceleration. Similarly, analysis is performed to derive component requirements from other system performance requirements related to fuel economy, fuel emissions, reliability, and cost. The requirements for ride comfort may require multiple analyses that address human factors, considerations related to road vibration, acoustic noise propagation to the vehicle's interior, space–volume analysis, and placement of displays and controls.

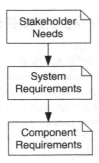

FIGURE 1.7

Stakeholder needs flow down to system and component requirements.

The system design alternatives are evaluated to determine the system solution that achieves a balanced design while addressing multiple competing requirements. In this example, the requirements to increase the vehicle acceleration and improve fuel economy represent competing requirements, which are subject to trade-off analysis. This may result in evaluating alternative engine design configurations, such as a 4-cylinder versus a 6-cylinder engine. The alternative designs are then evaluated based on criteria that are traceable to the system requirements and effectiveness measures. The preferred solution is validated with the stakeholders to ensure that it addresses their needs.

The component requirements are input to the *Component Design, Implementation, and Test* process from Figure 1.1. The component developers provide feedback to the systems engineering team to ensure that component requirements can be satisfied by their designs. Some components may be procured rather than developed, so designers need to understand the difference between what has been specified and what can be supplied. The assessment of the system and component design and reallocating the requirements are part of an iterative process that is often required to achieve a balanced system design solution.

The system test cases are defined to verify that the system satisfies its requirements. As part of the *System Integration and Test* process, the verified components are integrated into the system, and the system test cases are executed to confirm that system requirements are satisfied.

As indicated in Figure 1.7, requirement traceability is maintained between the *Stakeholder Needs,* the *System Requirements,* and the *Component Requirements* to ensure design integrity. For this example, the system and component requirements—such as vehicle acceleration, vehicle weight, and engine horsepower—can be traced to the stakeholder needs associated with vehicle performance and fuel economy.

A systematic process to develop a balanced system solution that addresses diverse stakeholder needs becomes essential as system complexity increases. An effective application of systems engineering requires maintaining a broad system perspective that focuses on the overall system goals and the needs of each stakeholder, while maintaining attention to detail and rigor that will ensure the integrity of the system design. SysML is intended to enable this process by providing a coherent and consistent model of the system that supports the analysis, specification, design, and verification activities described above.

1.4 MULTIDISCIPLINARY SYSTEMS ENGINEERING TEAM

To represent the broad set of stakeholder perspectives, systems engineering requires participation from many engineering and non-engineering disciplines. The participants must have an understanding of the end-user domain, such as the drivers of the car, and the domains that span the system lifecycle, such as manufacturing and maintenance. The participants must also have knowledge of the system's technical domains, such as the power and steering subsystems, and an understanding of the specialty engineering domains, such as reliability, safety, and human factors, to support the system design trade-offs. In addition, they must have sufficient participation from the component developers and testers to ensure the specifications are implementable and verifiable.

A **multidisciplinary systems engineering team** should include representation from each of these perspectives. The extent of participation depends on the complexity of the system and the knowledge of the team members. A systems engineering team on a small project may include a single systems engineer who has broad knowledge of the domain and can work closely with the component development teams and the test team. On the other hand, the development of a large system may involve a systems engineering team led by a systems engineering manager who plans and controls the system's engineering effort, and a chief systems engineer who has technical authority over the entire system design. This project may include tens or hundreds of systems engineers with varying expertise.

A typical multidisciplinary systems engineering team is shown in Figure 1.8. This group is sometimes called a Systems Engineering Integrated Team (SEIT). The *Systems Engineering Management Team* is responsible for the management activities related to planning and control of the technical effort. The *Requirements Team* analyzes stakeholder needs, develops the concept of operations, and specifies and validates the system requirements. The *Architecture Team* is responsible for synthesizing the system architecture by partitioning the system into components and defining their interactions and interconnections. This also includes allocating the system requirements and deriving technical specifications for these components.

The *Systems Analysis Team* is responsible for performing the engineering analysis on different aspects of the system, such as performance and physical characteristics, reliability, maintainability, and cost, to provide the rationale for the technical specifications. The *Integration and Test Team* is

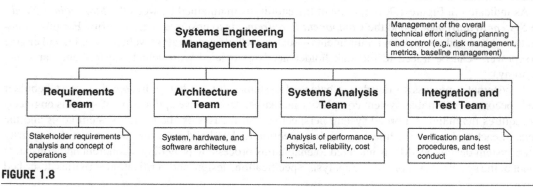

FIGURE 1.8

A typical multidisciplinary systems engineering team needed to represent diverse stakeholder perspectives.

responsible for developing test plans and procedures and for conducting tests to verify the requirements are satisfied. Many different organizational structures can provide these roles, and individuals may fill different roles on multiple teams.

1.5 CODIFYING SYSTEMS ENGINEERING PRACTICE THROUGH STANDARDS

As mentioned earlier, systems engineering is a widely accepted practice within the aerospace and defense industries to engineer complex, mission-critical systems that leverage advanced technology. These systems include land-, sea-, air-, and space-based platforms; weapon systems; command, control, and communications systems; and logistics systems

The complexity of systems being developed across industry sectors has dramatically increased due to the competitive demands and technological advances discussed earlier in this chapter. Specifically, many products incorporate the latest processing and networking technology, which has significant software content with substantially increased functionality. These products are often highly interconnected with increasingly complex interfaces. Establishing standards for systems engineering concepts, terminology, processes, and methods that help deal with this complexity is becoming increasingly important to the advancement and institutionalization of systems engineering across industry sectors and across international boundaries.

Systems engineering standards have evolved over the last several years. Figure 1.9 shows a partial taxonomy of standards that includes some of the systems engineering process standards, architecture

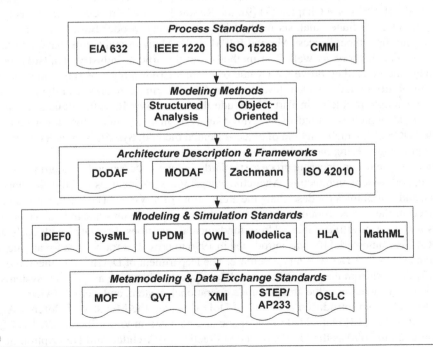

FIGURE 1.9

A partial systems engineering standards taxonomy.

frameworks, methods, modeling standards, and data exchange standards. A particular systems engineering approach may implement one or more standards from each layer of this taxonomy. Additional references to standards for systems modeling can be found in the Modeling Standards section of the *Systems Engineering Body of Knowledge* (SEBoK) [2].

Systems engineering process standards include EIA 632 [3], IEEE 1220 [4], and ISO 15288 [5]. These standards address broad industry needs and reflect the fundamental tenets of systems engineering, providing a foundation for establishing a systems engineering approach.

The systems engineering process standards share much in common with software engineering practices. Management practices for planning, for example, are similar whether they are for complex software development or systems development. As a result, the standards community has placed significant emphasis on aligning the systems and software standards where practical.

The systems engineering process defines what activities are performed but does not generally give details on how they are performed. A **systems engineering method** describes how the activities are performed and the kinds of systems engineering artifacts that are produced. An example of a systems engineering artifact is the concept of operations. As its name implies, the **concept of operations** defines what the system is intended to do from the user's perspective. It depicts the interaction of the system with its external systems and users but may not show any of the system's internal interactions. Different methods may use different techniques and representations to develop a concept of operations. The same is true for many other systems engineering artifacts.

Examples of systems engineering methods are identified in *Survey of Model-Based Systems Engineering (MBSE) Methodologies* [6] and include Harmony [7, 8], the Object-Oriented Systems Engineering Method (OOSEM; see Chapter 17) [9], the Rational Unified Process for Systems Engineering (RUP SE) [10, 11], the State Analysis method [12], the Vitech Model-Based Systems Engineering Method [13], and the Object Process Method (OPM) [14]. Many organizations have internally developed processes and methods as well. The methods are not official industry standards, but de facto standards may emerge as they prove their value over time. Criteria for selecting a method include its ease of use, its ability to address the relevant systems engineering concerns, and the level of tool support. The two example problems in Part III include the use of SysML with a functional analysis and allocation method, which is a kind of structured analysis method, and a top down scenario-driven method called OOSEM, which is a kind of object-oriented method. SysML is intended to support many different systems engineering methods.

In addition to systems engineering process standards and methods, several standard frameworks have emerged to support system architecting. An architecture framework includes specific concepts, terminology, artifacts, and taxonomies for describing the architecture of a system. The Zachman Framework [15] was introduced in the 1980s to define enterprise architectures; it defines a standard set of stakeholder perspectives and a set of artifacts that address fundamental questions associated with each stakeholder group. The C4ISR framework [16] was introduced in 1996 to provide a framework for architecting information systems for the US Department of Defense. The Department of Defense Architecture Framework (DoDAF) [17] evolved from the C4ISR framework to support architecting a system of systems (SoS) for the defense industry by defining the architecture's operational, system, and technical views.

The United Kingdom introduced a variant of DoDAF called the Ministry of Defence Architecture Framework (MODAF) [18] that added the strategic and acquisition views. The IEEE 1471-2000 standard was approved in 2000 as the "Recommended Practice for Architectural Description of Software-Intensive Systems" [19]. This practice provides additional fundamental concepts, such as the concept of view and viewpoint, that apply to both software and systems architecting. It was superseded by ISO/IEC 42010:2007 [20]. The Open Group Architecture Framework (TOGAF) [21] was originally approved in the 1990s as a method for developing architectures.

Modeling standards is another class of systems engineering standards that includes common modeling languages for describing systems. Behavioral models and functional flow diagrams have been de facto modeling standards for many years, and have been broadly used by the systems engineering community to support various kinds of structured analysis methods. The Integration Definition for Functional Modeling (IDEF0) [22] was issued by the National Institute of Standards and Technology in 1993.

The OMG SysML specification—the subject of this book—was adopted in 2006 by the Object Management Group as a general-purpose graphical systems modeling language that extends the Unified Modeling Language (UML). Several other extensions of UML have been developed for specific domains, such as the Unified Profile for DoDAF and MODAF (UPDM) [23] to describe system of systems and enterprise architectures that are compliant with DoDAF and MODAF requirements. The foundation for the UML-based modeling languages is the OMG Meta Object Facility (MOF) [24], a language that is used to specify other modeling languages.

Other relevant system modeling standards include Modelica [25], which is a simulation modeling language; the High Level Architecture (HLA) [26], which is used to support the design and execution of distributed simulations; and the Mathematical Markup Language (MathML), which defines a language for describing mathematical equations using the Extensible Markup Language (XML). The Architecture Analysis & Design Language (AADL) [27] standardized by the Society of Automotive Engineers (SAE) was originally developed for modeling embedded real-time systems. The Web Ontology Language (OWL) [28] is used to author ontologies that represent a set of concepts and the relationships between those concepts within a domain, such as systems engineering. Modelica and OWL are further discussed in Chapter 18, Section 18.4.

Model and data exchange standards is a critical class of modeling standards that supports model and data exchange among tools. Within the OMG, the XML Metadata Interchange (XMI) specification [29] supports the exchange of model data when using a MOF-based language such as UML, SysML, UPDM, or other UML extension. Another data exchange standard for systems engineering data is ISO 10303 (AP233) [30]. Other emerging data exchange standards include the web based exchange standards being developed through the Open Services for Lifecycle Collaboration (OSLC) [31] and the functional mock-up interface (FMI) standard, which supports co-simulation of interacting hardware and software components [32]. The data exchange standards are described in Chapter 18, Sections 18.4.3 and 18.4.4.

Additional modeling standards from the Object Management Group relate to **Model Driven Architecture** (MDA®) [33]. MDA comprises a set of concepts that include creating both technology-independent and technology-dependent models. The MDA standards enable transformation between models represented in different modeling languages as described in the MDA Foundation Model [34]. The OMG Query View Transformation (QVT) [35] is a modeling standard that defines a mapping language to specify language transformations precisely. MDA encompasses OMG modeling, metamodeling, and exchange standards from Figure 1.9.

The development and evolution of these standards are all part of a trend toward a standards-based approach to the practice of systems engineering. Such an approach enables shared understanding, common training, tool interoperability, reduced dependence on vendor specific solutions, and reuse of system specifications and design artifacts. This trend is expected to continue as systems engineering becomes prevalent across industries.

1.6 SUMMARY

Systems engineering is a multidisciplinary approach that is intended to transform a set of stakeholder needs into a balanced system solution that meets those needs. Systems engineering is a key practice to address complex and often technologically challenging problems. The systems engineering process includes activities to establish top-level goals that a system must support, specify system requirements, synthesize alternative system designs, evaluate the alternatives, allocate requirements to the components, integrate the components into the system, and verify that the system requirements are satisfied. It also includes essential planning and control processes needed to manage a technical effort.

Multidisciplinary teams are an essential element of systems engineering, because they address the diverse stakeholder perspectives and technical domains to achieve a balanced system solution. The practice of systems engineering continues to evolve, with an emphasis on dealing with systems as part of a larger interconnected system of systems. Systems engineering practices are becoming codified in various standards. This codification is essential to advancing and institutionalizing the practice across industry domains and geographic regions.

1.7 QUESTIONS

1. What are some of the demands that drive system development?
2. What is the purpose of systems engineering?
3. What are the key activities in the system specification and design process?
4. Who are typical stakeholders that span a system's lifecycle?
5. What are examples of different kinds of requirements?
6. Why is it important to have a multidisciplinary systems engineering team?
7. What are some of the roles on a typical systems engineering team?
8. What role do standards play in systems engineering?

MODEL-BASED SYSTEMS ENGINEERING

2

Model-based systems engineering (MBSE) applies systems modeling as part of the systems engineering process described in Chapter 1 to support analysis, specification, design, and verification of the system being developed. The primary artifact of MBSE is a coherent model of the system being developed. This approach enhances specification and design quality, reuse of system specifications and design artifacts, and communications among the development team.

This chapter summarizes MBSE concepts without emphasizing a specific modeling language, method, or tool. MBSE is contrasted with the more traditional document-based approach to encourage the use of MBSE and to highlight its benefits. Principles for effective modeling are also discussed.

2.1 CONTRASTING THE DOCUMENT-BASED AND MODEL-BASED APPROACH

The following sections contrast the document-based approach and the model-based approach to systems engineering.

2.1.1 DOCUMENT-BASED SYSTEMS ENGINEERING APPROACH

Traditionally, large projects have employed a **document-based systems engineering** approach to perform the systems engineering activities discussed in Chapter 1, Section 1.2. This approach is characterized by the generation of textual specifications and design documents, in hard-copy or electronic file format, that are then exchanged between customers, users, developers, and testers. System requirements and design information are expressed in these documents as text descriptions, graphical depictions generated from drawing tools, and tabular data and plots that may result from executing analysis models or derived from databases. A document-based systems engineering approach emphasizes controlling the documentation, ensuring the documentation is valid, complete, and consistent, and confirming that the developed system complies with the documentation.

In the document-based approach, specifications for a particular system, its subsystems, and its hardware and software components are usually depicted in a hierarchical tree called a **specification tree**. A **systems engineering management plan (SEMP)** describes how the systems engineering process is employed on the project, and how the engineering disciplines work together to develop the documentation needed to satisfy the requirements in the specification tree. Systems engineering activities are planned by estimating the time and effort to generate the documentation, and progress is measured by the state of completion of these documents.

Document-based systems engineering typically relies on the concept of operations document to define how the system supports the required mission or objective. Functional analysis is performed to

15

decompose the system functions and allocate them to the components of the system. Drawing tools—such as functional flow diagrams and schematic block diagrams—are used to capture the system design. These diagrams are stored as separate files and included in the system design documentation. Engineering trade studies and analyses are performed and documented by many different disciplines to evaluate and optimize alternative designs and allocate performance requirements. The analysis may be supported by individual analysis models for performance, reliability, safety, mass properties, and other aspects of the system.

Requirements traceability is established and maintained in the document-based approach by tracing requirements between the specifications at different levels of the specification hierarchy. Requirements management tools are used to parse requirements contained in the specification documents and to capture them in a requirements database. The traceability between requirements and design is maintained by identifying the part of the system or subsystem that satisfies the requirement, and/or the verification procedures used to verify the requirement, and then reflecting this traceability in the requirements database.

The document-based approach can be rigorous but has some fundamental limitations. The completeness, consistency, and relationships between requirements, design, engineering analysis, and test information are difficult to assess because the information is spread across several documents. Understanding a particular aspect of the system and performing the necessary traceability and change impact assessments become difficult. This, in turn, leads to poor synchronization between requirements, system level design, and lower-level detailed designs such as software, electrical, and mechanical design. It also makes it difficult to maintain or reuse the system requirements and design information for an evolving or variant system design. In addition, progress of the systems engineering effort is based on the documentation status, which is difficult to maintain and does not adequately reflect the quality of the system requirements and design. These limitations can result in inefficiencies that impact cost and schedule, and potential quality issues that often show up during integration and testing or—worse—after the system is delivered to the customer.

2.1.2 MODEL-BASED SYSTEMS ENGINEERING APPROACH

A model-based approach has been standard practice in electrical and mechanical design and other disciplines for many years. Mechanical engineering transitioned from the drawing board to increasingly more sophisticated two-dimensional and then three-dimensional computer-aided design tools beginning in the 1980s. Electrical engineering transitioned from manual circuit design to automated schematic capture and circuit analysis in a similar time-frame. Computer-aided software engineering became popular in the 1980s, using graphic models to represent software at abstraction levels above the programming language. The use of modeling for software development is becoming more widely adopted, particularly since the advent of the Unified Modeling Language in the 1990s.

The model-based approach is becoming more prevalent in systems engineering. A mathematical formalism for MBSE was introduced in 1993 by Wayne Wymore [36]. The increasing capability of computer processing, storage, and network technology along with emphasis on systems engineering standards has created an opportunity to significantly advance the state of the practice of MBSE. It is expected that MBSE will become standard practice in a similar way that it has with other engineering disciplines, and will become fully integrated into a broader model-based engineering approach.

"**Model-based systems engineering** (**MBSE**) is the formalized application of modeling to support system requirements, design, analysis, verification, and validation activities beginning in the conceptual design phase and continuing throughout development and later lifecycle phases" [37]. MBSE emphasizes the use of models to perform the systems engineering activities that have traditionally been performed using the document-based approach as described in the previous section. With MBSE, the output of the systems engineering activities is a coherent model of the system (i.e., system model) that is part of the engineering baseline, and the emphasis is placed on defining and evolving the model using model-based methods and tools. The intended result is enhanced specification and design quality, reuse of the system specification and design artifacts, and improved communications among the development team.

The System Model

The **system model** is generally created using a modeling tool and stored in a model repository. The system model includes system specifications, design, analysis, and verification information. The model consists of model elements that represent requirements, design, test cases, design rationale, and their interrelationships. Figure 2.1 shows the system model as an interconnected set of model elements that represent key system aspects as defined in SysML, including its structure, behavior, parametrics, and requirements. The multiple cross-cutting relationships between the model elements enable the system model to be viewed from many different perspectives that focus on different aspects of the system while maintaining consistency among the different views.

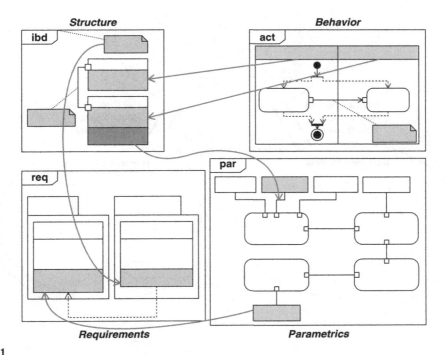

FIGURE 2.1

Representative system model example in SysML. (Specific model elements have been deliberately obscured and will be discussed in subsequent chapters.)

A primary use of the system model is to enable the design of a system that satisfies its requirements and meets its overall objectives. This model is an output from the system specification and design process that is discussed in Sections 1.2 and 1.3. Figure 2.2 depicts how the system model is used to specify the hardware and software components of the system. The system model includes component interconnections and interfaces, component interactions and the associated functions the components must perform, and component performance and physical characteristics. The textual requirements for the components may also be captured in the model and traced to system requirements.

The system model specifies the components of the system. The component specifications serve as inputs to procure and/or design a component. Component design models may be expressed in domain-specific modeling languages, such as UML for software design or computer-aided design and computer-aided engineering (CAD/CAE) models for hardware design. The information exchange between the system model and the component design models may be accomplished through the exchange mechanisms described in Chapter 18, Section 18.3, or by automatically generating the component specifications from the system model in more traditional document–based formats. The use of a system model

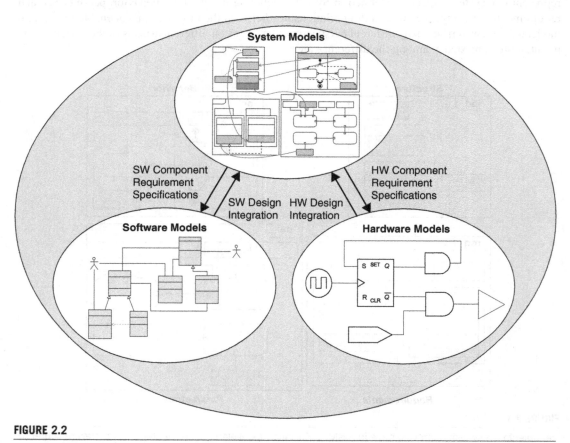

FIGURE 2.2

The system model is used to specify the components of the system.

provides a mechanism to specify and integrate subsystem and component designs into the system, and maintain traceability between the system and component requirements.

The system model can also be integrated with other engineering analysis and simulation models that perform computation and dynamic execution. The system model can be executed directly if the system modeling environment is augmented with an execution environment. A growing emphasis for the system model is its role in providing a common system description for integrating models created by other engineering disciplines, including hardware, software, testing, and other specialty engineering disciplines such as reliability, safety, and security. This is covered in Chapter 18, Section 18.2, as part of the discussion on specifying an integrated systems development environment.

The Model Repository

The system model contains model elements that are stored in a **model repository** and presented on diagrams with graphical symbols. The modeling tool enables the modeler to create, modify, and delete individual model elements and their relationships, and to store them in the model repository. The modeler uses the symbols on the diagrams to enter the model information into the repository and to view model information from the repository. The system specification, design, analysis, and verification information previously captured in documents is captured as the system model in the repository. The model can be queried and analyzed for a variety of purposes, including integrity checks of the system specification and design. The system model can be viewed in diagrams or in other combinations of graphical, tabular, and textual reports that are generated by querying the model and presenting the information in the desired form. These views enable understanding and analysis of different aspects of the system model.

Many of the modeling tools have a flexible and automated document-generation capability that can significantly reduce the time and cost of building and maintaining the system specification and design documentation from the system model. In this way, documents that may look similar to traditional document-based artifacts can continue to serve as an effective means for reporting the information. Document generation from the model is described in more detail in Chapter 18, Sections 18.2.2 and 18.4.5.

Model elements corresponding to requirements, design, analysis, and verification information are traceable to one another through their relationships, even though they are often presented on different diagrams. For example, an engine component in an automobile system model may have many relationships to other elements in the model. It is part of the automobile system, connected to the transmission, satisfies a power requirement, performs a function to convert fuel to mechanical energy, and has a weight property that contributes to the vehicle's weight. These relationships are part of the system model.

The modeling language imposes rules that constrain which relationships are valid. For example, the model should not allow a requirement to contain a system component or an activity to produce inputs instead of outputs. Additional model constraints may be imposed based on the MBSE method and other domain specific constraints that are employed. An example of a method-imposed constraint may be that all system functions must be decomposed and allocated to at least one component of the system. A domain specific constraint may be that a particular type of component must include certain kinds of properties, such as all electrical components must include predefined electrical characteristics. Modeling tools enforce constraints at the time the model is constructed, although when needed, it is also possible to run a model-checking routine that provides a report of any constraint violations.

This model provides much finer control of the information than is available in a document-based approach, where this information may be spread across many documents and the relationships may not be explicitly defined. The model-based approach promotes rigor in the specification, design, analysis, and verification process. It also significantly enhances the quality and timeliness of traceability and impact assessment over the document-based approach.

Transitioning to MBSE

Models and related diagramming techniques have been used as part of the document-based systems engineering approach for many years. They include functional flow diagrams, behavior diagrams, schematic block diagrams, N2 charts, performance simulations, and reliability models, to name a few. However, the use of models has generally been limited to supporting specific types of analysis or selected aspects of system design. Individual models have not been integrated into a coherent model of the overall system, and the modeling activities have not been fully integrated with other activities that form the systems engineering process. The transition from document-based systems engineering to MBSE is a shift in emphasis from controlling the documentation about the system to controlling the model of the system. MBSE integrates system requirements, design, analysis, and verification information to address multiple aspects of the system in a cohesive manner, rather than dealing with a disparate collection of individual models.

MBSE provides an opportunity to address many of the limitations of the document-based approach by providing a more rigorous means for capturing and integrating system requirements, design, analysis, and verification information, and facilitating the maintenance, assessment, communication, and exchange of this information across the system's lifecycle. Some of the MBSE potential benefits include the following:

* Enhanced communications
  * Shared understanding of the system across the development team and other stakeholders.
  * Ability to present and integrate views of the system from multiple perspectives.
* Reduced development risk
  * Ongoing requirements validation and design verification.
  * More accurate cost estimates to develop the system.
* Improved quality
  * More complete, unambiguous, and verifiable requirements.
  * More rigorous traceability between requirements, design, analysis, and testing.
  * Enhanced design integrity.
* Increased productivity
  * Faster and more comprehensive impact analysis of requirements and design changes.
  * More effective exploration of trade-space.
  * Reuse of existing models to support design evolution.
  * Reduced errors and time during integration and testing.
  * Automated document generation.
* Leveraging the models during downstream lifecycle phases
  * Support operator training on the use of the system.
  * Support diagnostics and maintenance of the system.
* Enhanced knowledge transfer
  * Efficient capture of domain knowledge about the system in a standardized form that can be accessed, queried, analyzed, evolved, and reused.

MBSE can provide additional rigor to the specification and design process when implemented using appropriate methods and tools. However, this rigor does not come without a price. Clearly, transitioning to MBSE underscores the need for up-front investment in processes, methods, tools, and training. It is expected that during the transition to a model-based approach, MBSE will be performed in combination with document-based approaches. For example, the upgrade of a large and complex legacy system still relies heavily on the legacy documentation, and only parts of the system may be modeled. Careful tailoring of the approach and scoping of the modeling effort is essential to meet the needs of a particular project. Considerations for transitioning to an MBSE approach are discussed in Chapter 19.

2.2 MODELING PRINCIPLES

The following sections provide a brief overview of some of the key modeling principles.

2.2.1 MODEL AND MBSE METHOD DEFINITION

A **model** is a representation of one or more concepts that may be realized in the physical world. The model generally describes a **domain of interest** where a domain may correspond to a particular application area (such as transportation) involving particular kinds of systems (such as automobiles) and particular facets of a system (such as vehicle performance). A key feature of a model is that it is an abstraction that does not contain all the detail of the modeled entities within the domain of interest, but only the details needed to address the intended use of the model. Models can be abstractions, such as quantitative, logical, and/or geometric representations, as well as concrete, physical scale models. The abstract representation may be expressed in combinations of text (such as the text statements in a programming language), mathematical equations, graphical symbols (such as nodes and arcs on a graph), and geometric layouts (such as a CAD model). A common example of a model is a blueprint of a building and a scaled prototype physical model. The building blueprint is a specification for one or more buildings that are built. The blueprint is an abstraction that does not contain all the building's detail, such as the detailed characteristics of its materials. Similarly, the scaled prototype is a representation of the actual building to be built that does not contain all the details of the building, such as the building materials. However, these models serve their intended use for specifying and visualizing the structure to be built.

A system model expressed in SysML is analogous to a building blueprint that specifies a system to be implemented. The SysML model represents the behavior, structure, properties, constraints, and requirements of the system. SysML has a semantic foundation that defines the kind of model elements and their relationships that can appear in the system model. The model elements that constitute the system model are stored in a model repository and can be presented graphically as well as in tables and other forms. A SysML model can also be integrated with other analysis and design models to represent other aspects of the system.

A **method** is a set of related activities, techniques, conventions, representations, and artifacts that implement one or more processes and is generally supported by a set of tools. A **model-based systems engineering method** is a method that implements all or part of the systems engineering process and produces a system model as one of its primary artifacts. Chapter 3, Section 3.4, provides a simplified MBSE method, while Chapter 16 and Chapter 17 provide detailed examples of applying two different MBSE methods.

2.2.2 THE PURPOSE FOR MODELING A SYSTEM

The purpose for modeling a system for a particular project must be clearly defined in terms of how various stakeholders intend to use the model, including the contributors and consumers of the model content. The stakeholders and their intended uses evolve across the lifecycle of the system's development, imposing an evolving set of requirements on the use of the model. For example, during the early conceptual design phase of a system, the intended use of the model may be to support the evaluation of alternative system design concepts. During this activity, emphasis may be placed on system sizing, high-level system functionality, and critical system properties. During later phases, the intended use may be to specify the hardware and software components of the system, where the emphasis is placed on specifying the behavior of the software and hardware components. As the detailed design proceeds, the intended use of the model may be to support component design integration and system/subsystem verification. The intended use for modeling a system is associated with the systems engineering activities the model is intended to support across the system lifecycle, and may include the following uses:

- Characterize and assess an existing system
- Specify and design a new or modified system
  - Represent a system concept.
  - Specify and validate system requirements.
  - Synthesize system designs.
  - Specify component requirements.
  - Maintain requirements traceability.
- Evaluate the system
  - Conduct system design trade-offs.
  - Analyze system performance requirements or other quality attributes.
  - Verify that the system design satisfies its requirements.
  - Assess the impact of requirements and design changes.
  - Estimate the system cost (e.g., development cost, lifecycle cost).
- Train users on how to operate or maintain a system
- Support system maintenance and/or diagnostics

2.2.3 MODEL VALIDATION

Model validation is the process for determining the extent to which the model accurately represents the domain of interest (e.g., the system and its environment) to meet the model's intended use. For analysis models, the validation is often accomplished through static checks of the model and through review by domain experts of the input data and assumptions, the model, and the analysis results. The results of the analysis are generated from executing the model and are compared with real-world results when such data is available.

A system model in SysML represents a description of the system and its environment that must be a sufficiently accurate representation to fulfill its intended use. The model's accuracy is dependent on the quality of the source information used to generate the model, the validity of the assumptions regarding the applicability of the source information, and the extent to which the source information and assumptions are properly captured in the model. As with analysis models, the system model validation can be performed by a combination of model checks and domain expert review. In addition, the system model can be used as an input to other analysis models and simulations that can be executed and validated, thus providing a further means for validating the system model.

Validating that a model is sufficient to meet its intended use also requires consideration of the inherent capabilities and limitations of the modeling language. This depends on the expressiveness and precision of the language. For example, a modeling language that only represents process and/or functional flow may not have the capability to represent system performance and physical characteristics and the equations that govern them.

2.2.4 ESTABLISHING MODEL QUALITY CRITERIA

Quality criteria can be established to assess how well a model meets its intended use. However, one must first distinguish between a good model and a good design. One can have a good model of a poor design or a poor model of a good design. A good model is judged on how well the model meets its intended use. A good design is based on how well the design satisfies its requirements and the extent to which it incorporates quality design principles. As an example, one could have a good model that provides an accurate representation of a chair that has been validated for its intended use. However, the chair's design may be a poor design if it does not have structural integrity. A good model can meet its intended use by providing visibility to aid the design team in identifying design issues and assessing design quality. The selected MBSE method and tools should facilitate a skilled and knowledgeable team to develop both a good model and a good design.

The following questions can be used to assess a model's ability to meet its intended use and to derive quality attributes for the model. The quality attributes in turn can be used to establish preferred modeling practices. The modeling tool can assist the implementation of these practices by providing model checking and reports that facilitate assessment of the quality attributes.

Is the model's purpose well defined?

The model's purpose must be clearly stated, as described in Section 2.2.2, for both the near- and long-term use of the model. This should include identifying representative stakeholders, such as different disciplines involved in the development process, and their intended use of the model throughout the system lifecycle. (Note: The stakeholders and their intended use can be defined as stakeholder viewpoints.)

Is the model's scope sufficient to meet its intended use?

The scope of the model should be sufficient to meet the intended use of the model as described above. The model's scope can be defined in terms of the model's breadth, depth, and fidelity, which evolve across different phases of development. This scope should be balanced with the available schedule, budget, skill levels, and other resources. Understanding the model's purpose and scope provides the basis for establishing realistic expectations and the required level of resources for the modeling effort.

- *Model breadth.* The breadth of the model must be sufficient for the intended use. This is accomplished by determining which parts of the system need to be modeled. This can be determined by the extent of the system requirements that the model must address. For example, if new functionality is being added to an existing system, one may choose to focus on modeling only those portions needed to support the new functionality. In an automobile design, for example, if the emphasis is on new or modified requirements for fuel economy and acceleration, the model may focus on elements related to the power train, with less focus on the braking and steering subsystems. This does not imply that other parts of the system are not impacted by the change, but the scope of the modeling effort is limited to represent the new functionality.

- *Model depth.* The depth of the model must be sufficient for the purpose, which is determined by the level of the system design hierarchy that the model must encompass. For a conceptual design or initial design iteration, the model may only address a high level system design. In the automobile example, the initial design iteration may only model the system to the engine black box level, whereas if the engine is subject to further development, a future design iteration may require the model to include the engine components.
- *Model fidelity.* The fidelity of the model must support the required level of detail. For example, a simple activity diagram with control flows may be sufficient for describing the initial functions a system or subsystem is required to perform. Additional model details may be required to execute the behavior in order to specify the software requirements fully. As another example, a low-fidelity model for modeling interfaces may only represent the data definitions and source and destination of the flows, whereas a higher-fidelity model may represent the message structure, communication protocol, and detailed communication path. A further example is a low fidelity model to analyze system performance versus a higher fidelity model that includes more detailed timing information, system performance characteristics, and constraints.

Is the model complete relative to its scope?

A necessary condition for the model to be complete is that its breadth, depth, and fidelity match its defined scope. Other completeness criteria may relate to other quality attributes of the model described below (e.g., whether the naming conventions have been properly applied) and design completion criteria (e.g., whether all design elements are traced to a requirement).

Is the model well-formed?

A well-formed model conforms to the rules of the modeling language. For example, the rules in SysML allow a component to satisfy a requirement but do not allow a requirement to satisfy a component. The modeling tool should enforce the constraints imposed by the rules of the modeling language and/or provide a report of violations.

Is the model consistent?

In SysML, some rules are built into the language to ensure model consistency. For example, type checking can help determine whether interfaces are compatible or whether units are consistent among different properties. Additional constraints can be imposed by the MBSE method used. For instance, a method may impose a constraint that logical components can only be allocated to hardware and equipment, software, or operational procedures. These constraints can be expressed in the object constraint language (OCL) [38] or some other constraint language and enforced by the modeling tool.

Enforcing constraints assists in maintaining consistency across the model, but it does not prevent design inconsistencies. A simple example may be that two modelers inadvertently give two different names to what is intended to be the same component. The model treats these as different components. This type of inconsistency should surface through the model and design reviews and reports. However, the likelihood of inconsistencies increases when multiple people are working on the same model. A combination of well-defined model conventions and a disciplined process can reduce the likelihood of this happening.

Is the model understandable?

The system model is intended to be interpretable by both humans and computers. Many factors can contribute to the understandability of the model by humans. In addition to the underlying semantics of the model, the way in which the information is presented is also important to human understanding. An understandable model should include views of the model that contain the information appropriate for the particular stakeholder's intended use.

The understandability can be enhanced by controlling what and how information appears on the diagrams and other reports. Often, the model contains a lot of detail, but only selected information is relevant to communicate a particular aspect of the design. The information on the diagram can be controlled by using the tool capability to elide (hide) nonessential information and display only the information relevant to the diagram's purpose. Again, the goal is to avoid information overload for the reviewer of the model.

The layout of the diagram does not generally contain semantic information but can impact how well the model is understood. For example, an activity diagram that represents a sequence of actions may be laid out in different ways. The layout is generally more understandable if the position of the actions on the diagram align with the action sequence.

The use of icons—such as the use of an icon for a particular kind of component (e.g., pump, valve)—can also aid in understanding. Also, tabular views may be preferred over diagrammatic views when presenting certain types of information to some stakeholders. Other factors that contribute to understandability are the use of modeling conventions and the extent to which the model is self-documenting, as described next.

Are modeling conventions documented and used consistently?

Modeling conventions and standards are critical to ensuring consistent representation and style across the model. This includes establishing naming conventions for each kind of model element, diagram names, and diagram content. Naming conventions may include stylistic aspects of the language, such as when to use uppercase versus lowercase and when to use spaces. The conventions and standards should also account for tool-imposed constraints, such as limitations in the use of alphanumeric and special characters. It is also recommended that a template be established for each kind of diagram so that a consistent style can be applied. Standard report formats from the model should also beinstituted.

A domain specific vocabulary that reflects the core domain concepts and their relationships can be defined more formally. The formal representation may be referred to as an ontology, a conceptual model, or a metamodel. This representation can then be used to define domain specific extensions to the language. An example of an ontology is described in Chapter 18, Section 18.4.4.

Is the model self-documenting?

The use of annotations and descriptions throughout the model can help to provide value-added information if applied consistently. This can include capturing the rationale for design decisions, listing issues or problem areas for resolution, and providing additional text descriptions for model elements. This information may also be included in documentation that is automatically generated from the model. However, this information must also be maintained as part of the model, so careful consideration should be given to what information is captured and how.

Does the model accurately reflect the domain of interest?

This is best answered by establishing a model validation approach as described in Section 2.2.3. The accuracy of this description is dependent on the quality of the source information, the validity of the assumptions regarding the applicability of the source information, and the extent to which the source information and assumptions are properly captured in the model, as well as the inherent capabilities and limitations of the modeling language. The quality of the source information and the validity of the assumptions are primarily assessed through subject matter review. The assessments of the extent to which the source information and assumptions are properly captured in the model is determined by assessing other quality attributes described above as well as further expert review.

Does the model integrate with other models?

The system model may need to integrate with electrical, mechanical, software, test, and engineering analysis models as referred to in Section 2.1.2. The required integration is dependent on the specific modeling languages, tools, and methods being used. The modeling information to be exchanged, its presentation, and the mechanisms for information exchange must be determined. For example, the approach for passing information from the system model using SysML to a software model using UML may require establishing a relationship between the software design elements in the UML model and the software specification elements in the SysML model. In other cases, this may require the exchange of selected information though a file or through the application programming interface of the modeling tools. The approach for integrating models and tools is discussed in Chapter 18.

2.2.5 MODEL-BASED METRICS

As noted in Section 2.2.4, there is a distinction between a good model and a good design. Applying the model quality criteria in Section 2.2.4 should help to meet the intended use of the model. However, the application of these criteria does not explicitly reflect the quality of the design. For example, a model of component requirements can be complete relative to its scope, well formed, consistent, understandable, well documented, validated, and integrated with other models, but not necessarily result in quality requirements. Such results are dependent on the skill and knowledge of the system engineering team.

Measurement data collection, analysis, and reporting can be used as a management technique throughout the development process to assess design quality and progress. This in turn is used to assess technical, cost, schedule status, and risk, and to support ongoing project planning and control. **Model-based metrics** can provide useful data that can be derived from a system model expressed in SysML. Such data can help answer the questions below and assess the design quality and progress. The data can be collected over time to provide additional insights through assessment of the data trends and statistical distributions.

What is the quality of the design?

Metrics can be defined to measure the quality of a model-based system design. Some of these metrics—such as assessing requirements satisfaction, requirements verification, and technical performance measurement—are based on metrics that have been traditionally used in document-based designs. Other metrics may include indicators of how well the design is partitioned and measures of complexity.

A SysML model can include explicit relationships that can be used to measure the extent to which the requirements are satisfied. The model can provide granularity by identifying model elements that satisfy specific requirements along with the supporting rationale. The requirements traceability can be established from mission requirements down to component requirements. Other SysML relationships can be used in a similar way to measure which requirements have been verified. This data can be extracted directly from the model or indirectly from a requirements management tool that is integrated with the SysML modeling tool.

A SysML model can include critical properties that are monitored throughout the design process to assess technical risks and to determine the impact of requirements and design change impacts on these critical properties. Typical properties may include performance properties, such as response time, throughput, and accuracy; physical properties, such as weight, size, and power; and other properties, such as reliability and cost. The SysML model can also include parametric relationships between the properties that are used to integrate with other analysis models. These properties can be monitored using standard technical performance measurement techniques supported by analysis models to compute the property values and sensitivities.

Design partitioning can be measured in terms of the level of cohesion and coupling of the design. Coupling can be measured by the number of interfaces or through more complex measures of dependencies between model elements. Cohesion metrics measure the extent to which a component can perform its functions without requiring access to external data. The object-oriented concept of encapsulation reflects this concept.

What is the progress of the design and development effort?

Model-based metrics can be defined to assess design progress relative to the completion criteria for the design. The quality attributes in the previous section refer to whether the model is complete relative to the defined scope of the modeling effort. This is necessary—but not sufficient—to assess design completeness. The extent to which the system design satisfies the system requirements is a measure of design quality and design completeness. The components interfaces, behavior, and properties must be sufficiently specified to assess whether the system design satisfies its requirements, and can be assessed in terms of model-based metrics. Other metrics may include the number of use-case scenarios that have been completed or the percent of logical components that have been allocated to physical components.

Other metrics for assessing progress include the extent to which components have been verified and integrated into the system and how well the system has been verified to satisfy its requirements. Test cases and verification status can be captured in the model and used as a basis for this assessment.

What is the estimated effort to complete design and development?

The Constructive Systems Engineering Cost Model (COSYSMO) is used for estimating the cost and effort of performing systems engineering activities. This model includes both sizing and productivity parameters, where the size estimates the magnitude of the effort and productivity factors are applied to arrive at a labor estimate to do the work.

When using model-based approaches, sizing parameters can be identified in the model in terms of the number of different modeling constructs, which may include the following:

- Model elements;
- Requirements;
- Use cases;
- Scenarios;
- System and component states;
- System and component interfaces;
- System and component activities or operations;
- System and component properties;
- Components by type (e.g., hardware, software, data, operational procedures);
- Constraints; and
- Test cases.

The metrics should also account for relationships between these model elements, such as the number of requirements that are satisfied, the number of requirements that are verified, the number of use cases that are realized, and the number of activities that are allocated to blocks.

The MBSE sizing parameters are integrated into the cost model. The parameters may have complexity factors associated with them as well. For example, the complexity of a use case may be indicated by the number of actors participating in the interaction. Additional factors to be considered are the amount of reuse and modification of existing models versus creating new models.

Sizing and productivity data need to be collected and validated over time to establish statistically meaningful data and cost estimating relationships to support accurate cost estimating. However, early users of MBSE can identify sizing parameters that contribute most significantly to the modeling effort, and use this data for local estimates and to assess productivity improvements over time.

2.2.6 OTHER MODEL-BASED METRICS

The previous discussion is a sampling of some of the model-based metrics that can be defined. Many other metrics can also be derived from the model, such as the stability of the number of requirements, design changes over time, and potential defect rates. The metrics can also be devised to establish benchmarks by which to measure the MBSE benefits as described in Section 2.1.2, such as the productivity improvements resulting from MBSE over time. These metrics should be defined and captured to support the business case for MBSE. Chapter 19, Section 19.1.1, includes a discussion of additional metrics related to deploying MBSE in an organization.

2.3 SUMMARY

The practice of systems engineering is transitioning from a document-based approach to a model-based approach, just as many other engineering disciplines—such as mechanical and electrical—have already done. MBSE offers significant potential benefits that enhance specification and design quality and consistency, reuse of the specification and design artifacts, and communication among the development team, yielding overall improvements in quality and productivity, while reducing development risk. The emphasis for MBSE is on producing and controlling a coherent system model, and using this model to specify and design the system.

System modeling can support many intended uses, such as evaluating alternative system design concepts or specifing the hardware and software components of the system. A good model meets its intended use, and a validated model accurately represents a system's domain of interest sufficient for its intended use. Although, a good model does not necessarily imply a good design, it should provide the information necessary for a skilled and knowledgeable design team to develop a quality design that satisfies its requirements.

The scope of the model should support its intended use within the resource constraints of the modeling effort. Quality attributes of a model—such as model consistency, understandability, and well-formedness—and modeling conventions can be used to assess the model quality and to derive preferred modeling practices. MBSE metrics can also be used to assess design quality, determine progress and risk, and support management of the development effort.

2.4 QUESTIONS

1. What are some of the primary distinctions between MBSE and a document-based approach?
2. What are some of the benefits of MBSE over the document-based approach?
3. Where are the model elements of a system model stored?
4. Why should a model be validated?
5. What constitutes a good model?
6. What is the difference between a good model and a good design?
7. Which aspects of the model can be used to define the scope of the model?
8. What are some of the key quality criteria a model should satisfy?
9. What are examples of questions that MBSE metrics can help answer?
10. What are possible sizing parameters that could be used to estimate an MBSE effort?

GETTING STARTED WITH SysML

3

This chapter provides an introduction to SysML and guidance on how to begin modeling with it. The chapter provides a brief overview of SysML, then introduces a simplified version of the language known as SysML-Lite, along with a simplified example and tool tips on how to capture the model in a typical modeling tool. This chapter also introduces a simplified model-based systems engineering (MBSE) method that is consistent with the systems engineering process described in Chapter 1, Section 1.2. The chapter finishes by describing some of the challenges involved in learning SysML and MBSE.

3.1 SysML PURPOSE AND KEY FEATURES

SysML[1] is a general-purpose graphical modeling language that supports the analysis, specification, design, verification, and validation of complex systems. These systems may include hardware and equipment, software, data, personnel, procedures, facilities, and other elements of human-made and natural systems. The language is intended to help specify and architect systems and to specify components that can then be designed using other domain-specific languages, such as UML for software design, VHDL for electrical design, and three-dimensional geometric modeling for mechanical design. SysML is intended to facilitate the application of an MBSE approach to create a cohesive and consistent model of the system that yields the benefits described in Chapter 2, Section 2.1.2.

SysML can represent the following aspects of systems, components, and other entities:

- Structural composition, interconnection, and classification;
- Flow-based, message-based, and state-based behavior;
- Constraints on the physical and performance properties;
- Allocations between behavior, structure, and constraints; and
- Requirements and their relationship to other requirements, design elements, and test cases.

---

[1]OMG Systems Modeling Language (OMG SysML™) is the official name of the language, but it is referred to as SysML for short. Additional information on SysML can be found at the official OMG SysML website at http://www. omgsysml.org.

3.2 SysML DIAGRAM OVERVIEW

SysML includes nine diagrams, as shown in the taxonomy in Figure 3.1. Each diagram kind is summarized here, along with its relationship to UML diagrams:

- *Package diagram* – presents the organization of a model in terms of packages that contain model elements (same as UML package diagram).
- *Requirement diagram* – presents text-based requirements and their relationships to other requirements, design elements, and test cases to support requirements traceability (not in UML).
- *Activity diagram* – presents flow-based behavior indicating the order in which actions execute based on the availability of their inputs, outputs, and control, and how the actions transform the inputs to outputs (modification of UML activity diagram).
- *Sequence diagram* – presents behavior in terms of a sequence of messages exchanged between systems or parts of systems (same as UML sequence diagram).
- *State machine diagram* – presents behavior of an entity in terms of its transitions between states triggered by events (same as UML state machine diagram).
- *Use case diagram* – presents functionality in terms of how a system is used by external entities (i.e., actors) to accomplish a set of goals (same as UML use case diagram).
- *Block definition diagram* – presents structural elements, called blocks, and their composition and classification (modification of UML class diagram).
- *Internal block diagram* – presents interconnection and interfaces between the parts of a block (modification of UML composite structure diagram).
- *Parametric diagram* – presents constraints on property values, such as F = m * a, used to support engineering analysis (not in UML).

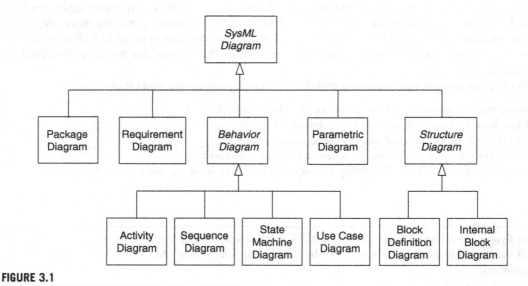

FIGURE 3.1

SysML diagram taxonomy.

A diagram presents selected model elements from the system model. The kinds of model elements and associated symbols (e.g., diagram elements) that can appear on a diagram are constrained by the diagram's kind. For example, an activity diagram can include diagram elements that present actions, control flow, and input/output flow (i.e., object flow), but not diagram elements for connectors and ports. Tabular presentations, such as allocation tables, are also supported in SysML as a complement to diagrams.

3.3 INTRODUCING SysML-Lite

SysML-Lite is introduced here as a simplified version of the language to help users start modeling with SysML. It is not referenced in the SysML specification. It includes six of the nine SysML diagrams and a small subset of the available language features for each diagram kind. SysML-Lite provides significant modeling capabilities. This section provides a brief introduction to SysML-Lite, including a simple example to highlight its features. Tool tips to assist new modelers in the use of a typical modeling tool are also covered.

3.3.1 SysML-Lite DIAGRAMS AND LANGUAGE FEATURES

The six kinds of diagrams that are part of SysML-Lite are highlighted in Figure 3.2. Each diagram contains a header that identifies the diagram kind and other information about the diagram that is explained in Chapter 5, Section 5.2. In particular, SysML-Lite includes:

* package diagrams to present the model organization;
* requirement diagrams to present text-based requirements and their relationships;
* activity diagrams to present the behavior of the system and its components;
* block definition diagrams to present the system hierarchy;
* internal block diagrams to present the system interconnection; and
* parametric diagrams to present the relationship among system properties to support engineering analysis.

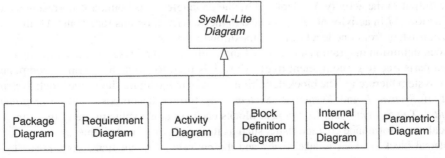

FIGURE 3.2

SysML-Lite includes six of the nine SysML diagrams and a subset of the language features. It is intended to introduce new modelers to SysML while providing substantial modeling capabilities.

This set of diagrams provides a model user with substantial capability for modeling systems that covers many of the classical systems engineering diagrams and more.

SysML-Lite includes a small subset of the language features for each of the six SysML diagrams. Some of the features of SysML-Lite are presented in the diagrams in Figure 3.3. The precise subset of SysML language features can be adapted as needed. The figure also shows thick lines with arrowheads that are not part of the language but highlight some of the important cross diagram relationships. These relationships generally support classical systems engineering methods, such as functional decomposition and allocation.

The package diagram, labeled *pkg*, is used to organize the **model elements** contained in the model. In this diagram, the *System Model* appears in the diagram header and contains packages for *Requirements*, *Behavior*, *Structure*, and *Parametrics*. Each of these packages, in turn, contains model elements that are presented on the requirement diagram, activity diagram, block definition diagram, internal block diagram, and parametric diagram, respectively. Note that model elements for both the block definition diagram and internal block diagram are contained in the *Structure* package.

The requirement diagram is labeled *req* and presents a simple hierarchy of text-based requirements that are typically part of a specification document. The top level requirement named *R1* contains two requirements, *R1.1* and *R1.2*. The corresponding requirement statement for *R1.1* is captured as a text property of the requirement and corresponds to the text that would be found for this requirement in a specification document.

The activity diagrams are labeled *act*. The activity diagram named *A0* presents the interaction between *System 1* and *System 2*. The initial node (shown as the filled dark circle) and final node (shown as the bulls-eye) indicate the start and finish of the activity, respectively. The activity specifies a simple sequence of actions, beginning with the execution of action *:A1*, which is followed by the execution of action *:A2*. The colon (*:*) in the action names and in other symbols indicates a particular usage associated with a reusable definition, which is described in Chapter 4, Section 4.3.12 and further described in Chapter 7, Section 7.3.1 and Chapter 9, Section 9.4.2. The output of *:A1* and the input of *:A2* are depicted by rectangles on the action boundary called pins. In addition, the activity partitions labeled *:System 1* and *:System 2* are responsible for performing the actions that are enclosed by the partitions. The action called *:A1* satisfies the requirement *R1.2*, which is represented by the *satisfy* relationship.

The action called *:A1* in the activity diagram *A0* is decomposed in the activity diagram called *A1* into actions *:A1.1* and *:A1.2*. These actions are performed by *:Component 1* and *:Component 2*, respectively. The output of the activity *A1*, depicted by the rectangle on its boundary, corresponds to the output pin of action *:A1* in activity *A0*. As indicated in the activity diagrams for *A0* and *A1*, the outputs and inputs are consistent from one level of decomposition to the next.

The block definition diagram is labeled *bdd* and is often used to describe the hierarchy of a system, similar to a parts tree (e.g., equipment tree). A block is used to define a system or component at any level of the system hierarchy. The block definition diagram in the figure shows the block *System Context* composed of *System 1* and *System 2*. *System 1* is further decomposed into *Component 1* and *Component 2*. The *System 1* and *Component* blocks each contain a value property that can correspond to a physical or performance characteristic, such as its weight or response time.

The internal block diagram is labeled *ibd* and the enclosing diagram frame corresponds to *System 1*. This diagram shows how the parts of *System 1* are interconnected. The small squares on *System 1* (i.e,, the frame) and its parts (i.e., *:Component 1* and *:Component 2*) are called ports and represent their interfaces. The lines connecting the ports are called connectors. *System 1* is also shown as the

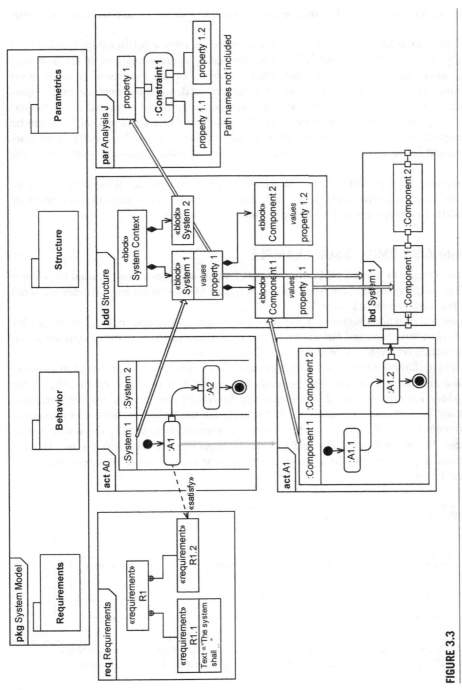

FIGURE 3.3

Simplified diagrams highlighting some of the language features for each kind of diagram in SysML-Lite.

activity partition in the activity *A0*, and the components are similarly shown as activity partitions in the activity *A1*.

The parametric diagram is labeled *par* and is used to describe parametric relationships that are used in engineering analysis, such as performance, reliability, and mass properties analysis. In this example, the parametric diagram includes a single constraint called *Constraint 1* that expresses an equation or set of equations. The small squares flush with the inside of the constraint depict the parameters of the equation. The properties of the system and component blocks can be bound to the parameters of the equations to establish an equality relationship. In this way, the parameters of a particular analysis can be aligned with the properties of the system design. Often, a single constraint is used to specify an analysis in terms of its input and output parameters, without specifying the detailed equations contained by the analysis.

In the above diagrams, only a small subset of the SysML language features are illustrated to indicate some of the key constructs used to model systems. The following simplified model of an air compressor illustrates how SysML-Lite diagrams and language features can be applied.

3.3.2 SysML-Lite AIR COMPRESSOR EXAMPLE

The following is an example of using SysML-Lite to model an air compressor that is used to power a pneumatic tool. This model is highly simplified for the purposes of illustration and includes the same kind of diagrams that were shown in Figure 3.3.

Figure 3.4 shows the package diagram for the *Air Compressor Model* and includes packages for *Requirements*, *Behavior*, *Structure*, and *Parametrics*. This model organization follows a similar pattern as described in the section on SysML-Lite above and shown in Figure 3.3.

The *Requirements* package contains a set of requirements that would generally be found in a system specification for the air compressor. The requirements are captured in the requirement diagram in Figure 3.5. The top level requirement called *Air Compressor Specification* contains a functional requirement to compress air, performance requirements that specify the maximum pressure and maximum flow rate, a requirement to specify storage capacity, power requirements to specify the source power needed to compress the air, and reliability and portability requirements. The text for the *Storage Capacity* requirement appears in the diagram, whereas the text for the other requirements is not displayed to reduce the clutter.

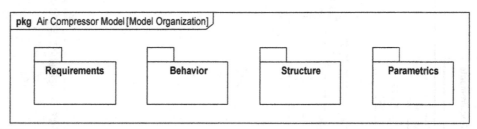

FIGURE 3.4

This package diagram is used to organize the *Air Compressor Model* into packages for *Requirements, Structure, Behavior,* and *Parametrics*. Each package contains model elements that can be related to model elements in other packages.

The *Behavior* package contains an activity diagram, shown in Figure 3.6, called *Operate Air Tool*, that specifies how the *Air Compressor* interacts with the external systems, including the *Air Tool*, the *Atmosphere*, and indirectly with the *Operator*. The *Air Compressor* and the external systems are shown as activity partitions. The *Air Compressor* performs the function (i.e., action) called *Compress Air*, which has a *low pressure air* input and a *high pressure air* output. The activity begins at the initial node (i.e., dark-filled circle), and then the *Operator* executes the *Control Tool* action. The activity completes its execution at the activity final node (i.e., bulls-eye symbol), after the *Operator* completes the *Control Tool* action. The *Compress Air* action is further decomposed in Figure 3.9.

The *Structure* package contains the blocks presented in the block definition diagrams in Figure 3.7 and Figure 3.8. The block definition diagram in Figure 3.7 called *Air Compressor Top Level* includes a block called the *Air Compressor Context* that is composed of the *Air Compressor* and the entities that are external to the *Air Compressor* representing the user, external system, and the physical environment. In this example, the user is the *Operator*, the external system is the *Air Tool*, and physical environment is the *Atmosphere*. The block definition diagram in Figure 3.8 is called *Air Compressor System Hierarchy*. The *Air Compressor* block in this figure is the same block that is shown in Figure 3.7, but this figure shows that the *Air Compressor* block is composed of components that include the *Motor Controller*, *Motor*, *Pump*, and *Tank*. The *Air Compressor*, *Motor*, *Tank*, and *Pump* all include value properties that are used to analyze the flow rate requirements.

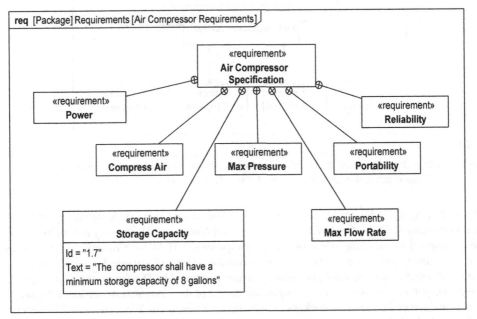

FIGURE 3.5

This requirement diagram presents the requirements contained in the *Requirements* package to specify the *Air Compressor*. Each requirement can include the requirements text that is typically found in a specification document.

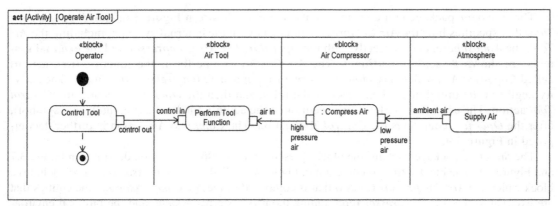

FIGURE 3.6

This activity diagram specifies the interaction between the *Air Compressor*, *Operator*, *Air Tool*, and *Atmosphere* to perform the *Operate Air Tool* activity.

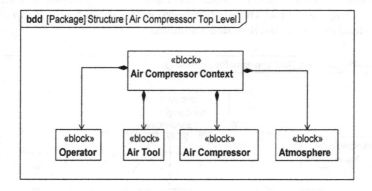

FIGURE 3.7

This block definition diagram shows the *Air Compressor*, *Operator*, *Air Tool*, and *Atmosphere* as blocks. The *Air Compressor Context* block provides the context for the *Air Compressor*.

The activity diagram in Figure 3.9 decomposes the action called *Compress Air* from Figure 3.6 to specify how the components of the *Air Compressor* interact to compress the air. The activity partitions in this activity diagram correspond to the components of the air compressor. The *Motor Controller* performs actions to *Sense Pressure* and *Control Motor*. The *Motor* performs the action to *Generate Torque*, the *Pump* performs the action to *Pump Air*, and the *Tank* performs the action to *Store Air*. The *low pressure air* input and *high pressure air* output are consistent with the input and output of the *Compress Air* action in Figure 3.6. This activity is contained in the *Behavior* package along with the *Operate Air Tool* activity in Figure 3.6.

The internal block diagram named *Interconnection* in Figure 3.10 shows how the components of the *Air Compressor* from Figure 3.8 are interconnected. The diagram frame corresponds to the *Air Compressor* block and the ports on the diagram frame depict the external interfaces of the *Air Compressor*. The ports on the parts represent the component interfaces, and the connectors connect the ports to one

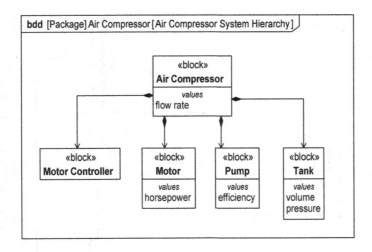

FIGURE 3.8

This block definition diagram shows the *Air Compressor* and its components. The *Air Compressor* block is the same block that is shown in Figure 3.7.

another. The component parts shown on the internal block diagram are contained in the *Structure* package along with the blocks on the block definition diagram.

The block definition diagram called *Analysis Context* in Figure 3.11 is used to define the context for performing the flow rate analysis. In particular, it includes a block called *Flow Rate Analysis* to represent the analysis. This block is composed of a constraint block called *Flow Rate Equations*, which contains the equations used to analyze *flow rate*. In this particular example, only the parameters of the flow rate equations are shown, and not the equations. The *Flow Rate Analysis* block also refers to the *Air Compressor Context* block from Figure 3.7, which is the subject of the analysis.

Defining the *Analysis Context* enables a parametric diagram to be created for the *Flow Rate Analysis* block as shown in Figure 3.12. The diagram shows the value properties of the *Air Compressor* and its parts, including *flow rate*, tank *volume* and *pressure*, motor *horsepower*, and pump *efficiency*, and the binding of these properties to the parameters of the *Flow Rate Equations*. The flow rate analysis equations can be solved by an analysis tool to determine the property values for the *Air Compressor* and its parts. The analysis context pattern is described further in Chapter 8, Section 8.10 and Chapter 17, Section 17.3.6.

This air compressor example illustrates how a system can be modeled with a subset of SysML diagrams and language features called SysML-Lite. Even a simple model such as this can contain many model elements and quickly become difficult to manage. A modeling tool is needed to efficiently build a model that is self consistent and to manage complexity. The following section describes how a typical SysML modeling tool is used to build this model.

3.3.3 SysML MODELING TOOL TIPS

This section provides a brief introduction on how to start modeling with a typical **SysML modeling tool**. The question of how to start modeling often arises when one uses a modeling tool for the first time. Although various tools may have significant differences, the tools typically share much

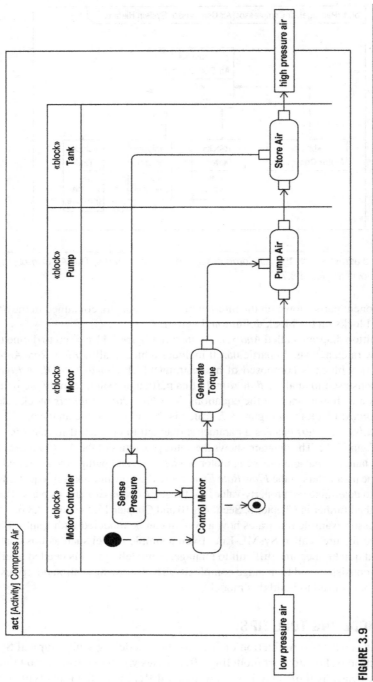

FIGURE 3.9

This activity diagram shows how the components of the *Air Compressor* interact to perform the *Compress Air* action from Figure 3.6.

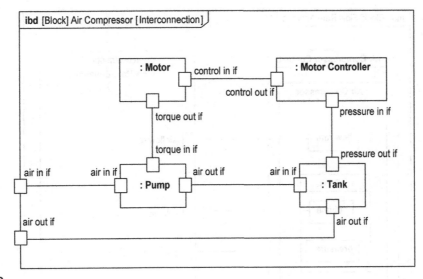

FIGURE 3.10

This internal block diagram shows how the components of the *Air Compressor* are interconnected via their ports, which specify the component interfaces.

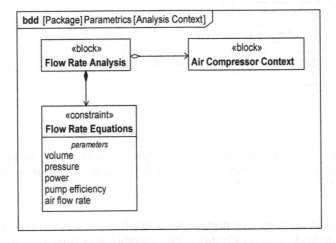

FIGURE 3.11

This block definition diagram is used to specify the *Flow Rate Analysis* in terms of a constraint block that defines the equations and parameters for the analysis (equations not shown), and the *Air Compressor Context*, which is the subject of the analysis.

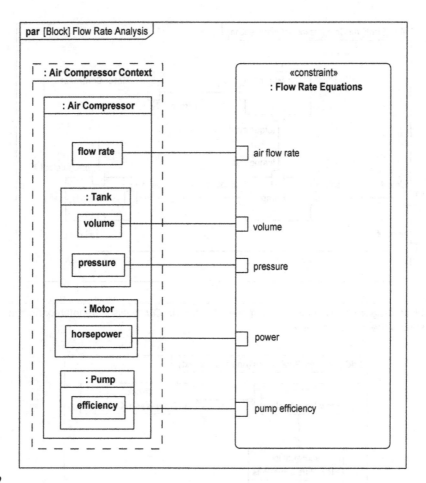

FIGURE 3.12

This parametric diagram shows the *Flow Rate Analysis* and how the parameters of the equations are bound to the properties of the design. Once captured, this analysis can be provided to an analysis tool to perform the analysis. The equations are not shown in the figure.

in common from a user interface perspective. As a result, once a modeler learns how to build a SysML model in one tool, it generally takes considerably less time to learn how to model in another tool.

The tool interface

The user interface for a typical modeling tool is shown in Figure 3.13, and includes a diagram area, a pallet (also known as toolbox), a model browser, and a toolbar. The diagram appears in the diagram area. The pallet includes diagram elements that are used to create or modify a diagram. The pallet is typically context sensitive such that the diagram elements that appear in the pallet depend on the

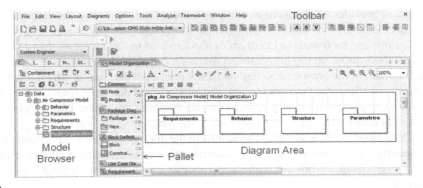

FIGURE 3.13

A typical SysML modeling tool interface consists of a diagram area, a pallet or toolbox, a model browser, and a toolbar. The model browser shows the hierarchy of model elements that are contained in the model.

diagram that is being viewed in the diagram area. For example, if a block definition diagram is being viewed in the diagram area, then the pallet will contain blocks and other elements used on a block definition diagram, whereas if an activity diagram is being viewed, the pallet will include actions and other elements used on an activity diagram. The model browser is a third part of the user interface. It presents a hierarchical view of the model elements contained in the model. A typical view of the browser shows the model elements grouped into a package hierarchy, where each package appears as a folder that can be expanded to view its contents. A package may contain other nested packages. The toolbar contains a set of menu selections that support different user actions related to file management, editing, viewing, configuring tool features, and other actions. Many modeling tools also enable further tool customization, such as the ability to develop scripts that perform additional model checking.

Some basic tool functionality includes adding a diagram; adding elements and relationships to the diagram; navigating between the diagram and the browser; deleting elements from the diagram and/or browser; and adding, modifying, and deleting details of a particular model element.

To create a new diagram, a modeler selects a diagram kind and names the diagram. There are often multiple ways to select a diagram kind, such as from a diagram menu or a diagram icon from the toolbar. The new diagram appears in the diagram area without any content. The diagram header information is visible and includes the diagram kind, the diagram name, and other information about the diagram frame.

The modeler can then drag a diagram element from the pallet onto the diagram in the diagram area and name the new element. Once this is done, the corresponding model element appears in the browser. Alternatively, the modeler can add the new model element directly in the browser, then drag this model element onto the diagram. A model element appears in only one place in the browser, but may appear on zero, one, or more diagrams.

Other diagram elements can be added to the diagram in a similar way. Allowable relationships between elements can be added by selecting the relationship symbol from the pallet and dragging it from one element to another. Alternatively, many tools provide a context sensitive menu to select the relationship from one element and drag it to the other element. The relationship appears in the browser like other model elements.

A modeling tool provides mechanisms to navigate between the symbol on the diagram and the corresponding model element in the browser. This can be convenient, because a large model may contain hundreds of diagrams and thousands or hundreds of thousands of model elements. Most tools allow the modeler to select the symbol on the diagram and find its location in the browser. A modeler can also select a model element in the browser and find its location on each diagram in which it appears.

The modeling tool allows the modeler to show and hide selected details of the model on any particular diagram. This is important for managing the complexity of the diagrams. The modeler only shows what is considered important to support the purpose of the diagram.

If the modeler wishes to delete a model element from the diagram, the tool may prompt the modeler whether to delete the model element from the diagram only or to delete the model element from the model as well by removing it from the browser. A modeler can also delete a model element directly from the browser.

A modeling tool has many other capabilities that enable a modeler to develop and manage a system model. Once the model element is created, the modeler can typically select the model element and open its specification, where details of the model element can be added, modified, or deleted. The modeler can also select a model element on the diagram and query the modeling tool to show all of the directly related model elements that can appear on that particular kind of diagram.

It is also worth noting that the modeling tool is often used in conjunction with a configuration management tool to put the model under configuration control. This is particularly important when modeling as part of a distributed team where multiple people are working on the same model. In such cases, a typical configuration management tool will allow read and/or write privileges to be assigned to a user to control access to different parts of the model. Once this is done, a modeler with read privileges assigned to a particular part of the model can view that part of the model, while a modeler with write privileges can also check out and modify that part of the model.

Chapter 18 describes how the SysML modeling tool integrates into a systems development environment with many other tools, including configuration management, requirements management, hardware and software design, and analysis tools. It also includes suggested criteria for selecting a SysML modeling tool.

Building the model

The following illustrates how to build the *Air Compressor Model* introduced in Section 3.3.2 in a typical modeling tool. Each tool will have a particular style of user interface, and different modeling guidelines and MBSE methods may suggest various ways to get started. The following example provides a representative starting point, which can be further adapted to the specific modeling tool, modeling guidelines, and MBSE method.

The modeler must first install and configure the modeling tool so that it can be used to build a model that is expressed in SysML. Many SysML tools also support UML and perhaps other modeling languages, so the modeler may be required to select and apply the SysML profile (refer to Chapter 15, Section 15.5 for a discussion of profiles). Once this is done, a modeler can create a new project and name it. In this example, the project is named Air Compressor Project.

As indicated in Figure 3.13, the first step in building the model is to create the top level package called the *Air Compressor Model* in the browser. The modeler can then select this package in the browser and create nested packages for *Requirements*, *Behavior*, *Structure*, and *Parametrics* (sometimes called *Analysis*). Alternatively, the modeler can create a new package diagram (as shown in Figure 3.13) by dragging new packages from the pallet onto the diagram and naming them accordingly.

The modeler can now begin to populate the packages with model elements by creating the diagrams in Figure 3.5 through Figure 3.12. For this example, the sequence for creating the diagrams will mirror the ordering of the figures, but the sequence can vary depending on the MBSE method, the availability of information, and/or user preference. Some elements used on a particular diagram may be created on another diagram. The modeler may partially complete one diagram, switch to another diagram to add elements, and then return to the original diagram to use those elements. In other words, modeling can be a highly iterative process where various parts of the model are created on one diagram, and used on other diagrams.

The modeler creates the requirements diagram shown in Figure 3.5 by selecting the *Requirements* package in the browser, creating a new requirement diagram, and naming it *Air Compressor Requirements*. Once the diagram appears in the diagram area, the modeler can drag new requirements from the pallet onto the diagram and name them to correspond to the requirements in the figure. The top level parent requirement, called *Air Compressor Specification*, can be connected to each of its child requirements with the cross hair symbol by using the context sensitive menu on the parent or child. The text for the requirement statement can be added to the *Storage Capacity* requirement by opening the specification for this model element and adding the text to the text property. Additional diagram presentation options may be required to display or hide the text on the diagram.

The modeler next creates the top level activity diagram *Operate Air Tool* shown in Figure 3.6. This is done by selecting the *Behavior* package, creating a new activity diagram, and naming the diagram *Operate Air Tool*. The modeler may drag actions from the pallet onto the activity diagram, along with the initial and final nodes, and connect the actions with the appropriate flow. The control flow is used to connect the initial node to *Control Tool*, and another control flow connects *Control Tool* to the activity final node. The object flows connect the outputs from one action to the input of another. The inputs and outputs are the small rectangles on the actions called pins, and can be created by selecting an input pin or output pin from the context sensitive menu. The activity partitions can be added after the *Air Compressor* and external entities have been defined, which is done in the next step of this process.

The modeler next creates the block definition diagram for the *Air Compressor Context* shown in Figure 3.7. This is accomplished by selecting the *Structure* package in the browser, creating a new block definition diagram, and naming it *Air Compressor Top Level*. A new block can be dragged from the pallet onto the diagram and called *Air Compressor Context*. The other blocks can then be defined similarly. The composition relationship between the *Air Compressor Context* block and the other blocks can be established using the context sensitive menu to select the composition relationship designated by the black diamond on one end of the line. Alternatively, the composition relationship can be selected from the pallet.

Once the blocks are defined, the activity partitions (i.e., swim lanes) that correspond to the blocks in the activity diagram in Figure 3.6 can be added. This activity diagram specifies the interaction between the *Air Compressor*, *Operator*, *Air Tool*, and *Atmosphere* to perform the *Operate Air Tool* activity. The previously created activity diagram, *Operate Air Tool,* can be viewed by selecting it from the *Behavior* package in the browser. The modeler then drags the activity partitions from the pallet onto the diagram and ensures that the actions are enclosed by the partitions as shown in the figure. In order to define an activity partition that corresponds to a particular block, the modeler opens the activity partition specification, then selects the particular block that is represented by the partition. For example, the activity partition that encloses *Compress Air* corresponds to the *Air Compressor* block. In this way, each action is placed within the activity partition corresponding to the block that is responsible for performing the action.

The modeler can then decompose the system into its component parts by creating the block definition diagram shown in Figure 3.8. This is done by selecting the *Structure* package, creating a new block definition diagram, and naming it *Air Compressor System Hierarchy*. New blocks can be dragged from the pallet onto the diagram and named. The relationships are established in a way similar to that described for the block definition diagram called *Air Compressor Top-Level* in Figure 3.7. The ports on each of the blocks can then be created by dragging a port from the pallet onto the block or—alternatively—by selecting a block, opening its specification, and adding the ports. In addition, the properties of the block can be added by selecting the block on the diagram or in the browser, opening the block's specification, adding the property, and naming it. In Figure 3.8, the ports are included in the model but are not shown to further simplify the diagram.

The modeler next creates the activity diagram to *Compress Air* as shown in Figure 3.9. This activity represents the decomposition of the *Compress Air* action that the *Air Compressor* performs in the *Operate Air Tool* activity in Figure 3.6. The modeler selects the *Compress Air* action in the *Operate Air Tool* activity, and then creates a new activity diagram named *Compress Air*. The tool is expected to ensure that the inputs and outputs to this activity are consistent with the input and output pins for the *Compress Air* action. This activity diagram shows how the components of the *Air Compressor* perform the *Compress Air* activity. The actions, flows, and activity partitions contained within this activity will be created in a similar way as for the *Operate Air Tool* activity. The activity partitions correspond to the component blocks from the *Air Compressor System Hierarchy* block definition diagram.

The modeler next creates the internal block diagram shown in Figure 3.10 to show how the parts of the *Air Compressor* are connected to one another. This is accomplished by selecting the *Air Compressor* block from the *Structure* package in the browser and creating a new internal block diagram. Some tools automatically populate the internal block diagram with the parts of the block that are typed by the component blocks in the *Air Compressor System Hierarchy* block definition diagram. A summary explanation of types is included in Chapter 4, Section 4.3.12, and a detailed treatment of this topic is provided in Chapter 7. The ports on the parts may not be visible on the diagram, even if they have been previously defined in the model. Many tools require the modeler to select the part and activate a menu item to display the ports. The ports can be connected to one another once the ports are visible on the diagram. A modeler may also connect the parts without ports, and add or connect to ports later if desired.

The modeler next creates the block definition diagram in Figure 3.11 to define the *Flow Rate Analysis* in terms of analysis constraints and the subject of the analysis. This is done by selecting the *Parametrics* package in the browser, creating a new block definition diagram, and naming the diagram *Analysis Context*. The *Flow Rate Analysis* block is created, and the *Air Compressor Context* block that is contained in the *Structure* package is dragged onto the diagram and referenced by the *Flow Rate Analysis* block using the aggregation relationship with the white diamond. A new constraint block is dragged from the pallet and named *Flow Rate Equations*. The *Flow Rate Analysis* block is related to the constraint block with a composition relationship (black diamond). The parameters of the flow rate equations are added to the constraint block in a way similar to the adding of properties to blocks as described earlier. The equations can be defined as part of the constraint block as well.

The modeler next creates the parametric diagram shown in Figure 3.12 in the Parametrics package. The constraint property, which is typed by the *Flow Rate Equations* constraint block, and a part, which is typed by the *Air Compressor Context* block, are dragged from the browser onto the diagram. The tool may automatically populate the diagram in the same way it does with parts. The *Air Compressor Context* is selected on the diagram, and its nested parts and properties are displayed. Different tools accomplish this in different ways. Once this is done, the value properties contained in the *Air Compressor*, *Tank*, *Motor*, and *Pump* can be connected to the parameters of the *Flow Rate Equations* constraint.

Creating this example in the modeling tool is a first step to learning how to model. Once this is understood, one can learn additional SysML language features and explore additional tool capabilities, such as diagram layout functions, documentation and report generation, and model execution. The automobile example in Chapter 4 introduces the remaining three SysML diagrams and additional language features that can serve as a next step in the learning process. The language features are described in detail in the chapters in Part II.

3.4 A SIMPLIFIED MBSE METHOD

In addition to learning the modeling language and tools, a modeler must apply a model-based systems engineering (MBSE) method that adheres to sound systems engineering and modeling practices in order to build quality system models. SysML provides a means to capture the system modeling information without imposing a specific MBSE method.

The selected **MBSE method** determines the modeling activities that are performed, the ordering of the activities, and the kinds of modeling artifacts produced. For example, traditional structured analysis methods can be used to decompose the functions and then allocate the functions to components. Alternatively, one can apply a scenario-driven method that derives the system functionality by analyzing the scenarios and the interactions among the parts. The two methods may involve different activities and produce different combinations of diagrams to present the system specification and design information. Several MBSE methods are documented in the *Survey of Model-based Systems Engineering Methodologies* [6]. Chapters 16 and 17 provide two examples using different MBSE methods.

The top level activities for a simplified MBSE method are highlighted in Figure 3.14. The activities are consistent with the systems engineering process introduced in Chapter 1, Section 1.2. The system model represents the system specification and design information, and is the primary artifact produced by this method. This method includes one or more iterations of the following activities to specify and design the system:

- *Organize the Model.*
  - Define the package diagram to organize the system model.
- *Analyze Stakeholder Needs* to understand the problem to be solved, the goals the system is intended to support, and the effectiveness measures needed to evaluate how well the system supports these goals and satisfies the stakeholder needs.
  - Identify the stakeholders and the problems to be addressed.
  - Define the domain model (e.g., block definition diagram) to identify the system and external systems and users.
  - Define the top level use cases to represent the goals the system is intended to support.
  - Define the effectiveness measures (moes) that can be used to quantify the value of a proposed solution for the stakeholders.

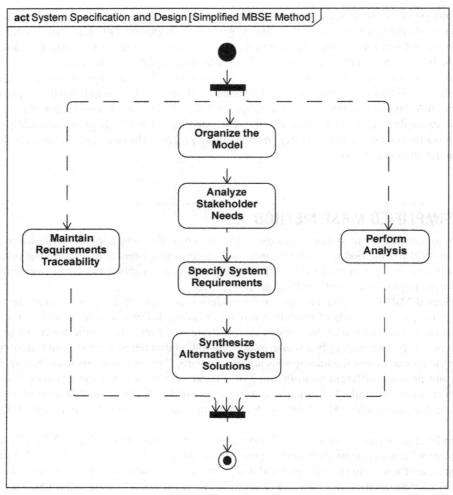

FIGURE 3.14

A simplified MBSE method that is consistent with the systems engineering process described in Chapter 1, Section 1.2. The method is used to produce the modeling artifacts that constitute the system model.

- *Specify System Requirements*, including the required system functionality, interfaces, physical and performance characteristics, and other quality characteristics to support the goals and effectiveness measures.
  - Capture text-based requirements that support the system goals and effectiveness measures in a requirement diagram.
  - Model each use-case scenario as an activity diagram to specify the system behavior requirements.
  - Create the system context diagram (internal block diagram) to specify the system external interfaces.

- *Synthesize Alternative System Solutions* by partitioning the system design into components that can satisfy the system requirements.
  - Decompose the system using the block definition diagram.
  - Define the interaction among the parts using activity diagrams.
  - Define the interconnection among the parts using the internal block diagram.
- *Perform Analysis* to evaluate and select a preferred system solution that satisfies the system requirements and maximizes the effectiveness measures.
  - Capture the analysis context (block definition diagram) to identify the analysis to be performed, such as performance, mass properties, reliability, cost, and other critical properties.
  - Capture each analysis as a parametric diagram.
  - Perform the engineering analysis to determine the values of the system properties (Note: the analysis is performed using engineering analysis tools).
- *Maintain Requirements Traceability* to ensure the proposed solution satisfies the system requirements and associated stakeholder needs.
  - Capture the traceability between the system requirements and the stakeholder needs (e.g., use cases, measures of effectiveness) on a requirements diagram.
  - Show how the system design satisfies the system requirements on a requirements diagram or table.
  - Identify test cases needed to verify the system requirements on a requirements diagram or table and capture the verification results.

Other systems engineering management activities—such as planning, assessment, risk management, and configuration management—are performed in conjunction with the modeling activities described above. The next chapter includes a simplified example that illustrates many of the model-based artifacts that are generated when applying a MBSE method such as the one described in this section. More detailed examples of how SysML can be used to support a functional analysis and allocation method and an object-oriented systems engineering method (OOSEM) are included in the modeling examples in Part III, Chapters 16 and 17, respectively.

3.5 THE LEARNING CURVE FOR SysML AND MBSE

Learning SysML and MBSE requires a commitment similar to what is expected when learning modeling for mechanical, electrical, software, and other technical disciplines. The challenges to learning SysML and MBSE have additional factors that contribute to its learning curve. In particular, a major focus for model-based systems engineering approaches is the ability to understand a system from multiple perspectives and to ensure integration across the different perspectives. In SysML, the system requirements, behavior, structure, and parametrics each represents different aspects of the system that need to be understood both individually and together.

Each of the individual perspectives introduces its own complexity. For example, the modeler may represent behavior using activity diagrams to specify precisely how a system responds to a stimulus. This involves specifying the details of how the system executes each use-case scenario. The activity diagrams may be integrated into a composite system behavior that is captured in a state machine diagram. Representing detailed behavior and integrating different behavior formalisms, such as activity diagrams and state machines, can introduce complexity.

As stated above, the modeler must maintain a consistent model that reflects many different perspectives. SysML is often used to express hierarchies for requirements, behavior, structure, and parametrics. Each hierarchy must be self consistent, such as the different levels of the behavior and structure hierarchy. The model must also be consistent across the different hierarchies. Some of these relationships are highlighted in the examples in Sections 3.3.1–2. Additional discipline-specific views— such as a safety view, reliability view, security view, or manufacturing view—may span requirements, behavior, structure, and parametrics. Again, ensuring consistency among these cross-cutting views introduces additional complexity to system modeling and MBSE.

SysML is a more complex language than some of its predecessors, such as IDEF0. It provides significant expressive capabilities to represent the various perspectives described above. SysML is also a typed language, which can significantly enhance reuse. For example, a SysML model can differentiate a front wheel from a rear wheel of a vehicle, while reusing the same definition of wheel. As a typed language, SysML also enables more effective integration with analysis models by providing the capability to describe complex data structures, such as the position of the system in terms of its x, y, and z coordinates with their respective units. These capabilities do not come without some added complexity. As the language evolves, it is anticipated that the tools will hide some of the complexity, and other enhancements will make the language more intuitive, such as increased emphasis on domain specific symbology.

An effective MBSE approach not only requires a language such as SysML to be capable of representing systems but also requires a method that defines the activities and artifacts, as well as a tool to implement the modeling language and method. The language, method, and tool each introduce their own concepts that must be learned to master model-based systems engineering. The language, method, and tool must be further adapted to a particular application domain, such as to the design of aircraft, automobiles, telecommunication systems, medical devices, and others, which introduces further complexities.

Additional modeling challenges are associated with scaling the modeling effort to larger projects. Challenges of managing the model come into play. Multiple modelers may be in multiple locations using different tools. Disciplined processes and tools are needed to manage changes to the models. The SysML model must integrate with many different kinds of models, such as analysis models; electrical, mechanical, and software design models; and verification models. The integration and management of the different models, tools, and other engineering artifacts is another challenge associated with MBSE.

Model-based systems engineering formalizes the practice of performing systems engineering. The complexity and associated challenges for learning MBSE reflect the inherent complexity and challenges of applying systems engineering to the development of complex systems. Some of this complexity was highlighted in the automobile design example in Chapter 1, Section 1.3, independent of the MBSE approach. When starting out on the MBSE journey, it is important to set expectations for the challenges of learning MBSE and how to apply it to a domain of interest. In addition to reaping the potential benefits of MBSE described in Chapter 2, embracing these challenges and becoming proficient in SysML and MBSE can provide a deeper understanding of systems and systems engineering concepts.

3.6 SUMMARY

SysML is a general-purpose graphical language for modeling systems that may include hardware and equipment, software, data, people, facilities, and other elements within the physical environment. The language supports modeling of requirements, structure, behavior, and parametrics to provide a robust description of a system, its components, and its environment.

The language includes nine diagram kinds each with many features. The semantics of the language enable a modeler to develop an integrated model of a system, where each kind of diagram can present a different view of the system being modeled. The model elements on one diagram can be related to model elements on other diagrams. The diagrams enable capturing the information in a model repository and viewing the information from the repository, to help specify, design, analyze, and verify systems. To facilitate the learning process, SysML-Lite was introduced, which includes six of the nine SysML diagrams and a relatively small subset of the language features for each diagram kind. Learning how to model this subset of the language in a modeling tool can provide a sound foundation on which to build.

The SysML language is a critical enabler of MBSE. Effective use of the language requires a well-defined MBSE method. This chapter introduced a simplified MBSE method to aid in getting started, but SysML can be used with a variety of MBSE methods.

SysML enables representation of a system from multiple perspectives. Each of the individual perspectives may be complex in its own right, but ensuring a consistent model that integrates across the different perspectives introduces additional challenges to learning SysML and MBSE. When learning SysML as part of an overall MBSE approach, the process, methods, and tools introduce their own concepts and complexity. Using SysML in support of MBSE formalizes the practice of systems engineering. Ultimately, the challenges of SysML and MBSE reflect the inherent complexities of applying systems engineering to develop complex systems. The learning expectations should be set accordingly.

3.7 QUESTIONS

1. What are five aspects of a system that SysML can represent?
2. What is a package diagram used for?
3. What is a requirement diagram used for?
4. What is an activity diagram used for?
5. What is the block definition diagram used for?
6. What is an internal block diagram used for?
7. What is a parametric diagram used for?
8. What are some of the common elements of the user interface of a typical SysML modeling tool?
9. Which part of the user interface presents a hierarchical view of the model elements contained in the model?
10. What is the purpose of applying an MBSE method?
11. What are the primary activities of the simplified MBSE method?

DISCUSSION TOPICS

What are some factors that contribute to the challenges of learning SysML and MBSE, and how do they relate to the general challenges of learning systems engineering?

AN AUTOMOBILE EXAMPLE USING THE SysML BASIC FEATURE SET

This chapter introduces the **basic feature set** of SysML. The basic feature set applies to all nine SysML diagrams and provides an expanded subset of the language features beyond the features of SysML-Lite that were introduced in the previous chapter. The basic feature set provides significant functionality of the language without adding the complexity associated with the full feature set of SysML.

In this chapter, a system model of an automobile similar to the one that was introduced in Chapter 1, Section 1.3, illustrates the use of the basic feature set. This example includes references to the chapters in Part II that provide a more detailed description of the diagrams and language concepts. The subset of the SysML constructs that comprise the basic feature set are highlighted by shaded paragraphs in Part II and in the notation tables in Appendix A.

4.1 THE SysML BASIC FEATURE SET AND SysML CERTIFICATION

The basic and full feature set provides language functionality that can be learned in steps and are the basis for SysML certification. The SysML certification program is called the OMG Certified Systems Modeling Professional (OCSMP) [39]. The OCSMP has four levels of certification. The first two levels of certification cover the basic feature set of SysML. These two levels are referred to as Model User and Model Builder-Fundamental. A modeler certified at the Model User level is expected to be able to interpret SysML diagrams that use the basic feature set, while a modeler certified at the Model Builder-Fundamental level is expected to be able to build models that use the basic feature set. The third level covers the full feature set of SysML. An individual certified at this level is called a Model Builder-Intermediate and is expected to be able to build models that use the full feature set of SysML. The fourth level covers additional modeling concepts that extend beyond SysML.

4.2 AUTOMOBILE EXAMPLE OVERVIEW

The following simplified example illustrates how the basic feature set of SysML can be applied as part of a model-based approach to specify and design an automobile system. This example is similar to the automobile example that was introduced in Chapter 1, Section 1.3, which described how the systems engineering process can be applied to the specification and system level design of an automobile. In Chapter 1, no assumptions were made regarding the use of a model-based approach. The example in this chapter highlights how a typical MBSE method can be used to generate modeling artifacts to help specify and design a system. The MBSE method is similar to the one introduced in Chapter 3, Section 3.4. Chapters 16 and 17 introduce much more detailed examples of how MBSE methods can be applied.

This example illustrates most of the SysML basic feature set and includes at least one diagram for each SysML diagram kind. A few features in the example extend beyond the basic feature set of SysML—including continuous and streaming flows and generalization sets—because they illustrate important features for this particular example. These additional features are noted in the example where they are used. References are also included in this section to the chapters and sections in Part II that provide a detailed description of these features.

This example also includes user-defined language concepts referred to as **stereotypes**. Chapter 15 describes how stereotypes are used to customize the language for domain-specific applications. The user defined concepts used in this example are shown below using the name of the concept in brackets:

```
«hardware»
«software»
«store»
«system of interest»
```

All SysML diagrams include a **diagram frame** that encloses the diagram header and diagram content. The **diagram header** describes the kind of diagram, the diagram name, and additional information that provides context for the **diagram content**. Detailed information on diagram frames and diagram headers is described in Chapter 5, Section 5.2.

4.2.1 PROBLEM SUMMARY

This example describes the use of SysML to specify and design an automobile system. As mentioned earlier, the modeling artifacts included in this example are representative of the kinds of modeling artifacts that are generated from a typical MBSE method similar to the one described in Chapter 3, Section 3.4. Only a small subset of the system requirements and design are addressed in this example to highlight the use of the language. The diagrams used in this example are shown in Table 4.1.

A marketing analysis that was conducted indicated the need to increase the automobile's acceleration and fuel efficiency from its current capability. In this simplified example, selected aspects of the design are considered to support an initial trade-off analysis. The trade-off analysis includes an evaluation of alternative vehicle configurations that included a 4-cylinder engine and a 6-cylinder engine to determine if they can satisfy the acceleration and fuel efficiency requirement.

Table 4.1 Diagrams Used in Automobile Example

Figure	Diagram Kind	Diagram Name
4.1	Package diagram	Model Organization
4.2	Requirement diagram	Automobile System Requirements
4.3	Block definition diagram	Automobile Domain
4.4	Use case diagram	Operate Vehicle
4.5	Sequence diagram	Drive Vehicle
4.6	Sequence diagram	Turn On Vehicle
4.7	Activity diagram	Control Power
4.8	State machine diagram	Drive Vehicle States
4.9	Internal block diagram	Vehicle Context
4.10	Block definition diagram	Vehicle Hierarchy
4.11	Activity diagram	Provide Power
4.12	Internal block diagram	Power Subsystem
4.13	Block definition diagram	Analysis Context
4.14	Parametric diagram	Vehicle Acceleration Analysis
4.15	Timing diagram (not SysML)	Vehicle Performance Timeline
4.16	Block definition diagram	Engine Specification
4.17	Requirement diagram	Max Acceleration Requirement Traceability
4.18	Package diagram	Architect and Regulator Viewpoints

4.3 AUTOMOBILE MODEL
The following subsections describe the system model for the automobile example.

4.3.1 PACKAGE DIAGRAM FOR ORGANIZING THE MODEL
The concept of an integrated system model is a foundational concept for MBSE, as described in Chapter 2, Section 2.1.2. The model contains the model elements, which are stored in a model repository. A particular model element may appear on zero, one, or multiple diagrams. In addition, a model element often has relationships to other model elements that may appear on the same diagram or other diagrams.

A model organization is essential to managing the model. A well-organized model is analogous to having a set of drawers to organize your supplies, where each supply element is contained in a drawer, and each drawer is contained in a particular cabinet. The model organization facilitates understandability, access control, change management, and reuse of the model.

The package diagram for the automobile example is shown in Figure 4.1. The diagram kind is shown as *pkg* and the name of the diagram is *Model Organization*. The package diagram shows how the model is organized into **packages**. This model organization includes an expanded set of packages

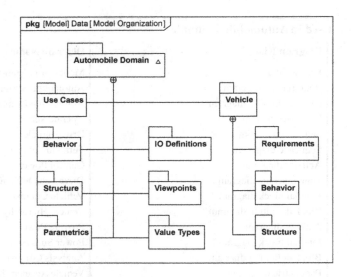

FIGURE 4.1

Package diagram showing how the model is organized into packages that contain the model elements that comprise the *Automobile Domain.*

over those that were introduced in the air compressor example using SysML-Lite in Chapter 3, Section 3.3.2. Each package **contains** a set of model elements, and each model element is contained in only one package. The package is said to own the elements that are contained within it. The package is also a namespace for the contained model elements, giving each model element a unique name within the model that is called its fully qualified name. A model element in one package can have relationships to model elements in other packages. Details on how to organize a model with packages are provided in Chapter 6.

The model organization for this example includes a package called the *Automobile Domain.* This package is the top-level model (designated by a triangle) that contains all the other model elements for the automobile example. The *Automobile Domain* contains nested packages for *Use Cases, Behavior, Structure, Parametrics, IO Definitions, Viewpoints, Value Types,* and *Vehicle.* The *Vehicle* package contains additional nested packages for *Requirements, Behavior,* and *Structure.* The *Use Cases, Behavior, Structure,* and *Parametrics* packages contain model elements about the vehicle context and its external environment, whereas the *Vehicle* package contains model elements about the vehicle design. The *IO Definitions* package contains elements to specify the interfaces, such as port definitions and inputs and output definitions. The *Viewpoints* package defines selected views of the model that address specific stakeholder concerns. The *Value Types* package contains definitions that are used to specify units for quantitative properties called **value properties**.

The rest of this example describes the content of these packages. Model elements contained in packages can be referenced by their fully qualified name as described above. The qualified name includes the path name relative to the model in which it is contained using a double colon (::) as a separator. For example, an activity called Provide Power in the vehicle behavior package in Figure 4.1 is designated as *Automobile Domain::Vehicle::Behavior::*Provide Power.

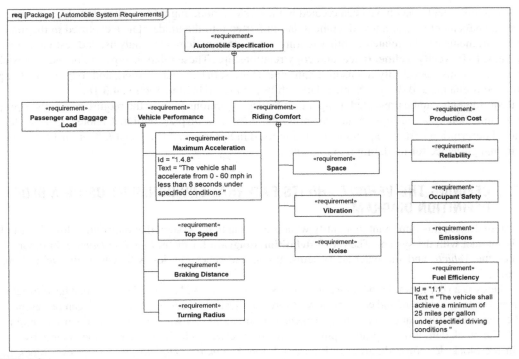

FIGURE 4.2

Requirement diagram showing the system requirements contained in the *Automobile Specification*.

4.3.2 CAPTURING THE *AUTOMOBILE SPECIFICATION* IN A REQUIREMENT DIAGRAM

The **requirement diagram** for the Automobile System is shown in Figure 4.2. The upper left of the diagram shows *req* to indicate its kind as a requirement diagram and displays the diagram name as *Automobile System Requirements*. The diagram header also indicates that the diagram frame corresponds to a *Package*.

The diagram presents the requirements that are typically captured in a text specification. The requirements are shown in a containment hierarchy to represent their parent–child relationships. The line with the crosshairs symbol at the top denotes **containment**. The *Automobile Specification* is the top-level requirement that contains the other requirements.

The *Automobile Specification* contains requirements for *Passenger and Baggage Load, Vehicle Performance, Riding Comfort, Emissions, Fuel Efficiency, Production Cost, Reliability,* and *Occupant Safety*. The *Vehicle Performance* requirement contains requirements for *Maximum Acceleration, Top Speed, Braking Distance,* and *Turning Radius*. Each requirement includes a unique identification and the text of the requirement, and can also include other user-defined properties that are typically associated with requirements, such as verification status and risk. The text for the *Maximum Acceleration* requirement is "The vehicle shall accelerate from 0 to 60 mph in less than 8 seconds under specified conditions" and the text for the *Fuel Efficiency* requirement is "The vehicle shall achieve a minimum of 25 miles per gallon under specified driving conditions."

The requirements may have been created in the SysML modeling tool or, alternatively, in a requirements management tool or a text document and imported into the model. Once captured in the model, the requirements can be related to other requirements, design elements, analysis, and test cases using **derive, satisfy, verify, refine, trace,** and **copy** relationships. These relationships can be used to establish requirements traceability to ensure requirements are satisfied and verified, and to manage change to the requirements and design. Some relationships are highlighted in Section 4.3.18.

Requirements can be presented using multiple display options to view the requirements, their properties, and their relationships. A tabular presentation is one display option. Chapter 13 provides a detailed description of how requirements are modeled in SysML, and Chapter 17, Section 17.3.7, gives additional guidance for modeling requirements.

4.3.3 DEFINING THE *VEHICLE* AND ITS EXTERNAL ENVIRONMENT USING A BLOCK DEFINITION DIAGRAM

In system design, it is important to identify what is external to the system that may either directly or indirectly interact with the system. The **block definition diagram** for the *Automobile Domain* in Figure 4.3 defines the *Vehicle* and the external systems, users, and other entities with which the vehicle may interact.

A **block** is a very general modeling concept in SysML that is used to model entities that have structure, such as systems, hardware and equipment, software, or physical object. That is, a block can represent any real or abstract entity that can be conceptualized as a structural unit with one or more distinguishing features. The block definition diagram captures the relation between blocks, such as a block hierarchy.

In the block definition diagram in Figure 4.3, the *Automobile Domain* is the top-level block that provides the context for the *Vehicle*. The *Automobile Domain* block is composed of other blocks that include the *Vehicle* block (designated as the «system of interest») and other blocks that are external to the *Vehicle*. The other blocks include the *Driver, Passenger, Baggage,* and *Physical Environment*.

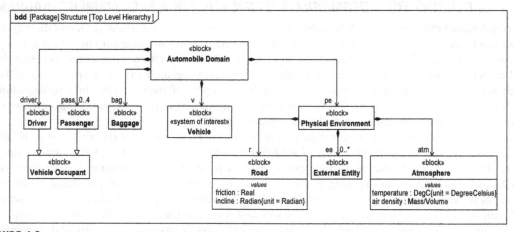

FIGURE 4.3

Block definition diagram of the *Automobile Domain* showing the *Vehicle* as the *system of interest*, along with the *Vehicle Occupants* and the Environment. Selected value properties for the *Road* and *Atmosphere* are also shown.

Notice that even though the *Driver, Passenger,* and *Baggage* are assumed to be physically enclosed by the *Vehicle,* they are not part of the *Vehicle,* and therefore are external to it.

This whole–part relationship is called a **composite association** and is indicated by the black diamond symbol and a line with the arrowhead pointing to the blocks that compose it. The name next to the arrow on the part side of the composite association identifies a particular usage of a block as described in Sections 4.3.10 and 4.3.12. The composition hierarchy is explained in Chapter 7, Section 7.3.1. It is different from containment (crosshair symbol), which connects parent to child requirements as shown in Figure 4.2. Requirement containment hierarchies are described in Chapter 13, Section 13.9.

The *Driver* and *Passenger* are **subclasses** of *Vehicle Occupant* as indicated by the hollow triangle symbol. This means that they inherit common features from *Vehicle Occupant.* In this way, a classification can be created by specializing blocks from more generalized blocks.

The *Physical Environment* is composed of the *Road, Atmosphere,* and multiple *External Entities.* The *External Entity* can represent any physical object, such as a traffic light or another vehicle, with which the *Driver* interacts. The interaction between the *Driver* and an *External Entity* can impact how the *Driver* interacts with the *Vehicle,* such as when the *Driver* sees the traffic light change from green to yellow or red, and then applies the brakes. The **multiplicity** symbol *0..** represents an undetermined maximum number of external entities. The multiplicity symbol can also express a positive integer such as 4, or a range, such as the multiplicity of *0..4,* for the number of *Passengers.*

Each block defines a structural unit, such as a system, hardware, software, data element, or other conceptual entity. A block can have a set of **features**. The features of the block include its **value properties** (e.g., weight), its **behavior** in terms of activities **allocated** to the block or **operations** of the block, and its interfaces as defined by its **ports.** Together, these features enable a modeler to specify the block at the level of detail that is appropriate for the intended use.

The *Road* is a block that has a value property called *incline* with units of *Radians* and a value property called *friction* that is defined as a real number. Similarly, *Atmosphere* is a block that has two value properties for *temperature* and *air density.* These value properties and others are used to support the analysis of vehicle acceleration and fuel efficiency, which are discussed in Sections 4.3.13–16.

The block definition diagram specifies the blocks and their interrelationships. It is often used in systems modeling to depict multiple levels of the system hierarchy from the top-level domain or context block (e.g., *Automobile Domain)* down to the blocks representing the vehicle components. Chapter 7 provides a detailed description of how blocks are modeled in SysML, including their features and relationships.

4.3.4 USE CASE DIAGRAM FOR *OPERATE VEHICLE*

The **use case diagram** for *Operate Vehicle* in Figure 4.4 depicts some of the high-level functionality involved in operating the vehicle. The **use cases** are contained in the *Use Cases* package and include *Enter Vehicle, Exit Vehicle, Control Vehicle Accessory,* and *Drive Vehicle.* The *Vehicle* is the **subject** of the use cases and is depicted as a rectangle. The *Vehicle Occupant* is an **actor** that is external to the vehicle and is shown as a stick figure. In a use case diagram, the subject (e.g., *Vehicle)* is used by the actor (e.g., *Vehicle Occupant)* to achieve the actor goals defined by the use cases (e.g., *Drive Vehicle).* The actors are allocated to the blocks with the same name in Figure 4.3 to establish equivalence between them. The allocation is not shown in the diagrams.

The *Passenger* and *Driver* are both a type of *Vehicle Occupant.* All vehicle occupants participate in entering and exiting the vehicle and controlling vehicle accessories, but only the *Driver* participates in *Drive Vehicle.*

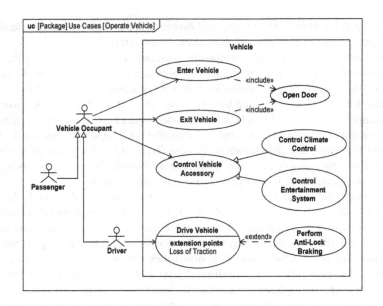

FIGURE 4.4

The use case diagram describes the major functionality in terms of how the *Vehicle* is used by the *Vehicle Occupants* to *Operate Vehicle*. The *Vehicle* and *Vehicle Occupants* are defined on the block definition diagram in Figure 4.3.

SysML provides the ability to specify relationships between use cases. The *Enter Vehicle* and *Exit Vehicle* use cases include the *Open Door* use case. The *Open Door* use case defines common functionality that is always performed when the *Enter Vehicle* and *Exit Vehicle* use cases are performed. *Enter Vehicle* and *Exit Vehicle* are referred to as the base use cases, and *Open Door* is referred to as the included use case. The relationship is called the **include** or **inclusion** relationship. The *Perform Anti-Lock Braking* use case extends the base use case called *Drive Vehicle*. Anti-lock braking is only performed under certain conditions as specified by the extension point called *Loss of Traction*. This relationship is called **extension** or **extends**, which relates the extending use case (i.e., *Perform Anti-Lock Braking*) to the base use case (i.e., *Drive Vehicle*). In addition to inclusion and extension relationships, use cases can be specialized as indicated by the subclasses of the *Control Vehicle Accessory* use case. The specialized use cases for *Control Climate Control* and *Control Entertainment System* all share the common functionality of *Control Vehicle Accessory* use case, but also have their own specific functionality associated with the particular accessory.

Use cases define the goals for using the system across the system lifecycle, such as the goals associated with manufacturing, operating, and maintaining the vehicle. The primary emphasis for this example is the operational use case for *Drive Vehicle* to address the acceleration and fuel efficiency requirements. Chapter 12 provides a detailed description of how use cases are modeled in SysML.

Use cases are often related to requirements, since use cases represent the high-level functionality or goals for the system. A use case often refines a set of requirements. Sometimes, a use case textual description is defined to accompany the use case definition. The steps in the use case description can also be captured as SysML requirements and related to the use case using a refine relationship.

The use cases are realized through interactions between the actors (e.g., *Driver)* and the subject (e.g., *Vehicle)* as described in the next section.

4.3.5 SPECIFYING *DRIVE VEHICLE* BEHAVIOR WITH A SEQUENCE DIAGRAM

The behavior for the *Drive Vehicle* use case in Figure 4.4 is shown in the **sequence diagram** in Figure 4.5. The sequence diagram specifies the **interaction** between the *Driver* and the *Vehicle* as indicated by the names at the top of the **lifelines.** Time proceeds vertically down the diagram. The first interaction is *Turn On Vehicle.* This is followed by *Driver* and *Vehicle* interactions to *Control Power, Control Brake,* and *Control Direction.* These three interactions occur in parallel as indicated by **par.** The **alt** on the *Control Power* interaction stands for alternative and indicates that the *Control Neutral Power, Control Forward Power,* or *Control Reverse Power* interaction occurs as a condition of the *vehicle state* shown in brackets. The state machine diagram in Section 4.3.8 specifies the *vehicle state.* The *Turn Off Vehicle* interaction occurs following these interactions.

The **interaction uses** in the figure each reference a more detailed interaction as indicated by **ref.** The referenced interaction for *Turn On Vehicle* is another sequence diagram that is illustrated in Section 4.3.6. The sequence diagrams for the *Drive Vehicle* and other referenced interactions are contained in the *Automobile Domain::Behavior* package. The references for *Control Neutral Power, Control Forward Power,* and *Control Reverse Power* are allocated to an activity diagram that is described in Section 4.3.7.

4.3.6 REFERENCED SEQUENCE DIAGRAM TO *TURN ON VEHICLE*

The *Turn On Vehicle* sequence diagram in Figure 4.6 is an interaction that is referenced in the sequence diagram in Figure 4.5. As stated previously, time proceeds vertically down the diagram. In this example, the sequence diagram shows the driver sending an *ignition on* **signal** to start the vehicle. The vehicle sends a *vehicle on* signal to the driver that the vehicle has started.

The sequence diagram can include multiple kinds of **messages.** In this example, the message is **asynchronous** as indicated by the open arrowhead. For asynchronous messages, the sender does not wait for a reply. A **synchronous** message is shown with a filled arrowhead. A synchronous message is an operation call that specifies a request for service, where the sender waits for a reply. The arguments of the operation call are the input data and return.

The example in Figure 4.6 is very simple. More complex sequence diagrams can include multiple message exchanges between multiple lifelines that represent interacting entities. The sequence diagram also provides additional capability to express behavior that includes other kinds of messages, timing constraints, additional control logic, and the ability to decompose the behavior of a lifeline into the interaction of its parts. Chapter 10 provides a detailed description of how interactions are modeled with sequence diagrams.

4.3.7 *CONTROL POWER* ACTIVITY DIAGRAM

The sequence diagram is effective for expressing behavior that emphasizes control flow and discrete signal flow, such as the *Turn On Vehicle* sequence diagram in Figure 4.6. However, behaviors that emphasize input and output flow as well as control flow, such as the interactions to *Control Power, Control Brake,* and *Control Direction,* can sometimes be more effectively expressed with activity diagrams.

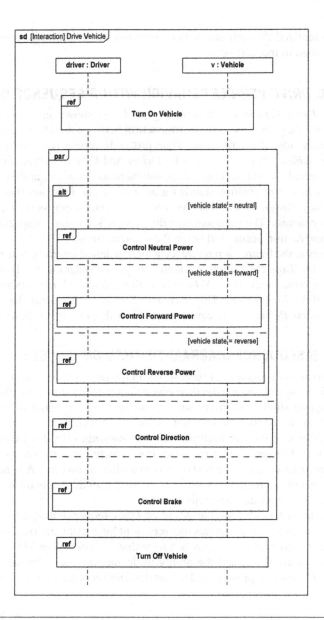

FIGURE 4.5

The *Drive Vehicle* sequence diagram describes the interaction between the *Driver* and the *Vehicle* to realize the *Drive Vehicle* use case in Figure 4.4.

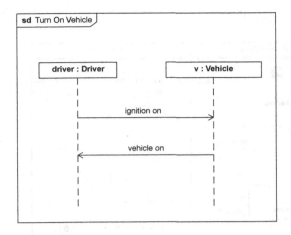

FIGURE 4.6

Sequence diagram for the *Turn On Vehicle* interaction that was referenced in the *Drive Vehicle* sequence diagram in Figure 4.5, showing the message from the *Driver* requesting *Vehicle* to start, and the *Vehicle* responding with the *vehicle on* reply.

The *Drive Vehicle* sequence diagram in Figure 4.5 includes the references to *Control Neutral Power*, *Control Forward Power*, and *Control Reverse Power*. Activity diagrams can be used to express the details of these interactions. To accomplish this, the *Control Neutral Power*, *Control Forward Power*, and *Control Reverse Power* interactions are **allocated** to a corresponding *Control Power* activity using the SysML allocate relationship (not shown). This activity is contained in the *Behavior* package of the *Automobile Domain*.

The **activity diagram** in Figure 4.7 shows the **actions** required of the *Driver* and the *Vehicle* to *Control Power*. The **activity partitions** (or **swim lanes**) correspond to the *Driver* and the *Vehicle*. The actions in the activity partitions specify functional requirements that the *Driver* and *Vehicle* must perform.

When the activity is initiated, it starts execution at the **initial node** (filled in circle), and then proceeds to the **fork node** to enable the start of both the *Control Accelerator Position* action and the *Control Gear Select* action that is performed by the *Driver*. The output of the *Control Accelerator Position* action is the *Accelerator Cmd*, which is a continuous input to the *Provide Power* action that the *Vehicle* must perform. The *Control Gear Select* action produces an output called *Gear Select*. The output of the *Provide Power* action is the continuous *torque out* to accelerate the *Vehicle*. When the *Ignition Off* signal is received by the *Vehicle* (called an **accept event action**), the activity terminates at the **activity final node** (bulls-eye symbol). Based on this scenario, the *Driver* is required to *Control Accelerator Position* and *Control Gear Select*, and the *Vehicle* is required to *Provide Power*. The *Provide Power* action is a **call behavior action** that invokes a more detailed behavior when it executes, which is shown in Figure 4.11. (Note: «continuous» is not part of the basic feature set.)

Activity diagrams include semantics for precisely specifying the behavior in terms of the flow of control and flow of inputs and outputs. A control flow is used to specify the sequence of actions and is depicted as a dashed line with an arrowhead (as shown in Figure 4.7) going to and from the fork node. An object flow is used to specify the flow of inputs and outputs, which are depicted by the rectangular

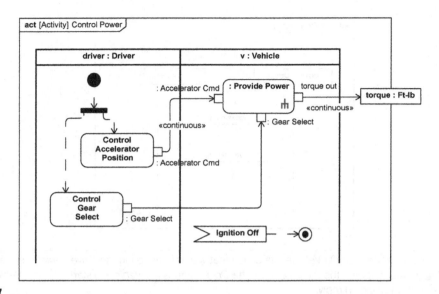

FIGURE 4.7

Activity diagram allocated from the *Control Neutral, Forward*, and *Reverse Power* interaction uses that are referenced in the *Drive Vehicle* sequence diagram in Figure 4.5. It shows the continuous *Accelerator Cmd* input and the *Gear Select* input from the *Driver* to the *Provide Power* action that the *Vehicle* must perform.

pins on the actions. The object flow (solid line with arrowhead) connects the output pin from one action to the input pin of another action. Chapter 9 provides a detailed description of how activities are modeled.

4.3.8 STATE MACHINE DIAGRAM FOR *DRIVE VEHICLE STATES*

The **state machine diagram** for the *Drive Vehicle States* is shown in Figure 4.8. This diagram shows the states of the *Vehicle* and the **events** that can **trigger** a **transition** between the **states**.

When the *Vehicle* is ready to be driven, it is initially in the *vehicle off* state. The receipt of the *ignition on* signal from the sequence diagram in Figure 4.6 is an event that triggers a transition to the *vehicle on* state. The text on the transition indicates that the *Start Vehicle* behavior is executed prior to entering the *vehicle on* state.

Upon entry to the *vehicle on* state, an **entry behavior** is performed, *Check Status*, to confirm the health of the vehicle. Following completion of the entry behavior, the *Vehicle* initiates the *Provide Power* behavior called a **do behavior** that is referred to in the activity diagram in Figure 4.7.

Once the *Vehicle* has entered the *vehicle on* state, it immediately transitions to the *neutral* state. A *forward select* event triggers a transition to the *forward* state if the **guard condition** *[speed>=0]* is true. The *neutral select* event triggers the transition from the *forward* state to return to the *neutral* state. The state machine diagram shows the additional transitions between the *neutral* and *reverse* states. An *ignition off* event triggers the transition back to the *vehicle off* state. Prior to exiting the *vehicle on* state and transitioning to the *vehicle off* state, the *Vehicle* performs an **exit behavior** to *Turn Off Accessories*. From the *vehicle off* state, the *Vehicle* can re-enter the *vehicle on* state when an *ignition on* event occurs.

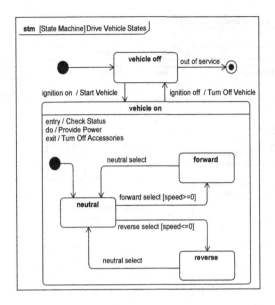

FIGURE 4.8

A state machine diagram that shows the *Drive Vehicle States* and the transitions between them.

This state machine can be owned by the *Vehicle* block, in which case it resides in the same package as the *Vehicle* block, or it can be owned by the vehicle's *Behavior* package and reside within that package.

A state machine can specify the lifecycle behavior of a block in terms of its discrete states and transitions, and is often used with sequence and/or activity diagrams, as shown in this example. State machines have many other features, which are described in Chapter 11, including support for multiple regions to describe concurrent behaviors and additional transition semantics.

4.3.9 *VEHICLE CONTEXT* USING AN INTERNAL BLOCK DIAGRAM

The *Vehicle Context* Diagram is shown in Figure 4.9. The diagram shows the interfaces between the *Vehicle*, the *Driver*, and the *Physical Environment* (i.e., *Road*, *Atmosphere*, and *External Entity*) that were defined in the block definition diagram in Figure 4.3. The *Vehicle* directly interfaces with the *Driver*, the *Atmosphere*, and the *Road*. The *Driver* interfaces with the *External Entities* such as a traffic light or another vehicle via the *Sensor Input* to the *Driver*. However, the *Vehicle* does not directly interface with the *External Entities*. The multiplicity on the *External Entity* is consistent with the multiplicity shown in the block definition diagram in Figure 4.3.

This context diagram is an **internal block diagram** that shows how the **parts** of the *Automobile Domain* block from Figure 4.3 are connected. It is called an internal block diagram because it represents the internal structure of a higher-level block, which in this case is the *Automobile Domain* block. The *Vehicle* **ports** are shown as the small squares on the boundary of the parts and specify interfaces with other parts. **Connectors** are shown as lines between the ports and define how parts connect to one another. Parts can also be connected without ports when the details of the interface are not of interest to the modeler as indicated by the connections to the *Atmosphere* and *External Entity*.

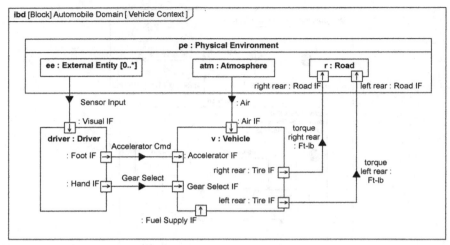

FIGURE 4.9

The internal block diagram for the *Automobile Domain* describes the *Vehicle Context*, which shows the *Vehicle* and its external interfaces with the *Driver* and the *Physical Environment* that were defined in Figure 4.3.

The external interfaces that enable the *Vehicle* to provide power are shown in Figure 4.9. The interfaces between the rear tires and the road are shown, since the *Vehicle* is assumed to be rear wheel drive. The interfaces to both rear tires are shown, because the power can be distributed differently to the left and right rear wheels depending on tire-to-road traction and other factors. The interfaces between the front tires and the road are not shown in this diagram. It is common modeling practice to present only the information relevant to the purpose of the diagram, even though additional information may be included in the model.

The black-filled arrowheads on the connector are called **item flows**. They represent the items flowing between parts. The items that flow may include mass, energy, and/or information. In this example, the *Accelerator Cmd* that was previously defined in the activity diagram in Figure 4.7 flows from the *Driver Foot IF* to the *Vehicle Accelerator IF,* and the *Gear Select* flows from the *Driver Hand IF* to the *Vehicle Gear Select IF.* The object flows that connect the inputs to the outputs on the activity diagram in Figure 4.7 can be **allocated** to the item flows on the connectors in the internal block diagram. Allocations are discussed as a general-purpose relationship for mapping one model element to another in Chapter 14.

SysML ports provide substantial capability to model interfaces. Ports can specify the items that can flow in or out of a part, and the services that are either required or provided by a part. The port provides a mechanism to integrate the behavior of the system with its structure by enabling access to a part's behavior and other features. (Refer to the discussion on ports in Chapter 7, Section 7.6.)

The internal block diagram enables the modeler to specify both the external and internal interfaces of a block and shows how its parts are connected. Details of how to connect parts on an internal block diagrams are described in Chapter 7, Section 7.3.

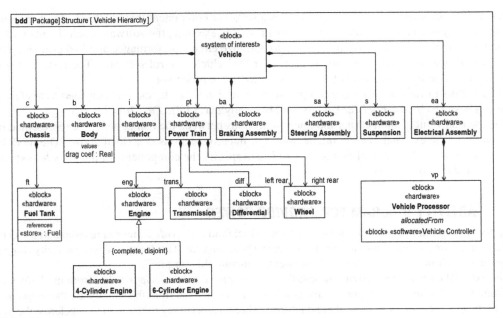

FIGURE 4.10

A block definition diagram of the *Vehicle Hierarchy* that shows the *Vehicle* and its components. The *Power Train* is further decomposed into its components, and the *Vehicle Processor* includes the *Vehicle Controller* software.

4.3.10 *VEHICLE HIERARCHY* REPRESENTED ON A BLOCK DEFINITION DIAGRAM

The example to this point has focused on specifying the vehicle in terms of its external interactions and interfaces. The *Vehicle* package shown in Figure 4.1 contains the description of the *Vehicle* and its parts in terms of its requirements, structure, and behavior. The *Vehicle* block is contained in the *Automobile Domain::Vehicle::Structure* package.

The *Vehicle Hierarchy* in Figure 4.10 is a block definition diagram that shows the decomposition of the *Vehicle* into its components. The *Vehicle* is composed of the *Chassis, Body, Interior, Power Train,* and other components. Each hardware component is designated as «hardware».

The *Power Train* is further decomposed into the *Engine, Transmission, Differential,* and *Wheel*. Note that the *right rear* and *left rear* indicate different usages of a *Wheel* in the context of the *Power Train*. Thus, each rear wheel has a different role and may be subject to different forces, such as is the case when one wheel loses traction. The front wheels are not shown in this diagram.

The *Engine* may be either 4 or 6 cylinders as indicated by the specialization relationship. The 4- and 6-cylinder engine configurations are alternatives being considered to satisfy the acceleration and fuel efficiency requirements. The *engine size* is *{complete, disjoint}*, which asserts that the 4- and 6-cylinder engines represent all possible engine types for this *Vehicle*, and that the 4- and 6-cylinder engines are mutually exclusive. (Note: This construct is called a **generalization set** and is not part of the SysML basic feature set.)

The *Vehicle Controller* «software» specifies a software component that is allocated to the *Vehicle Processor* as shown in its allocation compartment. In this example, the software controls many of the automobile engine and transmission functions to optimize engine performance and fuel efficiency, and the *Vehicle Processor* is the execution platform for the vehicle control software. The *allocatedFrom*, label indicates that the allocation is from the software to the processor.

The *Fuel* is shown in a *references* compartment of the *Fuel Tank* block. It is indicated as a reference because it is stored by the *Fuel Tank* but is not physically part of the *Fuel Tank*.

The internal vehicle interactions and interconnections between the components are represented in a way similar to the external *Vehicle* interactions and interconnections described above. The modeling artifacts for this next lower level of design are used to specify the components of the *Vehicle* system as described in the next sections.

4.3.11 ACTIVITY DIAGRAM FOR *PROVIDE POWER*

The activity diagram in Figure 4.7 shows that the vehicle must *Provide Power* in response to the driver accelerator command and generate *torque out* at the road surface. The *Provide Power* activity diagram in Figure 4.11 shows how the vehicle components generate this torque.

The external inputs to the activity include the *:Accelerator Cmd* and *:Gear Select* from the *Driver,* and *:Air* from the *Atmosphere* to support engine combustion. The outputs from the activity are the *torque right rear* and *torque left rear* from the right and left rear wheels respectively to the road to accelerate the *Vehicle.* The inputs and outputs for the *:Provide Power* action in Figure 4.7 are elaborated as a result of further refinement of the model, and now include *:Air* as an input, and torque from each rear wheel. Some of the other inputs and outputs, such as exhaust from the engine, are not included for simplicity. The activity partitions represent usages of the vehicle components shown in the block definition diagram in Figure 4.10.

The *Vehicle Controller* accepts *Driver* inputs including the *:Accelerator Cmd* and *:Gear Select,* and provides outputs to the *Engine* and *Transmission.* The *Fuel Tank* stores and dispenses the *:Fuel* to the *Engine.* The *:Fuel-Air Cmd* from the *Vehicle Controller* and *:Air* from the *Atmosphere* are inputs to the *Generate Torque* action. The engine torque is input to the *Amplify Torque* action performed by the *Transmission.* The amplified torque is input to the *Distribute Torque* action performed by the *Differential,* which distributes torque to the right and left rear wheels. The wheels *Provide Traction* to the road surface to generate the torque to accelerate the *Vehicle.* The *Differential* monitors and controls the difference in torque to the rear wheels. If one of the wheels loses traction, the *Differential* sends a *Loss of Traction* signal to the braking system to adjust braking. The *Loss of Traction* signal is sent using a send signal action.

A few other items are worth noting in this example. The flows are shown to be continuous for all but the *Gear Select.* The inputs and outputs continuously flow in and out of the actions. *Continuous* means that the delta time between arrival of the inputs or outputs approaches zero. Continuous flows build on the concept of streaming inputs and output parameters, which means that the inputs are accepted and outputs are produced while the action is executing. Conversely, nonstreaming inputs are only available prior to the start of the action execution, and nonstreaming outputs are produced only at the completion of the action execution. The ability to represent streaming and continuous flows adds a significant capability to classic behavioral modeling using functional flow diagrams. The continuous flows are assumed to be streaming but this is not shown in the diagram. (Note: Continuous and streaming are not part of the basic feature set.)

Modeling of activities provides the capability to specify behavior precisely in terms of the flow of control and data. This is explained in Chapter 9.

4.3.12 INTERNAL BLOCK DIAGRAM FOR THE *POWER SUBSYSTEM*

The previous activity diagram describes how the parts of the system interact to *Provide Power.* The parts of the system are represented by the activity partitions in the activity diagram. The internal block diagram for the *Vehicle* in Figure 4.12 shows how the parts are interconnected via their ports to achieve this functionality. This is a structural view of the system, as opposed to the behavioral view that was expressed in the activity diagram.

The internal block diagram shows the *Power Subsystem* that includes the parts of the *Vehicle* that interact to *Provide Power.* The frame of the diagram corresponds to the *Vehicle* black box. The ports on the diagram frame in Figure 4.12 correspond to the same ports shown on the *Vehicle* in the *Vehicle Context* diagram in Figure 4.9. The external interfaces are preserved as the internal structure of the *Vehicle* is further elaborated.

The *Engine, Transmission, Differential, right rear:Wheel* and *left rear:Wheel, Vehicle Processor,* and *Fuel Tank* are interconnected via their ports. The *Fuel* is stored in the *Fuel Tank* as indicated by «store». *Fuel* is shown as a dashed rectangle to indicate that the fuel is not part of the *Fuel Tank,* but is referenced by it. Only selected item flows are shown on the connectors. The item flows are allocated from the inputs and outputs on the *Provide Power* activity diagram in Figure 4.11.

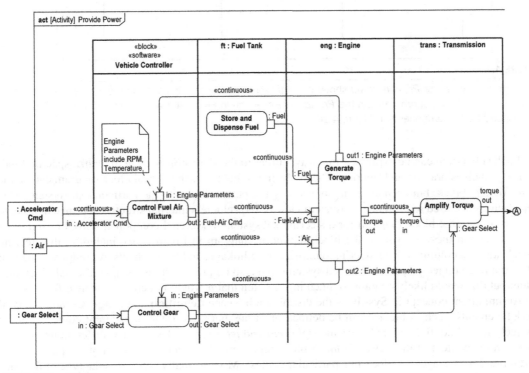

FIGURE 4.11   Cont'd

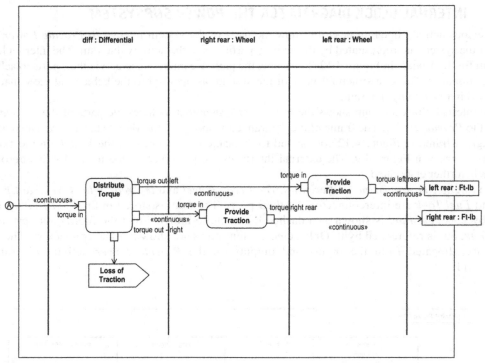

FIGURE 4.11

The activity diagram for *Provide Power* shows how the *Vehicle* components generate the torque to move the vehicle. This activity diagram realizes the *Provide Power* action in Figure 4.7 with activity partitions that correspond to the components in Figure 4.10.

Each subsystem can be expressed in a way similar to the *Power Subsystem* to realize specific functionality, such as braking and steering. The enclosing frame for each internal block diagram can be the same *Vehicle* block, but each diagram shows only the parts relevant to the particular subsystem. This approach can be used to present a subsystem view of the vehicle's internal structure. As an example, to express an internal block diagram for a steering subsystem, additional components would need to be defined beyond those shown on the block definition diagram in Figure 4.10, including the steering wheel, steering column, power steering pump, steering linkage, and front wheels. A composite view of all of the interconnected parts for all subsystems can also be presented on a single internal block diagram, but this would likely contain so much information that it would not communicate effectively.

An important concept in SysML is the distinction between **definition** and **usage**. Certain kinds of model elements, such as blocks, can be defined one time, but their usage in different contexts can be uniquely identified. In Section 4.3.10, the *right rear* and *left rear* are described as different usages of a *Wheel* in the context of the *Power Train*. A block represents the generic definition of the part, and the part represents a usage of a block in a particular context. More formally, a block is the type of the part, and a part is typed by a block.

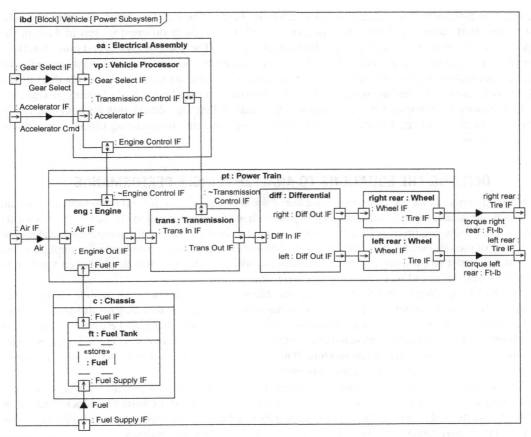

FIGURE 4.12

The internal block diagram for the *Power Subsystem* shows how the parts of the *Vehicle* that *Provide Power* are interconnected. The parts interact as specified by the activity diagram in Figure 4.11.

In Figure 4.10 and Figure 4.12, the *right rear* and *left rear* are different parts that represent distinct usages of *Wheel* in the context of the *Power Train*. Each usage of the block requires a composition relationship on the block definition diagram, such as the right rear wheel and left rear wheel in Figure 4.10. The colon (:) notation is used in Figure 4.12 to distinguish the part (i.e., usage) from the block (i.e., definition). The name to the right of the colon, *Wheel,* is the block. The names to the left of the colon, *right rear* and *left rear,* are particular parts or usages of *Wheel*. By convention, the usage names begin in lower case and the definitions begin with upper case.

A part enables the same block, such as a *Wheel,* to be reused in different contexts and be uniquely identified by its usage, such as *right rear* and *left rear*. Each part may be further redefined to have behaviors, value properties, and constraints that apply to its particular usage.

The concept of definition and usage applies to parts and blocks, but also applies to many other SysML language constructs. One example is that item flows can have both a definition and usage. For example, the item flow entering the fuel tank in Figure 4.12 can be *in: Fuel* and the item flow exiting the fuel tank can be *out : Fuel*. Both flows are defined by *Fuel*, but in and out represent different usages of *Fuel* in the *Vehicle* context (Note: the usages are not shown in the figure). The ports on blocks and pins on actions can also have definitions that specify detailed interface information that can be reused. As an example, the interface that enables the flow of 110 volt 60 cycle power can be defined one time and reused. For the *Automobile* example, most of the pins and ports have been typed and are contained in the *IO Definitions* package.

As mentioned previously, Chapter 7 provides the detailed language description for both block definition diagrams and internal block diagrams, and the key concepts for modeling blocks, parts, ports, and connectors.

4.3.13 DEFINING THE EQUATIONS TO ANALYZE VEHICLE PERFORMANCE

Critical requirements for the design of this automobile are to accelerate from 0 to 60 mph in less than 8 seconds, while achieving a fuel efficiency of greater than 25 miles per gallon. These two requirements impose conflicting requirements on the design space, because increasing the maximum acceleration capability of the vehicle can result in a design with lower fuel efficiency. Two alternative configurations (4- and 6-cylinder engine) are evaluated to determine which configuration is the preferred solution to meet the acceleration and fuel efficiency requirements.

The *4-Cylinder Engine* and *6-Cylinder Engine* alternatives are shown in the *Vehicle Hierarchy* in Figure 4.10. There are many possible impacts to the automobile design that may result from the selection of different engines, such as the impact on vehicle weight, body shape, and electrical power. This simplified example only considers some of the impacts on the *Power Subsystem*. The vehicle controller is assumed to control the fuel and air mixture. It also controls when the automatic transmission changes the gear to optimize engine and overall performance.

The *Analysis Context* block definition diagram in Figure 4.13 is used to define the equations for these analyses. This diagram introduces another kind of block called a **constraint block**. Instead of defining systems and components, the constraint block defines constraints in terms of reusable equations and their **parameter** definitions that can be used by one or more analyses.

In this example, the *Vehicle Acceleration Analysis* block is in the *Parametrics* package, as indicated by the diagram header, and comprises several constraint blocks that are used to analyze the vehicle acceleration. This analysis is performed to determine whether either the 4- or 6-cylinder vehicle configuration can satisfy its acceleration requirement. The constraint blocks define generic equations for *Gravitational Force, Drag Force, Power Train Force, Total Force, Acceleration*, and an *Integrator*. The *Total Force* equation, as an example, shows that *ft* is the sum of *fi, fj*, and *fk*. Note that the parameters are defined along with their units in the constraint block.

The *Power Train Force* is further decomposed into other constraint blocks that express the torque equations for the *Engine, Transmission, Differential*, and *Wheels*. The equations are not explicitly defined, but the critical parameters of the equations are identified. It is often useful in the early stages of an analysis to identify the critical parameters but defer definition of the equations until the detailed analysis is performed.

The *Vehicle Acceleration Analysis* block also references the *Automobile Domain* block that was originally shown in the block definition diagram in Figure 4.3. The *Automobile Domain* is the subject of the analysis. By referencing the *Automobile Domain*, the value properties of the *Vehicle* and the *Physical Environment* can be accessed and bound to the parameters of the generic equations, as described in the next section.

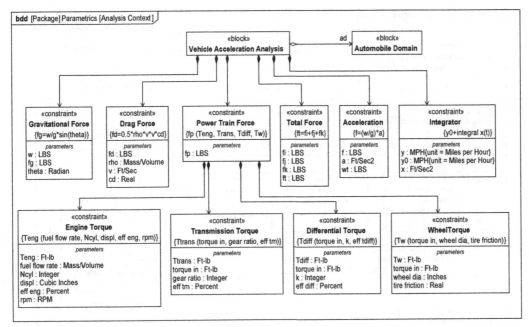

FIGURE 4.13

The block definition diagram for the *Analysis Context* that defines the equations for analyzing the vehicle acceleration requirement. The equations and their parameters are specified using constraint blocks. The *Automobile Domain* block from Figure 4.3 is referenced since it is the subject of the analysis.

4.3.14 ANALYZING VEHICLE ACCELERATION USING THE PARAMETRIC DIAGRAM

The previous block definition diagram defined the equations and associated parameters needed to analyze the system. The **parametric diagram** in Figure 4.14 shows how these equations are used to analyze the time for the *Vehicle* to accelerate from 0 to 60 mph and satisfy the maximum acceleration requirement. The diagram frame corresponds to the *Vehicle Acceleration Analysis* block from the block definition diagram in Figure 4.13.

The parametric diagram shows a network of constraints. Each constraint is a usage of a constraint block defined in the block definition diagram in Figure 4.13. The equations for some of the constraints are shown on this parametric diagram. The parameters of the equations are shown as small rectangles flush with the inside boundary of the constraint.

A parameter in one equation can be bound to a parameter in another equation by a **binding connector**. An example of this is the parameter *ft* in the *Total Force* equation, which is bound to the parameter *f* in the *Acceleration* equation. This means that *ft* in the *Total Force* equation is equal to *f* in the *Acceleration* equation.

The parameters can also be bound to **value properties** of blocks to equate the parameter of an equation to a value property of the system or environment. The value properties are shown as rectangles nested within the *ad:Automobile Domain*. An example is the binding of the coefficient of drag

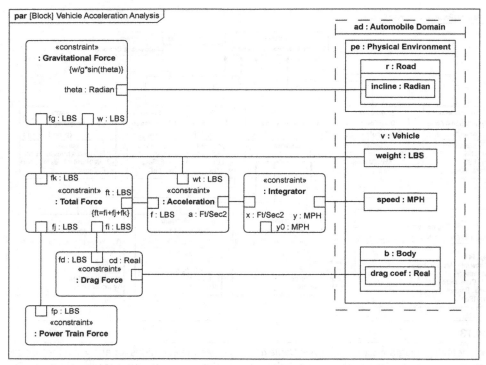

FIGURE 4.14

The parametric diagram that uses the equations defined in Figure 4.13 to analyze vehicle acceleration. The parameters of the equations are bound to other parameters and to value properties of the *Vehicle* and its *Physical Environment*, some of which were defined in Figure 4.3.

parameter *cd* in the *Drag Force* equation to the drag property called *drag coef,* which is a value property of the vehicle *Body*. Sometimes it is more convenient not to show the nested parts but identify the value properties using the dot notation. The drag coefficient would be shown as *ad.v.b.drag coef* to indicate that this is a value property of the body *b*, which is part of the vehicle *v* that is part of the Automobile Domain *ad*. Another example is the binding of the road *incline* angle to the angle *theta* in the gravity force equation. This binding enables values of parameters of generic equations to be set equal to values of specific value properties of the blocks. In this way, generic equations can be reused to analyze different designs by binding the parameters of the generic equations to value properties of different designs.

The parametric diagram and related modeling information can be used to specify an analysis that is executed in separate simulation or analysis tools as describe in Chapter 18, Sections 18.2.2 and 18.4. The simulation or analysis tools can be used to perform sensitivity analysis and determine the property values that are required to satisfy the acceleration requirements. In this example, only some of the vehicle properties are shown. However, a more complete depiction would show the binding of other vehicle value properties to other constraint parameters. Although not shown in Figure 4.14, the *Power*

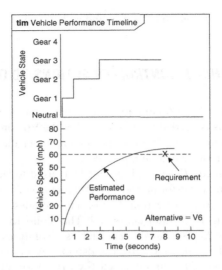

FIGURE 4.15

Analysis results from executing the constraints in the parametric diagram in Figure 4.14, showing the *Vehicle Speed* and *Vehicle State* as a function of time. This is captured in a UML timing diagram.

Train Force constraint includes nested constraints consistent with the constraint blocks that compose it from the *Analysis Context* block definition diagram in Figure 4.13.

In addition to the acceleration and fuel efficiency requirements, other analyses may address requirements for braking distance, vehicle handling, vibration, noise, safety, reliability, production cost, and others. These analyses can be performed to determine the required property values of the system components (e.g., *Body, Chassis, Engine, Transmission, Differential, Brakes, Steering Assembly*) to satisfy the overall system requirements. The parametrics enable the critical value properties of the system design to be identified and integrated with parameters in the analytical models. Details of how to model constraint blocks and their usages in parametric diagrams are described in Chapter 8.

4.3.15 ANALYSIS RESULTS FROM ANALYZING VEHICLE ACCELERATION

As mentioned in the previous section, the parametric diagram is expected to specify an analysis that is executed in an engineering analysis tool to provide the analysis results. This may be a separate specialized analysis tool, such as a simple spreadsheet or a high-fidelity performance simulation, or it may be a capability that the SysML modeling tool provides. The results from the execution then provide values that can be used to update the value properties in the SysML model.

The analysis results from executing the constraints in the parametric diagram are shown in Figure 4.15. This example uses the **UML timing diagram** to display the results. The timing diagram is not one of the SysML diagram kinds. It can be used with SysML, along with other more robust visualization methods such as response surfaces, to show multi-parameter relationships. In this timing diagram, the *Vehicle Speed* is shown as a function of time, and the *Vehicle State* is shown as a function of time. The *Vehicle* states correspond to nested states within the *forward* state in Figure 4.8. Based on the analysis performed, the 6-cylinder (V6) vehicle configuration is able to satisfy its acceleration requirement. A similar analysis showed that the 4-cylinder (V4) vehicle configuration does not satisfy the requirement.

4.3.16 DEFINING THE *VEHICLE CONTROLLER* ACTIONS TO OPTIMIZE ENGINE PERFORMANCE

The analysis results showed that the V6 configuration is needed to satisfy the vehicle acceleration requirement. Additional analysis is needed to assess whether the V6 configuration can satisfy the fuel efficiency requirement of a minimum of 25 miles per gallon under the stated driving conditions, as specified in the *Fuel Efficiency* requirement in Figure 4.2.

The activity diagram to *Provide Power* in Figure 4.11 is used to support the analysis needed to optimize fuel efficiency and engine performance. The :*Vehicle Controller* «software» is allocated to the *Vehicle Processor*, as described in Section 4.3.10, and includes an action to *Control Fuel Air Mixture* that controls the engine accelerator command. The inputs to this action include the *Accelerator Cmd* from the *Driver* and *Engine Parameters* such as revolutions per minute (rpm) and engine temperature from the *Engine*. The *Vehicle Controller* also includes the *Control Gear* action to determine when to change gears based on engine speed (i.e., rpm) to optimize performance and fuel efficiency. The specification of the *Vehicle Controller* software can include a state machine diagram that changes state in response to the inputs consistent with the state machine diagram in Figure 4.8.

The specification of the algorithms to realize the *Vehicle Controller* actions requires further analysis. The algorithm can be defined by further specifying the actions as mathematical and logical expressions that can be captured in a more detailed activity diagram or directly in code. A parametric diagram can also be developed to specify the algorithm performance requirements that constrain the input and output of the *Vehicle Controller* actions. For example, the constraints may specify the required fuel and air mixture as a function of rpm and engine temperature to achieve optimum fuel efficiency. The algorithms are used to control fuel flow rate and air intake, and perhaps other parameters, to satisfy these constraints. Based on the engineering analysis, whose details are omitted here, the V6 engine is able to satisfy the fuel efficiency requirements as well as the acceleration requirements, and is selected as the preferred vehicle system configuration.

4.3.17 SPECIFYING THE *VEHICLE* AND ITS COMPONENTS

The block definition diagram in Figure 4.10 defined the blocks for the *Vehicle* and its components. The model is used to specify the *Vehicle* and each of its components in terms of the functions they perform, their interfaces, and their performance and physical properties. Other aspects of the specification may include a state machine to represent the state-based behavior of the system and its components, and specification of the items that are stored by the system and its components, such as fuel in the fuel tank or data in computer memory.

A simple example is the specification of the *6-Cylinder Engine* block shown on the block definition diagram in Figure 4.16. The *Engine* block and the *6-Cylinder Engine* block were originally shown in the *Vehicle Hierarchy* block definition diagram in Figure 4.10.

In this example, the *Engine* hardware element performs a function called *generate torque*, which is shown as an operation of the block in the operations compartment. This operation corresponds to the *Generate Torque* action in Figure 4.11. The ports on the *Engine* specify its interfaces

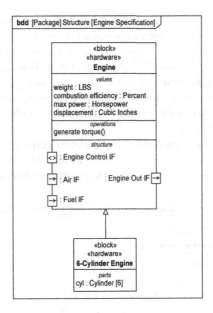

FIGURE 4.16

A block definition diagram that shows the *Engine* block and the features used to specify the block. This block was previously shown in the *Vehicle Hierarchy* block definition diagram in Figure 4.10.

as *Air IF, Fuel IF, Engine Control IF,* and *Engine Out IF.* Selected value properties of the engine are shown in the values compartment that represent its performance and physical properties, including its *displacement, combustion efficiency, max power,* and *weight.* Each value property is typed by a **value type** that specifies its data type (e.g., integer, real) and units (e.g., *Percent, Cubic Inches*).

The *6-Cylinder Engine* block is a subclass of the generic *Engine* block and inherits all of the features from *Engine.* However, the *6-Cylinder Engine* is a specialized engine that contains six *Cylinders,* as indicated in its parts compartment. In addition, the *6-Cylinder Engine* may define values for each value property contained in the generic *Engine,* such as the *max power* and *weight.* This information is derived from the parametric analysis discussed in Sections 4.3.13–15.

Other components of the vehicle can be specified in a similar way. If desired, text requirements can be written to correspond to the functional, interface, performance, and physical requirements associated with each block to create traditional text specifications from the model.

4.3.18 REQUIREMENTS TRACEABILITY

The *Automobile System Requirements* were shown in Figure 4.2. Capturing the text-based requirements in the SysML model provided the means to establish traceability between the text-based requirements and other specification, design, analysis, and verification elements of the model.

The requirements traceability for the *Maximum Acceleration* requirement is shown in Figure 4.17. This requirement traces to a *Market Analysis,* which was conducted in support of the system requirements analysis. The requirement is satisfied by the *Provide Power* activity that was shown in Figure 4.11. The *Max Acceleration* **test case** is also shown as the method to verify that the requirement is satisfied. In addition, the *Engine Power* requirement is derived from the *Maximum Acceleration* requirement and contained in the *Engine Specification*. The **rationale** for deriving the requirement refers to the *Vehicle Acceleration Analysis* parametric diagram in Figure 4.14. The *6-Cylinder Engine* block refines the *Engine Specification* by more precisely expressing the text requirements. The above relationships enable traceability from the system requirements with the supporting rationale to the system design, test cases, and analysis.

The direction of the arrows points from the *Provide Power* activity, *Max Acceleration* test case, and *Engine Power* requirement to the *Maximum Acceleration* as the source requirement. This is in the opposite direction from what is traditionally used to depict requirements flow-down. The direction reflects the

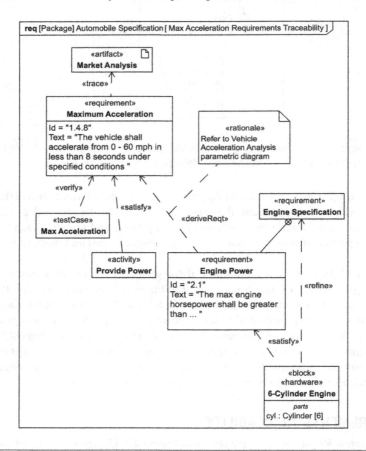

FIGURE 4.17

The requirement diagram showing the traceability of the *Maximum Acceleration* requirement that was displayed in the *Automobile Specification* in Figure 4.2. The traceability to a text-based requirement includes the design elements to satisfy it, other requirements derived from it, and a test case to verify it. Rationale for the deriveReqt relationship based on parametric analysis is also shown.

dependency of the design, test case, and derived requirement on the source requirement, such that if the source requirement changes, the design, test case, and derived requirement may also need to change.

The requirements are supported by multiple notation options including the direct, callout, and tabular presentation. Details of how SysML requirements and their relationships are modeled are described in Chapter 13.

4.3.19 VIEW AND VIEWPOINT

SysML includes the concept of **view** and **viewpoint** to reflect perspectives of different stakeholders. In Figure 4.18, the *Architect* and *Regulator* viewpoints reflect perspectives of the *System Architect* and *National Highway Traffic Safety Administration* stakeholders, respectively. These viewpoints include identification of the **stakeholders**, purpose, language, and methods for constructing a view of the model to address their concerns. In this example, the *System Architect* is concerned about the fuel economy versus acceleration trade-offs, and the *Government Regulator* is concerned about the vehicle's ability to meet safety requirements. The view is constructed by performing a query of the model that is specified by the viewpoint method and then presenting this information in a specified format. As indicated in the figure, the *Vehicle Performance* view **conforms** to the *Architect* viewpoint by providing traceability to the fuel efficiency and acceleration requirements and the associated design rationale in a requirements diagram. The *Vehicle Safety Regulations* view conforms to the *Regulator* viewpoint by providing the safety requirements, test cases, and test results in tabular format. The modeling tool can provide the query results to a rendering application to present the information in different formats, including documents with text, diagrams, tables, and plots.

Further details on modeling view and viewpoints can be found in Chapter 5, Section 5.6 and Chapter 15, Section 15.8.

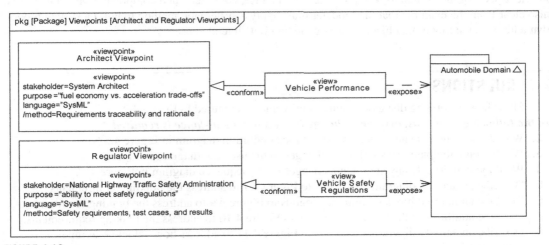

FIGURE 4.18

The package diagram showing the *Architect* viewpoint to address concerns related to fuel economy versus acceleration trade-offs, and a *Regulator* viewpoint to address concerns related to meeting safety requirements.

4.4 MODEL INTERCHANGE

An important aspect of systems modeling is the ability to exchange model information among tools. A SysML model that is captured in a model repository can be imported and exported from a SysML-compliant tool in a standard format called **XML metadata interchange** (XMI). This enables other tools to exchange this information if they also support XMI. Examples may be the ability to export selected parts of the SysML model to a UML tool to support software development of the *Vehicle Controller* software, or to import and export the requirements from a requirements management tool, or to import and export the parametric diagrams and related information to engineering analysis tools. The ability to achieve seamless model interchange capability may be limited by the quality of the model and by the limitations of tool conformance with the standard. Other interchange mechanism may use the tool's application programming interface (API) to access model information. Chapter 18, Section 18.3, includes a description of XMI and other data exchange mechanisms.

4.5 SUMMARY

The SysML basic feature set is a subset of the language features that applies to all nine SysML diagrams. It provides significant capability for representing systems, without introducing all of the language complexity associated with the full feature set. The basic feature set is required learning for the first two levels of SysML certification, called the Model User and Model Builder-Fundamental levels.

The automobile example demonstrates how a SysML model using the basic feature set can help to specify, design, analyze, and verify a system. It enables the requirements, behavior, structure, and parametric aspects of the system to be represented in a precise, consistent, and comprehensive manner. It is also clear from the example that the modeler must apply a systematic method to build a system model that addresses the modeling objectives associated with its intended use.

4.6 QUESTIONS

1. Show how a stopping distance requirement would be captured in Figure 4.2.

In the following questions, assume a change in the stopping distance is required.

2. Would you anticipate any changes to the block definition diagram in Figure 4.3?
3. Would you anticipate any significant changes to the use case diagram in Figure 4.4?
4. Would you anticipate any significant changes to the sequence diagram in Figure 4.5?
5. Describe an activity diagram analogous to Figure 4.7 to address the braking requirements.
6. Describe an internal block diagram analogous to Figure 4.9 to address the braking requirements.
7. Describe additions to the vehicle hierarchy in Figure 4.10 to address the braking requirements.
8. Describe an activity diagram analogous to Figure 4.11 to address how vehicle braking is performed.
9. Describe an internal block diagram analogous to Figure 4.12 for the vehicle braking subsystem.

10. Describe a block definition diagram analogous to Figure 4.13 to define the equations needed to analyze vehicle braking distance performance.
11. Describe a parametric diagram analogous to Figure 4.14 to describe the analysis used to analyze braking distance performance.

DISCUSSION TOPICS

What are some observations about the changes to the model that occur as a result of a requirements change such as the one described above (i.e., change in stopping distance)?

LANGUAGE DESCRIPTION

The chapters in Part II describe the SysML language and how it can be used to model a system. Chapter 5 introduces the SysML diagram taxonomy and the fundamental aspects of diagrams. Chapters 6–15 describe the language concepts and notation in detail. The ordering of the chapters is based on the logical development of the language concepts, including concepts for model organization, structure, behavior, allocation, requirements, and profiles. The ordering is not based on a systems engineering process.

Each chapter describes applicable language concepts, diagram notation, and example diagrams to illustrate how to create syntactically correct diagrams and models that conform to the language specifications.

THE SURVEILLANCE SYSTEM CASE STUDY

A single case study is used throughout this part of the book to help demonstrate the concepts in the SysML language.

CASE STUDY OVERVIEW

A company called ACME Surveillance, Inc., produces and sells surveillance systems. Their range of surveillance systems products is intended to provide security for either homes or small commercial sites. Their systems use sophisticated pan and tilt cameras to produce video images of the surrounding area. For a fee, they can be connected to a central monitoring service. ACME also produces the cameras and sells them as separate products for "do-it-yourself" enthusiasts.

A similar example is used in Chapter 17 to demonstrate the application of a model-based systems engineering method to the development of a residential security system.

FIGURE II.1 shows a typical surveillance system setup for a small commercial site. The system has four wall-mounted surveillance cameras, three connected into the company's Ethernet network and the fourth connected via a wireless access point. One office is used to house the monitoring station for the surveillance system, which is also connected to the office network. This particular monitoring station consists of one workstation and an additional screen. The office has a PBX that the monitoring station uses to communicate with its designated command center.

MODELING CONVENTIONS

When elements are named in the example model, the names chosen are generally valid English names. Whenever the names have more than one word, the words are separated by spaces. Names of model

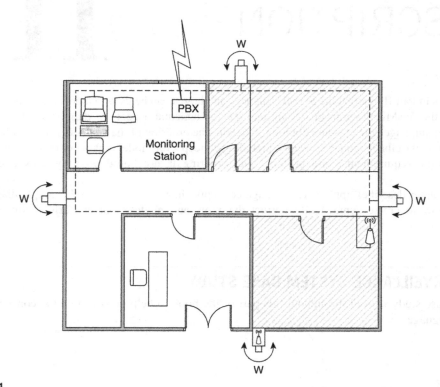

FIGURE II.1

Depiction of surveillance system example.

elements that represent definitions have the first letter of all words in uppercase. Names of features are all in lowercase. Definitions and features refer to certain kinds of model elements that are described in Chapter 7.

The following chapters contain numerous SysML diagrams used to illustrate the concepts in the language. With few exceptions, each diagram is accompanied by a description. To relate the description to the figures, names used in the diagram are presented in *italic* font. Terms in `monotype` refer to elements in the textual syntax of the language. Terms in **bold** are used to highlight fundamental concepts in the SysML language.

OCSMP CERTIFICATION COVERAGE AND SysML 1.3

The OMG Certified Systems Modeling Professional™ (OCSMP) Certification Program assesses a candidate's knowledge of model-based systems engineering concepts, particularly knowledge of SysML. The program will award the following four levels of certification based on passing an examination:

- OCSMP Model User
- OCSMP Model Builder – Fundamental
- OCSMP Model Builder – Intermediate
- OCSMP Model Builder – Advanced

The OCSMP Certification Program splits SysML into two feature sets: basic and full. The first two examination levels of the OCSMP Certification Program use a subset of SysML called the Basic Feature Set, whereas the third examination level uses the full set of SysML features. This part of the book is intended to provide a reference for the first three levels of certification. The fourth certification level addresses more general issues of system modeling that are discussed to some extent in parts I, III, and IV.

To help OCSMP candidates for the first two levels of examinations, paragraphs that describe features in the basic OCSMP feature set are shaded. The notation appendix uses the same convention.

OCSMP does not cover versions of SysML beyond version 1.2, but we nonetheless wanted to cover later developments in the book. For example, SysML 1.3 added some features and deprecated others. The deprecated features, which are all in Chapter 7, are retained but placed in a special section at the end of the chapter. Features added by SysML 1.3 are identified both in the text of the chapters and in the description column of the tables in the notation appendix. Similarly, SysML 1.4 changed the representation of views and viewpoints. A summary of the changes is provided in Chapter 15, Section 15.8.

VIEWING SysML MODELS WITH DIAGRAMS

5

A SysML model can represent many different aspects of a system, including its behavior, structure, requirements, and parametrics. Some of the basic concepts of models were introduced in Chapter 2, and Chapter 3 provided an introduction to SysML diagrams. This chapter discusses in detail how models expressed in SysML are visualized on diagrams and describes some of the common diagrammatic notations.

5.1 OVERVIEW

A diagram is a view of a model for a particular purpose. A diagram may allow a user to access the content of the model, provide inputs to the model, or both. SysML includes nine standard diagram kinds that present different views of the model. In addition to diagrams, SysML supports tabular, matrix, and tree views of the model.

A SysML diagram contains diagram elements or **symbols** that correspond to model elements contained in the model. The kind of diagram constrains the kind of model elements it can present and how they appear on that diagram. A model element may appear on any number of diagrams, and any changes to an element will be reflected in all the diagrams in which it appears.

SysML diagrams consist of a diagram frame and a content area. The diagram frame corresponds to a particular model element and sets the context for the diagram content. The diagram content is expressed using node symbols such as rectangles, ovals, and round-angles connected by line symbols. The diagram symbols can be adorned with text, icons, and tool-specific features, such as color and font.

SysML also includes some general purpose diagram elements to annotate the model and group model elements.

5.2 SysML DIAGRAMS

As noted in Chapter 2, Section 2.2.1, a model is a representation of one or more concepts that can be realized in the physical world. A SysML diagram provides a mechanism to present a focused view of a model for a specific purpose. The symbols on a diagram are mapped to model elements whose meaning is specified by the modeling language, in this case, SysML. The details of how SysML model elements are specified is discussed in Chapter 15, Section 15.2, and the remaining chapters in Part II describe the specific meaning of the symbols and their underlying model elements. These diagram concepts are further elaborated below.

5.2.1 DIAGRAM VERSUS MODEL

A simple example that highlights the distinction between model elements and a diagram that presents the model elements is shown in Figure 5.1. Some of the model elements that represent a *Vehicle* are shown in the browser view of a typical modeling tool. The model elements represent different concepts about the *Vehicle*, including selected vehicle components and the whole–part relationship between the *Vehicle* and its components. A view of the model elements is presented in a diagram, where the symbols on the diagram correspond to the model elements.

Note that only some of the model elements in Figure 5.1 are presented on the diagram. The diagram is a view of the model that is intended to address a particular purpose, and the modeler can choose what to present and what to hide (elide) on the diagram.

Another important aspect of a SysML model is that a particular model element can appear on zero, one, or many diagrams. For example, in Figure 5.2 a second diagram presents a view of the model that shows how an *Engine* is further composed of *cylinders* and *pistons*. The same model element *Engine* is thus presented on two different diagrams. If the model element is modified, the change will be reflected on all the diagrams that show the model element. For example, if we changed the model element name from *Engine* to *Motor,* the name would change on both diagrams as well as the browser. It should also be noted that the component called *Body* from Figure 5.1 is not presented on any diagram but is still contained in the model.

The same model element kind may map to more than one symbol. For example, various components of *Engine* are shown in Figure 5.3 using different symbols. *Engine* and *Cylinder* are shown using box symbols, but icons can also be used to visualize model elements, as illustrated for *Piston*. In

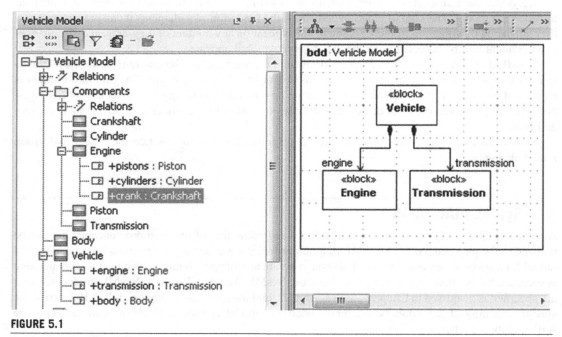

FIGURE 5.1

Distinction between model and diagram.

addition to being shown on separate symbols, *Piston* and *Cylinder* are shown in text strings in the parts compartment of the symbol for *Engine*. All of these symbolic presentations refer to the same model elements. The ellipsis in the parts compartment of *Engine* indicates that some entries are hidden (see Section 5.3.6 for further information).

There are ways to view a model other than with diagrams. For example, the same model elements may be presented in a tabular view. An example of this can be seen in Figure 5.10.

5.2.2 SysML DIAGRAM TAXONOMY

Figure 5.4 shows the SysML diagram taxonomy, which was previously summarized in Chapter 3, Section 3.2. Detailed diagram notation tables that describe the symbols used on SysML diagrams can be found in the Appendix of this book.

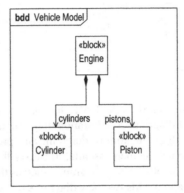

FIGURE 5.2

Engine shown on another diagram.

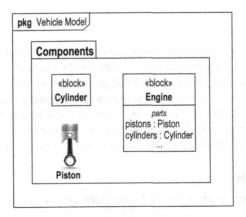

FIGURE 5.3

Different symbols for the same model element.

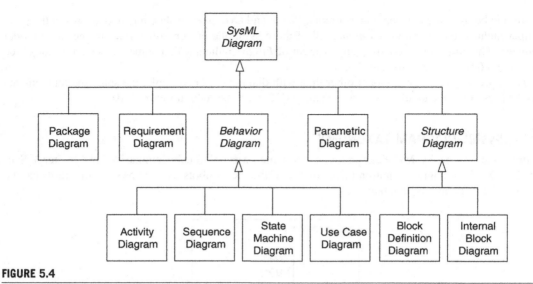

FIGURE 5.4

SysML diagram taxonomy.

SysML diagrams and notation are based on the UML diagrams and notation, although several of the UML diagrams, including the object diagram, collaboration diagram, deployment diagram, communication diagram, interaction overview diagram, timing diagram, and profile diagram were omitted from SysML. The omitted diagrams were not deemed essential to satisfy the requirements for modeling systems. SysML includes modifications to other UML diagrams, such as the class diagram, composite structure diagram, and activity diagram, and it adds two new diagrams for requirements and parametrics.

In addition to the graphical forms of representation used on SysML diagrams, SysML also identifies the need for tabular, matrix, and tree views of the model, examples of which are included in other chapters in Part II, including Chapters 13 and 14 on requirements and allocations, respectively.

5.2.3 DIAGRAM FRAMES

Every SysML diagram must have a **diagram frame** that encloses the diagram content. The diagram frame corresponds to a model element that provides the context for the diagram content. Certain diagrams can include symbols on the diagram frame to connect to other elements shown within the diagram frame.

The diagram frame is a rectangle with a diagram header containing standard information in the top left corner of the diagram. The rest of the area enclosed by the diagram frame is the content area, or canvas, where the symbols are shown. An optional diagram description, providing further details about the status and purpose of the diagram, can be attached to the diagram frame.

5.2.4 DIAGRAM HEADER

The **diagram header** is a rectangle with its lower right corner cut off. It includes the following information:

- *Diagram kind*—an abbreviation indicating the kind of diagram.
- *Model element kind*—the kind of model element to which the diagram frame corresponds.

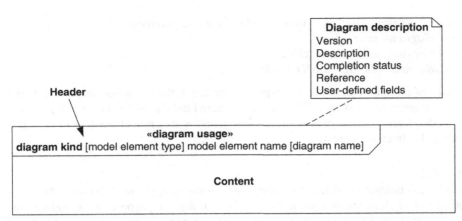

FIGURE 5.5

A diagram frame.

- *Model element name*—the name of the model element to which the diagram frame corresponds.
- *Diagram name*—the name of the diagram, which is often used to indicate the diagram purpose.
- *Diagram usage*—a keyword indicating a specialized use of a diagram.

An example of a diagram frame with a diagram header that includes all of the above information is shown in Figure 5.5.

Diagram kind

The **diagram kind** may take one of the following values, depending on the kind of diagram:

- Activity diagram—**act**
- Block definition diagram—**bdd**
- Internal block diagram—**ibd**
- Package diagram—**pkg**
- Parametric diagram—**par**
- Requirement diagram—**req**
- Sequence diagram—**sd**
- State machine diagram—**stm**
- Use case diagram—**uc**

Model element kind

Different diagram kinds have diagram frames that correspond to different kinds of model elements. The valid permutations are listed here by diagram kind:

- *Activity diagram*—activity
- *Block definition diagram*—block, constraint block, package, model, model library
- *Internal block diagram*—block
- *Package diagram*—package, model, model library, profile, view
- *Parametric diagram*—activity, block, constraint block

- *Requirement diagram*—package, model, model library, requirement
- *Sequence diagram*—interaction
- *State machine diagram*—state machine
- *Use case diagram*—package, model, model library

The choice of **model element kind** is explained further in the following chapters in Part II, where the individual diagrams are discussed. The model element kind should be shown in the header to avoid ambiguity if the diagram can represent more than one allowable model element kind. It also aids in understanding the diagram context.

Diagram name

Since a model can contain considerable amounts of information, the modeler may choose to include only selected model elements in a particular diagram for a given purpose, while hiding other model elements that may detract from this purpose. The **diagram name** is user defined and intended to provide a concise description of the diagram's purpose.

Diagram usage

The **diagram usage** indicates that a diagram is intended to support a specific use. The diagram usage name is included in the header in angle brackets called guillemets. For example, a use-case diagram may be referred to as a context diagram, where context diagram is the diagram usage name. This mechanism is further described as part of customizing the language in Chapter 15 Section 15.7.

5.2.5 DIAGRAM DESCRIPTION

The **diagram description** is an optional note attached either inside or outside of the diagram frame. It is intended to enable the modeler to capture additional information about the diagram. This information includes some predefined fields but also has provision for user-defined fields. The following are the predefined fields.

- *Version:* version of the diagram.
- *Completion status:* a statement by the diagram author about the completeness of the diagram relative to its intended completeness. It may include statements such as "in process," "draft," or "complete," and may also include a specific description of the information that is still missing from the diagram.
- *Description:* free text description of the diagram's content or purpose.
- *Reference:* references to other information about the diagram, or hyperlinks to related diagrams to aid in navigation.

5.2.6 DIAGRAM CONTENT

The **diagram content** area, sometimes called the **canvas,** contains elements that graphically represent model elements. The content area includes the diagram elements (symbols) that present the model elements of interest. As stated above, the kind of diagram constrains which kind of model elements can be shown and how they appear. Within the constraints of the diagram, the modeler determines which model elements to show and which to hide to achieve the diagram intent.

5.3 DIAGRAM NOTATIONS

SysML diagrams are composed of two kinds of diagram elements: nodes and paths. A node is a diagram element that generally appears as a shape, such as a rectangle or oval with a text label. The node may contain additional text strings and/or other graphical symbols that may correspond to other model elements. A path, also known as an edge, is a diagram element that generally appears as a line that may have additional adornments such as arrowheads and text strings.

5.3.1 KEYWORDS

SysML allows for the use of a **keyword** in **guillemets** (as «keyword») before the name of some model elements. A keyword on a symbol identifies the kind of model element to which it refers and is typically used to remove ambiguity when a particular symbol such as a rectangle or dashed line with an arrowhead can represent more than one kind of model element. For example, a rectangle is used to depict both a requirement and a block in SysML, but adding the keyword «requirement» or «block» to the rectangle eliminates the ambiguity.

5.3.2 NODE SYMBOLS

Node symbols are generally rectangular but may also be round-angles, ellipses, and other polygons. All node symbols have a name compartment that can be used to display the name string of the represented model element, along with any applicable keywords and properties. Some node symbols have extra compartments to display details of nested elements, either in textual or graphical form.

Figure 5.6 shows two examples of node symbols: a use case called *Fly Airplane* and the block *Airplane*. The *Airplane* symbol shows an internal compartment labeled *values* to store value properties.

5.3.3 PATH SYMBOLS

All path symbols are some kind of line, but they have different styles and ends depending on the modeling concept they represent. Paths may have a text adornment that contains their name string, keywords,

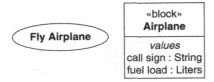

FIGURE 5.6

Examples of node symbols.

and additional properties, although this is often hidden. Additional textual information may also be shown on the ends of the lines when the model element requires it.

Figure 5.7 shows two examples of path symbols: an association and a generalization. The association symbol indicates that an *Airplane* has exactly two *wings*. The generalization symbol indicates that an *Airplane* is a kind of *Flying Thing*.

5.3.4 ICON SYMBOLS

Icons are typically used to represent a specific domain concept, such as a document, or perhaps a type of hardware component, such as a pump. A stereotype can specify an icon to be used as the symbol for the model element with the stereotype applied. If a model element symbolized by an icon has properties, these can be displayed in a text string floating near the object. Icons may also be displayed inside a node symbol or as adornments on line shapes. Figure 5.8 shows two examples of icons: a stick figure representing the actor *Pilot* and a small box containing an arrow that represents fuel flowing into the *Airplane* block.

5.3.5 NOTE SYMBOLS

A **note** symbol can be attached via a dashed line to a symbol of any model element or set of model elements. The note symbol is used to annotate the model with additional textual information that may include a hyperlink to a reference document. The note symbol is a rectangular box with a cutoff upper right corner containing textual information. A note symbol may be a graphical adornment on a diagram that does not correspond to any model element. Note symbols can also be used to display user-defined tags. They are used extensively in SysML to display cross-cutting information, such as traceability to requirements (see Chapter 13, Section 13.5.3) and allocations (see Chapter 14, Section 14.3). In these cases, the content of the note symbol does correspond to specific model elements.

Figure 5.9 shows two examples of note symbols. One note symbol is a description of the *Pilot*, and the other asserts that the Airplane's *call sign* satisfies the *Airplane Unique Identity* requirement.

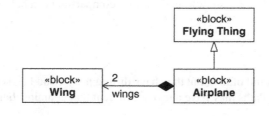

FIGURE 5.7

Examples of path symbols.

FIGURE 5.8

Examples of icon symbols.

5.3.6 OTHER SYMBOLS

SysML has a variety of other specific symbols and symbol styles that are listed here.

Ellipsis

A modeler may choose to present only a subset of the information about a model element on a given diagram. This is useful for reducing clutter and focusing on the diagram's purpose, but it can be helpful to someone viewing that diagram to know that there is information about a model element that could be shown but is hidden. SysML allows a modeler to optionally show an ellipsis at the bottom of a compartment on a symbol to indicate that not all of the potentially visible compartment elements are shown. An example of this can be seen in Figure 5.3.

Off-Page connectors

A path symbol between two node symbols corresponds to a relationship between the model elements that are depicted by the nodes. Sometimes, however, the diagram layout makes it difficult to connect the two nodes due to their placement on the diagram. In this case, SysML also allows a path symbol to be represented by two symbols. Each of these two symbols is connected at one end to a node symbol, while its other end is connected to a circle with a label inside. The combination of two of these "half-path" symbols with a common label is equivalent to a single traditional path symbol. Although this mechanism can be used within a single diagram, it is often used to visualize a path that connects two nodes on different diagrams; hence the circles are called "off-page connectors." The SysML specification advocates that this mechanism be used sparingly to avoid the construction of "spaghetti diagrams." Refer to the Appendix for an example of an off-page connector.

Decomposition and elaboration using the rake symbol

Certain symbols can be annotated with a rake symbol to indicate whether their corresponding model element is described by another diagram. Details of these symbols are given in the relevant chapters, but for completeness a summary of the symbols is offered here:

- Activity diagram – a call behavior action that can refer to another activity diagram.
- Internal block diagram – a part that can refer to another internal block diagram.
- Package diagram – a package that can refer to another package diagram.
- Parametric diagram – a constraint property that can refer to another parametric diagram.

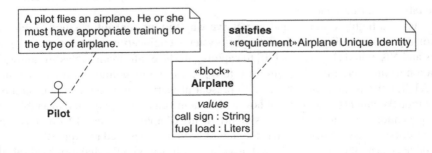

FIGURE 5.9

Examples of note symbols.

- Requirement diagram – a requirement that can refer to another requirement diagram.
- Sequence diagram – an interaction fragment that can refer to another sequence diagram.
- State machine diagram – a state that can refer to another state machine diagram.
- Use case diagram – a use case that is realized by other behavior diagrams (activity, state machine, sequence).

A modeler can indicate whether a given diagram will show symbol decomposition and, in addition, whether a given symbol on that diagram will show the rake symbol or not.

5.3.7 SYMBOL STYLE OPTIONS

- Constraint Property Shape – A modeler can indicate whether the node symbol for a constraint property (Chapter 8, Section 8.4) has rounded or square corners.
- Control Flow Style – A modeler can indicate whether the path symbol for a control flow (Chapter 9, Section 9.6) is a dashed or solid arrow.
- Line Jogs – A modeler can specify whether they wish to see line jogs, semi-circular hoops to indicate when two path symbols are crossing each other, on a diagram.

5.3.8 DIAGRAM LAYOUT

The diagram elements on a diagram must be arranged to ensure the diagram is well organized and communicates effectively. For example, the sequence of actions on an activity diagram may be arranged from top to bottom or from left to right to reflect their time ordering. The model does not require this, since the precedence relationships are part of the semantics, but arrangement may make it more human interpretable. The diagram layout is often performed manually by the modeler. However, SysML modeling tools generally provide an automatic diagram layout capability, which can reduce the time and effort for this part of the modeling activity. The sophistication of the layout algorithms and the complexity of the diagram determine the effectiveness for a particular application.

5.4 TABULAR, MATRIX, AND TREE VIEWS

SysML also includes nongraphical representations of model information that are often useful for efficiently displaying large amounts of information. The forms of nongraphical representation that SysML supports are tables, matrices, and trees.

A **table** can be a highly efficient and expressive way to represent information. Tables have been used traditionally for capturing a wide variety of systems engineering information, such as requirements tables and *N*-squared (N2) charts [40] to capture interface information. SysML allows the use of tabular notation as an alternative diagram form to represent the modeling information contained in a SysML model. Tabular formats may be used to present properties of model elements and/or relationships among model elements. The detail of how and what information is captured in a table is not specified, but tool vendors are encouraged to support them. Chapters 13 and 14 on requirements and allocations describe typical tabular formats that a tool vendor is expected to support.

When a table is used, the table is included in a diagram frame with the diagram kind **table** shown in the diagram label. Otherwise, the diagram label format is the same as that for any other kind of diagram. An example of a simple requirements table is shown in Figure 5.10.

id	req't name	req't text
4	Capacity	The Hybrid SUV shall carry 5 adult passengers, along with sufficient luggage and fuel for a typical weekend campout.
4.1	CargoCapacity	The Hybrid SUV shall carry sufficient luggage for 5 people for a typical weekend campout.
4.2	FuelCapacity	The Hybrid SUV shall carry sufficient fuel for a typical weekend campout.
4.3	PassengerCapacity	The Hybrid SUV shall carry 5 adult passengers.

table [Requirement] Capacity [Decomposition of Capacity Requirement]

FIGURE 5.10

Example of tabular format in SysML.

Matrices—identified by the diagram kind **matrix**—are very useful for describing relationships. Typically, the top row and first column of the matrix represent model elements, and its other cells describe a relationship between the row and column elements. An example of a matrix can be seen in Chapter 13, Figure 13.9, where the top row of the *satisfy dependency Matrix* lists requirements, the first column lists model elements, and the other cells indicate whether relationships exist between them. **Trees,** identified by the diagram kind **tree,** typically describe hierarchical and other kinds of relationships that are frequently presented using browser panes in SysML modeling tools.

5.5 GENERAL PURPOSE MODEL ELEMENTS

The following model elements can be used on all diagrams for a variety of purposes. Some other model elements, such as dependencies and allocations, can be used on all diagrams but those model elements tend to have more specific usage and are covered in other chapters.

5.5.1 COMMENT

A **comment** is a textual description that can be associated with any other model element. It can be shown on any diagram using a note symbol connected to a symbol representing the model element it describes. The major difference between a comment and a note symbol is that a comment is a model element that is part of the model, whereas a note symbol is a diagram annotation only.

5.5.2 ELEMENT GROUP

An **element group** provides a light weight mechanism for grouping model elements of any kind. It can be used for purposes like grouping elements that are associated with a particular release, a certain risk level, and/or a legacy design, to name a few examples. The members of an element group can be ordered.

An element group has a name and also includes the criterion for inclusion as a member of the group. It should be noted that SysML doesn't specify a semantic for the criterion. By grouping elements, the

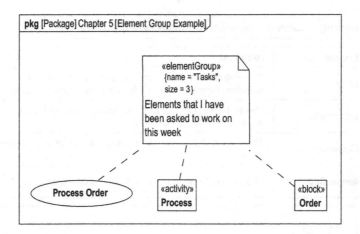

FIGURE 5.11

Example of an element group.

modeler simply asserts that the criterion of the group applies to the member. Model elements can appear in multiple element groups. The element group also includes a property that can be queried to reflect the number of members in the group.

An element group can have other element groups as members. However, group membership is not transitive. This is to say that if *model element 1* is a member of *element group A*, and *element group A* is a member of *element group B*, this does not imply that *model element 1* is a member of *element group B*. The rationale for non-transitivity of element groups can be explained by a simple example, where the membership criterion for *element group B* is all groups with 5 members or more, and the criterion for *element group A* is all blocks that are red. A particular red block is a member of *element group A*, but is not a member of *element group B*.

An element group is shown using a note symbol with the keyword «elementGroup» at the top of the symbol. The name and size of the group are shown in braces following the keyword. Inclusion of an element in the group is indicated by a dashed line from the group to the element. The criterion for the inclusion of an element in the group is shown in the body of the comment symbol.

Figure 5.11 shows an example of an element group on a package diagram. The group *Tasks* includes a use case (*Process Order*), an activity (*Process*) and a block (*Order*), making the size of the group *3*. The criterion is *Elements that I have been asked to work on this week*.

5.6 VIEW AND VIEWPOINT

SysML provides a mechanism, called a viewpoint, to specify customized views of a model beyond those offered directly by the language. SysML viewpoint and view constructs are consistent with the ISO-42010 [20] standard. A viewpoint describes the point of view of a set of stakeholders by framing their concerns along with the method for constructing an artifact that addresses those concerns. The view specifies the model content that is to be presented to the stakeholder in the artifact. Typical examples may include an operational, manufacturing, or security viewpoint. Viewpoints and the views that conform to them are important because they allow SysML concepts to be shown not just in the standard SysML diagrams but also in ways that are suitable to a specific purpose and audience.

Viewpoint and view are covered in detail in Chapter 15, Section 15.8, but it is worth noting that viewpoints are an important contributor to the topic addressed by this chapter, namely visualizing a SysML model. A viewpoint specifies the following:

- Its purpose;
- The stakeholders and concerns that are addressed;
- How the view content should be expressed (i.e. what modeling language is required for the information that will appear in the view?);
- The file format of the artifact that is produced from the view (e.g., set of slides in PowerPoint, a PDF file, a Word document, a web viewable format, etc.);
- How the information should be presented in the artifact (e.g., specifying that data values should be plotted on a graph or a particular tabular style, or that both English and Spanish text should be provided, or that photographs be shown in color with minimum dimensions of 100 millimeters square); and
- The method for producing an artifact from a view.

It is important to understand that while a view is a SysML construct that exists within a SysML model, artifacts produced from views potentially live outside of the modeling environment. For example, a movie or a PDF document generated from a view is not directly incorporated into a SysML model, while the view itself is.

5.7 SUMMARY

The ability for modelers and model stakeholders to visualize the content of models effectively is critical to the success of any modeling language. The following list summarizes the important aspects of model visualization in SysML:

- SysML has nine kinds of diagram that allow different aspects of a system model to be visualized graphically.
- Any SysML diagram will show only a subset of the elements in a model and model elements may appear in multiple diagrams.
- SysML also supports nongraphical views, such as matrices, trees, and tables.
- SysML supports custom visualizations through the viewpoint mechanism.

5.8 QUESTIONS

1. What is the difference between a diagram and a model?
2. What are the five elements of a diagram header and what are they used for?
3. What are the four kinds of symbols that can appear on a diagram?
4. When is a keyword needed as part of a graphical symbol?
5. What does an ellipsis indicate?
6. How are custom visualizations supported in SysML?

DISCUSSION TOPICS

Traditional engineering modeling tools show all relevant model elements in any given diagram, whereas SysML allows modelers to selectively hide detail. Discuss the relative benefits of these two approaches.

In addition to graphical representations of the model through diagrams, SysML supports the use of non-graphical representations such as tables and trees. Under which circumstances does it make sense to use these different representations?

ORGANIZING THE MODEL WITH PACKAGES

6

This chapter addresses the topic of model organization and describes the organizational capabilities provided by SysML. In SysML, the fundamental unit of model organization is the package.

6.1 OVERVIEW

A SysML model of a complex system can contain thousands or even millions of model elements. In SysML, each model element is contained within a single container that is called its owner or parent. Contained elements are often called the child elements. When a container is deleted or copied, its child elements are also deleted or copied. Some child elements can also be containers, which leads to a nested containment hierarchy of model elements.

Packages are one example of a container. The model elements contained within a package are called packageable elements, examples of which are blocks, use cases, and activities. Since packages are also packageable elements, they can support package hierarchies. A model is a special kind of package that contains a set of model elements describing a domain of interest.

In addition to having a place in a containment hierarchy, each model element with a name—called a named element—must also be a member of a namespace. A namespace enables its members to be uniquely identified within it by name. A package is a namespace for the packageable elements it contains. A packageable element has a fully qualified name to unambiguously locate it in the package hierarchy of a model.

An import relationship allows elements contained in one package to be imported into another package so that they can be referenced simply by their names within that package. SysML also contains a relationship between named elements called a dependency, which can be specialized as needed to reflect more specific semantics.

This chapter describes how model elements are organized to enhance modeling effectiveness. An effective model organization facilitates reuse of model elements, easy access, and navigability among model elements. It can also support configuration management of the model and exchange of modeling information with other tools, as described in Chapter 18. The importance of maintaining a well-defined model organization increases with the size of the model, but even small models benefit from consistently applied organizational principles. The specific criteria for partitioning the model are methodology dependent, but some examples of model organization principles are included later in this chapter.

Because reuse is so important in modeling, SysML includes the concept of a model library, which is specifically intended to contain model elements that can be shared within and between models. Model libraries are more fully described in Chapter 15.

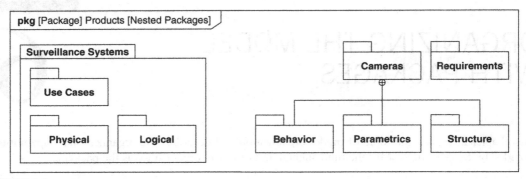

FIGURE 6.1

An example package diagram.

6.2 THE PACKAGE DIAGRAM

The model elements contained within a package can be shown on a **package diagram.** The complete diagram header for a package diagram is as follows:

```
pkg [model element kind] package name [diagram name]
```

The diagram kind is **pkg**, and the *model element kind* can be model, package, or model library. An example of a package diagram is shown in Figure 6.1. It shows several levels of the package hierarchy for the *Products* package of the ACME Surveillance Systems model. The notation tables for package diagrams are included in Table A.1 of the Appendix.

6.3 DEFINING PACKAGES USING A PACKAGE DIAGRAM

SysML models are organized into a hierarchical tree of packages that are much like folders in a computer directory structure. Packages are used to partition elements of the model into coherent units that can be subject to access control, model navigation, configuration management, and other considerations.

A **package** is a container for other model elements. It has a name and an optional **URI**, which uniquely identifies the package as a web-accessible resource, and is thus useful when packages are used widely within or between organizations. Any model element is contained in exactly one container, and when that container is deleted or copied, the model element it contains is deleted or copied along with it. This pattern of containment means that any SysML model is a tree hierarchy of model elements.

Model elements that can be contained in packages are called **packageable elements** and include blocks, activities, and value types, among others. Packages are themselves packageable elements, which allows packages to be hierarchically nested. The containment rules and other related characteristics of other kinds of packageable elements are described in the relevant chapters.

A **model** in SysML is a top-level package in a nested package hierarchy. In a package hierarchy, models may contain other models and packages. The choice of model content and detail—for example, whether to have a hierarchy of models—is dependent on the method used. Typically, however, a model is understood to represent a complete description of a system or domain of interest for some purpose, as described in Chapter 2.

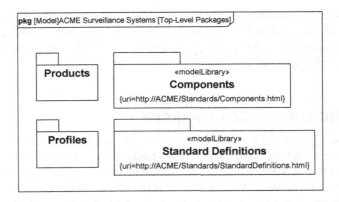

FIGURE 6.2

Package diagram for the surveillance system model.

A model has a single primary hierarchy containing all elements. Its organizing principle is based on what is most suitable to meet the needs of the project.

Often a package is constructed with the intent that its contents will be reused in many models. SysML contains the concept of a **model library**—a package that is designated to contain reusable elements. A model library is depicted as a package symbol with the keyword «modelLibrary» above the package name, as shown in Figure 6.2 for *Components* and *Standard Definitions*. See Chapter 15, Section 15.3 for more details on model libraries.

The diagram content area of a package diagram shows packages and other packageable elements within the package designated by the frame. Packages are displayed using a folder symbol, where the package name and keywords can appear in the tab or the body of the symbol. The URI, if specified, appears in braces after the package name.

If a model appears on a package diagram, which may happen when there is a hierarchy of models, the standard folder symbol includes a triangle in the top right corner of the symbol's body.

The package diagram in Figure 6.2 shows the top-level packages within the corporate model of *ACME Surveillance Systems*, as specified in the diagram header. The user-defined diagram name for this diagram is *Top-Level Packages,* indicating that the purpose of this diagram is to show the top level of the model's package structure. In this example, the model contains separate package hierarchies for:

- The company's products;
- Standard off-the-shelf components;
- Standard engineering definitions such as SI units—from the French *Système International d'Unités* (also known as International System of Units); and
- Any specific extensions required to support domain-specific notations and concepts (extensions to SysML, called profiles, are described in detail in Chapter 15).

The *Components* and *Standard Definitions* packages both have URIs because they are widely used within *ACME Surveillance Systems* and therefore need to be uniquely identified and web accessible across company projects.

Each package should contain packageable elements consistent with the model organization approach. These elements can then be represented as needed on different SysML diagrams including structure, behavior, parametric, and requirement diagrams, as described in Chapter 3, Section 3.2 and in more detail in later chapters.

6.4 ORGANIZING A PACKAGE HIERARCHY

As described previously, a model is organized into a single hierarchical structure of packages. The top-level package is a model that generally contains packages at the next level of the model hierarchy, as shown in Figure 6.2. These packages in turn often contain subpackages that further partition model elements into logical groupings. A well-defined model organization becomes increasingly important as the number of model elements increase. Figure 6.3 motivates the use of a nested package structure by contrasting such a structure with a similar flattened model organization shown in Figure 6.4. It is evident that large models can quickly become difficult to manage if not partitioned into subpackages.

The approach to model organization is a critical choice facing the modeler because it impacts reuse, access control, navigation, configuration management, data exchange, and other key aspects of the development process. For example, a package may be the unit of the model to which access privileges are assigned, granting only selected users the ability to modify its contents. In addition, when a particular package is checked out to modify its contents, other users may be excluded from making changes until the package is checked in. A poorly organized model also makes it difficult for users to understand and navigate the model.

The model hierarchy should be based on a set of organizing principles. The following are some possible ways to organize a model:

- By system hierarchy (e.g., system level, element level, component level);
- By process lifecycle, where each model subpackage represents a stage in the process (e.g., requirements analysis, system design);

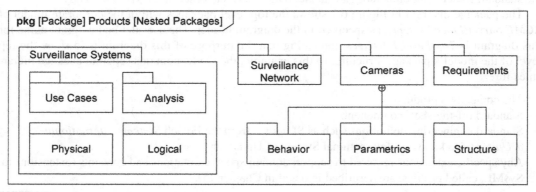

FIGURE 6.3

Showing nested packages on a package diagram.

- By teams that are working on the model (e.g., Requirements Team, Integrated Product Team (IPT) 1, 2);
- By the kind of model elements it contains (e.g., requirements, behavior, structure);
- By model elements that are likely to change together;
- By model elements organized to support reuse (e.g., model libraries);
- By other logical or cohesive groupings of model elements based on defined model-partitioning criteria; and
- A combination of the preceding principles.

Containment relates parents to children within a package hierarchy. Several levels of containment hierarchy can be shown on the package diagram using containment between container elements and their contained elements. Containment is shown as a line with a crosshair at the container (parent) end, but with no adornment on the ends associated with the contained elements (children). Each parent–child containment relationship can be shown as a separate path, but typically they are shown as a tree with one crosshair symbol and many lines radiating from it. An alternative representation of containment is to show the nested model elements enclosed within the body of the package symbol.

Figure 6.3 shows the four packages contained within the *Products* package of the corporate model: *Surveillance Systems, Surveillance Network, Cameras,* and *Requirements.* This example uses both notations for package containment. Different organizational principles are used for the *Products, Cameras,* and *Surveillance Systems* packages. The *Products* package is organized to contain packages for the three primary product lines that the company offers, with an additional package for all requirements specifications. The *Cameras* package hierarchy is organized by modeling artifact kind, and as such it contains packages to capture the structural, behavioral, and parametric aspects of the camera. The *Surveillance Systems* package hierarchy is organized based on architectural principles that require a *Logical Architecture* package, a *Physical Architecture* package, and a *Use Cases* package. It also contains an *Analysis* package for various kinds of analyses and their outcomes.

The containment hierarchy is generally one of the primary browser views visible in a tool. Figure 6.5 provides an example of the expanded browser view corresponding to the model organization from Figure 6.3. The containment hierarchy generally expands as the model evolves to include other nested

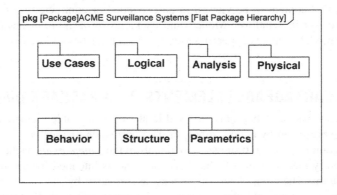

FIGURE 6.4

Alternate model with flat package hierarchy.

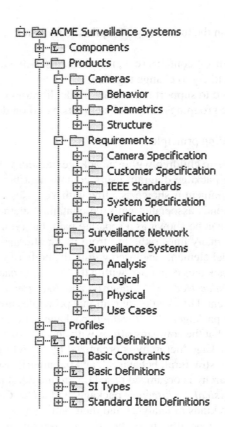

FIGURE 6.5

Browser view of the model's package hierarchy.

packages containing a variety of different model elements. A tool generally enables the containment hierarchy and associated content to be viewed in an expanded or contracted form from the browser, similar to the file browser in Windows. Models and packages form the branches of the containment hierarchy with other model elements appearing as lower-level branches and leaves.

6.5 SHOWING PACKAGEABLE ELEMENTS ON A PACKAGE DIAGRAM

In addition to packages, package diagrams are used to show packageable elements. Packageable elements are normally represented by node symbols or their corresponding icons.

The package diagram in Figure 6.6 shows more details of the *Components* package from Figure 6.2, which is a model library that contains off-the-shelf components intended for use in building cameras and surveillance systems. The components are blocks, as indicated by the «block» keyword, and are contained in the *Components* model library, as indicated in the diagram label. The diagram only shows some of the model elements within the model library to reduce clutter. As explained in Chapters 2 and

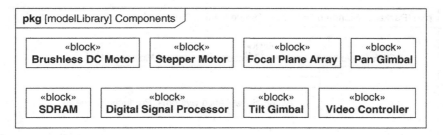

FIGURE 6.6

Showing the contents of the components package using a package diagram.

5, diagrams are simply views of the underlying model and may not show all possible contents that can appear on the diagram. The diagram name is also elided but could have been included to highlight the diagram purpose.

6.6 PACKAGES AS NAMESPACES

In addition to acting as a container for packageable elements, a package is a **namespace** for all named elements within it. Most SysML model elements may have names, although a few kinds of model element, such as a comment, cannot be named. A namespace applies a set of uniqueness rules to distinguish between the different named elements contained within it. The uniqueness rule for packageable elements in packages is simply that each element of a given element kind must have a unique name.

As stated earlier, a package hierarchy can include multiple levels of nested packages, meaning that a model element can be contained within a package that is contained in an arbitrary number of higher-level packages. Containment between a parent and child is unambiguously represented in a tool's browser view of the model.

A model element can appear on a diagram whose frame may or may not designate its parent namespace. However, a model element that is shown on a diagram that does not correspond to its parent may give the false impression that the model element is contained within the namespace designated by the diagram frame. The solution is to show a **qualified name** in the symbol for that model element. If the model element is nested within the containment hierarchy of the package designated by the diagram, then the qualified name shows the relative path from that package to the contained element. If the model element is not nested within the package designated by the diagram, the qualified name contains the full path from the root model to the element.

The qualified name for a model element always ends with the model element name, preceded by a path, with each containing namespace in the path delimited by a double-colon symbol (::), so that when reading the qualified name, the path is resolved from left to right. For example, a model element X that is contained within package B, which in turn is contained within package A, is represented as $A::B::X$.

Figure 6.7 shows some examples of the use of qualified names in a package diagram that corresponds to the *Standard Definitions* package shown in Figure 6.2. The symbol named *Basic Definitions::Waypoint* denotes a value type called *Waypoint* within a package called *Basic Definitions*, within the *Standard Definitions* package. *Waypoint* is used later to specify the scan pattern of a

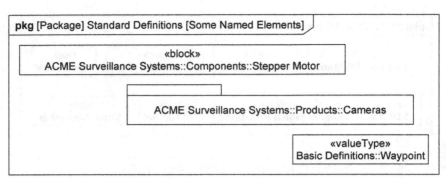

FIGURE 6.7

Using qualified names to represent model elements within a containment hierarchy.

surveillance camera. The other two symbols represent model elements that are external to *Standard Definitions* package and therefore have fully qualified names that correspond to the path name from the corporate model, *ACME Surveillance Systems*.

In a package hierarchy, each model element can be uniquely identified by its qualified name regardless of the diagrams in which it appears. Note that many SysML tools hide qualified names by default to reduce diagram clutter.

6.7 IMPORTING MODEL ELEMENTS INTO PACKAGES

Depending on the organization of a model, model elements from different packages and different models are often related to one another. For example, one model may contain a set of components that another model may want to reuse.

An import relationship is used to include an element or collection of elements belonging to a source namespace into another namespace, called the target namespace. The names of imported element names become part of the target namespace. The qualified name of the imported element is based on where the element resides within the target namespace, and so does not require a qualified name when shown on a diagram that designates the target namespace.

A **package import** imports an entire package, which means that all the model elements of the source package are imported into the target namespace. An **element import** imports a single model element, and may be used when it is unnecessary and possibly confusing to import all the elements of a package.

A name clash occurs when two or more model elements in the target namespace would have the same names as the result of imports. An element import has an alias field that can be used to provide an alternate name for a model element to prevent a name clash in the target namespace. The rules on name clashes are as follows:

- If an imported element name clashes with a child element of the target namespace, that element is not imported unless an alias is used to provide a unique name.
- If the names of two or more imported elements clash, then neither can be imported into the target namespace.

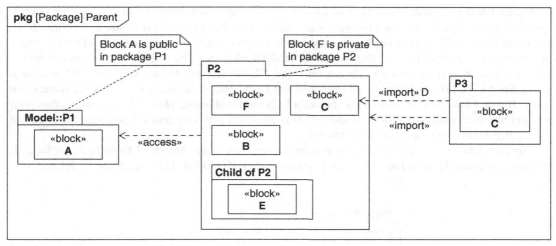

FIGURE 6.8

Illustration of «import» and «access».

The named elements recognized within a namespace—whether through direct containment or as a result of being imported—are called **members.** Members have a **visibility,** either public or private, within their namespace. The default visibility for a member of a namespace is public. The visibility of a member determines whether it can be imported into another namespace. A package import only imports members with public visibility in the source package into the target namespace. Furthermore, an import relationship can state whether the imported names should be public or private within the target namespace.

When access control on a model is enforced by a modeling tool, an imported element can only be changed in the source package, although any changes made to the element are visible in any diagrams representing the target package.

The import relationship is shown using a dashed arrow labeled with the keyword «import». The arrow's head points to the source from which names are being imported, and its tail points to the target namespace into which the names are to be imported. The arrow points either to an individual model element (element import) or to an entire package (package import). The keyword «access» is used instead of «import» when elements are to be imported as private members of the target namespace.

Figure 6.8 shows three packages (*P1, P2,* and *P3*) in the diagram corresponding to package *Parent.* The package called *Model::P1* is not contained in the diagram's context, and so its qualified name has to be used. *Model::P1* contains one block, called *A,* with public visibility (SysML does not have a graphical notation for visibility, hence the notes attached to the symbols). Package *P2* privately imports *P1* and contains a set of blocks, *B* and *C,* which are defined with public visibility, and *F,* which is defined with private visibility. *P2* also contains a nested package called *Child of P2,* which in turn contains a single public block, *E.* Package *P3* defines a public block, *C,* and imports the whole package *P2,* but also imports block *C* as a separate element with the alias *D* to avoid a name clash. Note that the alias *D* is annotated on the import relationship.

Figure 6.9 demonstrates the effect of import relationships on naming. It shows a diagram corresponding to package *P3* showing the names of various model elements from Figure 6.8. Blocks *B, C,* and *D* (an alias for *P2::C*) can be shown using simple names because they are members of the *P3*, either by direct containment or because they were imported. Block *E* has to be qualified by its parent *Child of P2*, whose name is visible because *P3* has imported *P2*. Block *F* has to be qualified by *P2* because it was defined to be private and so is not imported, but *P2* is visible because it is in the same namespace as *P3*. Block *A* has to be qualified by its parent's fully qualified name, *Model::P1*, because although it was defined with public visibility, *Model::P1* was imported privately into *P2* and was therefore not visible in *P2* and so was not imported into *P3*.

Figure 6.10 shows some of the import relationships within the *Standard Definitions* package. It contains an example of a reusable model library called *ISO80000*. (This package is defined as a

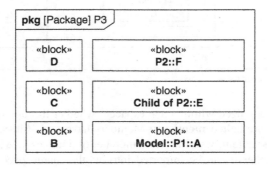

FIGURE 6.9

Naming in package *P3*.

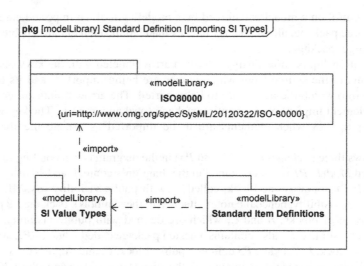

FIGURE 6.10

Importing a library of SI unit types into the Standard Item Definitions package.

non-normative model library in Annex E.6 of the SysML specification.) In order to make *ISO8000* web accessible, it has a URI. *ISO80000* is imported into the *SI Value Types* model library, which provides a common set of units for use throughout the model. *SI Value Types* is in turn imported for use within many other packages, one of which is the *Standard Item Definitions* model library, which contains definitions of information, material, and energy flowing through the surveillance systems.

6.8 SHOWING DEPENDENCIES BETWEEN PACKAGEABLE ELEMENTS

A **dependency** relationship can be applied between named elements to indicate that a change in the element on one end of the dependency may result in a change in the element on the other end of the dependency. The model elements at the two ends of the dependency are called client and supplier. The client is dependent on the supplier, such that a change in the supplier may result in a change in the client.

A dependency between packages is used when the content of one package is dependent on the content of another package. For example, the software applications in the application layer of the system software may depend on the software components within the system software's service layer. This may be expressed in a model of the software architecture by a dependency between the package that represents the application layer (client) and the package that represents the service layer (supplier).

Dependencies are often used to specify a relationship early in the modeling process that is subsequently replaced or augmented when the precise nature of the relationship is better defined. There are various kinds of dependency that can be used on the package diagram and selected other diagrams. The following is a list of the more common kinds of dependencies:

- **Use** – indicates that the client uses the supplier as part of its definition.
- **Refine** – indicates that the client represents an increase in detail compared to the specification of the supplier, such as when detailed physical and performance characteristics are included in a component definition. This relationship is often used in requirements analysis, as described in Chapter 13, Section 13.13.
- **Realization** – indicates that the client realizes the specification expressed in the description of the supplier, such as when an implementation package realizes a design package.
- **Trace** – indicates that there is a linkage between the client and supplier without imposing the more significant semantic constraints of a more precise relationship. This relationship is often used in requirements analysis, as described in Chapter 13, Section 13.14.
- **Allocate** – indicates that one model element is allocated to another. This relationship is described in Chapter 14.

A dependency is represented by a dashed line with an open arrowhead pointing from the client to the supplier. The kind of dependency is indicated by a keyword in guillemets.

Figure 6.11 shows some of the kinds of dependency relationships in the *Camera Performance* package. The constraint block *Video Stream Rate* is a more precise representation (refinement) of the *Video Performance* requirement. *Video Stream Rate* uses a definition of megabits per second (*Mbps*) as part of its definition. The activity *Generate Video Outputs* is traced to the *Video Stream Rate* because if this constraint changes, the performance of the activity may need to be reevaluated. *Generate Video Outputs* is allocated to *Camera* to indicate that the camera is responsible for performing that activity. Details of these various model elements are described in later chapters.

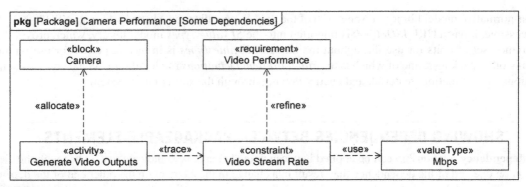

FIGURE 6.11

Example of dependencies used when documenting camera performance.

6.9 SUMMARY

A well-defined model organization is essential to ensuring that the model is partitioned into model elements that support reuse, access control, navigability, configuration management, and data exchange. Different organizing principles can be applied to establish a consistent package hierarchy with nested packages, each of which contains logical groupings of packageable elements. The following list summarizes the important aspects of model organization.

- The principal SysML organizing construct is called a package. Package diagrams are used to describe this model organization in terms of packages, their contents, and relationships.
- A model is a kind of package that represents a domain of interest for a given purpose. Models are the roots of package hierarchies. If the domain of interest is sufficiently complex, it may contain submodels.
- Package hierarchies are based on the concept of containment or ownership of packageable elements. An essential aspect of containment is that the packageable elements in a package get deleted or copied with their container. Examples of packageable elements are blocks, activities, and value types. A model has a single containment hierarchy, which therefore imposes a single organizational perspective on the model. The containment hierarchy in a model often drives the principal browser view in a modeling tool.
- Packages are also namespaces for a set of named elements called members. A namespace defines a set of rules for uniquely identifying an individual member. The namespace rule for packages is that a member must have a unique name within its package.
- The names of symbols on a diagram must allow a viewer to explicitly understand where the represented element is within the model containment hierarchy. If a symbol represents a member of the package that the diagram frame designates, then its name (and sometimes keyword) is all that is required. Otherwise a qualified name is required, which is a concatenation of the member's name and a path of all the namespaces between the member and the root model or diagram context.
- SysML provides a mechanism to import the members from a package or another model into a namespace, either as a whole package or as individual model elements. The visibility of the member in its source package governs whether it is a member of the target namespace. The

qualified name of the imported element is based on where the element resides within the target namespace.

- Model elements depend on each other in various ways. The dependency relationship between a supplier and a client element indicates that the client element is subject to change if the supplier element changes. Different kinds of dependencies are identified with a keyword and are used for specific purposes such as refinement, allocation, and traceability.

6.10 QUESTIONS

1. What is the diagram kind for a package diagram?
2. Which kinds of model element can be designated by a package diagram?
3. What is the generic term for model elements that can be contained in packages?
4. Where does a model appear in a package hierarchy?
5. Name three potential organizing principles that might be used to construct the package hierarchy of a model.
6. How can one show on a package diagram that one package contains another?
7. Which rule does a package enforce for the named elements that are its members?
8. How can one tell by looking at a package diagram that a model element represented on the diagram is a member of the package that is designated by the diagram frame?
9. Write down the qualified name for a block B1 contained in a package P1, which in turn is contained in a model M1.
10. A package P1 contains three elements—block B1, block B2, and block B3—all with public visibility, and a package P4 with private visibility. Another package P2 contains a package called B1 and two blocks called B2 and B4. If package P2 imports package P1 with public visibility, list all the members of P2.
11. If an empty package P9 imports P2 (as defined in Question 10) with public visibility, list all the members of P9.
12. What is an alias used for?
13. Name three common kinds of dependency.
14. How are dependencies shown on a package diagram?

DISCUSSION TOPIC

For a model that you are trying to build, discuss the kind of model organization that is appropriate for it.

MODELING STRUCTURE WITH BLOCKS

7

This chapter addresses the modeling of system structure in terms of hierarchy and interconnection, and the characterization of system structure using value properties. It introduces blocks, the principle structural construct of SysML, and the two types of diagrams used to represent structure, the block definition diagram and the internal block diagram. These representations are a formalization of traditional systems engineering block diagrams to enable a more precise representation of interfaces and other aspects of system structure.

7.1 OVERVIEW

The block is the modular unit of structure in SysML that is used to define a type of system, component, component interconnection, or item that flows through the system, as well as external entities, conceptual entities, or other logical abstractions. A block describes a set of instances that share the block's definition. A block is defined by its features, which may be subdivided into structural features and behavioral features.

The block definition diagram is used to define blocks and the relationships between them, such as their hierarchical relationship. It can also be used to specify instances of blocks, including their configurations and data values. The internal block diagram is used to describe the structure of a block in terms of how its parts are interconnected.

Properties are the primary structural feature of blocks. This chapter describes the different kinds of properties, including those that represent parts, references, and values. Parts are used to describe the composition hierarchy of a block and define a part in the context of its whole. Value properties describe quantifiable physical, performance, and other characteristics of a block such as its weight or speed. A value property is defined by a value type that describes its valid range of values, along with its quantity kind (e.g., length) and its units (e.g., feet or meters). Value properties can be related using parametric constraints as discussed in Chapter 8.

Behaviors associated with a block define how the block responds to stimuli. The different behavioral formalisms—including activities, interactions, and state machines—are discussed in Chapters 9 through 11, respectively. The behavioral features of a block, which include operations and receptions, provide a mechanism for external stimuli to invoke these behaviors.

Parts can be connected on an internal block diagram using connectors to enable interactions between them, including relaying items that flow in and out of them and invoking behaviors.

Ports are structural features of a block that specify access points at which the block can interact with other blocks.

As of SysML 1.3, flow ports and flow specifications were deprecated in favor of full and proxy ports. SysML 1.3 also introduced additional capabilities for ports, such as the ability to nest ports, and the ability to specify other types of interfaces, such as mating surfaces.

115

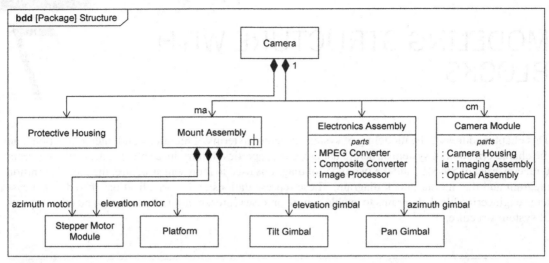

FIGURE 7.1

Example block definition diagram.

In addition to composition hierarchies, blocks can be organized into classification hierarchies that allow blocks to be defined in terms of their similarities and differences. Within a classification hierarchy, a block can specialize another more general block that allows it to inherit features from the general block and to add new features specific to it.

Instance specifications can be used to identify specific configurations of blocks, including the values of its value properties.

7.1.1 BLOCK DEFINITION DIAGRAM

The **block definition diagram** is used to define blocks in terms of their features and their structural relationships with other blocks. The complete header for a block definition diagram is as follows:

```
bdd [model element kind] model element name [diagram name]
```

The diagram kind is bdd and the *model element kind* that corresponds to the diagram frame can be a package, a block, or a constraint block.

Figure 7.1 shows an example block definition diagram containing some of the most common symbols. The diagram shows two levels of the composition hierarchy of an ACME *Camera*. The notation used in the block definition diagram to describe blocks and their relationships is shown in the Appendix, Tables A.3 through A.6.

7.1.2 INTERNAL BLOCK DIAGRAM

The **internal block diagram** or ibd resembles a traditional system block diagram and shows the connections between parts of a block. The internal block diagram header is depicted as follows:

```
ibd [block] block name [diagram name]
```

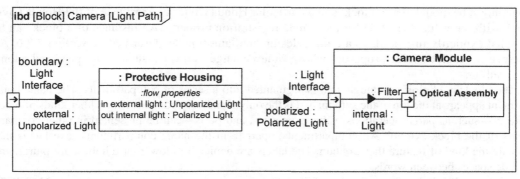

FIGURE 7.2

Example internal block diagram.

The frame of an internal block diagram always corresponds to a block, so the model element kind is often elided in the diagram header. The *block name* is the name of the block that is designated by the frame.

Figure 7.2 shows an example internal block diagram containing some common symbols. The diagram describes part of the internal structure of the *Camera* and how light flows in and through various intermediate parts to the *Optical Assembly*.

The notation used in the internal block diagram to describe the usage of blocks (called parts) and their interconnections is shown in the Appendix, Tables A.6, A.11, and A.12. Internal block diagram notation can also be shown in the structure compartment of a block on a block definition diagram. Figures 7.26 and 7.27 both provide examples of this.

7.2 MODELING BLOCKS ON A BLOCK DEFINITION DIAGRAM

The **block** is the fundamental modular unit for describing system structure in SysML. It can define a type of logical or conceptual entity; a physical entity (e.g., a system); a hardware, software, or data component; a person; a facility; an entity that flows through the system (e.g., water); or an entity in the natural environment (e.g., the atmosphere or ocean). Blocks are often used to describe reusable components that can be used in many different systems. The different kinds of block features used to define the block are described later and are broadly classified as structural features, behavioral features, and constraints.

A block is a type, that is, a description of a set of similar **instances** or **objects**, all of which exhibit common characteristics. A block owns a set of features that describe the characteristics of its instances. Structural features define its internal structure and properties. Behavioral features define how it interacts with its environment or modifies its own state. An example of a block is an automobile that may include physical, performance, other properties (e.g., weight, speed, odometer reading), and vehicle registration number, and also may include definitions of how it responds to steering and throttle commands. Each instance of the automobile block will include these features and may be uniquely identified by the value of some of its properties. For example, a Honda

Civic might be modeled as a block, and a particular Honda Civic is an instance of the Honda Civic block with the value A1F R3D for its vehicle registration property. An instance of a block can be modeled explicitly in SysML as a unique design configuration, as described in Section 7.7.6. An instance can include value properties whose values change over time, such as its speed and odometer reading.

The block symbol is a rectangle that is segmented into a series of compartments. The name compartment appears at the top of the symbol and is the only mandatory compartment. Other kinds of block features—such as parts, operations, value properties, and ports—can be presented in other compartments of the block symbol. All compartments, apart from the name compartment, have labels that indicate the kind of feature they contain. The labels are depicted in lower case italics, are plural, and include spaces between words.

Names on block definition diagrams follow the same convention as package diagrams. Model elements that are either directly contained in or imported into the namespace corresponding to the diagram are designated just by their names. Other model elements must be designated by their qualified names in order to clearly identify their location in the model hierarchy.

Any rectangle on a block definition diagram is interpreted by default as representing a block, but the optional keyword «block» may be used, preceding the name in the name compartment, if desired. To reduce clutter, the convention used in this chapter is that the «block» keyword is only used if blocks appear on the same block definition diagram as other model elements that are depicted as rectangles.

Figure 7.3 shows a block definition diagram that has three blocks in the company's corporate model, called *ACME Surveillance Systems*. The names of the blocks are fully qualified with their path to show where they are located within the package hierarchy of the model, which is shown in Chapter 6, Figure 6.5. The blocks shown cover a range of uses: *Camera* is a description of an ACME product; *Stepper Motor Module* is an off-the-shelf component used in ACME's cameras; and *Video* is used to describe the video images that the cameras produce.

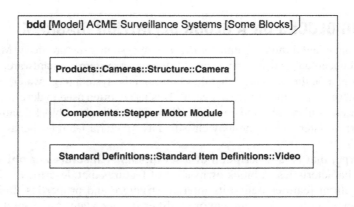

FIGURE 7.3

Blocks on a block definition diagram.

7.3 MODELING THE STRUCTURE AND CHARACTERISTICS OF BLOCKS USING PROPERTIES

Properties are structural features of a block. A property has a type that defines its characteristics, which may be another block, or some more basic type such as an integer. This section describes three categories of property and their uses.

- Part properties (parts for short) describe the decomposition of a block into its constituent elements. These are described in Section 7.3.1.
- Reference properties are properties whose values refer to parts of other blocks. Reference properties are described in Section 7.3.2.
- Value properties describe the quantifiable characteristics of a block, such as its weight or velocity, and are described in Section 7.3.4.

More advanced topics related to properties include the following:

- Property derivation, static properties, and read only properties are described in Section 7.3.4.
- Property redefinition and subsetting are defined in Sections 7.7.1 and 7.7.6, respectively.
- Property ordering and uniqueness are defined in Chapter 8, Section 8.3.1.

The *properties* compartment of a block can display its properties of any kind.

7.3.1 MODELING BLOCK COMPOSITION HIERARCHIES USING PARTS

Parts describe composition relationships between blocks. This kind of hierarchical composition of blocks is often seen in a bill of materials (also known as a parts list or equipment tree). A composition relationship is also called a whole–part relationship. A part is usually typed by a block, although it can also be typed by an actor as described in Chapter 12, Section 12.5.1.

A part identifies the usage of its type in a context. The key distinction between a part and an instance of a block is that the part describes an instance or instances of a block in the context of an instance of its composite block, whereas an instance does not require a context.

An instance of a composite block may include multiple instances of the block at the part end. The potential number of instances is specified by the multiplicity of the part, which is defined as follows:

- A lower bound (minimum number of instances) that may be 0 or any positive integer. The term "optional" is often used for multiplicities when the lower bound is 0, because an instance of the whole is not obliged to include any instances of the block at the part end.
- An upper bound (maximum number of instances) that may be 1, many (denoted by "*"), or any positive integer equal to or greater than the lower bound.

A part is a feature of a block, and as such can be listed in a separate parts compartment within a block. The parts compartment is labeled with the keyword *parts* and contains one entry for each part in the block. Each entry has the following format:

```
part name: block name [multiplicity]
```

The upper and lower bounds of a multiplicity are typically combined into one expression with the format lower bound..upper bound, except when both bounds have the same value, in which case that value is shown. If no multiplicity is shown on the part end, a value of 1 is assumed.

Figure 7.4 shows a simple example of an automobile with four wheels, in which each usage of *Wheel* is uniquely identified by a part. In this case, the *Automobile* is the whole and the wheels are represented as parts. Each of the four wheels has a common block definition, *Wheel,* with certain characteristics (e.g., *size, pressure*), but each wheel can have a unique **usage** or **role** in the context of a particular automobile. The front wheels have a different role than the rear wheels and may have different values for their pressure. Each wheel may also behave differently when the car is turning or accelerating and be subject to different constraints. Similarly, the front wheels on a front wheel-drive vehicle may have a different role than front wheels on a rear wheel-drive vehicle.

A part defines a set of instances that belong to an instance of the whole or composite block. If a block is part of more than one composite block, the SysML semantics are that an instance of that block is part of at most one block instance at any time. An example is an engine that can be part of two different types of vehicle, such as an automobile and a truck. However, any given instance of engine can only be part of one vehicle instance at a time. This rule implies that at the instance level the composition hierarchy is a strict tree, because an instance may have at most one parent.

Typically, a whole–part relationship means that certain operations that apply to the whole may also apply to each of its parts. For example, if a whole represents a physical object, a change in position of the whole could also change the position of each of its parts. A property of the whole, such as its mass, could also be inferred from its parts. However, these inferred characteristics must be specified in the model generally by using constraints as described in Chapter 8.

When blocks represent components of physical systems, the whole–part relationships can sometimes be considered an assembly relationship, where an instance of the block on the whole end is assembled from instances of the block on the part ends. The implications of whole–part relationships for software relate to creating and returning memory locations for computation. For software objects, a

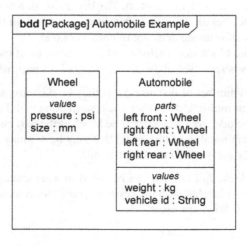

FIGURE 7.4

An automobile with four wheels described as separate parts.

typical interpretation for the whole–part relationship is that create, delete, and copy operations of the whole also apply to all of its parts. As an example, the whole–part semantics specify that when an instance at the whole end is destroyed, the instances at the part end will also be destroyed.

Composite associations

A **composite association** relates two blocks in a whole–part relationship. It has two ends, one describing the whole and the other describing the part. A part is owned by the block at the whole end of the association. The upper bound of the multiplicity at the whole end is always 1 because an instance of a part may only exist in one whole at any one time. However, the lower bound of the multiplicity at the whole end may be 0 or 1. A value of 1 means that instances of the block at the part end must always be composed from instances of the block at the whole end, whereas a value of 0 means that an instance of the block at the part end can exist even if no whole exists. In the latter case, an instance of a block at the part end may be composed within many other block instances over time, but it is still mandated that the instance is only part of one instance at any given time. For example, an instance of an engine may physically exist on its own or be part of an instance of an automobile or a truck at any given time.

A composite association is shown as a line between two blocks with various adornments at its ends. The whole end of a composite association is adorned by a black diamond. A shorthand notation can be used to represent a block that has many composite associations by showing a single black diamond with a series of lines connecting to the part ends of each composite association.

Each end of the composite association may show a name and a multiplicity, among other adornments. When the multiplicity for an end is not shown, the default interpretation is a whole end multiplicity of 0..1 and a part end multiplicity of 1. If a name appears as an adornment on the part end, it is the name of the corresponding part, although parts do not need to be named. Association ends can also show adornments corresponding to other features of the property they represent, as described later in this chapter. In the most common use of composite associations, the whole end of the composite association is generally not named and the part end has the part name and an open arrowhead. The absence of an arrowhead on the part end indicates the presence of a reference property as defined in Section 7.3.2.

The parts compartment of a block can show the parts represented at the part end of the composite associations. Typically on any given diagram, the part is shown either in a parts compartment or as an association end, but not both.

Figure 7.5 shows a portion of the top two levels of the composition hierarchy for a *Camera*. The composite associations for *Camera* and *Mount Assembly* are shown. The parts of the *Camera Module and Electronics Assembly* are shown in compartments. Although multiple levels of decomposition can be shown on a single diagram, this can increase the clutter even for relatively simple systems. As a result, a common practice is to show only a single level of decomposition on a particular diagram. Note that the diagram frame corresponds to the *Structure* package, as indicated in the diagram header, which contains all the blocks shown in the figure.

There are different philosophies on which parts should have names. In this chapter, except where stated, the following naming philosophy is used:

1. Names are used to distinguish two parts with the same type (block). An example of this is the use of names for *Stepper Motor Module* to distinguish the two parts, *elevation motor* and *azimuth motor*.

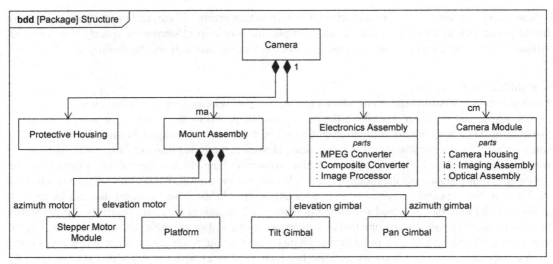

FIGURE 7.5

Showing a block composition hierarchy on a block definition diagram.

2. A part is given a name when the name of the type does not adequately describe the role the part plays. Examples of this are the names *elevation gimbal* and *azimuth gimbal*, since the block names *Tilt Gimbal* and *Pan Gimbal* do not explicitly describe the plane in which the gimbals move in the *Camera* application.

3. A part is not named when the type (block) name provides sufficient information to infer the role of the part. Examples of this are *Protective Housing* and *Electronics Assembly*. This is often the case when a block has been explicitly created to represent this part. This should also apply to *Mount Assembly, Camera Module,* and *Imaging Assembly*, but names were used to illustrate the part name notation in Figure 7.8 and Figure 7.54.

If the part has been given a name, it is referenced when describing the figure; otherwise the block name is used.

The lack of multiplicity adornments on all part ends in this figure indicate that there is exactly one instance of each part in the composition hierarchy of *Camera*. The multiplicity adornment on their whole end indicates that the *Electronics Assembly, ma,* and *cm* are always part of a *Camera*, whereas the block *Protective Housing* may be used in other blocks. All the parts of *ma* are typed by reusable blocks that have uses in many other contexts. The *Electronics Assembly* and *cm* are each shown with a parts compartment that lists their parts. None of the parts of the *Electronics Assembly* have a name, and they all have the default multiplicity of 1.

Modeling parts on an internal block diagram

In addition to appearing on a block definition diagram, parts can be shown on another diagram called the internal block diagram, which presents a different visualization of block composition. The internal block diagram enables parts to be connected to one another using connectors and ports as described later.

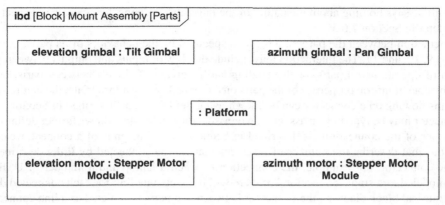

FIGURE 7.6

An internal block diagram for the *Mount Assembly*.

The relationship between composition—as shown on a block definition diagram and on an internal block diagram—is as follows:

- The whole end or composite (block) is designated by the diagram frame on the internal block diagram with the block name in the diagram header. It provides the context for all the diagram elements on the diagram.
- A part, shown either as a part end of a composite association whose whole end is the composite block or in the parts compartment of the composite block, appears as a box symbol with a solid boundary within the frame of the internal block diagram. The name string of the box symbol is composed of the part name followed by a colon followed by the type of the part. Either the part name or the type name can be elided.

The multiplicity of each part may be shown in the top right corner of the part symbol or in square brackets after the type name. If no multiplicity is shown, then a multiplicity of 1 is assumed.

Figure 7.6 is an internal block diagram derived from the composite associations whose whole end is *Mount Assembly* from Figure 7.5. The diagram header identifies *Mount Assembly* as the enclosing block that provides the context for the five parts shown in the diagram. In this case, the multiplicities are not shown, indicating that the multiplicity is the default value of 1. (See Figure 7.13 for an example of non-default multiplicity.) Note that this is a simplified form of internal block diagram for illustration.

A modeler may choose to indicate on a particular part symbol whether the internal structure of the block that types the part is further described by an internal block diagram. If they so choose and the block in question has an associated internal block diagram, then the symbol contains a rake icon in its bottom right corner. The rake icon on the *residence* part in Figure 7.13 indicates that that block is further elaborated in an internal block diagram, in this case shown in Figure 7.42.

Connecting parts on an internal block diagram

An internal block diagram can be used to show connections between the parts of a block. A **connector** is used to connect two parts and provides the opportunity for those parts to interact, although the connector alone says nothing about the nature of the interaction. Connectors can also connect ports, as described later in Section 7.6.3.

The interaction between the parts of a block is specified by the behaviors of its parts, as described in Chapters 9, 10, and 11. The interaction may include the flow of inputs and outputs between parts, the invocation of operations on parts, or the sending and receiving of signals between parts, or may be specified by constraints on properties of the parts on either end. When appropriate, the nature and direction of items flowing on a connector can be shown using item flows, as described in Section 7.4.3.

A connector may be typed by an association or association block that allows further definition of the characteristics of the connection, as described in Section 7.3.3. The ends of a connector can include multiplicities that describe the number of instances that can be connected by **links** described by the type of the connector. For example, the connection between a laptop and a number of USB devices might be modeled as a single connector, but there will be a separate link for each connected device.

On an internal block diagram, the connector between two parts is depicted as a line connecting two part symbols. A part can connect to multiple parts, but a separate connector is required for each connection. The full form of the connector name string is as follows:

```
connector name: association name
```

The ends of a connector can include an arrowhead, which means that the association that typed the connector had the equivalent adornment. This is not usually shown, however, and should not be confused with flows. The ends of the connector can be adorned with the name and multiplicity of the connector ends. If no multiplicity is shown, then a multiplicity of 1 is assumed. When connector symbols cross each other, their intersection can be designated by a semi-circular jog to distinguish the two connectors.

The internal block diagram for the *Camera* is shown in Figure 7.7. The *Protective Housing* that protects the camera internals is mechanically connected to the *Mount Assembly* (*ma*). The *Mount Assembly* provides the platform for the *Camera Module* (*cm*) and *Electronics Assembly,* which are connected to pass electrical signals that allow the camera to function. The connectors in this example have names, indicating that they are mechanically connected (*m1* to *m3*) or electrically connected (*e1*), but

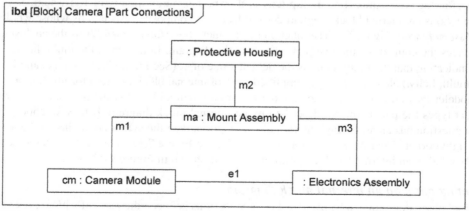

FIGURE 7.7

Connecting parts on an internal block diagram.

the names have no semantic implications. Meaningful semantics can be added by typing connectors, as described in Section 7.3.3, or by using a domain-specific profile as described in Chapter 15. All the connectors have default multiplicity implying one-to-one connections.

Modeling nested structures and connectors

Sometimes it is necessary to show multiple levels of nested parts within a system hierarchy on an internal block diagram. The nested parts can be represented by showing part symbols within part symbols, as shown in Figure 7.8. SysML also introduces an alternative notation to designate a nested part (also shown in the figure) in which each level of nesting of the part is separated by a period (dot) within the name string of a single part symbol. The symbol's name string, with **dot notation**, represents the path in the decomposition hierarchy from the level of the context block for the diagram down to the nested part. In Figure 7.8, the *azimuth gimbal* is represented as a nested rectangle within the *ma:Mount Assembly* symbol, and also represented using the dot notation with the higher-level part name, *ma,* and a dot preceding the part name, *azimuth gimbal.* It is expected that only the dot notation or the nested part notation is used on a diagram to depict a particular part.

Connectors can connect parts at different levels of nesting without directly connecting to the intermediate levels of nested parts. For example, a tire can be connected directly to a road without requiring intermediate connectors at each level of nesting from the vehicle to the suspension, the suspension to the wheel, and the wheel to the tire. The connector simply crosses the nested part boundaries in order to directly connect the tire to the road. Blocks have a special Boolean property called **isEncapsulated,** which if true prohibits connectors from crossing boundaries without connecting to any intermediate nested parts. It is often the case that connections are initially specified between top-level parts, and then as the internal details of the parts become known, connectors are specified between lower-level elements. It is a modeling choice as to whether the outer connectors are removed or kept.

Connectors with nested ends are shown in the same way as normal connectors except that they cross the boundaries of part symbols. The isEncapsulated property on a block is shown if true and not shown if false. If shown, it appears in the name compartment in braces before the block name.

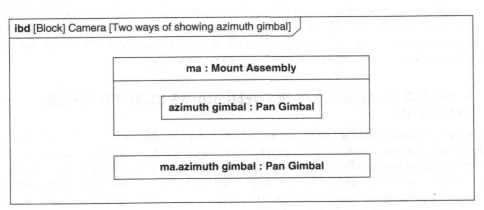

FIGURE 7.8

Showing deep-nested parts on an internal block diagram.

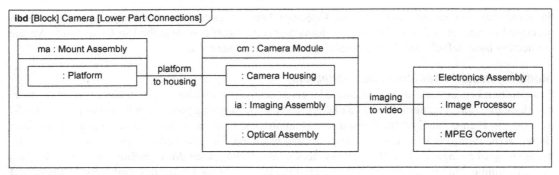

FIGURE 7.9

Nested connectors on an internal block diagram.

Figure 7.9 includes a more detailed look at the connections within the subassemblies in Figure 7.7. After further investigation, connector *m1* has been augmented with a connector, called *platform to housing,* whose nested ends directly connect the *Platform* of *ma* (the *Mount Assembly*) to the *Camera Housing* of the *cm* (the *Camera Module*). Similarly, the electrical connector, *e1,* has been augmented with a connector called *imaging to video* that connects the *Imaging Assembly* (*ia*) of *cm* to the *Image Processor* of the *Electronics Assembly.*

When a connector at one level of the structure is used to add more detail about a connector at some higher level, there are potential issues with maintaining the resulting model. For example, if the *m1* connector from Figure 7.7 is removed from the model, should *platform to housing* be removed as well? If this kind of relationship is important, then an association block can be used to show decomposition of the connector in a similar way that blocks show the decomposition of parts. Association blocks are described in Section 7.3.3. The use of ports is also important for addressing this kind of issue as described in Section 7.6.

Binding connectors

A **binding connector** is a special kind of connector that constrains its ends to have the same value. It is fundamental to the construction of parametric models (see Chapter 8) but also has uses in structural modeling with internal block diagrams. Two specific examples are the binding of proxy ports to parts (see Section 7.6.3) and the use of bound references to specify variation in blocks (see Section 7.7.4).

A binding connector is shown using the connector notation introduced above, except that the connector path optionally has the keyword «equal» shown near its center.

7.3.2 MODELING RELATIONSHIPS BETWEEN BLOCKS USING REFERENCE PROPERTIES

Reference properties, sometimes shortened to just **references,** enable an instance of a block that contains the reference property to refer to an instance of the block which types the reference property. The composition semantics of whole–part relationships, as described by parts, define a specific relationship between an instance of the block at the whole end and an instance of the block at the part end, as described in the previous section. An example of this is the destruction semantics, which specify that destroying an instance of the block at the whole end also destroys the instances of the blocks at the part ends. For reference properties, the destruction semantics associated with composition do not apply. There is also no constraint on the number of blocks that can have reference properties that refer to the same instance. This provides significant utility as described next.

Reference properties can be used to describe a logical hierarchy that references blocks that are part of other composition hierarchies. Reference properties can thus be used to cut across the tree structure of a composition hierarchy, which allows additional decomposition views besides the primary system whole–part hierarchy. This logical hierarchical organization can be represented on both the block definition diagram and internal block diagram. Binding connectors can be used to constrain the reference properties in a logical hierarchy to have the same value as a specific part in a composition hierarchy. Another use of reference properties is to model stored items (e.g., water stored in a tank). The water is not part of the tank in the same way that a valve is a part of the tank. For this case, the water may be owned by another block and shown as a reference property of the tank.

Like parts, reference properties can be listed in a separate compartment within a block. The references compartment is headed by the keyword *references* and contains one entry for each reference property in the block, with the same presentation as parts.

Reference associations

The composite association was discussed earlier in this chapter as representing a hierarchy of blocks. **Reference associations** are used on a block definition diagram to capture a different relationship between blocks, in which the block on one end of the association is referenced by the block on the other end. A reference association can specify a reference property on the blocks at one or both ends.

A reference association is represented as a line between two blocks. The black diamond that represents a composite association is not used. When there is a reference property on only one end, the line has an open arrowhead on the end of the association pointing from the owner of the reference property to the type that is referenced. There is no arrowhead on the end of the association that owns the reference property. If the reference association is bidirectional (i.e., has reference properties at both ends), then there are no arrowheads on either end. Multiplicities on the ends of reference associations have the same form as for composite associations.

One end of a reference association may be represented by a white diamond. SysML assigns the same meaning to the association whether the white diamond is present or not. However, the white diamond symbol is intended to be used with an applied stereotype that may specify unique semantics for a particular domain.

Composite associations can also define reference properties. If there is no arrowhead on the part end of a composite association, then the block typing the part has a corresponding reference property whose name is given at the whole end of the composite association.

Figure 7.10 shows a block called *Mechanical Power Subsystem* that uses reference associations to reference the *Power Supply* of the *Camera*, its powered mechanical components, including the motors in the various assemblies, and the *Distribution Harness*. The *Distribution Harness* itself has references to other harnesses that are part of the different assemblies in the *Camera*. In the composition hierarchy for the *Camera*, the components are part of a number of different assemblies, some of which are shown in Figure 7.5. The *Mechanical Power Subsystem* represents a logical aggregation of these components that interact to provide power to the rest of the camera. The white diamond adornment is used in this example to emphasize the hierarchical nature of the *Mechanical Power Subsystem*, but this emphasis is strictly notational and has no semantic implications.

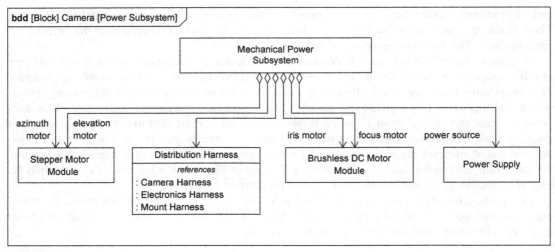

FIGURE 7.10

Reference associations on a block definition diagram.

Different model-based methods may include a block such as the *Mechanical Power Subsystem* in different parts of the model structure. Here it is contained in the *Camera* block itself, but it could just as easily have been placed in a special package of similar subsystems. An instance of *Mechanical Power Subsystem* does not show up in the equipment tree for the *Camera* but is more like a cross-cutting view of a portion of the equipment tree.

Reference associations are also used to represent associations between blocks for other purposes, such as those that might be used in the classical entity-relationship-attribute (ERA) kind of data modeling or more general class modeling.

Modeling reference properties on internal block diagrams

Reference properties are depicted in a similar fashion to parts when shown on the internal block diagram, except that their box symbol has a dashed instead of a solid boundary. Otherwise they have similar adornments and can be connected in the same way as any part symbol.

Figure 7.11 shows the connections between the reference properties of the *Mechanical Power Subsystem* used to support power transfer within the subsystem. In this case, a single *power source* provides all the power needs of the mechanical parts of the camera through the *Distribution Harness*.

7.3.3 USING ASSOCIATIONS TO TYPE CONNECTORS BETWEEN PARTS

Just as blocks can be used as the types of parts to model the structure of a system, **associations** can be used as the types of connectors to model the connections between parts. Associations can be used in two ways: to define how blocks can be validly connected, and to define details, including further structure, of those connections.

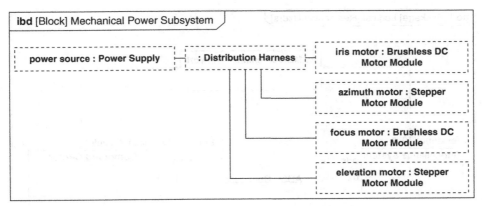

FIGURE 7.11

Reference properties and their interconnections on an internal block diagram.

Typing connectors by associations to assert compatibility

One use of a typed connector is to assert compatibility between the parts it connects by requiring that the parts at either end of the connector satisfy the constraints imposed by the association that types it. For a connector to be typed by an association, the connected parts must have a type that is compatible with the ends of that association. A compatible part type is either the same type as the association end or a specialization of that type.

A disciplined process may require all connectors be typed to ensure the compatibility of their ends. In such a process, a library of associations with compatible end types is provided, and every connector must be typed by an association from this library, which ensures that only parts that were intended to be connected can be. It is assumed in this process that the compatibility of the features of end types has also been validated (see Sections 7.4.3 and 7.5.4).

An association defines the multiplicity of block instances on each of its ends. Although connectors may have their own multiplicities, their lower and upper bounds are constrained to be within the multiplicity defined for the ends of the association that types it.

Figure 7.12 shows the part of the *ACME Surveillance Network* that deals with residential users. An Asynchronous Digital Subscriber Line (ADSL) connection is used to connect several *Surveillance Systems* to the *Command Center,* as shown by the association *ADSL Connection.* The ends of *ADSL Connection* represent reference properties of the blocks at each end and are named *adsl dte* and *adsl dce,* indicating the respective roles of the related blocks. A *Surveillance System* is a data terminator and thus has higher download than upload capacity and must be related, via its reference property *adsl dce,* to exactly one *Command Center.* A *Command Center* is related, via its reference property *adsl dte,* to zero or more *Surveillance Systems.*

Figure 7.13 shows the residential part of the *ACME Surveillance Network* on an internal block diagram. It shows the *residential surveillance center* connected to a set of *residences.* The connector, *res comms,* is typed by the *ADSL Connection* and so must conform to both the types of its ends and their multiplicities, which it does. In this case the connector does not further restrict the multiplicity stated on the association so there is no need to add multiplicities to the connectors. For an example of connectors with multiplicities, see Figure 7.42.

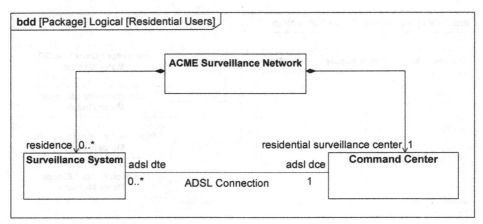

FIGURE 7.12

A reference association between two blocks.

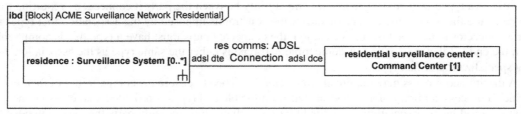

FIGURE 7.13

Connector typed by an association.

Using association blocks to define the structure of connectors

More detail can be specified for connectors by typing them with **association blocks.** An association block, as the name implies, is a combination of an association and a block, so it can relate two blocks together but can also have internal structure and other features. The internal structure can be used to decompose the connector that is typed by the association block.

Each end of the association block is represented by a special kind of property called a **participant property**, which is analogous to a reference property. This enables the blocks at the ends of the association block to be referenced by the association block, without being part of the association block. This in turn ensures association blocks are not confused with other parts of the system composition hierarchy.

Association blocks are shown on block definition diagrams as an association path with a block symbol attached to it via a dashed line. The name of the association block is shown in the block symbol rather than on the association path.

Figure 7.14 shows a refinement to Figure 7.12 in which *ADSL Connection* is now an association block. The figure also shows additional internal structure inside *Surveillance System* and *Command Center*: an *ADSL Modem* and an *ADSL Gateway,* respectively. These new parts are used to handle the ADSL communication between them, as shown in Figure 7.15.

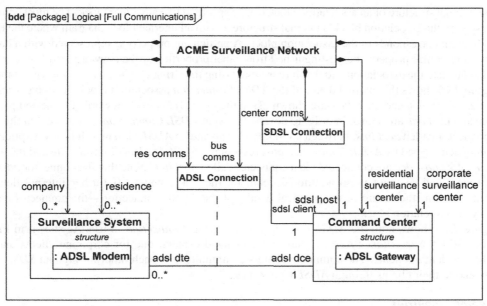

FIGURE 7.14

Using association blocks to relate blocks.

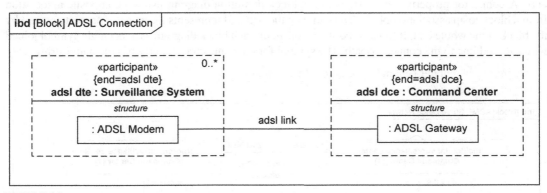

FIGURE 7.15

The internal structure of an association block.

Figure 7.14 also includes another association block, *SDSL Connection. SDSL Connection* represents the use of a Synchronous Digital Subscriber Line (SDSL) between *Command Centers,* but the parts required to support SDSL are not shown. In addition, the figure shows further aspects of the *ACME Surveillance Network* related to corporate customers and the connectors, *res comms, bus comms* and *center comms* used to connect them. Refer to the next section on connector properties for further discussion of these.

The internal structure of an association block can be specified like any other block. The most common way to specify the association block's internal structure is with an internal block diagram where the frame of the diagram corresponds to the association block. A participant property is represented with a dashed box, like a reference property, but distinguished from other properties by the keyword «participant». It may also indicate the association end that it represents using the string end = property name in braces.

Figure 7.15 shows the internal detail of the *ADSL Connection* association block. Its two participant properties—*adsl dce* and *adsl dte*—are shown using the «participant» keyword. The nested parts of *adsl dte* and *adsl dce* are shown in order to describe how an *ADSL Connection* is achieved, in this case via a connector called *adsl link,* between an *ADSL Modem* and an *ADSL Gateway*. It is now explicit that every connector typed by *ADSL Connection* ensures that the *ADSL Modem* of its *adsl dte* and the *ADSL Gateway* of its *adsl dce* are connected via a connector called *adsl link*. Note that the connector *adsl link* is not typed, and so there is no additional detail on the link's nature. If further internal detail is required—such as the nature of the physical details of the ADSL connection—the connector can be typed by an association block.

Figure 7.16 shows both the *ADSL Connection* and *SDSL Connection* in use. As shown in Figure 7.14, the *ACME Surveillance Network* has two command centers: one for corporate clients and the other for residential clients. The command centers communicate to each other through an *SDSL Connection* and to their clients through *ADSL Connections*.

Connector properties

As noted previously, a connector can be typed by an association or association block and is a feature of a block. SysML allows a connector typed by an association block to be represented by a **connector property**. A connector property can be shown on a block definition diagram using a composite association from a block to an association block. The name on the part end represents a connector property owned by the block at the whole end. It can also be shown on an internal block diagram as a rectangle symbol joined with a dotted line to the connector path. The symbol for the connector property has the name string:

```
«connector» connector name: association name
```

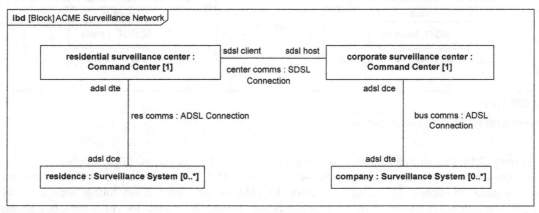

FIGURE 7.16

Example of an ACME surveillance network with two command centers.

Figure 7.14 shows three connector properties: *res comms* and *bus comms*, typed by *ADSL Connection*, and *center comms*, typed by *SDSL Connection*.

7.3.4 MODELING QUANTIFIABLE CHARACTERISTICS OF BLOCKS USING VALUE PROPERTIES

Value properties are used to model the quantitative characteristics of a block, such as its weight or speed. They can also be used to model vector quantities, such as position or velocity. Whereas the definition of a part or reference property is based on a block, the definition of a value property is based on a value type that specifies the range of valid values the property can take when describing an instance of its owning block. SysML defines the concepts of unit and quantity kind that can be used to further characterize a value type, although a value type does not require a quantity kind or unit. Value properties can have default values associated with them, and they can also define a probability distribution for their values.

Modeling value types on a block definition diagram

Value types are used to describe the values for quantities. For example, value properties called *total weight* and *component weight* might be typed by a value type called *kilograms* (kg) whose value can be any real number greater than or equal to 0. The intent of the value type is to provide a uniform definition of a quantity that can be shared by many value properties. Value type definitions can be reused by typing multiple value properties with the same value type.

A value type describes the data structure for representing a quantity and specifies its allowable set of values. This is especially important when relying on computers to operate on the values to perform various computations. A value type can be based on the predefined value types that SysML provides, or new value types can be defined. The following are the different categories of value type:

- A **primitive type** supports the definition of scalar values. *Integer, String, Boolean,* and *Real* are predefined primitive types in SysML.
- An **enumeration** defines a set of named values called literals. Examples of enumerations are colors and days of the week.
- A **structured type** represents a specification of a data structure that includes more than one data element, each of which is represented by a value property. *Complex* is a predefined structured type provided by SysML. Another example may be a value type called *Position* with value properties for *x*, *y*, and *z*.

Value types represent values, not entities, and so unlike blocks they have no concept of identity. In particular this implies that two instances of a value type are identical if they have the same values, which is not true of instances of blocks.

Value types are represented on a block definition diagram by a box symbol with a solid boundary. The name compartment of a value type has the keyword «valueType» preceding its name.

The symbol representing an enumeration has a single compartment, labeled *literals*, listing all the literals of the enumeration and the keyword «enumeration» preceding its name in the name compartment. The symbol representing a structured type also has a single compartment labeled *values* that lists the nested value properties of the value type, using the same compartment notation as shown for other value properties.

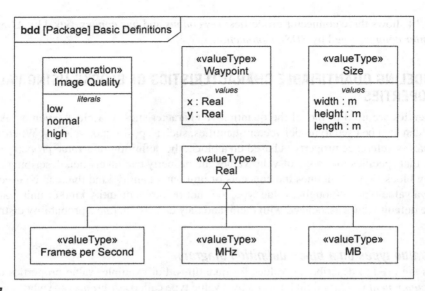

FIGURE 7.17

Definition of basic value types in a block definition diagram.

Figure 7.17 shows some value types in the *Basic Definitions* package. *Size* is a structured type, with three nested value properties: *width, height,* and *length*; they are typed by another value type *m* (for meters). The definition of *m* includes its unit and is shown later in Figure 7.19. *Image Quality* is an enumeration used to specify the quality of image captured by the camera, which can be used to control how much data are required to capture each video frame. The other value types are all real numbers and so are specializations of the SysML value type *Real*. In this case the specialization is simply stating that the values for *MHz, MB,* and *Frames per Second* are real numbers. See Section 7.7 for further discussion on the meaning and notation for specialization.

Adding units and quantities to value types

SysML defines the concepts of unit and quantity kind as shareable definitions that can be used consistently across a model, or captured in a model library that can be reused across a set of models. A **quantity kind** identifies a kind of physical quantity such as length, whose value may be stated in terms of defined **units** (e.g., meters or feet). To cover all potential situations, a unit can be associated with multiple quantity kinds, although typically a unit will be associated to just one. Often, equations can be expressed in terms of quantities that include quantity kinds without specifying units. Both quantity kinds and units can have symbols, such as those shown in Figure 7.18, which SysML model editors and other tools can use in place of the full names of quantity kinds and units.

In developing a system model, it is critical to ensure that the units of system data are compatible, and simply using a name or even a model library is not sufficient to identify a unit or quantity kind uniquely if many organizations and project teams are collaborating on a system development. SysML units and quantity kinds also include a **definitionURI**, which can be used to relate them to a unique web reference, so that definitive comparisons can be performed.

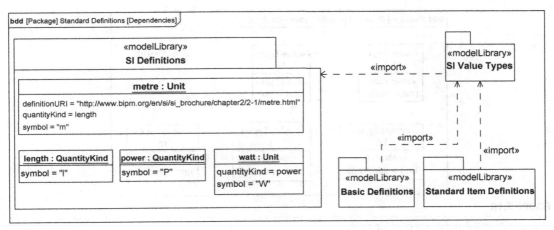

FIGURE 7.18

Importing the SI definitions defined by SysML.

A value type that represents a physical quantity may reference a quantity kind and/or unit as part of its definition, and thus assign units and quantity kinds to any value property that it types.

Both units and quantity kinds are shown on a block definition diagram using a box symbol. They have their name and type (unit or quantity kind), underlined and separated by a colon, shown in the name compartment, and their different slots shown in a compartment.

The SI standard for units and quantity kinds

The International System of Units (**SI**) is a standard for units and quantity kinds published by the International Standards Organization (ISO). The complete set of SI quantity kinds and units are described in a model library called *ISO80000* in Annex E.6 of the OMG SysML specification, based on a sophisticated foundation library that supports quantitative analysis. This model library can be imported into any model to allow the SI definitions to be used as is or as the basis for defining more specialized units and quantity kinds. Although this model library is a non-normative part of the SysML specification that is not required for tool vendor conformance, it is anticipated that many SysML modeling tools will include this library and possible extensions. All units and quantity kinds in the *ISO80000* model library have a definition URI taken from http://www.bipm.org/.

Figure 7.18 shows some of the definitions in the *SI Definitions* model library in the *Standard Definitions* library of ACME Surveillance Systems. All of the units and quantity kinds shown have definition URIs, although only the one for *metre* is displayed in the figure. *SI Value Types* is a locally defined model library that imports *SI Definitions* in order to define a set of SI value types for this application based on the SI units and quantity kinds.

Some of the value types in the *SI Value Types* model library are shown in Figure 7.19, using unit definitions imported from the *SI Definitions* package. This enables a consistent representation of quantities that can be checked for compatibility of quantity kinds and consistency of units. Although not shown here, all the value types in this figure are defined to be real numbers.

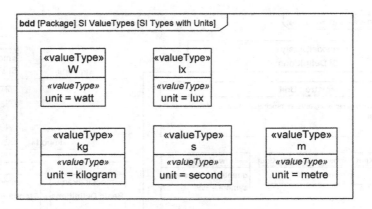

FIGURE 7.19

Using units in the definition of value types.

Adding value properties to blocks

Once value types have been defined, they can be used to type the value properties of blocks. Value properties can have multiplicity and are shown in a compartment of their owning block similar to other properties. The values compartment has the label *values*.

Figure 7.20 shows a block definition diagram containing three blocks with value properties: *Camera, Electronics Assembly,* and *Optical Assembly.* Some of the value properties, such as the *clock speed* and *memory* of *Electronics Assembly,* are typed with the value types specified in Figure 7.17. Others are typed with value types shown in Figure 7.19. For example, the *sensitivity* of the *Camera* is typed by *lux,* which measures luminance. The names of value types are not limited to alphanumeric characters. For example, *pan field of regard* in *Camera* is typed by the character "°," which is a symbol for degrees.

Read only and static properties

Properties can be specified as read only, which means that their values cannot change during the lifetime of their owner. A **read only property** is indicated using the keyword `readOnly` in braces at the end of the property string.

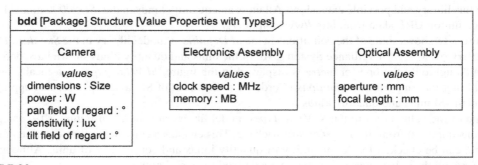

FIGURE 7.20

Use of a value type to type a value property on a block definition diagram.

A property can also be specified as static, which means that its value is the same across all instances described by this block. A **static property** is often used to describe some configuration characteristic that has the same value for a particular type, such as the number of sides of a cube. Static properties are shown by underlining the name string of the property.

Derived properties

Properties can be specified as derived, which means that their values are derived from other values. In software systems, a **derived property** is typically calculated by the software in the system. In physical systems, a property is typically marked as derived to indicate that the values of derived properties are calculated based on analysis or simulation, and may well be subject to constraints as described in Chapter 8, Section 8.3.1. By definition, constraints express noncausal relationships between properties, but derived properties can be interpreted as dependent variables, and thus allow the equations expressed in constraints to be treated as mathematical functions.

A derived property is indicated by placing a forward slash (/) in front of the property name.

Figure 7.21 shows *Optical Assembly* with an additional property *f-number,* which is marked as derived. It also shows a constraint between *focal length, aperture,* and *f-number* that can be used— given *focal length* and *aperture*—to calculate the value of *f-number.*

Modeling property values and distributions

A **default value** can be assigned to a property as part of its property string in the appropriate compartment of a block, using the following syntax:

```
property name: type name = default value
```

The **initial values** for a part can be specified using a dedicated compartment labeled *initial Values.* The initial values override the default values of the properties in the block that types the part. If no initial value is defined, the default value is used for properties of the part. The initial values compartment can be used on the part but cannot be used on the block.

A value property whose range of values can be described by a **probability distribution** rather than a single value is called a **distributed property**. Annex E.7 of the OMG SysML specification defines some commonly used probability distributions in a model library that can be reused. The following notation is used to represent a distributed property:

```
«distributionName» {p1=value, p2 = value ...} property name : type name
```

Optical Assembly
constraints   {f-number == aperture/focal length}
values   aperture : mm   focal length : mm   /f-number : Real

FIGURE 7.21

Example of derived property.

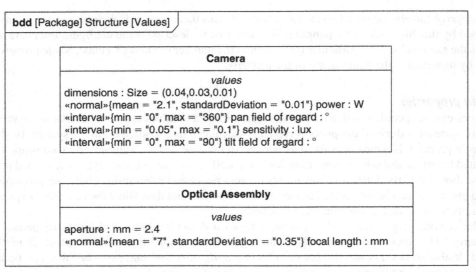

FIGURE 7.22

Examples of property values and distributions.

The tags *p1*, *p2*, and so on characterize the probability distribution. For example, a *mean* and *standard deviation* are properties that characterize a normal distribution, while a *min* and *max* value characterize an interval distribution.

Figure 7.22 shows a number of distributed properties, including *pan field of regard* and *focal length*. The *pan field of regard* is the size of the arc that the camera can view while panning. It is defined as an interval distribution with a minimum of 0° and a maximum of 360° because the actual field of regard will depend on where the camera is installed. The focal length of the *Optical Assembly* is defined as a normal distribution with a mean of 7 millimeters and a standard deviation of 0.35 millimeters. This is intended to accommodate differences arising from the combination of minor deviations in the placement of lenses and mirrors during manufacturing.

The distributions of both *pan field of regard* and *focal length* are distributions over the whole population of cameras and optical assemblies. The *dimensions* of the *Camera* and *aperture* of the *Optical Assembly* have default values: a simple scalar value for *aperture* and a value for each of the constituent value properties of *dimensions*.

7.4 MODELING FLOWS

Defining the flows between different parts of a system can provide an abstract view of their interactions. Flows may be physical in nature. For example a water pump might specify that water can flow in and out of the pump and that electrical power can flow in. Often, in electronic systems, it is information and/or control that flows, such as a signal from a radar system that represents the position and velocity of a target, or a signal resulting from a button being pressed on a keyboard.

Item is the general term used to define things that flow. Blocks may contain special properties, called flow properties, that define the items that can flow into or out of that block. In addition, item flows specify what actually does flow on connectors between parts.

7.4.1 MODELING ITEMS THAT FLOW

An **item** is used to describe a kind of entity that flows. It may be a physical flow, which includes matter and energy, as well as a flow of information. Items may be blocks, value types, or signals. When items are modeled as blocks, they typically include value properties that describe characteristics of the item, such as the temperature and pressure for a block that represents flowing water. An item may have significant internal structure, such as an automobile that flows through an assembly line or a complex message sent across a data bus. A flow may also be simplified to represent just a quantifiable property (e.g., water temperature), in which case the item can be represented as a value type instead of a block.

The flow of control and/or information can also be represented by signals. These signals may be used to control the behavior of a part that is the target of the signal flow. SysML allows—but does not require—that SysML implementations generate events when signals flow into or out of a block via flow properties. These events can be accessed by behaviors of a block and therefore may be used to control the behavior of a part that is the target of the signal flow (see Chapters 9, 10, and 11 for more detail on how these events are accessed).

Items can be defined at different levels of abstraction and may be refined throughout the design process. For example, an alert flowing from a security system to an operator may be represented as a signal at a high level of abstraction. However, in exploring the nature of how that alert is communicated in detail, the item may be redefined. If the alert is communicated as an audio alarm, for example, it may be redefined as a block that contains properties representing the amplitude and frequency of the sound.

Figure 7.23 shows part of the *Standard Item Definitions* model library that includes the items that flow in cameras. The items shown are modeled as blocks and contain value properties that describe their characteristics. The *Light* block defines its radiant *flux* in terms of Watts (*W*) and the *illuminance* in terms of *lux*. The *MPEG4* block defines the *frame rate* in *hertz* and number of *lines* in a frame.

7.4.2 FLOW PROPERTIES

A block may contain flow properties that specify what can flow in or out of the block. Each **flow property** has a name, type, multiplicity, and direction. The type of the flow property can be a block, value type, or signal depending on the specification of what can flow. The multiplicity of the flow property defines how many values it may contain as part of an instance of its owning block.

The flow properties of a block are shown in a special compartment labeled *flow properties,* with each flow property shown in the format:

```
direction property name: item type[multiplicity]
```

The direction of the flow property can be one of in, out, or inout.

The block diagram in Figure 7.24 shows two pieces of optical equipment, a *Light Source* and a *Light Sensor*. The *Light Source* outputs a *beam* of *Light*, and the *Light Sensor* accepts *incoming light*. The flow properties of both blocks are typed by the *Light* block shown in Figure 7.23.

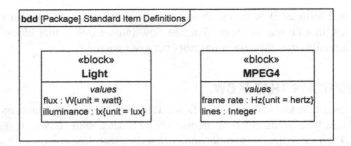

FIGURE 7.23

Items that flow in the *Camera* system.

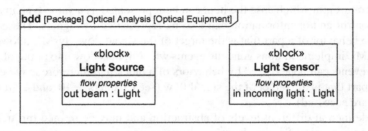

FIGURE 7.24

Flow properties on blocks.

7.4.3 MODELING FLOWS BETWEEN PARTS ON AN INTERNAL BLOCK DIAGRAM

A flow occurs as a result of a value (or values if the multiplicity of the property is greater than 1) being assigned to a flow property, which must have out or inout direction, on one end of a connector (the source). The assigned value is propagated across a connector or connectors to compatible flow properties, which must have in or inout direction, on connected parts.

Flow property compatibility

The ability of items to flow across connectors between parts is dependent on the flow properties specified on the parts at either end of the connector. For a flow to occur from a source part to a target part, both ends of the connector must have a flow property with at least a compatible type and direction. The flow property types are compatible if the type of the target flow property is either the same as or a generalization of the source flow property. Their directions are compatible if both properties have direction inout, or their directions are the opposite of each other. If more than one flow property matches based on type and direction, then compatible flow properties are determined based on their names.

The internal block diagram in Figure 7.25 shows *Light Source* and *Light Sensor* from Figure 7.24 connected inside a block called *Light Test*. The types and directions of their flow properties are compatible, allowing *Light* to flow from the *Light Source* to the *Light Sensor*.

The block definition in diagram Figure 7.26 extends the definition of *Light* from Figure 7.24 to include *Polarized Light*, which has additional properties, and *Unpolarized Light* (see Section 7.7.1 for a discussion of classification). It shows a specific light source, a *Lamp* and a *Polarized Light Sensor*.

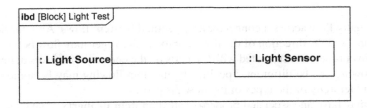

FIGURE 7.25

Connected parts with flow properties.

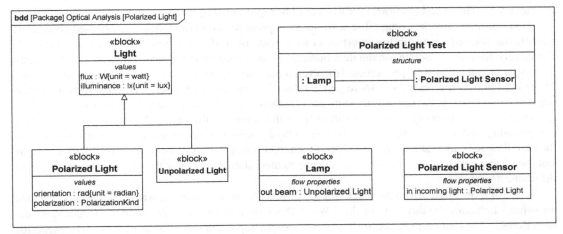

FIGURE 7.26

Connected parts with incompatible flow properties.

The *beam* emitted from the *Lamp* has type *Unpolarized Light* and so is incompatible with the *incoming light* property of the *Polarized Light Sensor*. Note that this is an abstraction, and it is probably more accurate to suggest that the *Polarized Light Sensor* will generate incorrect results in the presence of *Unpolarized Light*. A SysML modeling tool is expected to provide a notification of the incompatibility through a message or a change in the color of the connector.

Flow property propagation

If a part is connected to multiple parts that have compatible flow properties and/or any given connector represents multiple links, then a value assigned to an out flow property on that part is propagated across all links; this is sometimes called fan-out. The opposite case, sometimes called fan-in, occurs when an in flow property on the part is compatible with many out flow properties on connected parts. SysML does not define the assignment of multiple inflowing values to a single flow property. For example, the flow property may have a multiplicity equal to the number of sources of incoming flows, or the flow property may have a multiplicity of 1 and some form of averaging might take place. The language can be extended using a profile, as described in Chapter 15, to clarify the intent and meaning.

Item flows

The items that actually flow across a connector are specified by **item flows**. An item flow specifies the type of item flowing and the direction of the flow. For example, water may flow between a pump and a tank. While the flow properties associated with the parts on the ends of connectors define what can flow, the actual item flowing can be different. Specifically, the item flowing may be some other element in the generalization hierarchy of the types of the flow properties.

An item flow may have an associated property, called an **item property**, contained in the enclosing block, which identifies a specific usage of that item in the context of the enclosing block. In particular, multiple item properties may have the same type, but each item property represents a different usage. For example, the water flowing into a pump is one usage of water, while the water flowing out of the pump is another usage. The in and out flowing water would be represented by different item properties.

The item flow must be compatible with the flow properties on either end of its related connector. SysML has relaxed compatibility constraints to provide flexibility for how item flows are modeled. Effectively, the only constraint on the item flowing is that it must be in the same classification hierarchy as its source and target flow properties. However, a common approach to compatibility is that the type of the item flow is the same as or more general than the source flow property, and that the type of the target flow property is the same as or more general than that of the item flow. In other words, the flow is specified more generally as you transition from the source to the target. A simple example of this compatibility pattern is for the type of the source flow property to be intrusion alert status, the type of the item flow to be alert status, and the type of the target flow property to be status. Intrusion alert status can then leave a source part, cross the connector as alert status, and enter the part on the other side of the connector as status.

Item flows are represented as black-filled arrowheads on a connector, where the direction of the arrowhead indicates the direction of flow. When there are multiple item flows on a connector, all the item flows in the same direction are shown in a comma-separated list floating near the arrowhead for the appropriate flow direction. Each item flow has a type name and item property name, if it is defined. Item flows with opposite directions can be shown on a single connector.

Figure 7.27 shows the items flowing between various kinds of light sources and light sensors. A new kind of *Polarized Light*, *Coherent Light,* is added, which is the output from the *Laser* light source. The structure compartment of block *Laser Test* shows three parts typed by *Laser* and three by *Polarized Light Sensor.* The connectors between them show three possible item flows. The top two item flows illustrate the expected compatibility mode. The flow between *l1* and *s1* has item *Coherent Light*, which is the same as source flow property *beam*; the target flow property *incoming light* (from Figure 7.26) is *Polarized Light*, which is more general than the item flowing. The flow between *l2* and *s2* has type *Polarized Light*, which is more general than the source flow property and the same as the target flow property. Also illustrated, between *l3* and *s3* is the least constrained case, where the item flowing is *Light*, the root of the classification hierarchy. This last case does not adhere to the pattern noted above, but remains valid.

Items can also flow between connected reference properties. Figure 7.28 shows the flow of electricity, represented by the block *DC*, through the *Mechanical Power Subsystem* block first shown in Figure 7.11. The overall flow is from *power source* through the *Distribution Harness* to the various motors. Each item flow is represented by a corresponding item property owned by *Mechanical Power Subsystem.*

Item properties can be constrained in parametric equations, as described in Chapter 8. For an example of this, see Figure 16.22 in Chapter 16.

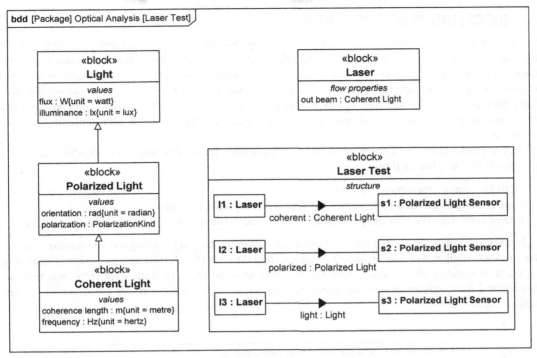

FIGURE 7.27

Item flows between parts.

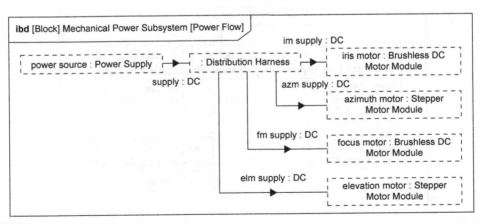

FIGURE 7.28

Item flows between reference properties.

7.5 MODELING BLOCK BEHAVIOR

Blocks provide a context for behaviors, which is the SysML term covering any and all descriptions of how the block deals with inputs, outputs, and changes to its internal state. A block may designate one behavior as its main or classifier behavior, which starts executing when the block is instantiated. Other behaviors may be designated as methods, which provide the detail of how service requests are handled. These two kinds of behaviors may in turn invoke other behaviors of the block. Behaviors have parameters that are used to pass items into or out of the behavior before, after, and sometimes during execution.

As Chapters 9 through 11 describe, there are three main behavioral formalisms in SysML: activities, state machines, and interactions.

- Activities transform inputs to outputs.
- State machines are used to describe how the block responds to events.
- Interactions describe how the parts of a block interact with one another using message passing.

SysML recognizes two other forms of behavior within the language. An **opaque behavior** is represented as a textual expression in some language external to SysML. A **function behavior** is similar to an opaque behavior with the added restriction that it is not allowed to affect the state of its owning block directly and may only communicate using parameters. Function behaviors are often used to define mathematical functions.

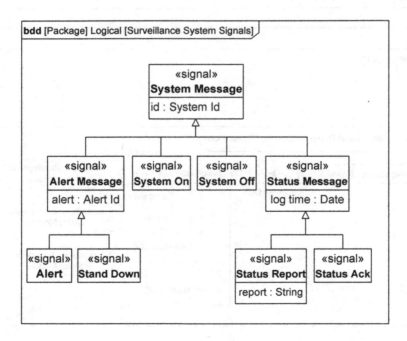

FIGURE 7.29

A signal classification hierarchy.

The behaviors of a block can be shown in compartments of a block symbol. The *classifier behavior* compartment shows the name of the classifier behavior, and the *owned behaviors* compartment shows the names of all the other behaviors that the block owns. The *Surveillance System* block in Figure 7.30 shows the name of its classifier behavior, which is a state machine called *Surveillance System*, and two of its owned behaviors, *Monitor Site* and *Handle Status Request*. These behaviors appear later in Chapters 9, 10, and 11.

7.5.1 MODELING THE MAIN BEHAVIOR OF A BLOCK

The **main behavior** (also called **classifier behavior**) of a block starts executing at the beginning of the block's lifetime and generally terminates at the end of its lifetime, although it may terminate before then. Depending on the nature of the block, the choice of formalism for the classifier behavior is between state machines (if the block is largely event-driven) and activities (if the block is largely used

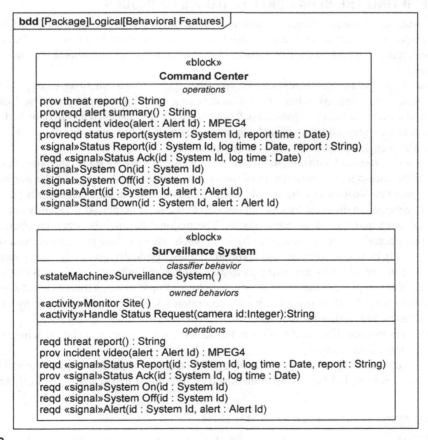

FIGURE 7.30

Blocks with behavioral features.

to transform input items to output items). A popular hybrid approach is to use a state machine to describe the states of a block and to specify an activity that executes when a block is in a given state or when it transitions between states. Behavior can also be specified independent of a block and can be allocated to blocks or parts of blocks.

When a block has a main behavior and also has parts with behaviors, the modeler should ensure that the behavior is consistent between the whole and the parts at each level of the system hierarchy. A main behavior may act as a controller that plays an active role in coordinating the behaviors of its parts. In this case, the behavior of the block is its main behavior, which is augmented by the main behaviors of its parts. Another approach is for the classifier behavior of the block to be an abstraction of the behavior of its parts, which is often called the black box view. In this case, the main behavior of the block represents a specification that the parts must realize. The behavior of the parts, often termed the white box view, interact in such a way that the black box behavior is preserved.

7.5.2 SPECIFYING THE BEHAVIORAL FEATURES OF BLOCKS

Along with structural features, blocks can also own **behavioral features** that describe which requests a block can respond to. A behavioral feature may have an associated method that is a behavior invoked when the block handles a request for the feature. There are two types of behavioral features: operations and receptions.

An **operation** is a behavioral feature that is typically triggered by a synchronous request (i.e., when the requester waits for a response). Each operation defines a set of **parameters** that describes the arguments passed in with the request, or passed back out once a request has been handled, or both. Note that an operation may be triggered by an asynchronous request (i.e., when the requester does not wait). In that case, no arguments are passed back to the requester.

A **reception** is associated with a **signal** that defines a message with a set of attributes that represent the content of the message; the parameters of the reception must be the same as the attributes of the associated signal. The attributes of the signal thus indirectly define the set of arguments passed in with the request. Receptions in different blocks can respond to the same signal, so frequently used messages can be defined once and reused in many blocks. The major difference between an operation and a reception is that operations may be triggered by both synchronous and asynchronous requests whereas receptions may only be triggered by an asynchronous request. Typically, an operation triggers an immediate response from the block by executing its associated method, whereas requests for receptions are handled by the block explicitly accepting the request, for example, when a transition between states in the state machine for a block is triggered by the reception's signal, or when an activity of the block includes an accept signal action for the signal.

Behavioral features are discussed further in the activity, interaction, and state machine chapters—Chapters 9 through 11, respectively.

Signals are defined using a box symbol with a solid outline and the keyword «signal» before the signal name. A signal symbol has a single unlabeled compartment that contains its attributes with the form:

```
attribute name: attribute type [multiplicity]
```

Figure 7.29 shows a set of signals that are used by a surveillance system. The signals are organized into a classification hierarchy, with each new layer in the hierarchy adding a new signal attribute (see Section 7.7 for a discussion of classification). For example, the *Status Report* signal has three attributes: *report*, which it defines directly; *log time*, from its relationship to *Status Message*; and *id*, from its relationship to *System Message*.

Operations and receptions are shown in a separate compartment of a block labeled *operations* and are described by their signature. The signature for an operation is a combination of its name along with parameters, and optional return type as follows:

```
operation name (parameter list):return type
```

The parameter list is comma-separated with the format:

```
direction parameter name: parameter type
```

Parameter direction may be in, out, or inout.

The signature for a reception is a combination of its name and a list of parameters as follows (the reception's name is always the name of its associated signal):

```
«signal» reception name (parameter list)
```

As of SysML 1.3, a block must designate whether it makes requests or handles requests for the behavioral features it defines. Requests for a **provided behavioral feature** are handled by the defining block. If a block defines a **required behavioral feature,** it indicates that it expects some external entity to handle any requests it makes for the feature. Behavioral features may be both required and provided.

A provided behavioral feature is indicated by the keyword prov preceding the signature of the feature. A required behavioral feature is indicated by the keyword reqd. The keyword provreqd indicates that a feature is both provided and required. If no keyword is shown, the feature is assumed to be provided.

Figure 7.30 shows a view of the services provided and required by *Surveillance System* and *Command Center*. They both have the same set of receptions, which correspond to the signals described in Figure 7.29. Most of the receptions defined by the *Surveillance System* are required, which means that it expects its environment to accept the signals it sends out, with the exception that it expects to receive *Status Ack* signals and so provides a reception for them. The reverse is true for *Command Center*, which only has one required reception; the rest are provided as indicated by the absence of a keyword. In addition, *Surveillance System* provides an operation to get the video related to any incident that it has reported, and the *Command Center* requires such an operation. The *Command Center* provides an on-demand *threat report*, detailing currently known issues; the *Surveillance System* requires such an operation. The *Command Center* also provides and requires two other operations, *alert summary* and *status report*, which are used to communicate between command centers and by external agencies investigating incidents.

7.5.3 MODELING BLOCK-DEFINED METHODS

Some behaviors owned by the block only execute in response to a particular stimulus, specifically when a request is made via a provided behavioral feature (operation or reception). Such a behavior is called a **method,** and it is related to the behavioral feature that was requested.

Unlike the main block behavior, methods typically have a limited lifetime, starting their execution following the stimulus, performing their allotted task, and then terminating, perhaps returning some results. Methods are usually specified using activities, opaque behaviors, or function behaviors.

It should be mentioned that not all behavioral features require methods. Requests associated with behavioral features can be handled directly by behaviors using the specialized constructs such as an accept event action, described in Chapter 9, Section 9.7, and a state machine trigger, described in Chapter 11, Sections 11.4.1 and 11.5. A behavioral feature cannot be related to both a method and these other constructs.

SysML supports the notion of **polymorphism,** which means that many different blocks may respond to the same stimulus, but each may do so in a specific way, by invoking a specific method. Polymorphism is strongly associated with classification, as described in Section 7.7.

7.5.4 ROUTING REQUESTS ACROSS CONNECTORS

Requests for behavioral features may be communicated across connectors between parts and references. When the behavior of a block makes a request for a required behavioral feature, then that request is communicated across any connector whose other end is targeted by the request. Any such target must have a provided behavioral feature (i.e., operation or reception) of the same kind with a compatible signature.

The signatures of two features must match all the following criteria below to be compatible. Firstly, the feature kind, parameter names, and parameter directions must be the same. Secondly, the type, multiplicity, ordering, and uniqueness characteristics of parameters must be compatible, which as a general rule means that input parameter characteristics on provided features must be the same or more general than the corresponding characteristics of required features, and that output parameter characteristics on provided features must be the same or more specialized than the corresponding characteristics of required features. For types, general and specialized refer to their position in a classification hierarchy. For multiplicity, a broader range (i.e., more values) is considered more general. For ordering, unordered is considered more general, and for uniqueness, nonunique is considered more general. For a discussion of ordering and uniqueness please refer to Chapter 8, Section 8.3.1.

As with flow properties, if a part is connected to multiple other parts or if a connector between a part and another part represents multiple links, then requests can be routed across many links whose ends have compatible behavioral features. If there are multiple links that fan-in, then the requests either immediately trigger the execution of a method per the request or they are queued until a behavior accepts them. If there are multiple links that fan-out, then an outgoing request is propagated across all links whose ends are targets of the request. However, SysML does not define the mechanism by which multiple return values are handled by the behavior that made the request. This is left to be specified by an execution profile.

As can be seen from Figure 7.30, *Command Center* and *Surveillance System* have a number of compatible behavioral features that can form the basis of communication between the two. Command centers can also communicate using *alert summary* and *status report*, which are both provided and required. By contrast, according to the definition in Figure 7.30, two connected surveillance systems would have nothing to say to one another. A typical configuration of these blocks is shown in Figure 7.16 in which the connector between *residence* and *residential surveillance center* has multiple links, which means that *residential surveillance center* needs to support fan-in requests for the operations and receptions that it provides.

7.6 MODELING INTERFACES USING PORTS

Modeling interfaces is a critical aspect of systems modeling. SysML allows modelers to specify a diverse set of interfaces, including mechanical, electrical, software, and human–machine interfaces. In addition, interfaces that specify information flow must be capable of specifying both the logical content of the information and the physical encoding of the information in bit, bytes, and other signal characteristics. Although system interfaces may be specified simply using the features of blocks and connectors between parts, SysML also introduces the concept of ports, which allow a more robust and flexible definition of system interfaces.

A **port** represents an access point on the boundary of a block and on the boundary of any part or reference typed by that block. A block may have many ports that specify different access points. Ports can be connected to one another by connectors on an internal block diagram to support the interaction between parts.

SysML 1.3 introduced two new kinds of ports called full ports and proxy ports. A **full port** is equivalent to a part on the boundary of the parent block that is made available as an access point to and from the block. A full port is typed by a block and can have nested parts and behaviors, and can modify incoming and outgoing flows like any other part. A full port can represent a physical part such as an electrical connector or a mechanical interface assembly, and therefore is a part in the system parts tree. The other kind of port is a **proxy port**. By contrast, a proxy port does not constitute a part of its parent block, but instead provides external access to and from the features of its parent block or the block's parts without modifying its inputs or outputs. A proxy port is essentially a pass through or relay that specifies what features of the owning block can be accessed at the port. A proxy port is typed by an interface block that specifies the features that can be accessed via the port. The interface block cannot have internal behavior or parts (or full ports), but may contain nested proxy ports.

Both proxy and full ports can support the same set of features, which are behavioral features and any kind of property (except proxy ports do not support parts). In either case, users of a block are only concerned with the features of its ports, regardless of whether the features are exposed by proxy ports or handled by full ports directly.

The decision on whether to use ports and which kind of port to use is a methodological question that often relates to how a block is intended to be used. A proxy port is often used to specify the system as a black box, in which case the interface specification does not specify any internal structure of the system. On the other hand, a full port is used to specify the interface in terms of an actual part of the system and enable that part to modify the inputs and outputs to the owning block. The choice between full and proxy ports is considered by some to be a design decision. To support this approach, a port can be created and connected without being designated as either a full or proxy port, allowing the decision to be deferred.

The concept of proxy ports and full ports was added in SysML 1.3 and was intended to replace the flow port and standard port concepts in SysML 1.2. In general, proxy ports provide the full functionality of SysML 1.2 flow ports and standard ports, but also add capability for nesting ports and for specifying nonflow properties. In SysML 1.3 and SysML 1.4, flow ports and standard ports are retained in the language, but the intent is to remove them in a future version. A discussion of these deprecated features is provided in Section 7.10.

7.6.1 FULL PORTS

Full ports are similar to parts, in that they are included in the parts tree of their owning block. Unlike parts, however, they are shown graphically on the boundary of their parent. An external connector can connect to a full port even if its parent block is encapsulated (i.e., isEncapsulated is set to true per Section 7.3.1), whereas connections to nested parts cannot be made if a block is encapsulated. Full ports are typed by blocks and can possess the full set of features available to any other block.

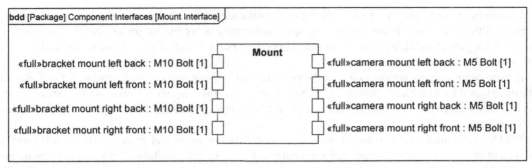

FIGURE 7.31

A block with full ports.

Full ports are shown as rectangles (typically square) intersecting the boundary of their parent symbol. The name, type, and multiplicity of the port are shown in a string either inside or floating near the port symbol in the form:

```
«full» port name: block name[multiplicity]
```

When a port's type has flow properties, an arrow inside the port's symbol can be used to provide information about their direction. If all flow properties have direction in, then the arrow faces inwards. If all flow properties have direction out, then the arrow faces outwards. If there is a mix of directions or all flow properties have direction inout, then two opposing arrowheads are used. If desired, the symbol for a full port can include the same set of compartments as a part symbol.

Ports of all kinds can be shown in a compartment on a block symbol labelled *ports*, using the string:

```
direction port name: block name[multiplicity]
```

Direction is only shown when the port's type has flow properties. A separate compartment labelled *full ports* just shows full ports.

Figure 7.31 shows a block definition diagram depicting a *Mount* block. The *Mount* has four mounting points (*Bolts*) that are intended to be used to attach the *Mount* to a bracket, and another four to attach the *Mount* to a camera. As indicated by the «full» keyword, the mounting points are represented as full ports, typed by two blocks, *M10 Bolt* and *M5 Bolt* (10 mm and 5 mm respectively). The bracket mounting needs larger bolts and so the bracket mounting points are larger in diameter, as indicated by the name of the port types.

Full ports can contain nested ports, whose types may contain ports themselves, thus leading to a nested full port hierarchy of arbitrary depth. Nested ports are shown as rectangles intersecting the boundary of their parent port symbol. They may be placed anywhere on the boundary with the caveat that they may not also intersect the symbols representing elements higher in the port nesting hierarchy. A full port can also have nested proxy ports. In this case for example, the full port may represent a physical connector, but the proxy ports are used to specify selected features of the connector, such as its pin out specifications.

Figure 7.32 shows a block definition diagram that describes the mounting interface for the ACME cameras. This particular diagram shows how the *Camera* is fixed in place. It has a full port called *mount* typed by the *Mount* block described in Figure 7.31. The ports of *Mount* can be seen on the boundary of

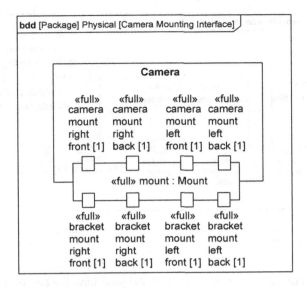

FIGURE 7.32

A full port with nested ports.

their parent port. Although nested ports of full ports can be placed anywhere on the boundary of their parent symbol (with the caveat noted above), the nested ports of *mount* have been placed so that those intended to be connected externally are shown on the outside and those intended to be connected internally are shown on the inside.

7.6.2 PROXY PORTS

A proxy port differs from a full port in that it does not represent a distinct part of the system, but is a modeling construct that exposes features of either its owning block or parts of that block. Proxy ports are typed by **interface blocks**, a specialized form of block that does not contain any internal structure or behavior. Whereas a full port is similar to a part, a proxy port is similar to a reference property, which provides access to a selected set of features of its owning block or its parts.

An interface block is shown by a block symbol with the keyword «interfaceBlock» and can include compartments for its features, excluding a parts compartment and full ports compartment.

Proxy ports, like full ports, are shown as rectangles intersecting the boundary of their parent symbol. The name, type, and multiplicity of the port are shown in a string floating near the port in the form:

```
«proxy» port name: interface block name[multiplicity]
```

Proxy port symbols can contain compartments that list their various features, including properties, nested ports, and behavioral features.

Block symbols can list their proxy ports in a *proxy ports* compartment, using the string:

```
direction port name: interface block[multiplicity]
```

Figure 7.33 shows several interface blocks on a block definition diagram. They all represent the physical interfaces that are needed to physically connect a camera to its environment. Interface blocks

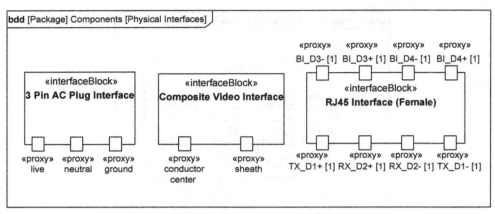

FIGURE 7.33

Interface blocks with proxy ports.

can only contain proxy ports and not full ports, so all the ports have the keyword «proxy». Figure 7.37 shows two examples of the proxy ports compartment.

As stated above, interface blocks can own proxy ports, enabling proxy ports to have further nested proxy ports. Nested ports on proxy ports are shown in a similar fashion to nested ports on full ports, with the exception that the nested ports of proxy ports are always shown on the outside boundary of their parent symbol.

Figure 7.34 shows the interface blocks from Figure 7.33 in use to depict the physical interface to a *Wired Camera* (the keywords «full» and «proxy» are elided on all the ports to reduce clutter). The *Wired Camera* has three proxy ports for *ethernet*, *power*, and *video*, and a full port for the *mount*, as shown in Figure 7.32. Note that the bracket mounting points—but not the camera mounting points—are shown on *mount*, because this diagram is intended to show only the external interface of the camera.

Behavior ports

A proxy port can be defined to be a **behavior port**, which indicates that it provides access to features of its owning block rather than to the features of some internal part of the owning block. The flow properties of a behavior port can be mapped to the parameters of the block's main (or classifier) behavior. SysML does not explicitly state how this should be done, allowing modelers using different methods or operating in different domains to establish different approaches. (See Section 7.5.1 for a description of the main behavior for a block.) Compatibility between features on a behavior port and features on its owning block are similar to those for features across connectors, except that for features with direction (i.e., flow properties and behavioral features), the directions must be the same as opposed to the opposite of each other.

A behavior of a block can both send and receive information through an arbitrarily nested behavior port by explicitly specifying the path to the port either when accepting events corresponding to features on the port or when sending signals or calling operations See Chapter 9, Sections 9.7 and 9.11.2 for further discussion on this.

A small round angle symbol (similar in form to an action or state) connected to a proxy port indicates that it is a behavior port. For an example of this notation, see Figure 7.46.

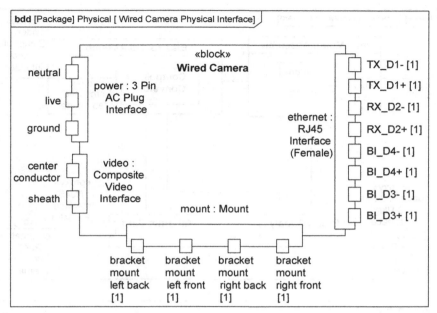

FIGURE 7.34

A block with nested ports.

7.6.3 CONNECTING PORTS

When a block has ports, the ports can also be depicted on the part and reference properties that are typed by this block on an internal block diagram. Ports can be connected either to other ports or directly to parts using connectors. A port can be connected to more than one other port or part, although each connection requires a separate connector.

In terms of feature compatibility, there is no difference between connecting to a full port and proxy port from an external perspective. However, the internal connections to proxy ports have different characteristics than the internal connections to full ports. An internal connector is one that connects a port to a part owned by the same block that owns the port. An external connector is one that connects a port to a part or port owned by some other block. The major difference between connecting full ports and proxy ports internally is the determination of feature compatibility, which is discussed in the sections below. Proxy ports that are behavior ports cannot be connected internally to parts of the owning block.

The notation for connectors was introduced in the Connecting Parts on an Internal Block Diagram subsection of Section 7.3.1. Ports shown on the diagram frame of an internal block diagram represent the ports on the enclosing block designated by the diagram frame.

In Figure 7.35, the ports on the diagram frame correspond to the ports on the *Wired Camera* block. Figure 7.35 shows how the ports of *Wired Camera* are connected internally. The *Electronics Assembly* and *Mount Assembly* (*ma*) are custom assemblies. The modeler decided not to encapsulate them, so their internal parts are connected directly from the outside without connecting through an intermediate

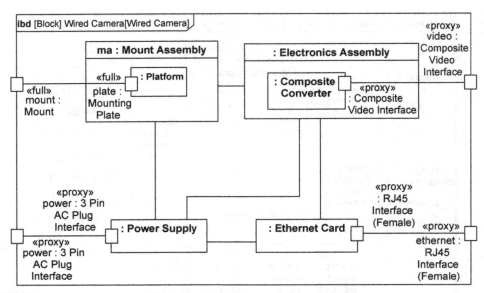

FIGURE 7.35

Connecting ports internally to a block.

port on their boundary. The *video* port of *Wired Camera* is connected directly to the *Composite Converter* part of *Electronics Assembly*. Similarly, the *mount* port is connected to the *Platform* part within the *Mount Assembly*. The *Power Supply* and *Ethernet Card* blocks are off-the-shelf components that are encapsulated, so they must be connected via their ports and do not allow direct connection to their internal parts. The *ethernet* port of *Wired Camera* is connected to a port on the *Ethernet Card*, and the *power* port is connected to a port on the *Power Supply*.

Connecting full ports

Connecting full ports has the same implications and constraints as connecting parts. In particular, the rules for determining the compatibility of behavioral features and flow properties for connected full ports is the same as that for parts, as described in Section 7.4.3.

Figure 7.36 shows the *Optical Assembly* being exercised in a test environment with the equipment defined in Figure 7.24. As can be seen from the directions of the flow properties on the connected ports and parts, *Light* can flow through the components of the *Optical Test Bench*. A *Light Source* emits a beam of light that falls on the *Filter* of the *Optical Assembly*. The *filtered light* output from the *Filter* is processed by optical components in the *Focusing Assembly* to yield *focused light*, which flows out from the *Optical Assembly* through a protective *screen*, and is incident on the *Light Sensor*. This sensor measures various properties of the light it receives.

When a full port represents a physical component with substructure, the port may be further decomposed with its own parts and ports. Connectors to and from the port then may need to be decomposed in order to show the details of how the port is connected. Decomposition of ports and connectors is described later in this section.

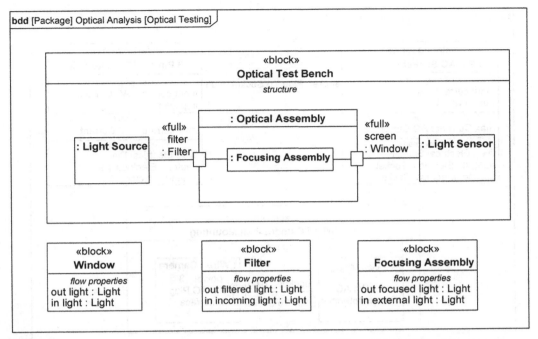

FIGURE 7.36

Connecting parts and full ports.

Connecting proxy ports

As stated above, the default compatibility rules for external connectors are the same for both proxy ports and full ports (and for parts, if encapsulation is not enforced). However, the compatibility rules for behavioral features and flow properties across internal connectors differ between full ports and proxy ports. Whereas internal connectors between full ports are still concerned with matching an outward flow from one part to an inward flow on another part, internal connectors to and from proxy ports are concerned with matching features on the type of the proxy port with corresponding features of the owning block or its parts. Because proxy port features represent the features of the internal parts to which they are connected, they require the behavioral features and flow properties to match (i.e., have the same rather than opposite directions) to be compatible.

Proxy ports can be connected internally to parts, full ports, or other proxy ports. If a proxy port is connected to a full port or part, the connector must be a binding connector, which indicates that the proxy port is literally a proxy for the full port or part, and does not itself represent a separate structural element.

In Figure 7.35, the *power* port on *Wired Camera* is connected to the *power* port on the *Power Supply* via an untyped internal connector. Both ports are typed by *3 Pin AC Plug Interface*, whose definition can be seen on Figure 7.37. The ends of the connector are feature compatible because both have a *current* flow property with compatible types and inout flow direction, and they both have a *power* flow property with compatible types and the same direction.

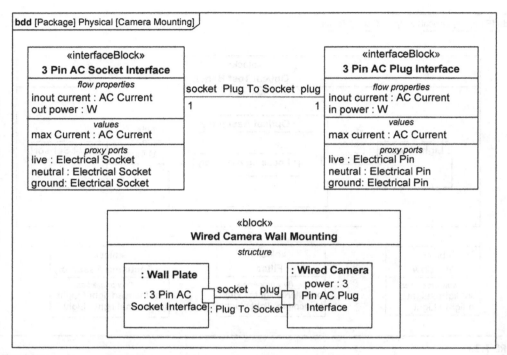

FIGURE 7.37

Connecting proxy ports with typed connectors.

The block definition diagram in Figure 7.37 shows the definitions of both *3 Pin AC Plug Interface* and *3 Pin AC Socket Interface* with an association, *Plug to Socket,* between them. It also shows a block called *Wired Camera Wall Mounting* with a structure compartment depicting how power is supplied to the camera. The external connector between wall and camera is typed by *Plug To Socket.* As discussed in Section 7.3.3, the ends of the connector are compatible with the ends of the connector's type. The ends of the connector also have compatible flow properties, including a *current* flow property whose types are the same and direction is inout and a *power* flow property whose types are the same and whose directions are the opposite of each other. They also both have *max current* value property whose type is *AC Current.* In this case, direction compatibility rules do not apply because it is not a directed feature.

Conjugating ports

When two blocks interact, they may exchange similar items but in opposite directions. Rather than creating two separate specifications for the proxy ports on the interacting blocks, SysML provides a mechanism called a **conjugate port** to reuse a single interface block for both ports. One port is set to be the conjugate of the other, which indicates that the direction of behavioral features and flow properties in the interface block is reversed with respect to this port. The conjugation also applies to nested ports, reversing the direction of any of their directed features, unless of course they themselves are conjugated to offset the reversal. Conjugation also affects the directional notation on port symbols, including inward and outward arrows on port symbols, reversing their direction.

Full ports, like parts, cannot be conjugated. The blocks that type full ports and parts contain behaviors that rely on directed features like flow properties and operations having a defined direction. Conjugation of the part or port typed by that block reverses the direction of these features, which violates the assumptions on which its internal behaviors are based.

Conjugated ports are indicated by placing a tilde (~) in front of the type of the port:

```
port name:~Interface Block Name.
```

An example of this notation can be seen in Figure 7.41.

Decomposing ports and connectors

As described in Sections 7.6.1 and 7.6.2, both kinds of ports may have nested ports, which may be separately connected. Figure 7.37 and Figure 7.35 showed an external connector and internal connector respectively to the *power* port of *Wired Camera*. The ends of each connector have nested ports (shown on Figure 7.34) which themselves can be connected. The connectors can be shown to connect directly to the nested ports, for example in Figure 7.35.

Alternatively, an association block can be used to specify this additional detail. Section 7.3.3 described the use of an association block for defining the internal structure of connectors. This internal structure can simply contain a set of connectors that define the connectors between nested ports of the association ends. When a connector is typed by an association block, the actual interaction between the connected ends will typically be handled by the internal structure of the association block, which may define a different set of rules for feature compatibility.

In Figure 7.38, the association on Figure 7.37 is replaced by an association block to show the connections between nested ports. The association block also adds a constraint that the *max current* of the *plug* must be greater than or equal to the *max current* of the *socket*. The connector on Figure 7.37 does not need to change.

Connectors between full ports can be typed by association blocks to show the structural details of how the connection is achieved. Figure 7.39 shows the definition of an association block, *Mount Interface*, which provides the detail of how a *Mount* and *Mounting Plate* are connected.

Figure 7.40 shows the internal block diagram for the *Mount Interface* association block, previously described in Figure 7.39. It shows that each *M5 Bolt* on the *Mount* is connected to an *M5 Hole* on the *Mounting Plate* and held in place with an *M5 Nut*.

The block diagram in Figure 7.41 shows part of a logical rather than physical view of a system. The interface block *Camera Interface* has two proxy ports, *video* and *control*, the first for digital video and the other for controlling the camera's operation. The interface block *Video Interface* types *video* and contains a single in flow property typed by *MPEG4*. The interface block *Control Interface* types the *control* port and contains a set of receptions and operations, all of which are required as described in Section 7.5.2. *Camera Interface* conjugates both its ports to specify an interface that can be used to type a port of *Camera*. The *video* port is shown in the proxy ports compartment as out even though its only flow property has direction in, because it is conjugated. *Camera* has a proxy port, *digital if*, typed by *Camera Interface*, which specifies the services required by a client of the *Camera*. The nested *video* port is shown with an outward facing arrow to indicate its effective direction.

The internal block diagram for *Surveillance System* in Figure 7.42 shows the communication between two components of the *Surveillance System*. As seen in Figure 7.41, *Camera* has a single

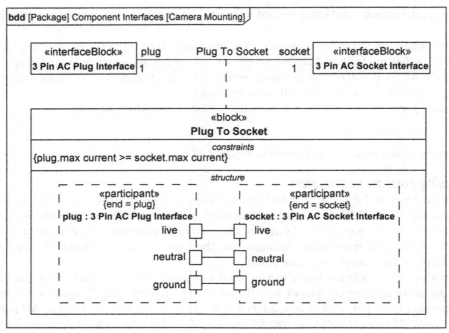

FIGURE 7.38

Connecting proxy ports in an association block.

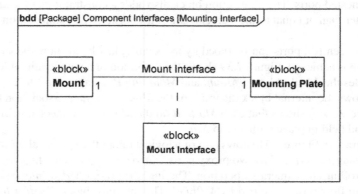

FIGURE 7.39

Defining a structural connection using an association block.

proxy port with two nested proxy ports, *control* and *video*, whereas *Monitoring Station* has two separate proxy ports. Nevertheless, these two sets of ports have compatible types and can be connected, because the *digital if* port of *Camera* is not conjugated, but its nested ports are, resulting in compatible conjugation. The same would be true if the *digital if* port was conjugated and the nested ports were not. The ports have various multiplicities, which is explained in the next section.

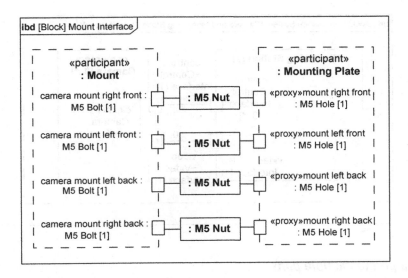

FIGURE 7.40

Showing structural connections in an association block.

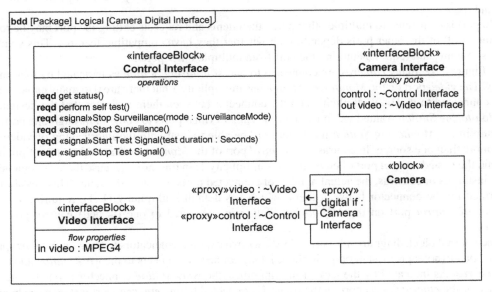

FIGURE 7.41

Defining nested ports with conjugation.

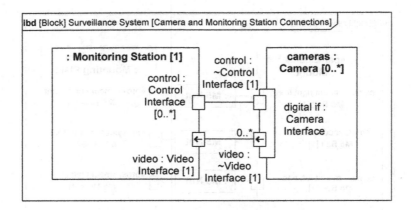

FIGURE 7.42

Connecting nested ports.

Connecting a port to multiple ports

As stated above, a port may be connected to many other ports. In addition, any connector may itself represent multiple links (i.e., connections between block instances). This is true of both internal and external connectors. The number of links on a connector is determined by the multiplicity of both the port and its owner.

If a port is connected to multiple other ports, then items and requests exiting the port may be routed to some or all of the other ports depending on whether they have compatible features. This similarly applies to items and requests entering the port from multiple other ports.

In Figure 7.42, many *cameras* are connected to one *Monitoring Station* as indicated by their multiplicity. The *video* port on the *Monitoring Station* has multiplicity 1 but there are 0 to many camera *video* ports connected to it. The multiplicities on the connector between them indicates that the designer of the *Monitoring Station* wanted video from all the camera *video* ports to come in through one port. The software in the *Monitoring Station* must therefore be able to deal with the interleaving of video data from more than one source. In contrast, the *control* port of the *Monitoring Station* has a multiplicity of 0..* and the nested *control* port of *cameras* has multiplicity 1. In this case, because there are potentially many instances of cameras, the actual number of connected ports might be the same. This possibility is confirmed by the connector between them, which has default multiplicity (1..1), requiring that one instance of *control* port on the *Monitoring Station* is connected to one (nested) *control* port on a *Camera*.

The internal block diagram in Figure 7.43 shows two external connectors to the *ethernet ports* proxy port of *router* (note: proxy stereotype is elided). One connector connects to the *work station* and one to the *cameras*. As indicated by the lack of multiplicities, the *work station* connector is one to one; one instance of the *ethernet ports* port on the router is connected to one *ethernet* port instance on the other end of the connection. However, the *camera* connector has a multiplicity of 4 on the *router* end, indicating that four instances of *ethernet ports* are connected via this connector. The *ethernet ports* has multiplicity 6. One is connected via the *work station* connector and 4 via the *camera* connector, leaving one spare port on the router. The caret shown before the name of *modem* and *workstation* indicates that they are inherited features. This notation is discussed in Section 7.7.

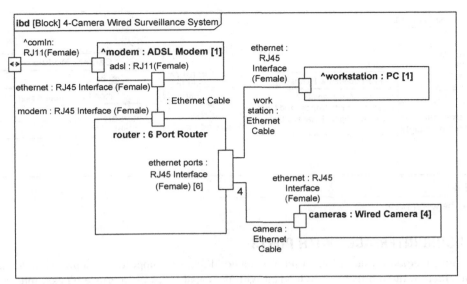

FIGURE 7.43

Connectors with non-default multiplicity.

SysML does not say anything about which port instances are connected by links, although when the connected ports and the connector all have the default multiplicity of 1, there is no ambiguity about which instances are connected. In other cases, such as in Figure 7.43, there is ambiguity as to which *ethernet ports* are connected to which cameras. If it is important to remove this ambiguity, either the design has to be elaborated to have an unambiguous configuration or additional data needs to be added via a profile.

7.6.4 MODELING FLOWS BETWEEN PORTS

As noted earlier in Section 7.4.3, item flows can be shown on connectors between parts. Item flows can also be shown on port-to-port connectors.

The same compatibility rules apply for parts and full ports, but the rules for connecting to proxy ports differ in the case of internal connectors. When an item flow appears on an internal connector from a proxy port, the matching rule for flow direction is the opposite of the rule for external connectors, although most other compatibility rules are the same. If the flow properties are unidirectional (i.e., not inout), the direction of the item flow must be the same as the direction of both the source and target flow properties.

Figure 7.44 shows the route that light takes from an external source to the *Optical Assembly* of the *Camera*. *Unpolarized Light* is incident on the *Protective Housing*, which through an unspecified means polarizes the light to reduce glare. The resulting *Polarized Light* then flows into the *Camera Module* through a proxy port, *light in*, which is a proxy for the full port *filter* on the *Optical Assembly*. Note that the label for the *flow properties* compartment of the *Protective Housing* part is prefixed by a colon. This is the standard mechanism for indicating that these are features of the block that types the part.

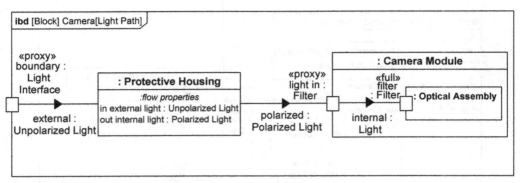

FIGURE 7.44

Item flows between ports.

7.6.5 USING INTERFACES WITH PORTS

An alternative method for describing a set of behavioral features supported by a port is to define them in an **interface**. Although they are redundant with the capabilities of interface blocks, interfaces are retained in SysML since they are used in UML, and some methods may choose to use the same modeling approach in both SysML and UML. One or more interfaces can be related to a port to define the behavioral features it provides or requires. Typically, an interface describes a set of behavioral features related to some specific service, such as tracking or navigation, but the allocation of the services offered by a block to its ports is a methodological question. Interface definitions can be reused as needed to define the interfaces of ports on many blocks.

Modeling interfaces

Interfaces are defined on a block definition diagram as box symbols with the keyword «interface» before their name. Interface symbols have an *operations* compartment like block symbols.

Figure 7.45 shows five interfaces that describe different logical groupings of services for aspects of the surveillance system. For example, *Test Tracking* contains a set of receptions that allow the reporting of progress during camera testing. The other interfaces support other services (e.g., user and route management).

Adding interfaces to ports

A **required interface** on a port specifies one or more operations required by behaviors of the block (or its parts). A **provided interface** on a port specifies one or more operations that a block (or one or more of its parts) must provide. A part that has a port with a required interface needs to be connected to another part that provides the services it needs, typically via a port with a provided interface. The compatibility of behavioral features on ports defined by interfaces is the same as for ports defined by interface blocks.

The required and provided interfaces of a port are represented by a notation called "ball-and-socket notation". An interface is represented by either a ball or socket symbol with the name of the interface floating near it. The ball depicts a provided interface, and the socket depicts a required interface. A solid line attaches the interface symbol to the port that requires or provides the interface. A port can have one

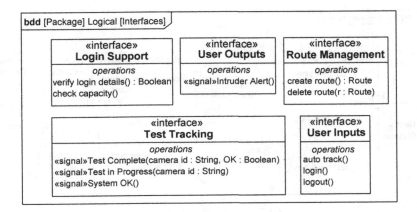

FIGURE 7.45

A set of interfaces used to define provided or required services.

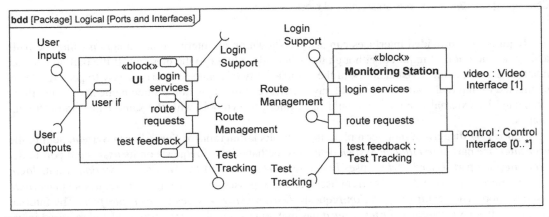

FIGURE 7.46

Defining a service-based interface using proxy ports.

or more required interfaces and one or more provided interfaces, and hence can be connected to multiple interface symbols.

Figure 7.46 shows the set of ports that define interface points on the blocks *UI* and *Monitoring Station*. *UI* has four ports: one that provides services, two that require services, and one that both provides and requires services. The port *test feedback* provides the services defined by the interface *Test Tracking*. The port *login services* requires the services defined by the interface *Login Support*. The port *user if* offers services defined in *User Inputs* and requires services defined by *User Outputs*. All of *UI*'s ports are behavior ports as indicated by the behavior port symbol. *Monitoring Station* has five ports. Two are defined using interface blocks as shown in Figure 7.41; the other three are defined using the interfaces defined in Figure 7.45.

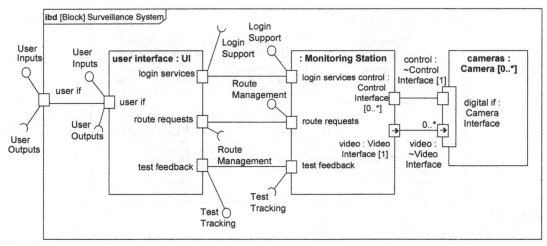

FIGURE 7.47

Connecting service-based ports on an internal block diagram.

Required and provided interfaces can also be shown on an internal block diagram using the ball-and-socket notation, if required, although this often adds clutter to the diagram. If the ball-and-socket notation is used, a quick visual check of the compatibility of connected ports is easy to perform. Ports connected by internal connectors should have interface symbols with the same name and shape. Ports connected by external connectors should have interface symbols with the same name and different shapes.

Figure 7.47 displays a more complete internal block diagram for *Surveillance System*, adding the *user interface* part. *Surveillance System* delegates the handling of requests on its *user login* port to the *user interface* part. *User interface* uses *Login Support* services of the *Monitoring Station,* via its *login services* port, to provide data on current users, and also passes route management requests via its *route requests* port. The *Monitoring Station* requests *Test Tracking* services of *user interface*. The internal connector from *Surveillance System.user if* has matching symbols for the provided and required interfaces on both ends. The external connectors between *user interface* and the *Monitoring Station* have opposite symbols. Note that the behavior port notation has been elided in this figure.

7.7 MODELING CLASSIFICATION HIERARCHIES USING GENERALIZATION

In SysML, a **classifier** is a type that may be used as the basis for more specific types. The classifiers so far encountered in this chapter are blocks, value types, interfaces, interface blocks, and signals.

The different kinds of classifiers can appear on a block definition diagram and can be organized into a classification hierarchy. In a classification hierarchy, each classifier is described as being more general or more specialized than another. Typically a general classifier contains a set of features that are common to more specialized classifiers. A more specialized classifier will **inherit** the common features from the more general classifier, and may contain additional features that are unique to it. The relationship between the general classifier and specialized classifier is called **generalization.** Different terms are used to identify the classifiers at the ends of a generalization relationship. In this chapter, the general classifier is called the **superclass**, and the more specialized classifier is called the **subclass.**

Classification can facilitate reuse when a subclass reuses the features of a superclass and adds it own features. The benefits of such reuse can be substantial when the superclass has significant detail or when there are many different subclasses.

This section deals initially with the inheritance of structural features (i.e., properties and ports) of a block, covering both the addition of features and the redefinition of existing features in subclasses. Although the focus for this section is on blocks and interface blocks, other classifiers with structural features—such as interfaces and value types—can also be organized in the same way. For example, a subclass of a more general value type may add specific units and quantity kinds.

In addition to classification for reuse, classification can also be used to describe specific configurations of a block, to identify unique configurations for testing, or to serve as the input to simulations or other forms of analysis.

Classification also applies to behavioral features and can be used to specialize blocks that respond to incoming requests in a particular way. Classification of behavioral features and the semantics implied by the use of classification are covered by numerous texts on object-oriented design, and so will not be dealt with in any detail here.

Generalization is represented by a line between two classifiers with a hollow triangular arrowhead on the superclass end of the relationship. Generalization paths may be displayed separately, or a set of generalization paths may be combined into a tree, as shown in Figure 7.48.

Figure 7.48 shows two subclasses of *Camera*: *Wired Camera* and *Wireless Camera.* Both of the subclasses require all the characteristics of *Camera* but add their own specialized characteristics as well. *Wired Camera* has both a wired *Power Supply* and a wired *Ethernet Card.* The *Wireless Camera* uses a *WiFi* (Wireless Ethernet) *Card* to communicate and is battery-driven. It also includes a value property for *battery life.*

It can be useful to show the inherited features in the symbol for the subclass, particularly if the subclass is shown on a separate diagram from its superclasses. In that case, the feature is shown prefixed by a caret (^) symbol. An example of this notation can be seen in Figure 7.43.

7.7.1 CLASSIFICATION AND THE STRUCTURAL FEATURES OF A BLOCK

Different blocks in a classification hierarchy have different structural features, with subclasses adding features not present in their superclasses. Not all features added in subclasses are new; some are introduced to override or otherwise change the definition of an existing feature, which is called **redefinition.**

When a feature from a superclass is redefined in a subclass, the original feature in the superclass is no longer available to the subclass. The more specific feature in the subclass, which is called the redefining feature, is used in place of the feature in the superclass, which is called the redefined feature. The feature in the subclass often has the same name as the feature in the superclass. When used in place of the redefined feature, the redefining feature may:

- Restrict its multiplicity (for example, from 0..* to 1..2, in order to reduce the number of instances or values that the feature can hold).
- Add or change its default value.

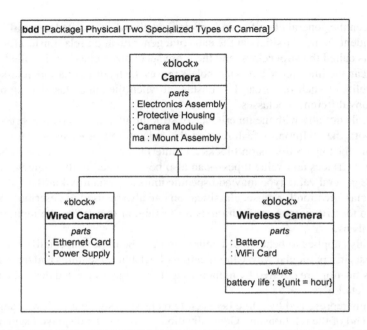

FIGURE 7.48

Example of block specialization.

- Provide a new distribution or change an existing distribution.
- Change the type of the feature to a more restricted type (in other words, a type that is a subclass of the existing type).

Redefinition is shown in braces after the name string of the redefining feature in the subclass, using the keyword `redefines` followed by the name of the redefined feature.

In the *Components* package, two motor modules are described for use in the system. Both motor modules share a number of features in common; for example, they both have some common value properties, such as *weight, power,* and *torque.* In Figure 7.49, a general concept of *Motor Module* is introduced to capture the common characteristics of the two motor modules.

In addition to value properties, *Motor Module* defines a common concept of a *control input* using a proxy port. The *Brushless DC Motor Module* and the *Stepper Motor Module* are represented as subclasses of this common concept with special features of their own, such as the *step size* and *position* output port for the *Stepper Motor Module.* In addition, the common properties from *Motor Module* have been redefined in the subclasses in order to place bounds on their values that are appropriate to the type of motor. The value properties are described by an «interval» probability distribution to represent the range of values they can have in their given subclass.

7.7.2 CLASSIFICATION AND BEHAVIORAL FEATURES

Just as the structural features of blocks and interface blocks can be organized into classification hierarchies, the behavioral features of blocks can be treated in a similar fashion. A summary description of

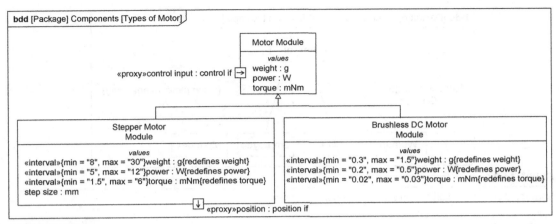

FIGURE 7.49

Showing a classification hierarchy on a block definition diagram.

the classification of behavioral features and corresponding behaviors is included here. A more complete discussion is beyond the scope of this book but can be found in many object-oriented design books.

General operations or receptions are described at an abstract level in the classification hierarchy, and more specific operations and receptions are described in more specialized blocks. As with structural features, the behavioral features of superclasses may be redefined in subclasses to modify their signature. Interfaces can also be classified and their behavioral features specialized in the same fashion as blocks.

The response of a block to a request for a behavioral feature may also be specialized. Although a behavioral feature may be defined in a general block, the method for that feature in a given specialization of the block may be unique to that block (see Section 7.5.3 for a discussion of methods). In software engineering, this phenomenon is called polymorphism—from the Greek for "many forms"—because the response to a request for a given behavioral feature may be different depending on the method that actually handles the request.

In object-oriented programming languages, polymorphism is handled by a dispatching mechanism. If a behavior sends a request to a target object, it knows the type (e.g., block) of the target object and that it can support the request. Due to specialization, however, the target object can be a valid subclass of the requested type, and may implement a different response to the request. The dispatching mechanism can ensure that the appropriate method is invoked to handle the request.

7.7.3 MODELING OVERLAPPING CLASSIFICATIONS USING GENERALIZATION SETS

Sometimes a subclass may include features from multiple superclasses. This is called **multiple generalization** or sometimes **multiple inheritance.** The subclasses of a given class may be organized into groupings based on how they can be used for further classification. For example, a superclass *Person* may have subclasses that represent the characteristics of an *Employee* OR a *Manager* in their job AND subclasses that represent the characteristics of a *Woman* OR a *Man* as their gender. This situation can be modeled using generalization sets, as shown in Figure 7.50.

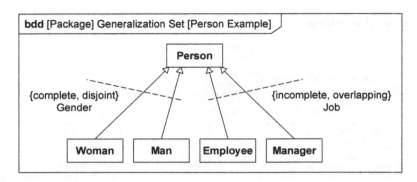

FIGURE 7.50

Showing a generalization set on a block definition diagram.

Generalization sets have two properties that can be used to describe coverage and overlap between their members. The **coverage** property specifies whether all the instances of the superclass are instances of one or another of the members of the generalization set. The two values of the coverage property are `complete` and `incomplete`. The **overlap** property specifies whether an instance of the superclass can only be an instance of at most one subclass in the generalization. The two values of the property are `disjoint` and `overlapping`.

A generalization set may be displayed on a block definition diagram by a dashed line intersecting a set of generalization paths. The name of the generalization set and the values of the overlap and coverage properties, shown in braces, are displayed floating near the line that depicts the generalization set. Alternatively, if the tree form of generalization notation is used, a generalization set may be depicted by a tree with the generalization set name and properties floating near the triangle symbol at its root. Figure 7.50 shows the dashed-line variant, and Figure 7.58 shows the tree variant.

Figure 7.50 shows the example of generalization sets described earlier. *Person* is subclassed by four subclasses in two generalization sets. *Gender* has two members, *Woman* and *Man,* and is both disjoint and completely covered because all instances of *Person* must be an instance of either *Woman* or *Man* but not both. *Job* has two members, *Employee* and *Manager,* and is overlapping and incompletely covered because an instance of *Person* may be an instance of both *Employee* and *Manager,* or neither.

7.7.4 MODELING VARIANTS USING CLASSIFICATION

The description and organization of product variants is a large and complex topic and requires solutions that cover many different disciplines, of which modeling is just one. Nonetheless, SysML contains concepts like classification and redefinition that can be used to capture some of the details and relationships needed to model variants. For example, classification can be used to model different variants of a block definition that represent alternative designs being evaluated in a trade study. This can be achieved by describing several specialized variants of a block as subclasses of a more general block, grouped into generalization sets. Note that multiple subclasses of a superclass can be recombined using multiple generalizations in subsequent levels of classification, but these must obey the specified overlap and coverage of their superclasses.

Figure 7.51 shows two mutually exclusive characterizations of the *Camera:* its intended location and the way that it connects with a controller. Each characterization in this case has two variants. There are two intended locations, indicated by the generalization set *Location,* served by either an *Internal*

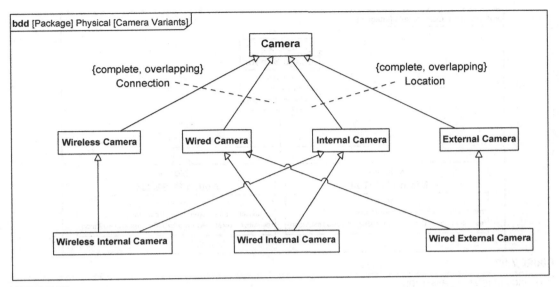

FIGURE 7.51

Modeling variant configurations on a block definition diagram.

Camera or an *External Camera.* There are also two intended modes of connection, indicated by the *Connection* generalization set, served by the *Wired Camera* and *Wireless Camera* originally shown in Figure 7.48. Three further variants, *Wired Internal Camera, Wireless Internal Camera,* and *Wired External Camera,* are created by multiple generalization from these four. The features of the blocks are hidden to reduce clutter.

Bound reference

Sometimes, the variation between two variant systems is nested deep within the composition hierarchy of the system, such as different types of *Wheels* in a *Vehicle.* In this case, it is convenient to refer to different *Vehicle* variants that have different types of *Wheels,* without having to display the entire *Vehicle* composition tree to show the variation. In particular, it is desirable to refer to the *Wide Wheel Vehicle* variant and the *Standard Wheel Vehicle* variant. This becomes increasingly useful as more variation is introduced, such as the case with a *High Performance Vehicle* variant that includes wide wheels, a larger engine, and stiffer suspension.

The concept of bound reference provides a mechanism to support a compact way to describe variants such as these. In particular, it enables the variations for the *High Performance Vehicle* variant to be displayed in the *High Performance Vehicle* block, without having to show composition hierarchy with all the deeply nested variant parts. The way this is accomplished is described below.

A **bound reference** is a reference property of a block that is bound using a binding connector to some other nested property within the composition hierarchy of the block. The properties that are connected using binding connectors must have compatible types and multiplicities. In this way, a bound reference can be a property of a high-level block in a composition tree (such as a *Vehicle*), which is constrained to be equal to a deeply nested part or property within the composition tree (such as a *Wheel*).

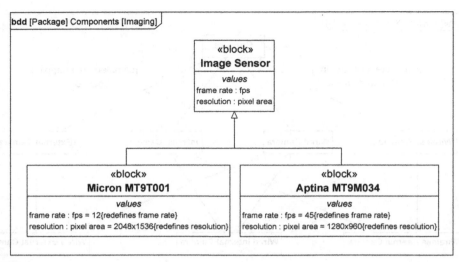

FIGURE 7.52

Two kinds of Imaging Assembly.

When the block is subclassed to create a variant, such as a *High Performance Vehicle* variant, each bound reference can be redefined to correspond to the selected variant part or property. The selected variant part or property must conform to the redefinition rules described in the previous section.

A bound reference is a reference property and thus has the same notation as a reference property. It is distinguished by the keyword «boundReference». A block can have a separate compartment for bound references, labeled *bound references*, which is convenient for identifying its variant parts, Each entry in the compartment has the following prefix in addition to standard property syntax:

```
{/bindingPath = property list; lower=integer;upper=integer}
```

Property list is simply a comma-separated list of the properties in the path of the property to which the reference is bound.

The imaging assembly of the camera contains a sensor, among other elements. There are many potential choices for such a sensor, two of which are shown in Figure 7.52. The *Micron M9T001* supports up to 2048×1536 pixels at a frame rate of 12 frames per second; the *Aptina MT9M034* supports up to 1280×960 pixels at 45 frames per second. The *Camera* block features a reference property called *sensor*, which is bound to the property *Camera::cm.ia.sensor*, as shown in Figure 7.53. Adding this bound reference to *Camera* allows different configurations, such as a *Low Fidelity Camera* and a *High Fidelity Camera*, to be specified by modifying the type of *sensor*, as shown in Figure 7.54.

Bound references can also be bound to full ports. Figure 7.55 shows the *Bracket* used to attach a *Camera* to a wall as part of a *Camera Assembly*. The *Camera* end of the *Bracket* is fixed to fit with the *Mount* of the *Camera*, as shown in Figure 7.32. However, the wall end of the bracket can have a variable number of holes of various sizes to suit different materials. This flexibility can be achieved by connecting a bound reference to the *holes* on the *Wall Mount*. Two potential variations of the *Camera Assembly* are shown in Figure 7.56: *Solid Wall Camera Assembly*, with 4 *M5 Holes* and a *Dry Wall Camera Assembly* with 6 *M10 Holes*.

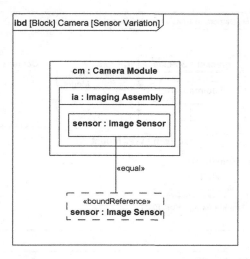

FIGURE 7.53

Adding a bound reference to support variants.

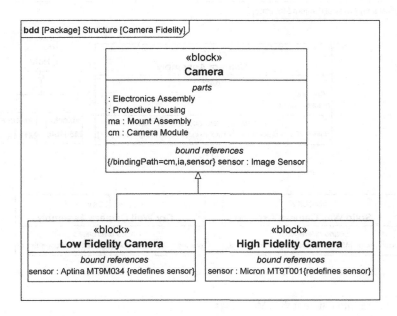

FIGURE 7.54

Using a bound reference to describe two variants of Camera.

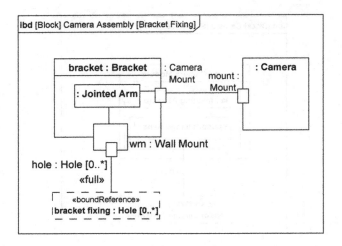

FIGURE 7.55

Using a bound reference to support port variation.

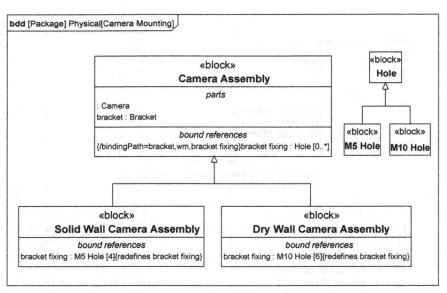

FIGURE 7.56

Two variants of Camera with different Wall Mountings.

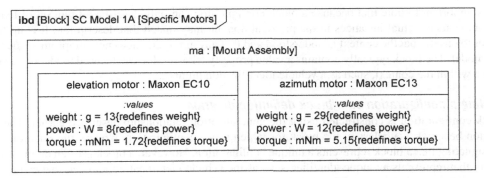

FIGURE 7.57

Property-specific types.

7.7.5 USING PROPERTY-SPECIFIC TYPES TO MODEL CONTEXT-SPECIFIC BLOCK CHARACTERISTICS

A **property-specific type** is used to designate properties of a block or value type that are further specialized for localized use within an internal block diagram. This might happen, for example, when one or more properties of a part have different distributions than in their original type. The property-specific type implicitly creates a subclass of the block that types the part to add the unique characteristics. The presence of a property-specific type is indicated by including the type name of a property in brackets. Compartments can be used to depict the unique features of the type for each part-specific property, such as the value properties for the different motors' weights in the following example. Note that if a compartment on a part symbol is used to show features of its type, the compartment label is prefixed by a colon.

Figure 7.57 shows a small fragment of a particular model of surveillance camera, the *SC Model 1 A*, which specializes *Camera*. In the *SC Model 1 A*, the generic *Stepper Motor Module* used in the *Mount Assembly* (*ma*) of *Camera* has been replaced by a specific motor module containing a *Maxon EC10* and a *Maxon EC13*. To do this replacement, rather than specifically create a block that represents this variant of *Mount Assembly*, a property-specific type is used. Significant properties of the *Maxon EC10* and Maxon EC13 are shown in the *:values* compartments of the parts.

7.7.6 MODELING BLOCK CONFIGURATIONS AS SPECIALIZED BLOCKS

A **block configuration** describes a specific structure and specific property values intended to represent a unique instance of a block in some known context. For example, a block configuration may be used to identify a particular aircraft in an airline company's fleet by its call sign and to provide other characteristics specific to that aircraft. In that example, the call sign is intended to consistently identify the same aircraft even though the values of other properties may change over time. Block configurations can also be used to identify the state of some entity at a given point in time. Extending the example of the aircraft, it might be important for an air-traffic control simulation to describe a **snapshot** of an aircraft's position, velocity, fuel load, and so on at certain critical analysis stages.

It is important to note that because a block configuration can only describe a finite set of features and values, many actual instances in the physical domain may match that description. It is up to the modeler to ensure that the context is understood and that any ambiguity does not compromise the value of the model. The block typically contains a value property whose value can be used to identify a single instance within the context, such as a vehicle identification number.

Modeling a configuration on a block definition diagram

A block configuration is constructed using the generalization relationship described earlier. The configuration becomes a subclass of the block for which it is a configuration. No specific notation exists for designating that a block represents a unique configuration. However, a block is often defined with a property that represents a unique identifier, such as the vehicle identification number, that can be used when modeling configurations. Often it is useful to introduce a generalization set for block configurations to distinguish them from other specializations of that block.

A useful characteristic of the SysML property concept is the ability to state that one property may **subset** one or more other properties, either in its owning class or in one of that class's superclasses. For example, if a block for *Vehicle* contains a property called *w:Wheel [4]* corresponding to four wheels, then an individual *wheel* property, such as the *right front wheel*, is a subset of the original *wheel* property. In this example, the *right front wheel* is called the subsetting property and *wheel* is the subsetted property. The subsetted property is retained and not replaced as it is in redefinition.

Subsetting is shown in braces after the name string of the subsetting property using the keyword subsets followed by the names of the subsetted properties.

Two configurations of the company's popular *4-Camera Wired Surveillance System* are shown in Figure 7.58. The values for *location* in each case give the addresses of the installations. It is intended that within the context of the ACME business, the specific values for *location* are enough to uniquely identify the instance of one of their surveillance systems. The company also offers an optional service package, and the *service level* provides details of the level of service offered. *Business Gold* includes hourly visits by a security agent outside office hours. *Household 24/7* ensures a response to any alert within 30 minutes, 24 hours a day and 7 days a week.

The *4-Camera Wired Surveillance System* specializes *Surveillance System* and redefines its *cameras* part with a new part, also called *cameras*. The new part has a new type, *Wired Camera*, which is a subclass of the original type, *Camera*. It has also a new multiplicity of 4 that restricts the upper number of instances held by *cameras* to 4 from the original upper bound of "*," and also raises the lower bound to 4.

To describe specific configurations, *AJM Enterprises System* and *Jones Household System* specialize the *4-Camera Surveillance System* and redefine or subset some of its properties. Two value properties, *location* and *service level,* are redefined in order to provide specific values. If a property has an upper bound of greater than 1 and it is important to identify the characteristics of each instance of the property, a new subset property can be created to identify explicitly one of the set of instances held by the property in order to define its specific characteristics. In Figure 7.58, the *cameras* part is subsetted by parts that represent individual cameras in the configuration. In *AJM Enterprises System,* the new parts are called *front, reception, store room,* and *computer room,* based on their location within the company's building.

The set of configurations of the *4-Camera Surveillance System* is grouped by a generalization set called *Configurations. Configurations* is disjoint, because an instance of *4-Camera Wired Surveillance*

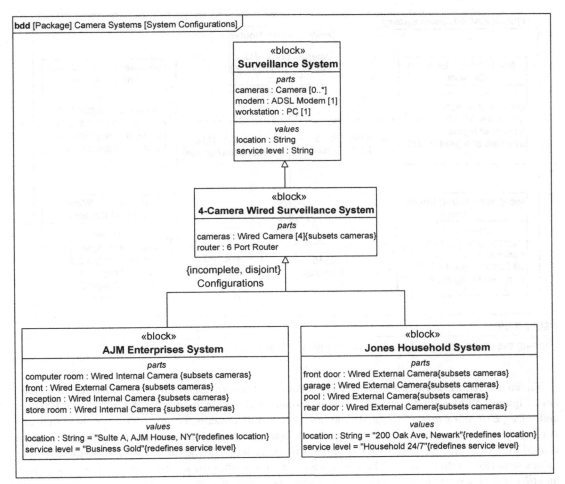

FIGURE 7.58

Modeling different configurations of a block on a block definition diagram.

System must be either an *AJM Enterprises System* or a *Jones Household System*, but not both. *Configurations* is incomplete because there may be other configurations of *4-Camera Wired Surveillance System*.

Modeling configuration details on an internal block diagram

When a block has been used to describe a configuration, the internal block diagram for that block can be used to capture the specific internal structure (e.g., precise multiplicities and connections) and values unique to that configuration's properties. In particular, this should include the value of a property that uniquely identifies the entities in the configuration (e.g., name, serial number, call sign). A unique design configuration can be created by defining an identification property for each part in the block that corresponds to the unique identification of the enclosing block.

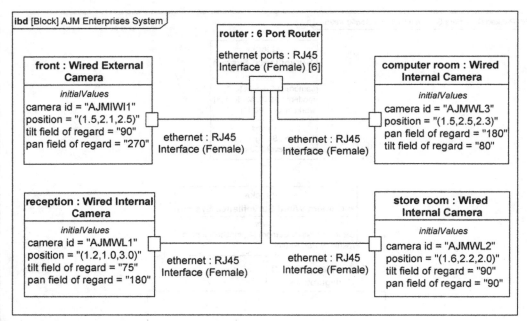

FIGURE 7.59

Showing the configuration of a block on an internal block diagram.

Given that *AJM Enterprises System* is a subclass of *4-Camera Surveillance System*, it has four cameras. Figure 7.58 identified a number of wired camera variants, including the *Wired Internal Camera* and *Wired External Camera*, to satisfy the installation requirements. Figure 7.59 shows how they are configured, including initial values for significant value properties. The *camera id* property of *Camera* is used to store unique identifiers for the cameras in the system, and the four cameras have these unique values stenciled on their casing. The configuration also describes the *position* and *field of regard* (*pan* and *tilt*) of each camera to facilitate coverage analysis as part of a security viewpoint.

7.8 MODELING BLOCK CONFIGURATIONS USING INSTANCES

As described in Section 7.7.6 it is possible to model a configuration of a block by specializing it and adding configuration-specific information to the specialized block. This is particularly useful if the configuration adds structural or data constraints not present in the more general block. However, if a configuration simply consists of a set of values for value properties, an **instance specification** can be used.

An instance specification is shown on a block definition diagram as a rectangular symbol containing an underlined name string with the following format:

```
instance name : block name.
```

The symbol contains a single compartment listing values for any specific properties that override any established initial values. Instance specifications can be nested to mirror the composition of blocks.

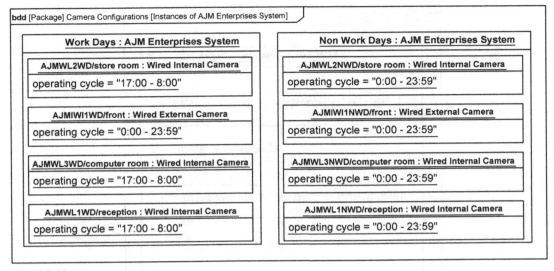

FIGURE 7.60

Describing block configurations with instances.

When an instance specification symbol is nested, its name string may also show the name of the part (or reference) to which this instance specification corresponds, using the following notation:

```
instance name/property name : block name.
```

Figure 7.60 describes two instances of the *AJM Enterprises System*, showing the operating cycle in two different circumstances: work days and non-work days. It has been decided that the internal cameras will be turned off during working hours on work days in order to cut costs. The value for *operating cycle* of the external camera (*front*) in the *Work Days* instance specification is set to *0:00–23:59*, and the value for the internal cameras is *17:00–8:00*. In the *Non-Work Days* instance specification, the values for all cameras are set to *0:00–23:59* to maintain full coverage.

Instance specifications can be connected by links, which represent instances of associations between blocks. A link is shown on a block definition diagram as a line between two instance specifications, whose ends and adornments are the same as those of the association of which it is an instance.

Figure 7.61 shows a configuration of the *ACME Surveillance Network*, originally introduced in Figure 7.13. It shows two instances of *Surveillance System*, *Smith Residence* and *O'Brien Residence*, both representing the *residence* property and connected to an instance of *Command Centre* called *CC*, representing the *residential surveillance center*, by instances of the *ADSL Connection* association.

7.9 SEMANTICS OF BLOCKS

A SysML model can be used to specify the structure and behavior of a system, as discussed throughout Part II of this book. Often a SysML model is used simply to facilitate communication among project teams, but sometimes the model is intended to be interpreted by machines or computer programs to simulate the system that it specifies. This latter category of model is often called an **executable**

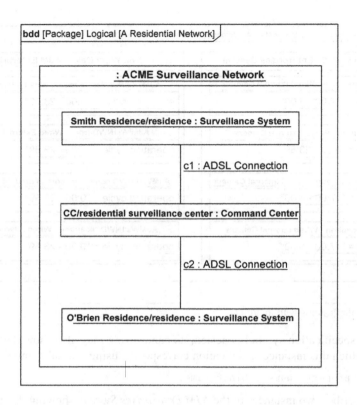

FIGURE 7.61

Describing links between instances.

specification because it contains all the information necessary for a machine to execute it. The construction of executable specifications requires the modeling formalism (SysML in this case) to have semantics defined precisely enough to allow execution of the model.

7.9.1 THE FOUNDATIONAL UML SUBSET (fUML)

In 2010, the OMG adopted a specification for a subset of UML called **Foundational UML** (or **fUML**, for short), which selects a subset of UML 2 and specifies foundational execution semantics for it [42]. Foundational UML is contained within UML4SysML, the subset of UML on which SysML is based, and so SysML modelers can also use Foundational UML to specify the semantics of SysML precisely.

The initial specification for Foundational UML defined:

- A subset of the abstract syntax of UML 2, covering basic structural concepts like classes and associations and behavioral concepts associated with activities;
- An execution model that defined an operational semantics for that UML 2 subset;
- A library of classes, data types, and behaviors to define basic functionality such as the manipulation of basic data types and input and output; and

- A formal (declarative) definition of the semantics of the execution model, expressed using **PSL** [43], a standard execution constraint language, against a smaller subset of UML called **base UML** or **bUML.**

Several execution engines based on the Foundational UML standard are available. There are two aspects of execution: the way the specification of structure relates to construction of instances of a system and the way specified behaviors affect the state of these instances. Section 9.14 in Chapter 9 describes how SysML supports the execution of activities using Foundational UML. The rest of this section covers the semantics of structure (i.e., blocks).

In 2013, the OMG adopted a specification called **Precise Semantics of UML Composite Structures** [44], which extends Foundational UML to specify the semantics of composite structures—including parts, ports, and connectors—which are fundamental to SysML. It also added a specific (informative) Annex which included the semantics of the following SysML concepts:

- Flow properties, including the flow of blocks, data, and signals;
- Proxy ports, particularly behavior ports; and
- Constraint blocks

However, there are number of significant exclusions in the structural part of Foundational UML that affect SysML Blocks:

- Association classes, which enable association blocks;
- Instance specifications;
- Default property values; and
- Subsetted, redefined, and distributed properties

The Foundational UML specification is continuing to be updated and over time should address some of these gaps.

The OMG has also adopted a complementary specification to Foundational UML called the **Action Language for Foundational UML** or **Alf** [45], for short. Alf is a textual concrete syntax for Foundational UML modeling elements. It is particularly useful when describing the detailed behavior of activities, which can be somewhat cumbersome when expressed graphically, and so is covered in Chapter 9, Section 9.14.2, which describes activities.

7.10 DEPRECATED FEATURES

Version 1.3 of SysML deprecated a number of features of blocks and ports that were in version 1.2. "Deprecated" means they are still formally a part of the language, but they are intended to be removed in a future revision. The SysML 1.3 blocks and ports subsume the SysML 1.2 functionality. This section describes the deprecated features for the sake of completeness and because the current OCSMP examination is based on SysML 1.2. The following features are covered:

- The flow port concept, whose capabilities were subsumed by proxy ports. **Atomic flow** ports have been removed from SysML.
- The flow specification concept, whose capabilities were subsumed by the interface block.

The notation for these features is shown in the Appendix, Table A.7.

7.10.1 FLOW PORTS

A **flow port** is used to describe an interaction point (or connection point) for items flowing in or out of a block. It is used to specify what input items can be received by the block and what output items can be sent by the block. It specifies this through its type. Like other structural features of a block, a flow port can have a multiplicity that indicates how many instances of the port are present on an instance of its owning block. A flow port can be typed by a flow specification.

Flow specification

A **flow specification** is defined on a block definition diagram. The flow specification includes flow properties that correspond to individual specifications of input and/or output flow. Each **flow property** has a type and a direction (in, out, or inout). The type of the flow property can be a block, value type, or signal depending on the specification of what can flow.

When two blocks interact through connectors, they may exchange similar items but in opposite directions. Rather than creating two separate flow specifications for the flow ports on the interacting blocks, flow ports can be conjugated to reuse a single flow specification for both ports. One port is set to be the conjugate of the other, which indicates that the direction of all flow properties in the flow specification is reversed with respect to the second port.

A flow specification is shown as a box symbol with the keyword «flowSpecification» above the name in the name compartment. The flow properties of a flow specification are shown in a special compartment labeled *flow properties,* with each flow property shown in the format:

```
direction property name: item type[multiplicity]
```

A flow port is indicated by two angle brackets facing each other (<>) drawn inside the port symbol. Flow ports can be listed in a special compartment labeled *flow ports* in their owning block. A flow port is shown in the format:

```
port name: flow specification name[multiplicity]
```

A conjugate flow port is indicated by placing a tilde (~) in front of the flow port's type.

Connecting flow ports on an internal block diagram

Like other ports, flow ports are shown on the boundaries of parts and reference properties on an internal block diagram and can be connected using connectors.

7.11 SUMMARY

SysML structure is primarily represented on block definition diagrams and internal block diagrams. The following are key concepts related to modeling structure:

- The block is the fundamental unit of structure in SysML and is represented on the block definition diagram and the frame of an internal block diagram. Blocks own and are defined by their features. A block provides the description for a set of uniquely identified instances that all have the features defined by the block. A block definition diagram is used to define a block, its characteristics, and its relationship to other blocks, as well as other types of classifiers such as interface blocks, interfaces, value types, and signals. Instance specifications and links between them can also be shown on block definition diagrams. An internal block diagram is used to describe the internal structure of a block.

- Blocks have a number of structural and behavioral features that comprise its definition. Properties describe a block's structural aspects in terms of its relationship to other blocks and its quantifiable characteristics. Ports describe a block's interface as a set of access points on its boundary. Behavioral features declare the set of services that characterize the blocks response to stimulus.

- A part is used to describe the hierarchical composition (sometimes called whole–part relationships) of block hierarchies. Using this terminology, the block or other classifier that owns the property is the whole, and the property is the part. Any given instance of the block that types a part may only exist as part of at most one instance of a whole at any instant of time. Composite associations are used to express the relationship of the part to the whole, in particular, whether blocks that type the part always exist in the context of an instance of the whole or may exist independently of the whole.

- A reference property allows blocks to refer to other blocks. Reference properties support the creation of logical hierarchies and associated internal block diagrams that can augment a composite hierarchy.

- Value properties represent quantifiable characteristics of a block, such as its physical and performance characteristics. Value properties are typed by value types. A value type provides a reusable description of some quantity and may include units and quantity kinds that characterize the quantity. A value property may have a default value a probability distribution.

- SysML has two different types of ports: a full port and a proxy port. A full port is typed by a block and is similar to a part except it is shown graphically on the boundary of its owning block. Proxy ports are typed by interface blocks that specify the black-box interface. They are similar to reference properties in that they do not exist in a block's part tree but serve as access points to the features of their owning block or its parts. They serve as a pass-through for inputs and outputs without modifying them. Both full ports and proxy ports support nesting of ports.

- A block has two kinds of behavioral features, operations and receptions, which enable the block to respond to stimuli. Operations describe synchronous interactions in which the requester waits for the request to be handled; receptions describe asynchronous behaviors in which the requester can continue without waiting for a reply. Behavioral features may be realized by methods, which are the behaviors that handle the requests. Requests for behavioral features may also be handled directly by the main (or classifier) behavior, typically an activity or state machine, as described in Chapters 9 and 11.

- The concepts of classification and generalization sets describe how to create classification hierarchies of blocks and other classifiers such as value types and signals. Classifiers specialize other classifiers in order to reuse their features and add new features of their own. Generalization sets group the subclasses of a given superclass according to how they partition the instances of their superclass. Subclasses may overlap, which means that a given instance can be described by more than one subclass. Subclasses may have complete or partial coverage of the superclass, depending on whether the subclasses define all possible subclasses of the superclass or not, and whether all instances are described by one of the subclasses in the set or not.

- Features of classifiers can be related in various ways within a classification hierarchy. All features of classifiers can be redefined by their subclasses in order to restrict certain of their characteristics, such as multiplicity or default value. Structural features may be defined to have the subset of values of some other feature in the same classifier or superclass. This has a particular use in identifying a specific member of a collection in order to define characteristics that are specific to it. This variation may either be performed using a new classifier or in a local context using a property-specific type.

- Blocks can be used to describe configurations, in which case the features of the block are defined in enough detail to identify a specific configuration of the block in the real world of the system. Alternatively, if the configuration does not require the application of further constraints on the structure or values of the block, an instance specification can be used.
- SysML 1.3 deprecated the flow port concept in favor of the proxy port, although it is still in the language. A flow port specifies what can flow in or out of a block. The proxy port supports the functionality of flow ports and more.

7.12 QUESTIONS

1. What is the diagram kind of a block definition diagram, and which model elements can it represent?
2. What is the diagram kind of an internal block diagram, and which model elements can it represent?
3. How is a block represented on a block definition diagram?
4. Name three categories of block property.
5. Which type of property is used to describe composition relationships between blocks?
6. What is the commonly used term for properties with a lower multiplicity bound of 0?
7. What is the default interpretation of the multiplicity for both ends of an association when it is not shown on the diagram?
8. Draw a block definition diagram using composite associations for blocks "Boat," "Car," and "Engine," showing that a "Car" must have one "Engine," and a "Boat" may have either one or two "Engines."
9. Give two situations in which the use of role names for the part end of a composite association should be considered.
10. How are parts shown on an internal block diagram?
11. What does the presence of a connector between two parts imply?
12. Draw an internal block diagram for the "Boat" from Question 8, but with an additional part "p" of type "Propeller." Add a connector between the "Engine" part (using its role name from Question 8 if you provided one) and "p," bearing in mind that one "Propeller" can be driven by only one "Engine."
13. What are the two graphical mechanisms that can be used to represent properties nested more than one level deep on an internal block diagram?
14. What is the major difference between parts and references?
15. What is the difference in representation between the symbol for composite association and reference association on a block definition diagram?
16. What is an association block?
17. How are the quantitative characteristics of blocks described?

18. What are the three categories of value types?
19. Apart from the definition of a valid set of values, what can value types describe about their values?
20. A block "Boat" is described by its "length" and "width" in "Feet" and a "weight" in "Tons." Draw a block definition diagram describing "Boat," with definitions of the appropriate value types, including units and quantity kinds.
21. What is a derived property?
22. How are probability distributions—such as an interval distribution—for a property represented in the values compartment on a block definition diagram?
23. Which SysML concepts can be used to represent items (i.e., things that flow)?
24. What does an item flow define?
25. How is a proxy port specified?
26. A block "Boat" takes "fuel" and "cold water" as inputs and produces "exhaust gases" and "warm water" as outputs. Show "Boat" on a block definition diagram with inputs and outputs as proxy ports, with accompanying definitions. Demonstrate the use of both port icons and the proxy ports compartment.
27. What is the difference between proxy and full ports?
28. What is the rule for assessing the compatibility of an item flow on a connector between two ports?
29. What is a behavior port on a block used for?
30. Name all five kinds of behaviors supported by SysML.
31. What are the behavioral features of blocks used for?
32. What is a method?
33. What do the required interfaces of a port specify?
34. What do the provided interfaces of a port specify?
35. Describe the ball-and-socket representation for the interfaces of ports.
36. Name four types of classifiers encountered in this chapter.
37. Name three aspects of a redefined property that a redefining property can change.
38. How is a generalization relationship represented on a block definition diagram?
39. When specifying a generalization set, what is the coverage property used to define?
40. How are generalization sets represented on a block definition diagram?
41. What is a bound reference used for and how is it shown on an internal block diagram?
42. If one property is defined to be a subset of another, what is the relationship between the elements of the subsetted property and the elements of the subsetting property?
43. Name two ways in SysML of specifying a block configuration.

DISCUSSION TOPICS

Modeling variants is of significant importance in the system engineering process. Discuss for a system known to you how you might model system variants.

Reference properties can be used to model cross-cutting hierarchies that correspond to specific subsystems, such as electrical, mechanical, etc. Discuss how you would organize a model to include these subsystem definitions.

MODELING CONSTRAINTS WITH PARAMETRICS

8

This chapter describes how to model constraints on the performance and physical properties of systems and their environment in SysML. This allows SysML models to support a wide array of engineering analyses and simulations.

8.1 OVERVIEW

A typical design effort includes the need to perform many different types of engineering analyses, such as trade studies, sensitivity analysis, and design optimization. It may include the analysis of performance, reliability, cost, and physical properties of the system under consideration. SysML supports this type of analysis through the use of parametric models.

Parametric models constrain the properties of a system, which can then be evaluated by an appropriate analysis tool. Constraints are expressed as equations, with the parameters of the equations being bound to the properties of the system being analyzed. Each parametric model can capture the specification of one or more engineering analyses of a design. A parametric model which captures multiple engineering analyses—such as performance, reliability, and cost—can be analyzed to evaluate a particular design alternative, to support trade-off analysis, or optimize a design based on multiple criteria.

SysML introduces the constraint block to support the construction of parametric models. A constraint block is a special kind of block used to define equations so that they can be reused and interconnected. Constraint blocks have two main features: a set of parameters and an expression that constrains those parameters. Constraint blocks follow the pattern of definition and use that applies to blocks and parts as described in Chapter 7. A use of a constraint block is called a constraint property and is analogous to a part property. The definition and use of constraint blocks is represented on a block definition diagram and parametric diagram, respectively. The semantics and notation of constraint blocks in SysML were heavily influenced by Russell Peak's work on Constrained Objects [46].

8.1.1 DEFINING CONSTRAINTS USING THE BLOCK DEFINITION DIAGRAM

Constraint blocks and their relationships are defined on block definition diagrams, similar to the way blocks are defined. An example of a block definition diagram containing constraint blocks is shown in Figure 8.1.

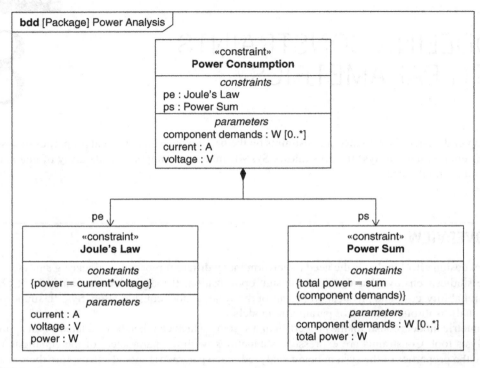

FIGURE 8.1

Example block definition diagram with constraint blocks.

This figure shows three constraint blocks. *Joule's Law* and *Power Sum* are leaf constraint blocks that each define an equation and its parameters. *Power Consumption* is a constraint block comprising *Joule's Law* and *Power Sum* to build a more complex equation.

The diagram elements for defining constraint blocks in the block definition diagram are shown in the Appendix, Table A.8.

8.1.2 THE PARAMETRIC DIAGRAM

Parametric diagrams are used to create systems of equations that can constrain the properties of blocks. The complete header for a parametric diagram is as follows:

```
par [model element kind] model element name [diagram name]
```

The diagram kind is **par**, and the *model element kind* can be either a block or a constraint block.

Figure 8.2 shows a parametric diagram for the constraint block *Power Consumption* from Figure 8.1. The constraint properties *ps* and *pe* are usages of the constraint blocks *Power Sum* and *Joule's Law*, respectively. The parameters of the constraint properties *ps* and *pe* are bound to each other and to the parameters of *Power Consumption*, which are shown flush with the diagram frame. The diagram elements of the parametric diagram are shown in the Appendix, Table A.13.

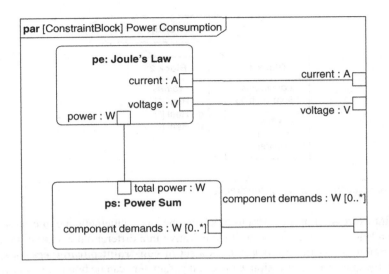

FIGURE 8.2

A parametric diagram used to construct systems of equations.

8.2 USING CONSTRAINT EXPRESSIONS TO REPRESENT SYSTEM CONSTRAINTS

SysML includes a generic mechanism for expressing constraints on a system as text expressions that can be applied to any model element. SysML does not provide a built-in constraint language because it is expected that different constraint languages—such as the Object Constraint Language (OCL), Java, or MathML—will be used as appropriate to the domain. The definition of a **constraint** should include the language used to enable the constraint to be evaluated.

Constraints may be owned by any element that is a namespace, such as a package or block. If the element that owns the constraint can include compartments, such as a block, the constraint can be shown in a special compartment labeled *constraints*. A constraint can also be shown as a note symbol attached to the model element(s) it constrains, with the text of the constraint shown in the body of the note. The constraint language is shown in braces before the text of the expression, although it is often elided to reduce clutter.

Figure 8.3 shows examples of the different constraint notations used in SysML that constrain the properties of a block. *Block 1* has an explicit compartment for the constraint, which in this case is expressed using Java. *Block 2* has a constraint that is shown in an attached note and is expressed in the constraint language of a specialized analysis tool called MATLAB.

8.3 ENCAPSULATING CONSTRAINTS IN CONSTRAINT BLOCKS TO ENABLE REUSE

SysML also includes a constraint block that extends the generic constraint concept. A **constraint block** encapsulates a constraint to enable it to be defined once and then used in different contexts, similar to the way parts represent usages of blocks in different contexts. The concept equivalent to the part is called a **constraint property.**

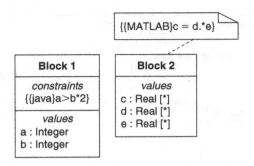

FIGURE 8.3

Example of the two notations for showing constraints.

The constraint expression of a constraint block can be any mathematical expression and may have an explicit dependency on time, such as a time derivative in a differential equation. In addition to the constraint expression, a constraint block defines a set of **constraint parameters**—a special kind of property used in the constraint expression. Constraint parameters can be bound to other parameters and to properties of the blocks. Constraint parameters do not have direction to designate them as dependent or independent variables with respect to the constraint expression. Instead, the interpretation of the dependencies between parameters is based on the semantics of the language used to specify the constraint expression. For example, in the C programming language, the expression $a = b + c$ is an assignment statement which states that a is dependent on the value of b and c, whereas the expression $a == b + c$ is a declarative statement and does not identify the dependent versus independent variables of the constraint.

Like other properties, each parameter has a type that defines the set of values that the parameter can take. Typically, parameters are value types that represent scalars or vectors. Through its value type, the parameter can also have a specific unit and quantity kind. Parameters can also support probability distributions like other properties.

8.3.1 ADDITIONAL PARAMETER CHARACTERISTICS

Properties whose multiplicity has an upper bound greater than 1 have two characteristics that are useful when defining collections. Modelers can specify whether the collection is **ordered** and whether the values in the collection must be **unique.** Ordered in this case means that the members of the collection are mapped to the values of a positive integer: member 1, member 2, and so on. The means by which the order is to be determined would have to be specified by an additional constraint or by using a behavior that builds the collection. In a unique collection, all of the collection's values must be different. These two characteristics are useful in specifying constraint parameters.

Another useful characteristic of properties is that they can be marked as derived (see the Derived Properties section in Chapter 7, Section 7.3.4). If a property is marked as derived, it means that its value is derived, typically from the values of other properties. This characteristic has two uses in specifying parametric models. First, if the calculation underlying an equation is known to be implemented as a function, a derived parameter can be used to identify the dependent variable. An example of this can be seen in Figure 8.4. Second, when the modeler wishes to guide the equation solver, derived properties

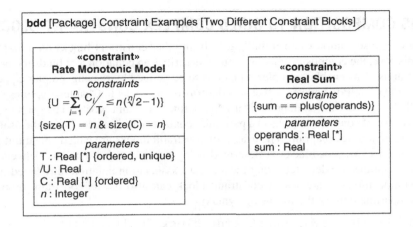

FIGURE 8.4

Two reusable constraint blocks expressed on a block definition diagram.

can indicate the values in a given analysis that need to be determined by solving the equation. An example of this can be seen later in Figure 8.16.

A constraint block is defined in a block definition diagram, as shown in Figure 8.4. The diagram header is the same as any other block definition diagram, specifying the package or block to which the diagram frame corresponds. The name compartment of the constraint block includes the keyword «constraint» above the name to differentiate it from other elements on a block definition diagram. The constraint expression is defined in the *constraints* compartment of the constraint block, and the constraint parameters are defined in the *parameters* compartment using a string with the following format:

```
parameter name: type[multiplicity]
```

Indications of ordering and uniqueness appear as keywords in braces after the multiplicity. The ordering indication is either ordered or unordered; the uniqueness indication is either unique or nonunique. In practice, unordered and nonunique are often indicated by the absence of a keyword. A derived property is shown with a forward slash (/) before its name.

Figure 8.4 shows two constraint blocks, *Real Sum* and *Rate Monotonic Model*. *Real Sum* is a simple reusable constraint where one parameter, *sum*, equals the sum of a set of operands, as expressed in the constraint in the constraints compartment. *Rate Monotonic Model* is also reusable but more specialized; it describes the equations underlying the rate monotonic analysis approach to scheduling periodic tasks on a processing resource. *T* represents the periods of the tasks, *C* represents the computation load of the tasks, and *U* represents the utilization of the processing resource. The constraint language is not shown in either case, but it can be seen that the constraint for *Real Sum* is expressed in a C-like syntax. The utilization constraint for *Rate Monotonic Model* is expressed using a more sophisticated equation language, which has the capability to be rendered using special symbols. Both mechanisms are equally acceptable in a SysML constraint block.

Both *T* and *C* are ordered collections, as indicated by the ordered keyword. The values of *Ti* are required to be unique because each task must have a different rate for the analysis to be correct. Parameter *n* specifies the number of tasks and an additional constraint is used to constrain the size of both *T* and *C* to be *n*. *U* is always the dependent variable in the underlying calculation and so is marked as derived.

8.4 USING COMPOSITION TO BUILD COMPLEX CONSTRAINT BLOCKS

Modelers can compose complex constraint blocks from other constraint blocks on a block definition diagram. In this case, the composite constraint block describes an equation that binds the parameters of its child constraints. This enables complex equations to be defined by reusing simpler equations.

The concept of definition and usage that was described for blocks in Chapter 7 applies to constraint blocks as well. A block definition diagram is used to define constraint blocks. The parametric diagram represents the usage of constraint blocks in a particular context. This is analogous to the usage of blocks as parts in an internal block diagram. The usages of constraint blocks are called constraint properties.

Composition of constraint blocks is described using composite associations between constraint blocks. The associations are depicted using the standard association notation introduced in Chapter 7 to represent composition hierarchies. A constraint block can also list its constraint properties in its *constraints* compartment using the following syntax:

```
constraint property : constraint block [multiplicity]
```

Figure 8.5 shows the decomposition of a *Power Consumption* constraint block into two other constraint blocks, *Joule's Law* and *Power Sum*. The role names on the component end of the compositions

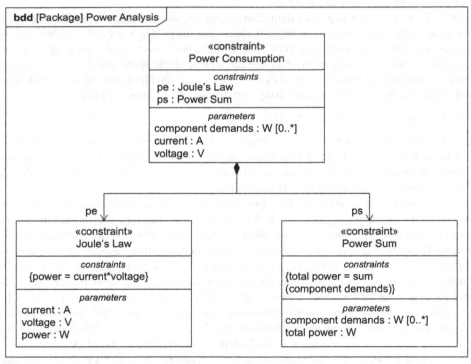

FIGURE 8.5

A hierarchy of constraints on a block definition diagram.

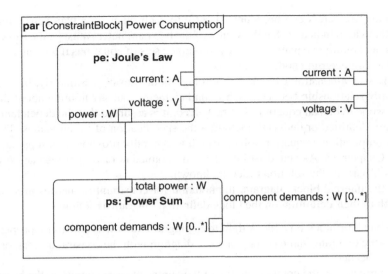

FIGURE 8.6

Internal details of the power consumption equation using a parametric diagram.

correspond to constraint properties. Property *pe* is a usage of the *Joule's Law* constraint block, which describes the standard power equation. Property *ps* is a usage of the *Power Sum* constraint block, which equates the *total power* demand to a set of *component demands*. *Power Consumption* uses these equations to relate the demands of a set of components to the required *current* and *voltage* of a power supply.

The *Joule's Law* and *Power Sum* constraint blocks feature their equations in their *constraints* compartments, whereas *Power Consumption* lists its constituent constraint properties. Note that in this example, the constituent constraints of *Power Consumption* are represented both in its *constraints* compartment and as association symbols. Typically, in a given diagram only one form of representation is used.

A modeler may choose to indicate on a particular constraint property symbol whether the internal structure of the constraint block that types it is further described by a parametric diagram. If the constraint block has an associated parametric diagram, then the symbol for the constraint property contains a rake symbol in its bottom right corner. The constraint block *Power Consumption* in Figure 8.7 has a rake symbol, indicating that it is further elaborated, in this case by the parametric diagram in Figure 8.6.

8.5 USING A PARAMETRIC DIAGRAM TO BIND PARAMETERS OF CONSTRAINT BLOCKS

As with blocks and parts, the block definition diagram does not show all the required information needed to interconnect its constraint properties. Specifically, it does not show the relationship between the parameters of constraint properties and the parameters of their parent and siblings. This additional information is provided on the parametric diagram using binding connectors, which express equality relationships between their two ends, as discussed in Chapter 7, Section 7.3.1.

Two constraint parameters can be bound directly to each other on a parametric diagram using a binding connector, which indicates that the values of the two parameters must be the same. This enables a modeler to connect multiple equations to create complex sets of equations if a parameter in one equation is bound to a parameter in another equation.

The parameters of a constraint block say nothing about causality. Similarly, binding connectors express an equality relationship between their bound elements, but say nothing about the causality of the equation network. When an equation is to be solved, it is assumed that the dependent and independent variables are identified or deduced, including the specification of initial values. This is typically addressed by a computational equation solver, which is generally provided in a separate analysis tool, as discussed in Chapter 18. As stated earlier, derived parameters or properties can be used to guide equation solvers if parts of the solution order are known.

Just as with the internal block diagram, the notation for constraint properties in a parametric diagram relates back to their definition on the block definition diagram as follows:

- A constraint block or block on a block definition diagram that owns constraint properties can be designated as the diagram frame of a parametric diagram with the constraint block or block name in the diagram header.
- A constraint property on the component end of the composite association on the block definition diagram may appear as a constraint property symbol within a frame designating the constraint block on the composition end. The name string of the symbol uses the colon notation previously described for parts in Chapter 7, Section 7.3.1:

```
constraint property name: constraint block name
```

When a composite association is used, the constraint property name corresponds to the role name on the component end of the association just as with parts. The type name corresponds to the name of the constraint block on the component end of the association.

The frame of a parametric diagram corresponds to a constraint block or a block. If the parametric diagram designates a constraint block, then its parameters are shown as small rectangles flush with the inner surface of the frame. The name, type, and multiplicity of each parameter are shown in a textual label floating near the parameter symbol.

On a parametric diagram, a constraint property (as described in Chapter 5, Section 5.3.7) may be shown either as a round-cornered rectangle (round-angle) symbol or as a rectangle with the keyword «constraint». The name and type of the property is shown inside the symbol, although either the property name or the type name can be elided if desired. The constraint expression itself can be elided, but if shown, it may appear either inside the round-angle or attached via a comment symbol to the round-angle. The parameters of the constraint property are shown flush with the inside surface of the constraint property symbol.

Figure 8.6 shows an example from the surveillance system, where the *Power Consumption* composite constraint block, originally introduced in Figure 8.5, is depicted as the context of a parametric diagram. The diagram shows how the parameters of constraint properties *ps*, a usage of *Power Sum*, and *pe*, a usage of *Joule's Law*, are bound together. As stated earlier, the names in the constraint property symbols are produced from the component ends of the associations on the block definition diagram. The *voltage* and *current* parameters of *pe* are bound to the *voltage* and *current* parameters of the block *Power Consumption* (hence shown on the frame boundary). The *power* parameter of *pe* is bound to the total cumulative power of all the powered equipment, calculated by *ps* from the set of *component demands* (also a parameter of *Power Consumption* and shown on the frame boundary). When all of the bindings between parameters are considered, the composed constraint for *Power Consumption* can be expressed as *{sum(component demands)=current*voltage}*.

It should be noted that although this is just a trivial example, it does highlight how parametric models can be used to construct more complex equations from reusable constraint blocks

8.6 CONSTRAINING VALUE PROPERTIES OF A BLOCK

Value properties of a block can be bound directly to other value properties with a binding connector to assert that their values are equal. However, more complex constraints on value properties can be expressed using constraint blocks. This is achieved by building a composition hierarchy of constraint blocks using a block definition diagram. In a parametric diagram, the block is designated by the enclosing frame and the constraint properties represent usages of the constraint blocks. The parameters of the constraint properties are bound to the value properties of the block using binding connectors.

In a parametric diagram for a block, a value property is depicted as a rectangle displaying its name, type, and multiplicity. A nested value property within a part hierarchy can be shown nested within its containing part symbol or can be shown using the dot notation that was described in Chapter 7, Section 7.3.1. An example of binding nested value properties using the part hierarchy notation is shown in Figure 8.7, and an example using the dot notation is shown in Figure 8.8.

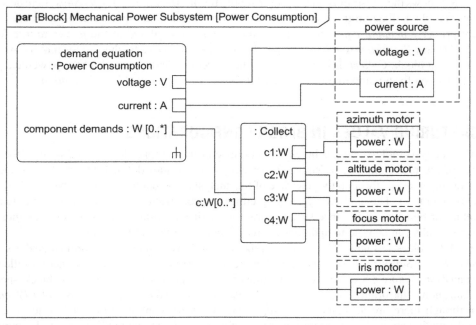

FIGURE 8.7

Binding constraints to properties on a parametric diagram.

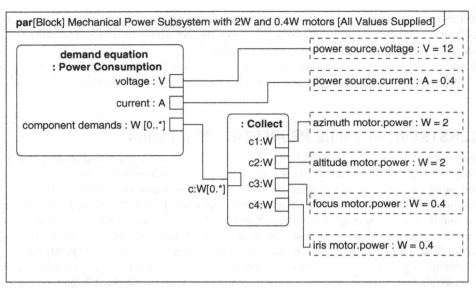

FIGURE 8.8

Describing a specific analysis configuration.

Figure 8.7 shows the constraints on the power supply for the *Mechanical Power Subsystem* described by the internal block diagram in Figure 7.11. The *Power Consumption* constraint block is used, via a constraint property *demand equation,* to relate the *current* and *voltage* of the *power source* for the *Mechanical Power Subsystem* to the load imposed on the *power source* by the various motors. An additional constraint block, *Collect,* is used to collect the power demand values of all the powered devices into one collection for binding to the *component demands* parameter of *demand equation.*

8.7 CAPTURING VALUES IN BLOCK CONFIGURATIONS

To allow an analysis tool to evaluate blocks containing constraint properties, at least some of the value properties of the block under analysis need to have specific values defined. Often, these values are provided during analysis through the interface of the analysis tool, but they can also be specified using a block configuration. This is done by creating either a specialization of the block with the required initial values or by using an instance specification to describe an instance of the block. In either case, the analysis results can be used to update the value properties of the configuration.

Although the block in Figure 8.7 contains all the relationships required to perform an analysis of the *Mechanical Power Subsystem* block, the related properties do not have values, and so there is little scope for direct analysis. Figure 8.8 shows a configuration of the *Mechanical Power Subsystem* block, specified as a specialization of the original block and called *Mechanical Power Subsystem with 2W and 0.4W motors.*

Even though there are no mandatory naming standards for configurations, it is often useful to include information about the configuration as part of its name. Note that in this case, all the values for the related properties are shown and so the *demand equation* constraint property simply acts as a check that the values are consistent. In other analysis scenarios, one or more properties may not have a value, in which case an equation-solving tool would be used to rearrange the constraint expression to compute the missing value or values or to report an error if a value cannot be determined.

8.8 CONSTRAINING TIME-DEPENDENT PROPERTIES TO FACILITATE TIME-BASED ANALYSIS

A value property is often a time-varying property that may be constrained by ordinary differential equations with time derivatives or other time-dependent equations. There are two approaches to representing these time-varying properties. The first, as illustrated in Figure 8.9, is to treat time as implicit in the expression. This can help reduce diagram clutter and is often an accurate representation of the analysis approach with time provided behind the scenes by the analysis tool.

Figure 8.9 shows the calculation of the *angular position,* in *Radians,* of the *azimuth gimbal* over time. The equation simply integrates the *angular velocity* of the *azimuth motor* over time to establish the angular position, *pos.* The initial value of *azimuth motor.angular velocity* in this case could be interpreted as a constant value depending on the semantics of the analysis.

Another approach to the representation of time is to include a separate time property that explicitly represents time in the constraint equations. The time property can be expressed as a property of a reference clock with specified units and quantity kind. The time-varying parameters in the constraint equations can then be bound to that time property. Local clock errors, such as clock skew or time delay, can also be introduced by defining a clock with its own time property that is related to some reference clock through additional constraint equations.

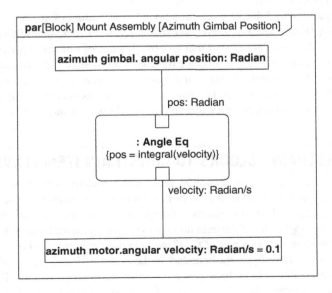

FIGURE 8.9

Using a time-dependent constraint.

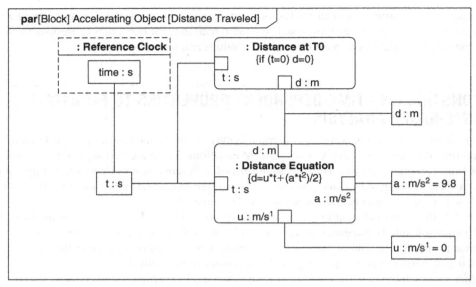

FIGURE 8.10

Explicitly representing time in a parametric diagram.

In Figure 8.9, time was implicit and initial conditions were defined by the default value of the velocity property. Figure 8.10 shows an example of the alternate approach of explicitly showing time, and uses constraints on values to express conditions at time zero.

The figure shows the standard distance equation bound to the values of an object under acceleration. The block *Accelerating Object* contains a reference to a *Reference Clock,* whose *time* property is bound to *t,* a value property of *Accelerating Object* that records passage of time as experienced by the object. The acceleration *a,* initial velocity *u,* and distance traveled *d* are bound to the *Distance Equation* along with time *t.* An additional constraint, *Distance at T0,* is used to specify the initial distance of the object (i.e., at time zero), which in this case is 0. The value of property *a* is specified with a default value that represents the constant value of acceleration due to gravity. Property *u* has a default value of 0.

8.9 USING CONSTRAINT BLOCKS TO CONSTRAIN ITEM FLOWS

A powerful use of constraint blocks is to show how properties associated with the flow of matter, energy, or information is constrained. To achieve this, item flows (or more accurately the item properties corresponding to item flows) can be shown on parametric diagrams and bound to constraint parameters.

Figure 8.11 shows the amplitudes of the item flows shown on the internal block diagram in Figure 7.44. *External* is the item flow from the boundary of the *Camera* to the *Protective Housing,* and *polarized* is the item flow from the *Protective Housing* to the boundary of the *Camera Module, cm.* The *Protective Housing* provides a value for acceptable loss of light power (flux) in value property *loss.* The *Camera* owns a loss equation, *Loss Eq,* to constrain the relative values of the light *flux* before and after passing through the *Protective Housing.* The *loss* parameter in *Loss Eq* is bound to the *loss* property of the *Protective Housing.*

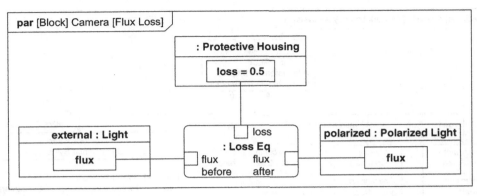

FIGURE 8.11

Constraining item flows.

8.10 DESCRIBING AN ANALYSIS CONTEXT

A constraint property that constrains the value properties of a block can, as discussed earlier, be part of a block's definition and thus shown in its constraints compartment. This works well when the constrained properties are intrinsically related in this way in all contexts. What often occurs, however, is that the constraints on block properties vary depending on the analysis requirements. For example, a different fidelity of analysis may be applied to the same system block depending on the required accuracy of the value of key properties. This type of scenario requires a more flexible approach such that the properties of the block can be constrained without the constraint being part of the block's definition. This approach effectively decouples the constraint equations from the block whose properties are being constrained, and thus enables the constraint equations to be modified without modifying the block whose properties are being constrained. An alternative approach is to specialize the block under analysis and add different constraints to each subclass that are relevant to different analyses.

To follow this approach, a modeler creates an **analysis context,** which composes both the block whose properties are being analyzed and all the constraint blocks required to perform the analysis. Libraries of constraint blocks may already exist for a particular analysis domain. These constraint blocks are often called **analysis models** and may be very complex and supported by sophisticated tools. The general analysis models in these libraries may not precisely fit a given scenario, and the analysis context may contain other constraint blocks to handle transformations between the properties of the block and the parameters of the analysis model. An analysis context is modeled as a block with associations to the block being analyzed (i.e., subject of the analysis), the chosen analysis model, and any intermediate transformations. By convention, the block being analyzed is referenced by the analysis context block because there may be many different analysis contexts for the block being analyzed. A white diamond symbol or a simple association with no end adornment is used to represent a reference from the analysis context block to the subject of the analysis. Composite associations are used between the analysis context and the analysis model and any other constraint blocks. An example of an analysis context is shown in Figure 8.12.

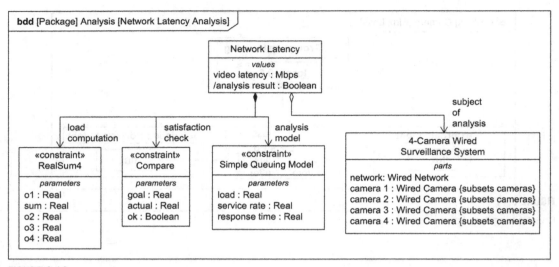

FIGURE 8.12

An analysis context shown on a bdd (constraint equations not shown).

Figure 8.12 shows the analysis of network throughput for a *4-Camera Wired Surveillance System*. The analysis context is called *Network Latency*, which references the *subject of analysis*, a *4-Camera Wired Surveillance System*. The analysis context also contains an *analysis model*, in this case a *Simple Queuing Model*, and uses the basic constraints *RealSum4* and *Compare* to perform a *load computation* and a *satisfaction check*, respectively. *Network Latency* contains two value properties: *video latency*, specified in *Mbps*, and *analysis result*, which is intended to be a computed value and hence is derived. In this case, the equations that define the constraints are not shown.

In Figure 8.13, the bindings needed to perform the analysis are shown. The parameters of the *analysis model* are bound to the properties of the *subject of analysis*. The loads on the system from all four cameras in the *subject of analysis* are summed to establish the total *load* using *load computation*. The *network bandwidth* of the *subject of analysis* is used to establish the *service rate* for the *analysis model*. The *response time*, calculated using *analysis model*, is then compared to the required *video latency* using *satisfaction check*. The *video latency* is a refinement of the requirement *Required Network Throughput* to establish the *analysis result* (see Chapter 13 for a discussion of requirements). The *analysis result* is derived to indicate that its value needs to be calculated. If the *analysis result* is true, then the network satisfies the requirement.

It is common practice for a single constraint block to represent a complex engineering analysis as a black box, without showing all the internal complexity of the composition. In this way, the constraint block specifies the input and output parameters of the analysis, and often defers to an appropriate analysis tool to provide detailed equations that relate the input and output parameters. The name of the constraint block is generally the name of the analysis, such as *Power Analysis*, *Power Analysis Model*, or *Power Analysis Equations*.

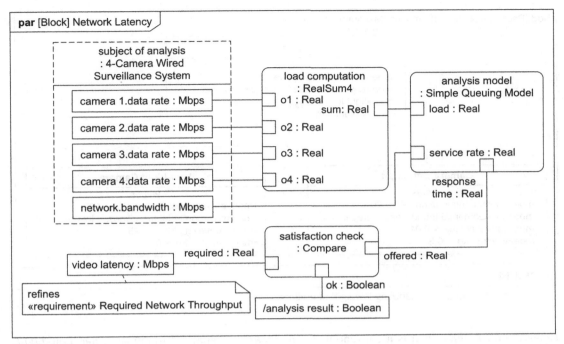

FIGURE 8.13

Binding values in an analysis context.

8.11 MODELING EVALUATION OF ALTERNATIVES AND TRADE STUDIES

A common use of constraint blocks is to support trade studies. A **trade study** is used to compare a number of alternative solutions to see whether and how well they satisfy a particular set of criteria. Each solution is characterized by a set of **measures of effectiveness** (often abbreviated "moes") that correspond to the evaluation criteria and have a calculated value or value distribution. The moes for a given solution are then evaluated using an **objective function** (often called a cost function or utility function), and the results for each alternative are compared to select a preferred solution.

Annex E.4 of the SysML specification introduces some concepts to support the modeling of trade studies. A moe is a special type of property. An objective function is a special type of constraint block that expresses an objective function whose parameters can be bound to a set of moes using a parametric diagram. A set of solutions to a problem may be specified as a set of blocks that each specialize a general block. The general block defines all the moes that are considered relevant to evaluating the alternatives, and the specialized blocks provide different values or value distributions for the moes.

A moe is indicated by the keyword «moe» in a property string for a block property. An objective function is indicated by the keyword «objectiveFunction» on a constraint block or constraint property.

Figure 8.14 shows two variants of a *Camera* intended to provide a solution to operate in low-light conditions. These variants are shown using specialization (as described in Chapter 7) and are called

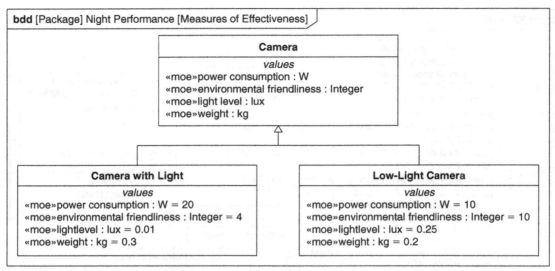

FIGURE 8.14

Two variants of a camera for handling low-light conditions.

Camera with Light, which is a conventional camera with an attached illuminator, and *Low-Light Camera*, which is designed to work at much lower levels of ambient light. Four relevant measures of effectiveness, indicated by the keyword «moe», are used to conduct the trade studies. Note that the moes in the specialized blocks are redefinitions of those in *Camera*. The redefinition keywords have been elided to reduce clutter.

A trade study is typically described as a type of analysis context, which references the blocks that represent the different alternatives. It also contains constraint properties for the objective function (or functions) to be used to evaluate the alternatives, and a means to record the results of the evaluation, typically value properties that capture the score for each alternative.

Figure 8.15 shows the definition of *Night Performance Trade-off*—a trade study for evaluating the nighttime performance of two camera variants. As indicated by its associations, *Night Performance Trade-off* contains two constraint properties, both typed by objective function *NP Cost Function* and two reference properties, one typed by *Low-Light Camera* and the other by *Camera with Light*. The intent of the analysis is that the equations be solved for *option 1* and *option 2*, and so they are shown as derived.

Figure 8.16 shows the internal bindings of the trade study *Night Performance Trade-off*. One use of the objective function *NP Cost Function, cf1,* is bound to the value properties of the *Low-Light Camera*, and the other, *cf2,* is bound to the *Camera with Light*. The *score* parameters of *cf1* and *cf2* are bound to two value properties of the context called *option 1* and *option 2*, which are the dependent variables in this particular analysis. In this case, using the values provided in Figure 8.14 for the measures of effectiveness of the two solutions, the scores are *400* for *option 1* and *450* for *option 2*, indicating that the *Low-Light Camera* is the preferred solution. Additional constraint blocks can be specified to relate the moes to other properties in the system (refer to Chapter 17, Section 17.3.6 for an example).

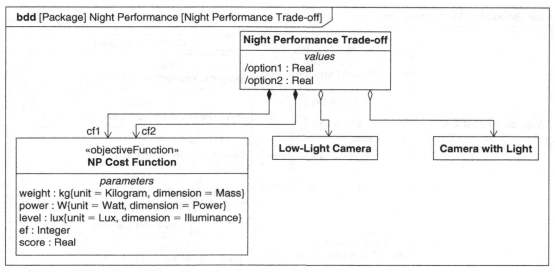

FIGURE 8.15

A trade study represented as an analysis context.

8.12 SUMMARY

Constraint blocks are used to model constraints on the properties of blocks to support engineering analyses, such as performance, reliability, cost, and mass properties analysis. The following are key aspects of constraint blocks and their usages:

- SysML includes the concept of a constraint that can correspond to any mathematical or logical expression, including time-varying expressions and differential equations. SysML does not specify a constraint language but enables the language to be specified as part of the definition of the constraint.
- SysML provides the ability to encapsulate a constraint in a constraint block so that it can be reused and bound with other constraints to represent complex sets of equations. A constraint block defines a set of constraint parameters related to each other by a constraint expression. Parameters may have types, units, quantity kinds, and probability distributions. The block definition diagram is used to define constraint blocks and their interrelationships. In particular, a composite association can be used to compose constraint blocks to create more complex equations. Constraint blocks can be defined in model libraries to facilitate specific types of analysis.
- Constraint properties are usages of constraint blocks. The parametric diagram shows how constraint properties are connected by binding their parameters to one another and to the value properties of blocks using binding connectors. Binding connectors express equality between the values of the constraint parameters or value properties at their ends. In this way, constraint blocks can be used to constrain the values of block properties. The specific values needed to support the evaluation of the constraints for a block are typically specified by a

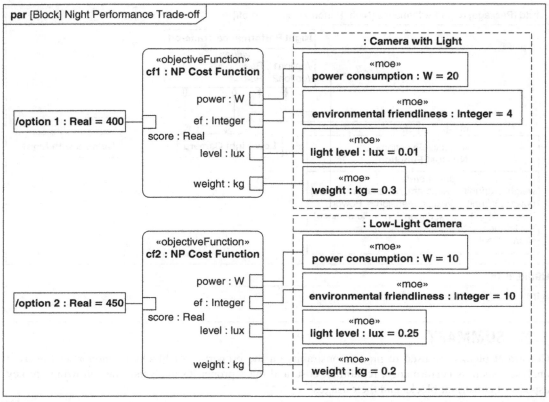

FIGURE 8.16

Trade-off results between the two low-light camera variants.

configuration of that block, using either a specialization of the block or an instance specification.

- An analysis context is a block that provides the context for a system or component that is subject to analysis. The analysis context is composed of the constraint blocks that correspond to the analysis model and references the system being analyzed. A parametric diagram whose frame designates the analysis context is used to bind the relevant properties of the block and the parameters of the analysis model. The analysis context can be passed to an engineering analysis tool to perform the computational analysis, and the analysis results can be returned as values of properties of the analysis context.
- A common and useful form of analysis used by systems engineers is the trade study, which is used to compare alternative solutions for a given problem based on some criteria. A moe ("measure of effectiveness") is used to define a property that needs to be evaluated in a trade study, and a constraint block, called an objective function, is used to define how the solutions are evaluated.

8.13 QUESTIONS

1. What is the diagram kind of a parametric diagram, and which kinds of model element can it represent?
2. If a constraint parameter is ordered, what does that imply about its values?
3. If a constraint parameter is unique, what does that imply about its values?
4. How are constraint parameters represented on a block definition diagram?
5. How is the composition of constraints represented on a block definition diagram?
6. How are constraint properties represented on a parametric diagram?
7. How are constraint parameters represented on a parametric diagram?
8. What are the semantics of a binding connector?
9. How can constraint blocks be used to constrain the value properties of blocks?
10. A block "Gas" has two value properties, "pressure" and "volume," that vary inversely with respect to each other. Create an appropriate constraint block to represent the relationship, and use it in a parametric diagram for "Gas" to constrain "pressure" and "volume."
11. What are the two approaches to specifying parametric models that include time-varying properties?
12. How are composite associations and reference associations typically used in an analysis context?
13. What is a measure of effectiveness and what is it used for?
14. What is an objective function and how is it represented on a block definition diagram and a parametric diagram?

DISCUSSION TOPICS

Under what circumstances is it useful or necessary to use derived properties or parameters in parametric models?

What are the relative merits of using constraint blocks to specify parametric equations as part of the definition of a block versus applying an externally defined parametric model to an existing block?

MODELING FLOW-BASED BEHAVIOR WITH ACTIVITIES

This chapter describes concepts needed to model behavior in terms of the flow of inputs, outputs, and control using an activity diagram. An activity diagram is similar to a traditional functional flow diagram but with many additional features to precisely specify behavior. Activities can also depict behavior performed by specific blocks or parts, which may represent a system or its components.

9.1 OVERVIEW

In SysML, an activity is a formalism for describing behavior that specifies the transformation of inputs to outputs through a controlled sequence of actions. The activity diagram is the primary representation for modeling flow-based behavior in SysML and is analogous to the functional flow diagram that has been widely used for modeling system behavior. Activities provide enhanced capabilities over traditional functional flow diagrams, such as the capability to express their relationship to the structural aspects of the system (e.g., blocks, parts) and the ability to model continuous flow behaviors. The semantics of a selected subset of activities are defined by the fUML specification [42] so they can be executed by an execution environment.

Actions are the building blocks of activities and describe how activities execute. Each action can accept inputs and produce outputs, called tokens. The tokens are placed on input and output buffers called pins until they are ready to be consumed. These tokens can correspond to anything that flows, such as information or a physical item (e.g., water). A certain class of actions, termed invocation actions, can invoke other activities that are further decomposed into other actions. In this way, invocation actions can be used to compose activities into activity hierarchies. Other actions are used to specify the leaf level of behavior, such as sending a signal or reading a property value.

The concept of object flow describes how input and output items flow between actions. Object flows can connect the output pin of one action to the input pin of another action to enable the passage of tokens. Flows can be discrete or continuous, where continuous flow represents the situation when the time between tokens is effectively zero. Complex routing of object tokens between actions can be specified by control nodes.

The concept of control flow provides additional constraints on when, and in which order, the actions within an activity will execute. A control token on an incoming control flow enables an action to start execution, and a control token is offered on an outgoing control flow when an action completes its execution. When a control flow connects one action to another, the action at the target end of the control flow cannot start until the source action has completed. Control nodes, such as join, fork, decision, merge, initial, and final nodes, can be used to route control tokens to further specify the sequence of actions.

The sending and receiving of signals is one mechanism for communicating between activities executing in the context of different blocks and for handling events such as timeouts. Signals are sometimes used as an external control input to initiate an action within an activity that has already started.

Streaming pins allow new tokens to flow into and out of an action while it is executing, whereas nonstreaming pins only accept and produce tokens at the start and end of execution. SysML also offers more advanced activity modeling concepts, such as extensions to flow semantics to deal with interrupts, flow rates, and probabilities.

SysML provides several mechanisms to relate activities to the blocks that perform them. Activity partitions are used to partition actions in an activity according to the blocks that have responsibility for executing them.

Alternatively, an activity may be specified as the main behavior of a block, which describes how inputs and outputs of the block are processed. An activity can also be specified as the method for an operation of the block that is invoked as a result of a service request for that operation. When the behavior of a block is specified using a state machine, activities are often used to describe the behavior of the blocks when the state machine transitions between states, or the behavior of the block when it is in a particular state.

Other traditional systems engineering functional representations are also supported in SysML. Activities can be represented on block definition diagrams to show activity hierarchies similar to functional hierarchies. Activity diagrams can also be used to represent Enhanced Functional Flow Block Diagrams (EFFBDs) [49].

9.2 THE ACTIVITY DIAGRAM

The principal diagram used to describe an activity is called an **activity diagram**. An activity diagram defines the actions in an activity along with the flow of input/output and control between them. The complete diagram header for an activity diagram is as follows:

act [*model element kind*] activity name [diagram name]

The diagram kind for an activity diagram is **act** and the *model element kind* can be an activity or control Operator.

Figure 9.1 shows an activity diagram for the activity *Log On* with some of the basic activity diagram symbols. *Log On* includes call actions that invoke other activities, such as action *a2* that invokes the *Read User Data* activity. Actions have input and output pins, shown as small rectangles, to accept tokens that may represent units of information, matter, or energy. Pins are connected using object flows and control flows (solid and dashed lines respectively). The notation for activity diagrams is shown in the Appendix, Tables A.14 through A.17.

Figure 9.2 shows an example of an activity hierarchy that can be represented on a block definition diagram. The activity hierarchy provides an alternative view of the actions and invoked activities shown on activity diagrams, but it does not include the flows between the actions and other activity constructs such as control nodes. The structure of the hierarchy is shown using composite associations from a parent activity—in this case, *Generate Video Outputs*—to other activities such as *Process Frame*. The role names on the associations, such as *a2*, correspond to the names of the actions used to invoke the activities in the activity diagram. The notation required to show activity hierarchies on block definition diagrams is described in the Appendix, Table A.9.

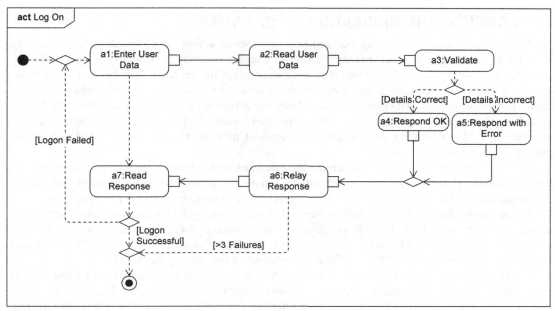

FIGURE 9.1

An example activity diagram.

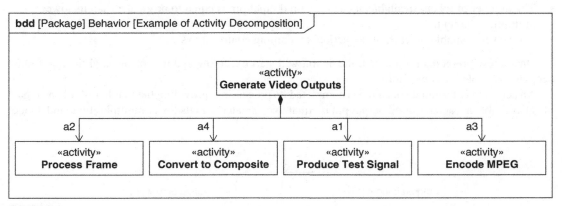

FIGURE 9.2

An example of an activity hierarchy in a block definition diagram.

9.3 ACTIONS—THE FOUNDATION OF ACTIVITIES

As described previously, an activity decomposes into a set of **actions** that describe how the activity executes and transforms its inputs to outputs. There are several different categories of actions in SysML described in this chapter, but this section provides a summary of the fundamental behavior of all actions. SysML activities are based on token-flow semantics related to Petri-Nets [47, 48]. **Tokens** hold the values of inputs, outputs, and control that flow from one action to another. An action processes tokens placed on its **pins.** A pin acts as a buffer where input and output tokens to an action can be stored prior to or during execution; tokens on input pins are consumed, processed by the action, and placed on output pins for other actions to accept.

Each pin has a multiplicity that describes the minimum and maximum number of tokens that the action consumes or produces in any one execution. If a pin has a minimum multiplicity of zero, then it is optional, marked by the keyword optional in guillemets. Otherwise, it is said to be required.

The action symbol varies depending on the kind of action, but by default it is a rectangle with round corners. The pin symbols are small boxes flush with the outside surface of the action symbol and may contain arrows indicating whether the pin is an input or output. Once a pin is connected to a flow and the direction of flow becomes obvious, the arrow notation in the pin may be elided.

Figure 9.3 shows a typical action, called *a1,* with a set of input and output pins. One input pin and one output pin are required; that is, they have a lower multiplicity bound greater than zero. The other two pins are optional; that is, they have a lower multiplicity bound of zero. The action also has one incoming control flow and one outgoing control flow shown as an arrow with a dashed line. (See Section 9.6 for a detailed description of control flows.) As long as its owning activity is executing, an action will begin execution when tokens are available on all its required inputs, including its control inputs as follows.

- The number of tokens available at each required input pin is equal to or greater than its lower multiplicity bound.
- A token is available on each of the action's incoming control flows.

Once these prerequisites are met, the action will start executing and the tokens at all its input pins become available for consumption.

An action may terminate once it has completed its processing, providing the number of tokens it has made available at each required output pin is equal to or greater than its lower multiplicity bound. Once

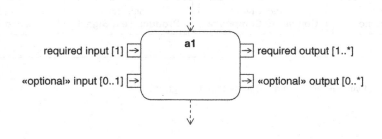

FIGURE 9.3

An action with input and output pins and input and output control flow.

the action has terminated, the tokens at all its output pins become available to other actions connected to those pins. In addition, a control token is placed on each outgoing control flow.

Object and control tokens are routed using control nodes that can buffer, copy, and remove tokens. For more information, see Section 9.5 for object flow and Section 9.6 for control flow.

The preceding paragraphs described the basic semantics of actions, but the following additional semantics are discussed later in this chapter:

- Different kinds of actions perform different functions, and some—particularly the call actions discussed in Section 9.4.2—introduce additional semantics such as streaming.
- SysML allows control tokens to disable as well as enable actions, but actions need control pins to support this, as described in Section 9.6.2.
- SysML also includes continuous flows that are addressed in Section 9.9.1.
- Actions can be contained inside an interruptible region, which, when interrupted, will cause its constituent actions to terminate immediately. Interruptible regions are described in Section 9.8.1.

The relationship between the semantics of blocks and activities is discussed in Section 9.11.

9.4 THE BASICS OF MODELING ACTIVITIES

Activities provide the context in which actions execute. Activities are used—and more importantly reused—through call actions. Call actions allow the composition of activities into arbitrarily deep hierarchies that allows an activity model to scale from descriptions of simple functions to very complex algorithms and processes.

9.4.1 SPECIFYING INPUT AND OUTPUT PARAMETERS FOR AN ACTIVITY

An activity may have multiple inputs and multiple outputs called **parameters.** Note that these parameters are not the same as the constraint parameters described in Chapter 8. Each parameter may have a type, such as a value type or block. Value types range from simple integers to complex vectors and may have corresponding units and quantity kinds. Parameters can also be typed by a block that may correspond to a structural entity, such as fluid flowing through a hydraulic system or an automobile part flowing through an assembly line. Parameters have a direction that may be in, out, or both.

Parameters also have a multiplicity that indicates how many tokens for this parameter can be consumed as input or produced as output by each execution of the activity. The lower bound of the multiplicity indicates the minimum number of tokens that must be consumed or produced by each execution. As with pins, if the lower bound is greater than zero, then the parameter is said to be **required;** otherwise, it is said to be **optional.** The upper bound of the multiplicity specifies the maximum number of tokens that may be consumed or produced by each execution of the activity.

Activity parameters are shown on an activity diagram using **activity parameter nodes.** During execution, an activity parameter node contains tokens that hold the arguments corresponding to its parameter. An activity parameter node is related to exactly one of the activity's parameters and must have the same type as its corresponding parameter. If a parameter is marked as inout, then it needs at least two activity parameter nodes associated with it, one for input and the other for output.

A parameter may be designated as streaming or nonstreaming, which affects the behavior of the corresponding activity parameter node. An activity parameter node for a **nonstreaming** input parameter may only accept tokens prior to the start of activity execution, and the activity parameter node for a nonstreaming output parameter can only provide tokens once the activity has finished executing. This contrasts with a **streaming** parameter, where the corresponding activity parameter node can continue to accept input tokens or produce output tokens throughout the activity execution. Streaming parameters add significant flexibility for representing certain kinds of behavior. Parameters have a number of other characteristics described later in this chapter.

Activity parameter node symbols are rectangles that straddle the activity frame boundary. Each symbol contains a name string composed of the parameter name, parameter type, and parameter multiplicity:

```
parameter name: parameter type[multiplicity]
```

If no multiplicity is shown, then the multiplicity 1..1 is assumed. An optional parameter is shown by the keyword «optional» above the name string in the activity parameter node. Conversely, the absence of the keyword «optional» indicates that the parameter is required.

Additional characteristics of the parameter, such as its direction and whether it is streaming, are shown in braces either inside the parameter node symbol after the name string or floating close to the symbol.

There is no specific graphical notation to indicate the direction of an activity parameter node on its symbol, although the direction of the parameter can be shown textually inside the symbol. Some modeling guidelines suggest that input parameter nodes are shown on the left of the activity and output parameter nodes on the right. Once activity parameter nodes have been connected by flows to nodes inside the activity, the activity parameter node direction is implicitly defined by the arrow direction on the object flows.

Figure 9.4 shows the inputs and outputs of the *Operate Camera* activity that is the main behavior of the camera (refer to Chapter 7 Section 7.5.1 for a description of main behavior). As can be seen from the notation in the parameter nodes, *Light* from the camera's environment is available as input using the *current image* parameter and two types of video signal are produced as outputs

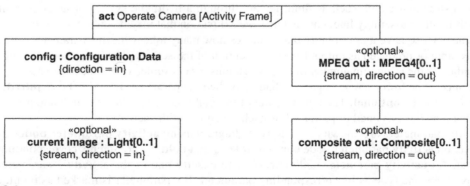

FIGURE 9.4

Specifying an activity using a frame on an activity diagram.

using the *composite out* and *MPEG out* parameters. The input parameter *config* is used to provide configuration data to the camera when it starts.

The activity consumes a stream of inputs and produces a stream of outputs as it executes, as indicated by the {stream} annotation on the main parameter nodes. The other parameter, *config*, is not streaming because it has a single value that is read when the activity starts. As stated earlier, when the multiplicity is not shown, for instance on parameter *config*, this indicates a lower bound and upper bound of one. The other parameters are streaming and there is not a minimum number of tokens consumed or produced, so they are shown as «optional».

9.4.2 COMPOSING ACTIVITIES USING CALL BEHAVIOR ACTIONS

An important kind of action is the **call behavior action,** which invokes a behavior when it executes. The invoked behavior is assumed to be an activity in this chapter, although it can be other kinds of SysML behavior. A call behavior action has a pin for each parameter of the called behavior, and the characteristics of those pins must match the multiplicity and type of their corresponding parameters on the invoked behavior. The name string of a pin has the same form as the name string for an activity parameter node symbol but floats outside the pin symbol.

If an activity parameter on the invoked activity is streaming, then the corresponding pin on the call behavior action also has streaming semantics. As stated earlier, tokens on nonstreaming pins, such as those shown in Figure 9.3, can only be available to the action for processing at the start (in the case of input pins) or the end (in the case of output pins) of the action execution. By comparison, tokens continue to be available through streaming pins while their owning action is executing, although the number of tokens consumed or produced by each execution is still governed by its upper and lower multiplicity bounds. As a result, it is generally appropriate to define an unlimited upper bound for streaming parameters.

The name string of a pin may include characteristics of the corresponding parameter, such as streaming. An alternative notation for a streaming pin is to shade the pin symbol.

The call behavior action symbol is a round-cornered box containing a name string with the name of the action and the name of the called behavior (e.g., activity) separated by a colon as follows:

    action name : behavior name.

The default notation includes just the action name without the colon or the behavior name. When the behavior name is shown and the action is not named, the colon is included to differentiate this notation from the default. A rake symbol in the bottom right corner of a call behavior action symbol indicates that the activity being invoked is described on another diagram.

To transform light into video signals, the *Operate Camera* activity invokes other activities that perform various subtasks using call behavior actions, as shown in Figure 9.5. The action name strings take the form *: Activity Name*, indicating that the actions do not have names. The parameter nodes and pins are optional in this case because the corresponding actions can start executing even if they have no tokens. This figure shows just activity parameter nodes and actions with their inputs and outputs. Note that the types of the pins have been elided here to reduce clutter.

All the invoked activities consume and produce streams of input and output tokens, as indicated by the {stream} annotation on the pins of the actions. *Collect Images* is an analog process performed by the camera lens. *Capture Video* digitizes the images from the outside world to a form of video output. *Generate Video Outputs* takes the internal video stream and produces MPEG and composite outputs for transmission to the camera's users.

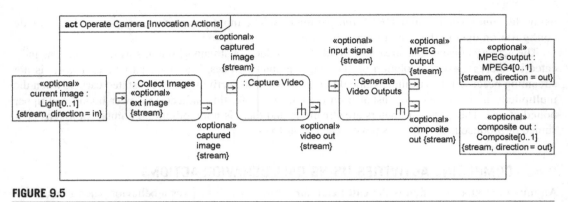

FIGURE 9.5

Invocation actions on an activity diagram.

9.5 USING OBJECT FLOWS TO DESCRIBE THE FLOW OF ITEMS BETWEEN ACTIONS

Object flows are used to route input/output tokens that represent information and/or physical items between object nodes. Activity parameter nodes and pins are two examples of object nodes. Object flows can be used to route items from the parameters nodes on the boundary of an activity to/from the pins on its constituent actions or to connect pins directly to other pins. In all cases, the direction of the object flow must be compatible with the direction of the object nodes at its ends (i.e., in or out), and the types of the object nodes on both ends of the object flow must be compatible with each other.

An object flow is shown as an arrow connecting the source of the flow to the destination of the flow, with its head at the destination. When an object flow is between two pins that have the same characteristics, an alternative notation can be used where the pin symbols on the actions at both ends of the object flow are elided and replaced by a single rectangular symbol, specifically called an object node symbol. In this case, the object flow connects the source action to the object node symbol with an arrowhead on the object node symbol end, and then connects the object node symbol to the destination action, with an arrowhead at the destination end. The object node symbol has the same annotations as a pin symbol, because it actually represents the pins on the source and destination actions.

In Figure 9.6, the actions of *Operate Camera* shown in Figure 9.5 are now interconnected by object flows to establish the flow from light entering the camera to the output of video images in the two required formats. The incoming light represented by the parameter called *current image* flows to the *:Collect Images* action; its output, *captured image,* is the input to *:Capture Video* (note the use of a rectangle symbol for this object node). *:Capture Video* produces video images, via its *video out* pin, which in turn becomes the input for *:Generate Video Outputs. :Generate Video Outputs* converts its input video signal into MPEG and composite outputs that are then routed to corresponding output parameter nodes of *Operate Camera*.

In Figure 9.6, the actions have no names, which is indicated by the presence of a colon in the name string of the action symbols. See Figure 9.8 for an example where the actions are named.

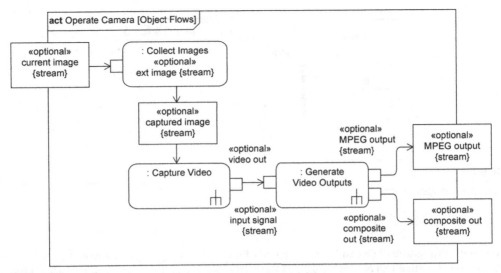

FIGURE 9.6

Connecting pins and parameters using object flows.

9.5.1 ROUTING OBJECT FLOWS

There are many situations where simply connecting object nodes using object flows does not allow an adequate description of the flow of tokens through the activity. SysML provides a number of mechanisms for more sophisticated expressions for routing flows. First, each object flow may have a guard expression that specifies a rule to govern which tokens are valid for the object flow. In addition, several constructs in SysML activities called collectively **control nodes** provide more sophisticated flow mechanisms, including:

- A **fork node** has one input flow and one or more output flows—it replicates every input token it receives onto each of its output flows. The tokens on each output flow may be handled independently and concurrently. Note that this replication of tokens does not imply that the items represented by the tokens are replicated. In particular, if the represented item is physical, replication of that physical object may not even be possible.
- A **join node** has one output flow and one or more input flows—its default behavior for object flows is to produce output tokens only when an input token is available on each input flow. Once this occurs, it places all input object tokens on the output flow. This has the important characteristic of synchronizing the flow of tokens from many sources. Note that this applies only to object tokens; the handling of control tokens is different, as described in Section 9.6.

    The default behavior of join nodes can be overridden by providing a join specification that specifies a logical expression that the arrival of tokens on the input flows must satisfy in order to generate an output token on the output flow.
- A **decision node** has one input and one or more output flows—an input token can only traverse one output flow. The output flow is typically established by placing mutually exclusive guards on all outgoing flows and offering the token to the flow whose guard expression is satisfied.

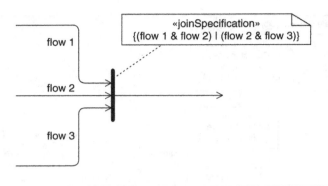

FIGURE 9.7

Example of a join specification.

The guard expression else can be used on one of the node's outgoing flows to ensure that there is always one flow that can accept a token. If more than one outgoing object flow can accept the token, then SysML does not define which of the flows will receive the token.

A decision node can have an accompanying decision input behavior that is used to evaluate each incoming object token. Its result can be used in guard expressions

- A **merge node** has one output flow and one or more input flows—it routes each input token received on any input flow to its output flow. Unlike a join node, a merge node does not require tokens on all its input flows before offering them on its output flow. Rather, it offers tokens on its output flow as it receives them.

Fork and join symbols are shown as solid bars, typically aligned either horizontally or vertically. Decision and merge symbols are shown as diamonds. Where forks and joins or decisions and merges are adjacent (i.e., would be connected by just a flow with no guards), they can be shown as a single symbol with the inputs and outputs of both connected to that symbol. Figure 9.12, later in the chapter, contains an example of a combined merge and decision node.

Join specifications and decision input behaviors are shown in notes attached to the relevant node.

Figure 9.7 shows an example of a join specification. The join node has three input flows—*flow 1, flow 2,* and *flow 3*—and the join specification states that output tokens are produced if input tokens are received on both *flow 1* and *flow 2,* or on both *flow 2* and *flow 3.* The expression uses the names of flows, so the flows must be named in this situation. Another use of flow names is to support flow allocation (see Chapter 14, Section 14.7). Figure 9.12 shows an example of a decision input behavior.

In Figure 9.8, the activity *Generate Video Outputs* accepts an input video signal and outputs it in appropriate formats for external use, in this case *Composite* video and *MPEG4.* The *a1:Produce Test Signal* action allows *Generate Video Outputs* to generate a test signal if desired. See the specification of *Produce Test Signal* later in Figure 9.14 to see how the activity knows when to generate the signal. The test signal, when generated, is merged into the stream of video frames using a merge node, and this merged stream is then converted into video frames by *a2:Process Frame.* Note that if tokens are produced on both the *input signal* parameter node and the *test signal* pin, then they will be interleaved into the *raw frames* pin by the merge node. That is the desired behavior in this case. If it is not the desired

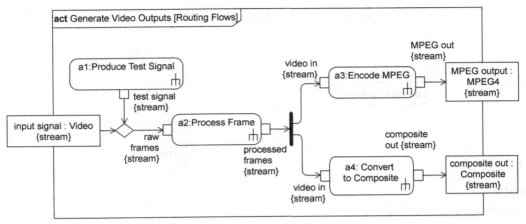

FIGURE 9.8

Routing object flows between invocations.

behavior, an additional control, such as a specific test mode, would be needed to ensure that incoming token streams were exclusive.

Once processed, the tokens representing the processed frames are then forked and offered to two separate actions: *a4:Convert to Composite* that produces the *composite out* output and *a3:Encode MPEG* that produces the *MPEG* output. These two actions can continue in parallel, each consuming tokens representing frames and performing a suitable translation. Note that the fork node does not imply that the frame data is copied (although they may be) but merely that both *a3:Encode MPEG* and *a4:Convert to Composite* have access to the data via their input tokens.

In this example, the name strings of the call behavior actions include both the action name and activity name, when arguably the actions need not be named. This helps to demonstrate the mapping from activities on this activity diagram to the same activities represented on the block definition diagram in Figure 9.26.

9.5.2 ROUTING OBJECT FLOWS FROM PARAMETER SETS

The parameters of an activity can be grouped together into **parameter sets,** which must have only input or only output parameters as members. When an activity is invoked that has input parameter sets, the parameter nodes corresponding to at most one input parameter set can contain tokens. When an activity that has output parameter sets completes, the parameter nodes corresponding to at most one output parameter set can contain tokens. A given parameter may be a member of multiple parameter sets.

Each set of parameters is shown by a rectangle on the outer boundary of the activity, which partially encloses the set of parameter nodes that correspond to parameters in the set. These rectangles can overlap to reflect the overlapping membership of parameter sets.

Figure 9.9 shows an activity called *Request Camera Status* with two distinct sets of outputs. When presented with a *camera number* as input, *Request Camera Status* will return an *error* and a *diagnostic* if there is a problem with the camera, or a *power status* and *current mode* if the camera is operational.

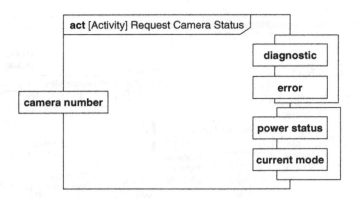

FIGURE 9.9

An activity with parameter sets.

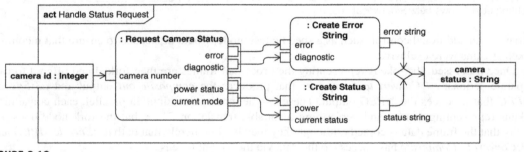

FIGURE 9.10

Invoking an activity with parameters sets.

If an invoked activity has parameter sets, then the groupings of pins corresponding to the different parameter sets are shown on the call behavior action, using notation similar to parameter sets on activities.

Figure 9.10 shows the object flow for an activity *Handle Status Request* that reads a *camera id* and writes a *camera status*. It invokes *Request Camera Status* with a *camera number* and expects one of two sets of outputs that correspond to two parameter sets: an *error* and a *diagnostic* or a *power status* and *current mode*. These two sets of outputs are used by two different string-formatting functions, *Create Error String* and *Create Status String*. Whichever formatting function receives inputs produces an output string that is then conveyed via a merge node to the *camera status* output parameter node.

9.5.3 BUFFERS AND DATA STORES

Pins and activity parameter nodes are the two most common kinds of object nodes, but there are cases when additional constructs are required. A **central buffer node** provides a store for object tokens outside of pins and parameter nodes. Tokens flow into a central buffer node and are stored there until they flow out again. It is needed when there are multiple producers and consumers of a single-buffered

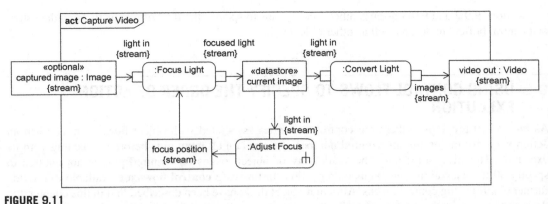

FIGURE 9.11

Using a data store node to capture incoming light.

stream of tokens at the same time. This contrasts with pins and activity parameter nodes, which have either a single producer or single consumer for each token.

Sometimes activities require the same object tokens to be stored for access by a number of actions during execution. A kind of object node called a **data store node** can be used for this. Unlike a central buffer node, a data store node provides a copy of a stored token rather than the original. When an input token represents an object that is already in the store, it overwrites the previous token. Data stores can provide tokens when a receiving action is enabled, thus supporting the pull semantics of traditional flow charts.

Data store nodes and central buffer nodes only store tokens while their parent activity is executing. If the values of the tokens need more permanent storage, then a property should be used. The language includes primitive actions, described in Section 9.14.3, which can be used to read and write property values.

Both data store nodes and central buffer nodes are represented by a rectangle with a name string, with the keywords «datastore» and «centralBuffer» above the name string. Their names have the same form as pins, buffer or store name: buffer or store type, but without multiplicity. An example of a central buffer node is shown in Figure 9.19.

Figure 9.11 describes the internal behavior of the *Capture Video* activity. Light entering the camera lens is focused by the action *:Focus Light,* which produces an image that is stored in a data store node called *current image.* The image stored in *current image* is then used by two other actions: *:Convert Light,* which samples the images to create video frames, and *:Adjust Focus,* which analyzes the current image for sharpness and provides a *focus position* to *:Focus Light.* The use of a data store node here facilitates the transition between the analog nature of the incoming light from the lens and the digital nature of the video stream. (See Figure 9.17 for an enhanced version of this diagram, including flow rate information.) In this case, the data store may be allocated to the focal plane array of the camera along with the *:Convert Light* action (see Chapter 14, Section 14.7 for a description of allocation).

The object node symbol called *focus position* is input to *Focus Light,* whereas *:Convert Light* and *:Adjust Focus* receive their input from a data store node. The notation for the object node representation of flows and the representation of buffer nodes is quite similar, but buffer nodes always have the keyword «datastore» or «centralBuffer» above their name.

Sections 9.9.2 and 9.9.3 discuss other mechanisms to specify the flow of tokens through data store and central buffers nodes, as well as other object nodes.

9.6 USING CONTROL FLOWS TO SPECIFY THE ORDER OF ACTION EXECUTION

As mentioned previously, there are control semantics associated with object flow, such as when an action waits for the minimum required number of tokens on all input pins before proceeding with its execution. However, sometimes the availability of object tokens on required pins is not enough to specify all the execution constraints on an action. In this case **control flows** are available to provide further control using control tokens. Although object flows have been described first in this chapter, the design of an activity need not necessarily start with the specification of object flows. In traditional flow charts, it is often the control flows that are established first and the routing of objects later.

In addition to any execution prerequisites established by required input pins, an action also cannot start execution until it receives a control token on all input control flows. When an action has completed its execution, it places control tokens on all outgoing control flows. The sequencing of actions can thus be controlled by the flow of control tokens between actions using control flows.

An action can have more than one control flow input. This has the same semantics as connecting the multiple incoming control flows to a join node, and connecting the output control flow from the join node to the action. Similarly, if an action has more than one control flow output, it can be modeled by connecting the action via an outgoing control flow to a fork node with multiple control flow outputs. As described in Section 9.6.2, control tokens can be used to disable actions as well as enabling them.

9.6.1 DEPICTING CONTROL LOGIC WITH CONTROL NODES

All the constructs used to route object flows can also be used to route control flows. In addition, a join node has special semantics with respect to control tokens; even if it consumes multiple control tokens, it emits only one control token once its join specification is satisfied. Join nodes can also consume a mixture of control and object tokens, in which case once all the required tokens have been offered to the join node, all the object tokens (but none of the control tokens) are offered on the outgoing flow.

In addition to the constructs described in Section 9.5.1, there are some special constructs that provide additional control logic:

- *Initial node*—when an activity starts executing, a control token is placed on each initial node in the activity. The token can then trigger the execution of an action via an outgoing control flow. Note that although an initial node can have multiple outgoing flows, a control token will only be placed on one. Typically, guards are used when there are multiple flows in order to ensure that only one is valid, but if this is not the case, then the choice of flow is arbitrary.
- *Activity final node*—when a control or object token reaches an activity final node during the execution of an activity, the activity execution terminates.
- *Flow final node*—control or object tokens received at a flow final node are consumed but have no effect on the execution of the enclosing activity. Typically they are used to terminate a particular sequence of actions without terminating an activity. An example of when a flow final node is used

is when a fork node has two output flows to two concurrent actions. If one of the action terminates but the other continues as part of a processing chain, a flow final node can be used to indicate that one action has completed its execution without terminating the activity.

A control flow can be represented either by using a solid line with an arrowhead at the destination end like an object flow or, to more clearly distinguish it from object flow, by using a dashed line with an arrowhead at the destination end. An initial node symbol is shown as a small solid black circle. The activity final node symbol is shown as a bulls-eye, Examples of the initial and activity final nodes are shown in Figure 9.12.

The flow final node symbol is a hollow circle containing an X. Figure 9.21 contains an example of a flow final node.

The console software provides the capability to drive a camera through a preset scan route, as shown in Figure 9.12. The activity *Follow Scan Route* will follow a route that is a set of positions for the camera defined in terms of pan-and-tilt angles. It has one input parameter, the *route* as a fixed-length collection of positions with size *route size*. When started, the activity resets its *count* property, then iterates over all points in the route—incrementing *count* for every point. It terminates when the return value of the associated decision input behavior evaluates to false (and thus satisfies the *[false]* rather than the *[true]* guard) indicating that the last point in the route is reached. The decision input condition is an opaque expression written in Alf (see Section 9.14.2 for a description of the Alf programming language). As with constraints, the language used to specify the action can be added in braces before the expression. The *Position Camera* activity is invoked for each position token offered on the *route* parameter. Control flows dictate the order in which the activity executes.

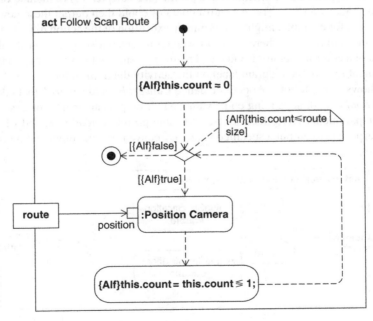

FIGURE 9.12

Control flow in activities.

Note that in this case there is a combined merge and decision symbol that accepts two input control flows and has two output control flows: one leads to an activity final node and the other leads into another iteration of the algorithm. The activity's *count* property is initialized and incremented using actions *this.count = 0;* and *this.count = this.count + 1;* these are opaque actions; that is, their function is expressed in some language external to SysML (in this case Alf).

9.6.2 USING CONTROL OPERATORS TO ENABLE AND DISABLE ACTIONS

An action with nonstreaming inputs and outputs typically starts once it has the prerequisite incoming tokens and terminates execution when it completes the production of its outputs. However, the completion of the action execution may need to be controlled by a control input, particularly if the action is a call action with streaming inputs and/or outputs. To achieve this, a value can be sent via a control flow to the action to enable or disable its invoked activity. SysML provides a specific control enumeration for this called **ControlValue,** with values `enable` and `disable`. For an action to receive this control input, it needs to provide a control pin that can receive it. A control value of `enable` has the same semantics as the arrival of a control token, and a control value of `disable` will terminate the invoked activity.

A special behavior called a **control operator** produces control values via an output parameter, typed by `ControlValue`. A control operator can include complex control logic and can be reused in many different activities via a call behavior action. A control operator is also able to accept a control value on an appropriately typed input parameter and will treat it as an object token rather than a control token.

The control value type could be extended in a profile (see Chapter 15) to include other control values in addition to `enable` and `disable`. A control operator could then output these new values. A control value of `suspend`, for example, might not terminate execution of the action like `disable`. The action would allow execution to resume where it left off when it received a `resume` control value.

The definition of a control operator is indicated by the presence of the keyword «`controlOperator`» as the model element kind in the diagram label on the activity diagram frame.

Figure 9.13 shows a simple control operator, called *Convert Bool to Control,* that takes in a *Boolean* parameter called *bool in* and, depending on its value, either outputs an `enable` or `disable` value on its *control out* output parameter. The values are created using primitive actions, called value specification actions, whose purpose is to output a specified value. By convention, the input and output pins of these

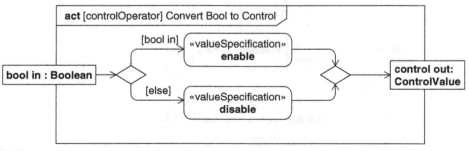

FIGURE 9.13

Using a control operator to generate a control value.

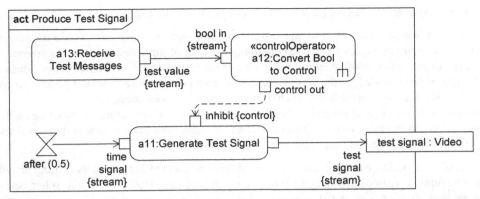

FIGURE 9.14

Using a control operator to control the execution of an activity.

actions are elided. (See Section 9.14.3 for a discussion of primitive actions.) *Convert Bool to Control* is a generally useful control operator that can be reused in many applications.

A control operator is a kind of behavior and so may be invoked using a normal call behavior action. A call behavior action that invokes a control operator has the keyword «controlOperator» above its name string. A control pin symbol is a standard pin symbol with the addition of the property name control in braces floating near the pin symbol.

A test signal is not always wanted on the video output. A mechanism to inhibit test signal production is shown in Figure 9.14. The *Convert Bool to Control* control operator shown in Figure 9.13 reads a *Boolean* flag *test value* from the activity *Receive Test Messages* to generate an enable or disable value on a pin called *control out*. This pin in turn is connected via a control flow to the *inhibit* pin of the *Generate Test Signal* activity. *Generate Test Signal* interprets this input as a control value because *inhibit* is a control pin, as indicated by the annotation {control}. When *Generate Test Signal* is enabled, it reads the time at 2 Hz from an accept time event action (see Section 9.7 for a discussion of time events). The activity *Receive Test Messages* is defined in Figure 9.24.

9.7 HANDLING SIGNALS AND OTHER EVENTS

In addition to obtaining inputs and producing outputs using its parameters, an activity can accept signals using an **accept event action** for a signal event (commonly called an **accept signal action**) and send signals using a **send signal action.** Communication can then be achieved between activities by including a send signal action in one activity and an accept signal action for a signal event representing the same signal in another activity. More typically, signals are sent from or received by the instances of the blocks that own and execute the activities, as described in Section 9.11.2. Communication via signals takes place asynchronously; that is, the sender does not wait for the signal to be accepted by the receiver before proceeding to other actions.

An accept signal action can output the received signal on an output pin. A send signal action has one input pin per attribute of the signal to be sent and one input pin to specify the target for the signal.

The accept event action can accept others kinds of events, including:

- A time event, which corresponds to an expiration of an (implicit) timer. In this case the action has a single output pin that outputs a value containing the time of the accepted event occurrence.
- A change event, which corresponds to a certain condition expression (often involving values of properties) being satisfied. In this case there is no output pin, but the action will generate a control token on all outgoing control flows when a change event has been accepted.
- A change event can also be related to the change in the value of a structural feature (e.g., a flow property). When the value of the structural feature changes, both the previous and new values of the feature are presented on output pins.

An accept event action with no incoming control flows is enabled as soon as its owning activity (or owning interruptible region; see Section 9.8.1) starts to execute. However, unlike other actions, it remains enabled after it has accepted an event and so is ready to accept others.

As of SysML 1.3, both send signal actions and accept event actions can be sent and received, respectively, through ports, including nested ports. See Chapter 7, Section 7.6 for a description of ports. An accept event action can specify that it accepts an event from a particular port, such as a signal arriving at a given port. A send signal action can specify that its signal must be sent through a particular port.

A send signal action is represented by a rectangle with a triangle attached on one end, and an accept event action is represented by a rectangle with a triangular section missing from one end. When the event accepted is a time event, the accept event action may be shown as an hourglass symbol (see Figure 9.14).

Also as of SysML 1.3, if an event is accepted through a port, the path to the port is given as a prefix to the name string of the accept event action with the format: «from» (portname, ...). If a signal is to be sent through a port, the path to the port is given as a prefix to the name string of the accept event action with format: via portname, ...

Figure 9.15 shows how MPEG frames are transmitted over the surveillance camera network. The *Transmit MPEG* activity first sends a *Frame Header* signal to indicate that a frame is to follow. It then executes *Send Frame Contents,* which splits the frame into packets and sends them. When *Send Frame Contents* finishes, it outputs a *packet count* and two signaling actions are performed: a *Frame Footer* signal is sent and then an accept signal action waits for a *Frame Acknowledgment* signal. Once the *Frame Acknowledgment* signal has been received, the *Check Transmission* activity is invoked to check the packet count returned with the acknowledgment against the count provided as an output of *Send Frame Contents.* If the packet counts match, then transmission is deemed to have succeeded and the variable *transmission OK* is set to true. This variable is then tested on the outgoing guards of a decision node and, if true, the activity terminates; otherwise the frame is resent, having previously been stored.

9.8 STRUCTURING ACTIVITIES

There are various ways in which the actions in an activity can be grouped together to obtain specific execution semantics. Interruptible regions allow the execution of a set of nodes to be interrupted. Structured activity nodes provide an alternate mechanism to activities for executing a set of actions with common inputs and outputs as a single group.

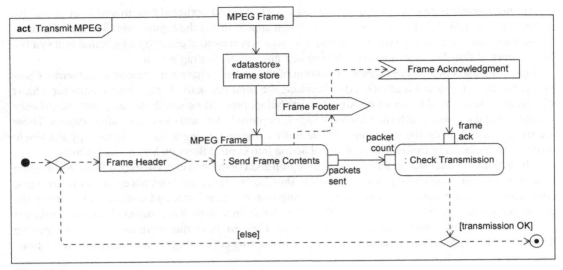

FIGURE 9.15

Using signals to communicate between activities.

9.8.1 INTERRUPTIBLE REGIONS

All the action executions within an execution of an activity are terminated when the activity is terminated. However, there are some circumstances when the modeler wants only a subset of the action executions to be terminated.

An **interruptible region** can be used to model this situation. An interruptible region groups a subset of actions within an activity and includes a mechanism for interrupting execution of those actions, called an **interrupting edge,** whose source is a node inside the interruptible region and whose destination is a node outside it. Both control and object flows can be designated as interrupting edges. Normal (i.e., noninterrupting) flows may have a destination outside the region as well; tokens sent on these flows do not interrupt the execution of the region.

When an interruptible region is entered, at least one action within the region starts to execute. An interruption of an interruptible region occurs whenever a token is accepted by an interrupting edge that leaves the region. This interruption causes the termination of all actions executing within the interruptible region, and execution continues with the activity node or nodes that accepted the token from the interrupting edge. (It can be more than one node because the interrupting edge can connect to a fork node.)

A token on an interrupting edge often results from the reception of a signal, either by the activity containing the interruptible region or the block that owns the activity, if it has one. In that case, the signal is received by an accept signal action within the interruptible region that offers a token on an outgoing interrupting edge to some activity node outside the region. Special semantics are associated with accept event actions contained in interruptible regions. As long as they have no incoming edges, the accept event action does not start to execute until the interruptible region is entered, as opposed to the normal case where the accept event action starts when the enclosing activity starts.

An interruptible region is notated by drawing a dashed round-cornered box around a set of activity nodes. As of SysML 1.2, the name of the region can appear inside the region, which is useful if there are multiple interruptible regions. An interrupting edge is represented either by a lightning bolt symbol or by a normal flow line with a small lightning bolt annotation floating near it.

Figure 9.16 shows a more complete definition of the overall behavior of the camera, *Operate Camera,* previously shown in Figure 9.6. After invoking the *Initialize* activity, the camera waits for a *Start Up* signal to be received by an accept signal action before proceeding simultaneously with the primary activities that the camera performs: *Collect Images, Capture Video,* and *Generate Video Outputs.* These are triggered, following the acceptance of the *Start Up* signal, using a fork node to copy the single control token emerging from the accept signal action into control flows ending on each action.

The actions are enclosed in an interruptible region and continue to execute until a *Shut Down* signal is accepted by an accept signal action. When a *Shut Down* signal has been accepted, an interrupting edge leaves the interruptible region, all the actions within it terminate, and control transitions to the action that invokes the *Shutdown* activity. Once the *Shutdown* activity has completed, a control token is sent to an activity final node that terminates *Operate Camera.* Note that there are other flows leaving the interruptible region, but because they are not interrupting edges, they do not cause its termination.

9.8.2 USING STRUCTURED ACTIVITY NODES

Activities are inherently concurrent in nature with the execution of actions only governed by the availability of object and control tokens. However, if the modeler wishes to execute a set of actions within an activity as a group, SysML offers a **structured activity node**. A structured activity node can have a

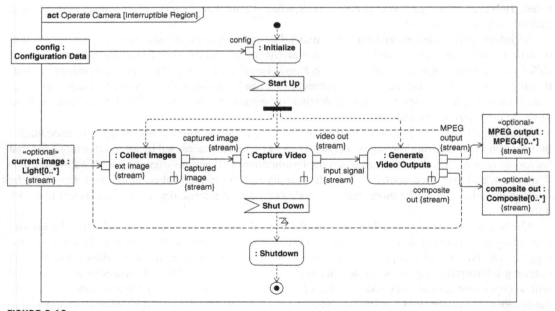

FIGURE 9.16

An interruptible region.

set of pins through which tokens flow to and from its internal actions. A structured activity node, like an action, cannot start until it has the required number of object and control tokens on its inputs, and only delivers tokens on its outputs when all of its internal actions have completed their execution. A structured activity node is often used in preference to an activity when its actions are unlikely to be reused in more than one context. The content of a structured activity node is shown in the same diagram as the owning activity whereas the content of a called behavior is typically not.

There are three specialized kinds of structured activity node:

- A **sequence node**, which executes its actions one after the other in a defined order;
- A **conditional node**, which contains a number of groups of actions that are executed only under certain conditions;
- A **loop node**, which contains a set of actions that are executed repeatedly;

A sequence node is the simplest specialized form of structured activity node, containing just a single grouping of actions. A successor action in the sequence cannot start to execute until its predecessor has completed its execution, even if all of its other execution prerequisites (see Section 9.3) have been met.

A conditional node contains a set of **clauses,** each containing a test and a body. It is similar to an if statement in a programming language like Java. When the conditional node starts to execute, the tests of all the clauses are executed and if one of the tests yields a true result then the body of its clause is executed. The body of only one clause can execute; the choice of which body to execute if more than one test yields true is not defined by the language. However, the modeler may specify an evaluation order for the clauses, which allows them to determine the outcome in such cases. There is a special clause, called the **else clause,** whose test always yields true, that will be selected for execution if no other clause is executed.

A loop node contains three sections, the setup, the test and the body. It is similar to the while and for statements in a programming language like C. The setup is performed once on entry to the node. After setup, the body of the node is executed while the test yields true; the test may either be executed before the body or after the body. A loop node can contain loop variables, similar to those provided in the C programming language, which are accessible to the setup, test, and body sections of the node.

A structured activity node is shown as a rounded rectangle with a dashed boundary and the keyword «structured» above its name string. SysML defines no graphical notation for sequence, conditional or loop nodes, but the Action Language for Foundational UML (Alf), described in Section 9.14.2, does provide a textual syntax for them.

9.9 ADVANCED FLOW MODELING

In SysML, there is a default assumption that tokens flow at the rate dictated by the executing actions and that tokens flowing into an object node flow out in the same order and with equal probability. SysML offers constructs to deal with situations when these assumptions are not valid.

9.9.1 MODELING FLOW RATES

Any streaming parameter can have a rate property that specifies the expected rate at which tokens flow into or out of a related pin or parameter node. Flows can also have a rate property that specifies the expected number of tokens that flow per time interval, that is, the expected rate at which they leave the source node and arrive at the target node.

The rate property can represent a continuous or discrete rate. Continuous flow is a special case that indicates that the expected rate of flow is infinite or conversely that the time between token arrivals is zero. In other words, there are always newly arriving tokens available at whatever rate the tokens are read. When a discrete rate is specified, the value is only the statistically expected rate value. The actual value may vary over time, only averaging out to the expected value over long periods.

A continuous rate is indicated by the keyword «continuous» above the name string of the corresponding symbol. A discrete rate is indicated by the keyword «discrete». A specific discrete rate is specified using the property pair rate = rate value in braces either inside or floating alongside the corresponding symbol.

In Figure 9.17, the object flows associated with light in the *Capture Video* activity are continuous. The *Focus Light* and *Adjust Focus* actions invoke analog processes with continuous inputs and outputs, as indicated by the appearance of the keyword «continuous» on object nodes associated with those actions, including the *current image* data store. However, the images generated by the *Convert Light* action must be produced at a rate of 30 frames per second, as indicated on the *video out* parameter node.

9.9.2 MODELING FLOW ORDER

As described earlier in this chapter, tokens can be queued at pins or other object nodes as they await processing by the action, subject to a specified **upper bound**. When the upper bound of an object node is greater than one, the modeler can specify the order in which its tokens are read using the **ordering property** of the node that can take values of ordered, FIFO (first-in/first-out), LIFO (last-in/first-out), or unordered. If the ordering property is specified as ordered, the modeler must provide an explicit selection behavior that defines the ordering. This mechanism can be used to select the token based on some value, such as priority, of the represented object.

In a case when an offered token would cause the number of tokens to exceed the upper bound of the object node, a modeler can choose to **overwrite** tokens already there or to discard the newly arrived tokens.

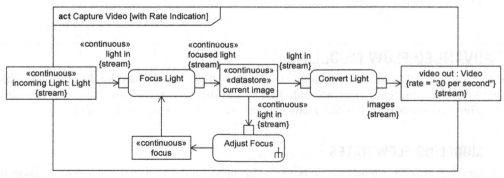

FIGURE 9.17

Use of continuous flows and discrete flows with rate information.

The notation for ordering is the name value pair `ordering = ordering value` placed in braces near or inside the object node. If no ordering is shown, then the default `FIFO` is assumed. The keyword «overwrite» is used to indicate that a token arriving at a full node removes a token that is already present before adding itself to the node in accordance with its ordering property. The token removed is the one that has been in the object node the longest. For `FIFO` ordering, this is the token that is next to be selected; for `LIFO` it is the token that would be last to be selected. Alternatively, the keyword «noBuffer» can be used to discard newly arriving tokens that are not immediately processed by the action.

9.9.3 MODELING PROBABILISTIC FLOW

When appropriate, a flow can be tagged with a probability to specify the likelihood that a given token will traverse a particular flow among available alternative flows. This is typically encountered in flows that emanate from a decision node, although probabilities can also be specified on multiple edges going out of the same object node (including pins). Each token can only traverse one edge with the specified probability. If **probabilistic flows** are used, then all alternative flows must have a probability and the sum of the probabilities of all flows must equal 1.

Probabilities are shown either on activity flow symbols or parameter set symbols as a property/value pair `probability = probability value` enclosed in braces floating somewhere near the appropriate symbol.

Figure 9.18 shows the activity diagram for *Transmit MPEG*, first introduced in Figure 9.15. In this example, the probability of successful transmission has been added. The two flows that correspond to successful and unsuccessful transmission have been labeled with their relative probability of occurrence.

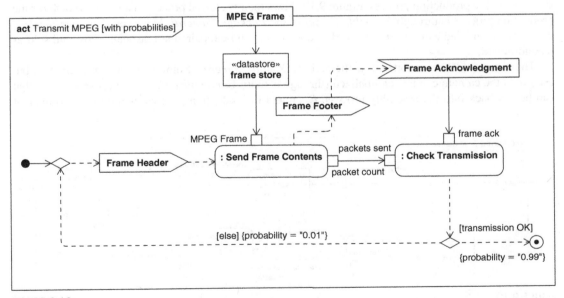

FIGURE 9.18

Probabilistic flow.

9.10 MODELING CONSTRAINTS ON ACTIVITY EXECUTION

The basic constraints on activity execution were covered in Section 9.3. This section describes modeling techniques that can be used to specify further execution constraints.

9.10.1 MODELING PRE- AND POST-CONDITIONS AND INPUT AND OUTPUT STATES

An action is able to execute when all of the prerequisite tokens have been offered at its inputs, and similarly may terminate when it has offered the postrequisite tokens on its outputs. However, sometimes additional constraints apply that are based on the values of those tokens or conditions currently holding in the execution environment. These constraints can be expressed using **pre-** and **post-conditions** on the actions and, in the case of call actions, on the behaviors they invoke.

In the specific case when an object represented by a token has an associated state machine, an object node may explicitly specify the required current state or states of that object in a **state constraint.**

The display of pre- and post-conditions depends on whether they are specified against the behavior or the action. Pre- and post-conditions on behaviors (in this case activities) are specified as text strings placed inside the activity frame, preceded by either the keyword «precondition» or «postcondition». Pre- and post-conditions on actions are placed in note symbols attached to the action, with the keyword «local-Precondition» or «localPostcondition» at the top of the note preceding the text of the condition.

A state constraint on an object node is shown by including the state name in square brackets underneath the name string of the symbol for that object node. This is equivalent to a local pre-condition or post-condition on the owning action requiring the specified state.

Although ACME Surveillance Systems does not manufacture the cameras, they do want to have some say in the production process. Figure 9.19 shows their preferred process. The optimal path for the production process is through *Assemble Cameras* and *Package Cameras*. However, their experience is that some assembled cameras do not work properly but can be repaired at reasonable cost and sold as reconditioned.

The repair process is modeled as the activity *Repair Cameras*. Some cameras are unfixable, but even then the camera can be cannibalized (through activity *Cannibalize Cameras*) for spare parts that can be fed back into the assembly process. A camera in production progresses through a number of

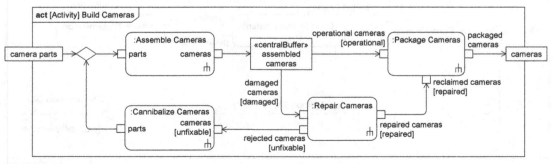

FIGURE 9.19

Example of using states on pins.

states (see Chapter 11 for a description of state machines) as it moves through production, and different activities require or provide cameras in specific states. *Assemble Cameras* may produce cameras faster than they can be packaged or repaired, so they are placed in a buffer called *assembled cameras*. From there they either progress directly to *Package Cameras* if their state is *operational*, or, they progress to *Repair Cameras* if their state is *damaged*. *Repair Cameras* accepts cameras in the *damaged* state, and they are either *repaired* or deemed *unfixable* when the activity has completed.

Note that the activity *Build Cameras* models the process of building cameras, using tokens to represent cameras. In this example, the flow of tokens could mirror quite closely the flow of physical cameras through a production system. The central buffer node might be allocated to a storage rack, for example.

The previous discussion described how the states on input and output pins could be used to specify pre-conditions and post-conditions, respectively. A constraint on the input and output relationship can also be specified, in effect, by combining a pre-condition and post-condition. These constraints might, for example, express the relationship between the pressure of some incoming gas and the temperature readings provided by some outgoing electrical signal. Alternatively, this could be used to express an accuracy or time constraint associated with the action or activity. The constraint can be captured using a constraint block to support further parametric analysis.

9.10.2 ADDING TIMING CONSTRAINTS TO ACTIONS

SysML provides a specialized form of constraint that can be used to specify the duration of an action's execution. The constraint is shown using standard constraint notation, a note attached to the action which is constrained.

Figure 9.20 shows an additional timing constraint on frame transmission. It is used to indicate that the action which invokes the *Send Frame Contents* activity has at most 10 milliseconds to execute.

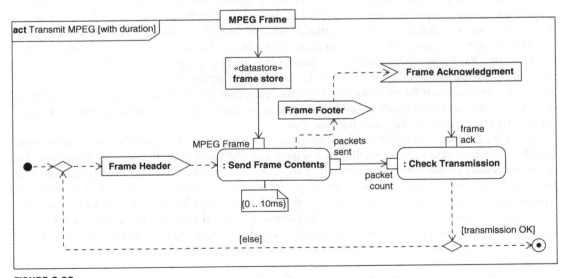

FIGURE 9.20

Adding timing constraints to actions.

9.11 RELATING ACTIVITIES TO BLOCKS AND OTHER BEHAVIORS

Activities are often specified independently of structure (i.e., blocks), and their execution semantics do not depend on the presence of blocks. However, as the system design progresses, the relationship between the behaviors of a system, expressed in this case using activities, and the structure of a system, expressed using blocks, needs to be established.

Different methods approach this in different ways. A classical systems engineering functional decomposition method allocates the functions to components as described in the method in Chapter 16. Other methods approach this somewhat differently by establishing a system hierarchy and driving out the scenarios defined by the interaction between components as described in the method in Chapter 17.

SysML has two mechanisms to relate blocks and activities. The first is the use of an activity partition to assert that a given block (or part) is responsible for the execution of a set of actions. The second is for a block to own an activity, as introduced in Chapter 7, Section 7.5.1, and use this as a basis for specifying aspects of the block's behavior.

9.11.1 LINKING BEHAVIOR TO STRUCTURE USING PARTITIONS

A set of activity nodes—in particular call actions—can be grouped into an **activity partition** (also known as a **swim lane**) that is used to indicate responsibility for execution of those nodes. A typical case is when an activity partition represents a block or a part and any behaviors invoked by call actions in that partition are the responsibility of the block or the part. The use of partitions to indicate which behaviors are the responsibilities of which blocks specifies the functional requirements of a system or component defined by the block.

Activity partitions are depicted as rectangular symbols that physically encompass the action symbols and other activity nodes within the partition (the so-called "swim lane" notation). Each partition symbol has a header containing the name string of the model element represented by the partition. In the case of a part or reference, the name string consists of the part or reference name followed by the type (block) name, separated by a colon. In the case of a block, the name string simply consists of the block's name. Partitions can be aligned horizontally or vertically to form rows or columns, or optionally can be represented by a combination of horizontal and vertical rows to form a grid pattern. An alternative representation for an activity partition for call actions is to include the name of the partition or partitions in parentheses inside the node above the action name. This can enable the activity to have a more efficient layout than the swim lane notation.

Figure 9.21 contains an example of partitions taken from the model of an ACME surveillance system. It shows how new intruder intelligence is analyzed and handled by the *security guard* and the *company security system* within some overall system context. Once the security guard has received new intelligence (signal *Intruder Intel*), he or she may need to address two concerns in parallel, so the token representing the signal is forked into two object flows. If the intruder has moved, then a *Move Joystick* action is performed to follow him or her. If the intruder is deemed to have moved out of range of the current camera, then a *Select Camera* activity is performed to select a more appropriate camera. In both cases, a flow final node is used to handle the tokens referencing the signal data when no action is required.

The *company security system* stores the currently selected camera in a data store node. It uses this information when it reacts to joystick commands by sending *Pan Camera* and *Tilt Camera* commands

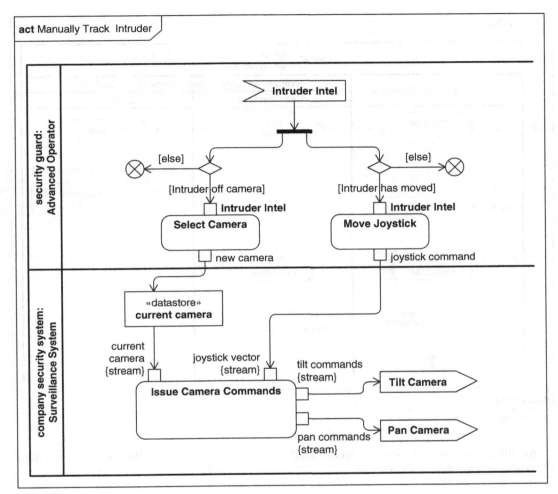

FIGURE 9.21

Activity partitions.

to the selected camera. *Security guard* and *company security system* are parts, as indicated by the name strings in the partition headers.

Partitions themselves may have subpartitions that can represent further decomposition of the represented element. Figure 9.22 shows the process for an *Operator* (*security guard*) logging in to a *Surveillance System* (*company security system*). The *security guard* enters his or her details, which are read by the *User Interface*, part of the *company security system,* and validated by another part, the *Controller,* which then responds appropriately. The *User Interface* and the *Controller* are represented by nested partitions within *company security system.* In this case, the *security guard* and the *company security system* are themselves shown as nested partitions of a block representing the context for both the surveillance system and its users.

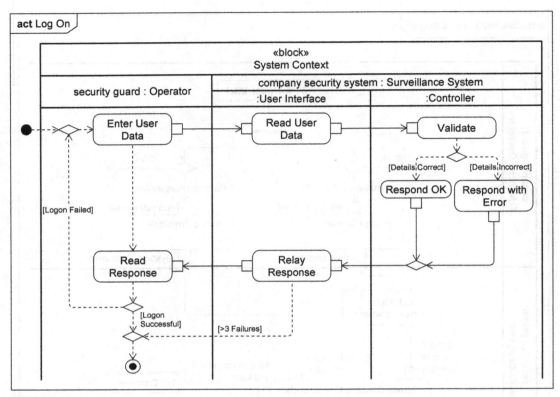

FIGURE 9.22

Nested activity partitions.

An allocate activity partition is a special kind of partition that can be used to perform behavioral allocation, as described in Chapter 14.

9.11.2 SPECIFYING AN ACTIVITY IN A BLOCK CONTEXT

In SysML, activities can be owned by blocks, in which case an instance of the owning block executes the activity. For a block, an activity may either represent the implementation of some service, which is termed a method (see Chapter 7, Section 7.5.3), or it may describe the behavior of the block over its lifetime, which is termed the classifier behavior or the main behavior (see Chapter 7, Section 7.5.1). During execution of an activity, an instance of its owning block provides its execution context. The execution of the activity can access stored state information from the instance and has access to its queue of requests.

Activities as block behaviors

When an activity serves as a classifier behavior, parameters of the activity may be mapped to flow properties of ports on the owning block. SysML does not explicitly say how flow properties are matched to parameters because there are many different approaches, depending on method and domain. An obvious strategy is to

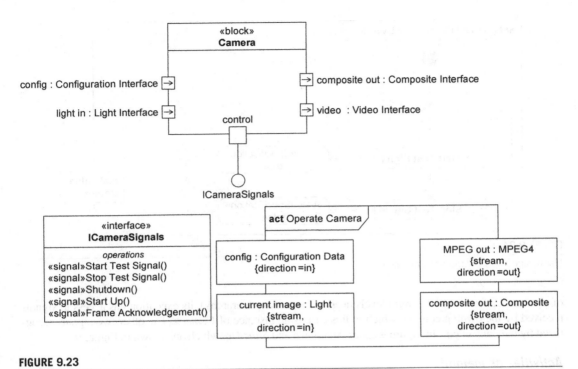

FIGURE 9.23

A block with proxy ports and a block behavior.

match parameters to flow properties based on at least type and direction. If this still results in ambiguity, the names can also be used to confirm a match. Allocation can also be used to express the mapping.

Figure 9.23 shows a block called *Camera* that describes the design for one of ACME's surveillance cameras. It has four proxy ports, three of which allow light to flow into the camera and video to flow out in either *Composite* or *MPEG4* format. The fourth allows configuration data to be passed to the camera. It also has a port with a provided interface that supports a set of control signals used to control the operation of the camera. The block behavior of the camera is the activity *Operate Camera* that has appeared in a number of previous figures, most recently Figure 9.16. In Figure 9.23, the parameters of the activity match, and can therefore be bound to, flow properties of the proxy ports of the *Camera* block. (Note that the interface blocks for the proxy ports have not been shown here, but *Video Interface* was shown in Chapter 7, Figure 7.41).

In Figure 9.23, there is no direct correspondence between the *control* port on *Camera* and a parameter or parameters on its block behavior *Operate Camera*. However, when an activity acts as the behavior for a block, it can accept signals received through ports on the block, as long as the block declares a reception for that signal. These signals can be accepted using an accept event action within the activity.

Figure 9.24 shows the specification of the activity *Receive Test Messages* that is invoked as part of *Produce Test Signal,* as shown on Figure 9.14. Once the activity starts, it simply waits for *Start Test Signal* using an accept signal action, then waits for *Stop Test Signal,* and then repeats the sequence. The accept signal actions trigger value specification actions via control flows that create the right Boolean value, and these values are merged into a *test value* output. Because *Receive Test Messages* executes as part of the execution

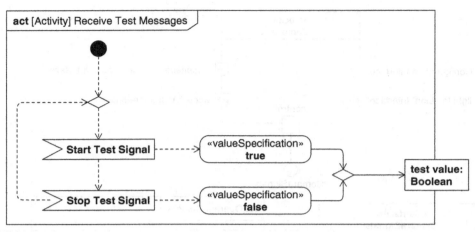

FIGURE 9.24

Using signals to control activity flow.

of *Operate Camera* (albeit several levels deep in the activity hierarchy), its execution has access to signals received by the owning context, which in this case is an instance of *Camera*. The other two signals recognized by the *control* port in Figure 9.23 are *Shutdown* and *Start Up,* which are shown in Figure 9.16.

Activities as methods

When used as a method of an owning block, an activity needs to have the same signature (i.e., same parameter names, types, multiplicities, and directions) as the associated behavioral feature of the block. There are two kinds of behavioral feature. An operation supports synchronous requests and asynchronous requests. A reception only supports asynchronous requests. A reception indicates that the object can receive signals of a particular kind, as the result of a send signal action (see Section 9.7). A method is invoked when the owning block instance (object) consumes a request for its associated behavioral feature. The activity executes until it reaches an activity final node, when the service is deemed to be handled, and if the request is synchronous, any output (including return) arguments are passed back to the initiator of the request.

SysML has a specific action to invoke methods via operations, called a **call operation action.** This has pins matching the parameters of the operation, and one additional input pin used to represent a target, which must provide the operation. When the action is executed, it sends a request to the target object, which handles the request, perhaps by invoking the method of the operation being called. The action passes its parameters as input arguments and returns any output arguments.

Just as a signal can be sent through a port, an operation can be called through a port. The path to the port is shown in the symbol for the call operation action with the format:

```
via port name, ...
```

If an activity that is invoked as the result of a call operation action has streaming parameters, then the pins of the call operation action may consume and produce tokens during execution of the activity. However, in a typical client/server approach to system design, all parameters are nonstreaming to fit more easily into a client/server paradigm.

Figure 9.25 shows the *Surveillance System* block with one of its ports, called *status*. The status port provides an interface *Camera Status* that includes an operation called *get camera status* as shown, with

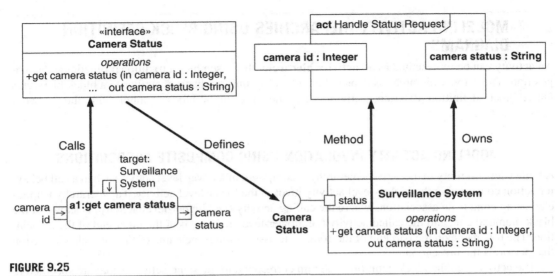

FIGURE 9.25

A block with behavioral features and associated methods.

an input parameter called *camera id* and an output parameter called *camera status*. The activity *Handle Status Request,* shown originally in Figure 9.10, is designated to be the method of *get camera status,* so it has the same parameters. A call operation action called *a1* for *get camera status* is shown, with pins corresponding to the two parameters and a pin to identify the *target,* that is, the *Surveillance System* to which the request must be sent. The call operation action will result in the invocation of *Handle Status Request* with an argument for *camera id,* and it will expect a response on *camera status.*

9.11.3 RELATIONSHIP BETWEEN ACTIVITIES AND OTHER BEHAVIORS

SysML has a generic concept of behavior that provides a common underlying base for its three specific behavioral formalisms: activities, state machines, and interactions. This provides flexibility to select the appropriate behavioral formalism for the modeling task. A call behavior action or call operation action in an activity can be used to invoke any kind of behavior. However, the design and analysis method must further specify the semantics and/or constraints for a call action to call a state machine or an interaction from an activity, since this is not currently fully specified. We expect future versions of SysML and perhaps domain-specific extensions to provide more precise semantics.

State machines may use any SysML behavior to describe what happens when a block is in certain states and when it transitions between states. In practice, activities are often used to describe these behaviors as follows:

- What happens when a state machine enters a state (called an entry behavior).
- What happens when a state machine exits a state (called an exit behavior).
- What happens while a state machine is in a state (called a do behavior).
- What happens when a state machine makes a transition between states (called a transition effect).

State machines are discussed in Chapter 11.

9.12 MODELING ACTIVITY HIERARCHIES USING BLOCK DEFINITION DIAGRAMS

An activity can be represented as an **activity hierarchy** that resembles a traditional functional decomposition. The activity hierarchy is depicted on a block definition diagram similar to a block hierarchy. On a block definition diagram, activities are shown using a block symbol with the keyword «activity».

9.12.1 MODELING ACTIVITY INVOCATION USING COMPOSITE ASSOCIATIONS

A higher-level activity in the activity hierarchy is composed of a lower-level activity, when a call behavior action contained in the higher-level activity invokes the lower-level activity. The hierarchy is modeled using composite associations where the calling activity (i.e., higher-level activity) is shown at the black diamond end, and the called activity (i.e., lower-level activity) is at the other end of the association. The role name on the part end of the composite association is the name of the call behavior action that performs the invocation.

The activities in the block definition diagram correspond to the same activities that are specified in activity diagrams. However, the parts in the block definition diagram have no explicit relationship to the call behavior actions in the activity diagrams, other than being given the same name. A part can refer to a call behavior action in the activity diagram by applying the **adjunct property** stereotype. The call behavior action that is referred to must be contained in the activity on the whole end of the composite association and invoke the activity on the part end of the association. An adjunct property can be indicated on a block definition diagram by the keyword «adjunct».

Figure 9.26 shows the activity hierarchy on a block definition diagram for *Generate Video Outputs,* as described in Figure 9.8. The adjunct properties are applied to the properties on the part end

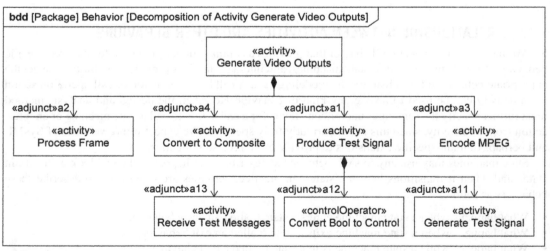

FIGURE 9.26

An activity hierarchy modeled on a block definition diagram.

of the composite associations, which have same name as the call behavior actions that they refer to.

9.12.2 MODELING PARAMETER AND OTHER OBJECT NODES USING ASSOCIATIONS

A block definition diagram cannot represent flows from an activity diagram, but it can include parameters and object nodes. By convention, the relationship from activities to object nodes is represented with a reference association versus a composite association. This is because the tokens contained within the object nodes are references to entities that are not "part" of the executing activity, and they are not necessarily destroyed when the execution of the activity terminates. The activity is shown at the white diamond end, the object node type is shown at the part end, and the role name at the part end is the name of the object node. Properties of the object node may be shown floating near the corresponding role name.

Figure 9.27 shows the hierarchy of activities for the *Capture Video* activity originally shown in Figure 9.11, including its own parameter nodes and the parameter nodes of its various subactivities. The data store *current image* is also shown. The adjunct property stereotypes have been elided from the properties *cv1*, *cv2*, and *cv3* to simplify the diagram.

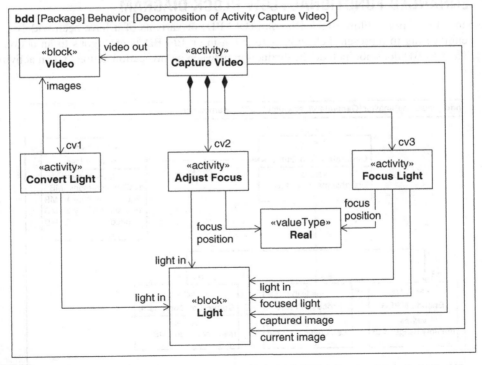

FIGURE 9.27

An activity hierarchy with parameters.

9.12.3 ADDING PARAMETRIC CONSTRAINTS TO ACTIVITIES

It is sometimes useful to specify performance constraints of an activity execution, such as resource usage (e.g., processor time) or other characteristics (e.g., average execution time, accuracy). Activities can be treated as blocks and thus can own value properties. Constraint blocks can then be used to constrain their values by binding them to constraint parameters.

On a block definition diagram, an activity can be shown as a block with all of the compartments that a block symbol has, including its value properties. A parametric diagram can depict this activity enabling the use of constraint properties to bind its value properties.

Figure 9.28 shows a block definition diagram for the *Generate Video Outputs* activity and associated actions (adjunct stereotype not shown), with additional value properties to capture memory usage. It also shows a constraint block called *Memory Use* with four parameters: three that represent memory use and a fourth that represents available memory. Its constraint asserts that the total memory use must be less than the available memory.

Figure 9.29 shows the parametric diagram for *Generate Video Outputs* using the *Memory Use* constraint block. Its parameters are bound to the properties that represent available memory and memory use of *Generate Video Outputs* activity and the activities that comprise it.

9.13 ENHANCED FUNCTIONAL FLOW BLOCK DIAGRAM

The Enhanced Functional Flow Block Diagram (**EFFBD**) or variants of it have been widely used in systems engineering to represent behavior. A function in an EFFBD is analogous to an action in an activity. The EFFBD does not include the distinction between an invocation action and an activity.

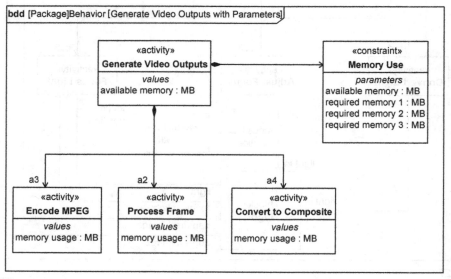

FIGURE 9.28

A bdd describing value properties and constraints for an activity.

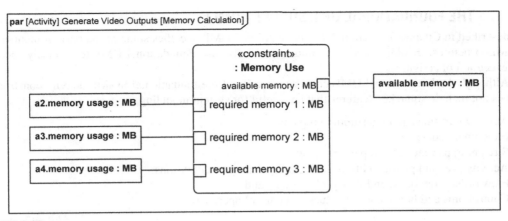

FIGURE 9.29

A parametric diagram describing constraints on an activity.

Most of the functionality of an EFFBD can be represented as a constrained use of a SysML activity diagram. The constraints are documented in Annex E.2 of the SysML specification [1]. Using the keyword «effbd» in the diagram header of an activity indicates that the activity conforms to the EFFBD constraints. These constraints preclude the use of activity partitions and continuous and streaming flows, as well as many other features within activity diagrams.

Some EFFBD semantics are not explicitly addressed by the activity diagram. In particular, a function in an EFFBD can only be executed when all triggering inputs, the control input, and the specified resources are available to the function. A "resource" is not an explicit construct in SysML, but resource constraints can be modeled using pre- and post-conditions and parametrics as described in the previous section. Triggering inputs in EFFBDs correspond to "required inputs" in activity diagrams, non-triggering inputs correspond to "optional inputs," and control inputs correspond to control flow in activity diagrams. The detailed mapping between EFFBD and activity diagrams, along with an example of the mapping in use, is described in SysML and UML 2.0 Support for Activity Modeling [49].

9.14 EXECUTING ACTIVITIES

This section describes how SysML supports the execution of activities using Foundational UML (previously discussed in Chapter 7, Section 7.9.1).

In order for an activity to be executed, the complete detail of all its processing—such as the transformation of property values—must be specified precisely. SysML includes a set of primitive actions that support basic object manipulation such as creation, deletion, access to properties, object communication, and others. Foundational UML provides executable semantics for these actions.

SysML also allows modelers to include "opaque" constructs in their models. These are constructs whose specification is expressed as text using some language other than SysML. These opaque constructs are often used to specify executable behavior using a programming language and are normally accompanied by technologies for performing the execution, as discussed in Chapter 18. An important use of opaque constructs is to include behavior expressed in a language called Alf, which is a text-based concrete syntax for Foundational UML.

9.14.1 THE FOUNDATIONAL UML SUBSET (fUML)

As described in Chapter 7, Section 7.9.1, Foundational UML specifies some of the basic semantics of SysML structures. In addition, system modelers can also use Foundational UML to precisely specify the execution of activities.

Although the Foundational UML covers a majority of the fundamental SysML activity constructs, it does not include some key features that are useful for system modeling, such as:

- Activity partitions and interruptible regions;
- Flow final nodes;
- Streaming parameters and parameter sets;
- Activity pre- and post-conditions and local pre and post conditions;
- Flow order, flow rates, and flow probabilities; and
- Control pins and hence control values and control operators.

9.14.2 THE ACTION LANGUAGE FOR FOUNDATIONAL UML (Alf)

The OMG has also adopted a complementary specification to Foundational UML called the **Action Language for Foundational UML**, or **Alf** [45] for short. Alf is a textual concrete syntax for Foundational UML modeling elements. The key use of Alf is to act as the textual notation for specifying executable behaviors in UML, such as methods for class operations, the behavior of a class, or transition effects on state machines. Alf also provides an extended notation that may be used to represent a limited subset of structural modeling elements. Because the SysML structural and behavioral constructs, such as block and activity, are based on UML, Alf can be used to specify those aspects of SysML models.

The Alf syntax primarily reflects a C legacy that should make it familiar to Java, C++, and C# programmers. However, Alf also adopts a number of syntactic conventions from OCL [38] to capitalize on its strength in the manipulation of sequences of values.

The execution semantics for Alf are given by mapping the Alf concrete syntax to the abstract syntax specified by Foundational UML. The result of executing a fragment of Alf text is thus given by the semantics of the Foundational UML model to which it is mapped.

Alf is integrated into activities using either an opaque behavior or an opaque action. When used to specify an opaque behavior, it may be invoked by a call behavior action. An opaque action specified in Alf can be inserted into an activity and related to other actions in the activity.

Figure 9.30 shows the activity *Position Camera* from Figure 9.12, specified using Alf. In this case, *Position Camera* has a single opaque action whose language is defined to be Alf and whose body is an Alf statement. It ensures that *position* is within range and invokes the camera device driver with the (potentially altered) position.

9.14.3 PRIMITIVE ACTIONS

SysML includes a set of primitive actions and precise definitions and notations for them based on Foundational UML and Alf. Other system engineering tools could specify alternative semantics and notations that could be mapped to these primitive actions.

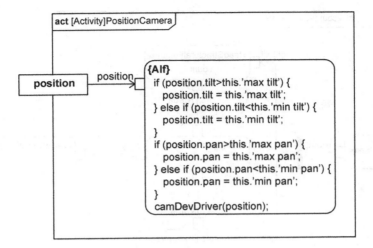

FIGURE 9.30

An activity specified using Alf.

Some of these primitive actions have been described previously in this chapter:

- Accept event actions respond to events in the environment of the activity.
- Send signal actions support communication between executing behaviors using messages.
- Call actions allow an activity to trigger the invocation of another behavior and to provide it with inputs and receive outputs from it.

In addition, there are a number of actions that have a more localized effect, such as updating properties and creating or destroying objects. These actions can be broadly categorized as:

- Object access actions, which allow properties of blocks and the variables of activities to be accessed.
- Object update actions, which allow those same elements to be updated or added to.
- Object manipulation actions, which allow objects themselves to be created or destroyed.
- Value actions, which allow the specification of values.

Note that the set of actions defined in SysML does not include fundamental operations such as mathematical operators. A set of these operators are provided in the Foundational Model Library of Foundational UML, but for external execution domains, these have to be provided as libraries of opaque behaviors—or more likely function behaviors—suitable for the domain. Opaque behaviors and function behaviors are referenced in Chapter 7, Section 7.5.

SysML provides an optional notation for primitive actions. Primitive actions are shown using an action symbol (round-cornered rectangle) with the kind of action shown in guillemets, along with a set of pins that are appropriate to the action.

Figure 9.31 shows an alternate representation of the Alf expression *this.count = this.count + 1* in the algorithm in Figure 9.12 using primitive actions instead of the opaque action. The resulting activity fragment first has to execute a `readSelf` action to establish the context indicated by *this*. Having obtained this, a `readStructuralFeature` action is used to obtain the value of the *count* property of the

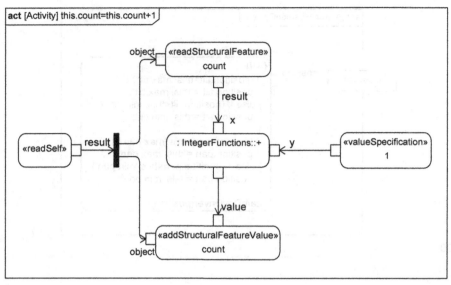

FIGURE 9.31

Example of primitive actions.

context (the executing activity). The value of the *count* property is then passed to a call of the + function behavior in the Foundational UML *Integer Functions* package. The other input is provided by a `value-Specification` action that outputs the value 1. The result of the addition is then offered to an `addStructuralFeatureValue` action that updates the *count* property. Using primitive actions to create models can be quite arduous; Alf or other textual representations are a more compact means for specifying low-level behavior.

9.14.4 EXECUTING CONTINUOUS ACTIVITIES

When a model is used as a blueprint for a system, it is expected that continuous activities will be implemented by physical devices such as motors, sensors, or humans. In this case, the specification of the activity may be a set of equations, or it may simply be allocated to some component that is already known to provide the appropriate behavior. Both Alf and parametric constraints as described in Section 9.12.3 can be used to specify these equations.

It is often important to simulate these continuous activities prior to building the system itself. A number of different technologies exist to execute models of continuous activities and their corresponding equations. They typically impose restrictions on the constructs that can be used in the activity's definition (e.g., no token buffering) and have their own specialized libraries of functions that need to be integrated into the model. They often also require additional constructs and semantics. In SysML, these artifacts can be provided using a profile. More information on profiles can be found in Chapter 15, and a discussion of integrating SysML with external tools such as simulation tools can be found Chapter 18.

9.15 SUMMARY

Activities provide a means of describing flow-based behavior, which are represented on both the activity diagram and the block definition diagram.

- An activity represents a controlled sequence of actions that transform its inputs to its outputs. The inputs and outputs of an activity are called parameters.
- An activity is composed of actions that represent the leaf level of its behavior. An action consumes input tokens and produces output tokens via its pins.
- Actions are connected by flows. There are two kinds of flow:
  - Object flows route object tokens between the input and output pins of actions. The flowing tokens may need to be queued or stored for later processing. Specialized nodes called central buffer nodes and data stores can store tokens. Input and output pins can also queue tokens. Depending on the domain, flows may be identified as streaming and continuous, which is particularly useful for describing physical processes.
  - Control flows transfer control from one action to other actions using control tokens.
- Control nodes—including join, fork, decision, and merge—allow flows to be split and merged in various ways. There are also specialized control nodes that describe what happens when an action starts and stops. These are the initial node, activity final node, and flow final node.
- Actions come in many different categories, from primitive actions, such as updating variables, to the invocation of entire behaviors.
  - Call actions are an important category of action because they allow one activity to invoke the execution of another (or in principle any kind of behavior). The pins of call actions correspond to the parameters of the called entity. A call behavior action allows an activity to include the execution of another activity as part of its processing. A call operation action allows an activity to make a service request on another object that can trigger the execution of some activity to handle the request. Operation calls make use of the dispatching mechanism of SysML blocks to decouple the caller from knowledge of the invoked behavior.
  - Send signal actions and accept event actions allow the activity to communicate via signals rather than just through its parameters. When the activity is executing in the context of a block, the activity can accept signals sent either to the block or sent directly to the activity.
- Activity partitions provide the capability to assign responsibility for actions in an activity diagram to the blocks or parts that the partitions represent.
- Structured activities allow modelers to group actions that need to execute together, including conditional execution.
- Block definition diagrams are used to describe the hierarchical relationship between activities and the relationship of activities to their inputs and outputs. The use of a block definition diagram for this purpose is similar to a traditional functional hierarchy diagram.

- The behavior of actions and activities can be constrained in a variety of ways including:
  - Adding pre- and post-conditions to the execution of an activity or action, including the state of token values.
  - Adding a constraint on the duration of an action execution.
  - Constraining properties of the activity, such as latency or resource use, on a parametric diagram.
- A constrained use of activity diagrams can provide equivalent behavioral models as Enhanced Functional Flow Block Diagrams (EFFBDs), which have been widely used for system behavior modeling.
- Activities may be described as stand-alone behaviors independent of any structure, but they often exist as the main behavior of a block. Activities within a block can communicate using signals, accepting signals that arrive at the block boundary, and sending signals to other blocks. The parameters of a main behavior may also be mapped directly to flow properties on the ports of its parent block. In this case, flows to and from activity parameter nodes are routed directly through the ports.
- An activity can also be used to implement the response to a service request when the arguments of the request are mapped to the activity's parameters. As discussed in Chapter 11, activities are often used to describe the processing that occurs when a block is transitioning between states and what the block does while in a particular state.
- SysML includes a subset of UML called Foundational UML or fUML, for which a formal executable semantics is defined. The subset includes basic UML structural elements such as classes and associations and also almost all of UML activities. SysML also incorporates a text-based concrete syntax for this subset, called the Action Language for Foundational UML, or Alf. SysML models based on this subset can be executed and various simulation tools based on fUML are available.

9.16 QUESTIONS

1. What is the diagram kind of the activity diagram, and what kinds of model elements does the frame correspond to?
2. How are an action and its pins typically represented on an activity diagram?
3. What does action *a1* in Figure 9.3 require to start executing?
4. How are the parameters of activities shown on activity diagrams?
5. What is the difference in semantics between a streaming and nonstreaming parameter?
6. How are parameters with a lower-multiplicity bound of 0 identified on an activity diagram?
7. Draw an activity diagram for an activity "Pump Water," which has a streaming input parameter "w in" typed by block "Water" and a streaming output parameter "w out," also typed by "Water."
8. How are the set of pins for a call behavior action determined?
9. What is an object flow used for and how is it represented?
10. How does the behavior of a join node differ from that of a merge node?
11. How does the behavior of a fork node differ from that of a decision node?
12. What are parameter sets used for and how are they represented, both in the definition and invocation of an activity?

13. Figure 9.10 only shows the object flows between the call behavior actions. What else does it need in order to perform as the method for the *get camera status* in Figure 9.25? Draw a revised version of Figure 9.10 with suitable additions.

14. What is the difference between a data store node and a central buffer node?

15. What is the difference in behavior between a flow final and an activity final node?

16. How is an initial node represented on an activity diagram, and what sort of flows can be connected to it?

17. What special capability does a control operator have?

18. An action "pump" invokes the activity "Pump Water" from Question 7 and can be enabled and disabled by the output of a control operator. What additional features does "pump" need in order to enable this?

19. Another action "provide control" calls a control operator called "Control Pump" with a single output parameter of type "Control Value." Draw an activity diagram to show how the actions "pump" and "provide control" need to be connected in order for "provide control" to control the behavior of "pump."

20. Name three kinds of events that can be accepted by an accept event action.

21. How can an interruptible region be exited?

22. What would be the appropriate construct to describe a group of actions that need to be executed together repeatedly while some condition holds?

23. What does a flow rate of "25 per second" on an activity edge indicate about the flow of tokens along that edge?

24. How would a modeler indicate that new tokens flowing into a full object node should replace tokens that already exist in the object node?

25. If a call behavior action is placed in an activity partition representing a block, what does this say about the relationship between the block and the called behavior?

26. Name the two different roles that an activity can play when owned by a block.

27. Describe the four ways in which activities can be used as part of state machines.

28. An action "a1:GetFrameBuffer" must take less than 10ms to execute. Show how this is specified on an activity diagram.

29. Draw an activity diagram fragment that executes either an action with the Alf expression "count=count+1" or an action with the Alf expression "count=count−1" based on whether count is greater than zero. Use a decision input behavior to make the decision.

DISCUSSION TOPIC

Discuss the various ways that activities with continuous flows may be executed.

MODELING MESSAGE-BASED BEHAVIOR WITH INTERACTIONS

10

This chapter discusses the use of sequence diagrams to model how parts of a block interact by exchanging messages.

10.1 OVERVIEW

In Chapter 9, behavior was modeled using activity diagrams, which represent a controlled sequence of actions that transform inputs to outputs. In this chapter, an alternative approach to representing behavior is introduced. This approach uses sequence diagrams to represent the **interaction** between structural elements in a model as a sequence of message exchanges. The interaction can be between the system and its environment or between the components of a system at any level of a system hierarchy. A message can represent the invocation of a service on a system component or the sending of a signal.

This representation of behavior is useful when modeling service-oriented concepts, when one part of a system requests services of another part. A service-oriented approach can represent discrete interactions between software components, when one software component requests a service of another and when the service is specified as a set of operations. However, the sequence diagram is not limited to modeling interactions between software components, and has found broad application in modeling system-level behaviors. A sequence diagram can be written as a specification of how parts of a system should interact, and can also be used as a record of how the parts of a system do interact.

The structural elements of a block are represented by lifelines on a sequence diagram. The sequence diagram describes the interaction between these lifelines as an ordered series of occurrence specifications that describe different kinds of occurrences, such as the sending and receiving of messages, the creation and destruction of objects, or the start and end of behavior executions.

Many of the occurrence specifications on a sequence diagram are associated with the exchange of messages between lifelines. There are several different kinds of messages, including both synchronous messages (the sender waits for a response) and asynchronous messages (the sender continues without waiting for a response). A sending occurrence specification marks when the message is sent by the sending lifeline, and a receiving occurrence specification marks when the message is received by the receiving lifeline. On reception of a message, the receiving lifeline may start the execution of a behavior that implements the operation or signal reception referenced in the message. The receipt of a message may also trigger the creation or destruction of the receiving lifeline.

To model ordering of occurrences more complex than simple sequences, interactions can include specialized constructs called combined fragments. A combined fragment has an operator and a set of operands, which may be primitive interaction fragments such as occurrence specifications, or may themselves be combined fragments, thus forming a tree of interaction fragments. There are a number of operators that describe different ordering semantics, such as parallel, alternative, and iterative ordering of their operands.

Interactions themselves can also be composed to handle large scenarios or to allow reuse of common interaction patterns. An interaction may reference another interaction to abstract away the detail of some segment of the interaction between multiple lifelines, or to reference an interaction between the parts of a particular lifeline.

An interaction executes in the context of an instance of its owning block, each lifeline in the interaction represents a single instance that is owned by the instance of its owning block. Occurrences happen as the instances execute their behavior and send and receive requests corresponding to operation calls and signals. As an interaction executes, it observes the occurrences and compares them to its own definition of occurrence ordering.

The sequence of occurrences for a given scenario of interest, in this case the lifetime of the interaction, is called a trace. Each interaction can define a set of valid traces and a set of invalid traces. A valid trace is one in which the occurrences are consistent with the ordering defined by the interaction. On the other hand, the use of the neg interaction operator indicates that any trace that is consistent with its operand is invalid. The assert operator states that if a trace is not consistent with its operands then it is invalid. If an assert operator is not used, then inconsistent traces are deemed to be undecided (i.e. neither valid or invalid).

10.2 THE SEQUENCE DIAGRAM

A **sequence diagram** represents an interaction. The complete diagram header for a sequence diagram is as follows:

    sd [interaction] interaction name [diagram name]

The diagram kind for a sequence diagram is **sd** and the model element kind that corresponds to its frame can only be *interaction*.

Figure 10.1 shows a sequence diagram with examples of many of the symbols. It shows an interaction between an *Advanced Operator* and the *Surveillance System* during the handling of an intruder alert. The notation for the sequence diagram is shown in detail in the Appendix, Tables A.18 through A.20.

10.3 THE CONTEXT FOR INTERACTIONS

The context for an interaction execution is an instance of the block that owns the interaction. As the instance (including instances of all its parts) is executing, any currently executing interactions observe the events occurring as a result of the execution of other behaviors, such as state machines or activities. As with other kinds of behavior, an interaction can either be the classifier behavior for a block, or an owned behavior of the block invoked by a specific invocation action. If an interaction is a classifier behavior, it starts executing when an instance of the block is created; if the interaction is an owned behavior, it begins execution when it is invoked. Interactions end their execution after they complete the execution of their last fragment.

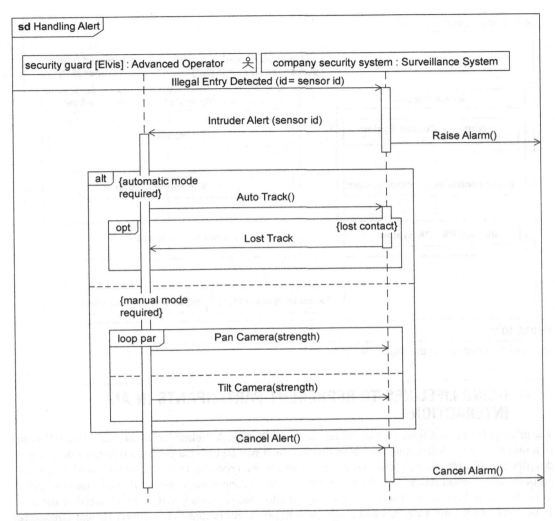

FIGURE 10.1

An example sequence diagram.

Figure 10.2 shows an internal block diagram of the *System Context* block that contains all the significant participants in the interactions that are described in the figures in this chapter. *System Context* is the context for a specific usage of a *Surveillance System* called *company security system*. In addition to the *company security system,* the context contains other parts, including a *regional HQ,* a set of *Perimeter Sensors,* an *Alarm System,* and a *security guard,* which correspond to entities that are external to the *company security system.* The diagram also shows the internal parts of the *Alarm System* and the *company security system* whose behavior is specified in the following interactions. The interaction lifelines can also represent reference properties, but this does not affect the notation or the semantics of the interaction.

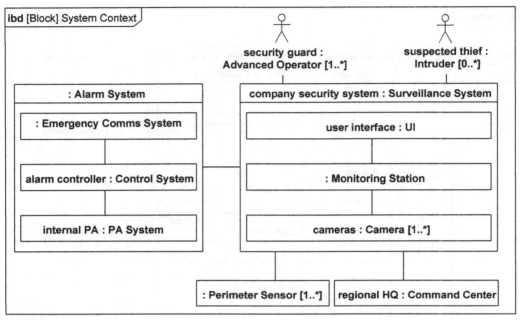

FIGURE 10.2

Internal block diagram of the interaction context.

10.4 USING LIFELINES TO REPRESENT PARTICIPANTS IN AN INTERACTION

The principal structural feature of an interaction is the **lifeline.** A lifeline represents the relevant lifetime of a property of the interaction's owning block, which will be either a part or a reference property, as described in Chapter 7. As explained there, a part can be typed by an actor, which enables actors to participate in interactions as well. However, since an actor cannot support operations, its use has restrictions. To avoid these restrictions, an actor may be allocated to a block that is used instead of the actor as the type of the part. Lifelines can also represent ports, but because proxy ports typically just relay messages, they rarely contribute much to the understanding of an interaction, and so are rarely used.

When an instance of its owning block executes an interaction, each lifeline denotes an instance of some part of the block (see Chapter 7 for a definition of block semantics). Thus, when the lifeline represents a property with multiplicity greater than 1, an additional **selector expression** should be used to explicitly identify one instance. Otherwise, the lifeline is taken to represent an arbitrarily selected instance. The selector expression can take many forms depending on how instances are identified in this part. For example, it may be an index into an ordered collection, a specific value of some attribute of the part's block, or a more informal statement of identity.

A lifeline is shown using a rectangle (the head) with a dashed line descending from its base (the tail). The head contains the name and type—if applicable—of the represented property, separated by a colon.

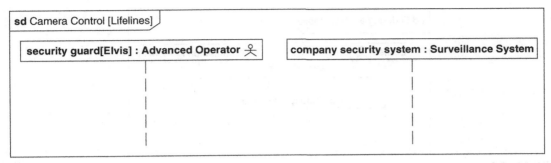

FIGURE 10.3

An interaction with lifelines.

The selector expression, if present, is shown in square brackets after the name. The head may indicate the kind of model element it represents using a special shape or icon.

Figure 10.3 shows a simple sequence diagram with a diagram frame and two lifelines. One represents the *Surveillance System* under consideration, called *company security system,* and the other lifeline represents an *Advanced Operator,* called *security guard.* Because, the *security guard* from Figure 10.2 has an upper bound greater than 1, the lifeline also contains a selector called *Elvis* to specify exactly which instance is interacting. The *security guard* is shown with a small actor icon to indicate that it is a user of the *Surveillance System.*

10.4.1 OCCURRENCE SPECIFICATIONS

A lifeline is related to an ordered list of **occurrence specifications** that describe what can happen to the instance represented by the lifeline during the execution of the interaction. When an interaction is executed, the set of occurrences ordered in time is called a **trace.** A comparison of the order and structure of the specifications and actual occurrences determines whether the trace is consistent with the interaction. Different kinds of occurrence specifications describe different kinds of occurrences. Three categories of occurrence are relevant to interactions:

- The sending and receiving of messages;
- The starting and ending of the execution of actions and behaviors; and
- The creation and destruction of instances.

Constructs like messages and interaction operators—described later in this chapter—provide further order and structure to these occurrence specifications.

10.5 EXCHANGING MESSAGES BETWEEN LIFELINES

Messages can be exchanged between the instances represented by lifelines to achieve interactions. A message can be sent from a lifeline to itself to represent a message that is sent and received by the same instance.

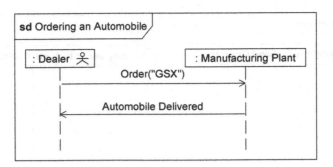

FIGURE 10.4

A simple example of message exchange.

A message represents an invocation or request for service from the sending lifeline to the receiving lifeline, or the sending of a signal from the sending lifeline to the receiving lifeline. A message is shown on a sequence diagram as a line with different arrowheads and annotations depending on the kind of message.

Messages are sent by behaviors that are executing on a lifeline, or more precisely by invocation actions, such as send signal or call operation actions, within those behaviors. (See Chapter 9, Section 9.7 for more information on send signal actions.) Receipt of a message by a lifeline can trigger the execution of a behavior, or it may simply be accepted by a currently executing behavior (refer to Section 10.5.4). Note that there may be a delay between the time a message is sent and the time it is received and handled.

Although messages are often used to model information passed between computer systems and their users, they may also indicate the passage of material or energy. An interaction in a radar-tracking system might represent the detection of a target and the response to that detection. The request for manufacture of a car and the subsequent delivery of that car to a dealer might be modeled as an interaction between the dealer and the manufacturer, as shown in Figure 10.4.

10.5.1 SYNCHRONOUS AND ASYNCHRONOUS MESSAGES

The two basic kinds of messages are asynchronous and synchronous. A sender of an asynchronous message continues to execute after sending the message, whereas a sender of a synchronous message waits until it receives a reply from the receiver that it has completed its processing of the message before continuing execution.

Asynchronous messages correspond to either the sending of a signal or to an asynchronous invocation (or call) of an operation. A synchronous message corresponds to the synchronous invocation of an operation on the receiver. In the case of an operation call, the reply to the sender can be indicated using a separate message from the receiver back to the sender. See Chapter 7, Section 7.5.2 for a description of the behavioral features of blocks.

Call messages and send messages can include arguments that correspond to the input parameters of the associated operation, or attributes of the sent signal. Arguments can be literal values, such as numbers or strings; attributes of the part represented by the sending lifeline; or parameters of the currently executing behavior. A reply message can include arguments that correspond to output parameters or the return value of the called operation. When an operation returns a value, the features to which the output parameters and return value are assigned can be indicated. A feature can either be an attribute of the calling lifeline or a local attribute or parameter of the caller's current execution.

The presence of a message implies two occurrences. One is related to the sending of the message by the instance corresponding to the sending lifeline. The other is related to the receipt of the message by the instance corresponding to the receiving lifeline. As one might expect, the sending occurrence has to happen before the receiving occurrence.

Messages are represented by arrows between lifelines. The tail represents the occurrence corresponding to the sending of the message, and the head represents the occurrence corresponding to the receipt of the message. The shape of the arrowhead and the line style of the arrow line indicate the nature of the message as follows:

- An open arrowhead means an **asynchronous message.** Input arguments associated with the message are shown in parentheses as a comma-separated list after the message name. The name of the operation parameter or signal attribute to which an argument corresponds may be included (followed by an equal sign) before the argument:

```
parameter name = value
```

If this notational option is not used, all the input arguments must be listed in the appropriate order.

- A closed arrowhead means a **synchronous message.** The notation for arguments is the same as for asynchronous messages.
- An arrowhead on a dashed line shows a **reply message.** Output arguments associated with the message are shown in parentheses after the message name, and the return value, if any, is shown after the argument list. The feature to which the return value is assigned is shown (followed by an equal sign) before the message name:

```
feature name = message name (arguments) : return value
```

As with input arguments, output arguments can be preceded by name of their corresponding parameters separated by an equal sign. In the rare case that both the parameter name and assigned feature are required, the following syntax is used:

```
feature name = parameter name: argument
```

Figure 10.5 shows a sequence of messages exchanged between the two lifelines introduced in Figure 10.3. The *security guard* first selects camera *CCC1*. After selecting the camera, the guard issues a *get current status* request to retrieve that camera's current status, to which the system responds *"OK."* Note that although the *company security system* does not provide an explicit confirmation to the *security guard* that the camera has been selected, the system does not handle the *get current status* request until after it has received (and processed, as shown in Figure 10.7) the *select camera* request. The *company security system* obtains the status from the selected camera by issuing a subsidiary *get status* request to itself, providing the *id* of the currently selected camera. Having obtained an *"OK"* status, the *security guard* then commands the system to move the camera by giving a *pan camera* order (probably via a joystick). He asks for the status again, which this time is *"Moving."*

10.5.2 LOST AND FOUND MESSAGES

Normally, message exchange is deemed complete; that is, it has both a sending and receiving occurrence. However, it is also possible to describe lost messages with no receiving occurrence and found messages with no sending occurrence. This capability is useful, for example, to model message traffic across an unreliable network and to model how message loss affects the interaction.

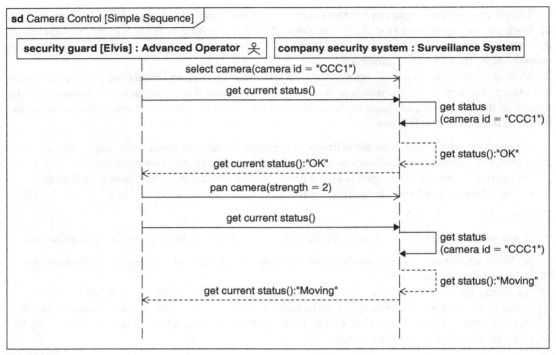

FIGURE 10.5

Synchronous and asynchronous messages exchanged between lifelines.

The notation for lost messages is an arrow with the tail on a lifeline and the head attached to a small black circle. The notation for found messages is the reverse—the tail of the arrow attached to a small black circle and the head attached to a lifeline. An example can be seen in the Appendix, Table A.17.

10.5.3 WEAK SEQUENCING

An interaction imposes the most basic form of order on the messages and other occurrences that it contains, called **weak sequencing.** Weak sequencing means that the ordering of occurrences on a lifeline must be followed, but other than the constraint that message receive occurrences are ordered after message send occurrences, there is no ordering between occurrences on different lifelines.

The messages on the sequence diagram in Figure 10.6 impose an order on send and receive occurrences; for example, *A.send* happens before *A.receive* and *B.send* happens before *B.receive*. Lifelines also impose an order on occurrences, so *lifeline 3* states that *A.receive* happens before *B.send*. However, nothing is said about the ordering of *B.send* and *D.send* on *lifeline 3* and *lifeline 2*, respectively. Note also that it is not the messages that are sequenced but their send and receive occurrences. For example, *B.send* happens before *C.send*, but *B.receive* happens after *C.receive*. This phenomenon is sometimes referred to as **message overtaking** and is dealt with in more detail in Section 10.6.

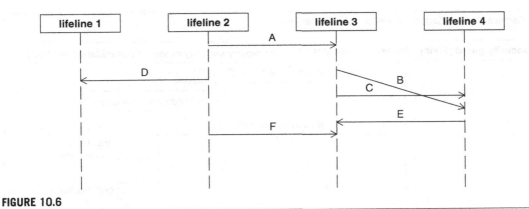

FIGURE 10.6

Explanation of weak sequencing.

10.5.4 EXECUTIONS

The receipt of a message by a lifeline may trigger the **execution** of a behavior in the receiver. In this case, the receiving lifeline executes the behavior (called the method) for the behavioral feature that the message represents. Alternatively, the message receipt may simply trigger a change in a currently executing behavior, such as a state machine or activity, and cause it to execute other actions. The arguments contained in a call or send message are passed to the behavior that handles it. If and when a reply message is sent, the output arguments are provided to the execution that sent the corresponding synchronous call message.

Lifelines can send messages to themselves. This may cause a new execution to be started, nested within the current execution.

Lifelines are hosts to executions, either of single actions or entire behaviors. The extent to which executions are modeled is left to the modeler. Typically an execution start occurrence is coincident with a message receipt occurrence, but it does not have to be in all cases (i.e., the execution can occur later due to message scheduling delays). When an execution is triggered by the receipt of a synchronous message, the execution end occurrence may be coincident with the sending of a reply message.

Activations are rectangular symbols overlaid vertically on lifelines. They correspond to executions and begin at the execution's start occurrence and end at the execution's end occurrence. Activations are opaque and may either be grey or white; this shading does not affect their meaning. When executions are nested, the activations are stacked from left to right. If an execution is triggered by the receipt of a message, the arrow is attached to the top of the activation. If an execution ends with the sending of a reply message, then the tail of the reply arrow is attached to the bottom of the activation. An alternate notation for activations is a box symbol overlaid crosswise on the lifeline with the name of the behavior or action inside.

Figure 10.7 shows the same interaction as Figure 10.5 but with activations added. The relevant behaviors and actions on the *company security system* and *security guard* lifelines are now explicit. The *select camera* operation tells the *company security system* to store the *id* of the selected camera. In a change from Figure 10.5, the action executed to store the camera id, *current camera = camera id,* is explicitly shown here using box notation. The processing of *get current status* causes a new execution

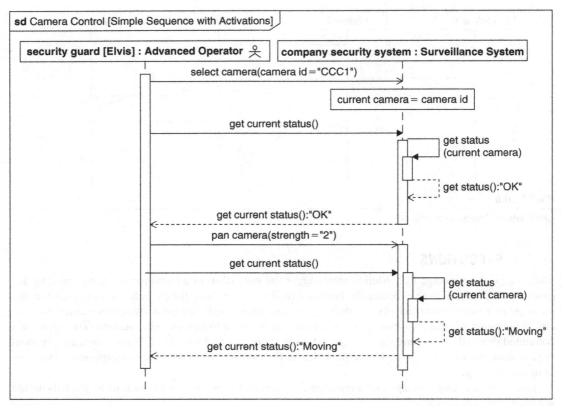

FIGURE 10.7

Lifelines with activations.

to start that is triggered by a *get status* message with the previously stored *camera id* as an argument. This new execution ends with a status reply of *"OK."* After the *pan camera* command triggers the execution of a behavior to move the camera (which takes some time), another *get status* message triggers a nested execution that returns the result *"Moving."* The execution on the *security guard*'s lifeline continues throughout the interaction, even while waiting for a response from the *company security system.*

10.5.5 LIFELINE CREATION AND DESTRUCTION

In an interaction, the creation and destruction of the instances represented by lifelines can be represented by special kinds of messages. A **create message** represents the creation of an instance and so is the first occurrence on the lifeline representing the instance. A **deletion message** ends in a special kind of occurrence called a **destruction occurrence**, which must be the last occurrence on a lifeline. A destruction occurrence can also occur in isolation to indicate some undefined (presumably internal) cause of destruction. These occurrences generally apply to the allocation and release of memory to

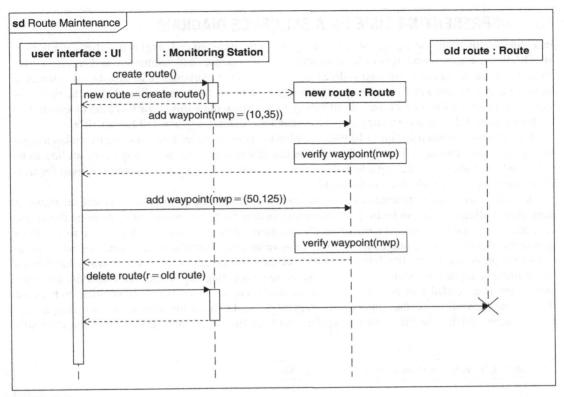

FIGURE 10.8

Create and destroy messages.

execute software instances. However, they can also be used to indicate the addition or removal of a physical part of a system from a scenario.

The notation for a create message is a dashed line with an open arrowhead, terminating on the header box of the lifeline being created, which is moved down in the sequence diagram to accommodate the notation. The dashed tail of the lifeline is drawn as normal. The create message's name and input arguments are displayed in the same way as those of a call message. The notation for a destroy occurrence is a cross at the end of a lifeline.

The sequence diagram in Figure 10.8 shows how new routes are created and destroyed by a surveillance system. A *Route* is a set of pan-and-tilt angle pairs that a surveillance camera follows when in an automated surveillance mode. In this case the *user interface* component communicates with the *Monitoring Station* to perform the route maintenance operations. First, the *user interface* calls the *create route* service offered by the *Monitoring Station,* which in turn creates a new route and returns a reference to the *user interface* via the *new route* attribute. The *user interface* then interacts with this new route in order to add waypoints. Finally, when the route is complete (only some of the waypoints are shown here), it uses the *delete route* service to delete *old route.* Note that the execution of action *verify waypoint* is shown using box notation.

10.6 REPRESENTING TIME ON A SEQUENCE DIAGRAM

In a sequence diagram, time progresses vertically down the diagram and, as stated earlier, occurrences on a lifeline are correspondingly ordered in time. In addition, the send occurrence and receive occurrence for a single message are also ordered in time. However, particularly in distributed systems, a message may be overtaken by a subsequent message sent from the same lifeline; that is, the first message may arrive after receipt of the second message. Sequence diagrams allow this kind of situation to be drawn using a downward-slanting arrow between two lifelines, as shown in Figure 10.9.

The sequence diagram in Figure 10.9 shows what happens when an *Alert* message overtakes a regular *Status Report* message. This may be because the *Status Report* message is queued, waiting to be processed, perhaps due to having a lower priority, or it may be that a manual process is used for handling status reports, which slows their handling.

In addition to relative ordering in time, time can be represented explicitly on sequence diagrams. A **time observation** refers to an **instant** in time corresponding to the occurrence of some event during the execution of the interaction, and a **duration observation** refers to the time taken between two instants during the execution of the interaction. A **time constraint** and a **duration constraint** can use observations to express constraints involving the values of those observations. A time constraint identifies a constraint that applies to a single occurrence on the sequence diagram. A duration constraint identifies two occurrences, called start and end occurrences, and expresses a constraint on the duration between them. A duration constraint can apply to any element deemed to have duration, such as a message or an execution, in which case the constraint applies between the occurrences that bracket the element's

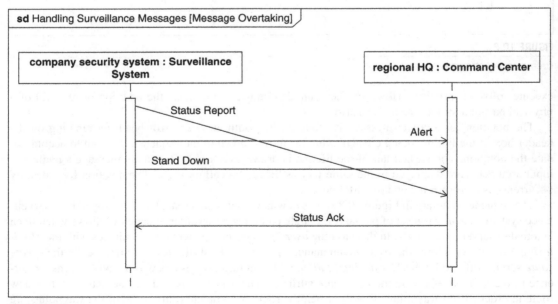

FIGURE 10.9

Message overtaking scenario.

duration. The expressions used for time observations and constraints make no assumption regarding the source of time, such as a reference clock, or how time is computed.

A time constraint is shown using a standard constraint expression in braces attached by a line to the constrained occurrence. A duration constraint is shown by a double-headed arrow between the two constrained occurrences with the constraint floating near it, also expressed in standard constraint notation (i.e., in braces). A duration constraint may also be shown as a standard constraint floating close to an element such as a message or an interaction use (see Section 10.8). Observations are shown in a way similar to constraints, but instead of an expression in braces, an observation has the name of the observation followed by an equal sign and then an expression indicating how the value for the observation is obtained. The actual language used to express observations and constraints, including default time units, must be stated as part of the observation or constraint.

Figure 10.10 shows a scenario in which the *Monitoring Station* is asked by the *user interface* to test the system's cameras. The *Monitoring Station* in turn requests each camera to perform a self-test and awaits the result. While waiting for a response from each camera, the controller component internal to the *Monitoring Station* needs to provide a progress indication to the *user interface,* so it uses

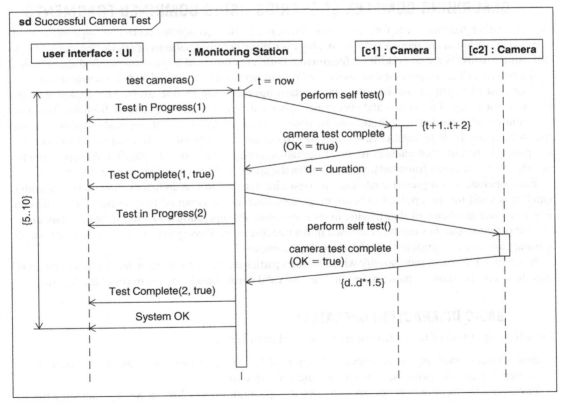

FIGURE 10.10

Representing time on a sequence diagram.

asynchronous messages to interleave communication. In this case, the communication between the *Monitoring Station* and the cameras is over a network, and the communication between the controller and *user interface* is local. As a result of network delays, the *Monitoring Station* receives the response from the camera after the progress message is sent. Note that although sloping lines are used here to indicate the passage of time, the slope has no formal semantic implication. The only timing implications are expressed using the time and duration constraints and the ordering of occurrences.

A number of observations and constraints on this interaction are expressed in a time unit of seconds. A time observation, *t,* is taken at the point when the first self-test message is sent using the expression $t = now$. A time constraint indicates that the message receipt must occur between 1 and 2 seconds after *t.* The duration between sending and receipt of the first self-test response message is observed via a duration observation *d,* and there is a constraint on the second response message to not exceed 1.5 times the first duration. The total time taken between the user interface requesting a test command and the completion of both camera self-tests should be between 5 and 10 seconds, as indicated by the duration constraint on the left of the diagram.

10.7 DESCRIBING COMPLEX SCENARIOS USING COMBINED FRAGMENTS

As stated earlier, the most basic form of an interaction is a weak sequence of occurrences—generally read from top to bottom of the sequence diagram. However, more complex patterns of interaction can be modeled using constructs called **combined fragments.** Different combined fragments specify different rules for the ordering of messages and their associated occurrences, such as parallel and alternative traces.

A combined fragment consists of an **interaction operator** and its **operands.** An interaction operand defines a group of messages and occurrence specifications that span one or more lifelines. The start of execution of a particular operand can be time-ordered relative to other operands. An interaction operator defines the logic used to time-order the execution of the operands. An example of an operator is a parallel operator that enables multiple operands to begin execution in parallel. An operand can include other combined fragments, which enables the specification of complex control logic.

Each operand has a **guard** containing a constraint expression that indicates the conditions under which it is valid for the operand to begin execution. Each guard is bound to a single lifeline and can only reference attributes of that lifeline in its constraint. The operands may themselves contain combined fragments, and thus can be composed into a tree hierarchy. During execution of an interaction, all operands use weak sequencing semantics on their contents.

A combined fragment must specify which lifelines participate in the interaction defined by its operands. Only the occurrences on the participating lifelines are valid when considering the traces of the fragment.

10.7.1 BASIC INTERACTION OPERATORS

The following subset of interaction operators is used most frequently:

- **Seq**—weak sequencing, as described in Section 10.5.3. Weak sequencing is the default form of sequencing for all operands, so is rarely indicated explicitly.
- **Par**—an operator in which operands can occur in parallel, each following weak sequencing rules. There is no implied order between occurrences in different operands. This operator has an alternate shorthand notation when applied to a single lifeline, called a **coregion,** where the operands are bracketed by vertical square brackets instead of a frame.

- **Alt/else**—an operator in which exactly one of its operands will be selected based on the value of its guard. The guard on each operand is evaluated before selection, and if the guard on one of the operands is valid, then that one is selected. If more than one operand has a valid guard then the selection is nondeterministic. An optional else fragment is valid only if none of the guards on the other operands are valid.
- **Opt**—a unary operator that is equivalent to an alt with only one operand. This implies that the operand is either executed or skipped depending on the validity of the guard.
- **Loop**—an operator in which the trace represented by its operand repeats until its termination constraint is met. A loop may define lower and upper bounds on the number of iterations as well as the guard expression. These bounds are documented in brackets after the loop keyword in the fragment label as (`lower bound, upper bound`), where the upper bound may have the value * indicating an unlimited upper bound.

A combined fragment is shown using a frame whose label indicates the kind of operator and sometimes other information, depending on the kind of operator.

Alt and par operators have multiple horizontal partitions separated by dashed lines that correspond to their operands. Other operators have just a single partition. Messages, activations, and possibly other combined fragments are nested within each operand. Guards are shown in braces overlapping the lifeline to which it is bound. When an operator has a single operand that is itself a combined fragment, the frames of the operator and operand can be merged into one. The frame label for the merged frame is used to indicate all the operators, such as **loop par.**

The frame symbol for the combined fragment must not obscure the lifelines that participate in its interaction, so the tails of the participating lifelines are visible on top of the frame. The frame does obscure the lifelines that do not participate in the fragment's interaction.

In Figure 10.11, lifelines 1 through 3 participate in the **opt** fragment, but only lifelines 1 and 4 participate in the **loop** fragment. To maintain the current layout, lifelines 2 and 3 are obscured by the **loop** frame to indicate that they do not participate.

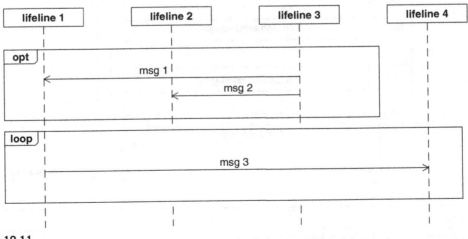

FIGURE 10.11

Example of overlapping and nonoverlapping lifelines.

Figure 10.12 shows what happens when an intruder is detected and tracked by the *company security system*. The interaction is started when some lifeline external to this interaction detects a potentially illegal entry into the monitored areas. This triggers the system to alert the user (the *security guard*) with the id of the sensor and raise the alarm. The *security guard* then attempts to find and track the intruder and eventually (in this case) cancels the alert.

Within this sequence, the **alt** operator indicates that the *security guard* has a choice between using the system's auto-track feature and manually tracking the intruder. In the automatic case, the system

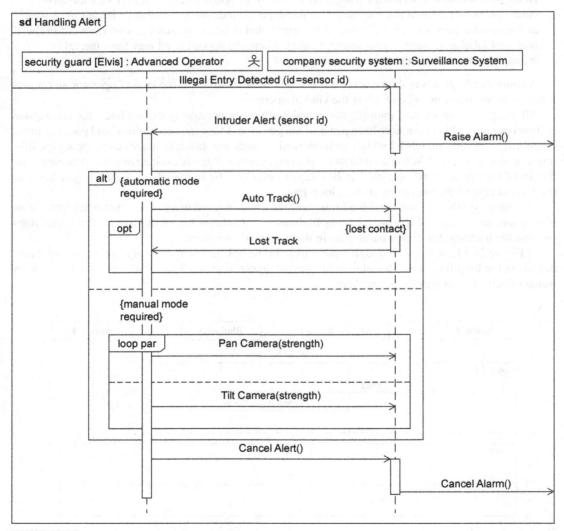

FIGURE 10.12

Complex interactions described using interaction operators.

attempts to acquire and track a target. Failure to acquire a target or loss of an acquired target is indicated by a *Lost Track* message. In the manual-tracking case, the *security guard* uses an input device to repeatedly pan and tilt the cameras, as indicated by the **loop par** fragment.

In all scenarios, the *security guard* is responsible for canceling the alert, which prompts the *company security system* to cancel the alarm. In this figure, the *Illegal Entry Detected, Raise Alarm,* and *Cancel Alarm* messages start or terminate at gates on the frame to interact with lifelines outside the current interaction (see Section 10.8 for a description of gates).

10.7.2 ADDITIONAL INTERACTION OPERATORS

The following are other interaction operators that are less commonly used.

- **Strict**—like seq except that the occurrences represented by its operands are sequenced in order across all participating lifelines. The strict rule does not apply to the operands of any nested combined fragments.
- **Break**—an operator whose operand is executed rather than the remainder of the enclosing fragment. This is often used to represent the handling of exceptional scenarios.
- **Critical**—an operator in which the sequence of operands must take place with no interleaving of other occurrences, at least within the participating lifelines of the fragment. This may be used when some higher-level **par** operator indicates that interleaving can occur, and this operator is used to constrain the interleaving.
- **Neg**—an operator in which the traces described by its operand are deemed invalid.

There are cases in interaction modeling when covering all potential message occurrences is very onerous, such as when there are a large number of occurrences related to messages that are not relevant to the scenario being described. Consider and ignore operators allow occurrences and messages that have been explicitly ignored (or not considered) to be interleaved with valid traces of their operand:

- **Consider**—only consider messages for a specified set of operations and/or signals. All occurrences corresponding to other messages are ignored; that is, they are not considered when analyzing a trace using the operator's operand. Only considered messages can appear in the operand.
- **Ignore**—do not consider messages for a specified set of operations and/or signals. Occurrences corresponding to ignored messages are not considered when analyzing a trace. Ignored messages cannot appear in the operand.

Unlike other operators, which determine either valid or invalid (in the case of neg) traces but not both, the `assert` operator provides a mechanism to assert that those traces that are not valid according to its operand are definitely invalid. This is a very powerful construct but can present challenges when there are many occurrences and the modeler wishes to use assert to cover traces with only some of them. With other interaction operators, traces that include occurrences that do not match their operands do not count as either valid or invalid, whereas with assert they are deemed invalid, which may not be desired. For this reason, fragments with consider and ignore operators are often used with assert to reduce the set of occurrences that are relevant so that a valid/invalid decision can be trusted.

For consider and ignore operators, messages to be considered or ignored are shown in braces following the keyword in the fragment label.

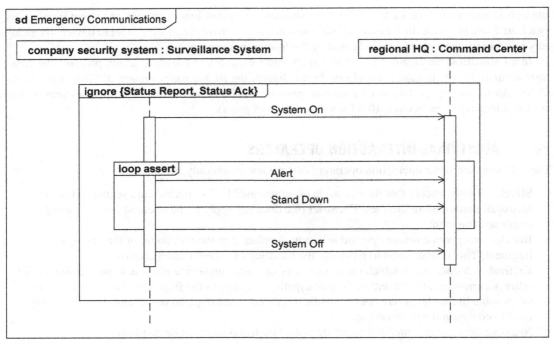

FIGURE 10.13

Message-filtering scenario.

Figure 10.13 describes the sequence of messages exchanged when the *company security system* is communicating with the *regional HQ* in an emergency. Alerts only happen while the surveillance system is on, so the *regional HQ* can discount any alerts apparently received when the system is off (although they may wish to investigate why they happened). When a valid *Alert* message has been sent, no other messages are allowed until a *Stand Down* message has been received. Any other trace is invalid, and an `assert` operator is used to ensure this. However, there are always regular status updates and acknowledgments between any surveillance system and the *regional HQ*, and these should not be deemed to constitute an invalid trace. By enclosing the `assert` operator in an `ignore` fragment that lists *Status Report* and *Status Ack*, the occurrence of these state update messages does not create an invalid trace.

10.7.3 STATE INVARIANTS

It is often useful to augment the message-oriented expression of valid traces by adding constraints on the required state of a lifeline at a given point in a sequence of occurrences. This can be achieved using a **state invariant** on a lifeline. The invariant constraint can include the values of properties or parameters, or the state (of a state machine) that the lifeline is expected to be in.

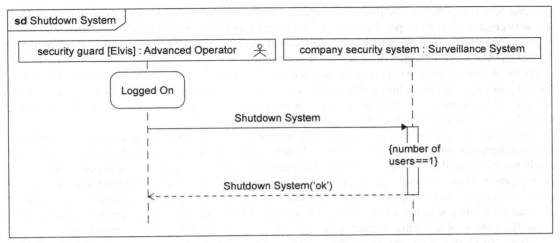

FIGURE 10.14

State invariants.

The notation for state invariants is an expression in braces shown on the lifeline that is constrained. If the invariant specifies the state of a state machine, it is shown as a state symbol on the lifeline.

Figure 10.14 shows a scenario for shutting down the system. The state invariant on the *security guard*'s lifeline indicates that the guard has to be logged on for the *Shutdown System* message to be valid. The state invariant on the *company security system* lifeline indicates that for a shutdown request to be valid, the number of users must be one; that is, no other users are currently logged on. A valid trace ends with a reply of *"OK"* to the *security guard*.

10.8 USING INTERACTION REFERENCES TO STRUCTURE COMPLEX INTERACTIONS

In most systems engineering projects, the size of systems and hence the size of interactions often become very large. There are also many patterns of interaction—or example, initialization and shutdown—which are used many times as parts of different scenarios.

To support large-scale uses of interactions, an interaction may include an **interaction use** that references an interaction described on another sequence diagram. Interaction uses can be nested, because a referenced interaction can in turn reference another. This capability significantly enhances the scalability of interactions. It also facilitates reuse since an interaction can be used (i.e., referenced) by more than one using interaction. The using interaction identifies the participants in the referenced interaction. The using interaction's definition must have lifelines that represent all the participants in the referenced interaction but may include additional lifelines as well.

To allow messages to pass into and out of an interaction when it is being used by another, an interaction can have connection points, called **formal gates,** at its boundary. There is a gate for every message that enters or leaves the interaction at its boundary. When the interaction is used, the using interaction has **actual gates** that correspond one-to-one with the formal gates of the used interaction. The messages arriving or leaving the actual gates must match those arriving or leaving at their corresponding formal gates in terms of name, direction, kind, and values.

In the definition of an interaction, messages can connect to the frame of the interaction. There is a formal gate at each connection point, although no symbol represents the gate itself. Gates can be named, but the name is typically not shown. An example of messages connecting to the frame at the formal gates of an interaction is shown in Figure 10.12.

Interaction uses are shown as frames with the keyword ref in the frame label. The body of the frame contains the name of the referenced interaction. Messages that terminate/start at the boundary of the frame imply the presence of actual gates. Lifelines that participate in the nested interaction are obscured by the frame symbol. Note that this is opposite to the way participants are shown on combined fragments, where participants are not obscured. A modeler may choose to indicate on a particular interaction use symbol whether the internal structure of the referenced interaction is further described by another sequence diagram. If so, the symbol for that interaction use contains a rake symbol in its bottom right corner.

Figure 10.15 shows an interaction that references four other interactions, as indicated by ref. The first-referenced interaction describes the *company security system* being set up by the *security guard*.

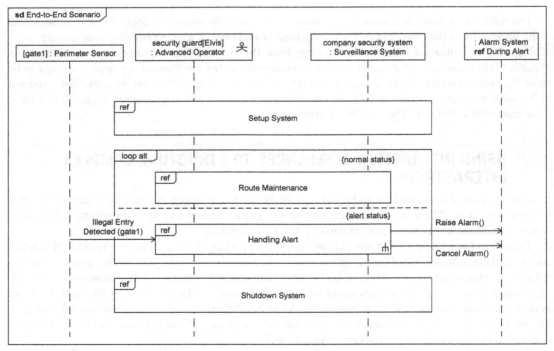

FIGURE 10.15

Reference to another interaction.

During the guard's shift, one of two things is shown as potentially occurring. If things are quiet (normal status), the guard might perform some maintenance on the automated surveillance routes (the scenario in Figure 10.8); otherwise, the guard and the system might handle an alert (the scenario from Figure 10.12). These two alternatives may occur repeatedly, as indicated by the **loop alt** fragment, until the guard shuts down the system. To use the *Handling Alert* interaction, this interaction needs to attach compatible messages to all its gates. The rake symbol in the use of *Handling Alert* indicates that it is described by a sequence diagram (Figure 10.12)

Interactions, like other behaviors, can have parameters. Any use of an interaction must provide arguments corresponding to the interaction's input parameters and may expect to obtain arguments corresponding to its output parameters. Parameters may be typed by blocks or value types and may be used wherever values of that type are valid, for example, in invariants and as arguments to and from messages.

An interaction's parameters appear in the diagram label using the same syntax as is used to describe operations (see Chapter 7, Section 7.5.2). The interaction use symbol can specify arguments to the used interaction using the same notation as is used for operation call and reply messages (see Section 10.5.1). Examples of this notation are shown in the Appendix, Table A.18.

10.9 DECOMPOSING LIFELINES TO REPRESENT INTERNAL BEHAVIOR

As described above, the property that a lifeline represents is a usage of a block, which may itself have nested properties. A lifeline may be decomposed to show lifelines corresponding to those properties.

A sequence diagram includes the provision to decompose a lifeline and further elaborate the interaction among its parts. For example, a sequence diagram may be used to represent a system as a single lifeline, interacting with its environment. This is often referred to as a black-box interaction, when the internal behavior of the system is hidden and only external behavior is visible. The system lifeline can then be decomposed to specify a nested interaction between its parts that supports the black-box interaction.

The interaction between these parts is defined by a separate interaction referenced by the parent lifeline that is being decomposed. The referenced interaction includes formal gates that correspond to the sending or receiving of messages on the parent lifeline. The messages at the gates of the referenced interaction must be compatible with the messages of the parent lifeline, and the message send and receive occurrences must occur in the same order as on the parent lifeline. Only lifelines representing properties of the block that is the type of the parent lifeline may appear in the referenced interaction.

A **lifeline decomposition** is shown by adding the name of the referenced interaction below the name of the lifeline, prefixed by the keyword `ref`. The same name is used in the frame label of the referenced interaction.

Figure 10.16 shows the decomposition of the black-box lifeline for the *Alarm System* from Figure 10.15. It shows how the *Alarm System* handles alerts. When the *alarm controller* receives a *Raise Alarm* message, it requests an announcement on the *internal PA*. It then alerts all the registered emergency services through the *Emergency Comms System*, providing a *location* and a

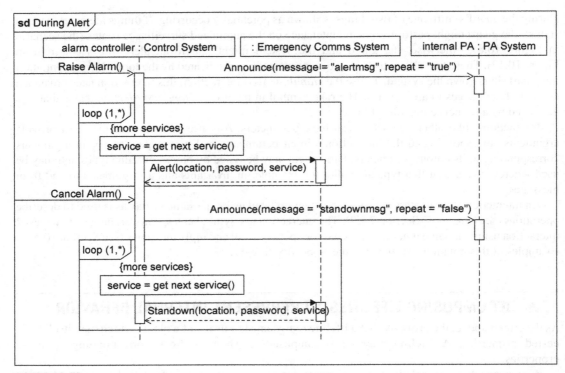

FIGURE 10.16

A decomposed lifeline.

password to authenticate the alert. When the *Cancel Alarm* message is received, the *alarm controller* requests another announcement and then sends a request to the emergency services to stand down. At least one emergency service must be alerted, but the maximum number may depend on circumstances.

There is an alternative to using the reference sequence diagram for representing a nested interaction. This is accomplished by showing the lifeline and its nested parts on the same sequence diagram, with the black-box lifeline shown on top of the lifelines corresponding to the nested parts. The header boxes of the parts are attached to the underside of the parent lifeline's header box. The nested lifelines can be used to show interactions that occur within the parent lifeline or to send and receive messages directly to and from other external lifelines.

Figure 10.17 shows a white-box view of what happens when the *security guard* wishes to log in to the *company security system*. The two significant parts of the *company security system*—the *user interface* and the *Monitoring Station*—are shown underneath the lifeline of the *company security system*. In this scenario, a *login* message is received by the *user interface* and requests the *Monitoring Station* to verify it. The *user interface* then checks that the maximum number of logins has not been exceeded and returns control to the *security guard*.

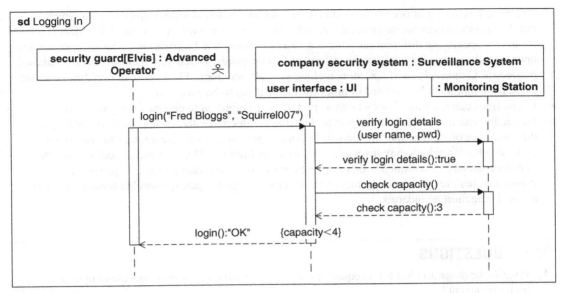

FIGURE 10.17

Inline nesting of lifeline decomposition.

10.10 SUMMARY

Sequence diagrams describe interactions, which are used to capture system scenarios as a set of specified occurrences across several parts of the system, represented by lifelines. An interaction is specified using occurrence specifications, which are organized into a hierarchy, and ordered by interaction operators. When an interaction executes, it evaluates the set of event occurrences generated by instances of its lifelines and determines whether they are valid. The most significant source of occurrences is the exchange of messages between lifelines, which may trigger executions. The following list highlights key aspects of interactions:

- Lifelines represent parts (or references) of the block that owns the interaction. During execution, a lifeline may represent only one instance; so when the part has an upper bound greater than 1, an additional selector expression is required to specify exactly one of all the instances that may be represented by the part. Lifelines may run from the top to the bottom of a sequence diagram, indicating that the parts they represent exist before and after the execution of the interaction. They also may start and/or end within the sequence diagram, indicating the creation or destruction of instances during execution of the interaction. Lifelines may be physically nested on a diagram to show a white-box view of the interactions within that lifeline. State invariants on the lifelines assert conditions that must hold at that point in the interaction's execution for the current trace to be valid.
- Messages are exchanged between lifelines and typically represent an invocation of an operation or a sending of a signal. Messages do not represent data flows, but the flow of data (or other items such as matter or energy) can be captured via arguments of the message. Messages are sent and received by behaviors executing on the lifelines and can be either asynchronous (sender continues executing) or synchronous (sender waits for a response).

- The default ordering of occurrences imposed by an interaction is weak sequencing, in which unrelated occurrences are sequenced within but not across lifelines. A combined fragment is a means for specifying different ordering semantics. A combined fragment includes an operator and operands; the operator identifies the ordering of its operands, which may themselves be combined fragments. Commonly used operators include **par, alt,** and **loop.** Each operand may have a guard expression that must be satisfied in order for the operand to be executed.
- Interactions can use other interactions as part of their definition to enhance scalability. An interaction can use another interaction to describe the internal interactions of one of its lifelines; this enables a black-box specification style. An interaction can also use another to specify part of its total behavior, which may involve a number of its lifelines. This decomposition is either done to reduce the size of a sequence diagram or to reuse some common interaction pattern. Interaction frames can feature connection points on their perimeter, called gates, to enable messages to pass across interaction boundaries.

10.11 **QUESTIONS**

1. What is the diagram kind for a sequence diagram, and which kind of model element does its frame represent?
2. What is the context for an executing interaction?
3. Draw a sequence diagram with two lifelines: one representing a part with no name, typed by the actor "Customer," and the other with the name "m," typed by the block "Vending Machine."
4. What is a selector expression used for?
5. Which kinds of occurrence are relevant when specifying interactions?
6. List the different kinds of messages that can be exchanged between lifelines.
7. On the diagram from Question 3, add a message from the "Customer" lifeline to the "Vending Machine" lifeline representing the signal "Select Product" with the argument "C3."
8. What does the term "message overtaking" mean?
9. How is an action or behavior execution represented on a sequence diagram?
10. What is an observation and how is it used?
11. In the diagram from Question 7, observe the current time (provided by the "clock" function) when the "Select Product" message is sent.
12. How is a combined fragment represented on a sequence diagram?
13. Name four common interaction operators.
14. In the diagram from Question 7, change "Select Product" from a signal to an operation on "Vending Machine" and show two different replies: if the machine has stock, then it replies with the return string "Stock Available"; otherwise, it replies with the string "Sold Out."
15. Messages M1 and M2 from lifeline L2 can occur in any order on lifeline L1. Show two different ways that this can be expressed on a sequence diagram.
16. Are the lifelines that participate in a combined fragment shown in front of or behind the frame box for the combined fragment?
17. Which messages are valid inside an ignore fragment?
18. What does a state invariant specify?

19. What are gates used for?
20. Name two ways of showing the interaction between the children of a lifeline.
21. Are the lifelines that participate in an interaction use shown in front of or behind the frame box for the interaction use?

DISCUSSION TOPIC

Sequence diagrams can be used to capture test specifications or test results. What differences would you expect to see between sequence diagrams used for these two purposes?

MODELING EVENT-BASED BEHAVIOR WITH STATE MACHINES

This chapter describes how to use state machines to model the behavior of blocks as they respond to internal and external events.

11.1 OVERVIEW

State machines are typically used in SysML to describe the state-dependent behavior of a block throughout its lifecycle, which is defined in terms of its states and the transitions between them. A state machine for a block may start, for example, when it initiates power up, then transition through multiple states in response to different stimuli, and terminate when it completes power down. The state machine defines how the block's behavior changes as it transitions between different states and while the block is in different states. State machines in SysML can be used to describe a wide range of state-related behavior, from the behavior of a simple lamp switch to the complex modes of an advanced aircraft.

State machines are normally owned by blocks and execute within the context of an instance of that block, but a state machine can also be owned by a package. The behavior of a state machine is specified by a set of regions, each of which contains its own states. The states in any one region are exclusive; that is, when the region is active, exactly one of its substates is active. A region normally has an initial pseudostate, which is the place the region starts executing when it first becomes active. When a state is entered, an (optional) entry behavior (e.g., an activity) is executed. Similarly, an optional exit behavior is executed on exit. While in a state, a state machine can execute a do behavior. A region also normally has a final state that signifies that the region has completed. Change of state is effected by transitions that connect a source state to a target state. Transitions are defined by triggers, guards, and effects. The trigger indicates an event that can cause a transition from the source state, the guard is evaluated in order to test whether the transition is valid, and the effect is a behavior executed once the transition is triggered. Triggers may be based on a variety of events such as the expiration of a timer or the receipt of a signal by the state machine's owning object.

Operation calls on the owning block are also valid trigger events for transitions. Junction and choice pseudostates support the construction of compound transitions between states, with multiple guards and effects.

State machines in different blocks may interact with one another by either sending signals or invoking operations. For example, the state machine of one block can send a signal to another block as part of a transition effect or state behavior. The event corresponding to the receipt of this signal by the receiving block can trigger a state transition in its state machine. Similarly, a state machine in one block may call an operation on another block that causes an event that triggers a transition.

273

State hierarchies occur when a state contains its own regions. A state with just one region is the most common case and is called a composite state. A state with more than one region is called an orthogonal composite state. Finally, a kind of state called a submachine state may reference another state machine. To model state hierarchies effectively, additional constructs are needed. Fork and join pseudostates are needed to specify transitions into and out of orthogonal composite states. Entry and exit point pseudostates can be used to add connection points for transitions on the boundary of a state or state machine.

State machines may also specify constraints within states or on transitions. The constraints may specify equations that correspond to different behaviors or different levels of performance that must be true in different states.

State machines can be used with other behaviors. For example, a state machine can use an activity or other behavior to specify what happens within a state, on entry, on exit, or on transition between states. State machines can also be used within interactions (see Chapter 10, Section 10.7.3) and activities (see Chapter 9, Section 9.11.3) to constrain certain aspects of their behavior. The integration of the semantics of different kinds of behaviors is sometimes complex and should be used with care.

11.2 STATE MACHINE DIAGRAM

State machine diagrams are sometimes referred to as **state charts** or state diagrams, but the actual name in SysML is the state machine diagram. The complete diagram header for a state machine diagram is as follows:

```
stm [stateMachine] state machine name [diagram name]
```

The diagram kind for a state machine diagram is **stm**, and the model element kind is always stateMachine. Because of this, the model element kind in square brackets is usually elided.

Figure 11.1 shows many of the basic notational elements for describing state machines. It describes a state machine for an ACME *Surveillance System*. It starts in the *idle* state, runs through a series of states during its

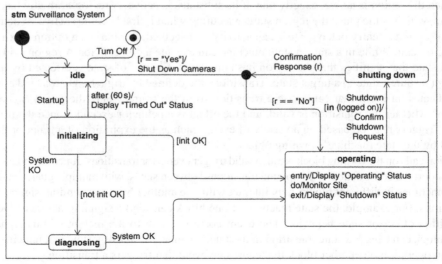

FIGURE 11.1

A state machine.

lifecycle, and finally ends up at *idle* again, when it may receive a *Turn Off* signal that causes it to complete its behavior. The notation for state machine diagrams is shown in the Appendix, Tables A.21 through A.23.

11.3 SPECIFYING STATES IN A STATE MACHINE

A **state machine** is a potentially reusable definition of some state-dependent behavior. State machines typically execute in the context of a block, and events experienced by the block instance may cause state transitions.

11.3.1 REGION

A state machine can contain one or more regions, which together describe the state-related behavior of the state machine. Each **region** is defined in terms of states and **pseudostates** and the transitions between them. An active region has exactly one active state within it at a given time. The difference between a state and a pseudostate is that a region can never stay in pseudostate, which merely exists to help determine the next active state. If a state machine contains a single region, it typically is not named, but if there are multiple regions, they are often named.

A state machine with multiple regions may describe some concurrent behavior happening within the state machine's owning block. This may represent an abstraction of the behavior of different parts of the block, as discussed in Chapter 7, Section 7.5.1. For example, one part of a factory may be storing incoming material, another turning raw material into finished products, and yet another sending out finished goods. The state machine may also include concurrent behaviors—such as a camera being panned and tilted at the same time—that are performed by multiple parts. If the parts' behaviors are specified, the relationship between the state machine for the parent block and the behaviors of its parts should also be specified. States can also contain multiple regions, as described in Section 11.6.2, but this section describes **simple states** only (i.e., states with no regions and therefore without nested states).

The initialization and completion of a region are described using an initial pseudostate and final state, respectively. An **initial pseudostate** is used to determine the initial state of a region. The outgoing transition from an initial pseudostate may include an effect (see Section 11.4.1 for a detailed discussion of transition effects). Such effects are often used to set the initial values of properties used by the state machine. When the active state of a region is the **final state**, the region has completed, and no more transitions take place within it. Hence, a final state can have no outgoing transitions.

The **terminate pseudostate** is always associated with the state of an entire state machine. If a terminate pseudostate is reached, then the behavior of the state machine terminates. A terminate pseudostate has the same effect as reaching the final states of all the state machine's regions. The termination of the state machine does not imply the destruction of its owning object, but it does mean that the object will not respond to events via its state machine.

If a state machine has a single region, it is represented by the area inside the frame of the state machine diagram. Multiple regions are shown separated by dashed lines.

The notation for the concepts introduced thus far is as follows:

- An initial pseudostate is shown as a filled circle.
- A final state is shown as a bulls-eye (i.e., a filled circle surrounded by a larger hollow circle).
- A terminate pseudostate is shown as an X.

11.3.2 STATE

A **state** represents some significant condition in the life of a block, typically because it represents some change in how the block responds to events and what behaviors it performs. This condition can be specified in terms of the values of selected properties of the block, but typically the condition is expressed in terms of implicit state variable(s) for each region. It is helpful to use the analogy that the block is controlled by a switch. Each state corresponds to a switch position for the block, and the block can exhibit some specified behavior in each switch position. The state machine defines all valid switch positions (i.e., states) and transitions between switch positions (i.e., state transitions). If there are multiple regions, each region is controlled by its own switch with its switch positions corresponding to its states. The switch positions can be specified by a form of truth table—similar to how logic gates can be specified—in which the current states and transitions define the next state.

Each state may contain **entry** and **exit behaviors** that are performed whenever the state is entered or exited, respectively. In addition, the state may contain a **do behavior** that executes once the entry behavior has completed. The do behavior continues to execute until it completes or the state is exited. Although any SysML behavior can be used, entry and exit behaviors and do behaviors are typically activities or opaque behaviors.

A state is represented by a round-cornered box containing its name. Entry and exit behaviors and do behaviors are described as text expressions preceded by the keywords entry, exit, or do and a forward slash. There is some flexibility in the content of the textual expression. The text expression typically is the name of the behavior, but when the behavior is an opaque behavior, the body of the opaque behavior can be used instead (refer to Chapter 7, Section 7.5 for a description of an opaque behavior).

Figure 11.2 shows a simple state machine for the *Surveillance System*, with a single *operating* state in its single region. A transition from the region's initial pseudostate goes to the *operating* state. On entry, the *Surveillance System* displays that it is operational on all operator consoles, and on exit, it displays a shutdown status. While the *Surveillance System* is in the *operating* state, it performs a do activity of its standard function to *Monitor Site*, which is monitoring the building where it is installed for any unauthorized entry. When in the *operating* state, a *Turn Off* signal triggers a transition to the final state, and because there is only a single region, the state machine terminates.

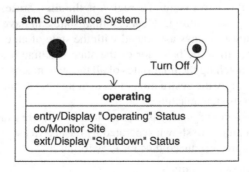

FIGURE 11.2

A state machine containing a single state.

11.4 TRANSITIONING BETWEEN STATES

A **transition** specifies when a change of state occurs within a state machine. State machines always run to completion once a transition is triggered, which means that they are not able to consume another trigger event until the state machine has completed the processing of the current event.

11.4.1 TRANSITION FUNDAMENTALS

A transition may include one or more triggers, a guard, and an effect as described next.

Trigger

A **trigger** identifies the possible stimuli that cause a transition to occur. SysML has four main kinds of triggering events.

- A **signal event** indicates that a new asynchronous message corresponding to a signal has arrived. A signal event may be accompanied by a number of arguments that can be used in the transition effect.
- A **time event** indicates either that a given time interval has passed since the current state was entered (relative) or that a given instant in time has been reached (absolute).
- A **change event** indicates that some condition has been satisfied (normally that some specific set of attribute values hold). Change events are discussed in Section 11.7.
- A **call event** indicates that an operation on the state machine's owning block has been requested. A call event may also be accompanied by a number of arguments. Call events are discussed in Section 11.5.

Once the entry behavior of a state has completed, transitions can be triggered by events irrespective of what is happening within the state. For example, a transition may be triggered while a do activity is executing, in which case the do activity is terminated.

By default, events must be consumed when they are presented to the state machine, even if they do not trigger transitions. However, events may be explicitly deferred while in a specific state for later handling. The deferred event is not consumed as long as the state machine remains in that state. As soon as the state machine enters a state in which the event is not deferred, the event must be consumed before any others. The event triggers a transition or it is consumed without any effect.

Transitions can also be triggered by internally generated **completion events.** For a simple state, a completion event is generated when the entry behavior and the do behavior have completed.

Guard

The **transition guard** contains an expression that must evaluate to true for the transition to occur. The guard is specified using a constraint, introduced in Chapter 8, Section 8.2, which includes a textual expression to represent the guard condition. When an event satisfies a trigger, the guard on the transition is evaluated. If the guard evaluates to true, the transition is triggered; if the guard evaluates to false, then the event is consumed with no effect. Guards can test the state of the state machine using the operators **in** (state x) and **not in** (state x).

Effect

The third part of the transition is the **transition effect.** The effect is a behavior, normally an activity or an opaque behavior, executed during the transition from one state to another. For a signal or call event, the arguments of the corresponding signal or operation call can either be used directly within the transition effect or be assigned to attributes of the block owning the state machine. The transition effect can be an arbitrarily complex behavior that may include send signal actions or operation calls used to interact with other blocks.

If the transition is triggered, first the exit behavior of the current (source) state is executed, then the transition effect is executed, and finally the entry behavior of the target state is executed.

A state machine can contain transitions, called internal transitions, which do not effect a change in state. An internal transition has the same source and destination and, if triggered, simply executes the transition effect. By contrast, an external transition with the same source and destination state—sometimes called a transition-to-self—triggers the execution of that state's entry and exit behaviors as well as the transition effect. One frequently overlooked consequence of internal transitions is that, because the state is not exited and entered, timers for relative time events are not reset.

Transition notation

A transition is shown as an arrow between two states, with the head pointing to the target state. Transitions-to-self are shown with both ends of the arrow attached to the same state. Internal transitions are not shown as graphical paths but are listed on separate lines within the state symbol, as shown in Figure 11.9.

The definition of the transition's behavior is shown in a formatted string on the transition with the list of triggers first, followed by a guard in square brackets, and finally the transition effect preceded by a forward slash. Section 11.4.3 describes an alternate graphical syntax for transitions.

The text for a trigger depends on the event, as follows:

* *Signal and call events*—the name of the signal or operation followed optionally by a list of attribute assignments in parentheses. Call events are typically distinguished by including the parentheses even when there are no attribute assignments. Although this is a useful convention, it is not part of the standard notation.
* *Time events*—the term `after` or `at` followed by the time. `after` indicates that the time is relative to the moment when the state is entered. `at` indicates that the time is an absolute time.
* *Change events*—the term `when` followed by the condition that has to be met in parentheses. Like other constraint expressions, the condition is expressed in text with the expression language optionally in braces.

The effect expression may either be the name of the invoked behavior or contain the text of an opaque behavior.

When an event is deferred in a state, the event is shown inside the state symbol using the text for the trigger followed by a "/" and the keyword defer. See Figure 11.12 for an example.

Transitions can also be named, in which case the name may appear alongside the transition instead of the transition expression. A name is sometimes a useful shorthand for a very long transition expression.

Figure 11.3 shows a more sophisticated state machine for the *Surveillance System* than in Figure 11.2, with all the principal states and the transitions between them. In contrast to Figure 11.2, the initial pseudostate now indicates that the region starts at the *idle* state. The final state is now also reached from the *idle* state, but it is still triggered by the receipt of a *Turn Off* signal. Once processing is complete in the *initializing* state (refer to Figure 11.14 to view inside the *initializing* state), a completion event for *initializing* will be

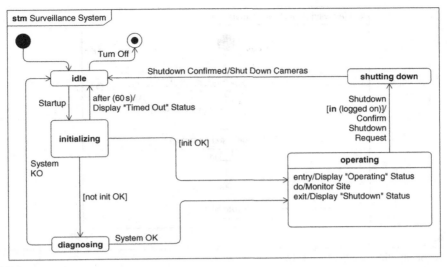

FIGURE 11.3

Transitions between states.

generated that triggers the two outgoing transitions. If the condition variable *init OK* is true, the system enters the *operating* state. Otherwise, the system enters the *diagnosing* state in which an operator will look at the error logs and try to manually initialize the system. Just in case something happens and the test procedure does not complete, the system has a time-out after 60 seconds, which returns the system to the *idle* state.

From the *diagnosing* state, the operator indicates success using the signal *System OK,* which allows the system to enter the *operating* state. The signal *System KO* indicates that the system is beyond operator repair and causes a transition back to *idle.* From the *operating* state, a *Shutdown* signal will cause a transition to the *shutting down* state, as long as the operating state is in substate *logged on* (refer to Figure 11.9 for a view inside the *operating* state). As part of shutting down, the system requests a confirmation and will only exit the *shutting down* state when it receives a *Shutdown Confirmed* signal, whereupon it executes the *Shut Down Cameras* activity.

Unless the graphical notation for transitions is being used (see Section 11.4.3), transition effect—with the exception of opaque behaviors—are specified on separate diagrams appropriate to the kind of behavior. Figure 11.4 shows the activity diagram for the *Shut Down Cameras* activity.

When invoked as a transition effect, *Shut Down Cameras* loops over all known cameras and sends each a *Shutdown* signal. Note that the activity does not include an accept event action; this would leave the invoking state machine in an ambiguous (mid-transition) state when waiting for new events to occur.

11.4.2 ROUTING TRANSITIONS USING PSEUDOSTATES

There are a variety of situations when a simple transition directly between two states is not sufficient to express the required semantics. SysML includes a number of pseudostates to provide these additional semantics. This section introduces junction and choice pseudostates, which support compound transitions between states.

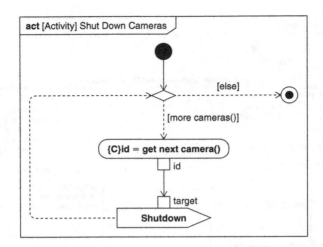

FIGURE 11.4

Defining a transition effect using an activity.

A **junction pseudostate** is used to construct a compound transition path between states. The compound transition allows more than one alternative transition path between states to be specified, although only one path can be taken in response to any single event. Multiple transitions may either converge on or diverge from the junction pseudostate. When there are multiple outgoing transitions from a junction pseudostate, the selected transition will be one of those whose guard evaluates to true at the time the triggering event is processed. If more than one guard evaluates to true, SysML does not define which one of the valid transitions is chosen for execution. If a particular compound transition path includes more than one junction between two states, all the guards along that path must evaluate to true before the compound transition is taken.

The **choice pseudostate** also has multiple incoming transitions and outgoing transitions and, like the junction pseudostate, is part of a compound transition between states. The behavior of the choice pseudostate is distinct from that of a junction pseudostate in that the guards on its outgoing transitions are not evaluated until the choice pseudostate has been reached. This allows effects executed on the prior transition to affect the outcome of the choice. When a choice pseudostate is reached in the execution of a state machine, there must always be at least one valid outgoing transition. If not, the state machine is invalid. A technique that is often used to ensure the validity of a choice pseudostate is to use a catch-all guard on no more than one outgoing transition. This is specified using the keyword `else`. Whether a compound transition contains junction pseudostates, choice pseudostates, or both, any possible compound transition must contain only one trigger, normally on the first transition in the path.

The various routing pseudostates are represented as follows:

- A junction pseudostate is shown, like an initial pseudostate, as a filled circle.
- A choice pseudostate is shown as a diamond.

Figure 11.5 completes the state machine for the *Surveillance System* shown in Figure 11.3. The handling of shutdown has been improved to describe what happens if the operator does not actually

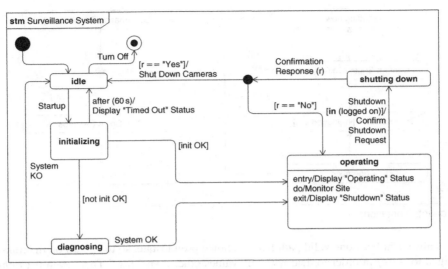

FIGURE 11.5

Routing transitions.

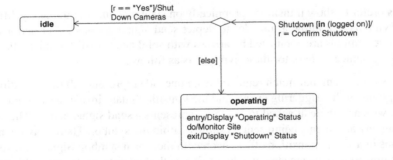

FIGURE 11.6

Specifying shutdown using a choice pseudostate.

want to shut down the system after all. The argument of the *Confirmation Response* signal, which takes values of *"Yes"* or *"No"* is mapped to attribute *r*. The transition triggered by the *Confirmation Response* signal now ends at a junction, with two outgoing transitions with different guards. If *r* == *"Yes"* then the system shutdown proceeds; if *r* == *"No,"* then the system returns to the operating state.

The transition from shutting down to idle/operating could be specified using a junction pseudostate in Figure 11.5 because the value of *r,* needed to determine the complete transition path, was available as part of the transition's trigger. However, Figure 11.6 shows another approach to system shutdown without a *shutting down* state. Here, the confirmation request is made as an effect of the transition out of the *operating* state, so the value of *r* is not known until after the first leg of the compound transition has been taken. In this case, a choice pseudostate is needed to allow the value of *r* returned from *Confirm Shutdown* to be used in the guard conditions on its exit transitions. As noted earlier, the modeler must ensure

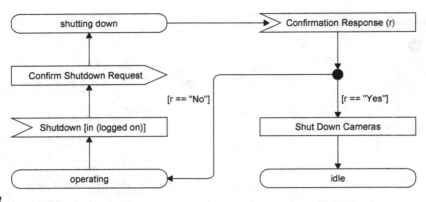

FIGURE 11.7

Transition-oriented notation.

that there is always at least one valid path from a choice pseudostate, so the guard on the transition has been changed to *[else]* in order to deal with any values other than *"Yes."* Then, even if *Confirm Shutdown* unexpectedly returns a value other than *"Yes"* or *"No,"* the state machine will still operate.

11.4.3 SHOWING TRANSITIONS GRAPHICALLY

Some modelers prefer to show transitions graphically on state machine diagrams. SysML introduces a set of special symbols that allow a modeler to depict send signal actions, other actions, and triggers graphically. These symbols are connected by arrows with solid heads to differentiate them from transition arrows. The graphical syntax for these symbols is as follows:

- A rectangle with a triangular notch removed from one side represents all the transition's triggers, with descriptions of the triggering events and the transition guard inside the symbol.
- A rectangle with a triangle attached to one side represents a send signal action. The signal's name, together with any arguments being sent, is shown within the symbol. There may be many send signal actions in a single transition effect, each with their own symbol. Signals are very important when communicating between state machines (hence the separate treatment of this action).
- Any other action in the transition effect is represented by a rectangle containing text that describes the action to be taken. There may be many actions as part of a transition effect, each with its own symbol.

Figure 11.7 shows the use of transition notation to provide an equivalent definition of the transitions between *operating, idle,* and *shutting down,* originally shown on Figure 11.5.

11.5 STATE MACHINES AND OPERATION CALLS

State machines can respond to operation calls on their parent block via call events. A call event may either be handled in a synchronous fashion—that is, the caller is blocked while waiting for a response—or asynchronously, which results in similar behavior to the receipt of a signal. The state machine executes all behaviors triggered by the call event until it has reached another state, and then returns any outputs created by those behaviors to the caller.

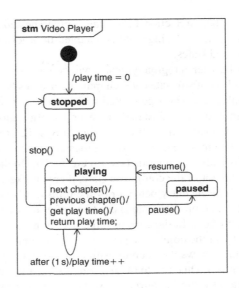

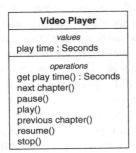

FIGURE 11.8

A state machine driven by call events for operations on its owning block.

One of the components used by the surveillance system's operators is a video player that allows them to review recorded surveillance data. The *Video Player* block, shown in Figure 11.8, provides a set of operations in its interface to control playback. Although many of the operations do not return data, it makes sense for any client of *Video Player* to wait until a request for these operations has been processed; hence, it makes sense for its interface to be defined using operations. The response of the block to requests from these operations is defined using the state machine shown in Figure 11.8, in which call events related to the operations are used as triggers on transitions. Calls to the *play, stop, pause,* and *resume* operations cause call events that trigger transitions between the various states of *Video Player.* Calls to the operations *next chapter, previous chapter,* and *get play time* cause call events that trigger internal transitions to state *playing.* To simplify the example, Figure 11.8 does not show many of the transition effects, but it does show how a request on *get play time* gets its return argument.

11.6 STATE HIERARCHIES

Just as state machines have regions, so can states; such states are called **composite** or **hierarchical states.** These allow state machines to scale to represent arbitrarily complex state-based behaviors. This section discusses composite states with single and multiple regions, as well as the reuse of an existing state machine to describe the behavior of a state.

11.6.1 COMPOSITE STATE WITH A SINGLE REGION

Arguably the most common situation is a composite state that has a single region. A state nested within the region can only be active when the state enclosing the region is active. Thus, the switch position analogy described in Section 11.3.2 can apply to nested states by requiring that the switch position corresponding to the enclosing state be enabled in order to enable the switch positions corresponding to any of its nested states.

As stated earlier, a region typically will contain an initial pseudostate and a final state, a set of pseudostates, and set of substates, which may themselves be composite states. If the region has a final state, then a completion event is generated when that state is reached.

When an initial pseudostate is missing from a region in a composite state, the initial state of that region is undefined, although extensions to SysML are free to add their own semantics. However, a composite state may be porous, which means transitions may cross the state boundary, starting or ending on states within its regions (see Figure 11.10). In the case of a transition ending on a nested state, the entry behavior of the composite state, if any, is executed after the effect of the transition and before the execution of the entry behavior of the transition's target nested state. In the opposite case, the exit behavior of the composite state is executed after the exit behavior of the source nested state and before the transition effect. In the case of more deeply nested state hierarchies, the same rule can be applied recursively to all the composite states whose boundaries have been crossed.

Figure 11.9 shows the decomposition of the state *operating* from Figure 11.5 into the substates of one of its regions. On entry to the *operating* state, two entry behaviors are executed: the entry behavior of *operating, Display "Operating" status; logged in = 0,* and then the entry behavior of *logged off, Display "Logged Off."* This is because on entry, as indicated by the initial pseudostate, the initial substate of *operating* is *logged off.*

When in state *logged off,* a *Login* signal will cause a transition to the *logged on* state and will increment the value of *logged in.* While in the *logged on* state, repeated *Login* and *Logout* signals will increment and decrement the value of *logged in,* often as internal transitions without a change of state. However, if a *Logout* signal is received when the value of *logged in* is 1, then the signal will trigger a transition back to *logged off.* The entry behavior for *logged on* records the time in the variable *time on,* and its exit behavior uses that to display the *Session Length.*

The do activity *Monitor Site* executes as long as the state machine for the *Surveillance System* is in the *operating* state or until it reaches its own activity final. State *operating* does not have a final

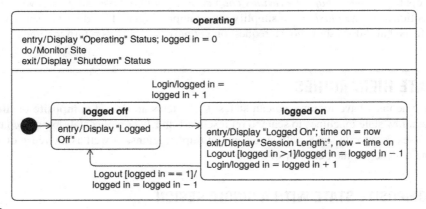

FIGURE 11.9

States nested within a composite state.

state, and so a completion event is never generated (as described above). As can be seen in Figure 11.5, this state is exited when a *Shutdown* signal is presented.

11.6.2 COMPOSITE STATE WITH MULTIPLE (ORTHOGONAL) REGIONS

A composite state may have many regions, which may each contain substates. A composite state with more than one region is sometimes called an **orthogonal composite state.** When an orthogonal composite state is active, each region has its own active state that is independent of the others, and any incoming event is independently analyzed within each region. A transition that ends on the composite state will trigger transitions from the initial pseudostate of each region, so there must be an initial pseudostate in each region for such a transition to be valid. Similarly, a completion event for the composite state will occur when all the regions are in their final state.

When an event is associated with triggers in multiple orthogonal regions, the event may trigger a transition in each region, assuming the transition is valid based on the other usual criteria. A simple example of this scenario is shown later in Figure 11.11.

Note that a transition can never cross the boundary between two regions of the same composite state. Such a transition, if triggered, would leave one of the regions with no active state, which is not allowed.

In addition to transitions that start or end on the composite state, transitions from outside the composite state may start or end on the nested states of its regions. In this case, one state in each region must be the start or end of one of a coordinated set of transitions. This coordination is performed by a fork pseudostate in the case of incoming transitions and a join pseudostate for outgoing transitions.

A **fork pseudostate** has a single incoming transition and as many outgoing transitions as there are orthogonal regions in the target state. Unlike junction and choice pseudostates, all outgoing transitions of a fork are part of the compound transition. When an incoming transition is taken to the fork pseudostate, all the outgoing transitions are taken. Because all outgoing transitions of the fork pseudostate have to be taken, they may not have triggers or guards but may have effects.

The coordination of outgoing transitions from an orthogonal composite state is performed using a **join pseudostate** that has multiple incoming transitions and one outgoing transition. The rules on triggers and guards for join pseudostates are the opposite of those for fork pseudostates. Incoming transitions of the join pseudostate may not have triggers or a guard but may have an effect. The outgoing transition may have triggers, a guard, and an effect. When all the incoming transitions can be taken and the join's outgoing transition is valid, the compound transition can occur. Incoming transitions occur first followed by the outgoing transition.

A fork and join pseudostate is shown as a vertical or horizontal bar with transition edges either starting or ending on the bar. An example of this can be seen in Figure 11.10, which shows a possible decomposition of the *operating* state from Figure 11.5.

The presence of multiple regions within a composite state is indicated by multiple compartments within the state symbol, separated by dashed lines. The regions can optionally be named, in which case the name appears at the top of the corresponding compartment. All nodes within such a compartment are part of the same region. As an alternative to showing the name of a state in a compartment, its name can be placed in a tab attached to the outside of the state symbol. An example of this can be seen in Figure 11.11.

Figure 11.10 shows a further elaboration of the *operating* state shown in Figure 11.9. In this elaboration, the *logged on* state has two orthogonal regions. One region, called *alert management*, specifies

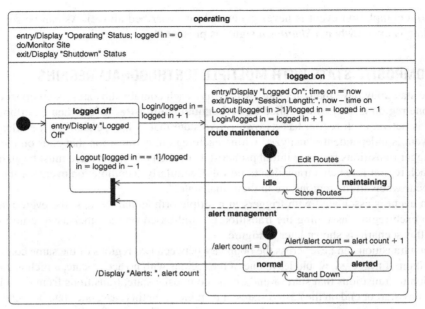

FIGURE 11.10

Entering and leaving a set of concurrent regions.

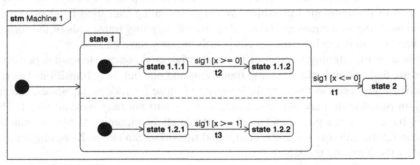

FIGURE 11.11

Illustration of transition firing order.

states and transitions for *normal* and *alerted* modes of operation; the other region, called *route mainte-nance,* specifies states and transitions for updating the route (i.e., pan-and-tilt angles) when the auto-matic surveillance feature of the system is engaged. As before, in state *logged off,* the receipt of a *Login* signal triggers transition to *logged on.* Based on the initial pseudostates in the two regions, the two initial substates of *logged on* are *idle* for region *route maintenance* and *normal* for region *alert manage-ment.* The receipt of an *Alert* signal triggers the transition from *normal* to *alerted* in *alert management.*

Similarly, the receipt of an *Edit Routes* signal triggers the transition from *idle* to *maintaining* in *route management.*

To ensure appropriate operator oversight of the system, the last operator can only log off if the *logged on* state is in substates *idle* and *normal.* This constraint is specified using a join pseudostate whose outgoing transition is triggered by a *Logout* signal with a guard of *logged in* = = *1.* The two incoming transitions to the join pseudostate start on *idle* and *normal,* so even if there is a *Logout* signal and the number of logged on operators is one, the outgoing transition from the join pseudostate will be valid only if the two active substates of *logged on* are *idle* and *normal.* Because the transitions from *idle* and *normal* cross the boundary of state *logged on,* its exit behavior is executed before any effects on the transitions. After evaluating that the guard condition on the transition evaluates to true, the order of execution triggered by the valid *Logout* signal is:

*   exit behavior of *logged on*—Display *"Session Length:", now-time on*;
*   incoming transition effect to join—Display *"Alerts:," alert count*;
*   outgoing transition effect from join—*"logged in = logged in—1"*; and
*   Entry behavior of logged off—Display *"Logged Off".*

Having elaborated the *operating* state, it is apparent that the transitions *Logout [logged in > 1]* and *Login* are rightly internal transitions rather than transitions-to-self. Transitions-to-self always exit and reenter the state, which in this case would reset the substates of *route maintenance* and *alert management*; obviously, this is not desirable in the middle of an intruder alert.

11.6.3 TRANSITION FIRING ORDER IN NESTED STATE HIERARCHIES

It is possible that the same event may trigger transitions at several levels in a state hierarchy, and with the exception of concurrent regions, only one of the transitions can be taken at a time. Priority is given to the transition whose source state is innermost in the state hierarchy.

Consider the state machine *Machine 1,* shown in Figure 11.11, in its initial state (i.e., in state 1.1.1 and 1.2.1). The signal *sig1* is associated with the triggers of three transitions, each with guards based on the value of variable *x.* Note that, in this case, the transitions have both a name and a transition expression, whereas a transition edge normally would show one or the other. This has been done to help explain the behavior of the state machine. The following list shows the transitions that will fire upon receipt of *sig1* based on values of *x* from −1 to 1:

*   *x* equals −1—transition *t1* will be triggered because it is the only transition with a valid guard;
*   *x* equals 0—transition *t2* will be triggered because, although transition *t1* also has a valid guard, state *1.1.1* is the innermost of the two source states; or
*   *x* equals 1—both transitions *t2* and *t3* will be triggered because both their guards are valid.

The normal rules for execution of exit behaviors apply, so, before the transition from *state 1* to *state 2* can be taken, any exit behavior of the active nested states of *state 1,* as well as the exit behavior *of state 1,* must be executed.

The example in Figure 11.11 is fairly straightforward. Assessing transition priority is more complex when compound transitions and transitions from within orthogonal composite states are used. However, the same rules apply.

11.6.4 USING THE HISTORY PSEUDOSTATE UPON RETURN TO A PREVIOUSLY INTERRUPTED REGION

In some design scenarios, it is desirable to handle an exception event by interrupting the behavior of the current region, responding to the event, and then returning back to the state that the region was in at the time of the interruption. This can be achieved by a kind of pseudostate called a **history pseudostate.** A history pseudostate represents the last active state of its owning region, and a transition ending on a history pseudostate has the effect of returning the region to that state. An outgoing transition from a history pseudostate designates a default history pseudostate. This is used when the region has no previous history or its last active state was a final state.

The two kinds of history pseudostate are deep and shallow. A **deep history pseudostate** records the states of all regions in the state hierarchy below and including the region that owns the deep history pseudostate. A **shallow history pseudostate** only records the top-level state of the region that owns it. As a result, the deep history pseudostate will enable a return to a nested state, while a shallow history pseudostate will enable a return to only the top-level state.

A history pseudostate is described using the letter "H" surrounded by a circle. The deep history pseudostate has a small asterisk in the top right corner of the circle.

The *Surveillance System* supports an emergency override mechanism, as shown in Figure 11.12. In a change from Figure 11.10, the reception of an *Override* signal with a valid password will always cause a transition from the *logged on* or *logged off* states, even if there is an ongoing alert. This transition is routed out of the enclosing *operating* state via an exit point pseudostate to the *emergency override activated* state (see a discussion of this at the end of Section 11.6.5). However, once the emergency is over, a *Resume Operation* signal needs to restore the *operating* state completely to its previous state so that the system can continue with its interrupted activities. To achieve this, the transition triggered

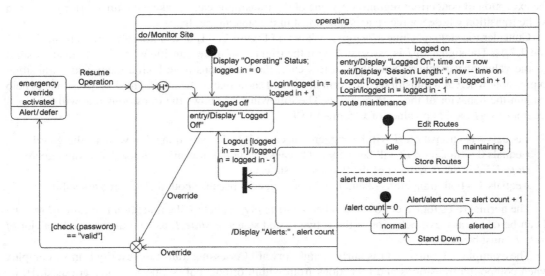

FIGURE 11.12

Recovering from an interruption using a history pseudostate.

by the *Resume Operation* signal ends (via an entry-point pseudostate) on a deep history pseudostate, which will restore the complete previous state of *operating*, including substates. By comparison, if a shallow history pseudostate was used, and the previous substate of *operating* was *logged on,* then the state machine would return to the initial states of logged on rather than previously active substates of *logged on.* If there is no previous history, the default state is *Logged Off.*

Alert events are deferred in the *emergency override activated* state so that they can be handled, if appropriate, in the resumed *operating* state.

11.6.5 REUSING STATE MACHINES

A **submachine state** is a kind of state that references a state machine that can be reused by other submachine states. A transition ending on a submachine state will start its referenced state machine. Similarly, when the referenced state machine completes, it will generate a completion event that can trigger transitions whose source is the submachine state. Modelers can also benefit from two additional kinds of pseudostates, called **entry** and **exit-point pseudostates**, which allow the state machine to define additional entry and exit points that can be accessed from a submachine state.

Entry and exit points on state machines

For a single-region state machine, entry- and exit-point pseudostates are similar to junctions; that is, they are part of a compound transition. Their outgoing guards have to be evaluated before the compound transition is triggered, and only one outgoing transition will be taken. On state machines, entry-point pseudostates can only have outgoing transitions, and exit-point pseudostates can only have incoming transitions.

Entry- and exit-point pseudostates are described by small circles that overlap the boundary of a state machine or composite state. An entry-point symbol is hollow, whereas an exit-point symbol contains an X.

Figure 11.13 shows a state machine for testing cameras, called *Test Camera,* which uses the graphical form for specifying transitions. From the entry-point pseudo state, the first transition simply sets the *failures* variable to 0 and ends on a choice pseudostate. On first entry, the state machine will always take the *[else]* transition, which will result in the sending of a *Test Camera* signal with the current camera number *(ccount)* as its argument. The state machine then stays in the *await test result* state until a *Test Complete* signal with argument *test result* has been received. The transition triggered by a *Test Complete* signal ends on a junction that either leads to the exit-point pseudostate *pass* (if the test passed) or back to the initial choice pseudostate (if the test failed), incrementing the *failures* variable on the way. If the camera has failed its self-test more than three times, then the transition with guard *[failures > 3]* will be taken to exit-point *fail.*

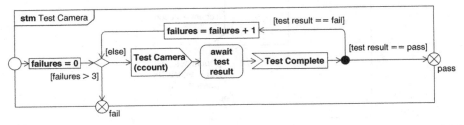

FIGURE 11.13

A state machine with entry and exit points.

Submachine states

A submachine state contains a reference to another state machine that is executed as part of the execution of the submachine state's parent. The entry- and exit-point pseudostates of the referenced state machine are represented on the boundary of the submachine state by special nodes called **connection points**. Connection points can be the source or target of transitions connected to states outside the submachine state. A transition whose source or target is a connection point forms part of a compound transition that includes the transition to or from the corresponding entry- and exit-point pseudostate in the referenced state machine. An example of this can be seen in Figure 11.14. In any given use of a state machine by a submachine state, only a subset of its entry and exit-point pseudostates may need to be externally connected.

A submachine state is represented by a state symbol showing the name of the state, along with the name of the referenced state machine, separated by a colon. A submachine state also includes an icon shown in the bottom right corner depicting either a simple state machine or a rake to be consistent with the representation of diagram decomposition in other diagrams. Connection points may be placed on the boundary of the submachine state symbol. These symbols are identical to the entry- and exit-point pseudostate symbols used in the referenced state machine. Note that only those connection points that need to be attached to transition edges need be shown on the diagram. Figure 11.14 shows the

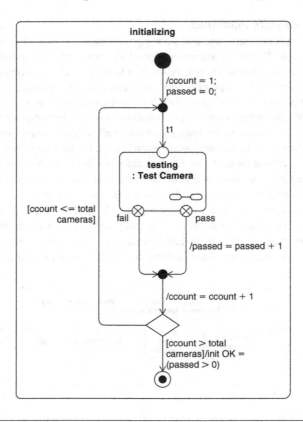

FIGURE 11.14

Invoking a substate machine.

initializing state of the *Surveillance System*. On entry, *ccount* (a property of the owning block that counts the number of cameras tested) and *passed* (a property that counts the number of cameras that passed their self-test) are initialized to 1 and 0, respectively. A junction pseudostate follows, which allows the algorithm to test as many cameras as required. To test each camera, the *testing* state uses the *Test Camera* state machine. The transition leaving the *pass* exit-point pseudostate has an effect that adds one to the *passed* variable; the transition leaving its *fail* exit-point pseudostate does not. Both transitions end in a junction whose outgoing transition increments the count of cameras tested. This transition ends on a choice, with one outgoing transition looping back to test another camera if *[ccount < = total cameras]* and the other reaching the final state of *initializing*. On the transition to the final state, the effect of the transition sets the *init OK* variable to true if at least one camera passed its self-test or false otherwise.

As stated earlier, entry- and exit-point pseudostates form part of a compound transition that, in the case of submachine states, incorporates transitions (and their triggers, guards, and effects) from both containing and referenced state machines. Looking at both Figure 11.13 and Figure 11.14, the compound transition from the initial pseudostate of state *initializing* will be as follows:

1. Initial pseudostate of the (single) region owned by state *initializing*
2. Transition labeled with effect *ccount = 1; passed = 0*
3. Transition named *t1*
4. Transition with effect *failures = 0*
5. Transition with guard *[else]* (at least this time)
6. (Graphical) transition with effect send *Test Camera* signal with argument *ccount*
7. State await test result.

Entry- and exit-point pseudostates on composite states

Entry-point and exit-point pseudostates can be used on the boundaries of composite states as well as a state machine. If the composite state has a single region, they behave like junctions. If the composite state has multiple regions, they behave like forks in the case of entry-point pseudostates and joins in the case of exit-point pseudostates. For entry-point pseudostates, the effects of their outgoing transitions execute after the entry behavior of the composite state. For exit-point pseudostates, their incoming transitions execute before the composite state's exit behavior. An example of entry-point and exit-point pseudodstates can be seen in Figure 11.12

11.7 CONTRASTING DISCRETE AND CONTINUOUS STATES

The examples shown so far in this chapter have been based on discrete semantics, specifically state machines in which the triggering event is a specific stimulus (i.e., a signal, an operation call, or the expiration of a timer). SysML state machines can also be used to describe systems with transitions that are driven by the values of either discrete or continuous properties. Such transitions are triggered by change events.

A trigger on a transition may be associated with a **change event** whose change expression states the conditions, typically in terms of the values of properties, which will cause the event to occur and hence trigger the transition. The change expression has a body containing the expression and an indication of the language used, which allows a wide variety of possible expressions.

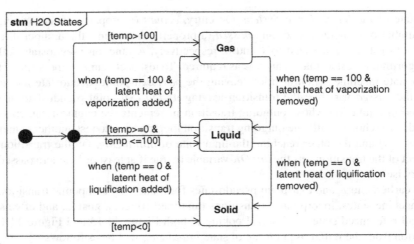

FIGURE 11.15

State machine for H_2O.

The state machine H_2O *States,* shown in Figure 11.15, defines the transitions between *Solid, Liquid,* and *Gas* states. These represent discrete states of H_2O, while the values of its properties, such as temperature and pressure, represent continuous state variables. Specific values for the variable *temp,* plus other conditions (e.g., the withdrawal or addition of energy), define the expressions for the change events and guards on the transitions. Implicitly, therefore, the values of its state variables are used to determine the discrete states of H_2O and the transitions between those states. Similarly, the discrete state of other continuous systems can be defined in terms of values of selected continuous properties of the system.

11.8 SUMMARY

A state machine is used to describe the behavior of a block in terms of its states and the transitions between them. State machines can be composed hierarchically like other SysML behavioral constructs, enabling arbitrarily complex representations of state-based behavior.

The significant state machine concepts covered in this chapter include the following:

- A state machine describes a potentially reusable definition of the state-dependent behavior of a block. Each state machine diagram describes a single state machine.
- Each state machine contains at least one region, which itself can contain a number of states and pseudostates, as well as the transitions between them. During execution of a state machine, each of its regions has a single active state that determines the transitions that are currently viable in that region. A region can have an initial pseudostate and final state that correspond to its beginning and completion, respectively.
- A state is an abstraction of some significant condition in the life of a block and specifies the effect of entering and leaving that condition and what the block does while it is in that condition using behaviors such as activities.

- Transitions describe valid state changes and under what circumstances those changes will happen. A transition has one or more triggers, a guard, and an effect. A trigger is associated with an event, which may correspond either to the reception of a signal (signal event) or operation call (call event) by the owning block; the expiration of a timer (time event); or the satisfaction of a condition specified in terms of properties of the block and its environment (change event). A transition can also be triggered by a completion event that occurs when the currently active state has completed.
- A guard expresses any additional constraints that need to be satisfied if the transition is to be triggered. If a valid event occurs, the guard is evaluated and, if true, the transition is triggered. Otherwise the event is consumed with no change in state. A transition can include a transition effect that is described by a behavior such as an activity. If the transition is triggered, the transition effect is executed.
- A state may specify that certain events can be deferred, in which case they are only consumed if they trigger a transition. Deferred events are consumed on transition to a state that does not further defer them.
- In a number of circumstances, simple transitions between states are not sufficient to specify the required behavior. Junction and choice pseudostates allow several transitions to be combined into a compound transition. Although the compound transition can include only one transition with triggers, it can have multiple transitions with guards and effects. Junction and choice pseudostates can have multiple incoming transitions and outgoing transitions. They are used to construct complex transitions that have more than one transition path, each potentially having its own guard and effect. History pseudostates allow a region to be interrupted and then subsequently to resume its previously active state or states.
- States may be composite with nested states in one or more regions. Just like state machines, during execution an active state will have one active substate per region. Composite states are porous; that is, transitions can cross their boundaries. Special pseudostates called fork and join pseudostates allow transitions to and from states in multiple regions at once. A given event may trigger transitions in multiple active regions.
- State machines may be reused via submachine states. Interactions with the reused state machine take place via transitions to and from the boundary of the corresponding submachine state, either directly or through entry- and exit-point pseudostates.
- Change events are driven by the values of variables of the state machine or properties of its owning block. In addition to discrete systems, change events can trigger transitions in continuous systems, in which transitions between the system's discrete states are triggered by changes in the values of continuous state variables. In this case, a behavior is a constraint on one or more state variables that must be true within a given state.

11.9 QUESTIONS

1. What is the diagram kind for a state machine diagram?
2. Which kinds of model element may a state machine region contain?
3. What is the difference between a state and a pseudostate?
4. A state machine has two states, "S1" and "S2." How do you show that the initial state for this machine is "S1"?

5. What is the difference between a final state and a terminate pseudostate?
6. A state has three behaviors associated with it. What are they called and when are they invoked?
7. What are the three components of a transition?
8. Under what circumstances does a completion event get generated for a state with a single region?
9. What is the difference in behavior between an internal transition and an external transition with the same source and target state?
10. What would the transition string for a transition look like if triggered by a signal event for signal "S1" with guard "a > 1" and an effect "a = a + 1"?
11. Draw the same transition using the graphical notation for transitions.
12. Where and how is a deferred event represented?
13. What is the difference between a junction and a choice pseudostate?
14. If a state has several orthogonal regions, how are they displayed?
15. What is the difference between a shallow and deep history pseudostate?
16. How can a state machine be reused within another state machine?
17. How are entry- and exit-point pseudostates represented on a state machine?
18. Under what circumstances will a given change event occur?

DISCUSSION TOPIC

State machines describe the behavior of blocks, but so do activities (via the use of activity partitions). Discuss approaches to ensuring that the two descriptions of behavior are consistent when both are used to describe the behavior of the same block.

MODELING FUNCTIONALITY WITH USE CASES

This chapter describes how to model the high-level functionality of a system with use cases.

12.1 OVERVIEW

Use cases describe the functionality of a system in terms of how it is used to achieve the goals of its various users. The users of a system are described by actors, which may represent external systems or humans who interact with the system.

Actors can be classified using generalization. Use cases can also be classified using generalization, but in addition, one use case may include or extend other use cases. Actors are related to the use cases in which they participate. The relationships between the system under consideration, its actors, and its use cases are described on a use case diagram.

Use cases have been viewed as a mechanism to capture system requirements in terms of the uses of the system. SysML requirements can be used to capture text requirements more explicitly with relationships to use cases and other model elements (refer to Chapter 13 for a discussion on requirements). The steps in a use case description can also be captured as SysML requirements.

Different methodologies apply use cases in different ways [50]. For example, some methods require a use case description for each use case captured in text, which may include pre- and post-conditions, and primary, alternative, and exceptional flows. Use cases are generally elaborated with detailed descriptions of their behavior, using activities, interactions, and/or state machines.

12.2 USE CASE DIAGRAM

On a **use case diagram,** the frame corresponds to a package, model, model library, or block, and the content of the diagram describes a set of actors and use cases and the relationships between them. The complete diagram header for a use case diagram is as follows:

```
uc [model element kind] model element name [diagram name]
```

The diagram kind for a use case diagram is **uc**, and the *model element kind* is a package model, model library, or block.

Figure 12.1 shows an example of a use case diagram containing the key diagram elements, a system (i.e., subject), a use case, and some actors. The diagram shows the main use case for the *Surveillance System* and the participants in that use case. The notation for use case diagrams is shown in the Appendix, Table A.24.

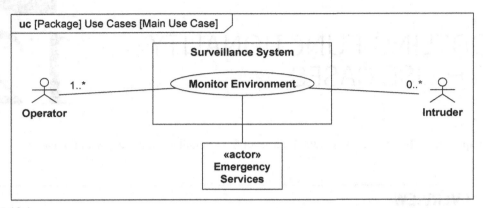

FIGURE 12.1

Example use case diagram.

12.3 USING ACTORS TO REPRESENT THE USERS OF A SYSTEM

An **actor** is used to represent the role of a human, an organization, or any external system that participates in the use of some system. Actors may interact directly with the system or indirectly through other actors.

It should be noted that "actor" is a relative term, because an actor who is external to one system may be internal to another. For example, assume individuals in an organization request services from an internal help desk department that provides IT support for the organization. The help desk is considered the system and the members of the organization who are requesting service are considered the actors. However, these same individuals may in turn be providing services to an external customer. In that context, the individuals who were previously considered actors relative to the help desk are considered part of the system relative to the external customer. A similar analogy can be drawn for a subsystem, when the subsystem can be viewed as external (i.e., an actor) to another subsystem but internal to the system.

Actors can be classified using the standard generalization relationship. Actor classification has a similar meaning to the classification of other classifiable model elements. For example, a specialized actor participates in all the use cases that the more general actor participates in.

An actor is shown either as a stick figure with the actor's name underneath or as a rectangle containing the actor's name below the keyword «actor». The choice of symbol is dependent on the tool and method being used. Actor classification is represented using the standard SysML generalization symbol—a line with a hollow triangle at the general end.

The *Use Cases* package for the *Surveillance System* contains descriptions of the system's actors. Five actors are shown in Figure 12.2. The actors include an *Operator* who operates the system and a *Supervisor* who manages the system. There is also an *Advanced Operator* whose role is a specialized version of the *Operator* because that role has additional specialized skills. Note that an *Intruder* is also modeled as an actor. Although strictly speaking not a user, an intruder does interact with the system and is an important part of the external environment to consider. Also of interest are the *Emergency Services* to whom incidents may need to be reported. This actor could have been modeled using an actor stick-figure symbol but wasn't because it is an organization composed of people, systems, and other equipment.

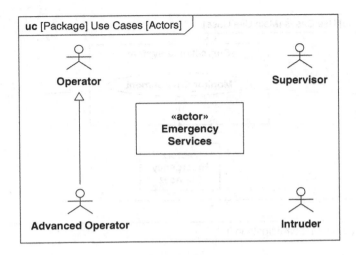

FIGURE 12.2

Representing actors and their interrelationships on a use case diagram.

12.3.1 FURTHER DESCRIPTIONS OF ACTORS

Although not defined in SysML, many methods suggest additional descriptive properties that can apply to actors as users of a system. Examples include the following:

- The organization of which the actor is a part (e.g., procurement);
- Physical location;
- Skill level required to use the system; and
- Clearance level required to access the system.

12.4 USING USE CASES TO DESCRIBE SYSTEM FUNCTIONALITY

A **use case** describes the goals of a system from the perspective of the users of the system. The goals are described in terms of functionality that the system must support. Typically, the use case description identifies the goal(s) of the use case, a main pattern of use, and a number of variant uses. The system that provides functionality in support of use cases is called the **system under consideration** and often represents a system that is being developed. The system under consideration is sometimes referred to as the **subject** and is represented by a block. We will use the term system or subject interchangeably to denote the system under consideration.

A use case may cover one or more **scenarios** that correspond to how the system interacts with its actors under different circumstances.

Actors are related to use cases by **communication paths,** which are represented as associations, with some restrictions. The association ends can have multiplicities, in which the multiplicity at the actor end describes the number of actors involved in each use case. The multiplicity at the use case end describes the number of instances of the use case in which the actor or actors can be involved at any one

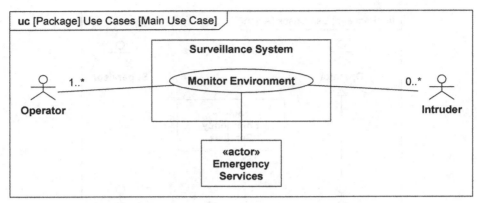

FIGURE 12.3

A use case and the actors that participate in it.

time. Composite associations in either direction are not permitted since actors are not part of use cases and use cases are not part of actors.

Neither actors nor use cases may own properties, so role names on associations do not represent reference properties as they might on block definition diagrams. The role name on an actor end can be used to describe the role an actor plays in the associated use case whenever it is not obvious from the actor's name. The role name on the use case end can be used to describe the relevance of the use case functionality to the associated actor.

A use case is shown as an oval with the use case name inside it. Associations between actors and use cases are shown using standard association notation. The default multiplicity of the association ends, if not shown, is "0..1." Associations cannot have arrowheads in use case diagrams because neither actors nor use cases may own properties. The subject of a set of use cases can be shown as a rectangle enclosing the use cases, with the subject's name centered at the top.

The use cases owned by a model element can be shown in a specific compartment labeled *owned use cases*.

Figure 12.3 shows the central use case of the *Surveillance System,* called *Monitor Environment.* The main actors associated with *Monitor Environment* are the system's *Operator,* the *Intruder,* and the *Emergency Services.* The multiplicities on the associations indicate that there must be at least one *Operator* and potentially many *Intruders.* The *Emergency Services* are also associated with the *Monitor Environment* use case, although they may not be active participants unless an *Intruder* is detected and reported.

12.4.1 USE CASE RELATIONSHIPS

Use cases can be related to one another by classification, inclusion, and extension.

Inclusion and extension

The **inclusion** relationship allows one use case, referred to as the **base use case,** to include the functionality of another use case, called the **included use case.** The included use case is always performed

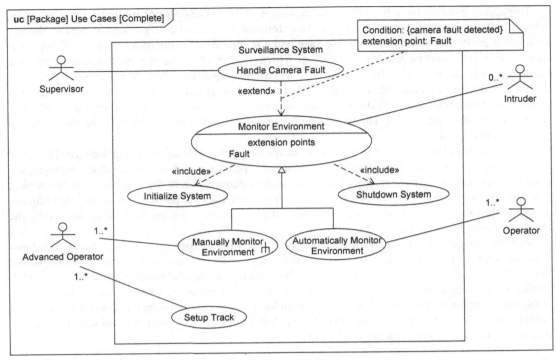

FIGURE 12.4

A set of use cases for the *Surveillance System.*

when the base use case is performed. A behavior that realizes the base use case often references the behavior of the included use case, as described in Section 12.5.

It is implicit in the definition of inclusion that any participants of a base use case may participate in an included use case, so an actor associated with a base use case need not be explicitly associated to any included use case. For example, as shown in Figure 12.4, the *Operator* implicitly takes part in *Initialize System* and *Shutdown System* through their association with *Monitor Environment.*

Included use cases are not intended to represent a functional decomposition of the base use case, but rather are intended to describe common functionality that may be included by other use cases. In a functional decomposition, the lower-level functions represent a complete decomposition of the higher-level function. By contrast, a base use case and its included use cases often describe different aspects of the required functionality. For example, in the case of *Monitor Environment* in Figure 12.4, the key monitoring function is described by the base use case, and additional functionality is described by the included use cases *Initialize System* and *Shutdown System.*

A use case can also extend a base use case using the **extension** relationship. The **extending use case** is a fragment of functionality that is not considered part of the base use case functionality. It often describes some exceptional behavior in the interaction, such as error handling between subject and actors that does not contribute directly to the goal of the base use case.

To support extensions, a base use case defines a set of **extension points** that represent places where the base use case can be extended. An extension point can be referenced as part of the use case description. For example, if the use case had a textual description of a sequence of steps, the extension point could be used to indicate at which step in the sequence an extending use case would be valid. An extension has to reference an extension point to indicate where in the base use case it can occur. The conditions under which an extension is valid can be further described by a constraint. The constraint is evaluated when the extension point is reached to determine whether the extending use case occurs. The presence of an extension point does not imply that there will be an extension related to it.

Unlike an included use case, the base use case does not depend on an extending use case. However, an extending use case may be dependent on what is happening in its base use case; for example, the extending use case may assume that some exceptional circumstance in the base use case has arisen. There is no implication that an actor associated with the base use case participates in the extending use case, and the extended use case in fact may have entirely different participants, as demonstrated by the use case *Handle Camera Fault* in Figure 12.4.

Inclusion and extension are shown using dashed lines with an open arrowhead at the included and extended ends, respectively. An inclusion line has the keyword «include» and an extension line has the keyword «extend». The direction of the arrows should be read as tail end includes or extends head end. Thus, a base use case includes an included use case, and an extending use case extends a base use case. A use case may have an additional compartment under its name compartment that lists all its extension points. The extension line can have an attached note that names its extension point and shows the condition under which the extending use case occurs.

Classification

Use cases can be classified using the standard SysML generalization relationship. The meaning of classification is similar to that for other classifiable model elements. One implication, for example, is that the scenarios for the general use case are also scenarios of the specialized use case. It also means that the actors associated with a specialized use case can also participate in scenarios described by a general use case. Classification of use cases is shown using the standard SysML generalization symbol.

Figure 12.4 shows a use case diagram containing the complete set of use cases for the *Surveillance System*. As part of *Monitor Environment,* all *Operators* are allowed to oversee the automatic tracking of suspicious movements in the *Automatically Monitor Environment* use case —that is, when the system controls the cameras. This allows the security company to use junior or less highly trained employees for this purpose. *Advanced Operators* can participate in the *Manually Monitor Environment* use case, when they control the cameras manually using a joystick. *Advanced Operators* also have the option to set up surveillance tracks for the cameras to follow.

The complete specification for *Monitor Environment* also includes system initialization and shutdown as indicated by the include relationships between *Monitor Environment* and *Initialize System* and *Shutdown System*.

The *Fault* extension point represents a place in the *Monitor Environment* use case where camera fault might be handled. The *Handle Camera Fault* use case extends *Monitor Environment* at the *Fault* extension point. It is an exceptional task that will only be triggered when camera faults are detected, as indicated by its associated condition, and may only be performed by the *Supervisor.*

12.4.2 USE CASE DESCRIPTIONS

A text-based **use case description** can be used to provide additional information to support the use case definition. This description can contribute significantly to the use case's value. The description text can be captured in the model as a single or multiple comments. It is also possible to treat each step in a use case description as a SysML requirement. A typical use case description may include the following:

- *Pre-conditions*—the conditions that must hold for the use case to begin.
- *Post-conditions*—the conditions that must hold once the use case has completed.
- *Primary flow*—the most frequent scenario or scenarios of the use case.
- *Alternate and/or exception flows*—the scenarios that are less frequent or other than nominal. The exception flows may reference extension points and generally represent flows that are not directly in support of the goals of the primary flow.

Other information may augment the basic use case description to further elaborate the interaction between the actors and the subject.

Here is an extract from the use case description for *Monitor Environment*:

Pre-condition

The *Surveillance System* is powered down.

Primary Flow

The *Operator* or *Operators* will use the *Surveillance System* to monitor the environment of the facility under surveillance. An *Operator* will initialize the system (see *Initialize System*) before operation and shut the system down (see *Shutdown System*). During normal operation, the system's cameras will automatically follow preset routes that have been set to optimize the likelihood of detection.

If an *Intruder* is detected, an alarm will be raised both internally and with a central monitoring station, whose responsibility it is to summon any required assistance. If available, an intelligent intruder tracking system—which will override the standard camera search paths—will be engaged at this point to track the suspected intruder. If an intelligent intruder tracking system is not available, the *Operators* are expected to maintain visual track of the suspected intruder and pass this knowledge on to the *Emergency Services* if and when they arrive.

Alternate Flow

Immediately after system initialization but before normal operation begins, it is possible that a fault will arise, in which case it can be handled (c.f. *Fault* extension point), but faults will not be handled thereafter.

Post-condition

The *Surveillance System* is powered down.

12.5 ELABORATING USE CASES WITH BEHAVIORS

The textual definition for a use case, together with the use case models described previously, can describe the functionality of a system. If desired, however, a more detailed definition of the use case may be modeled with interactions, activities, and/or state machines, which are described in Chapters 9 through 11. These are typically added to elaborate the requirements and the design after the use case definition has been reviewed and accepted. The choice of behavioral formalism is often a personal or project preference, but in general:

- Interactions are useful when a scenario is largely message-based.
- Activities are useful when the scenario includes considerable control logic, flow of inputs and outputs, and/or algorithms that transform data.
- State machines are useful when the interaction between the actors and the subject is asynchronous and not easily represented by an ordered sequence of events.

A modeler may choose to indicate on a particular use case symbol whether the behavior of that use case is further described by one of the behavior diagrams listed above. If the use case has an associated behavior diagram, then the symbol for that use case contains a rake symbol in its bottom right corner. The use case *Manually Monitor Environment* in Figure 12.4 has a rake symbol, indicating that it is further elaborated, in this case by the diagrams in Figures 12.6 and 12.7.

12.5.1 CONTEXT DIAGRAMS

When using interactions or activities, the lifelines and partitions represent participants in the use case. It is useful to create an internal block diagram where the enclosing frame corresponds to the **system context** and the subject and participating actors correspond to parts in the system context internal block diagram. To support this technique, actors can appear on a block definition diagram, and a part on an internal block diagram can be typed by the actor. Alternatively, the actors can be allocated to blocks using the allocate relationship described in Chapter 14, and then the parts representing actors can be typed by the block.

Figure 12.5 shows an internal block diagram that describes the internal structure of the block *System Context,* which represents the context for the *Surveillance System* and its associated use cases. The system under consideration, *Surveillance System,* is represented as part of the *System Context,* called *company security system.* Two of the actors, *Advanced Operator* and *Intruder,* who participate in the use cases, are also represented as parts *security guard* and *suspected thief,* respectively.

12.5.2 SEQUENCE DIAGRAMS

In addition to being described in a use case description, a use case can be elaborated by one or more interactions described by sequence diagrams. Different interactions may correspond to the (base) use case, any included use cases, and any extending use cases. The block that owns the interactions must have parts that correspond to the subject and participants, which can then be represented by lifelines in the interactions.

As stated earlier, an included use case must always occur as part of its base use case. As a result, an interaction describing an included scenario will typically be a mandatory part of the interaction representing a base scenario. This is typically indicated within the base scenario interaction, by referencing the interaction for the included scenario within a combined fragment with an operator such as seq, strict, or loop.

Strictly speaking, an interaction representing a base use case should be specified without reference to extending use cases, simply noting the extension points. However, a popular approach is to reference extending use cases as optional constructs in the interaction representing the base scenario. In this approach, an interaction corresponding to an extending use case is typically contained in an operand of

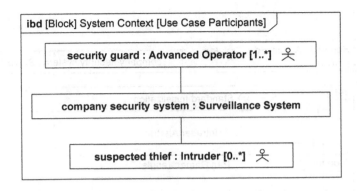

FIGURE 12.5

Context for use case scenarios.

a conditional operator, such as `break`, `opt`, or `alt`. The operand should be guarded using the constraint on the extension, if one is specified.

The block *System Context,* whose internal block diagram was shown in Figure 12.5, owns a number of interactions. The interaction describing the primary scenario of the *Manually Monitor Environment* use case, *Handling Alert,* is shown in Figure 12.6. In Figure 12.4, the *Manually Monitor Environment* use case included the *Initialize System* use case and the *Shutdown System* use case. The *Handling Alert* interaction includes corresponding uses of the interaction *Standard Initialization,* which is a scenario for the *Initialize System* use case, and the interaction *Standard System Shutdown,* which is a scenario for the *Shutdown System* use case.

In between these two interactions, the scenario describes how the security guard, *Honoria,* deals with an intruder alert. Because she is an *Advanced Operator,* she will manually control the cameras to track the suspected intruder. Interactions for the use case *Automatically Monitor Environment*, shown in Figure 12.4, do not include manual control of the cameras.

12.5.3 ACTIVITY DIAGRAMS

As mentioned previously, a use case scenario can also be described by an activity diagram, in which case the participants are represented as activity partitions. As with interactions, an activity can elaborate a base use case, included use cases, and extending use cases.

Figure 12.7 shows an alternate description of how manual tracking of suspected intruders is handled for the *Manually Monitor Environment* use case. Two activity partitions, representing the *security guard* and the *company security system,* are used to indicate which use case participant takes responsibility for which actions.

New intruder intelligence is analyzed. The control flow initiated by the reception of the intelligence is forked to address two concerns. If the intruder has moved, then a *Move Joystick* action is performed to follow the intruder. If the intruder appears to have moved out of range of the current camera, a *Select Camera* action is performed to select a more appropriate camera. In both cases, a flow final node is used to handle situations when no action is required. Meanwhile, this stream of

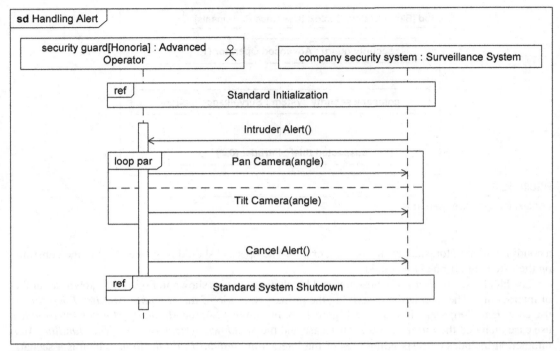

FIGURE 12.6

Scenario for a use case described by a sequence diagram.

inputs is turned into *Pan Camera* and *Tilt Camera* messages to the appropriate camera by the *Issue Camera Commands* action.

12.5.4 STATE MACHINE DIAGRAMS

State machines can also be used to describe scenarios. Some methods encourage the use of a single state machine to represent all possible scenarios of the use case, including exception cases, while other methods recommend that a separate state machine be used for each scenario. Note that when using a state machine, there are no language constructs that can be used to explicitly identify the parties responsible for taking actions. However, separate state machines may be defined for each participant, including the system of interest and the actors.

Figure 12.8 shows part of a state machine describing the *Manually Monitor Environment* use case. It shows three states: *operator idle, intruder present,* and *automatic tracking enabled.* When in the *operator idle* state, an *Intruder Alert* event causes the *Raise Alarm* message to be sent and a transition

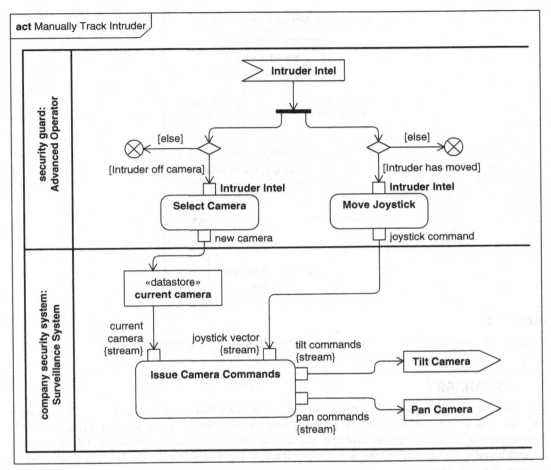

FIGURE 12.7

Using an activity to describe a scenario.

made to the *intruder present* state. Once in the *intruder present* state, the intruder can be manually tracked, but an *Auto Track* event will trigger a transition to *automatic tracking enabled* and prohibit manual tracking until a *Lost Track* event happens. In this way, a single state machine can represent multiple scenarios.

This description shares many of the signals with Figure 12.6, but it focuses on states rather than messages.

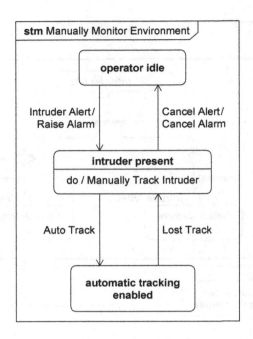

FIGURE 12.8

Using a state machine to describe the *Manually Monitor Environment* use case.

12.6 SUMMARY

Use cases are used to capture the functionality of a system needed to achieve user goals. A use case is often used as a means to describe the required functionality for a system and can augment SysML requirements to refine the definition of text-based functional requirements. The way in which use cases are employed is highly dependent on the method used. The following are the key use case concepts introduced in this chapter:

- A use case describes a particular use of a system to achieve a desired user goal. Use case relationships for inclusion, extension, and classification are useful for factoring out common functionality into use cases that can be reused by other use cases. An included use case is always performed as part of the base use case. A use case that extends the base use case is usually performed by exception and generally is not in direct support of the goals of the base use case.
- The system under consideration (also known as the subject) provides the functionality required by actors, expressed as use cases.
- Actors describe a role played by an entity external to the system and may represent humans, organizations, or external systems. Generalizations may be used to represent the classification relationships between different categories of actors. Associations relate actors to the use cases in which they participate.
- The functionality described by a use case is often elaborated in more detail using interactions, activities, and state machines. The selection of which behavioral formalisms are used and how they are used is often dependent on the particular method.

12.7 **QUESTIONS**

1. What is the diagram kind for a use case diagram, and to which model elements can the frame correspond?
2. What does an actor represent?
3. How are actors represented on a use case diagram?
4. If one actor specializes another, what does that imply?
5. What does a use case represent?
6. What is another term for the system under consideration?
7. How does a scenario differ from a use case?
8. How is an inclusion relationship represented?
9. Apart from a base and extending use case, which two other pieces of information might an extension relationship include?
10. If one use case specializes another, what does that imply about its scenarios?
11. How may use case participants and the system under consideration be represented on an internal block diagram?
12. How are use case participants and the system under consideration represented in interactions?
13. How are use case participants and the system under consideration represented in activities?

DISCUSSION TOPICS

Apart from those listed in Section 12.3.1 discuss two additional descriptive properties that would be useful for describing actors.

Apart from those listed in Section 12.4.2 discuss two additional descriptive properties that would be useful for describing use cases.

MODELING TEXT-BASED REQUIREMENTS AND THEIR RELATIONSHIP TO DESIGN

13

This chapter describes how text-based requirements are captured in the model and related to other model elements.

13.1 OVERVIEW

As stated in the SysML specification [1], a **requirement** specifies a capability or condition that must (or should) be satisfied, a function that a system must perform, or a performance condition a system must achieve.

Requirements come from many sources. Sometimes requirements are provided directly by the person or organization paying for the system, such as a customer who hires a contractor to build a house. At other times, requirements are generated by the organization that is developing the system, such as an automobile manufacturer that must determine consumer preferences for its product. The source of requirements often reflects multiple stakeholders. In the case of the automobile manufacturer, the requirements include government regulations for emissions control and safety in addition to the direct preferences of the consumers.

Irrespective of the source, it is common practice to group similar requirements for a system, element, or component into a **specification**. The individual requirements should be expressed in clear and unambiguous terms, sufficient for the developing organization to implement a system that meets stakeholder needs. The classic systems engineering challenge is to ensure that these requirements are consistent (i.e., not contradictory), feasible (i.e., solutions are within the realm of possibility), sufficiently complete and validated to reflect real stakeholder needs, and verified to ensure that the system design and its realization actually satisfy them.

Requirements management tools are widely used to manage both requirements and the relationships between them. Requirements are often maintained in a database. SysML includes a requirements modeling capability to provide a bridge between the text-based requirements that may be maintained in a requirements management tool and the system model. A combination of tool automation, the requirements management process, and configuration management processes are used to synchronize the requirements between the requirements management tool and the model. This capability is intended to significantly improve requirements management throughout the lifecycle of a system by enabling rigorous traceability between the text-based requirements and the model elements that represent the system design, analysis, implementation, and test cases.

Individual or groups of text requirements may be brought into the system modeling tool from a requirements management tool or from a text specification. Requirements may also be created directly in the system modeling tool. The specifications are typically organized in the model into a hierarchical package structure that corresponds to a specification tree. Each specification contains multiple requirements, such as a systems specification that contains the requirements for the system, or the component specifications that contain the requirements for each component. The requirements contained in each specification are often modeled in a tree structure that corresponds to the organizational structure of the text-based specification. The individual or aggregate requirements within the containment hierarchy can then be linked to other requirements in other specifications and to model elements that represent the system design, analysis, implementation, and test cases.

SysML includes requirements relationships for derivation, satisfaction, verification, refinement, and trace that support a robust capability for relating requirements to one another and to other model elements. In addition to capturing the requirements and their relationships, SysML includes the capability to capture the rationale or basis for a particular decision, and for linking the rationale to any model element. This includes linking the rationale to a requirement or to a relationship between the requirement and other model elements. A copy relationship is also provided to accommodate appropriate reuse of requirement text.

Each individual text requirement can be captured in the model as a SysML requirement. The requirement construct includes a name, a text string, and an id, and may also include additional user defined properties such as risk.

SysML provides multiple ways to capture requirements and their relationships in both graphical and tabular notations. A requirement diagram can be used to represent many of these relationships. In addition, compact graphical notations are available to depict the requirements relationships on any other SysML diagrams. SysML also supports tabular views of the requirements and their relationships. The browser view of the requirements that is generally provided by the tool implementer also provides an important mechanism for visualizing requirements and their relationships.

Use cases are used to support requirements analysis in many of the model-based approaches using UML and SysML. Different model-based methods may choose to leverage use cases in conjunction with SysML requirements. Use cases are typically effective for capturing the functional requirements but are not as well suited for capturing other requirements, such as physical requirements (e.g., weight, size, vibration), availability requirements, or other nonfunctional requirements. The incorporation of text-based requirements into SysML effectively accommodates a broad range of requirements.

Use cases—like any other model element—can be related to requirements using the requirement relationships (e.g., the refine relationship). In addition, use cases are often accompanied by a use case description (see Chapter 12, Section 12.4.2). The steps in the use case description can be captured as individual text requirements and then related to other model elements to provide more granular traceability between the use cases and the model.

13.2 REQUIREMENT DIAGRAM

Requirements captured in SysML can be depicted on a **requirement diagram,** which is particularly useful in graphically depicting hierarchies of specifications or requirements. Because this diagram can depict large numbers of relationships for a single requirement, it is useful in representing the traceability of a single requirement to examine how that requirement is satisfied, verified, and refined, and to examine its derived relationships with other requirements. The requirement diagram header is depicted as follows:

```
req [model element kind] model element name [diagram name]
```

The requirement diagram can represent a package or a requirement, as designated by the *model element kind* in square brackets. The *model element name* is the name of the package or requirement that sets the context for the diagram, and the *diagram name* is user defined and often describes the purpose of the diagram. Figure 13.1 presents an example of a requirement diagram that contains some of the most common symbols.

This example highlights a number of different requirements relationships and alternative notations. For example, *Camera* satisfies the requirement called *Sensor Decision.* In addition to the *satisfy* relationship, the figure also includes examples of *containment,* the *deriveReqt,* and the *verify* relationship. The relationships are depicted using a combination of the direct notation, compartment notation, and callout notation. Only one of these notations is typically used for a particular relationship. The relationships and notation options are discussed later in this chapter. Tables A.25 through A.27 in the Appendix contain a complete description of the SysML notation for requirements.

A requirement can be shown directly on block definition diagrams, package diagrams, and use case diagrams, along with its relationships to other model elements on the diagram. However, a requirement cannot be shown directly on other diagram kinds, such as internal block diagrams. For

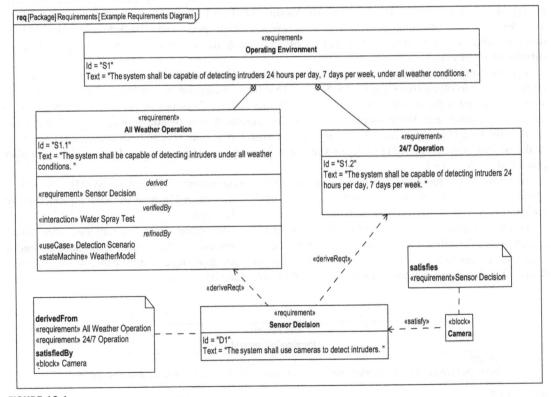

FIGURE 13.1

Generic example of a requirement diagram.

all diagram kinds, the relationships between a requirement and the other model elements can be represented using compartment and/or callout notations (see Sections 13.5.2 and 13.5.3 for examples). Alternative ways to view requirements are discussed in Section 13.7 (tabular views) and Section 13.9.1 (browser view).

13.3 REPRESENTING A TEXT REQUIREMENT IN THE MODEL

A **requirement** that is captured in text is represented in SysML as a «requirement». Each requirement includes predefined properties for a unique identifier and for a text string. Once captured, it can be related to other requirements and to other model elements through a specific set of relationships.

Figure 13.2 is an example of a text-based requirement called *Operating Environment* as represented in SysML. It is distinguished by the keyword «requirement» and contains—at a minimum—a name and properties for *id* and *text*. This same information can be displayed in a tabular format that is described later in this chapter.

Requirements can be customized by adding properties such as verification method, verification status, criticality, risk, and requirements category. The verifyMethod property, for example, may be typed by an enumeration called VerifiyMethodKind and include values such as inspection, analysis, demonstration, and test. A risk or criticality property may include the values high, medium, and low. A requirements category property may include values such as functional, performance, or physical.

An alternative method for creating requirements categories is to define additional subclasses of the requirement stereotype (see Chapter 15, Section 15.4 for a discussion of subclassing stereotypes). The stereotype enables the modeler to add constraints that restrict the types of model elements that can satisfy the requirement. For example, a functional requirement may be constrained so that it can only be satisfied by a behavioral model element such as an activity, state machine, or interaction. Annex E of the SysML specification [1] includes some non-normative requirement subclasses, which are also presented in Table 13.1.

As shown in the table, each category is represented as a stereotype of the generic SysML «requirement». Table 13.1 also includes a brief description of the category. Additional stereotype properties or constraints can be added as deemed appropriate for the application.

Other examples of requirements categories may include operational requirements, specialized requirements for reliability and maintainability, requirements for stores, control requirements, and a high-level category for stakeholder needs. Some guidance for applying a requirements profile follows. (General guidance on defining a profile is included in Chapter 15, Section 15.4.)

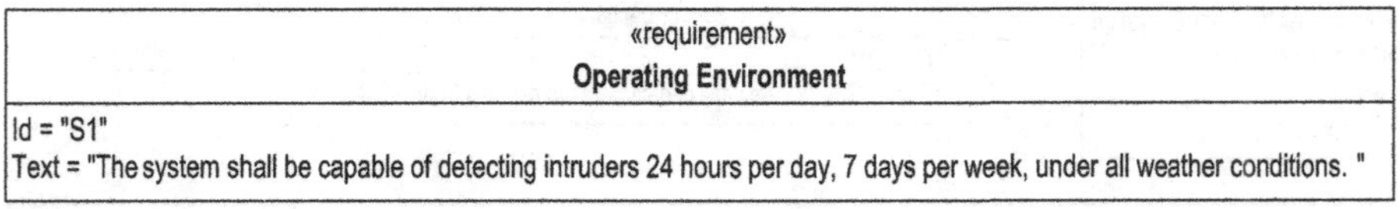

«requirement»
Operating Environment
Id = "S1"   Text = "The system shall be capable of detecting intruders 24 hours per day, 7 days per week, under all weather conditions. "

FIGURE 13.2

Example of a requirement as depicted in SysML.

Table 13.1 Optional Requirements Stereotypes from SysML 1.4 Annex E.3.2

Stereotype	Base Class	Properties	Constraints	Description
«extendedRequirement»	«requirement»	source: String risk: RiskKind verifyMethod: VerifyMethodKind	N/A	A mix-in stereotype that contains generally useful attributes for requirements.
«functionalRequirement»	«extendedrequirement»	N/A	Satisfied by an operation or behavior.	Requirement that specifies an operation or behavior that a system or part of a system must perform.
«interfaceRequirement»	«extendedrequirement»	N/A	Satisfied by a port, connector, item flow, and/or constraint property.	Requirement that specifies the ports for connecting systems and system parts and that optionally may include the item flows across the connector and/or interface constraints.
«performanceRequirement»	«extendedrequirement»	N/A	Satisfied by a value property.	Requirement that quantitatively measures the extent to which a system or a system part satisfies a required capability or condition.
«physicalRequirement»	«extendedrequirement»	N/A	Satisfied by a structural element.	Requirement that specifies physical characteristics and/or physical constraints of the system, or a system part.
«designConstraint»	«extendedrequirement»	N/A	Satisfied by a block or a part.	Requirement that specifies a constraint on the implementation of the system or system part, such as "the system must use a commercial off-the-shelf component."

- The categories should be adapted for specific applications or organizations and reflected in the profile. This includes agreement on the categories and their associated descriptions, stereotype properties, and constraints. Additional requirements categories can be added by further sub-classing the stereotypes presented in Table 13.1 or creating additional stereotypes at the peer level.
- Apply the more specialized requirement stereotype (e.g., functional, interface, performance, physical, design constraint) as applicable and ensure consistency with the description, stereotype properties, and constraints of these requirements.
- A specific text requirement can include the application of more than one requirement category, in which case each stereotype should be shown in a comma-separated list within guillemets (« »).

13.4 TYPES OF REQUIREMENTS RELATIONSHIPS

SysML includes specific relationships to relate requirements to other requirements as well as to other model elements. These include relationships for defining a requirements hierarchy, deriving requirements, satisfying requirements, verifying requirements, refining requirements, and copying requirements, as well as a general purpose trace relationship.

Table 13.2 summarizes the specific relationships, which are discussed later in this chapter. The *derive*, and *copy* relationships can only relate one requirement to another. The *satisfy, verify, refine*, and *trace* relationships can relate requirements to other model elements. *Containment* can be used to relate a requirement to another requirement or to another namespace like a block or a package.

When relating a requirement to a nested property, the specific path to the nested property should be used to avoid ambiguity if more than one path exists. This is described in more detail as it applies to the allocate relationship in Chapter 14, Section 14.10.

Table 13.2 Requirement Relationships and Compartment Notation			
Relationship Name	**Keyword Depicted on Relation**	**Supplier (arrow) End Callout/Compartment**	**Client (no arrow) End Callout/Compartment**
Satisfy	«satisfy»	Satisfied by «model element»	Satisfies «requirement»
Verify	«verify»	Verified by «model element»	Verifies «requirement»
Refine	«refine»	Refined by «model element»	Refines «requirement»
Derive Requirement	«deriveReqt»	Derived «requirement»	Derived from «requirement»
Copy	«copy»	(No callout)	Master «requirement»
Trace	«trace»	Traced «model element»	Traced from «requirement»
Containment (Requirement decomposition)	(Crosshair icon)	(No callout)	(No callout)

13.5 REPRESENTING CROSS-CUTTING RELATIONSHIPS IN SYSML DIAGRAMS

Relationships between requirements and other model elements can appear on various diagram kinds. These relationships can be shown directly if the requirement and related model elements are on the same diagram. If the related model elements do not appear on the same diagram as the requirements, they can still be shown by using the compartment or callout notation. The direct notation may be used, for example, to show a derive requirement relationship between two requirements on a requirement diagram. The compartment or callout notation can be used to relate a requirement to another model element without requiring both the requirement and the other model element to appear on the same diagram. An example is a block on a block definition diagram that uses its compartment to show a satisfy relationship to a requirement that is not displayed on the same block definition diagram.

In addition to these graphical representations, SysML provides a flexible tabular notation for representing requirements and their relationships. Note that the allocation relationship (described in Chapter 14) is represented using the same notational approaches that are described here.

13.5.1 DEPICTING REQUIREMENTS RELATIONSHIPS DIRECTLY

When the requirement and the model element to which it relates are shown on the same diagram, their relationship may be depicted directly. **Direct notation** depicts this relationship as a dashed arrow with the name of the relationship displayed as a keyword (e.g., «satisfy», «verify», «refine», «deriveReqt», «copy», and «trace»).

Figure 13.3 presents an example of a «satisfy» relationship between a *Camera* and a requirement, *Sensor Decision,* where the camera is part of the design that is asserted to satisfy the requirement. Note that the arrow points from the block to the requirement.

It is important to recognize the significance of the arrow direction. Since most requirement relationships in SysML are based on the UML dependency relationship, the arrow points from the dependent model element (called the client) to the independent model element (called the supplier). The general dependency relationship is described in Chapter 6 Section 6.8. The interpretation of this «satisfy» relationship is that the camera design is dependent on the requirement, meaning that if the requirement changes, the impact on the design must be assessed. Similarly, a derived requirement will be dependent on the source requirement that it is derived from. In SysML, the arrow direction is opposite of what has typically been used for requirements flow-down where the higher-level requirement points to the lower-level requirement.

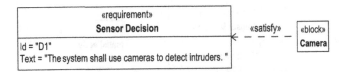

FIGURE 13.3

Example of direct notation depicting a satisfy relationship.

13.5.2 DEPICTING REQUIREMENTS RELATIONSHIPS USING COMPARTMENT NOTATION

Compartment notation is an alternative method for displaying a requirement relationship between a requirement and another model element that supports compartments, such as a block, part, or another requirement. This is a compact notation that can be used instead of displaying a direct relationship. It also can be used for diagrams that preclude display of a requirement directly, such as an internal block diagram. In Figure 13.4, the compartment notation is used to show the same satisfy relationship as the requirement from Figure 13.3. This should be interpreted as "the requirement *Sensor Decision* is satisfied by the *Camera.*" The compartment notation explicitly displays the relationship and direction (*satisfiedBy*), the model element kind (*«block»*), and the model element name (*Camera*).

Note that the description of the requirement compartment notation in the SysML specification [1] has been unclear and ambiguous, so many SysML tools do not implement it as described here. This will be corrected in a future version of the SysML specification.

13.5.3 DEPICTING REQUIREMENTS RELATIONSHIPS USING CALLOUT NOTATION

Callout notation is another notation for depicting requirements relationships. It is the least restrictive notation in that it can be used to represent a relationship between any requirement and any other model element on any diagram kind. This includes relationships between requirements and model elements such as pins, ports, and connectors that do not support compartments and therefore cannot use the compartment notation.

A **callout** is depicted as a note symbol graphically connected to a model element. The callout symbol references the model element at the other end of the relationship. The callout notation depicted in Figure 13.5 presents the same information as the compartment notation in Figure 13.4, and it should be interpreted as "the requirement *Sensor Decision* is satisfied by the *Camera.*"

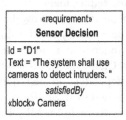

FIGURE 13.4

Example of compartment notation depicting a satisfy relationship.

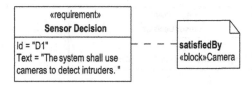

FIGURE 13.5

Example of callout notation depicting a satisfy relationship.

13.6 DEPICTING RATIONALE FOR REQUIREMENTS RELATIONSHIPS

A **rationale** is a SysML model element that can be associated with a requirement, a requirement relationship, or any other model element. As the name implies, a rationale is intended to capture the reason for a particular decision. Although a rationale is described here for requirements, it can be applied throughout the model to capture the basis for any type of decision. Rationale is based on Comment, which is discussed in Chapter 5, Section 5.5.1.

As presented in Figure 13.6, the rationale is expressed using a note symbol with the keyword «rationale». The text in the note symbol can either provide the rationale directly or reference an external document (e.g., a trade study or analysis report) or another part of the model such as a parametric diagram. The reference may include a hyperlink, although this is not explicit in the language. This particular example shows a reference to a trade study, *T.1*. The context for this particular rationale is presented in Figure 13.14 later in this chapter.

A **problem** is a model element similar to a rationale but used to flag design issues in the model. It can be associated with any model element and is expressed using a note symbol with the keyword «problem».

A rationale or problem can be attached to any requirements relationship or to the requirement. For example, a rationale or problem can be attached to a satisfy relationship and refer to an analysis report or trade study that justifies the assertion or raises the issue of whether a particular design satisfies the requirement. Similarly, the rationale can be used with other relationships, such as the derive relationship.

13.7 DEPICTING REQUIREMENTS AND THEIR RELATIONSHIPS IN TABLES

The requirement diagram has a distinct disadvantage when viewing large numbers of requirements. Large amounts of real estate are needed to depict and relate all the requirements needed to specify a system of even moderate complexity. The traditional method of viewing requirements in tables is a more compact representation than viewing them in a diagram. Modern requirements management tools typically maintain requirements in a database, and the results of queries to the database can be displayed clearly and succinctly in tables or matrices. SysML embraces the concept of displaying results of model queries in tables as well as using tables as a data input mechanism, but the specifics of generating tables is left to the tool implementer.

Figure 13.7 provides an example of a simple **requirements table** of the same requirements that were presented in Figure 13.1. In this example, the table lists the requirements in the *System*

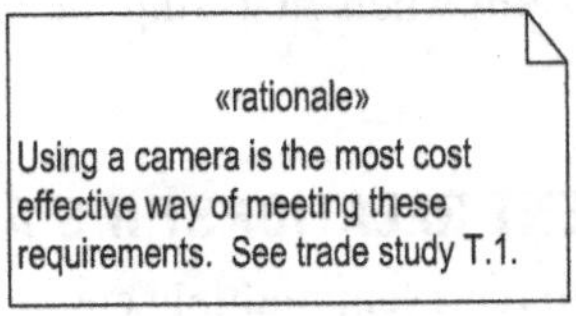

FIGURE 13.6

Example of rationale as depicted on any SysML diagram.

table [Package] System Specification [Decomposition of Top-level Requirements]		
id	name	text
S1	Operating Environment	The system shall be capable of detecting intruders 24 hours per day...
S1.1	All Weather Operation	The system shall be capable of detecting intruders under all weather...
S1.2	24/7 Operation	The system shall detect intruders 24 hours per day, 7 days per week
S2	Availability	The system shall exhibit an operational availability (Ao) of 0.999...

FIGURE 13.7

Example of requirements table.

table [Requirement] Camera Decision [Requirements Tree]					
id	name	relation	id	name	Rationale
D1	Sensor Decision	derivedFrom	S1.2	24/7 Operation	Using a camera is the most cost-effective way of meeting these requirements. See trade study T1.
		derivedFrom	S1.1	All Weather Operation	Using a camera is the most cost-effective way of meeting these requirements. See trade study T1.

FIGURE 13.8

Example of table following the deriveReqt relationship.

Specification package as indicated by the diagram header. Depending on its capability, a tool may also apply query and filter criteria to generate requirements reports from a query of the model. This report can represent a view of the model, as described in Chapter 5, Section 5.6. In addition, the tool may support editing requirements and their properties directly in the tabular view.

13.7.1 DEPICTING REQUIREMENT RELATIONSHIPS IN TABLES

A relationship path can be formed by selecting one or more requirements (or other model elements) and navigating the relationships from the selected requirement. This can be concisely shown in tables, as discussed in Chapter 5, Section 5.4. In the example presented in Figure 13.8, *D1* is the selected requirement. The path includes two deriveReqt relationships with directions as presented in Figure 13.14, as well as the rationale associated with each relationship.

The relationship paths can be arbitrarily deep. That is, they can navigate a single kind of relationship from one model element to the next or navigate different types of relationships from one model element to the next. This can be particularly useful when analyzing the impact of requirements changes across the model.

13.7.2 DEPICTING REQUIREMENT RELATIONSHIPS AS MATRICES

The tabular notation can also be used to represent multiple complex interrelationships between requirements and other model elements in the form of matrices. Figure 13.9 presents the result of a query in tabular (**matrix**) form. It depicts the satisfy and derive relationships. In this example, the requirements

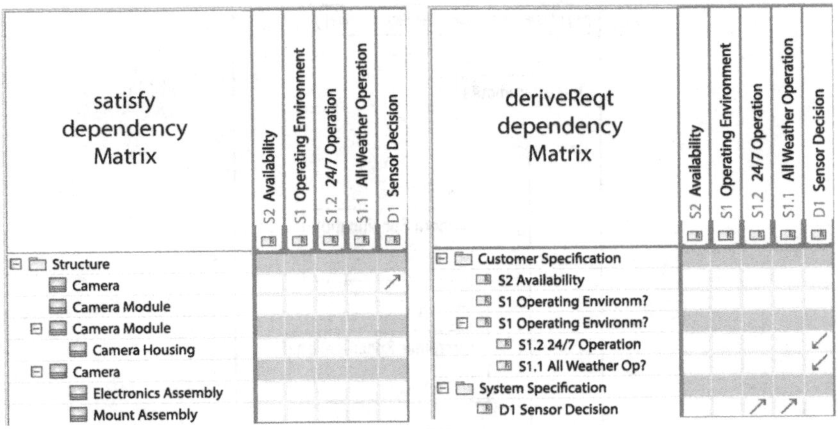

FIGURE 13.9

Example of tabular view of requirements as matrices tracing satisfy and derive requirement relationships, respectively.

are presented in the left column, and the model elements that have a derive or satisfy relationship are presented in the other columns. Filtering criteria can be applied to limit the size of the matrix. In this example, the requirements properties have been excluded, and only the derive and satisfy relationships have been included. These relationships are discussed later in this chapter. Again, this is an example of a mechanism that a tool vendor might use to construct a view of the model.

13.8 MODELING REQUIREMENT HIERARCHIES IN PACKAGES

Requirements can be organized into a package structure. A typical structure may include a top-level package for all requirements in the model. Each nested package within this package may contain requirements from different specifications, such as the system specification, element specifications, and component specifications. Each specification package contains the text-based requirements for that specification. This package structure may correspond to a typical specification tree that is a useful artifact for describing the scope of requirements for a project.

An example of a requirements package structure—or **specification tree**—is presented in the package diagram in Figure 13.10. The containment relationship, with the crosshairs symbol at the owning end, is used to indicate that the *Customer Specification* package, the *System Specification*, and the *Camera Specification* are contained in the *Requirements* package. An alternative representation for defining a specification tree on a requirement diagram using trace relationships between the specifications is described in Chapter 17, Section 17.3.7.

Organizing requirements into packages corresponding to various specifications provides familiarity and consistency with document-based approaches and facilitates configuration management of individual specifications at the package level. A specification document or report can be generated directly from the contents of the appropriate package but will require additional supporting text for headers, section introductions, and other aspects of document generation.

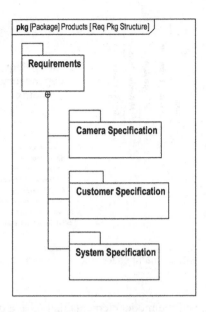

FIGURE 13.10

Example of a package structure for organizing requirements.

13.9 MODELING A REQUIREMENT CONTAINMENT HIERARCHY

Containment is used to represent how a compound requirement can be partitioned into a set of simpler requirements. Containment can be viewed as logically anding (conjunction) the contained requirements with the containing requirement. The partitioning of compound requirements into simpler requirements helps establish full traceability to show how individual requirements are the basis for further derivation and how they are satisfied and verified.

Figure 13.11 presents a requirement diagram with a simple containment hierarchy. The *Customer Specification* package from Figure 13.10 represents a top-level specification that serves as a container for all other customer-generated requirements. In this example, the *Customer Specification* package contains two other requirements, as depicted by the crosshairs symbol. Note that instead of using a package, a specification may be modeled as a «requirement» that contains a hierarchy of other requirements, such as that presented in Chapter 17, Figure 17.55. A typical specification may contain hundreds or thousands of individual requirements, but they generally can be organized into a hierarchy that corresponds to the organization of a specification document.

Figure 13.12 presents how containment hierarchies can be used to create multiple levels of **nested requirements.** In this example, the *Operating Environment* requirement contains two additional requirements for *All Weather Operation* and *24/7 Operation*.

13.9.1 THE BROWSER VIEW OF A CONTAINMENT HIERARCHY

As described in Chapter 3, Section 3.3.3, a typical modeling tool includes a model browser that can depict the requirements hierarchy. In Figure 13.13, the specification packages corresponding to the package diagram in Figure 13.10 are presented along with the requirements corresponding to the

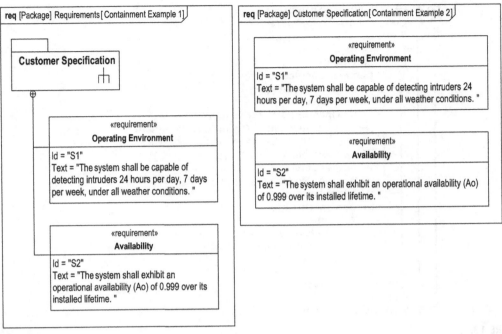

FIGURE 13.11

Two equivalent examples of requirements contained in a package.

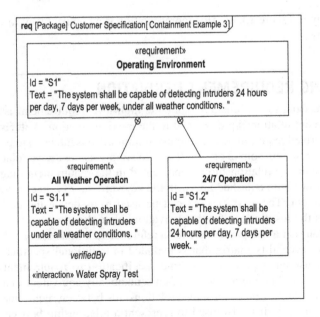

FIGURE 13.12

Example of requirements containment hierarchy.

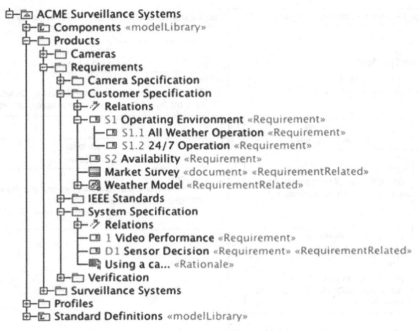

FIGURE 13.13

Example of requirements containment in a tool browser.

containment hierarchy in Figure 13.12. This representation is a compact way to view the requirements containment hierarchy.

13.10 MODELING REQUIREMENT DERIVATION

Deriving requirements from source, customer, or other high-level requirements is fundamentally different from the containment relationship described in the previous section. A **derive requirement relationship** between a derived requirement and a source requirement is intended to be based on an analysis. The derive requirement relationship is often referred to simply as the derive relationship.

An example of the derive relationship is represented in the requirement diagram in Figure 13.14. The relationship is shown with a dashed line with the keyword «deriveReqt» with the arrow pointing to the source requirement. The «rationale» can be used to associate the derive relationship to an analysis that provides the justification for the derivation. Note that the «rationale» has been associated with the derivation relationship and includes a reference to a trade study *T.1*.

The requirements traceability matrix that is included in traditional specification documents often shows relationships between requirements in one specification to requirements in other higher- or lower-level specifications. This relationship is often semantically equivalent to a set of SysML derive relationships. A derive relationship often shows relationships between requirements at different levels of the specification hierarchy. It is also used to represent a relationship between requirements at the

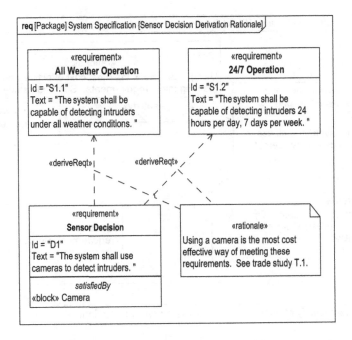

FIGURE 13.14

Example of «deriveReqt» relationship, with rationale attached.

peer level of the hierarchy but at different levels of abstraction. For example, the hardware or software requirements that are originally specified by the systems engineering team may be analyzed by the hardware or software team to derive more detailed requirements that reflect additional implementation considerations or constraints. The more detailed requirements from the hardware and software team may be related to the original requirements specified by the system team through derive relationships.

13.11 ASSERTING THAT A REQUIREMENT IS SATISFIED

The **satisfy relationship** is used to assert that a model element corresponding to the design or implementation satisfies a particular requirement. The actual proof that the assertion is true is accomplished by the verify relationship described in the next section. Figure 13.15 presents an example of a satisfy relationship.

The satisfy relationship is shown with a dashed line with the keyword «satisfy» with the arrow pointing to the requirement to assert that the *Camera* satisfies the requirement. The callout notation is also shown on both ends of the satisfy relationship. In practice, only one of these notations would be used to depict this relationship on a particular diagram. The «rationale» is associated with the satisfy relationship to indicate why this design is asserted to satisfy the requirement. In Figure 13.16, the same satisfy relationship from Figure 13.15 is presented on the block definition diagram using the compartment notation.

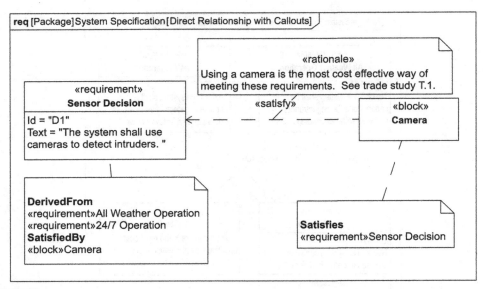

FIGURE 13.15

Example of requirement satisfy relationship and associated callout notation.

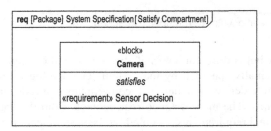

FIGURE 13.16

Example of satisfy relationship using compartment notation.

13.12 VERIFYING THAT A REQUIREMENT IS SATISFIED

The **verify relationship** is a relationship between a requirement and a test case or other model element that is used to verify that the requirement is satisfied. As stated in the previous section, the satisfy relationship is an assertion that the model elements representing the design or implementation satisfy the requirement, but the verify relationship is used to prove that the assertion is true (or false).

A **test case** specifies the input stimulus, conditions, and expected response to verify one or more requirements are satisfied. The test case can reference a documented verification procedure, or it can represent a model of the verification behavior, such as an activity, state machine, or interaction (sequence diagram). The results from performing the test case are called the verdict, which can include a value of none (test not completed yet), pass, fail, inconclusive, or error (i.e., an error in the testing environment).

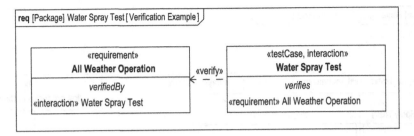

FIGURE 13.17

Example of verify relationship.

Figure 13.17 provides an example of the use of the verify relationship. The verify relationship is shown with a dashed line with the keyword «verify» with the arrow pointing from the *Water Spray Test* test case to the *All Weather Operation* requirement that is being verified. An alternative compartment notation for both the requirement and test case is also shown to depict this relationship.

A test case can be a behavior or an operation, which can be further elaborated using a sequence diagram, activity diagram, or state machine diagram to specify the test case method. An example of applying the test case keyword to an interaction (represented by a sequence diagram) is presented in Figure 13.18. This presents a *spray tester*, who is a *Test Technician*, using a *sprayer : Nozzle* to apply water to the *first production : Camera*, which is the **system under test** (designated by the keyword «sut»). Note that the *spray tester* is expected to disassemble and inspect the camera for water leakage before determining the test outcome. An example of a test case that is modeled as an activity can be found in Chapter 17, Figure 17.57.

In general, a test case that is modeled as a behavior can represent a measurement of almost any characteristic, including structural characteristics. For example, the test case could represent a behavior that measures system weight. In this sense, a test case is a general-purpose mechanism for verifying requirements. In addition, other model elements can be used to verify a requirement. An example may include using a constraint block to verify a requirement by analysis.

The use of test case in SysML is consistent with the UML Testing Profile [50]. This profile provides additional semantics for representing many other aspects of a test environment. The integration between the SysML modeling tools and verification tools is covered briefly in Chapter 18, Section 18.2.2 as part of the discussion on information flow between tools.

13.13 REDUCING REQUIREMENTS AMBIGUITY USING THE REFINE RELATIONSHIP

As discussed in Chapter 6, Section 6.8, the **refine relationship** provides the capability to reduce ambiguity in a requirement by relating a SysML requirement to another model element that clarifies and often formalizes the requirement. This relationship is typically used to refine a text-based requirement with some portion of the model, but it can also be used to refine a portion of the model with a text-based requirement. For example, a text-based functional requirement may be refined with a more precise representation, such as a use case and its realizing activity diagram. Alternatively, the model element or elements may include a fairly

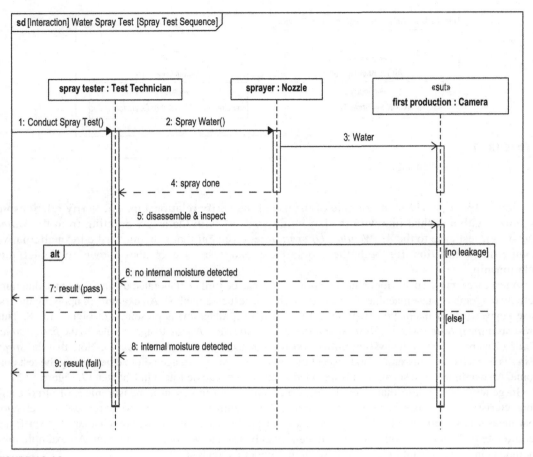

FIGURE 13.18

Example of a test case interaction depicted as a sequence diagram.

abstract representation of required system interfaces that can be refined by an interface's text specification that includes a detailed description of an interface protocol or a drawing of a physical interface envelope.

A refinement should clarify the requirement meaning or context. It is distinguished from a derive relationship in that a refine relationship can exist between a requirement and any other model element, whereas a derive relationship is only between requirements. In addition, a derive relationship is intended to impose additional constraints based on analysis.

An example of the refine relationship is provided in Figure 13.19. It presents how the *All Weather Operation* requirement is refined by a state machine that models weather conditions and transitions. The refine relationship is shown with a dashed line with the keyword «refine» with the arrow pointing from the element that represents the more precise representation to the element being refined. An alternative compartment notation is also shown to represent this relationship. Note that the *Weather Model* state machine only partially refines the requirement. The *Detection Scenario* use case might address, for example, specific detection expectations in each weather condition.

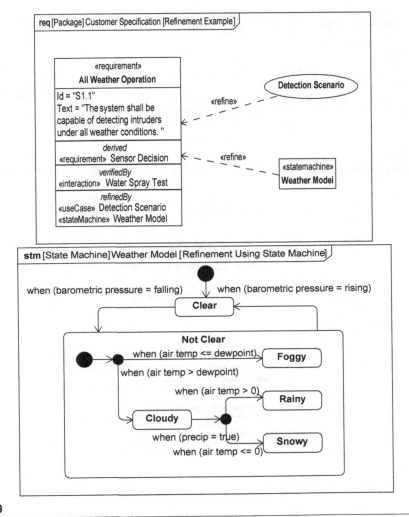

FIGURE 13.19

Example of refine relationship applied to requirement.

13.14 USING THE GENERAL-PURPOSE TRACE RELATIONSHIP

A **trace relationship** provides a general-purpose relationship between a requirement and any other model element. This is also discussed in Chapter 6, Section 6.8. The trace semantics do not include any constraints and therefore are quite weak. However, the trace relationship can be useful for relating requirements to source documentation or for establishing a relationship between specifications in a specification tree (refer to Chapter 17, Section 17.3.7).

As presented in Figure 13.20, the trace relationship is used to relate a particular requirement to a *Market Survey* that was conducted as part of the needs analyses. The trace relationship is shown with a dashed line with the keyword «trace» with the arrow pointing to the source document. The survey is represented as a user-defined model element with the keyword «document».

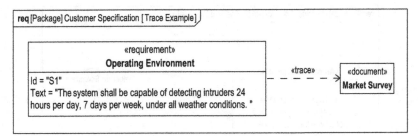

FIGURE 13.20

Example of trace relationship linking a requirement to an element representing an external document.

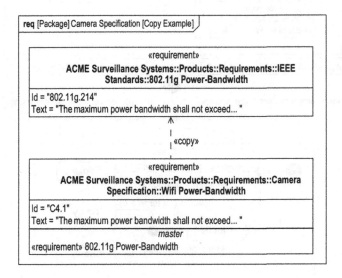

FIGURE 13.21

Example of a requirement copy relationship.

13.15 REUSING REQUIREMENTS WITH THE COPY RELATIONSHIP

The **copy relationship** supports reuse of requirements by explicitly relating a copy of a requirement to a source requirement. The text property of the copied requirement is a read-only copy of the text property of the source requirement, but the copied requirement has a different id and may be contained in a different namespace. Note that the copied requirement does not retain any of the relationships or rationale of the original requirement.

An example of a copy relationship is presented in Figure 13.21. The copy relationship is shown with a dashed line with the keyword «copy» with the arrow pointing from the copied requirement to the source requirement, also known as the **master requirement**. In this example, the source requirement being copied is a requirement from a technical standard that is reused in many different requirements specifications.

Note that requirements in SysML are precluded from having or typing part properties. This makes them different from blocks (see Chapter 7, Section 7.3.1). The standard mechanism for reusing requirements is the copy relationship.

13.16 SUMMARY

SysML can be used to model text-based requirements and relate them to other requirements and to other model elements. The following are some of the key requirements modeling concepts:

- The SysML requirement modeling capability serves as a bridge between traditional text-based requirements and the modeling environment. The requirements can be imported from a requirements management tool or text specification, or created directly in the modeling tool.
- A requirement includes a name, an id, and a text property at a minimum. Additional user defined properties such as risk and verification method can be included as well. Special kinds of requirements categories can also be created, in addition to the predefined categories in SysML (e.g., functional, interface, performance).
- Each specification is generally captured in a package. The package structure can correspond to a traditional specification tree. Each specification in turn includes a containment hierarchy of the requirements contained within the specification. The browser view in most tools can be used to view the requirements containment hierarchy.
- The individual or aggregate requirements contained in a specification can be related to other requirements in the same or other specifications, as well as to model elements that represent the design, analysis, implementation, and test cases. The requirements relationships include derive, satisfy, verify, refine, trace, and copy. These relationships provide a robust capability for managing requirements and supporting requirements traceability.
- There are multiple notational representations to enable requirements to be related to other model elements on other diagrams. These include direct notation, compartment notation, and callout notation. The requirement diagram is generally used to represent a containment hierarchy or to represent the relationships for a particular requirement or set of requirements. Tabular notations are also used to efficiently report requirements and their relationships.

13.17 QUESTIONS

1. What is the diagram kind of a requirement diagram?
2. Which kind of model element can the frame of a requirement diagram represent?
3. Which standard properties are expressed in a SysML requirement?
4. How can you add properties and constraints to a requirement?
5. What kind of requirement relationships can only exist between requirements?
6. Express in a sentence how you interpret Figure 13.3.
7. How do you express the requirement relationship in Figure 13.3 using call-out notation?
8. How do you express the requirement relationship in Figure 13.3 using compartment notation?
9. How do you represent a «deriveReqt» relationship between Reqt A and Reqt B in a matrix?

10. How do you represent the rationale for the derived requirement in Figure 13.14 that the derivation is based on the *xyz* analysis?
11. What is a satisfy relationship used for?
    a. To ensure a requirement is met
    b. To assert a requirement is met
    c. To more clearly express a requirement
12. What are the kinds of elements found on either end of a verify relationship?
13. What is used as a basis for a derived relationship?
    a. analysis
    b. design
    c. test case
14. Consider the requirement A with text that reads "The system shall do x and the system shall do y." How would you show the deconvolution of requirement A into two requirements, A.1 and A.2, using containment?
15. Which relationship would you use to relate a requirement to a document?
    a. deriveReqt
    b. satisfy
    c. verify
    d. trace
16. Why are requirements included in SysML? (This can be a discussion topic rather than a question.)

DISCUSSION TOPICS

What are different uses of a requirement diagram?
When would you use a requirement diagram versus a table?
How can requirements and use cases be used together?

MODELING CROSS-CUTTING RELATIONSHIPS WITH ALLOCATIONS

This chapter describes how the allocate relationship is used to map from one model element to another to support behavioral, structural, and other forms of allocation.

14.1 OVERVIEW

Beginning early in systems development, the modeler may need to relate elements in the system model in abstract, preliminary, and sometimes tentative ways. It is inappropriate to impose detailed constraints on the solution too early in the development of a system. Allocation is a mechanism for relating model elements in a way that provides guidance for the more rigorous relationships that are subsequently developed during model refinement. Additional user-defined constraints can augment the allocate relationship to add the necessary rigor as the design progresses. For example, an allocation of functions (e.g., activities) to components may be done early in the design process. As the design progresses, additional constraints are imposed to ensure that the activity inputs, outputs, and controls are explicitly allocated to component interfaces. With appropriate user-defined constraints, allocation can be used to help enforce specific system development methods to ensure the model's integrity.

The allocate relationship is used to support many forms of allocation, including allocation of behavior, structure, and properties. A typical example of behavioral allocation is the allocation of activities to blocks (traditionally called functional allocation), where each block is assigned responsibility for implementing a particular activity. An important distinction is made between allocation of definition (described in Section 14.5.2) and allocation of usage (described in Section 14.5.1). The concepts of definition (e.g., blocks) and usage (e.g., part properties) are explained in Chapter 7, Section 7.3.1. For functional allocation, allocating activities to blocks is an allocation of definition, and allocating actions to parts is an allocation of usage.

SysML includes several notational options to provide flexibility for representing allocations of model elements. The options include both graphical and tabular representations similar to those used for relating requirements. Figure 14.1 shows some of the graphical representations of allocation on an activity diagram, on an internal block diagram, and on a block definition diagram. A complete description of the SysML notation for allocations can be found in the Appendix, Table A.28.

14.2 ALLOCATE RELATIONSHIP

As referenced in Chapter 6, Section 6.8, an **allocate relationship** is a kind of dependency used to allocate one model element to another. An allocate relationship may be established between any two named model elements and provides a general purpose assignment mechanism. Responsibilities that are associated with one model element may be assigned to another model element, such as when an activity is allocated to a block. For this case, the block assumes responsibility for performing the activity. Every SysML allocate relationship has one "from" end and one "to" end, although a model element may be allocated from or to more than one model element. Model element *A* is said to be "allocated to" model element *B* when the model element at the "from" end of the allocate relationship (i.e., the client) is *A* and the model element at the "to" end of the allocate relationship (i.e., the supplier) is *B*. The supplier end of the relationship has an arrow. Additional constraints may be placed on allocations; for example, functional allocation may be constrained to occur only between blocks and activities. Section 14.4 discusses various kinds of allocation.

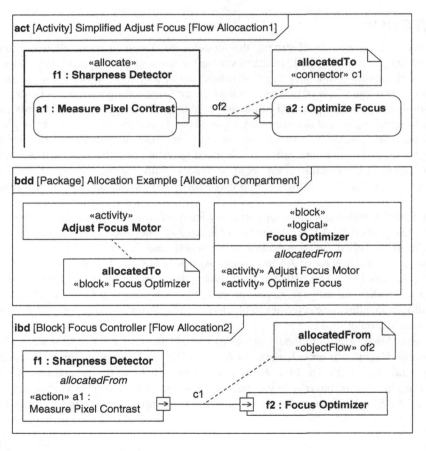

FIGURE 14.1

Examples of allocation on activity, block definition, and internal block diagrams.

14.3 **ALLOCATION NOTATION**

Several different notations can be used to represent allocation of one model element to another. The notations that SysML uses to represent allocate relationships are similar to the graphical and tabular notations used to represent requirements relationships, as described in Chapter 13, Section 13.5. Graphical notations include the direct notation, compartment notation, and callout notation.

When the model elements at both ends of the allocate relationship can be shown on the same diagram, the allocate relationship can be depicted directly, as indicated in Figure 14.2, using the keyword «allocate» on the relationship. Here, the *Adjust Focus Motor* activity is allocated to the *Focus Optimizer,* and the arrow represents the allocatedTo end of the relationship (i.e., supplier). Although functional allocation is depicted in this example, this representation is equally valid for other kinds of allocations.

As with requirements relationships, the model elements at either end of an allocate relationship may be on different diagrams. For these cases, compartment notation and callout notation can be used to identify the model element at the other end of the relationship.

The compartment notation identifies the element at the opposite end of the allocate relationship in a compartment of the model element, as shown in Figure 14.3. However, this can only be used when the model element can include compartments such as blocks and parts. It cannot be used for model elements that do not have compartments, such as connectors.

The callout notation shown in Figure 14.4 can be used to represent the opposite end of the allocate relationship for any model element whether it has compartments or not. Callout notation is represented as a note symbol that is attached to the model element via an anchor, like a comment. The callout notation specifies the kind and name of the model element at the other end of the allocate relationship. It also identifies which end of the allocate relationship applies to the attached model

FIGURE 14.2

Example directly depicting an allocate relationship, when both model elements appear on the same diagram.

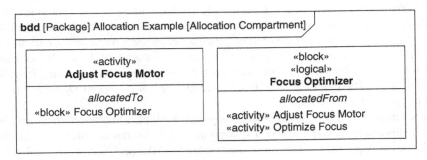

FIGURE 14.3

Example depicting an allocate relationship in compartment notation.

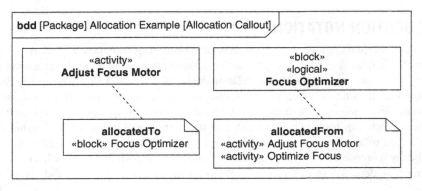

FIGURE 14.4

Example depicting an allocate relationship in callout notation.

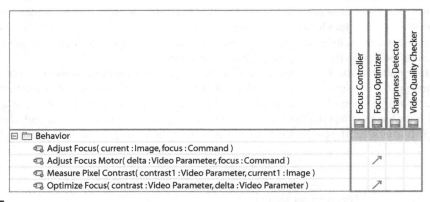

FIGURE 14.5

Example depicting allocate relationships in tabular matrix form.

element as indicated by the *allocatedTo* or *allocatedFrom*. This is similar to the callout notation for requirements relationships discussed in Chapter 13, Section 13.5.3. The callout notation is read by starting with the name of the model element that the callout notation attaches to, then reading the *allocatedTo* or *allocatedFrom,* and then reading the model element name in the callout symbol. For example, the allocate relationship in Figure 14.4 is read: "The activity *Adjust Focus Motor* is allocated to the block *Focus Optimizer*," and "the block *Focus Optimizer* is allocated from the activity *Adjust Focus Motor*." The latter could be interpreted as "The block *Focus Optimizer* is responsible for the activity *Adjust Focus Motor*."

A matrix notation can be used to simultaneously view multiple allocate relationships, as shown in Figure 14.5. In this example, activities are displayed in the left column and blocks are displayed in the top row. This format is not specifically prescribed by the SysML specification and will vary from tool to tool. The arrows in the cells of the matrix indicate the direction of the allocate relationships, consistent with those shown in Figure 14.3 and Figure 14.4.

This matrix or tabular form of representing allocations is particularly useful when a concise, compact representation is needed, and it is used often in this chapter to illustrate allocation concepts.

14.4 KINDS OF ALLOCATION

The following section describes different kinds of allocations, including allocation of requirements, behavior, flow, structure, and properties.

14.4.1 ALLOCATION OF REQUIREMENTS

The term **requirement allocation** represents a mechanism for mapping source requirements to other derived requirements, or mapping requirements to other model elements that satisfy the requirement. SysML does not use the «allocate» relationship to represent this form of allocation, but instead uses specific requirements relationships that are described in Chapter 13.

14.4.2 ALLOCATION OF BEHAVIOR OR FUNCTION

The term **behavioral allocation** generally refers to a technique for segregating behavior from structure. A common systems engineering practice is to separate models of structure (sometimes referred to as models of form) from models of behavior (sometimes referred to as models of function) so that designs can be optimized by considering several different structures that provide the desired emergent behavior and properties. This approach provides the required degrees of freedom—in particular, how to decompose structure, how to decompose behavior, and how to relate the structure and behavior to optimize designs based on trade studies among alternatives. The implication is that an explicit set of relationships must be maintained between behavior and structure for each alternative.

The behavior of a block can be represented in different ways. On a block definition diagram, the operations of a block explicitly define the responsibility the block has for providing the associated behavior (see Chapter 7, Section 7.5 for more on modeling behavior of blocks). In a sequence diagram, a message sent to a lifeline invokes the operation on the receiving lifeline to provide the behavior (see Chapter 10 for more on interactions). In activity diagrams, the placement of an action in an activity partition implicitly defines that the part represented by the partition provides the associated behavior. (See Chapter 9 for more on activities.)

In this chapter, the term behavioral allocation specifically refers to the concept of allocating behavioral model elements (activities, actions, states, object flow, control flow, transitions, messages, etc.) to structural models elements (blocks, parts, ports, connectors, item flows, etc.). The term **functional allocation** is a subset of behavioral allocation, and it refers specifically to the allocation of activities or actions (also known as functions) to blocks or parts, respectively.

14.4.3 ALLOCATION OF FLOW

Flow represents the transfer of energy, mass, and/or information from one model element to another. Flows are typically depicted as object flows from and to action pins on activity diagrams (as described in Chapter 9, Section 9.5) and as item flows between ports or parts on an internal block diagram (as described in Chapter 7, Section 7.4.3). **Flow allocation** is often used to allocate flows between activity diagrams and internal block diagrams.

14.4.4 ALLOCATION OF STRUCTURE

Structural allocation refers to allocating elements of one kind of structure to elements of another kind of structure. A typical example is a **logical–physical allocation,** where a logical block hierarchy is often built and maintained at an abstract level, and in turn is mapped to another physical block hierarchy at a more concrete level. **Software–hardware allocation** is another example of structural allocation. In SysML, allocation is often used to allocate abstract software elements to hardware elements. UML uses the concept of deployment to specify a more detailed level of allocation that requires software artifacts to be deployed to platforms or processing nodes. The transition from a SysML allocation to a UML deployment may be accomplished through model refinement and more detailed modeling and design of the software.

14.4.5 ALLOCATION OF PROPERTIES

Allocation can also be used to allocate performance or physical properties to various elements in the system model. This often supports the budgeting of system performance or physical property values to property values of the system components. A typical example is a weight budget in which system weight is allocated to the weights of the system's components. Once again, the initial allocation can be specified in more detail as part of model refinement using parametric constraints, as discussed in Chapter 8, Section 8.6.

14.4.6 SUMMARY OF RELATIONSHIPS ASSOCIATED WITH THE TERM "ALLOCATION"

Table 14.1 is a partial list of some uses for allocation in systems modeling.

Table 14.1 Various Uses of "Allocation" and How to Represent in SysML

Kind of Allocation	Reference	Relationship	From	To
Requirement allocation	Section 13.11	Satisfy	requirement	model element
	Section 13.10	DeriveReqt	requirement	requirement
	Section 13.13	Refine	model element requirement	requirement model element
Functional allocation	Section 14.6	Allocate	activity action	block part
Structural allocation (e.g., logical to physical, software to hardware)	Section 14.9	Allocate	block	block
	Section 14.10	Allocate	port	port
	Section 14.9	Allocate	item flow connector	item flow parts and connectors
Flow allocation	Section 14.7	Allocate	object flow object flow object flow	connector item flow item property
Property decomposition/allocation	Section 7.7	Binding connector	value property	parameter

14.5 PLANNING FOR REUSE: SPECIFYING DEFINITION AND USAGE IN ALLOCATION

The allocation of a model element to another model element establishes a relationship between them that can impact their reuse. For example, allocating a function to a component, such as allocating camera function to a mobile phone, may limit the ability to reuse the mobile phone for another application. This motivates the distinction between allocation of definition versus allocation of usage as described below.

The concept of definition and usage, relative to parts typed by blocks, is discussed in Chapter 7, Section 7.3.1. A block is defined in terms of its features. A part typed by a block represents a usage of that block in the context of an owning block. The distinction between definition and usage applies to any property, such as a constraint property typed by a constraint block or an item property typed by a block. The concept can also be applied to other elements such as a call behavior action and the activity it calls. The action can be viewed as a usage of the called activity in the context of an owning activity. Table 14.2 shows different kinds of diagrams, the model elements that represent usages on the diagrams, and the model elements that type or define them.

Allocation can be used to relate elements of definition (blocks, activities, etc.) or elements of usage (actions, parts, etc.) in various combinations. The following examples explicitly depict this concept for functional allocation, but it applies equally well to structural allocation (block to block, part to part, etc.). The concepts of definition and usage are a significant strength of SysML, but merit careful consideration during allocation to maintain model consistency.

14.5.1 ALLOCATING USAGE

As shown in Figure 14.6, **allocation of usage** applies when both the "from" and "to" ends of the allocate relationship relate usage elements such as parts, actions, and connectors. When allocating usage, nothing is inferred about any corresponding defining elements (blocks, activities, etc.) that may type or invoke the usage. This is similar to property specific types as described in Chapter 7, Section 7.7.5. Only the specific usage is affected by the allocation. For example, if an action on an activity diagram is allocated to a part on an internal block diagram, the allocation is specific to that part, and not to any other parts that are typed by the same block. If the modeler finds a large number of similar parts with

Table 14.2 Contextualized Elements Representing Usages and Their Definition

Diagram Kind	Model Element/Usage	Model Element/Definition
Activity diagram	action	activity
	object node/action pin	block
	activity edge (object flow, control flow)	(none)
Internal block diagram	part	block
	connector	association
	item flow	(none)
	item property	block
	value property	value type
Parametric diagram	Constraint property	constraint block

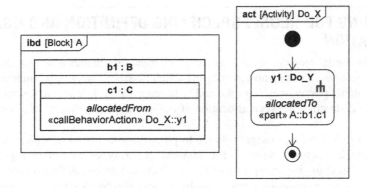

FIGURE 14.6

Allocation of usage. Functional allocation is shown here, but structural allocation is similar.

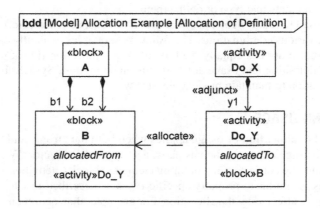

FIGURE 14.7

Allocation of definition.

similar allocated characteristics or functions, it may be appropriate to consider allocation of definition as described in Section 14.5.2.

SysML supports instance specifications, as described in Chapter 7, Section 7.8. Allocation to and from instance specifications can also be considered allocation of usage.

14.5.2 ALLOCATING DEFINITION

As shown in Figure 14.7, **allocation of definition** applies when both the "from" and "to" ends of the allocate relationship relate to elements of definition, such as blocks, activities, and associations. When allocating to an element that represents definition or classifier, such as a block, then the allocation applies to every property that is typed by the definition. For example, when a block

Table 14.3 Allocation Guidelines Table

Allocation of Usage	Allocation of Definition
Example: part to part, action to part, connector to connector, property to property	Example: block to block or activity to block
Applicability: when the allocation is not intended to be reused	Applicability: when the allocation is intended to apply to all usages
Discussion	Discussion
– Most localized with least implication on other diagrams and elements	– Allocation inferred to all usages
– Only way to allocate flows and connectors that have no definition	– Can result in over-allocation (more activities allocated to a part than necessary)
– Possible redundancy or inconsistency as parts/actions used in multiple places	– Not directly represented on an activity diagram with allocate activity partition (see Section 14.6.3)

is used to type several different parts, the result of any allocation to the block applies to all the parts that are typed by this block. Note that allocations are not inherited when a block is specialized.

14.5.3 ALLOCATING ASYMMETRICALLY

Asymmetric allocation is when one end of the allocate relationship relates to an element of definition, and the other end relates to an element of usage. Asymmetric allocation is used by exception; that is, it is not generally recommended because it can introduce ambiguity. Allocation of usage and allocation of definition are the preferred allocation approaches.

14.5.4 GUIDELINES FOR ALLOCATING DEFINITION AND USAGE

The significance of using allocation of usage and allocation of definition relationships is discussed in Table 14.3. The following conclusions can be drawn by examining these two approaches to allocation with respect to functional allocation, flow allocation, and structural allocation:

- Allocation of usage is localized to the fewest model elements and has no inferred allocations. It can be directly represented on diagrams of usage (e.g., internal block diagram or activity diagram). It is appropriate to start with allocation of usage and consider allocation of definition after each of the uses has been examined.
- Allocation of definition is a more complete form of allocation because it applies (is inferred) to every usage. Allocation of definition follows from allocation of usage, as it typically requires blocks or activities to be specialized or decomposed to the point where the allocation of definition is unique, and over-allocation (more allocations than really desired) is avoided. If a part requires a unique allocation, using allocation of definition requires the additional step of specializing the block to define the part uniquely and then allocating to (or from) that specialized block instead of to the part. This extra attention to refine the definition facilitates future reuse of definition hierarchies.

14.6 ALLOCATING BEHAVIOR TO STRUCTURE USING FUNCTIONAL ALLOCATION

Functional allocation is used to allocate functions to system components. Figure 14.8 defines a suitably complex behavioral hierarchy and a structural hierarchy to be used for the following functional allocation examples. Note that in this example, *Measure Pixel Contrast* is used by more than one activity, and *Sharpness Detector* is used by more than one block. See Chapter 9, Section 9.12 for modeling activity hierarchies on block definition diagrams and Chapter 7, Section 7.3.1 for modeling composition hierarchies on block definition diagrams.

The surveillance camera employs a passive autofocus system that uses pixel-to-pixel contrast as a way of determining how well the optics are focused, and then it generates a signal to adjust the focus motor accordingly. The *Adjust Focus* activity, then, can be composed of actions defined by three other activities: *a1 : Measure Pixel Contrast, a2 : Optimize Focus,* and *a3 : Adjust Focus Motor.* An activity diagram describing the behavior of the autofocus portion of the surveillance camera is depicted on the left side of Figure 14.9. Note that a separate activity to detect edges of objects in the video frame may also use the *Measure Pixel Contrast* activity, as shown in Figure 14.8.

A logical structure for the autofocus portion of the camera is also depicted in Figure 14.8. The *Focus Controller* block is composed of parts *f1 : Sharpness Detector* and *f2 : Focus Optimizer.*

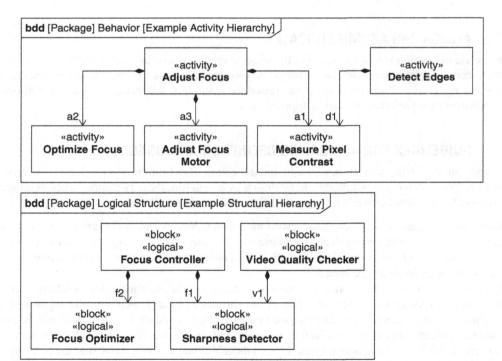

FIGURE 14.8

Example of behavioral and structural hierarchy definition.

Assume, hypothetically, that the block *Sharpness Detector* may also define a part used by some other logical block whose purpose is to check video quality.

14.6.1 MODELING FUNCTIONAL ALLOCATION OF USAGE

As discussed in an earlier section, functional allocation of usage (e.g., action to part) should be used over functional allocation of definition (e.g., activity to block) when the action is not intended to be reused by other usages of the block. Allocation of usage should also be considered if the action uses different inputs/outputs (i.e., pins) that may result in different interfaces on the associated block.

Figure 14.9 depicts functional allocation of usage. This example shows the use of the callout notation for representing allocations from the actions on the activity diagram to the parts on the internal block diagram. Note that action *a1 : Measure Pixel Contrast* on the activity diagram is allocated to part *f1 : Sharpness Detector,* but that none of the other actions are allocated. This is because their defining activities are allocated in Section 14.6.2, so it is not appropriate to also allocate the usage. Also, notice that object flow *of2* is allocated to connector *c1*. This kind of flow allocation can only be allocation of usage and is described in more detail in Section 14.7.3.

The allocation callouts on the internal block diagram are the reciprocal of the allocation callouts on the activity diagram. An allocation matrix is also provided as an alternative concise representation of the allocate relationships in the other diagrams.

14.6.2 MODELING FUNCTIONAL ALLOCATION OF DEFINITION

Allocation of definition between an activity and a block is used when each usage of the activity is allocated to a usage of the block. This can be depicted on block definition diagrams. The allocate

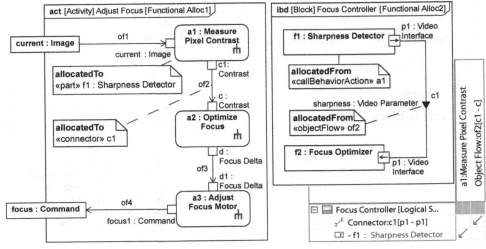

FIGURE 14.9

Example of functional allocation of usage, with allocation matrix.

relationship between an activity and a block can include the activity or block on the "to" or "from" end of the allocation, but the allocation is generally from an activity to a block.

Figure 14.10 shows an example of functional allocation of definition using the allocate relationship. Note that the activities *Optimize Focus* and *Adjust Focus Motor* are allocated to the block *Focus Optimizer*. The use of *Focus Optimizer* in the block *Focus Controller*—and everywhere else it is used—has an inferred allocation of these two activities. This allocation can later be realized by creating two operations for *Focus Optimizer* whose methods are *Optimize Focus* and *Adjust Focus Motor*. These new operations would then be available to every instance typed by *Focus Optimizer*.

Note that the activity *Measure Pixel Contrast* is not allocated to the block *Sharpness Detector,* even though a conceptual relationship exists between them. In this particular example, *Measure Pixel Contrast* is also used by the activity *Detect Edges,* which is a processing technique not associated with picture sharpness. *Measure Pixel Contrast* does not have any inferred allocation to *Sharpness Detector* when it is used in *Detect Edges,* thus allocation of definition is inappropriate. Allocation of usage is the correct technique in this case.

Figure 14.11 is a block definition diagram of a system similar to the water distiller example in Chapter 16. Note that the *Meter Flow* activity has been allocated to the block *Valve,* which infers that the *Meter Flow* activity applies to each usage of the *Valve* block. This is appropriate because every valve performs an activity to meter fluid flow. Note also that the activity *Boil Water* has been allocated to the block *Boiler,* which infers that all the usages of the *Boiler* can perform the activity *Boil Water.*

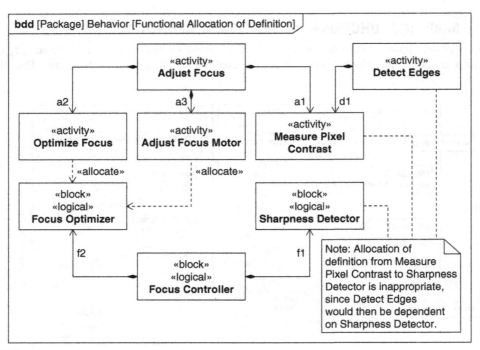

FIGURE 14.10

Example of functional allocation of definition.

Figure 14.12 is a block definition diagram describing a *Power Station,* and it uses many of the blocks previously defined for the *Distiller.* The allocation of definition to the *Boiler* and *Valve* referenced in Figure 14.11 is still valid. The part *stm gen : Boiler* has an inferred allocation from the *Boil Water* activity, and both the *feed* and *throttle* usages of *Valve* include an inferred allocation from the *Meter Flow* activity.

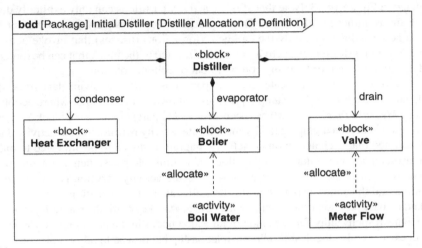

FIGURE 14.11

Functional allocation of definition from distiller example.

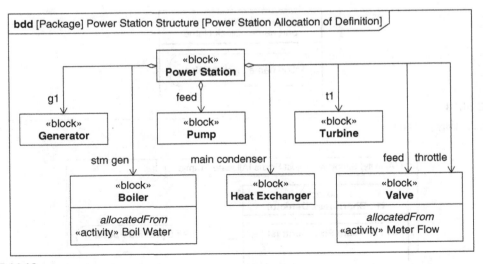

FIGURE 14.12

Implications of functional allocation of definition as seen in the power station example.

14.6.3 **MODELING FUNCTIONAL ALLOCATION USING ALLOCATE ACTIVITY PARTITIONS (ALLOCATE SWIM LANES)**

Activity partitions are discussed in Chapter 9, Section 9.11.1. An **allocate activity partition** is a special type of activity partition that is distinguished by the keyword «allocate». The presence of an allocate activity partition on an activity diagram implies an allocate relationship between any action node within the partition and the part or block represented by the partition (which appears as the name of the partition), as depicted in Figure 14.13. Note that allocate activity partitions can only explicitly depict allocation of usage or asymmetric allocation. This is because activities (definition) cannot be directly represented on activity diagrams; only the call behavior actions (usages) that invoke activities can. If allocation of definition is desired, the activity must be allocated to the block that can be directly depicted on a block definition diagram or by using compartment or callout notation.

Functional allocation using allocate activity partitions (allocate swim lanes) is depicted in Figure 14.14. This is a subset of the example previously shown in Figure 14.9, where action node *a1* (a usage of activity *Measure Pixel Contrast*) has been allocated to part *f1* (a usage of block *Sharpness Detector*). This allocation is depicted graphically by the allocate activity partition on the activity diagram.

We have assumed that each action on an activity diagram is meant to be allocated to only one part. If for some reason an action is intended to be allocated to multiple parts, then a new untyped part may be created that aggregates the parts in question. An allocate activity partition is used to represent this new aggregation, and the action is placed in this new allocate activity partition.

If a standard activity partition is used without the «allocate» keyword, the part or block represented by the partition retains responsibility for execution of all action nodes in the partition (see Chapter 9, Section 9.11.1). This does not employ the SysML allocate relationship but instead tightly couples the behavior definition to the structural definition. For example, when a call operation action is in a standard activity partition, most tools will automatically populate a corresponding operation in the block that represents the partition.

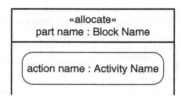

FIGURE 14.13

Allocate activity partition.

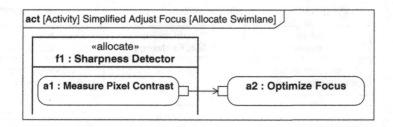

FIGURE 14.14

Simple example of functional allocation using an allocate activity partition (swim lanes).

14.7 ALLOCATING BEHAVIORAL FLOWS TO STRUCTURAL FLOWS

Flow between activities can either be control flow or object flow as described in Chapter 9, Section 9.5 and 9.6. The following sections address allocating object flow as represented on activity diagrams. Allocation of control flow may be depicted in a similar way as allocation of object flow. Flow allocation is typically an allocation of usage, because items that flow between model elements are usually specified in the context of their usage.

14.7.1 OPTIONS FOR ALLOCATING FLOW

Item flows are used to depict flow between parts on internal block diagrams, as described in Chapter 7, Section 7.4. Item flows can have an associated item property. The item flow represents the direction of flow and relates the item property to the connector, and the item property is the usage of the item that flows. Item properties can be defined (i.e., typed) by blocks just as parts are typed by blocks.

Chapter 9, Section 9.5 discusses the equivalent depiction of object flows (solid arrows on activity diagrams) in either action pin notation (small squares on the edges of action nodes) or object node notation (larger rectangles between action nodes). The object node notation on activity diagrams represents both an output pin and an input pin. To avoid ambiguity of the allocate relationship, it is recommended that action pin notation be used when performing flow allocation.

The following sections discuss allocating an object flow to a connector, allocating an object flow to an item flow, and allocating item properties between diagrams. Other kinds of flow allocation can be used as well, such as allocating an action pin to an item flow or an activity parameter node to a port. These additional allocations are an advanced topic that is a function of the specific design method used and are not discussed here.

14.7.2 ALLOCATING AN OBJECT FLOW TO A CONNECTOR

Figure 14.15 extends the example shown in Figure 14.14 and is also a subset of the example shown in Figure 14.9. The object flow *of2* is allocated to the connector *c1*. This is a convenient preliminary form of allocation to use before item flows have been defined or if item flows are not modeled. It can be ambiguous, however, if more than one item flow or item property is associated with the connector. Control flows can also be allocated to connectors, but the semantics and physical implications of allocating control flows are also highly dependent on the design method. Additional model refinement may be required before unambiguous control flow allocation can be achieved.

14.7.3 ALLOCATING OBJECT FLOW TO ITEM FLOW

Figure 14.16 depicts an alternative method of flow allocation from Figure 14.15. In this case object flow *of2* has been allocated to the item flow *if1*. This can be depicted on an activity diagram or internal block diagram using callout notation. In addition to the activity diagram, an allocation matrix is provided to explicitly show the allocate relationships. The nesting of the allocation matrix around the activity diagram is done solely for convenience and is not a standard SysML representation. This is a more specific form of allocation than object flow to connector, and it is unambiguous even if more than one item flow is associated with the connector. In general, activity edges that represent control flow or object flow can be allocated to item flows.

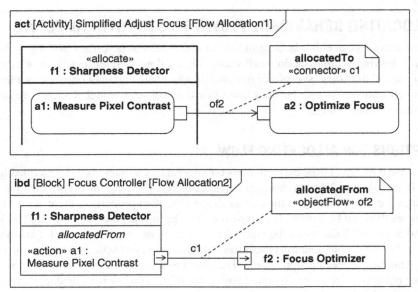

FIGURE 14.15

Object flow to connector allocation.

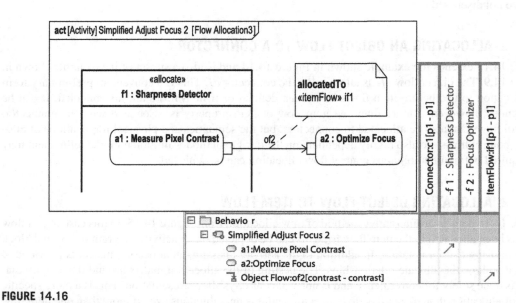

FIGURE 14.16

Object flow to item flow allocation with allocation matrix.

Allocating an object flow or control flow to an item flow does not affect the behavior represented on the activity diagram. If the modeling tool animates or executes the activity diagram, it is the object flow that will be part of that execution semantic, not the item flow.

When allocating object flows to item flows, it is important to ensure consistent typing. The built-in constraints on object flows ensure that the action pins on each end of the object flow are typed consistently. When allocating the object flow to an item flow, the type of the action pins associated with the object flow should be consistent with the conveyed classifier that types the item flow and any associated item property. This is an example of what might be expected from a model checker provided by the tool to reduce the likelihood of error and the workload of the modeler.

Rather than allocate the object flow to the item flow, it may be appropriate to allocate the object flow to the item property associated with the item flow. Figure 14.17 shows the results of this kind of allocation in the surveillance camera. This particular method of allocation is also used in the water distiller example in Chapter 16 because it ties the object flows in the functional model to specific properties of the water flowing through the system. The values of these properties are used for subsequent engineering analysis.

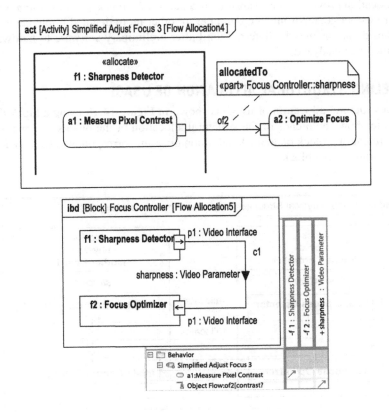

FIGURE 14.17

Object flow to item property allocation.

14.8 ALLOCATING BETWEEN INDEPENDENT STRUCTURAL HIERARCHIES

There are times to consider more than one model of structure. For example, it is a common practice to group capabilities, functions, or operations into an abstract or **logical structure** while maintaining a separate implementation-specific **physical structure**. An example of developing a logical architecture and allocating the logical components to the physical architecture can be found in Chapter 17, Section 17.3.5 (*Define Node Physical Architecture*) and in Figure 17.33. The logical to physical allocation provides an opportunity to address alternative allocations that are subject to trade study evaluation.

A particular method for logical architecture development should relate elements of logical structure with elements of physical structure. SysML allocation provides a mechanism to perform and analyze this mapping. Implementation of the physical structure may require further model development to realize the logical structure, but this development should wait until the logical-to-physical allocation is stable and consistent across the system model.

The physical structure may itself be divided into software structures and hardware structures. UML software modelers typically use deployment relationships to map software structures to hardware structures. SysML allocation provides a more abstract mechanism for this kind of mapping, which does not have to consider host–target environment, compiler, or other more detailed implementation considerations. These considerations may be deferred until after preliminary software-to-hardware allocation has been performed and analyzed.

14.8.1 MODELING STRUCTURAL ALLOCATION OF USAGE

An example of a structural allocation of usage is shown in Figure 14.18 using a block definition diagram. The diagram shows both ends of the structural allocation of the blocks' internal structure. The structure compartment of a block on a block definition diagram corresponds to what is depicted on the internal block diagram of that block.

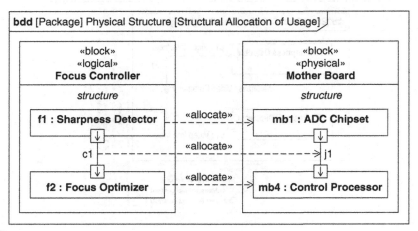

FIGURE 14.18

Structural allocation of usage example.

Allocation between parts in different structure compartments, as shown, can only depict allocation of usage. Likewise, allocation shown between connectors on internal block diagrams or structure compartments can only represent allocation of usage.

14.8.2 ALLOCATING A LOGICAL CONNECTOR TO A PHYSICAL STRUCTURE

A connector is used to connect parts or ports. A connector depicted in an abstract or logical structure may be allocated to one or more interfacing parts in a physical structure, such as a wiring harness, a bus, or a complex network.

The example in Figure 14.19 depicts the allocation of a connector in a logical structure—where physical connection details are not considered—to a physical part (*ea5 : PWB Backplane*) and the

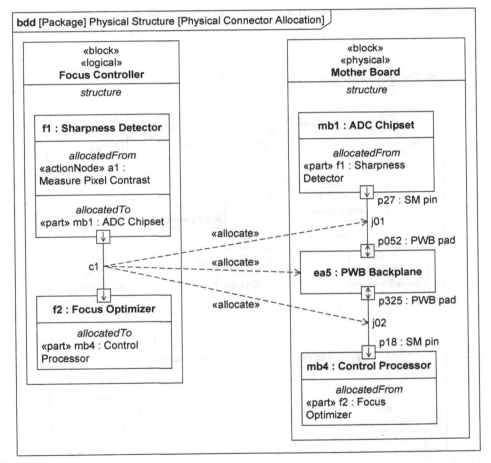

FIGURE 14.19

Refining a connector using allocation.

associated connectors. The use of allocation is an appropriate way to show the refinement of the logical connector without requiring undue extension of the logical architecture into implementation details. Any item flow on the logical connector can be allocated to multiple item flows in the physical structure, such as allocating an item flow on a logical connector to the item flows entering and exiting a cable.

14.8.3 MODELING STRUCTURAL ALLOCATION OF DEFINITION

Figure 14.20 shows structural allocation of definition for the autofocus portion of the surveillance camera. This is different from the allocation represented previously in Figure 14.18, which depicted allocation of usage. If a structural allocation is meant to apply to all its usages, then allocation of definition is appropriate. In this example, wherever the block *Vector Processor* is used, it will include the inferred allocation from *Image Processor*, even if it is not used in a *Mother Board*.

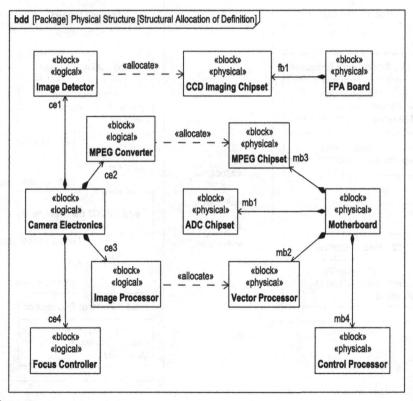

FIGURE 14.20

Depicting structural allocation of definition.

14.9 **MODELING STRUCTURAL FLOW ALLOCATION**

The item that flows, which may be represented by a block, can be used to type the flow on both an abstract (e.g., logical) internal block diagram and a concrete (e.g., physical) internal block diagram. This enables a common structural data model to be maintained between logical and physical hierarchies.

There may be good reasons, however, to establish separate abstract logical and physical data models. For example, a standard logical data model may be required, but the data-level implementation may need to be optimized. In the case in which an item flow depicted at an abstract level needs to be allocated to structures at a more concrete level, it may be necessary to decompose the abstract item flow so that it may be uniquely allocated. If a block is used to represent the item that flows at the abstract level, it can be decomposed into a set of blocks that represent the items that flow at the more concrete level. The abstract item flow can then be allocated to the more concrete item flows that use the appropriate blocks to type item properties.

Figure 14.21 shows how an item flow or item property at an abstract level can be allocated to an item flow or item property at a more concrete level. Note in the structural compartments of the *Focus Controller*

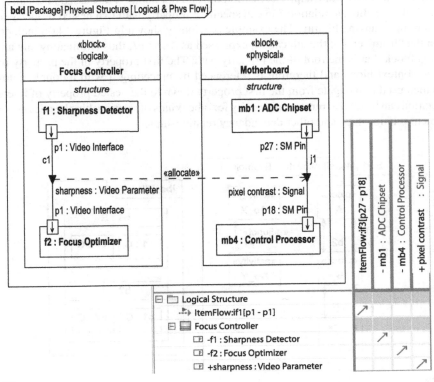

FIGURE 14.21

Example of structural flow allocation with allocation matrix.

and *Motherboard* blocks on the block definition diagram that only the names of the item properties are displayed, not the names of the item flows. It is possible to allocate from an item property on one diagram directly to an item property on another diagram, in this case *sharpness : Video Parameter* allocated to *pixel contrast : Signal*. Because the logical data model is independent of the physical data model, the types (conveyed classifiers) of each item property are different (*Video Parameter* and *Signal*). Note that allocation between item flows or item properties is most clearly represented on the allocation matrix. The name of the item flow in *Focus Controller* is *if1*. Likewise, the name of the item flow in *Mother Board* is *if3*.

14.10 ALLOCATING DEEPLY NESTED PROPERTIES

Special care may be required to avoid ambiguity when allocating deeply nested usages/properties such as parts and callBehaviorActions. The block definition diagram in Figure 14.22 presents a structural hierarchy and a behavioral hierarchy. When allocating callBehaviorAction *y1* specifically to part *c1*, the information on the block definition diagram can be ambiguous. The internal block diagram in Fig 14.22 presents the plausible internal structure of Block *A*, where both *b1* and *b2* include *c1* in their internal structure.

An allocate relationship can include a property path, which is a combination of namespace qualified name notation (::) discussed in Chapter 6, Section 6.6 and dot notation discussed in Chapter 7, Section 7.3.1. As a result, the allocate relationship can specify a property path to a nested property on either of its ends and remove any ambiguity. The example previously shown in Figure 14.06 includes a nested property on the "from" end of the allocation, expressed as *A::b1.c1*, thus eliminating any ambiguity. *A* is the context block that is the root of the property path. The first property in the property path is contained in the context block and therefore is referenced by preceding it with a double colon. The dot notation is then used to navigate from the first property down to the nested property of interest.

This notation can be used to remove ambiguity for other kinds of relationships besides allocation, such as requirement relationships and other dependency relationships.

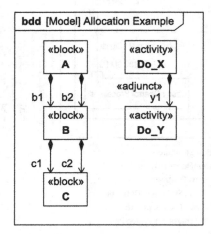 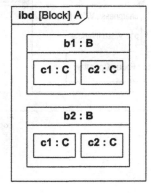

FIGURE 14.22

Example of potential ambiguity introduced by deeply nested parts. When allocating to part c1, which one is it?

14.11 EVALUATING ALLOCATION ACROSS A USER MODEL

The integrity and completeness of the allocate relationships are largely dependent on the system's stage of development. Since allocation may be used as an abstract prelude to more concrete relationships, the quality of allocation at a given point in time is assessed with respect to the system development method or strategy being employed.

14.11.1 ESTABLISHING BALANCE AND CONSISTENCY

The model can be assessed in terms of the completeness and consistency of the allocate relationships and the overall balance of the allocation as described next.

Completeness and consistency can be evaluated using user defined rules or constraints. In functional allocation, for example, allocation of a package of activities is said to be complete when each activity has an allocate relationship to a block in the model. It may not be judged to be consistent, for example, until the actions in the activities are depicted in a valid activity diagram. The inferred allocation to parts is depicted on a valid internal block diagram, and any object flows on the activity diagram are allocated to appropriate connectors on the internal block diagram. Consistency can also involve checking for circular allocations, redundant allocations, and what the modeler may define as inappropriate allocations (e.g., allocating an activity to another activity). Again, automated model checking is expected to assist with this.

Evaluating the balance of the allocation is more subjective and likely to require experience and judgment on the part of the modeler. One aspect of balance may involve assessing the level of detail represented by the model element at each end of the allocate relationship. For example, balance might involve either examining portions of the model that are rich in allocation to determine whether the level of detail is too high or assessing whether the allocation-poor portions of the model need further refinement. When evaluating functional allocation, for example, if a large number of activities are allocated to a single block but other blocks have few or no activities allocated, the modeler may ask: 1) Have the activities of the system been completely modeled? or 2) Has the structural design incorporated too much functionality into a single block? The answers to these questions will help determine the direction for the future modeling effort. For Question 1, it might mean fleshing out the activity model in other areas; for Question 2, it might involve decomposing the over-allocated block into lower-level blocks.

14.12 TAKING ALLOCATION TO THE NEXT STEP

Once allocation across the model is balanced and complete, each allocation may be refined by a more formal relationship that preserves and elaborates the constraints from the "from" end to the "to" end of the allocation. In this way, allocation is used to direct the system design activity through the model without prematurely deciding how the relationship between model elements will be refined. Of course, this is highly dependent on the modeling method.

SysML allocations allow the modeler to keep model refinement options open. For example, functional allocations can be refined by designating activities allocated to a block as methods called by operations of the block, which requires the additional step of creating the operations. Deferring the decision allows the modeler to work at a consistent level of abstraction, without prematurely committing to modeling details.

Even after the model is refined, it is appropriate to retain the allocate relationships, possibly capturing supporting «rationale» in the model to provide a history of how the model was developed. This can be very important information when considering reuse of the model on a different program or product.

14.13 SUMMARY

The allocate relationship provides significant flexibility for relating model elements to one another beginning early in the development process. Key concepts for modeling allocations include the following:

- An allocate relationship is a form of mapping between model elements that provides the capability to assign responsibility associated with one model element to another.
- Use of allocation enables certain implementation decisions to be deferred by specifying the model at higher levels of abstraction and then using allocations as a basis for further model refinement.
- There are many different kinds of allocation, including allocation of behavior, structure, and properties. Allocation supports traditional systems engineering concepts, such as allocating behavior to structure by allocating activities to blocks. Also supported are allocations of logical connectors to physical interfaces, software to hardware, object flows to item flows, and many others.
- A key distinction must be made between an allocation of definition and an allocation of usage. In allocation of definition, defined elements (e.g., activities) are allocated to other defined elements (e.g., blocks); allocation between the activity and the block is valid for all usages of the activity and all usages of the block, regardless of the context. For allocation of usage—such as when an action is allocated to a part—the allocation is only valid in the specific context of the part properties/roles and actions.
- An allocate activity partition provides an explicit mechanism to allocate responsibility of an action to a part.
- There are multiple graphical and tabular representations for representing allocations similar to those used for representing requirements relationships. Graphical representations include direct notation, compartment notation, and callout notation. Matrix and tabular representations can provide a compact form for representing multiple allocate relationships.

14.14 QUESTIONS

1. List four ways that allocations can be depicted on SysML diagrams.
2. Which kinds of model elements can participate in an allocate relationship in SysML?
3. Is the allocate relationship appropriate to use when allocating requirements?
4. List and describe three uses of the allocate relationship in SysML.

5. For each of the following allocate relationships, indicate whether they are allocation of definition or allocation of usage:
   a. action on activity diagram to part on internal block diagram
   b. activity to block
   c. object flow to connector
   d. activity parameter node to interface block
6. What is the significance of choosing an allocation of definition instead of an allocation of usage?
7. Should an object flow ever be allocated to a block? Explain your answer.
8. Should an activity ever be allocated to a part? Explain your answer.
9. Should a connector ever be allocated to a block? Explain your answer.
10. Describe what is being allocated in Figure 14.21 and its significance.

DISCUSSION TOPICS

What is the purpose of allocation? What role does it play in system development? How can good or poor allocation impact the overall quality of the system design?

Describe an appropriate next step after completing functional allocation. Which mechanisms are available to implement functionality in blocks?

CUSTOMIZING SysML FOR SPECIFIC DOMAINS

This chapter introduces metamodeling concepts that are typically of interest to language designers and provides an overview of the SysML language specification itself. It then describes how to customize SysML using profiles and model libraries to support a wide range of systems modeling domains. In addition, this chapter includes a discussion of SysML view and viewpoint, and how these constructs are used to customize the presentation of modeling information for different stakeholders.

15.1 OVERVIEW

SysML is a general-purpose systems modeling language that is intended to support a wide range of domain-specific applications such as the modeling of automotive or aerospace systems. The SysML language is described in a metamodel, whose elements—called metaclasses—describe concepts in the system modeling domain. Section 15.2 of this chapter provides an overview of both metamodeling and the SysML specification.

SysML has been designed to enable extensions that explicitly support specialized domains. An example may be a customization of SysML for the automotive domain that includes specific automotive concepts and representations of standard domain elements such as engines, chassis, brakes, roads, drivers, and passengers.

To accomplish this, SysML includes extension mechanisms called stereotypes, which are grouped into special kinds of packages called profiles. Stereotypes extend existing SysML language concepts with additional properties and constraints. SysML also supports model libraries—collections of reusable model elements commonly used in a particular domain. Profiles and model libraries are themselves contained in models, but they typically are authored by language designers rather than the general system modeler. The term "user model" refers to a model authored by a system modeler to describe a system or systems.

Model libraries provide constructs that can be reused by a model, such as blocks that specify reusable components, value types that define valid units, and quantity kinds for value properties. Profiles, on the other hand, provide constructs that extend the modeling language itself. For example, SysML is a profile of UML that extends basic constructs such as a UML class to create the concept of a SysML block.

Profiles and model libraries are often depicted on package diagrams (as described in Chapter 6) or block definition diagrams (as described in Chapter 7, with additional notations described in this chapter). The model element kinds corresponding to the frame of the package diagram are `profile` and `modelLibrary` respectively.

Figure 15.1 shows a package diagram with much of the notation used for defining stereotypes. This diagram contains the definitions of three stereotypes and their properties to support simulations. *Flow-Based Simulation* and *Flow Simulation Element* both extend the SysML *Activity* metaclass and add information

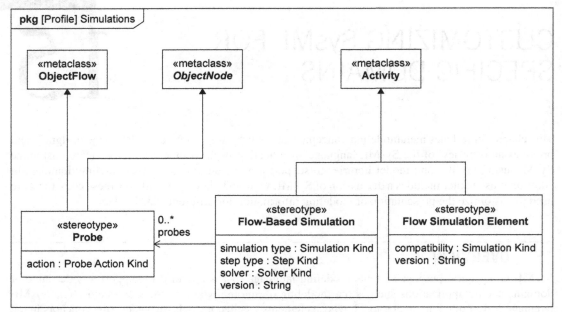

FIGURE 15.1

Example of a profile defined on a package diagram.

about the kind of simulation and how it executes. *Probe* extends both the *ObjectFlow* and *ObjectNode* meta-classes—part of the activity specification—and is used to tell the simulation which data to monitor.

Table A.2 in the Appendix shows the additional notation needed to represent the extensions for model libraries and profiles on a package diagram.

Figure 15.2 shows a model library of elements that are themselves extended using the stereotypes shown in Figure 15.1. The model elements in the *Flow Simulation Elements* model library are intended for use in building flow-based simulations. They are activities (i.e., model elements whose type is the metaclass *Activity* shown in Figure 15.1) with the stereotype *Flow Simulation Element* applied. Note that when stereotypes are applied, the keyword for a stereotype by convention has a different typographic style than the style of the stereotype's name and is described in Section 15.6. These activities can be invoked from actions owned by a flow-based simulation. The values for the stereotype's properties allow the simulation tool to determine their validity based on the kind of simulation required (e.g., continuous, discrete).

Table A.29 in the Appendix shows the additional notation needed on SysML diagrams to represent model elements that have been extended by stereotypes.

Sections 15.3 through 15.7 discuss model libraries and profiles in detail. Section 15.3 describes model libraries and their use in defining reusable components. Sections 15.4 and 15.5 cover the definition of stereotypes and the use of profiles to describe a set of stereotypes and supporting definitions. Sections 15.6 and 15.7 focus on the use of profiles and model libraries to build domain-specific user models.

Section 15.8 describes views and viewpoints, which can be used to present modeling information in ways other than those provided by the SysML language and are an important aspect of customizing the language. A viewpoint specifies how to produce a custom visualization of model information to address

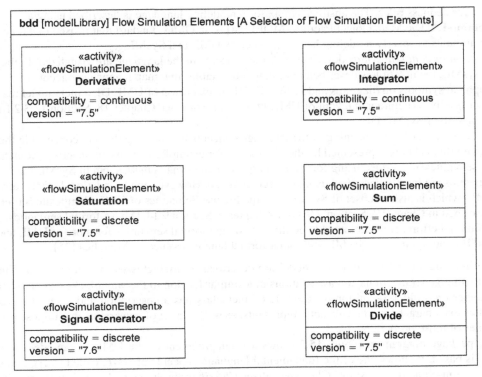

FIGURE 15.2

Example of the application of stereotypes to model elements.

a set of stakeholder concerns. A view conforms to a viewpoint and specifies the set of model elements that will be exposed in the visualization. Table A.30 in the Appendix shows the notation for representing views and viewpoints.

15.2 THE SysML SPECIFICATION AND LANGUAGE ARCHITECTURE

The SysML language itself is specified by extending UML using profiles and model libraries. This section introduces the fundamental concepts of modeling language design and then describes the architecture of SysML.

15.2.1 MODELING LANGUAGE DESIGN

The concepts needed to specify UML-based modeling languages, such as SysML, are discussed below. A modeling language specification has three parts:

- *Abstract syntax* describes the concepts in the language, the relationships between the concepts, and a set of rules about how the concepts can be put together, sometimes referred to as well-formedness rules. The abstract syntax for a modeling language is described using a **metamodel.** The Meta Object Facility (MOF) [24] is an OMG standard that is used to define metamodels to specify modeling languages such as UML and SysML.

- *Notation or concrete syntax* describes how the concepts in the language are visualized. In the case of SysML, the notation is described both in notation tables that map language concepts to graphical symbols on diagrams and in SysML DI, an extension of UML DI, a metamodel that describes the structure and layout of UML-based diagrams. See Chapter 18, Section 18.3.2 for a discussion of SysML DI.

- *Semantics* describe the meaning of the language concepts by mapping them to concepts in the domain that is being represented by the language—for example, systems engineering. Sometimes the semantics are defined using formal techniques, such as mathematics, but in SysML the semantics are mostly described using natural language. However, the foundational UML subset of UML, which is also a subset of SysML, and the Precise Semantics of UML Composite Structures (described in Chapter 7, Section 7.9.1 and Chapter 9, Section 9.14.1) have formal semantics. Additional efforts are anticipated to continue to define formal semantics for more of UML and SysML, and to integrate SysML with other formal languages such as Modelica [25].

The individual concepts in a metamodel are described by **metaclasses,** which are related to one another using generalizations and associations in a similar fashion to the way blocks can be related to one another on a block definition diagram. Each metaclass has a description and a set of metaclass properties that characterize the concept it represents, as well as a set of constraints that impose rules on the values of those properties.

The package diagram in Figure 15.3 shows a small fragment of the UML metamodel on which SysML is based. It shows one of the fundamental language concepts of *UML*, called *Class,* and some of its most important relationships. *Class* specializes *Classifier*, through which it gains the capability of forming classification hierarchies. The figure also shows the *Class* associations to *Property* and *Operation,* which between them define most of the important features of a *Class*. The figure also shows some metaclass properties such as the *isAbstract* metaclass property contained by *Classifier*.

Profiles and model libraries (discussed in detail in Sections 15.3–5) are used to add new capabilities to a modeling language. Profiles extend an existing metamodel, called a reference metamodel, with additional concepts called stereotypes, which have their own properties, rules, and relationships. They therefore allow the language defined by the original metamodel to be augmented with concepts for domains not covered by it directly. Model libraries can contain model elements that are described by metaclasses in the metamodel, or concepts that have been further extended by stereotypes in a profile.

A user model of a system contains model elements that are instances of the metaclasses and stereotypes that are defined in the language. For example, an instance of the metaclass *Package* is a particular package in the user model. These instances have references to other instances based on the metaclass properties and relationships defined in the metamodel.

These model elements are visualized using a concrete syntax (e.g., symbols on diagrams) as described in Chapter 5, Section 5.3. The symbols are mapped to metaclasses and stereotypes in the language so that each symbol represents a specific concept. For example, a block and its properties have a specific graphical representation as a box symbol with compartments.

Figure 15.4 shows a fragment of a block definition diagram for defining airplanes, along with the mapping to the metaclasses and stereotypes that represent the various concepts. *Airplane Model* is a

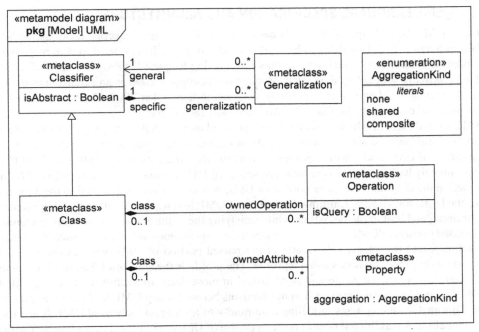

FIGURE 15.3

Fragment of *UML*, the underlying metamodel for SysML.

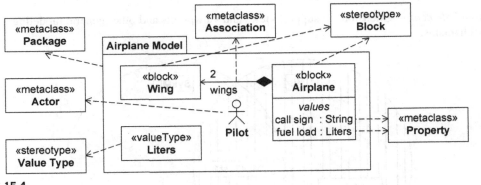

FIGURE 15.4

Relationship of metaclasses to model elements in the user model.

package containing *Airplane* and *Wing* blocks; *Pilot*, an actor (i.e., external to the system); and *Liters*, a value type. *Airplane* has two properties that describe two of its quantifiable characteristics: *call sign*, whose valid values are described by *String* (a primitive concept defined by SysML), and *fuel load*, with type *Liters*. *Airplane* has an association to block *Wing*, which describes part of its structure, in this case its (two) *wings*.

15.2.2 SysML LANGUAGE SPECIFICATION AND ARCHITECTURE

The official OMG SysML specification [1] defines a set of language concepts, using the architecture described in Section 15.2.1, which can be used to model systems. It was developed in response to the requirements specified in the UML for Systems Engineering Request for Proposal (UML for SE RFP) [52]. It was formally adopted by the Object Management Group in 2006 as an extension to the Unified Modeling Language [53] and became publicly available in September 2007. The SysML specification is maintained and evolved by the OMG SysML Revision Task Force.

SysML extends UML, which was originally specified as a modeling language for software design to support general-purpose software modeling. As indicated in the Venn diagram in Figure 15.5, SysML reuses a subset of UML and adds extensions to meet the requirements in the UML for SE RFP.

Approximately half of *UML* was reused. The subset of *UML* reused by *SysML* is called *UML4SysML* as indicated in the diagram. The other portion of UML was not viewed as essential to meet the requirements of the UML for SE RFP. Limiting the portion of UML that was used reduced the requirements for SysML training and tool implementation, while satisfying the requirements for systems modeling.

The reused portion of UML was in some cases used as-is without modification, such as interactions, state machines, and use cases. Other parts of the reused portion of UML were extended to address unique systems engineering needs using a profile. The profile is the standard UML mechanism used to specify extensions to the language and is described in more detail in Section 15.5. The profile-based approach was chosen over other extension mechanisms because many UML tools can interpret profiles directly. This enables the systems modeling community to leverage widely used UML-based tools for systems modeling. An additional benefit is that a profile of UML can be used in conjunction with UML to help bridge the gap between systems and software modeling.

The SysML profile is organized into the following discrete language units that extend UML to provide additional system modeling capabilities:

- *Model elements*—extensions to support views and viewpoints and other general modeling mechanisms.

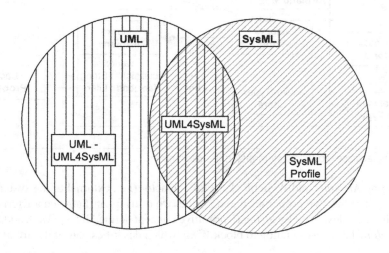

FIGURE 15.5

Relationship between SysML and UML.

- *Requirements*—extensions to support textual requirements and their relationships to each other and to models.
- *Blocks*—extensions to represent system structure and properties.
- *Activities*—extensions to support continuous behavior.
- *Constraint blocks*—extensions to model constraints and parametric models that support engineering analysis.
- *Ports and flows*—extensions to support flow of information, matter, and energy between system elements, as well as nested ports and other interface concepts needed to support the diversity of systems interfaces.
- *Allocations*—extensions to support mapping relationships between model elements

SysML also defines three model libraries:

- *PrimitiveValueTypes*—introduces a set of standard primitive values types including Real and Complex.
- *ControlValues*—introduces a value type called ControlValue, which is used by control operators (see Chapter 9, Section 9.6.2).
- *UnitAndQuantityKind*—introduces Unit and QuantityKind, which are used to express the units of value types (see Chapter 7, Section 7.3.4).

The SysML profile is intended to be applied strictly (see Section 15.6), which means that models developed using the SysML extensions may only use that subset of UML defined in UML4SysML. SysML as described in the specification is therefore the combination of UML4SysML and the SysML profile as indicated in Figure 15.5.

15.3 DEFINING MODEL LIBRARIES TO PROVIDE REUSABLE CONSTRUCTS

A **model library** is a special type of package that is intended to contain a set of reusable model elements for a given domain. Model libraries are not used to extend the language concepts of SysML, although model elements in the library may have stereotypes applied if they support a specialized domain, as shown in Figure 15.2. A model library can contain model elements of specifications similar to those found in a parts catalog, or they can contain model elements with wider applicability, such as the ISO80000 model library provided in the SysML specification.

Any packageable model element (see Chapter 6, Section 6.5), such as a block, a value type, an activity, or a constraint block, can be included in a model library. Elements in a model library may be contained directly in that library, or they may have been defined in other models or packages and imported. In the latter case, the model library acts as a mechanism to gather and organize elements from disparate sources for reuse.

The contents of a model library may be shown on a package diagram or block definition diagram using the standard symbols for those diagrams. When a model library is shown on a package diagram, it is designated by a package symbol with the keyword «modelLibrary» appearing above the name of the model library in the name compartment or tab of the package. (See Figure 15.11 for an example of the former notation.) When a model library corresponds to the frame of a diagram, modelLibrary is shown in square brackets in the diagram header as the model element kind.

The model library in Figure 15.6 defines a set of blocks to represent some very basic physical concepts intended to be specialized by domain-specific blocks. *Physical Thing* describes things with *mass* and *density* and provides a constraint on its mass via the constraint property *me*. The type of *me, Mass Equation,* defines a constraint which relates the *total* parameter to the sum of the parameter *componentMass*, a collection of component masses. The block *Moving Thing* specializes *Physical Thing* with properties of motion (e.g., *acceleration* and *velocity*). It also has a property *force,* which allows force to be applied to accelerate or decelerate a *Moving Thing*. Instead of modeling equations as constraints, the properties of *Moving Thing* are calculated using a simulation, as shown later in Figure 15.13.

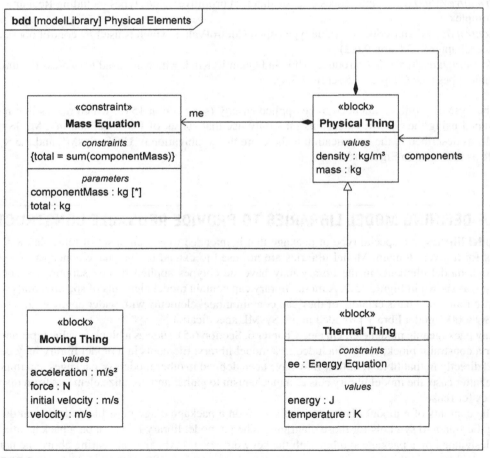

FIGURE 15.6

A model library defining some basic physical concepts.

15.4 DEFINING STEREOTYPES TO EXTEND SysML CONCEPTS

Whereas the elements of model libraries use existing language concepts to describe reusable constructs, **stereotypes** add new language concepts, typically to support a specific application domain. Stereotypes are grouped together in special packages called profiles. SysML itself is defined as a profile of UML and uses stereotypes to define system concepts such as block and requirement. Just as user models contain instances of metaclasses, they can also contain instances of stereotypes, although instances of stereotypes have special rules along with different conventions for how they are displayed.

A stereotype extends one or more metaclasses in a reference metamodel. In the case of SysML, the reference metamodel is the subset of UML called UML4SysML as described in 15.2.2. The relationship between a base metaclass and a stereotype is a kind of association called an **extension**. An extension is conceptually similar to a generalization in that it applies the stereotype's characteristics to the base metaclass. The choice of the base metaclass or metaclasses for a stereotype depends on the kind of concepts that need to be described. A language designer will identify a base metaclass with some of the characteristics needed to represent the new concept and then add or potentially remove other characteristics.

Metamodels, including UML, contain abstract metaclasses that cannot be instantiated directly in the user model but exist to provide a set of common characteristics that are specialized by concrete metaclasses that can be instantiated in the user model. A stereotype that extends an abstract metaclass or a concrete metaclass that is further specialized is equivalent to the stereotype extending all the specializations of that metaclass.

A **profile** is a special kind of package that contains stereotypes, metaclasses, and their interrelationships. A profile can be shown on a package diagram with `profile` as the model element kind that corresponds to the diagram frame. A metaclass is represented by a rectangle with the keyword «metaclass» centered at the top, followed by the name of the metaclass. A stereotype is represented by a rectangle with the keyword «stereotype» centered at the top, followed by the name of the stereotype. An extension relationship is depicted as a line with a filled triangle at the metaclass end.

Figure 15.7 shows a profile that contains a set of stereotypes that describe new concepts for representing flow-based simulation artifacts. The stereotype *Flow-Based Simulation* allows modelers to

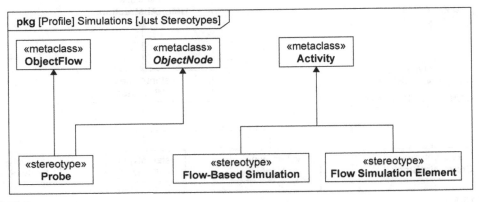

FIGURE 15.7

A package diagram containing stereotypes that support flow-based simulations.

define simulations of system flow. *Flow-Based Simulation* extends *Activity*, because activities already have a flow-based semantic and so have many of the right characteristics. The stereotype *Flow Simulation Element* is used to model a specialized form of activity that can be added to a flow-based simulation.

A very useful capability of simulations is to monitor the values of certain elements as the simulation runs. The *Probe* stereotype allows the modeler to indicate that certain elements of the simulation should be monitored. *Probe* extends both *ObjectFlow* and *ObjectNode* because these are both constructs through which values (as tokens) flow. *Probe* extends *ObjectNode*, which is an abstract metaclass as indicated by the use of italic font for its name. This means that all the concrete subclasses of *ObjectNode* (e.g., *DataStoreNode* and *ActivityParameterNode*) are implicitly extended as well. Note that this is an example of how extension and generalization differ. *Probe* is not a specialization of both *ObjectFlow* and *ObjectNode*; rather an instance of *Probe* may extend an instance of *ObjectFlow* or an instance of *ObjectNode* (or one of its concrete subclasses), but not both. The extension enables the properties and constraints of a *Probe* stereotype to be applied to an object flow or object node in the user model.

In addition to extending a metaclass, a stereotype can also be defined in the metamodel by specializing an existing stereotype or stereotypes using the generalization mechanism described in Chapter 7, Section 7.7.1. In this case the new stereotype inherits all the characteristics of the stereotypes it specializes, including extensions. The new stereotype can then add characteristics which are relevant to the new concept. Stereotypes may be abstract, which means they cannot be used directly in a user model, but can be specialized and their characteristics inherited. Stereotype specialization is shown using the standard generalization notation—a line with a hollow triangle at the general end.

Figure 15.8 shows an example from SysML of a stereotype that specializes another stereotype. *Block* extends the UML metaclass *Class*, and *ConstraintBlock* specializes *Block*. It inherits the property *isEncapsulated,* which indicates whether a connector can cross its boundary, from *Block.* The

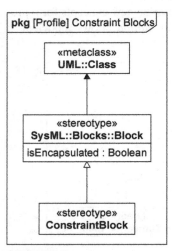
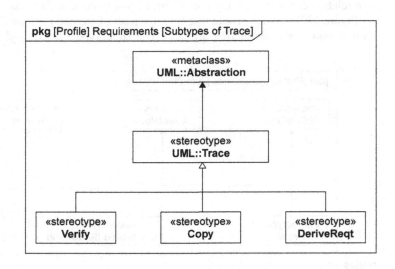

FIGURE 15.8

Specialization example from SysML.

following is a snippet of the description for *ConstraintBlock* in Section 10.3.2.1 of the SysML specification:

> *"A constraint block is a block that packages the statement of a constraint so it may be applied in a reusable way to constrain properties of other blocks."*

"SysML also reuses a stereotype from UML called *Trace*, and specializes it to represent relationships in the *Requirements* section of SysML.

15.4.1 ADDING PROPERTIES AND CONSTRAINTS TO STEREOTYPES

A stereotype definition can include both properties and constraints. Stereotypes that specialize other stereotypes inherit the properties and constraints of their general stereotype.

Stereotype properties are like metaclass properties; they represent metadata about the model element to which the stereotype is applied. The properties have a type that defines the kind of data that is represented. SysML defines a set of primitive types—String, Integer, Boolean, Real, and Complex—but profiles can add their own types or use types defined in model libraries.

It is important to distinguish between the properties of blocks and the properties of stereotypes. For example, a block *Vehicle* may have a property called *inspector*, which records who checked this instance of *Vehicle* as it came off the production line. At the same time, someone could extend the *Block* stereotype to include an *inspector* property, but this would record the identity of someone who checked the specification of the *Vehicle* block and have nothing to do with the instances described by the *Vehicle* block.

Constraints can be added to a stereotype to specify rules about valid uses of its properties or to restrict the use of an existing concept by further constraining the properties of the metaclasses that are extended. Constraints are specified using a textual expression in a specified language. The constraint language OCL [38] is often used for expressing constraints in profiles.

A stereotype may also include properties that are typed by either stereotypes or metaclasses. This allows instances of the stereotype in the user model to contain references to instances of other stereotypes and metaclasses in the user model. These properties can be defined in the metamodel using associations between the stereotype and other stereotypes or metaclasses, or simply as properties of the stereotype definition. Metaclasses in the reference metamodel cannot be modified by a profile. This means that an association between a stereotype and metaclass can define properties on the stereotype but not on the metaclass.

Stereotype properties and constraints are shown in a similar way to the properties and constraints of blocks (i.e., in compartments below the name compartment). Constraints can also be shown in note symbols attached to the constrained stereotype. In addition to properties and constraints, a stereotype definition may include an image that can optionally be displayed when the stereotype is applied to a model element. The iconic representation may be extremely useful for representing concepts in a particular domain.

Figure 15.9 shows the properties and constraints of the stereotypes first shown in Figure 15.7 and some enumerations that are needed to define some of those properties. The definition of *Flow-Based Simulation* includes three properties that govern the kind of simulation performed. *Simulation type* is typed by the enumeration *Simulation Kind*, which has two values, *discrete* and *continuous*, stating whether a continuous or discrete solution is required. *Step type* stipulates whether the simulation steps are fixed in size or can vary. *Solver* defines the kind of solver to be used. The definition of *Flow Simulation Element* includes a property called *compatibility*, which gives the kinds of simulation with which

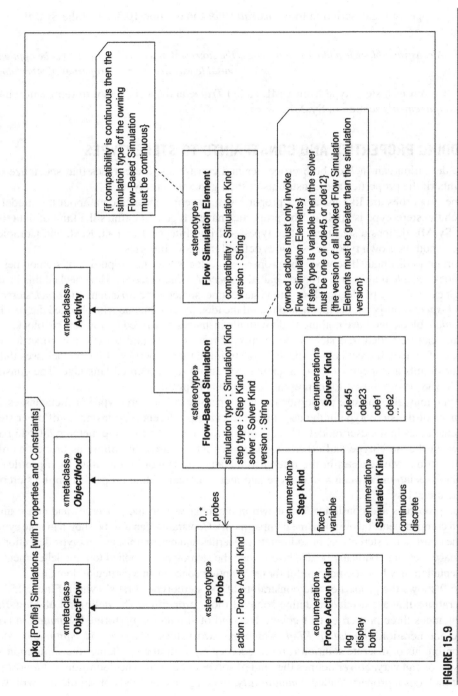

FIGURE 15.9

Providing additional detail for the flow-based simulation stereotypes.

it is compatible. A value of *continuous* means that this element can only be used in continuous simulations; a value of *discrete* means it can be used in both discrete and continuous simulations.

These stereotypes also define constraints that affect activities with the various stereotypes applied. A constraint on *Flow Simulation Element* states that an element whose *compatibility* property has the value *continuous* can be used only if the *simulation type* of their owning activity has the value *continuous*. Another constraint states that a *Flow Simulation Element* may be invoked only by an action contained in a *Flow-Based Simulation*. A constraint on *Flow-Based Simulation* states that a variable step solver (*ode45* or *ode23*) must be used if the value for *step type* is *variable*. (Note: *ode* refers to ordinary differential equations.)

Probe has a property *action* that indicates the action to take place for values on the monitored element. Its type, *Probe Action Kind*, can have three values: *display* means display values in a simulation window; *log* means log these values to a log file; *both* means do both. *Flow-Based Simulation* has a property *probes* that references all the probes defined within it, as indicated by the association between *Flow-Based Simulation* and *Probe*.

For practical reasons of tool implementation, stereotypes are not metaclasses but rather define additional elements that are created along with instances of metaclasses in the user model. However, some stereotypes are viewed more like metaclasses, while others are viewed more like ancillary constructs.

For example, a modeler probably intends to create a *Flow-Based Simulation* (see Figure 15.9) rather than create an *Activity* and then apply the *Flow-Based Simulation* stereotype to it. A *Flow-Based Simulation* has constraints placed on it that an activity is unlikely to satisfy. On the other hand, the stereotype *Audited Item* in Figure 15.15 is an example of a stereotype that is a provider of ancillary information. *Audited Item* adds auditing information to a model element and is only needed once auditing of the element has begun. It is therefore natural in this scenario to imagine creating an instance of *Classifier* (like a block) and only applying *Audited Item* at some later date.

In a user model, a stereotype can be applied to any model element that has a metaclass that the stereotype extends or to any model element whose metaclass is a subclass of a metaclass that the stereotype extends. Typically, it is the modeler who dictates whether a stereotype is used or not, but occasionally the profile designer may wish to enforce that every model element of a particular metaclass must have a specific stereotype applied. The extension is then said to be **required.** Required extensions can be useful when the use of the model depends on all model elements of a certain metaclass having some special characteristics. If the stereotype is required, then the property keyword {required} is shown near the stereotype end of the extension. Figure 15.15 shows an example of a required extension that adds configuration data—perhaps in conjunction with some configuration management tool—to all model elements of metaclasses that are deemed worthy of configuration control.

15.5 EXTENDING THE SysML LANGUAGE USING PROFILES

A profile is a kind of package used as the container for a set of stereotypes and supporting definitions. Typically a profile will contain a set of stereotypes that represent a cohesive set of concepts for a given modeling domain. More complex profiles may contain either subprofiles or subpackages that further divide the overall domain into subsets of related domain concepts. The difference between creating subprofiles and subpackages is that subprofiles may be applied apart from each other, whereas all of the subpackages of a profile are applied with their owning profile. So, if the intention of the profile authors is simply to partition a profile for ease of communication, then they should use subpackages, but if the subsets of the profile contents can be used independently of each other, then subprofiles should be used.

Profiles typically serve one of two potential uses: either the profile defines a set of concepts that support a new domain or it defines a set of concepts that add new information to a model in a domain that is already supported. It is often useful to keep this distinction in mind when creating a profile.

The former use is sometimes called a domain-specific language and offers a new set of language concepts that a modeler might use when building models in that domain. The *Simulations* profile shown in Figure 15.9 is an example of this use. A modeler will set out to build a simulation using language concepts in the *Simulations* profile and will think in terms of those concepts. In this kind of use, the stereotypes in the profile will predominantly resemble metaclasses, as described in the previous section.

In the latter use, a stereotype defines additional data that can be stored about existing model elements. A process or configuration management profile, such as the *Quality Assurance* profile shown later in Figure 15.15, is a good example of this use. Stereotypes from the *Quality Assurance* profile will be added to existing model elements when quality-assurance information about them is required, and removed if and when the information is no longer relevant.

15.5.1 REFERENCING A METAMODEL OR METACLASS FROM A PROFILE

Section 15.4 described how stereotypes are defined by either extending a metaclass or subclassing a stereotype. For a stereotype to extend a metaclass, the profile that contains the stereotype must include a reference to the metaclass, or a reference to the metamodel that contains the metaclass, using a special kind of import relationship called a **reference relationship** (see Chapter 6, Section 6.7 for a discussion on the import relationship). To specialize a stereotype contained in another profile, the profile must import the stereotype the profile that contains the stereotype. When a profile is importing an existing profile, metaclass references made by the imported profile are the basis for its reference metamodel, although it may reference additional metaclasses as well.

The notation for the reference relationship is a dashed arrow, annotated with the keyword «reference», with its head pointing at the referenced metaclass or metamodel. The import relationship is also shown as a dashed arrow with its head pointing toward the imported stereotype or profile, but it is annotated with the keyword «import».

In Figure 15.10, the *SysML* profile references the *UML* metamodel to extend its metaclasses. The «metamodel» keyword is used, and the triangle indicates that this is a model. The *Simulations* profile imports the *SysML* profile, and hence its reference metamodel is also *UML*. Stereotypes inside the *Simulations* profile can now extend metaclasses in *UML* (e.g., *Activity*) and subclass SysML stereotypes (e.g., *Block*).

15.6 APPLYING PROFILES TO USER MODELS IN ORDER TO USE STEREOTYPES

The two previous sections in this chapter have described how to define a profile and the stereotypes contained within the profile. For modelers to use constructs from the profile in their model, they need to apply the profile to their model or to a subpackage of their model. Once the profile has been applied, the

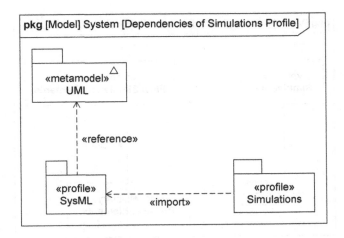

FIGURE 15.10

Defining the inputs required to specify the *Simulations* profile.

stereotypes and other model elements in the profile and the metaclasses from its reference metamodel may be used anywhere within the containment hierarchy of the model or package.

A profile is applied to a model or package using a **profile application** relationship. The user of the profile can choose whether to apply the profile strictly by using the **strict property** of the profile application relationship. A strict application implies that only metaclasses from the profile's reference metamodel can be used within the model or package applying the profile. This ensures that all profiles applied to a package or model must reference the same set of metaclasses. If the strict property is not set on the profile application, there is no restriction on which metaclasses can be used, and so a package or model may apply multiple profiles with different metaclasses. A modeler can add or remove a profile application relationship at any time. However, when a profile application is removed, any instances of stereotypes from the profile are also removed from the user model. Therefore, any such removal should be undertaken with care, and a backup copy of the model should be made.

Whenever possible, it is recommended that the reference model for a profile be constructed in such a way that the profile can be applied strictly (i.e., that it has all the constructs required to support the profile domain). If users need to use metaclasses other than those referenced by the profile, it is likely that the impact of using them in combination with profile concepts will not have been fully considered. The SysML profile has been defined to be applied strictly, but this restriction can be removed to use additional software-related concepts from the UML metamodel if supported by a well-thought out systems and software development methodology.

The notation for applying a profile to a user model or subpackage is a dashed arrow, labeled with the keyword «apply», whose head points toward the profile that is applied.

Figure 15.11 shows a package diagram that contains the *Physical Elements* model library. *Physical Elements* applies the *Simulations* profile so that elements within it can have simulation extensions applied. Note that the *Simulations* profile is applied strictly, which means that only metaclasses from its reference metamodel (via its import of *SysML* shown on Figure 15.10) can be used in the *Physical*

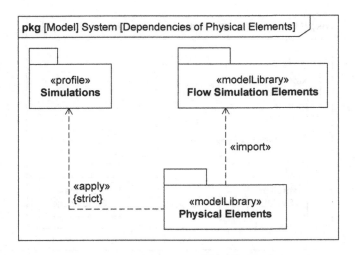

FIGURE 15.11

Applying the *Simulations* profile to a model and importing elements to support flow-based simulations.

Elements model library. *Physical Elements* also imports a model library called *Flow Simulation Elements* so that it can use the simulation elements it contains.

15.7 APPLYING STEREOTYPES WHEN BUILDING A MODEL

Once a user model has a profile applied to it, the stereotypes from the profile may be applied to model elements within that user model. How stereotypes are used depends on whether the intended purpose of the profile is a domain-specific language or a source of ancillary data and rules to support a particular aspect of the model. Although nothing in the specification of a profile differentiates the two cases, often tool vendors will add custom support tailored to the intended use when building the profile.

For a given stereotype, its extension relationships define the model elements that it can validly extend, subject to the model element satisfying any additional constraints that the stereotype specifies. A model element may have any number of valid stereotypes applied to it, in which case it must satisfy the constraints of each stereotype.

Although the intention of the SysML graphical notation for stereotypes—and the intention of many tool vendor implementations of profiles—is to hide these details and to provide a visualization that matches the modeler's expectation, the mechanics of how stereotypes are applied is worthy of some explanation. When a stereotype is applied to a model element in the user model (i.e., a metaclass instance), an instance of the stereotype is created in the user model and is related to the model element. Once an instance of the stereotype exists, the modeler can then add values for the stereotype's properties to the instance. An instance of a stereotype cannot exist without a related metaclass instance to extend, and therefore when a model element is deleted, all its related stereotype instances are also deleted.

Subject to these basic rules, how the modeler actually applies stereotypes is often governed by a modeling tool, based on the intended use of the stereotype. For example, the tool may create an instance of the stereotype and an instance of the base metaclass at the same time, or it may allow the modeler to create a model element first and then add and potentially remove the stereotype as separate actions.

Information from a stereotype is shown as part of the symbol of the model element to which it is applied or in a callout attached to the symbol. A stereotyped model element is shown with the name of the stereotype in guillemets (e.g., «stereotypeName»), followed by the name of the model element. The stereotype name may be capitalized and may contain spaces in its definition. However, the convention in SysML is for the stereotype name to be shown as a single word using camel case (the first letter of the name is lowercase, while the first letter of the second and subsequent words in the name are capitalized) when applied to a model element in a user model.

If a model element is represented by a node symbol (e.g., rectangle), the stereotype name is shown in the name compartment of the symbol. If the model element is represented by a path symbol (e.g., a line), the stereotype name is shown in a label next to the line and near the name of the element. Stereotype keywords can also be shown for elements in compartments before the element name.

If a model element has more than one stereotype applied, by default each stereotype name is shown on a separate line in a name compartment. If no stereotype properties are shown, multiple stereotype names can appear in a comma-separated list within one set of guillemets. See Figure 15.16 for an example of the application of multiple stereotypes. Whenever stereotypes are applied to a model element whose symbol normally has a keyword, its standard keyword is displayed before/above the stereotype keywords. The properties for a stereotype may be displayed in braces after the stereotype label or, if the symbol supports compartments, in a separate compartment with the stereotype name as the compartment label.

A stereotyped model element may also be shown with a special image that is part of the stereotype definition. For node symbols, that image may appear in the top right corner of the symbol, in which case it is often shown instead of the stereotype keyword. Alternatively, the image may replace the entire symbol.

Figure 15.12 shows some of the elements in the *Flow Simulation Elements* model library. They all have the *Flow Simulation Element* stereotype applied so that their *version* and *compatibility* properties can be specified. In this case *Derivative* and *Integrator* are only compatible with continuous simulations; the rest are compatible with discrete and continuous simulations. They all have version *"7.5"* except the *Signal Generator,* which has version *"7.6."* Note that because the underlying model elements are all activities, the keyword «activity» is shown, as described in Chapter 9, Section 9.12. These elements can be used in the construction of flow-based simulations.

The activity diagram in Figure 15.13 shows a simulation model of the motion of the *Moving Thing* block, first shown in Figure 15.6, using continuous semantics (the «continuous» keyword is elided in the figure). The activity *Motion Simulation* is the classifier behavior of *Moving Thing,* so the model shows what happens to it over its lifetime. The simulation calculates the values of acceleration, velocity, and distance over time. The algorithm first calculates the acceleration from the *mass* of the object (inherited from *Physical Thing)* and the *force* applied. It then integrates the acceleration to get the velocity. Finally, it integrates the sum of the velocity due to acceleration and the *initial velocity* to get

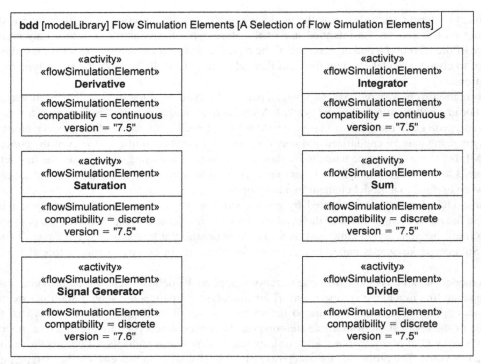

FIGURE 15.12

Defining a library of flow-based simulation elements using stereotypes to add simulation details.

the distance traveled, which is stored in data store *distance* (the initial state of the *integrator* activity is 0, so the initial value for *distance* is 0). The current values of acceleration and velocity from the simulation are used to update the relevant properties of a *Moving Thing*. In this simulation model, time is implicit to the calculation and is not shown.

Three probes are used over time to display the values of *acceleration*, *velocity*, and *distance*. The first two values are obtained via probes on object flows, and the third by a probe on a data store. Figure 15.14 shows *Motion Simulation* as an activity hierarchy (note that the adjunct keyword described in Chapter 9, Section 9.12.1 is not shown in this figure). This view is useful because it shows the properties of the simulation elements. *Motion Simulation* and its children in the activity hierarchy satisfy all the constraints imposed by the stereotypes *Flow-Based Simulation* and *Flow Simulation Element,* as defined in Figure 15.9:

- All the invoked activities of *Motion Simulation* are stereotyped by *Flow Simulation Element.*
- All the invoked activities have version numbers at least as high as *Motion Simulation* itself.
- The *ode45* solver is appropriate for a variable step continuous simulation.
- *Motion Simulation* is a continuous simulation, so both discrete and continuous *Flow Simulation Elements* are allowed.
- Data store *distance* is typed by the value type *m* (meters).

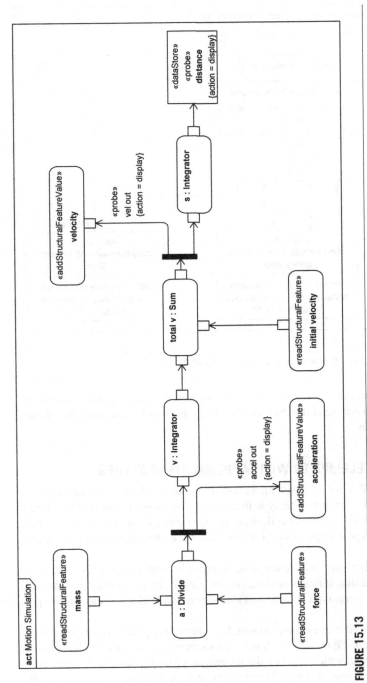

FIGURE 15.13

Using flow-based simulation stereotypes and library elements in the definition of a simulation.

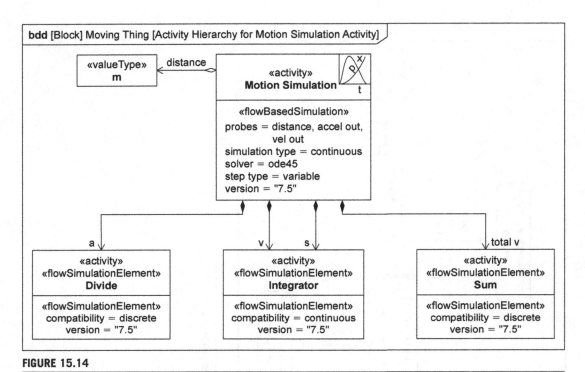

FIGURE 15.14

Block definition diagram showing the activity hierarchy for *Motion Simulation.*

Instead of showing the keyword «flowBasedSimulation» for *Motion Simulation,* this figure shows the stereotype's image in the top right corner of the symbol. The image is part of the stereotype's definition and is stored as part of the profile.

15.7.1 SPECIALIZING MODEL ELEMENTS WITH APPLIED STEREOTYPES

A potential area of confusion is the effect of specializing a classifier, such as a block, that has a stereotype applied to it in the user model. Applying a stereotype to a classifier does not imply that the stereotype is applied to subclasses of the classifier. If this is desired, the stereotype definition should include a constraint to ensure that the stereotype is applied to each subclass of the classifier that the stereotype is applied.

Even when a constraint forces subclasses to have the same stereotype as their superclasses, they do not inherit values for stereotype properties. If this is desired, the stereotype should include an additional constraint that every subclass has the stereotype applied and also inherits the values of the stereotype's properties.

Figure 15.15 and Figure 15.16 describe an example in which neither the applied stereotypes nor the values of their properties are inherited. Figure 15.15 shows two stereotypes from the profile *Quality Assurance.* The stereotype *Audited Item,* which extends the metaclass *Classifier* and can be applied to blocks among other model elements, is used when a classifier has been audited for quality—typically,

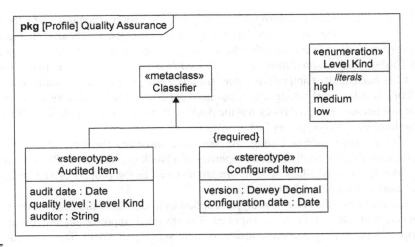

FIGURE 15.15

Definitions of two stereotypes used as part of quality assurance on a model.

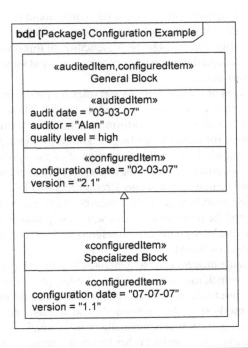

FIGURE 15.16

Application of quality-assurance stereotypes to two blocks, one of which specializes the other.

when it reaches a certain level of maturity. It has properties to capture the *audit date,* the *auditor,* and the *quality level* that may take values from *low* to *high.* The stereotype *Configured Item* contains properties that must be applied to every classifier, hence the presence of the {required} property.

Figure 15.16 shows the *Audited Item* and *Configured Item* stereotypes in use. In this case the block *General Block* has been audited and so has values for *audit date, auditor,* and *quality level.* Its subclass *Specialized Block* is still in early design, so it has not yet been audited. It clearly does not make sense to assume that just because *General Block* has the *Audited Item* stereotype applied to it that *Specialized Block* will also have this stereotype applied.

Even when a stereotype, such as *Configured Item,* is required and therefore applied to all blocks, it clearly is not the case that the configuration properties of a block (e.g., *General Block*) will be inherited by a subclass like *Specialized Block.* The information stored in the properties of *Configured Item* is specific to the model element to which it is applied.

Note that *General Block* has two stereotypes applied to it, demonstrating one of the notations that can be used where multiple stereotypes are applied. The keywords representing the two applied stereotypes both appear separated by a comma inside a single set of guillemets. The properties of the two stereotypes appear in separate compartments, labeled using the keyword of their owning stereotype.

15.8 DEFINING AND USING VIEWPOINTS TO GENERATE VIEWS OF THE MODEL

SysML models contain comprehensive descriptive information about the system and its environment that can be presented in SysML diagrams and tables as described throughout this part of the book. However, it is important to be able to customize the presentation of this information to support a diverse set of consumers. SysML has adopted the concepts of viewpoint and view from ISO-42010 (formerly IEEE-1471) [20] to address this need.

A **viewpoint** is a specification of the conventions and rules for producing artifacts that offer customized presentations of information contained in a SysML model. These presentations may contain SysML diagrams but in addition may present information in other forms including graphs, textual documentation, and other tabular formats. The artifacts produced by a viewpoint are intended to address the concerns of one or more stakeholders in the development of the system. A **stakeholder** is a role, group, or individual that has concerns that need to be addressed. For example, a security viewpoint may describe the production and presentation of a security report required by certification authorities. Multiple viewpoints may be needed to address all of the concerns of any given stakeholder. A **view** specifies a set of model elements that will be processed by a viewpoint to produce a specific artifact presenting information from those elements. Viewpoints can be referenced by multiple views to present information from different sets of model elements.

A viewpoint specifies both the process used to generate the artifacts and how the artifacts should be presented to the stakeholders, which may include figures, tables, plots, entire documents, presentation slides, or video. The process used to construct the artifacts is specified in an owned behavior of the viewpoint, identified as the **method** of the viewpoint's constructor operation. It may be expressed informally as a guide to producing the artifacts manually or in a formal language that can automatically produce the artifacts. The behavior may invoke other behaviors defined by both its owning viewpoint and other viewpoints.

A viewpoint is depicted by a box symbol with the keyword «viewpoint» at the top of its name compartment. The various properties of the viewpoint are shown in a second compartment, labelled «viewpoint», consisting of:

- The list of stakeholders for whom the viewpoint is intended;
- The set of concerns that the viewpoint addresses;
- The purpose of the viewpoint, which may state how stakeholder concerns have been addressed;
- The language used to describe the model content, which may be some profile of SysML;
- The method used to produce the viewpoint artifacts; and
- The presentation constraints of the generated artifacts, such as file format, language, etc.

Viewpoint concerns may also be shown in comment symbols linked to the viewpoint symbol. The constructor operation, which is always called *View*, can be shown in a separate compartment labeled *operations*.

The symbol for a stakeholder may either be a box symbol or an actor symbol. In the case of a box symbol, the symbol's name compartment contains the keyword «stakeholder» and a compartment labelled «stakeholder» that lists the stakeholder's concerns. In the case of an actor, the keyword and properties are listed before the actor name. As with viewpoint, the concerns of a stakeholder can also be shown in attached comment symbols.

The package diagram in Figure 15.17 shows a viewpoint called *ICD*, whose purpose is "*To document the interface of a block*". The sole stakeholder is the *System Architect*, who in this case is modeled as an actor. For the sake of completeness, the stakeholder concern addressed by the viewpoint is shown both in a separate comment symbol and in the viewpoint compartment, although typically only one rendering is used. The construction method is called *Generate ICD*.

In order to generate artifacts, the viewpoint method needs to be provided with a list of model elements whose information is to be queried for presentation. This list of model elements is specified by a view. When the view is instantiated, the method of the view's nominated viewpoint is invoked with the

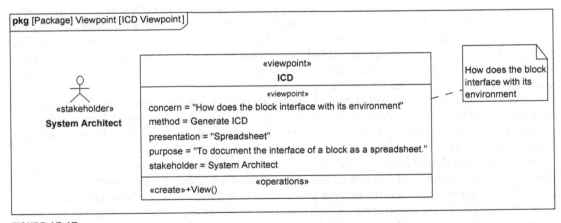

FIGURE 15.17

A viewpoint.

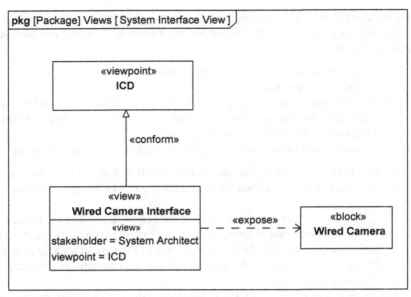

FIGURE 15.18
A view.

list of model elements to produce the artifacts for that view. The method describes how the model elements are navigated to extract the desired information.

A view is said to conform to the viewpoint that generates the view's artifacts. The set of model elements presented in the generated artifact are said to be exposed by the view. The conformance of a view to a viewpoint is expressed using a **conform** relationship from a view to a viewpoint. A view exposes a model element using an **expose** relationship, which relates a view to exposed model elements.

A view is shown as a box symbol with the keyword «view» at the top of its name compartment. Another compartment, labeled «view», shows the viewpoint to which this view conforms and the stakeholders of that viewpoint and hence the view. A conform relationship is shown as a dashed line with a hollow triangle at the viewpoint end and the keyword «conform» shown near the line. An expose relationship is shown as a dashed line with an open arrowhead pointing towards the element exposed with the keyword «expose» shown near the line.

Figure 15.18 shows a view, called *Wired Camera Interface*, which conforms to the *ICD* viewpoint. It exposes the *Wired Camera* block. Figure 15.19 shows an extract from the spreadsheet generated by the viewpoint method *Generate ICD* from *Wired Camera Interface*. It shows all of the ports of *Wired Camera* and their characteristics.

It is sometimes desirable to construct composite views that incorporate other views. To support this, a view may reference one or more views via its properties, each of which conforms to a viewpoint. The viewpoint to which the composite view conforms has access to these properties of the view and may invoke the constructors of their viewpoints to construct corresponding artifacts. Properties of the view can be ordered and this information can be used to order the presentation of the artifacts.

Component	Wired Camera		
Port Name	Port Type	Direction	Description
plug	3 Pin AC Plug Interface	inout	Power socket
mount	Bracket	inout	Mounting point
video	Composite Video Interface	out	Physical video out
ethernet	RJ45 Interface (Female)	inout	Network connection

FIGURE 15.19

An extract from an artifact generated from a view.

Figure 15.20 shows a view, called *Wired Camera Product Description*, which is composed of two further views: *Wired Camera Interface* (from Figure 15.18) and *Wired Camera Bill of Materials*, which describes the parts list for the *Wired Camera* so that a manufacturer knows how to build one. *Product Description*, the viewpoint to which *Wired Camera Product Description* conforms, can access its properties to construct a complete product description artifact.

SysML 1.4 introduced significant changes to view and viewpoint. The changes are summarized below:

- A viewpoint uses the same symbol as before, but viewpoint concerns can now be shown in separate comment symbols. The method of a viewpoint is now specified as the method of a constructor operation, whereas previously the method was defined as a string.
- A stakeholder is now represented by a separate model element, whereas previously stakeholders were listed solely as strings in a compartment of the viewpoint symbol.
- A view is now shown as a box rather than package symbol and can list the stakeholders of its viewpoint. Views can now own properties typed by views and participate in associations to other views.
- An expose relationship is now used instead of an import relationship to specify the set of model elements exposed by the view.
- The conform relationship now has a solid line with a hollow triangle at its head instead of a dashed line with an open arrowhead.

Annex C.5 of the SysML specification includes guidelines to transition earlier versions of SysML view and viewpoint to SysML 1.4.

15.9 SUMMARY

SysML is a general-purpose systems modeling language that includes built-in mechanisms, called model libraries and profiles, to customize the language. Model libraries and profiles can be used to support domain-specific modeling for many different domains. The following are some of the key concepts for domain-specific modeling:

- A modeling language is defined using a metamodel and contains a number of distinct language concepts, represented by metaclasses. Metaclasses have a set of properties and constraints on them. Metaclasses can also be associated with one another, thus allowing the language concepts to be related to one another. The underlying metamodel for SysML is a subset of UML called

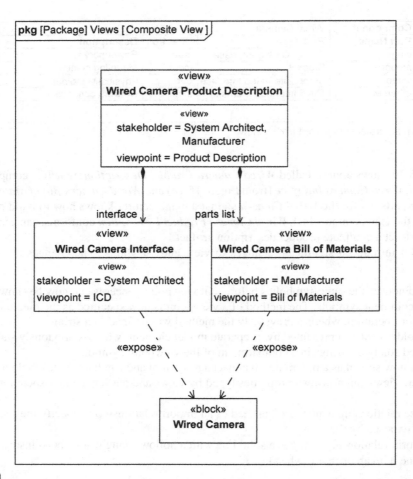

FIGURE 15.20

A composite view.

UML4SysML, an existing modeling language. UML4SysML contains the subset of UML concepts that are needed for systems modeling. SysML defines a graphical notation, based on UML, to represent the concepts in the metamodel.
- A model library is a special kind of package that contains model elements intended for reuse in multiple models. They can vary from very specific, such as representing a set of electronic components, to general, such as a definition of a common set of units and quantity kinds.
- A profile adds new concepts to a language (in this case SysML) by means of stereotypes. A profile extends a reference metamodel, which for SysML profiles is always its reference metamodel—UML. SysML itself is defined as a profile that extends UML, but it also makes the profile mechanism available to SysML modelers so that they may further extend the language. A profile can import another profile in order to reuse the stereotypes and metaclasses it contains.

- A stereotype can extend one or more metaclasses in the referenced metamodel. A stereotype can contain properties and constraints that may constrain both the values of its own properties and the property values of its base metaclasses. Even if a stereotype extends more than one metaclass, any given stereotype instance extends only one metaclass instance in the user model.
- User models contain model elements, which are instances of metaclasses contained in a metamodel or stereotypes from profiles. These model elements have values for the properties of their metaclasses or stereotypes and can be related according to the associations defined between their metaclasses or stereotypes.
- To use a profile, a modeler must apply it to his or her model or some subpackage of the model using a profile application relationship. A profile may be applied strictly, which means that model elements in the model or package that applies the profile may only be instances of metaclasses in the profile's reference metamodel.
- When a profile has been applied, stereotypes from that profile may be applied to appropriate model elements within it. More than one stereotype may be applied to a model element. Once a stereotype has been applied, modelers may provide values based on the stereotype's properties, and the constraints of the stereotype are applied to the model element. SysML includes a graphical notation that describes how a stereotyped model element appears in a diagram, which includes the use of special images or icons.
- SysML provides standard presentations of the model information, including SysML diagrams and tabular formats. SysML also includes the ability to generate customized visualizations to meet the needs of a broad set of stakeholders who may consume the information contained in SysML models. A viewpoint describes a set of rules for constructing such customized visualizations. A view conforms to a single viewpoint and identifies model elements that should be exposed in a specific visualization. Views may be composed of other views to allow the incremental definition of composite visualizations.

15.10 QUESTIONS

1. What does the abstract syntax of a modeling language describe?
2. What are the two parts of the SysML abstract syntax?
3. How are language concepts defined in a metamodel?
4. What is a profile and what does it contain?
5. What do the semantics of a modeling language describe?
6. Which kind of diagram is used to define model libraries and profiles?
7. List the three parts of a modeling language like UML and SysML.
8. What is the relationship between metaclasses in the metamodel and model elements in the user model?
9. What is a model library used for?
10. What is the relationship between a stereotype and its base metaclass called and how is it represented on a diagram?
11. Which rule applies to an association between a stereotype and a metaclass and why?
12. Which model elements can a profile contain?

13. What is the reference relationship used for?
14. What must modelers do before they can apply stereotypes to elements in their models?
15. On a diagram, how can a modeler tell that a stereotype has been applied to a model element?
16. How can the applied stereotype and stereotype property values for a graphical path (line) symbol be shown?
17. How can the applied stereotype and stereotype property values for a block symbol be shown?
18. When a block subclasses another block with a stereotype applied to it, which of the following describes the effect?
    a. The subclass automatically inherits the stereotypes applied to its superclass.
    b. The subclass automatically inherits the stereotypes applied to its superclass and also inherits the values of any stereotype properties.
    c. The subclass cannot inherit either applied stereotypes or the values of stereotype properties.
    d. The subclass can inherit applied stereotypes and the values of stereotype properties, but the stereotype has to be explicitly specified with a suitable constraint.
19. Name three properties of a viewpoint.
20. How do you represent a view V1, which conforms to a viewpoint VP1, on a package diagram?

DISCUSSION TOPICS

When adding new concepts to a language, when does it make sense to use a profile and when to use a model library?

What is the difference in meaning and use between a property of a stereotype and the property of a block?

EXAMPLES OF MODEL-BASED SYSTEMS ENGINEERING METHODS

Part III includes two examples to illustrate how SysML can support different MBSE methods. The first example (Chapter 16) is a functional analysis and allocation method to specify and design a water distiller system. The second example (Chapter 17) applies to the design of a security system consisting of a central monitoring station and multiple sites that are monitored. It uses a comprehensive object-oriented systems engineering method (OOSEM) and emphasizes how the language is used to address a range of systems engineering concerns, including black-box versus white-box design, logical versus physical design, and the design of distributed systems. While these two methods are considered representative of how MBSE with SysML can be applied to model systems, SysML is intended to support other MBSE methods as well.

PART

III

EXAMPLES OF
MODEL-BASED
SYSTEMS
ENGINEERING
METHODS

WATER DISTILLER EXAMPLE USING FUNCTIONAL ANALYSIS

This chapter contains an example that describes the application of SysML to the design of a water distiller intended for use in remote, undeveloped areas of the world. This example will start with a description of the problem and the model-based approach using a traditional functional analysis method, which is both familiar and intuitive to many practicing systems engineers. This approach is generally consistent with the simplified MBSE method introduced in Chapter 3, Section 3.4.

16.1 STATING THE PROBLEM—THE NEED FOR CLEAN DRINKING WATER

Consider the needs of a humanitarian organization dedicated to providing safe drinking water to the broadest possible spectrum of people, especially in impoverished parts of the world where it is not readily available. For purposes of this example, it is assumed that cost effectively supplying a sustainable long-term source of pure water in remote, impoverished areas is of paramount importance.

It is also assumed that studies have shown sources of water generally available in these target areas of the world, but because of viral and bacterial contamination, it is seldom safe to drink. Since the cost of transporting water to these remote areas over the long term would be prohibitive, the decision was made by this humanitarian organization to pursue the development of an extremely simple, inexpensive water purifier. Initial studies indicated that filter-based approaches to water purification are not sustainable, because of the limited effective lifetime of low cost viral grade filters, and the high logistical cost of maintaining a ready supply of replacement filters in remote areas.

This humanitarian organization is already making a substantial investment in deploying thousands of very simple solar powered low temperature evaporative stills, which have proven quite effective in sunny regions. They are now seeking an alternative for use in areas where a solar still is not suitable, such as under a forest canopy, in deep canyons, under predominantly overcast conditions, or in the presence of pathogens requiring high temperature sterilization. In particular, they seek to develop and deploy a large number of extremely simple thermal-powered, high-temperature (boiling) water distillers of a common design that is both economical to build and adaptable to the variety of energy sources anticipated in these remote areas. This example problem addresses the design and analysis of this thermal powered water distiller system.

Many assumptions are made regarding the feasibility of various solutions to make the scope of this sample problem manageable. The scope of this example is limited solely to the design of the distiller unit itself, but it is acknowledged that an actual solution must consider the greater issue of transportation, installation, logistics support, and operator training in order to meet the operational need.

16.2 DEFINING THE MODEL-BASED SYSTEMS ENGINEERING APPROACH

The selection of a model-based systems engineering approach depends largely on the nature of the problem to be solved, the expected outputs, and the resources available to work the problem. Note that while the steps are shown as a sequence, they are often performed in parallel and iteratively.

The nature of the water distiller system is neither complex nor software intensive. The selected MBSE method needs to provide a framework for specifying both the structure and operation of the system and for analyzing its performance. This leads to a method that supports functional analysis supported by domain experts to help define appropriate operational contexts. This example is generally consistent with the simplified MBSE method described in Chapter 3, Section 3.4, as outlined below.

- *Organize the model*—This is addressed in Section 16.3.
- *Elicit and analyze stakeholder needs*—This is addressed in Section 16.4.1, which focuses on capturing the stakeholder mission statement, top-level requirements, and assumptions. These are then used to establish the top-level system context and use cases.
- *Specify functionality, interfaces, physical, and performance characteristics*—The stakeholder needs are used as a basis to derive and elaborate specific system requirements. A hierarchy of system requirements for the system is proposed in Section 16.4.2. These in turn drive the system design. Required system behavior is addressed in Section 16.4.3, along with relationships and constraints on the resulting system.
- *Synthesize alternative solutions*—The initial goal during system synthesis, as covered in Section 16.5, is to determine the simple low cost system that meets the overall requirements. Performance of the resulting configuration is predicted using a heat balance analysis in Section 16.6.
- *Tradeoff analysis*—Tradeoffs should normally be considered whenever alternatives arise. This example discusses trading off fundamental behavior in Section 16.4.4 and examines alternatives to improve basic functionality and the user interface in Section 16.7.
- *Maintain traceability*—Traceability to system requirements is demonstrated throughout the process via requirement relationships and functional allocation. This is most evident in Sections 16.4.3 and 16.5.

16.3 ORGANIZING THE MODEL

A critical step prior to initiating a significant modeling effort is the establishment of the initial organization of the model, which is done by defining the model's overall package structure. The organization should also consider what model libraries may be leveraged for the development. Chapter 6, Section 6.4, includes a number of approaches that can be used to organize the model. Caution must be exercised when organizing the model to avoid prematurely constraining or biasing the design.

The package diagram in Figure 16.1 presents the organization for this model. The diagram header indicates that the context for this diagram is the root-level model *Distiller Project*. Each package on the diagram is contained within this model. The user-defined diagram name for this package diagram is *model organization,* which may be used to differentiate it from any other package diagram that designates the *Distiller Project* for its context. The conventions for diagram headers are used consistently throughout this example and are important for understanding the context of each diagram within the model organization. See Chapter 5, Section 5.2.3, for more information on diagram headers.

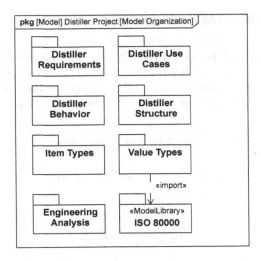

FIGURE 16.1

Package diagram of the organization of the distiller model.

The packages in this model are primarily organized based on the types of artifacts developed using the selected process, including requirements, use cases, and behavioral and structural models. The *Engineering Analysis* package includes the constraint blocks and parametric models used to analyze the performance.

Note that the *Value Types* package in Figure 16.1 imports the *ISO 80000* package, which is a reusable model library package available to multiple models. It contains a system of units and quantity-Kinds that is described in Chapter 7, Section 7.3.4, and Annex E of the OMG SysML specification [1]. The *Value Types* package uses the imported definitions of units and quantity kinds to create specific value types, which are then applied to value properties with consistent units throughout the model.

A package for *Item Types* is included to capture the types of things that flow in the system. Segregating item types into its own package allows the modeler to concentrate on defining the things that flow and leverage reuse libraries that may exist independent of where they flow or how they are used. This segregation is similar to establishing a reusable library of components. For this example, water and heat flow through the system. Providing a separate package for item types allows the modeler to consolidate all the relevant information about water, heat, and the other item types used in this model.

The browser of the modeling tool typically provides a view of these packages in a folder-like structure that is populated as the model is developed. It may be convenient to revise the organization of the model over time as the model is refined and updated. For example, after an initial design has been established, packages may be established for each component that is subject to further design and analysis.

16.4 ESTABLISHING REQUIREMENTS

The following sections describe how requirements are elicited and elaborated sufficiently to drive the design of the distiller system.

16.4.1 CHARACTERIZING STAKEHOLDER NEEDS

The requirements for the distiller system need to be captured and traced in the system model. Section 16.1 provides a set of mission statements that provide a basis for more specific mission requirements. These mission requirements are used to derive effectiveness measures and then through analysis lead to a comprehensive set of system requirements for the distiller specification. Figure 16.2 presents the package structure that accommodates these kinds of requirements. Figure 16.3 presents a table of

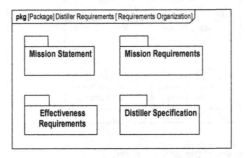

FIGURE 16.2

Organization of requirements for distiller problem.

table [Package] Mission Statement [Table of Mission Requirements]			
#	ID	Name	Text
1	MS.1	Safe Drinking Water	The client is a humanitarian organization dedicated to the purpose of providing safe drinking water to the broadest possible spectrum of people, especially in impoverished parts of the world where it is not readily available. For purposes of this project, we will assume that cost effectively supplying a sustainable long-term source of pure water in remote, impoverished areas is of paramount importance.
2	MS.1.1	Client Definition	The client is a humanitarian organization dedicated to ... providing safe drinking water to ... parts of the world where it is not readily available.
3	MS.2	Contaminated Sources	The client's studies have shown sources of water generally available in these target areas of the world, but because of viral and bacterial contamination, it is seldom safe to drink.
4	MS.3	Need for Purifier	Since the cost of transporting water to these remote areas over the long term would be prohibitive, the decision was made by the client to pursue the development of an extremely simple, inexpensive water purifier.
5	MS.4	Not a Filter	Initial studies have indicated that filter-based approaches to water purification are not sustainable, because of the limited effective lifetime of low cost viral grade filters, and the high logistical cost of maintaining a ready supply of replacement filters in remote areas.
6	MS.5	Economical Distiller	The client would like to explore the viability of developing and deploying a large number of extremely simple water distillers, of a common design which is both economical to build, and adaptable to use the variety of energy sources anticipated in remote areas. This project addresses the design and analysis of this water distiller system.
7	MS.5.1	Simple Distiller	The client would like ... extremely simple water distillers... economical ... and adaptable.
8	MS.5.2	Project Scope (1)	This project addresses the design and analysis of this water distiller system.
9	MS.6	Project Scope (2)	The scope of this project will also be necessarily limited solely to the design of the distiller unit itself.

FIGURE 16.3

Capture of mission statement as a set of requirements.

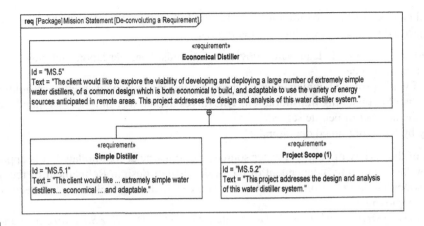

FIGURE 16.4

Decomposing a requirement using containment.

requirements from the original mission statement. The tabular format is an allowable notation in SysML and represents a traditional and convenient way to view requirements. This table is generated from requirements contained in the system model and contains the same information that can be shown in a requirement diagram: requirement id, name, and text. In this case, the table relies on the numbering to indicate the hierarchy that is captured in the model using containment, but this could have also been shown by level of indentation or another mechanism. Note that the identifiers for each of these requirements start with the letters "*MS*", to indicate that they represent parts of the mission statement.

Figure 16.4 presents how a compound mission statement requirement has been separated into simpler requirements, without adding to or changing its meaning. This process is often referred to as "requirements decomposition" but it is more accurately described as "requirement de-convolution." It is important to recognize that requirements de-convolution and system decomposition are very different kinds of relationships in SysML.

The purpose of the distiller system is to provide clean drinking water economically in a wide variety of remote, undeveloped areas. A survey of conditions in such areas leads to the following mission requirements, which are also captured in the model:

- Electrical power will generally not be available.
- Sources of heat for the distillation process will vary widely based on the climate, native vegetation, agricultural, and mineral resources of the region. Liquid fuel or solid fuel heaters may need to be accommodated.
- The source of unclean water may be still or flowing. In some cases, elevation will be sufficient to gravity feed water to the distiller. In other cases, water will need to be carried and poured into the distiller manually.
- Sufficient human resources will be available locally to operate the distiller, but it must be intuitive to operate by untrained personnel.
- The output of the distiller will feed local water distribution systems, which might include anything from storage tanks and pipelines to a series of hand carried water jars.

An initial analysis of these requirements yields the following set of effectiveness measures for the distiller project, which are also captured in the model:

- Sustained cost per unit of clean water provided. This must consider labor, fuel, power, consumables and maintenance.
- Quality of water provided, which must be above a minimum accepted safety threshold.
- Cost per distiller, including transportation. This drives the number of units that may be procured, and thus the number of people served.
- Usability by local, untrained operators.

Because of the variety of heat and water sources that must be accommodated, it is appropriate initially to view them as being independent of the basic distiller design. Refinement of the design may incorporate water handling equipment and heating sources, including fuel storage, if deemed appropriate for broad deployment.

The *Distiller System Context* block was created within the *Distiller Structure* package. Its internal block diagram is presented in Figure 16.5. Note that blocks representing *Water Source, Distiller, Heat Source,* and *Water Distribution System* were also created and used to type parts of the *Distiller System Context* block. Other properties are typed by the *Operator* and *Water User* actors contained in the *Distiller Use Cases* package. Flows in and out of the *Distiller* have been depicted using item flows, typed by appropriate item types (*H2O, Heat*) contained in the Item Types package.

The initial intent is to have the *Heat Source* procured locally, if possible, and thus minimize transportation costs. For this reason, the *Heat Source* will be modeled as if it were external to the *Distiller*. The *Water Source* may be any suitable body of water or a locally provided holding tank. Note that in addition to operating the *Distiller* itself, the operator(s) will also need to interact with the *Water Source* and the *Heat Source*.

An initial use case diagram for the distiller is presented in Figure 16.6. For purposes of this example, emphasis is placed on the operation of the *Distiller* itself. Distribution of clean water, along with transportation, setup, maintenance and takedown of the distiller are beyond the scope of this example. This

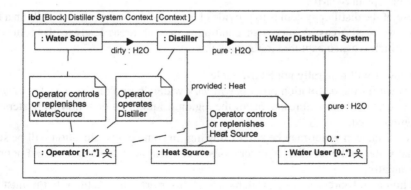

FIGURE 16.5

Establishing a context for the distiller system.

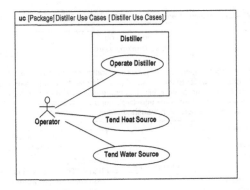

FIGURE 16.6

Establishing an initial set of use cases for the distiller system, based on system context.

context is restricted in order to present a compact, manageable example problem. A more complete treatment of the problem should also consider the customer's transportation and logistical resources, as well as suggest an approach for maintaining distillers and training operators. It is assumed that this broader context is considered only after a feasible point of departure design for the distiller has been achieved.

16.4.2 CHARACTERIZING SYSTEM REQUIREMENTS

This section describes the breakdown of stakeholder needs, assumptions, and constraints into a cohesive set of requirements. All essential requirements for the distiller are explicitly stated so that their satisfaction may be specifically related to the system design. Figure 16.7 presents the initial derivation of a requirement for the distiller to purify water, which was not explicitly stated in the mission requirements. Note that the rationale for this derivation is also stated.

The system requirements are derived from an analysis of each mission requirement. The resulting derivation of distiller system requirements is presented in Figure 16.8. The *External Heat Source*, *Gravity Feed*, *Cooling* and *Boiling* requirements, together with the previously identified *Purification* requirement, are used to drive the initial system design. Note that requirements that make up the distiller specification contain "*DS*" in their ID property.

Although multiple relationships from a requirements tree can be shown graphically on the requirement diagram, it is often more compact to view the information in tabular format. Figure 16.9 presents a table of the system requirements and their derivation. In addition to ID and name, the table captures the derive relationship. Tools are expected to provide the tabular format for editing and viewing requirements and other types of modeling information, as described in Chapter 5, Section 5.4.

Modelers may want to leverage the non-normative requirement types presented in Chapter 13, Section 13.3, and/or create user-defined extensions using the profile mechanism described in Chapter 15, Section 15.4.

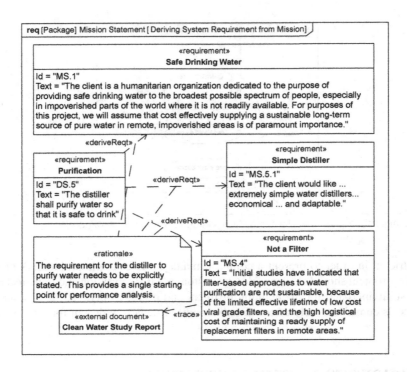

FIGURE 16.7

Establishing purification requirement.

16.4.3 CHARACTERIZING REQUIRED BEHAVIORS

This section describes techniques to characterize system behavior based on functional requirements. An initial decomposition of the *Distill Water* function is presented as a block definition diagram in Figure 16.10. The word "function" is used interchangeably with the word "activity" throughout this example. The boxes on the diagram are functions, not blocks, and they are named using verbs. The role names at the end of the composite association denotes the name of the call behavior actions contained in *Distill Water* that calls each associated activity (e.g., action *a2* calling activity *Boil Water*). The approach to decomposing activities is discussed in Chapter 9, Section 9.12.

A *satisfy* relationship is established between the *Boiling* requirement and the *Boil Water* function, and between the *Cooling* requirement and the *Condense Steam* function. The cooling requirement may not be fully satisfied simply by condensing the steam, because the resulting condensate may still be too hot to distribute easily. To simplify the initial analysis, it is assumed that the condensate is allowed to cool in the external collection device prior to distribution.

A *satisfy* relationship is also established between the *Purification* requirement and the top level *Distill Water* function. This relationship may later be augmented by additional satisfy relationships between requirements derived from Purification (e.g., minimum water temperature over minimum time) and additional functions of the distiller (e.g., monitor temperature, monitor flow rate).

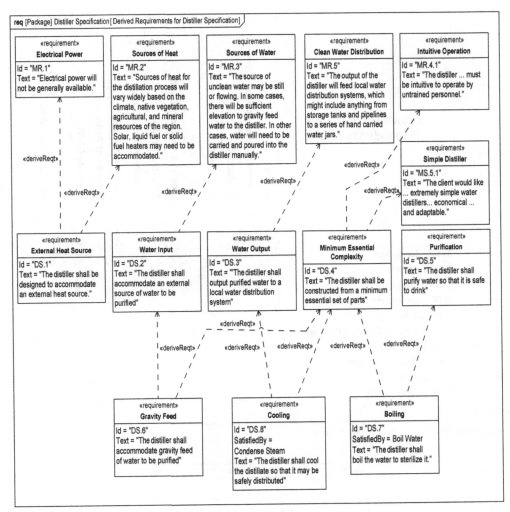

FIGURE 16.8

Derivation of initial distiller system requirements.

Heat Water is an essential function, even though it doesn't immediately satisfy a stated requirement. If we assume that the water from the source will be at ambient temperature, heating and boiling water must be distinguished because the mechanism of heat transfer is different. The function *Heat Water* raises the water's temperature without changing its state. The function Boil Water changes the water's state without changing its temperature. Nothing is implied about how or where these functions are performed, and in fact they might be performed by the same device (e.g., a pot on a stove). Nonetheless, they are two separate functions and must be treated accordingly.

Derive Requirement Dependency Matrix	DS.7 Boiling	DS.4 Minimum Essential Complexity	DS.5 Purification	DS.2 Water Input	DS.3 Water Output	MR.5 Clean Water Distribution	MR.1 Electrical Power	MR.4.1 Intuitive Operation	MR.2 Sources of Heat	MR.3 Sources of Water	MS.5.1 Simple Distiller	MS.4 Not a Filter	MS.1 Safe Drinking Water
⊟ 🗀 Distiller Specification													
🖼 DS.7 Boiling		↗	↗										
🖼 DS.8 Cooling		↗			↗								
🖼 DS.1 External Heat Source							↗		↗				
🖼 DS.6 Gravity Feed		↗		↗									
🖼 DS.4 Minimum Essential Complexity	↙							↗			↗		
🖼 DS.5 Purification	↙										↗	↗	↗
🖼 DS.9 Residue Removal	↗												
🖼 DS.2 Water Input										↗			
🖼 DS.3 Water Output					↗								

FIGURE 16.9

Tracking deriveReqt relationships in a matrix.

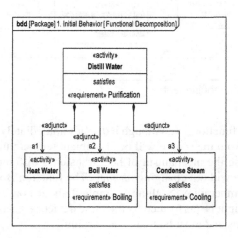

FIGURE 16.10

Initial decomposition of distiller functions.

H2O is modeled as a block in the Item Types package. The state of H2O as it flows through the distiller must be understood when analyzing the distiller's performance. The state machine in Figure 16.11 presents its state changes between gas (steam) and liquid as it proceeds through the *Distill Water* process. Latent heat of vaporization must be added to transition from liquid to gas. The same latent heat of vaporization must be removed when transitioning from gas to liquid.

The relationship of the three functions that compose the *Distill Water* function is captured in the activity diagram presented in Figure 16.12. The enclosing frame designates an activity called *Distill Water* as designated in the diagram header. As described in Chapter 9, Section 9.3, round-cornered boxes designate actions (usages) that can invoke activities (definitions). The dashed lines are control flows that define the sequence of actions; dashed lines are an optional notation in place of solid lines and help to distinguish control flow

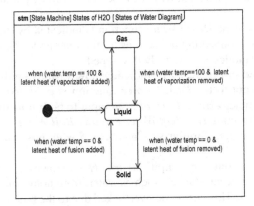

FIGURE 16.11

Representing states of H_2O.

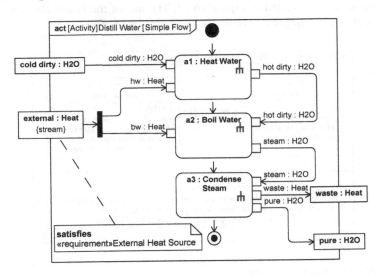

FIGURE 16.12

Initial activity diagram of *Distill Water*.

from object flow more clearly. Note that the flow of control presented in Figure 16.12 is a sequential process, where each action must complete before the next action begins. The actions and action pins include their role names (usages) and types (definitions) using the standard role name : Type Name notation.

The input and output activity parameters of the *Distill Water* function are typed by the blocks from the Item Types package (*Heat, H2O*). Use of item types in this way maintains a consistent representation of the things flowing in the system. The activity parameter *external : Heat* has a *satisfy* relationship to the distiller specification requirement *External Heat Source*, indicating that the heat is being generated external to the distiller system.

Each of the other functions that compose *Distill Water* has activity parameters identified that are typed by blocks in the Item Types package. The type of the pins on the call behavior actions on the activity diagram (*a1, a2, a3*) are consistent with the type of the activity parameters on the activities (i.e., functions) they call.

The sequence of actions for the *Distill Water* function is indicated by the control flow from the initial node, via the dashed lines connecting the actions, to the final node. This sequence is subsequently re-examined as the behavior model is more fully developed.

The object flow presented in Figure 16.12 indicates how various kinds and phases of water flow between the actions. The input to the *Distill Water* function is *cold dirty : H2O*, and the output is *pure : H2O*. The input parameter *external : Heat* is an input to both *Boil Water* and *Heat Water* functions. Because it is needed for both *a1 : Heat Water* and *a2 : Boil Water* sequentially, *external : Heat* must be a streaming parameter. Similarly, *Condense Steam* has *waste : Heat* as an output parameter.

The function *Boil Water* has only one output, *steam : H2O*. However, this does not account for the fact that boiling separates volatile substances, such as water, from nonvolatile substances, such as sediment, salts, metals, and nitrates. This cannot be overlooked due to the potential of using highly polluted sources of water. In order to accommodate the need to dispose of the accumulated residue, a new requirement is derived and a new function is proposed to be performed by the distiller. This, along with the associated rationale, is presented in Figure 16.13. The use of the *Drain Residue* function is presented in subsequent activity diagrams, starting with Figure 16.15

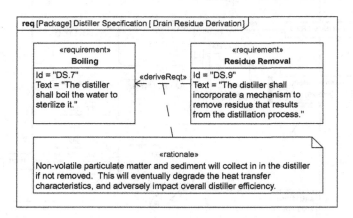

FIGURE 16.13

Derivation of the Drain Residue requirement.

16.4.4 **REFINING BEHAVIOR**

This section describes techniques for elaborating the distiller behavior and introduces behavioral allocation. After initially defining overall behavior, it is common to refine system behavior and system structure in parallel. One of the key tenets of functional decomposition is to consider behavior and structure independently (at least at a given level of abstraction) and to specifically allocate one onto the other. This segregation of concerns helps explore the variety of structural alternatives available to implement a particular functional need. In this example, alternative behavioral constructs that satisfy the requirements will be subject to trade-off, and the simplest possible structures that can effectively support those behaviors will be selected.

Batch and continuous distillers exhibit fundamentally different behaviors. The left side of Figure 16.14 presents a batch distiller that includes a boiler and a condenser. In batch process, the boiler is filled with water, and a heat source is used to heat the water in the boiler. Steam is then generated, and the distilled water is collected from the condenser. The process stops when there is no more water in the boiler; purifying more requires refilling the boiler with water. The right side of Figure 16.14 presents a continuous distiller that can have water flow through it continuously. It includes a boiler with an internal heating element and a heat exchanger that has cool liquid flowing in the coils and steam condensing around them.

The control flow presented previously in Figure 16.13 is consistent with the behavior of a batch distiller. Each action ends before the next one begins. When *Heat Water* is complete, the action *Boil Water* is initiated. When Boil Water is complete, *Condense Steam* is initiated. When these actions are complete, the *Distill Water* activity is complete, and a batch of pure water is available. The entire process must be started over to distill the next batch of water.

Figure 16.15 presents an activity model of continuous distiller behavior using the same actions identified previously and including *a4:Drain Residue*. Each action executes concurrently, and each action pin or activity parameter is {streaming}, meaning it provides or accepts objects while executing, and is stereotyped as «continuous», meaning that the time between sending and receiving objects is

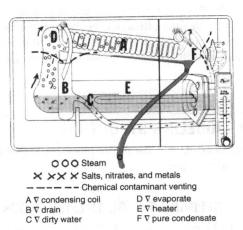

○ ○ ○ Steam
✕ ✕ ✕ ✕ Salts, nitrates, and metals
— — — — — — Chemical contaminant venting

A ▽ condensing coil   D ▽ evaporate
B ▽ drain   E ▽ heater
C ▽ dirty water   F ▽ pure condensate

FIGURE 16.14

A batch distiller (left) and a continuous distiller (right).

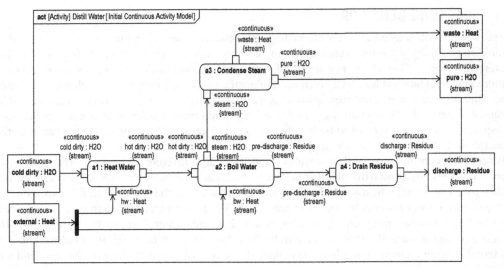

FIGURE 16.15

Initial continuous distiller activity diagram.

arbitrarily short. This accurately models the behavior of a distiller in which heat and water continuously flow through the system.

The activity models for batch and continuous may be built to execute and used as a basis for comparing performance of the two alternatives. This example assumes that a suitable quantitative comparison of these two approaches shows a greater sustained output of pure water from a continuous distiller, due to the additional time a batch distiller needs to cool down and refill. A design decision is made to proceed with design of a continuous distiller, and this rationale is documented in the model.

The *Distill Water* function has heat as both an input and an output. To simplify the functional design and improve distiller efficiency, the heat output by action *a3 : Condense Steam* is used as a source of heat for action *a1 : Heat Water*. Figure 16.16 presents a revised activity model of this kind of distiller behavior. Note that *waste : Heat* no longer appears as an output parameter of the *Distill Water* function.

16.5 MODELING STRUCTURE

This section describes the use of blocks, parts, and ports for modeling of the distiller's structure and behavioral allocation.

16.5.1 DEFINING THE DISTILLER'S BLOCKS IN THE BLOCK DEFINITION DIAGRAM

Figure 16.17 presents a block definition diagram for the distiller system. The diagram presents the block named *Distiller,* which is composed of a block named *Heat Exchanger,* a block named *Boiler,* and a block named *Valve.* The composition relationship shows that the *Distiller* is composed of one

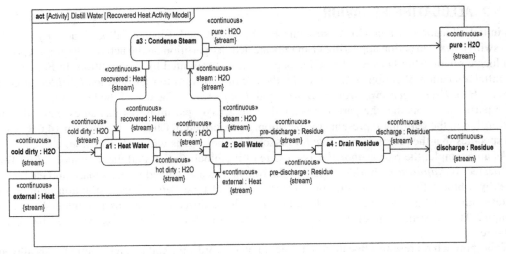

FIGURE 16.16

Continuous distiller activity diagram with recovered heat.

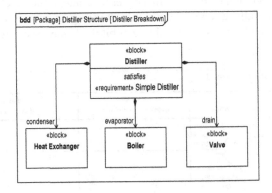

FIGURE 16.17

Initial *Distiller* structure.

Heat Exchanger that fulfills the role *condenser,* one *Boiler* that fulfills the role *evaporator,* and one *Valve* that fulfills the role *drain.*

The block *Distiller* shows a compartment indicating that it satisfies the requirement *Simple Distiller.* This does not mean, of course, that the *Distiller* always satisfies that original mission statement imperative, but rather that it is asserted to satisfy it, so that the requirement needs to be carefully considered when making decisions affecting the design of the *Distiller.* In keeping with the mission statement requirement *Simple Distiller,* the design philosophy for this project is to use the minimum number of parts necessary for effective operation. The three components shown are a good start at keeping the design simple. The required behaviors must now be mapped onto this structure and the resulting design analyzed for feasibility and performance.

16.5.2 ALLOCATING BEHAVIOR

The initial allocation of behavior to structure has been specified using the allocate activity partitions (i.e., swim lanes): an action appearing in an allocate activity partition on the activity diagram represents an allocate relationship between the action and the part represented by the partition. In Figure 16.18, the initial allocation of actions is specified by the use of partitions to represent the *Distiller* parts *condenser : Heat Exchanger, evaporator : Boiler,* and *drain : Valve.* The use of the keyword «allocate» in the partition means that the partition is an allocate activity partition that has an explicit allocation relationship to the part that represents the partition, as described in Chapter 14, Section 14.6.3. This in turn specifies that the part is responsible for performing the actions within its partition.

As an example, the part *evaporator* is a usage of the block *Boiler,* and the action *a2 : Boil Water* is allocated to *evaporator : Boiler.* Note that the role names are defined for each part, and each part is typed by a block. For example, the role *drain* is a part of type *Valve.* This distinction is important, because other valves with the same definition may have different roles, as is evident later in the example. The specification of the parts and blocks are described next as part of the distiller structure.

This approach represents allocation of usage. In other words, the call behavior action *a2* is allocated to the part *evaporator.* Nothing is said about the more general case between the activity *Boil Water* and the block *Boiler.* This allocation of usage applies only to the context of the activity *Distill Water* allocated within the context of the block *Distiller.* In a different context, the block *Boiler* may boil a different kind of fluid. Behavioral allocation of definition (allocating an activity to a block) should only be done if every use of a specific block is expected to exhibit the behavior of the allocated activity.

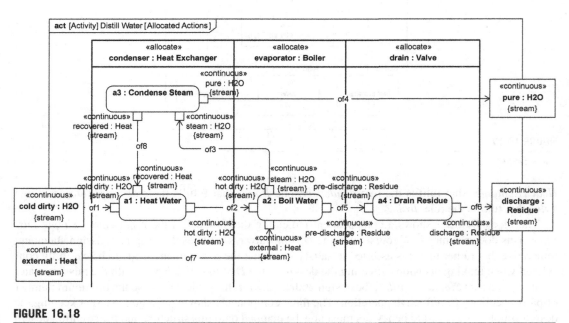

FIGURE 16.18

Distill Water activity model with actions allocated to parts of the *Distiller.*

Note that this allocation assumes a steady-state flow in which the evaporator is only boiling the water, not warming it; and that the condenser is only condensing the steam, not cooling the condensate. At sea level, this assumption means that the temperature of the water in *objectFlow of2* must be 100° C, and the temperature of the water in *objectFlow of4* must also be 100° C.

This significant simplifying assumption is not universally valid, especially during system startup, but it is proposed as a best-case efficient use of heat energy through the distiller and an appropriate starting point to evaluate the feasibility of this initial distiller design. Subsequent refinement of the distiller design should consider the cases where each of these temperatures is less than 100° C, with additional heating occurring in the evaporator and additional cooling occurring in the condenser.

16.5.3 DEFINING THE PORTS ON THE BLOCKS

An internal block diagram can be developed based on the block definition diagram to show how parts are connected to one another. However, before doing this, the blocks on the block definition diagram are further elaborated by identifying the ports on the blocks and their definitions so that the ports can be connected in the internal block diagram.

The ports are identified on the blocks on the block definition diagram in Figure 16.19. The ports in this example are all undefined ports (neither proxy ports nor full ports), which is legal in SysML and appropriate for this initial stage of design. Each port has been typed by an interface block, so that they specify the items that can flow in and out of the block and have no behaviors of their own. They are also unidirectional, meaning that the interface block that types the port have flow properties that flow in only one direction. Two kinds of interface blocks (or kinds of ports) have been created, one named *Fport* that has a flow property passing *Fluid* and one named *Hport* that has a flow property passing *Heat*. For both interface blocks, the default flow direction is *in*. The block *Valve* has ports for *in : Fport* and *out : ~Fport* (the conjugate of *Fport*, which reverses the direction of the flow property). Note that these port definitions apply to all uses of a two-port

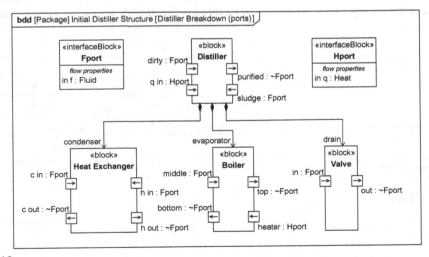

FIGURE 16.19

Distiller breakdown with ports.

valve. The *Heat Exchanger* has a cold loop (*c in* and *c out*) and a hot loop (*h in* and *h out*); a feature common to all counter-flow heat exchangers. Note that careful attention to specifying the port configurations can facilitate their reuse. The *Boiler* has 3 ports typed by *Fport* (*top*, *middle*, and *bottom*) and one typed *Heat* (*bottom*). The stratification of sediment and steam in an operating boiler makes it efficient to extract steam from the top, sludge from the bottom, and to inject feed water in the middle.

The next step is to show usage of these blocks in the context of the *Distiller* on an internal block diagram, including the connections and flows between them.

16.5.4 CREATING THE INTERNAL BLOCK DIAGRAM WITH PARTS, PORTS, CONNECTORS, AND ITEM FLOWS

Figure 16.20 presents an internal block diagram for the *Distiller* system. The diagram header identifies the enclosing block as the *Distiller*. The user-defined diagram name is *initial distiller internal configuration*. The parts represent how the blocks are used in the *Distiller* context and have the same role names as were shown on the block definition diagram. The ports are consistent with their definition on the block definition diagram. The allocation of actions to parts first presented on Figure 16.18 is also shown here using compartment notation on each of the three parts. These allocation relationships are explicitly depicted in the allocation compartments; *allocatedFrom* indicates the direction of the relationship—namely, *from* the elements specified in the compartment *to* the part.

The connectors between the parts and the item flows on the connectors on the internal block diagram represent information that is not available on the block definition diagram. The connectors relate the ports (both internal and external) and reflect the distiller's internal structure.

As discussed in Chapter 7, Section 7.4, item flows depict things flowing on connectors. They specify what flows and the direction of flow. In this example, all the blocks used to type things that flow are kept in the *Item Types* package. These are then used to type activity parameters, action pins, flow properties of interface blocks, and properties referenced by item flows (item properties), messages, signals, etc. Using a common repository for all of the kinds of things that flow is a key principle of effective interface management.

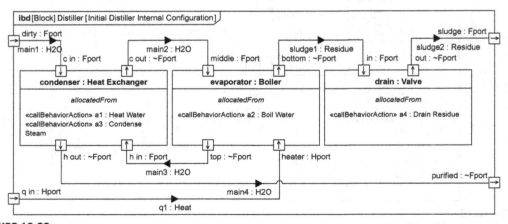

FIGURE 16.20

Initial distiller internal configuration with item flow and allocation.

A naming convention for item properties is used to identify the items flowing through the system. The main flow of water (*H2O*) through the *Distiller* is shown as follows: *main1* is the flow of *H2O* into the system and into the cold loop of the *consenser*; *main2* is the flow of *H2O* out of the cold loop of the *condenser* and into the *evaporator*; *main3* is the flow of *H2O* (steam) out of the *evaporator* and into the hot loop of the *condenser*; and *main4* is the flow of *H2O* (condensate or pure water) out of the *condenser* and out of the system. The flow of sludge has been similarly designated: *sludge1* flows out of the *evaporator* and into the *drain* valve, and *sludge2* flows out of the *drain* valve and out of the system. The only additional flow is *q1*, which represents heat flowing into the system and into the *evaporator*.

The *Distiller*'s structure is defined on the block definition diagram, and the connection and context of how these elements are used, along with the physical flows, are represented on the internal block diagram. The allocation of behavior (actions) to structure (parts) is in the context of the *Distiller* system, using allocate activity partitions presented in Figure 16.18. It is now appropriate to allocate the flow in the activity model to flow in the structural model.

16.5.5 ALLOCATION OF FLOW

In the activity diagram, the flows are as specified by the name and type of the action pins, and the object flows provide the context and connection between the pins. When specifying flows as part of the structure, ports specify what can flow on blocks and parts, and item flows specify what actually flows in the context of the owning block. In this example, object flows are allocated directly to item properties, requiring the type of the action pins connected by the object flow to be checked for consistency with the type of the item property. Each object flow on the activity diagram (Figure 16.18) is allocated to a corresponding unique item property on the internal block diagram (Figure 16.20). Subsequent analysis of system performance focuses on relevant characteristics of these item properties, such as temperature and mass flow rate.

The matrix presented in Figure 16.21 is used to depict flow allocation. The arrows in the matrix represent the direction of the allocation relationship. A matrix like this generally provides a more compact representation of flow allocation than callouts or compartments.

Allocation Matrix	- main1 : H2O	- main2 : H2O	- main3 : H2O	- main4 : H2O	-q 1 : Heat	- sludge 1 : Residue	- sludge 2 : Residue
Object Flow:of1[- cold dirty]	↗						
Object Flow:of2[hot dirty - hot dirty]		↗					
Object Flow:of3[steam - steam]			↗				
Object Flow:of4[pure -]				↗			
Object Flow:of5[pre-discharge - pre-discharge]						↗	
Object Flow:of6[discharge -]							↗
Object Flow:of7[- external]					↗		

FIGURE 16.21

Allocating flows from *Distill Water* object flows to *Distiller* properties.

16.6 ANALYZE PERFORMANCE

In this section, the *Distiller* performance is analyzed to determine the feasibility of the design.

16.6.1 ITEM FLOW HEAT BALANCE ANALYSIS

A key aspect of distiller performance is the appropriate balance of mass flow and heat flow through the system. To evaluate the flow balance, the analysis focuses on the physical flow of water and heat, as expressed by item properties on the internal block diagram. An alternative analysis approach that focused on the flows in the activity diagram was briefly explored but discarded in favor of the more intuitive approach of analyzing physical flow on the internal block diagram.

The feasibility of the design is assessed by fixing the mass flow rate of the H2O through the system and then analyzing the heat flow required for the associated H2O temperature and phase changes. This analysis is simplified by the fact that the entire system is isobaric; that is, the pressure throughout the system is assumed uniformly atmospheric.

Figure 16.22 depicts the parametric diagram used to support this analysis. The *Distiller Isobaric Heat Balance* block is designated by the diagram frame. Establishing a clear analysis context is important, especially early in the design process. This diagram is used to express simple mathematical relationships between the physical flows, consistent with the simplifying assumptions listed in Section 16.5.2. The twelve rectangular boxes on the left of the diagram (*main1.mass flow rate : gm/sec, main1. water temp : °C,* and so on) represent value properties (e.g., *mass flow rate*) within item properties (e.g., *main1*) on the *Distiller* internal block diagram (Figure 16.20). Note that each item property has associated value properties unique to its usage, such as temperature and mass flow rate. Specific heat and latent heat are common, invariant (read only) properties of H2O that also need to be considered in the analysis, so they are included as well. The round-angles on the right of the diagram represent constraint properties of the *Initial Distiller Analysis* block; each has a corresponding constraint expressed as a mathematical formula enclosed within curly brackets. Before the analysis can proceed, an instance of the entire distiller system must be created, thus providing slots for specific values for each of the value properties. The name of this instance of the distiller is *initial distiller.*

Based on the topology of the initial distiller design, the steady state mass flow rates *main1*, *main2*, *main3*, and *main4* must be equal. This equivalence is presented in Figure 16.22 by the value bindings between *initial distiller.main1.mass flow rate*, *initial distiller.main2.mass flow rate*, *initial distiller. main3.mass flow rate*, and *initial distiller.main4.mass flow rate.*

The system must concurrently heat water and condense steam as specified in the activity diagram. The single-phase heat transfer equation, which is applied when heating liquid water, relates mass flow rate, change in temperature, and specific heat to heat flow (*q rate*). Note that the constraint *heating feedwater : Single Phase Heat Xfer Equation* shows each of these parameters in small square boxes. Binding connectors are used to bind the value properties associated with the *main1* and *main2* mass flow rates and temperatures and the specific heat of water to the parameters of this constraint. The *q rate* from *condensing : Phase Change Heat Xfer Equation* is bound to an intermediate value property of distiller, *initial distiller.q_int : dQ/dt*, which is in turn the *q rate* for *s1 : Single Phase Heat Xfer Equation*. This is because the energy used to heat the water comes from condensing steam.

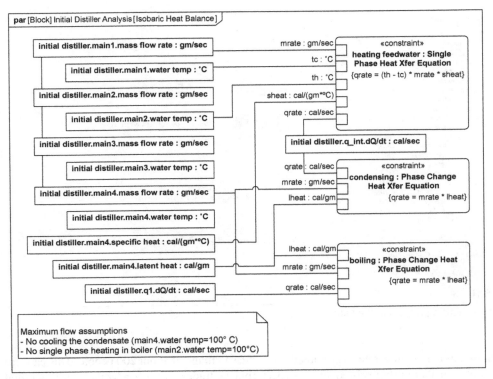

FIGURE 16.22

Defining parametric relationships as a prelude to analysis.

A simple phase change equation is used to determine how much heat needs to be extracted for a given mass flow rate of steam. In this example, the constraint block, *Phase Change Heat Xfer Equation*, is used both for condensing steam and for boiling water. This equation is defined only once as a constraint block, and it used to type the two constraints: *condensing* and *boiling*. Both *condensing* and *boiling* constraints have identical parameters but are bound to different properties. *Specific heat* and *latent heat* are bound as value properties of *main4* out of convenience; they are inherited from H2O and are constant across all four flows.

This parametric diagram defines the mathematical relationships between properties, but it does not execute the analysis. It explicitly constrains properties of the items that flow through the distiller. The next step is to perform the analysis by evaluating the equations.

16.6.2 RESOLVING HEAT BALANCE

An analysis tool (i.e., a constraint solver) is used to solve the constraints specified by the parametric diagram above. As shown in Figure 16.23, a typical mass flow rate through the system is set as a given parameter, and the input heat flow *q1* is the target value to be solved. 10gm/sec (approximately 36L/hr)

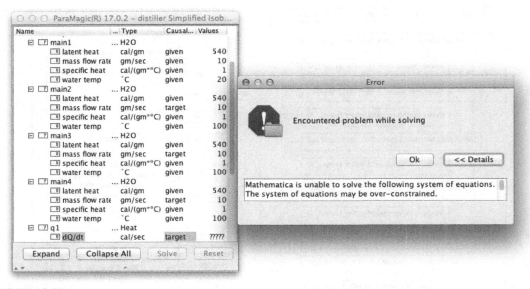

FIGURE 16.23

Analysis reveals a problem in the initial design.

was chosen as a mass flow rate large enough to service a village of about 200 people. This capacity will need to be revisited during subsequent cost/performance trades, but it is adequate for this initial heat balance analysis.

The values and equations are passed to the analysis tool to solve for the target value of input heat flow. In this case, an alert is generated indicating that the system of equations may be over constrained. A check reveals that the heat used to bring a fixed mass of feed water from 20 to 100° C is about 1/7th of the heat that must be removed from the same mass of steam to condense it fully. The cooling flow through the condenser is not enough to adequately condense the steam. Without a way to remove more heat from the steam, this is determined to be an infeasible design.

16.7 MODIFY THE ORIGINAL DESIGN

Since the analysis revealed a fundamental flaw in the original distiller design, this section describes modifications to the design to overcome performance limitations.

16.7.1 UPDATING BEHAVIOR

As presented in Figure 16.24, the design is modified by adding another part called *diverter assembly :*, which is represented as an allocate activity partition with an action to divert water called *a5 : Divert Feed*. This now allows excess heated water to exit the system without entering the boiler.

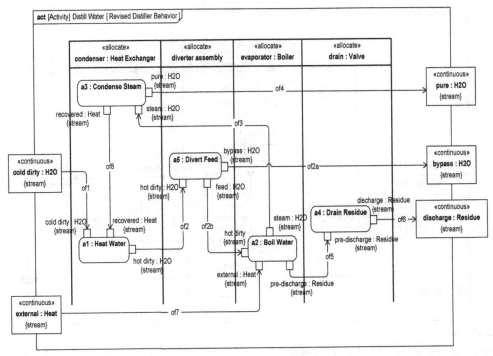

FIGURE 16.24

Revising behavior to accommodate diverting feed water.

16.7.2 UPDATING ALLOCATION AND STRUCTURE

The allocate activity partition corresponds to a new part, which includes another usage of the previously defined *Valve* block. This new part, its internal structure, and the associated flows are presented in the internal block diagram in Figure 16.25. This assembly is decomposed into a *splitter : Tee Fitting* to divert most of the flow out of the system (*m2.2 : H2O*), and a *feed : Valve* to throttle the water entering the boiler (*m2.1 : H2O*). The *diverter assembly : * is a simple collection of parts. The use of nested connector ends avoids the need to use flow ports on the *diverter assembly*.

Note how the block *Valve* has been reused. The *drain : Valve* and the *feed :Valve* each have two ports, both of which have the same definition but are connected differently.

This refined distiller design seems feasible and represents an adequate point of departure for a more detailed design. The previous parametric analysis is updated, and results are presented in Figure 16.26. The analysis tool is used to solve for the relative flow through the feed valve and is able to complete the calculation with no alerts or inconsistencies. Note that in a steady-state condition, the feed valve allows only 14.8% of the total flow to enter the boiler. This analysis establishes the maximum percentage of total flow that can feed the boiler. A more complete analysis of the distiller can now be performed, considering cooling of the condensate in the condenser and heating of water in the boiler as mentioned in Section 16.5.2. Elaborating this distiller model to this more general case is left as an

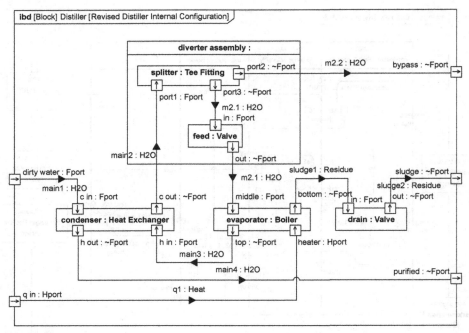

FIGURE 16.25

Revised distiller internal structure with flow diverter.

exercise for the student. Note that the structural design of the distiller may not need to change, but that the functional allocation and the parametric analysis will definitely need to be updated.

16.7.3 CONTROLLING THE DISTILLER AND THE USER INTERACTION

Up to this point, the design has not explicitly considered how the user interacts with the distiller. The design seems adequate for continuous operation, but the process of starting up and shutting down the distiller must now be specified.

A design excursion is proposed that considers how the distiller operability can be enhanced if a source of reliable electrical power is available. The availability of electrical power can facilitate control of the distiller in two ways: it allows for electric heating, and it also allows for a controller/processor to monitor the operation and perform routine adjustments to the distiller, thus greatly simplifying the operation of the distiller and minimizing the training and skill required. A control panel provides a uniform centralized operator interface for the distiller.

The original use case diagram presented in Figure 16.6 is still valid, but the *Operate Distiller* use case needs to be elaborated to address startup, steady-state operation, and shutdown using a control panel based interface. The use case description is as follows:

The *Operator* starts by turning the *Distiller* on and observes a *Power Lamp On*. When the *Distiller* reaches operating temperature, the *Operator* observes the *Operating Lamp On*; the distiller then cycles

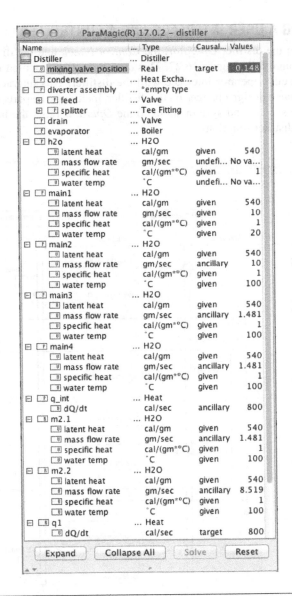

FIGURE 16.26

Analysis of revised distiller confirms benefit of flow diverter.

as it produces distilled water. The *Operator* turns the *Distiller* off, and the *Power Lamp Off* signal is returned by the *Distiller*.

The next section examines the interaction of the operator, control panel, and controller during distiller operation.

16.7.4 DEVELOPING A USER INTERFACE AND A CONTROLLER

The interaction between the distiller *Operator*, the *Control Panel*, and the distiller *Controller* is presented on a sequence diagram in Figure 16.27. This does not reflect detailed interactions of distilling water but rather the specific operator interface with the distiller. This interaction imposes additional requirements and associated design changes on the distiller, including the parts needed for the *Operator* to provide inputs to the system and system status to the *Operator* (e.g., the lamps), and for the automated control of some distiller functions.

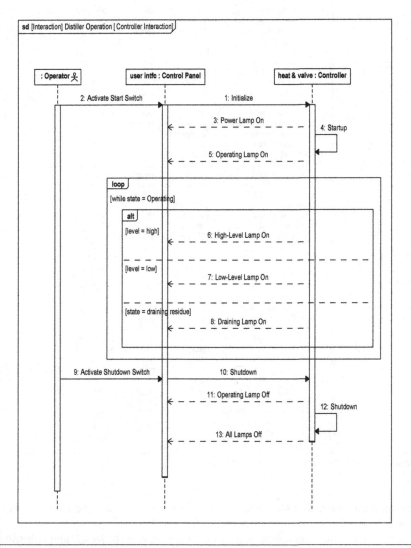

FIGURE 16.27

Defining operator interaction using a sequence diagram.

Figure 16.28 presents an internal block diagram that reflects the update to the design to realize the use case. A *Control Panel* has been added with the switches to turn the *Distiller* on and off and lamps that the operator observes. A *Controller* has been added to ensure that the valves are operated in the proper sequence and that the lamps are turned on and off.

Power input is provided to the heaters in the *Boiler* to convert electrical power to heat. It makes sense to use the controller to provide power to the *Boiler*. An interface block named *Boiler Signals* is used to specify the kind of signals expected to pass between the *Controller* and the *Boiler*. Flow properties in the *Boiler Signals* interface block may include information such as the position of float switches in the boiler to indicate whether the level is high or low.

Figure 16.29 presents the new interface blocks necessary for this advanced design. Note that *Boiler Signals* uses two flow properties, *control* and *status*, and the direction is appropriate for the *heat and valve : Controller* presented in Figure 16.28. The *evaporator : Boiler* uses a conjugate port with the same interface block as the port on the *Controller*. The *Cport* interface block includes a flow property for controlling one valve, and the *Pport* interface block includes a flow property for electric power.

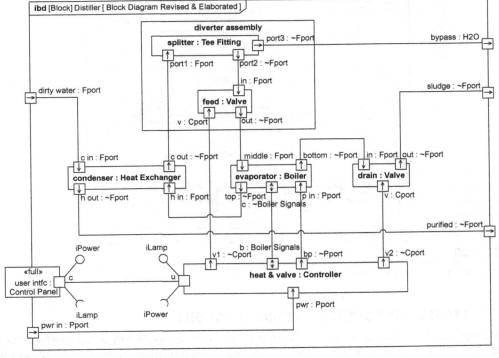

FIGURE 16.28

Distiller internal structure with controller and user interface.

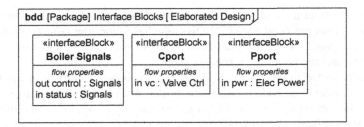

FIGURE 16.29

Interface block for boiler signals.

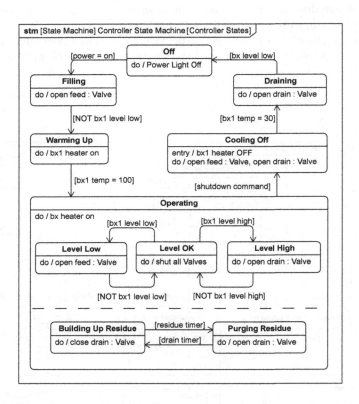

FIGURE 16.30

Controller state machine for distiller.

16.7.5 STARTUP AND SHUTDOWN CONSIDERATIONS

The startup, shutdown and other aspects of system control can be specified by a state machine diagram for the *Controller,* as presented in Figure 16.30. The states and transitions in the diagram are identified by examining the sequence diagram associated with the *Operate Distiller* use case.

Several things have to happen before transitioning the *Distiller* from the *Off* state, in which it is cold and dry, to the *On* state, where it begins producing clean water. The first step is to fill the boiler with water. While in the *Filling* state, the *feed : Valve* opens. As soon as the water level in the *Boiler* is adequate to cover the heater coils, the heater can be turned on without damage. The system can now enter the *Warming Up* state, where the boiler heaters are turned on and the boiler begins to warm up.

Once the boiler temperature reaches 100° C, the system enters the *Operating* state. In this state, the boiler heaters are still on, but two substates, *Controlling Boiler Level* and *Controlling Residue,* occur in parallel. In this example, control of residue relies on a simple timer to transition between the *Building Up Residue* substate when the *drain : Valve* is closed and the *Purging Residue* substate when the *drain : Valve* is open to dispose of the residue. The *Distiller* state machine periodically blows down the boiler to limit the sludge build up.

When controlling the water level in the *Boiler,* one of three substates exists: either *Level OK,* in which case the *drain : Valve* and *feed : Valve* both need to be closed; *Level Low,* in which the *feed : Valve* needs to be open; or *Level High,* where the *drain : Valve* needs to be open.

When operations are finished, the *Distiller* goes through a shutdown procedure. Otherwise, corrosion will severely limit the lifespan of the *Distiller.* The first step in this procedure is to cool the system. In the *Cooling Off* state, the heaters are turned off and the *feed : Valve* and the *drain : Valve* opened, allowing cool water to flow freely through the entire system. Once the boiler temperature reaches a safe level, the *Boiler* needs to be drained. In the *Draining* state, the *feed : Valve* is shut while the *drain : Valve* remains open and all water is drained out of the *Boiler.* Once the *Boiler* is empty, the *Distiller* power is safely switched off.

16.8 SUMMARY

This example presents how SysML can be used to model a system with a traditional functional analysis method. The example also illustrates its application to modeling physical systems with limited software functionality. Examples of each SysML diagram are used to support the specification, design, and analysis, along with leveraging some of the fundamental SysML language concepts such as the distinction between definition and use.

16.9 QUESTIONS

The following questions may best be addressed in a classroom or group project environment.

1. Evaluate the "significant simplifying assumption" mentioned in Section 16.5.2.
   a. Describe how the activity model depicted in Figure 16.24 should be modified to account for the fact that water may be heated in the evaporator and the condensate may be cooled in the condenser. In other words, the temperature of water entering the evaporator and the condensate leaving the condenser may be less than 100°C.
   b. Describe how the parametric model depicted in Figure 16.22 needs to be modified to accommodate these changes, and describe the overall impact of adding this fidelity to the heat balance.

2. The customer has introduced this new requirement: "The water distiller shall be able to operate at least 2 meters vertically above the source of dirty water." Show the impact of this new requirement on the system design, as expressed in each of the following modeling artifacts.

   a. Requirement diagram (relate new requirement to existing requirements).
   b. Activity diagram (define and incorporate new activities to support the new requirement).
   c. Block definition diagram (define and incorporate new blocks to support the new requirement).
   d. Internal block diagram (define flows and interfaces to any new parts necessary to support the new requirement, and any functional and flow allocations from the activity diagram).
   e. Parametric diagram (describe how the heat balance is affected by this new requirement).
   f. Use case diagram (describe any changes to the operational scenario).
   g. Sequence diagram (elaborate any changes to the *Operate Distiller* use case).
   h. State machine diagram (describe how the *Controller* state machine would be affected by the preceding design changes).

3. Concern has been expressed about the energy inefficiency of the revised distiller design, in that only 1/7th of the water entering the distiller actually emerges as clean water, and the rest is simply used for cooling. Lowering the pressure in the evaporator can significantly reduce the temperature at which the water boils, thus reducing the amount of energy used and also requiring less cooling water.

   a. Redesign the distiller so that the evaporator can operate at below atmospheric temperature. Update the activity model with any additional actions required and the structural model with any additional components required.
   b. Assume that the minimum safe temperature for boiling water in a distiller is 70° C. Update the parametric model to determine the steady state mixing valve position, using 70° C for the temperature of *main 2*, *main 3* and *main 4*, and keeping the other parameters the same as in Figure 16.26.

4. Discuss the applicability and physical significance of control flows in the distiller activity model as presented on Figure 16.12 and Figure 16.14. In which situations are control flows useful representations of behavior?

RESIDENTIAL SECURITY SYSTEM EXAMPLE USING THE OBJECT-ORIENTED SYSTEMS ENGINEERING METHOD

The example in this chapter describes the application of SysML to the development of a residential security system using the **Object-Oriented Systems Engineering Method** (OOSEM). A simplified version of this method is introduced in Chapter 3, Section 3.4, and a typical set of modeling artifacts resulting from its application is introduced in the Automobile example in Chapter 4, Section 4.3.

The application of OOSEM along with the functional analysis method in Chapter 16 is an example of how SysML is applied using a model-based systems engineering method. SysML can be applied with other methods as well. The intent of this chapter is to provide a robust model-based system specification and design method that readers can adapt to meet the needs of their application.

This chapter begins with a brief introduction to the method and how it fits into an overall development process, and then it shows how OOSEM is applied to the residential security example. The reader should refer to the language description in Part II for the foundational language concepts used to model this example.

17.1 METHOD OVERVIEW

This section provides an introduction to OOSEM. It includes the motivation and background for the method, a high-level summary of the system development process that provides the context for OOSEM, and describes the OOSEM system specification and design process that is part of the system development process.

17.1.1 MOTIVATION AND BACKGROUND

OOSEM is a top-down, scenario-driven process that uses SysML to support the analysis, specification, design, and verification of systems. The process leverages object-oriented concepts and other modeling techniques to help architect flexible and extensible systems that can accommodate evolving technology and changing requirements. OOSEM is also intended to ease integration with object-oriented software development, hardware development, and test processes.

In OOSEM and other model-based systems engineering approaches, the system model is a primary output of the system specification and design process. The model artifacts present different views of the system such as behavior, structure, properties, and traceability to its requirements. OOSEM helps ensure the various views provide a consistent representation of the system, as described in Chapter 2, Section 2.1.2.

417

OOSEM includes the fundamental systems engineering activities such as stakeholder needs analysis, requirements analysis, architecture design, trade studies and analysis, and verification. It has similarities with other methods such as the Harmony process [7, 8] and the Rational Unified Process for Systems Engineering (RUP SE) [10, 11], which also apply a top-down, scenario-driven approach that leverages SysML as the modeling language. OOSEM leverages object-oriented concepts such as encapsulation and specialization, but these concepts are applied at the system level somewhat differently than they are applied to software design. In particular, OOSEM integrates structured analysis concepts, such as data flow, with selected object-oriented concepts. OOSEM also includes modeling techniques, such as causal analysis, black box and white box descriptions, logical decomposition, partitioning criteria, node distribution, variant design, and enabling systems that span the life cycle, to deal with a broad spectrum of system concerns. In particular, OOSEM emphasizes the **separation of concerns** to manage complexity and integrate the concerns into a cohesive model of the system.

OOSEM was developed in 1998 [53,54] and further evolved as part of a joint effort between Lockheed Martin Corporation and the Systems and Software Consortium (SSCI), which previously was the Software Productivity Consortium [9]. Early pilots were conducted to assess the feasibility of the method [55], and then it was further refined by the INCOSE OOSEM Working Group beginning in 2002. In its original form, OOSEM utilized UML with nonstandard extensions to express many of the modeling artifacts. Tool support was substantially improved for OOSEM with the adoption of the SysML specification beginning in 2006.

17.1.2 SYSTEM DEVELOPMENT PROCESS OVERVIEW

The full system engineering **lifecycle process** includes processes for developing, producing, deploying, operating, supporting, and disposing the system. The successful output of the **development process** is a verified and validated system that satisfies the operational requirements, capabilities, and other lifecycle requirements for production, deployment, support, and disposal.

OOSEM is part of a development process that was originally based on the Integrated Systems and Software Engineering Process (ISSEP) [56]. A modified version of this process as it applies to OOSEM is highlighted in the *Develop System* process in Figure 17.1, and includes the management process, the system specification and design process, the development processes at the next level of design, and the system integration and verification process. In the figure, the development processes includes the development of the hardware, software, database, and operational procedures. More generally, this process can be applied recursively to multiple levels of a system's hierarchy in a way similar to a Vee development process [57], where the development process is applied to successively lower levels of the system hierarchy. This development process is different from a typical Vee process in that it applies both the management processes and the technical processes at each level of the Vee, whereas a typical Vee process applies only the technical processes at each level of the Vee.

Applying the process at each level result in the specification of elements at the next lower level of the system hierarchy. For example, applying the process at the system-of-systems (SoS) level results in the specification and verification of one or more systems. Applying the process at the system level results in the specification and verification of the system elements, and applying the process at the element level result in the specification and verification of the components. The hardware and software development processes are then applied at the component level to analyze the component requirements and to design, implement, and verify the components.

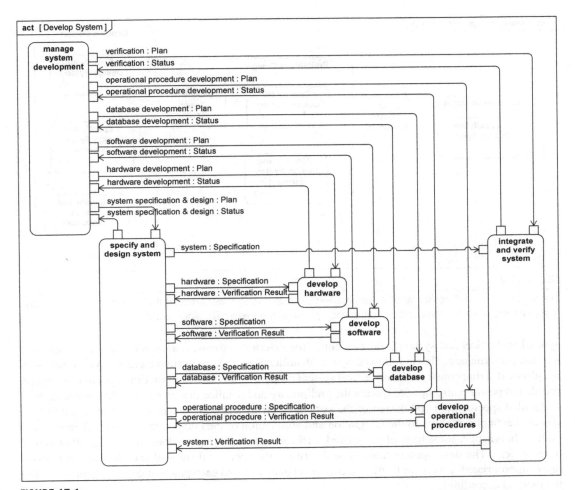

FIGURE 17.1

System development process.

The leaf level of the process is the level at which an element or component is procured or implemented. In the automobile design example in Chapter 4, if the automotive design team procures the engine, the team specifies the engine requirements as indicated in Figure 4.16 and verifies that the engine satisfies its requirements. On the other hand, if the engine is subject to further design, the process is applied to the next level of engine design to specify the engine components and verify that the components satisfy their requirements.

The development process may be applied iteratively throughout different phases of development including conceptual design, preliminary design, detailed design, and later phases as shown in Figure 17.2. However, the levels and detail of the specification and design process is generally adapted to the phase of development. For example, during the early conceptual design phase, the process is

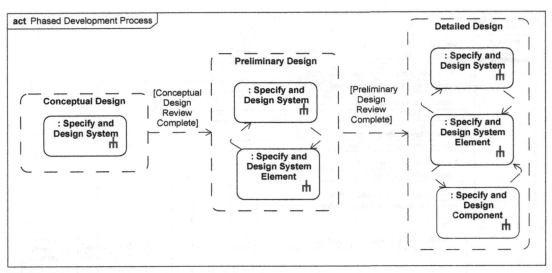

FIGURE 17.2

The specification and design activities are applied to progressively lower levels of the system design hierarchy (e.g., system, element, component) during each phase of the system development process.

applied at the SoS and system level to identify the external systems, critical mission parameters, and mission performance. This is followed by the identification of major system elements, key functionality, physical sizing constraints, and critical system properties such as response times, accuracies, range, speed, and power consumption. During the preliminary and detailed design phases, the emphasis shifts to detailed specification and design of the system elements and components respectively, and in later phases the emphasis shifts to the integration and verification of the components, system elements, and system. In practice, some level of design and verification activity is often done throughout all phases of development. The development team must determine the scope and rigor of specification and design that is appropriate for their application at each level of design and each phase of development, and tailor the method accordingly.

The following subsections provide a high-level summary of each process shown in the *Develop System* process in Figure 17.1.

Manage system development

This process includes project planning and controlling the execution of the work in accordance with the plan. Project control includes monitoring cost, schedule, and performance metrics to assess progress against the plan, to manage risk, and to control changes to the technical baseline. The model-based metrics described in Chapter 2, Section 2.2.5 can be used to support the management process.

The management process also includes selection of the lifecycle model, such as waterfall, incremental, or spiral, that defines the ordering of the activities for each level of design and for each phase of development. Use cases that are defined in the model provide units of functionality that can serve as an effective organizing principle for planning and controlling the scope of work to be accomplished for a particular development spiral or increment. For example, the design realization of selected mission use cases or the design of critical infrastructure elements that supports the realization of multiple use cases may take priority for a particular design increment.

The management process also includes tailoring the activities and artifacts defined by the systems engineering methods to meet the project's needs. Tailoring depends on the level of design and the phase of development as noted previously, plus a variety of other factors that may include the extent to which the system is a new design (i.e., unprecedented), the system size and complexity, the available time and resources, and the level of experience of the development team. As an example, a system design may be constrained to include significant legacy or predefined commercial off-the-shelf (COTS) components. This can significantly impact which activities are performed and the ordering of the activities. The activities may include early characterization of the COTS component capabilities in parallel with other system specification and design activities. The design emphasis is placed on how the COTS components interact to achieve the system requirements and how to interface with the COTS components.

Additional tailoring of the process and its artifacts may be required for specific domains at each level of the system's hierarchy. For example, applying the method to specify and design the power train, body, braking, and steering assembly of an automobile each include unique types of analysis that need to be performed and require specific design techniques and modeling artifacts.

Specify and design system

This process is implemented by OOSEM, which is summarized in Section 17.1.3, and applies to the left side of the Vee process. The system specification and design process includes activities to analyze the system requirements, define the system architecture, and specify the requirements for the next level of design. The next level of design performs a similar set of activities to satisfy its requirements. For more complex systems, there may be multiple intermediate levels of design, which are generically referred to as "element levels." The component level is typically the lowest level of design that the hardware, software, database, and operational procedures are designed, implemented, and tested. The specification and design activities also provide requirements and test cases as inputs to the Integrate and Verify process that is performed on the right side of the Vee process.

Develop hardware, software, database, and operational procedures

These development processes include the analysis and further refinement of the specification that is flowed down from the next higher level, and the design, supporting analysis, implementation, and verification of the components. For hardware, implementation is accomplished by fabricating and/or constructing the hardware components; for software, implementation is accomplished by generating code for the software components. If there are multiple intermediate levels of hardware and software, the development process in Figure 17.1 can be applied recursively to each intermediate level.

Integrate and verify system

This process integrates the system elements and/or components and verifies that the integrated design satisfies its requirements. The process includes developing verification plans, procedures, and methods (e.g., inspection, demonstration, analysis, testing), conducting the integration and verification, analyzing the results, and generating the verification reports. OOSEM supports the right side of the Vee by specifying the test cases at each level of design. The test cases are then used to develop the verification plans and procedures and the requirements for the verification system as described in Section 17.3.8,

Product integration and verification is performed as part of the processes on the right side of the Vee, where the physical hardware and software are integrated at each level, and the test cases are executed to verify that the component-, element-, and system-level requirements are satisfied. In a model-based approach, design integration and verification can also be performed early in the design process to gain confidence that the system, element, and components satisfy their requirements. This is sometimes called virtual integration and verification. This process is accomplished by integrating a lower-level design model into a higher-level design model and then verifying that the integrated model at each level satisfies its requirements through analysis. As an example, design integration and verification of an automobile design may include verifying the engine controller design model satisfies its requirements through analysis, and then integrating the engine controller design model into the engine design model. After verifying through analysis that the engine design satisfies its requirements, the engine design model is integrated into the automobile system design model, which is then verified. The integrated model is used to verify that the engine component designs satisfy their requirements, the engine design satisfies its requirements, and the automobile system design satisfies its requirements using a combination of design and analysis models.

17.1.3 OOSEM SYSTEM SPECIFICATION AND DESIGN PROCESS

Figure 17.3 is a high-level summary of the OOSEM *Specify and Design System* process. A simplified version of this process is introduced in Chapter 3, Section 3.4. The number in each action refers to the section number in this chapter where the action is further elaborated and described. The referenced section includes an activity diagram to show the next level of detail. To simplify the process description, the activity diagram includes neither the process iteration loops nor the input and output artifacts from each activity. However, the referenced sections in Figure 17.3 include a description and example of the modeling artifacts that are produced. The action names are shown in lower case, but the names of the corresponding activity names in the referenced sections start with upper case.

The *Set-up Model* activity establishes the basic prerequisites for developing the model, including establishing the modeling guidelines and organizing the model (refer to Section 17.3.1). The *Analyze Stakeholder Needs* activity characterizes the as-is system and enterprise, describes its limitations and potential improvement areas, and specifies the mission requirements that the to-be system must support (refer to Section 17.3.2). The *Analyze System Requirements* activity specifies the system requirements in terms of input and output responses and other black-box characteristics needed to support the mission requirements (refer to Section 17.3.3). The *Define Logical Architecture* activity decomposes the system into logical components and defines how the logical components interact to realize the system requirements (refer to Section 17.3.4). The *Synthesize Candidate Physical Architectures* activity allocates the logical components to physical components that are implemented in hardware, software, data, and procedures (refer to Section 17.3.5). The *Optimize and Evaluate Alternatives* activity is invoked throughout the process to perform engineering analysis that supports system design trade studies and design optimization (refer to Section 17.3.6). The *Manage Requirements Traceability* activity is used to manage traceability from the mission-level requirements to the component requirements (refer to Section 17.3.7). OOSEM also includes activities that support the *Integrate and Verify System* process (refer to Section 17.3.8). Each of these activities is applied to the residential security example in the rest of the chapter. The simplified MBSE method in Chapter 3, Section 3.4 excludes the logical architecture design activity, and only includes a subset of the other activities.

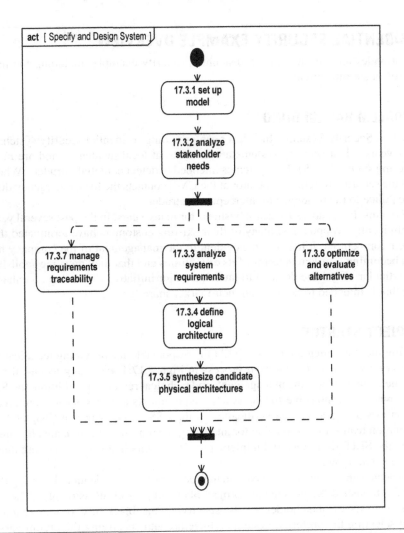

FIGURE 17.3

OOSEM *Specify* and *Design System* process. The action numbers refer to the subsection where the action is described.

When capturing this method for use by an organization or project, the level of detail of the process documentation should be tailored to address organizational and project needs. The documentation can be further elaborated to describe the detailed process description for creating each modeling artifact, such as a use case. In addition, the process flows can be further refined to reflect the design iterations and the flow of inputs and outputs. This level of detail is not included in any of the process flows in this example to simplify the process description. The process can be documented in a process modeling and/or process authoring tool and published to a web environment. This approach facilitates maintenance, the tailoring of the process, and the use of the process information. In the example below, the process model is contained in a package called *OOSEM Process*.

17.2 RESIDENTIAL SECURITY EXAMPLE OVERVIEW

This section provides an overview of the residential security example, including the problem background and project startup activities.

17.2.1 PROBLEM BACKGROUND

A company called Security Systems, Inc., has been providing residential security systems to the local area for many years. Their security systems are installed at local residences and are monitored by a central monitoring station (CMS). The system is intended to detect potential intruders. When an intruder is detected by the security system, an operator at the CMS contacts the local emergency dispatcher who dispatches the police to the residence to intercept the intruder.

Security Systems, Inc., had a successful business for many years. In the past several years, however, their sales significantly dropped, and many of their existing customers have terminated their contracts in favor of their competitors. It has become evident to the management of the company that their current system is becoming obsolete in terms of its capabilities and that they must reestablish their market position. In particular, they have decided to launch a major initiative to develop an enhanced security system (ESS) that is intended to help regain their market share.

17.2.2 PROJECT STARTUP

The Systems Engineering Integrated Team (SEIT) is responsible for providing technical management as part of the *manage system development* process in Figure 17.1, including technical planning, risk management, the technical baseline management, and technical reviews. In addition, the SEIT includes team members who are responsible for the system requirements analysis, system architecture design, engineering analysis, integration, and verification of the ESS, as described in Chapter 1, Section 1.4. The implementation teams are responsible for analyzing the requirements that are allocated to the ESS components by the SEIT, designing and implementing the components, and verifying that the components satisfy their requirements.

The SEIT selected an incremental development process as its lifecycle model. During the first increment, the SEIT established the incremental project plan and project infrastructure. The second increment includes analysis of stakeholder needs, specifying the black-box system requirements, and evaluating and selecting the preferred system architecture and specifying the preliminary component requirements for the proposed ESS solution. The follow-on increments focus on architecture refinement and implementing the component requirements needed to achieve incremental capabilities corresponding to selected ESS use cases.

As part of establishing the project plan and infrastructure during the first increment, the initial activities for the modeling effort included defining the modeling objectives; scoping the model to meet the objectives; selecting and tailoring the MBSE method; selecting, acquiring, and installing the tools; defining the schedule for the modeling activities and delivery of the modeling artifacts; staffing the effort; and providing the necessary training.

The SEIT selected OOSEM as their model-based systems engineering method in conjunction with SysML as their graphical modeling language. This was based on the results of an earlier pilot project to assess how well the method and tools would support their needs (refer to discussion on pilots in

Chapter 19, Section 19.1.4). They selected tools based on the tool selection criteria described in Chapter 18, Section 18.5. The systems development environment includes SysML modeling tools, a UML-based software development environment; hardware design tools; engineering analysis tools; testing tools; configuration management tools; a requirements management tool; and other project management tools for planning, scheduling, and risk management. The SEIT and selected members of other implementation teams received training in SysML, OOSEM, and the use of their selected tools.

17.3 APPLYING OOSEM TO SPECIFY AND DESIGN THE RESIDENTIAL SECURITY SYSTEM

The example in this chapter is intended to describe the modeling activities for the second increment. During this increment, the ESS modeling is initiated and used to specify and validate system requirements, architect the solution, and allocate requirements to the ESS hardware, software, and data components. The components are either developed by the implementation teams or procured as COTS products. It is anticipated that there will be significant software and database development, but the hardware components—such as sensors, cameras, processors, and network devices—are primarily COTS. The model is also used to develop new operational procedures for the customers and central monitoring station operators that define how to interact with the system.

The following subsections elaborate the *Specify and Design System* process and artifacts that were summarized in Section 17.1.3. The subsection numbers correspond to the numbers referenced in the actions in Figure 17.3. The activities—*Manage Requirements Traceability* and *Optimize and Evaluate Alternatives*—are included toward the end of this section, even though they occur as supporting activities throughout this process. The model objectives and scope for this example are intended to illustrate the approach by focusing on the intruder-monitoring thread and not elaborating other functionality of the system.

17.3.1 SETUP MODEL

Setting up the model is a critical first step in any modeling effort. This includes establishing the modeling conventions and standards, and organizing the model as shown in Figure 17.4.

Establish modeling conventions and standards

Modeling conventions and standards are needed to ensure that consistent presentation and style of modeling is applied across the model, and to help ensure the integrity of the model. The conventions and standards can be defined, documented, and shared at the organizational level, such that each individual project is able to use them as their starting point.

The conventions and standards include establishing naming conventions for diagrams and for model elements, such as package names. The conventions and standards also identify other stylistic aspects of the language, such as when to use upper case versus lower case and when to use spaces in the names, and also account for tool-imposed constraints, such as limitations on the use of alphanumeric and special characters. It is also recommended that a template be established for each diagram kind to highlight diagram layout standards. Additional guidelines can be developed to generate customized reports from the model, customize the language concepts and terminology through stereotypes, and develop customized scripts for model checking.

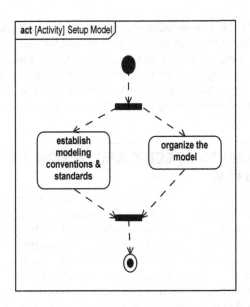

FIGURE 17.4

Set-up Model process.

Some example guidelines that are used in this example include the following:

Use of Upper and Lower Case
Upper case is used for the first letter of each word for all definitions/types, such as blocks and value types, and for packages and requirements, with a space between compound names that have more than one word.
Example: "Video Camcorder"
Lower case is used for all letters in names of parts, properties, item properties, actions, and states with a space between compound names that have more than one word.
Example: "record data" (this is an action name)
Verb/Noun Form—The verb/noun form is used to name activities, actions, and use cases.
Example: "Monitor Intruder" (this is an Activity Name)
Names of Port Types—Names of port types typically are appended with IF for interface.
Examples: *"Video IF"*
Tool-Specific Notation—The diagrams in this chapter are generated directly from a modeling tool with little post editing. Some of the notation may differ somewhat from the SysML specification that is described in Part II due to tool specific implementations. However, the guidelines should note any tool specific notations as distinct from the standard notation.
Model Element Descriptions—Another example of a modeling guideline is defining the appropriate level of text description for each model element. A standard text description may include a terse definition of the model element and possibly the source of the information. This can be captured as a comment or in the documentation field for the model element that most tools provide. If this is done properly, it can enhance the understandability and maintenance of the

Table 17.1 OOSEM-Specific Profile of SysML-User-Defined Stereotypes

OOSEM Stereotype	Base Class
«analysis»	Block, Property
«caused by»	Dependency
«configuration item»	Block, Property
«data»	Block, Part Property
«document»	Block
«failure mode»	Constraint Block
«file»	Block, Part Property
«hardware»	Block, Part Property
«logical»	Block, Part Property
«mop»	Property
«moe»	Property
«node logical»	Block, Part Property
«node physical»	Block, Part Property
«operator»	Block, Part Property
«procedure»	Block, Part Property
«software»	Block, Part Property
«status»	Property
«store»	Property
«system of interest»	Block, Part Property
«test component»	Block, Part Property
«test objective»	Comment, Requirement
«violates»	Dependency

model. This information can also support automated generation of documentation from the model, which can include both the diagrams and the text descriptions. Chapter 18, Section 18.4.5 describes how documents and other views can be automatically generated from the model.

Customized Stereotypes and Model Libraries—Projects often require customization of the language with specific stereotypes that are applicable to their domain and/or method. Table 17.1 contains a list of user-defined stereotypes for an OOSEM-specific profile of SysML that is used in this example. In addition to these stereotypes, a project using OOSEM may choose to define additional stereotypes and model libraries that are unique to their domain. The approach for defining a profile is described in Chapter 15, Section 15.4.

Some terms used in this example are unique to this method, including:

Domain—This term is used to represent the scope of the model.
Example: Operational Domain refers to the portion of the model that includes the operational system, users, and environment. The term *Operational Context* is a synonym for *Operational Domain*.
Enterprise—An aggregation of systems and users that work together to accomplish a goal. In OOSEM, the term *System-of-Systems* could be considered a synonym for *Enterprise*.

Example: Security Enterprise refers to the logical aggregation of the security system, emergency services, and the communication systems that collaborate to respond to emergencies.

Logical—An abstraction of a physical entity that is intended to capture its functionality but is not constrained by the specific technology or implementation.

Example: An *entry sensor* is a logical component that is an abstraction of a physical component such as an *optical sensor* or *contact sensor*.

Subsystem—A logical aggregation of components that either perform one or more system functions (Example A) or have a common feature among the parts (Example B).

Example A: A power management subsystem that is an aggregation of components that manage and distribute power

Example B: An electrical subsystem that is an aggregation of electrical components

Node—A partitioning of entities based on some criteria. A node in OOSEM is generally used to describe a distributed system where each node represents a partitioning of components based on their physical location. Nodes may also be defined based on other criteria such as organizational responsibility (e.g., the people and resources assigned to a particular department).

Example: The *Site Installation* nodes and the *Central Monitoring Station* node represent a set of components at different physical locations.

Mission—A primary task that the system(s) and enterprise are intended to support.

Example: The Enhanced Security System and Emergency Services support the mission to "Enhance security of life and property by providing emergency response for single-family residence, multi-family residence, and small business, to theft, burglary, fire, and health and safety."

Customized model scripts—A project can leverage the model in many ways to improve productivity, quality, and provide additional capabilities. This is often done through the development and use of customized scripts that most modeling tools support. The scripts can be used to implement validation rules that validate that the model conforms to the project guidelines. The scripts should be subject to proper development guidelines and made available in a common library to be applied consistently throughout the project and/or organization.

Organize the model

The model organization is recognized as a critical aspect of developing an effective system model. The complexity of the system model can quickly overwhelm the users of the model and become intractable, particularly for large distributed teams. This in turn can impact the ability of model developers to maintain a consistent model and to maintain control of the model baseline. Refer to Chapter 6 for considerations for how to organize the model with packages.

OOSEM includes a standard approach for how to organize the model that is defined by the package structure. The model organization builds on the concepts first introduced as part of SysML-Lite in Chapter 3, Section 3.3 and in Chapter 4, Section 4.3.1 but includes additional package structure to deal with more complex models.

The model organization typically includes a recursive package structure that mirrors the system hierarchy. A package may be defined for a block that is further decomposed. This package may contain nested packages for the blocks requirements, structure, and behavior, and may include additional nested packages for the blocks at the next lower level of system decomposition. The parametrics or analysis package may also be included at each level of the system hierarchy or maintained at the top level.

The model organization also includes other packages that are not nested within the packages at each level of the system hierarchy. These packages contain model elements that may be reused at multiple levels of the system hierarchy, such as packages for value types and viewpoints. These packages may contain their own hierarchy consisting of nested packages that may be independent of the system hierarchy.

The model organization for this example is highlighted by the package structure in the package diagram and browser view in Figure 17.5. The package diagram named *Model Organization* shown in the figure mirrors the model organization presented in the browser view.

The *OOSEM Profile Extensions* is one package, and the *Model* is the other package at the top level of the containment tree. The *Model* package contains packages for *Process Guidance, Security Domain as-is, Security Domain to-be, Value Types, and Viewpoints.*

The *Process Guidance* package provides a convenient mechanism to capture process definition, tool issues, and other process information that is captured by the systems engineering team throughout the modeling process. If the information is relevant across projects, it should be reflected in updates to the organization's standard processes. For this example, the package contains the activity diagrams that describe OOSEM, including the activity diagram in Figure 17.3, and the lower-level activities that are included in Section 17.3.1–7. Alternatively, other process-modeling tools can be used to capture the process information, which can be referenced from this package.

The *Security Domain as-is* package contains model information about the as-is domain to aid in understanding the limitations of the current system and enterprise and to identify the parts of the as-is model that may be reused in the to-be model.

The *Value Types* package contains value types with units and quantity kinds for use throughout the model. This package imports the ISO 80000 package (not shown), which contains a library of standard units and quantity kinds. Value types and the ISO 80000 model library are described in Chapter 7, Section 7.3.4.

The *Viewpoints* package contains viewpoints and associated views for different ESS stakeholders. Viewpoints and views are described in Chapter 15, Section 15.8. The viewpoints for this example are discussed in Section 17.3.5 under the subsection *Defining Other Architecture Views.*

The *Security Domain to-be* package contains nested packages that contain systems and enterprises that implement different lifecycle processes. In particular, it contains the *Installation* package and the *Operational* package, but could contain other packages for other lifecycle processes, such as Manufacturing, Support, and Disposal. Each of these packages contains model elements that specify the systems that implement a particular lifecycle process. For example, the *Installation* package contains model elements that specify and design the installation system and enterprise to implement the installation process. The model elements in this package represent the installers and the installation system, including the installation trucks and installation equipment. The *Installation* package is described in Section 17.3.9.

Most of the elaboration of this model is contained within the *Operational* package, since the focus of this example is on the design of the operational system called *ESS*. The *Operational* package contains nested packages for *Requirements, Structure, Use Cases, Behavior, Parametrics, Interface Definitions,* and the *ESS*, which is the system of interest. Some of the package names start with a number to establish the order in which they appear in the package hierarchy. However, these numbers are not included when they are referenced in the text below. The packages for other lifecycle processes are organized similar to the *Operational* package.

The *Operational* package contains model elements that describe different aspects of the operational domain. The *Requirements* package contains the mission requirements for the ESS. The *Structure*

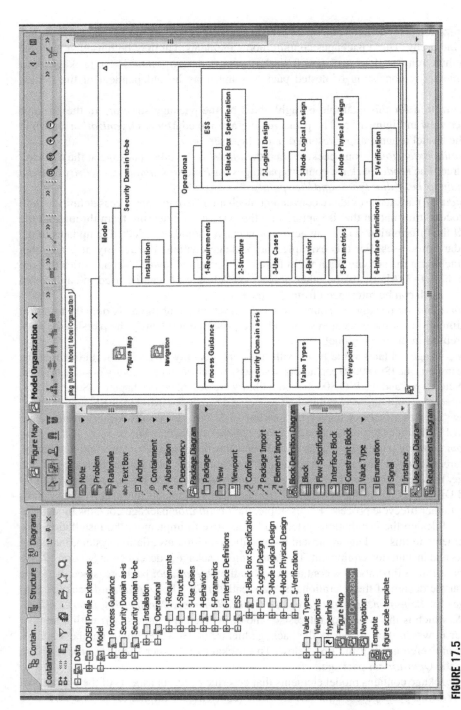

FIGURE 17.5

ESS *Model Organization.*

package defines the context for the *ESS*, including its external systems and users. The *Use Cases* package contains the enterprise use cases that the ESS must support. The *Behavior* package contains the mission scenarios for each use case. The *Parametrics* package contains the top level engineering analysis that support trade studies and design optimization.

The *Interface Definitions* package contains the input and output definitions and the port specifications that are used throughout the model. These definitions are not limited to a single level of the hierarchy and are therefore contained at the highest level at which they apply. The *ESS* package contains the model elements that represent the ESS. As shown in Figure 17.5, the ESS contains nested packages for its *Black Box Specification*, *Logical Design*, *Node Logical Design*, *Node Physical Design*, and *Verification*. The *Node Physical Design* contains nested packages for hardware, software, data, and operational procedures (not shown).

Each of the preceding packages contains model elements that are created by applying OOSEM to the specification and design of the system. The content of each package is described in the sections of this chapter that correspond to the OOSEM activity that the content is created.

Diagrams contained in particular packages are highlighted in the browser with special symbols that are unique to each tool. As an example, a symbol in Figure 17.5 towards the bottom of the browser refers to the *Model Organization* package diagram shown in the tool's diagram area.

As described in Chapter 5, Section 5.2, the diagram frame actually designates a model element. The model element that is designated by the diagram frame determines where the diagram appears in the browser hierarchy. In this case, the diagram frame corresponds to the *Model* as indicated in the diagram header, so the diagram symbol appears under the *Model* in the browser.

Model elements contained in one package can be related to model elements contained in another package. When a model element from another package appears on a diagram, its fully qualified name identifies the package that contains it. This enables each model element on a diagram to be uniquely identified, even if two model elements in different packages have the same name. The fully qualified name can be shown with the double-colon notation described in Chapter 6, Section 6.6. The fully qualified name is elided in figures throughout this chapter to reduce diagram clutter.

In order to ease the navigation of the model, it is sometimes useful to create a package diagram that contains hyperlinks to the diagrams of interest that facilitates navigation to selected modeling artifacts. The diagram symbol for the package diagram named *Navigation* is also shown in the browser. This diagram includes hyperlinks to other diagrams contained throughout the model to enable easy access to the diagrams without having to know the details of the package structure. An example of a diagram hyperlink icon is shown in the *Model Organization* package diagram in Figure 17.5. Clicking on this icon provides a hyperlink to the *Navigation* diagram.

17.3.2 ANALYZE STAKEHOLDER NEEDS

The *Analyze Stakeholder Needs* activity is referenced in Figure 17.3 and is shown in Figure 17.6. As mentioned previously, this simplified process flow does not include inputs and outputs or process iterations. Performing this activity provides the analysis to understand the stakeholder problems to be solved, specify the mission-level requirements that must be satisfied, and set the context for the system(s) needed to solve the problem.

This analysis includes assessing the limitations of the current systems by characterizing the as-is system and enterprise and by performing causal analysis to determine the limitations and

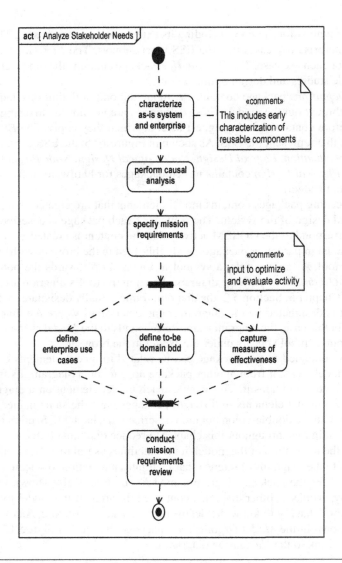

FIGURE 17.6

Analyze Stakeholder Needs activity to specify mission requirements.

potential improvement areas from the perspective of each stakeholder. Analysis results are used to derive mission requirements and overall objectives for the to-be system and enterprise that address the limitations of the current system and enterprise. The modeling artifacts generated from this activity include the causal analysis, mission requirements, the to-be domain model, the enterprise use cases, and the measures of effectiveness. A mission requirements review is conducted to validate that the mission requirements address the stakeholder needs and the proper context is set for the solution.

A stakeholder refers to any person or organization that has an interest in the ESS across its lifecycle, including ESS development, installation, operations, and support. The stakeholder identification includes users of the system, installers of the system, and participants involved in the development of the system. As the specification and design process progresses, additional stakeholders are identified, such as the police who respond to ESS alerts. The stakeholders and their concerns are explicitly captured in viewpoints, which are discussed at the end of Section 17.3.5.

For this example, OOSEM is applied to the design of a single system called ESS. The external systems, such as Emergency Services, are assumed to be specified and are not subject to further design As a result, there is little emphasis placed on developing the architecture at SoS or enterprise level. If SoS or enterprise architecting is required, then the OOSEM specification and design activities are first applied at the SoS level [58] and then recursively applied to the system and lower levels of design. In particular, the OOSEM activities following *analyze stakeholder needs* in Figure 17.3 would include activities to analyze SoS requirements, *define SoS logical architecture*, and *synthesize candidate SoS physical architectures*. The output from these activities is the SoS architecture, which is followed by analyzing the system requirements. As noted in Section 17.1.2, additional tailoring is required to adapt the method to each level of design.

Characterize as-is system and enterprise

The as-is system, users, and enterprise are characterized at a level sufficient to understand the stakeholders' concerns. This involves modeling the as-is system and enterprise only as needed to provide insight into the problem. If an as-is solution does not exist, there is obviously nothing to characterize, and one can proceed directly to specifying the mission requirements. However, a current set of users, systems, and enterprises are already in place, which provide a starting point for the analysis.

The *Operational Domain as-is* is shown in the block definition diagram in Figure 17.7. It includes a top-level block called the *Operational Domain as-is,* which provides the context for the other blocks in the domain. This block is decomposed into the *Security Enterprise as-is* and *Site as-is,* which has a multiplicity that indicates there can be from one to many sites.

In OOSEM, an enterprise block is established to represent an aggregation of systems and users that collaborate to achieve a set of mission objectives. In this example, the as-is enterprise includes the as-is security system, which is stereotyped as the «system of interest»; the *Emergency Services,* which includes the *Dispatcher* and the *Police*; and the *Communication Network,* which enables communication between the as-is security system and the *Emergency Services*. These blocks collaborate to monitor a residence for potential intruders.

The sites that are being protected are external to the enterprise. Each site is composed of a *Single-Family Residence* with one or more *Occupant*s and zero to many *Intruder*s.

The domain model described above helps establish the boundary between the system of interest and the external systems and users with which the system either directly or indirectly interacts. The as-is security system includes multiple site installations, as indicated by the multiplicity on the association end, and a single central monitoring station. Note that the site installation, which represents the security equipment that is installed at a site, is owned (black diamond) by the *Security System as-is* and is referenced (white diamond) by the *Single-Family Residence as-is*. The reference provides a mechanism to represent a more complex system boundary, where a part is owned by one block and referenced by another.

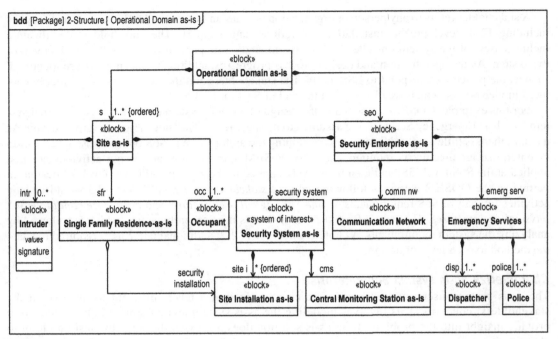

FIGURE 17.7

The as-is operational domain.

In Figure 17.8, an alternative depiction of the as-is domain shows the system and external systems in iconic form. This provides a means to communicate a simplified depiction of the as-is operational domain that can be annotated to represent selected interactions and relationships among the entities. The relationships between the entities could be expressed as associations, but for the purpose of this example, it is assumed that they are merely annotations on the block definition diagram. The relationships are expressed later as connectors with item flows on an internal block diagram.

Perform causal analysis

The as-is system and enterprise are analyzed to assess their capabilities and limitations and to identify potential improvement areas. Other sources of data may be required to support this analysis, including marketing data such as customer surveys and competitive data.

A useful technique for structuring the causal analysis is to use a fishbone diagram to present a tree of cause–effect dependencies. A fishbone diagram showing the causal analysis for the *Security Enterprise as-is* is shown in Figure 17.9. The root node of the tree represents a problem from the perspective of each stakeholder. This problem can be related to one or more measure of effectiveness (moe) that represents stakeholder value. The nodes of the tree can impact the root of the tree through their cause-effect dependencies.

Business sales are a moe of particular importance to the company owner, as well as to the investors of Security Systems, Inc., and *Lack of Sales* is the corresponding root of the tree. The cause–effect

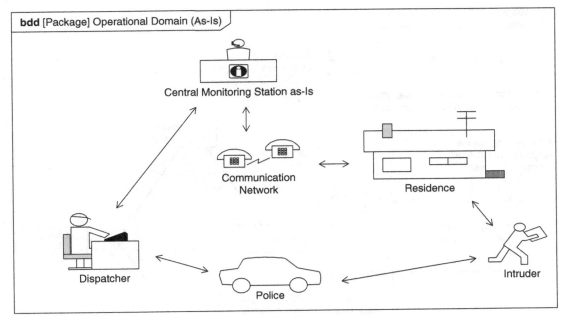

FIGURE 17.8

The as-is operational domain (iconic presentation).

dependencies show that sales are impacted by *Customer Satisfaction* and the *Market Size. Customer Satisfaction* is measured in terms of *System Cost* and *Security Effectiveness. System Cost* is measured in terms of its *Installation Cost* and *Service Cost. Security Effectiveness* is measured in terms of *response time, false alarms, missed detections,* and other parameters.

A similar causal analysis is performed for the other ESS stakeholders—including the customer, the police department, and internal stakeholders such as central monitoring station operators and system installers. The stakeholder concerns for the police department include the number of false alarms and the associated cost to the city of unnecessary deployment of resources. The cause–effect relationships for each stakeholder can be integrated into a composite fishbone diagram to provide a comprehensive multi-stakeholder view of the problems and potential contributing factors. The stakeholder viewpoints defined at the end of Section 17.3.5 should reflect these concerns.

In this example, the fishbone diagram is not expressed in SysML, but the diagram can be referenced under the *Parametrics* package. If this diagram needs to be expressed more formally, stereotypes can be defined to represent the relevant concepts, similar to the approach shown in Figure 17.21, which captures constraint violations and cause–effect dependencies to support identification of failures. This kind of modeling artifact can be used to support analysis of various kinds, including failure modes and effects analysis, fault tree analysis, risk analysis, and others.

Additional engineering analysis is performed to quantify the impact of the contributing parameters implied by the fishbone diagram, such as the contribution of response time, false alarm, and cost parameters to the moes. This analysis may include timeline analysis, reliability analysis, and lifecycle cost

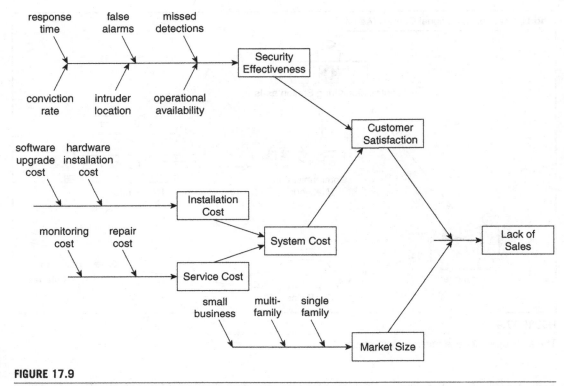

FIGURE 17.9

Causal analysis of the *Security Enterprise as-is* from the Company Owner perspective.

analysis. This analysis is captured in parametric diagrams as discussed later in this section and in Section 17.3.6.

For this example, a primary deficiency identified during the causal analysis is the limited functionality of the current security system relative to the competing systems. A stakeholder need is identified to extend the functionality beyond intruder detection to include protection for fire and medical emergencies. Also, it was determined that the market size for the security systems needs to be expanded to provide protection for multi-family residences and small businesses in addition to single-family residences.

Specify mission requirements

Based on the preceding analysis, a prioritized set of mission requirements is defined that address the limitations of the as-is domain. The mission requirements are captured as text requirements, as shown in the requirement diagram in Figure 17.10. The top-level mission requirement for the ESS includes the text statement, "Enhance security of life and property by providing emergency response for single-family residence, multi-family residence, and small business, to theft, burglary, fire, and health and safety." The mission requirements are contained in the *Operational::Requirements* package. The traceability between the mission requirements and lower-level requirements is discussed in Section 17.3.7.

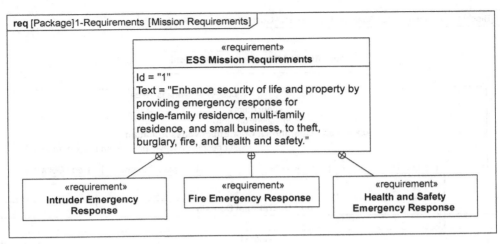

FIGURE 17.10

ESS mission requirements.

Capture measures of effectiveness (moe)

Moes are mission-level performance requirements that reflect value to the customer and other stakeholders. They are derived from the stakeholder needs analysis that includes causal analysis and other mission analysis. The moes for the ESS are the emergency response time, probability of intruder conviction, availability, and operational cost. The target value for each moe is established to address stakeholder needs and achieve a competitive advantage.

The moes are captured in the top-level parametric diagram in Figure 17.11. The «objective Function» defines the overall cost effectiveness of the design solution in terms of a weighted sum of the utility associated with each parameter of the objective function. The parameters of the objective function are bound to the moes, which are properties of the *Security Enterprise.*

Engineering analysis is performed throughout the development effort to support evaluation, selection, and optimization of the design solution in terms of the moes. A parametric diagram can be defined to support the analysis of each moe. The parametric diagram relates the moe to the lower-level parameters that impact the moe value. This provides a mechanism to flow down the moes to critical system parameters, also known as technical performance measures (tpms) or measures of performance (mops), as the model is further elaborated. This is discussed further in Section 17.3.6.

Define to-be domain model

Based on the preceding analysis, the scope for the to-be system and enterprise can be established. The block definition diagram for the to-be operational domain is shown in Figure 17.12. The diagram presents the hierarchy of blocks with the *Operational Domain* as the top-level block. This block is contained in the *Operational::Structure* package. The to-be operational domain includes significant changes from the as-is operational domain in Figure 17.7. The to-be operational domain reflects the broader set of mission requirements that were derived from the causal analysis.

The *Emergency Services* includes the *Fire Fighter* and *Paramedic* in addition to the *Police* and *Dispatcher* that were included in the as-is domain. The *Police, Firefighter,* and *Paramedic* are

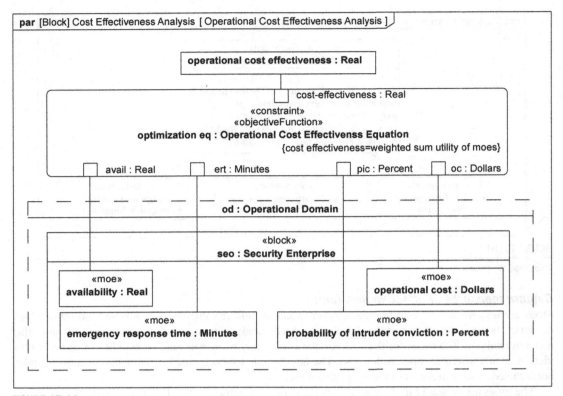

FIGURE 17.11

ESS top-level parametric diagram showing operational cost effectiveness and its relationship to the measures of effectiveness (moes).

subclasses of *Responder*. The *Multi-Family Residence*, *Small Business*, and *Single-Family Residence* are specializations of *Property* from the as-is domain. The *Physical Environment* is included because the system must now monitor the environment for fire.

More generally, capturing the physical environment and classifying the different types of environments are important considerations in the design of the system. As an example, the ESS environment may also include the electromagnetic environment induced by lightning. These effects are then subject to analysis and factored into the specification and design.

The *Security Enterprise* is responsible for satisfying the mission requirements and providing protection services to the customer and *Occupants*. The moes are a special kind of value property («moe») of the *Security Enterprise* block along with their corresponding units. Target values and/or value distributions can be specified as well. The *Security Enterprise* is composed of the *ESS*, *Emergency Services*, and *Communications Network*. The *ESS* replaces the as-is security system and is the «system of interest» for this development effort.

The *Investigator* investigates burglaries, thefts, and other mishaps to increase the probability of intruder conviction. This moe significantly impacts the specification and design of the *ESS* by requiring

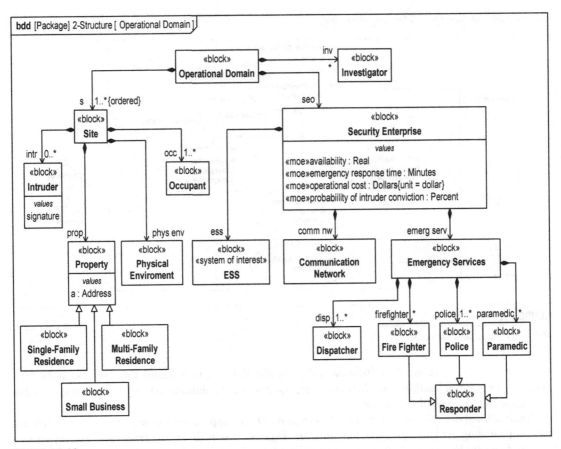

FIGURE 17.12

The to-be operational domain.

the *ESS* to capture and store information about emergency events that can be accessed by the *Investigator*.

As complexity increases, it may be necessary to create a separate block definition diagram of the specialization hierarchies for the external systems and users to reduce the amount of information shown on a single diagram.

Define enterprise use cases

As noted above, the *Security Enterprise* is responsible for satisfying the mission requirements. Mission objectives can be derived from the mission requirements in Figure 17.10 and used to define the *Security Enterprise* use cases. The mission objectives and associated use cases are to provide responses to intruders, fire, and medical emergencies, as shown in the use case diagram in Figure 17.13. Each use case is specialized from a more general use case called *Provide Emergency Response*.

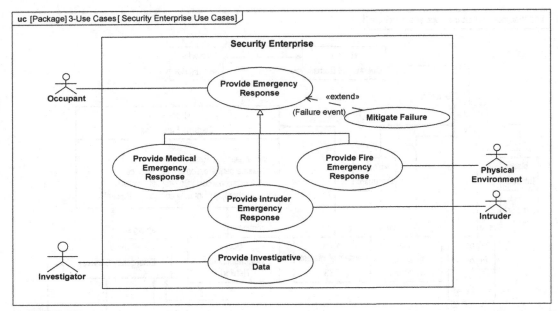

FIGURE 17.13

Security Enterprise Use Cases.

An extending use case called *Mitigate Failure* is also defined. Introducing this use case at the mission level provides a starting point for developing fault tolerant solutions to mitigate failure modes that can impact the success of the mission.

An additional use case, called *Provide Investigative Data,* supports post-emergency response actions, such as providing evidence to convict an intruder. This use case includes the *Investigator* as an actor.

The *Security Enterprise* is the subject in the use case diagram and is used by the actors to achieve the use case goals (i.e., mission objectives). The actors are allocated to the blocks that are external to the enterprise in the *Operational Domain* block definition diagram in Figure 17.12. The *Physical Environment* is also shown as an actor that participates in the *Provide Fire Emergency Response* use case to indicate its role as the source of the fire.

The use cases in this example refine the mission requirements using the refine relationship. An example of the refine relationship is shown in Figure 17.56. The use cases may also trace to other source documentation such as a concept of operations or marketing data. The enterprise use cases are further elaborated by mission scenarios that define the interaction between the actors and the enterprise or its parts. This analysis is used to help specify the ESS black-box requirements, as described in the next section.

Each use case may be augmented with a use case description (as discussed in Chapter 12, Section 12.4.2) that includes a textual description of the use case scenario. Many books are available that cover how to write and model use cases for software analysis [49]. The textual description can be captured as SysML requirements that can be traced to other model elements, such as specific actions in an activity diagram. The use case description may include additional information such as alternative flows and pre- and post-conditions.

17.3.3 ANALYZE SYSTEM REQUIREMENTS

The *Analyze System Requirements* activity is shown in Figure 17.14. This activity specifies the requirements for the system as a black box in terms of its input and output behavior and other externally observable characteristics. Scenario analyses for each of the enterprise use cases describe how the system interacts with the external systems and users identified in the domain model to achieve the mission objectives.

The scenarios are modeled using either activity diagrams with activity partitions or sequence diagrams. A system context diagram is described using an internal block diagram of the operational domain to define the interfaces between the system and the external systems and users. Critical system properties, which can impact the measures of effectiveness, are identified. Based on this analysis, the system is specified as a black box in terms of its system functions, interfaces, stores, and performance and physical properties. The system state machine specifies the conditions and events that trigger the functions or operations that the system performs in support of the use case scenarios. As described in Section 17.3.7, the text requirements to specify the system are related to the system black box and its features, and traceability is maintained from mission level down to component level.

In addition to specifying the black box, design constraints that are imposed on the system design, such as the required use of a COTS component, are also identified and captured and later integrated into the architecture. The identification of potential failures, based on analysis of the system functions, supports the development of a fault tolerant system design. Requirements variation analysis is performed to evaluate the probability that a requirement will change, and the results are used in the architecture activities to architect a robust solution that can accommodate the potential requirements change.

A system requirements review is conducted to validate that the requirements address the stakeholder needs and mission requirements and to ensure the quality of the requirements (e.g., sufficient, unambiguous and concise, verifiable). This review may be performed incrementally, perhaps at the completion of the analysis for each enterprise use case.

Define mission scenarios

In this activity, one or more mission scenarios are defined for each enterprise use case to specify the interaction between the system and the external systems and users to achieve the use case goals (i.e., mission objectives). The mission scenarios provide the basis for specifying the system behavioral requirements. A complete set of scenarios that correspond to each primary and alternative path for each use case are needed to specify the system requirements completely. Some refactoring of the use cases may be done to leverage common functionality that can be shared across different use cases. The selection of the use case scenarios should ensure sufficient coverage of the required functionality by considering the following:

- High likelihood scenarios;
- Performance stressing scenarios and scenarios that significantly impact the moes;
- Failure and exception scenarios;
- Critical system functionality;
- New system functionality; and
- Interactions that include all external systems and users.

The mission scenarios are modeled with activity or sequence diagrams. The activity partitions (also known as swim lanes) in the activity diagram or the lifelines in the sequence diagram represent the system and external systems and users from the to-be domain model. For this example, the mission

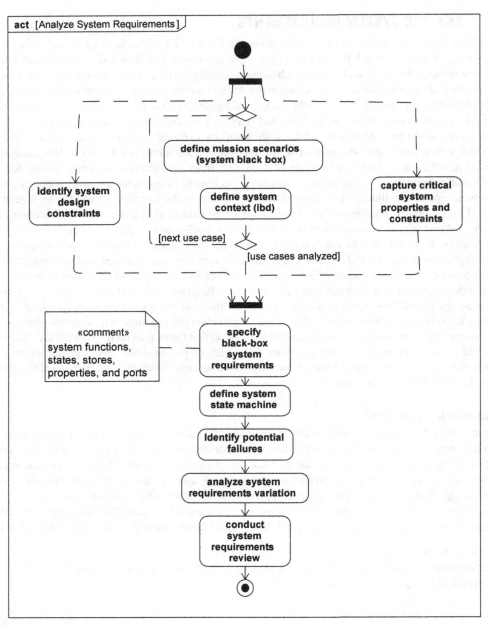

FIGURE 17.14

Analyze System Requirements activity to specify black-box system requirements.

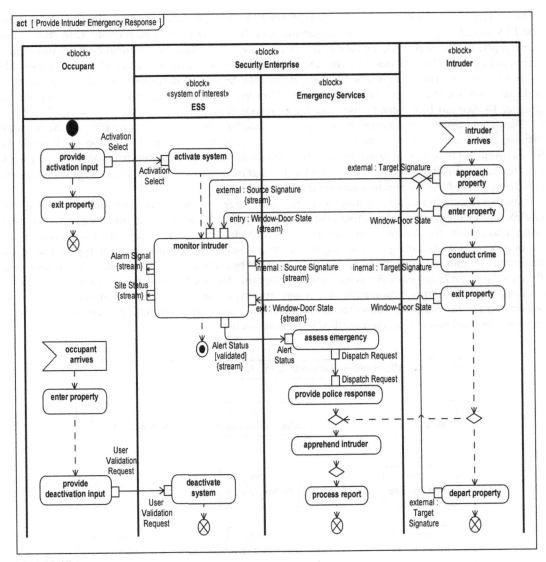

FIGURE 17.15

The *Provide Intruder Emergency Response* scenario realizes an enterprise use case.

scenarios are expressed with activity diagrams. The actions in the activity partition are performed by the entity that corresponds to the activity partition.

A representative enterprise use case scenario, called *Provide Intruder Emergency Response*, is shown in Figure 17.15. This scenario is contained in the *Operational::Behavior* package and corresponds to the *Provide Intruder Emergency Response* use case in Figure 17.13. The scenario is expressed by an activity diagram with activity partitions for the *ESS, Emergency Services, Occupant,* and *Intruder.* The *ESS* and *Emergency Services* are sub partitions of the *Security Enterprise.* (Note: If the method is being applied at the SoS level, then the *Enterprise* is treated as a black box without defining its subpartitions until the next level of design.) The actions in each activity partition specify what the corresponding block must do. The *ESS* must activate and deactivate the system in response to the *Occupant* input and must monitor the environment to detect an *Intruder.* The allocate activity partition described in Chapter 14, Section 14.6.3 can be used to allocate responsibility for the actions.

The accept event action represents the arrival of an *Intruder.* The streaming pins on the *monitor intruder* action indicate that the action continues to accept inputs and/or provide outputs as it monitors the environment to detect the *Intruder.* The *Alert Status* output from the *monitor intruder* action asserts that the output must be in the *validated* state for the alert message to be sent to the *Emergency Services,* which imposes additional requirements on the ESS.

Another feature in this activity diagram is the use of three flow final nodes (symbol with X inside of circle). One example shows the output control flow from *deactivate system* terminating on a flow final node. This enables the *deactivate system* action to complete without terminating the overall activity.

In order to specify the inputs and outputs of the actions fully, their pins must be typed. The block definition diagram in Figure 17.16 specifies the type of the input and output pins for the actions in the *Provide Intruder Emergency Response* activity diagram. The tool should perform type checking to confirm the compatibility between the output and input types, and provide a validation error if they do not conform to the matching rules. These types are also used to type the item properties in the corresponding internal block diagram described in the next section.

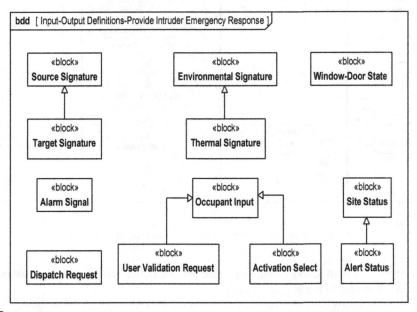

FIGURE 17.16

Input and Output Definitions for the *Provide Intruder Emergency Response* scenario.

Define system context

The *System Context* diagram is shown as an internal block diagram in Figure 17.17. This diagram depicts the *ESS* and its interfaces to the external systems and users that participate in the mission scenarios. The frame of the internal block diagram corresponds to the *Operational Domain* block. The parts of the *Operational Domain* correspond to the *Security Enterprise* and the enterprise actors from the block definition diagram in Figure 17.12. The parts typed by *ESS* and *Emergency Services* are

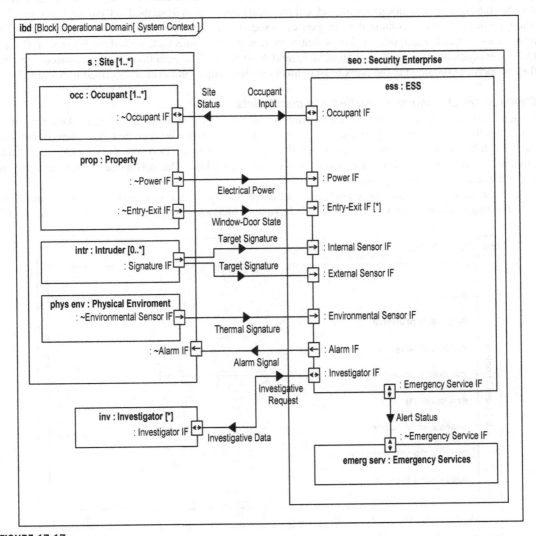

FIGURE 17.17

System Context showing the interfaces between the ESS and the external systems, users, and physical environment.

nested within the *seo:Security Enterprise*, and the parts typed by *Occupant, Property, Intruder*, and *Physical Environment* are nested within the *s:Site*. The input and output flows (i.e., object flows) from the *Provide Intruder Emergency Response* activity diagram in Figure 17.15 are allocated to item flows that flow across the connectors between the parts (refer to Chapter 14, Section 14.7). The item properties are typed by the type of the input and output pins from the activity diagram.

Ports are used to specify interfaces that describe how parts are connected to each other. The details are specified by the type of the port and in some cases by the type of the connector. The port types can specify detailed interface specifications for logical and physical interfaces as described in Chapter 7, Section 7.6. The type of the port can contain flow properties to specify the items that can flow through the port. The item flows indicate the types of things that flow across the connectors, including *Electrical Power, Occupant Input, Site Status, Target Signatures*, and *Alert Status*. The item flows on the connector and the flow properties contained in the ports must conform to the compatibility rules described in Section 7.4.3.

Capture critical system properties and constraints

Critical performance requirements can be captured as value properties of the system black box or of items that flow. For example, the required system response time may be specified as a value property of the system black box, and the max flow rate that the system can support may be specified as a value property of an item that flows in or out of the system black box. The performance requirements are derived based on engineering analysis.

One example of a performance analysis is a timeline analysis. The timing diagram in Figure 17.18 specifies the mission timeline for the *Provide Intruder Emergency Response* scenario in Figure 17.15.

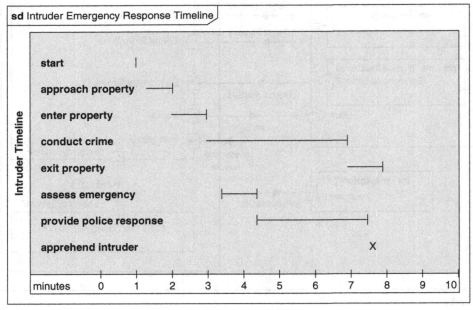

FIGURE 17.18

Intruder Emergency Response timeline.

The actions from the activity diagram are shown on the *y*-axis, and the required or assumed time to perform the actions are shown on the *x*-axis. The timeline is used to allocate time to each action in the scenario in order to satisfy the mission response time that was identified as a moe. In this example, the intruder detection response time is the time from the intruder entering the property until the ESS reports the alert to the Emergency Services. This is viewed as a critical system property, referenced as a measure of performance and expressed as «mop» in the model. The value for this property can be budgeted based on its impact on overall security effectiveness. Figure 17.18 is a UML timing diagram that is not part of SysML. A timeline is one of many presentations that can be used to visualize the results of an engineering analysis.

Other critical system properties that require analysis to satisfy requirements include *probability of intruder detection*, *probability of intruder identification*, and *probability of intruder false alarm*. The constraints on these properties are captured in parametric diagrams as part of the engineering analysis described in Section 17.3.6 and contribute to the moes in Figure 17.11.

Specify black-box system requirements

The application of OOSEM results in the specification of the system based on the scenario analysis and other engineering analyses performed, as described earlier in this section. The specification is often called a black-box specification in that it defines the system's externally observable behavior and physical characteristics. The black-box specification does not specify how the system achieves the externally observable behavior, which is defined by the system design. Design constraints may augment the black-box specification to constrain how the black-box requirements are implemented. An example is a design constraint to use a particular COTS component or a particular algorithm in the design.

The specification of a black box is expressed as a block with the following features:

- The required functions it must perform and the associated inputs and outputs. The required functions are modeled as activities that are allocated to the block or methods of the operation of the block. The associated inputs and outputs are the inputs and outputs to the action or operation that calls the activity.
- The required external interfaces that enable it to interact with other external systems and users. The interfaces are specified by the ports on the block and the associated port type.
- The required performance and quality characteristics that impact how well the functions must be performed or a physical characteristic such as its weight and size. These characteristics are specified as value properties typed by Value Types that define the units and quantity kind. The value properties may have deterministic values or probability distributions associated with their values. Constraints on value properties are captured using parametric constraints. OOSEM applies the «mop» stereotype to properties that are identified as critical (e.g., can significantly impact mission performance).
- The required control in terms of input events and pre-conditions that determine when functions are performed. The required control is expressed by a state machine for the block that specifies which activities are performed in response to different triggering events, and their associated guard conditions.
- The required items that the system must store including data, energy, and mass. The required stores can be modeled as reference properties of the block. OOSEM applies the «store» stereotype to these properties.

The specification features for the *ESS* block are shown in Figure 17.19. In this example, an operation is defined for the ESS block that corresponds to each action in the *ESS* activity partition in Figure 17.15. Additional operations are defined for each action in the other mission scenarios that are analyzed. The action in the ESS activity partition in the activity diagram can be a **call operation action**

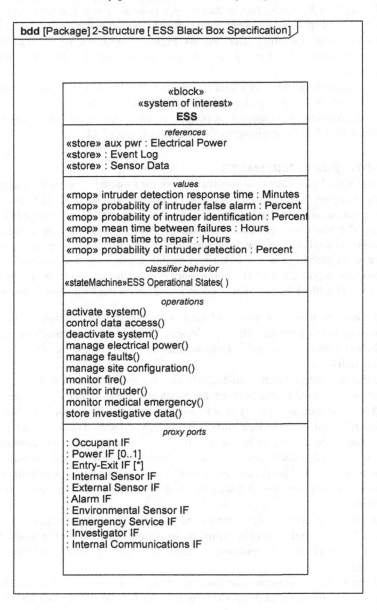

FIGURE 17.19

ESS black-box specification.

or a **call behavior action**. The call operation action calls an operation of the block. This method of the operation can be an activity. Alternatively, the action can be a call behavior action that calls an activity that is allocated to the *ESS* block. For this example, call behavior actions are used, but the call behavior actions are allocated to operations of the block with the same name. The activity that is called by the call behavior action is allocated to the block. This hybrid approach enables the operations to be used as a proxy for the actions, which can then be inherited and redefined.

The performance properties, such as *probability of intruder detection, probability of intruder false alarm, intruder detection response time,* and *mean time between failures,* are stereotyped as measures of performance «mop». Parametric constraints on these properties can support various engineering analysis. The ports and their types specify the system interfaces. The items that are stored, such as the *:Event Log, :Sensor Data,* and *aux pwr:Electrical Power* are reference properties that are stereotyped as «store». The state machine, shown in the classifier behavior compartment, is also part of the black -box specification and is discussed in the next subsection.

The black-box specification and its features can be related to the mission requirements as described in Section 17.3.7 using the appropriate requirements relationships. Traceability can be defined at a fine-grained feature level or at a less granular level depending on the need.

The black-box specification can be applied at any level of design, including system, element, and component levels. This approach to specifying features of a block is used later in the chapter to specify component requirements.

Define system state machine

The activity diagrams for each mission scenario define actions that the ESS must perform. The ESS state machine specifies the composite behavior that the ESS must perform based on the actions from all of the scenarios that the ESS participates in. The state machine specifies when the ESS performs specific actions. This is done by specifying when a state is entered and exited and enabling specific behaviors in specific states. The transition between states is triggered by events subject to the guard conditions, and the events are associated with the receipt of inputs (i.e., signal or call event), a change event, or time event. The details of state machines are discussed in Chapter 11.

The ESS evaluates the guard conditions in response to an input event to determine whether to transition to a next state. The guard conditions can specify conditions on the input values, current state, and resource availability. If the transition is triggered, the block executes the exit behavior from the current state, executes the transition behavior (i.e., effect), and enters the next state. It then executes the entry behavior of the next state followed by its do/behavior, which is defined by an activity. (Note: If the next state is a composite state, the ESS transitions from the initial pseudostate to its nested state.) The transition behavior may include a send signal action that can trigger a transition in an external system's state machine. The entry, exit, do, and transition behaviors can correspond to activities called by call behavior actions in the ESS activity partition. The system's logical and physical design must implement the control requirements imposed by the system state machine including receipt of inputs, evaluation of guard conditions, changes of state, and invocations of behavior.

A state machine specifies the control requirements as a series of statements as follows. If an input event occurs while in the current state and the guard conditions are satisfied, then the system transitions to the next state and executes the specified actions within the specified performance constraints. This transition logic can also be reflected in an activity diagram using constructs such as pre- and post-conditions on actions, guard conditions on control nodes, interruptible regions, accept event actions, and send signal actions.

A portion of the ESS state machine is shown in Figure 17.20. The state machine includes *power off*, *power up*, *power on*, and *power down* states. The *power on* state is a composite state with multiple regions for *activation-deactivation, intruder monitoring, fire monitoring, fault monitoring*, and *power source management*. The system has an active state in each of its orthogonal regions at any given time.

The system transitions from *deactivated* to *activated* based on the *Activate Select*. As shown in the *intruder monitoring* region, the ESS initially transitions to the *intruder nonalert* state. If an intruder is detected and the ESS is in the activated state, it sets the alarm and transitions to the *intruder alert* state. In the *intruder alert* state, the alert is initially *unvalidated*. Once the alert has been validated, the system transitions to the *validated* state and sends the validated intruder alert to *Emergency Services*.

Identify potential failures

A systematic approach to identify potential failure modes and/or off-nominal conditions is an essential step to achieve a fault tolerant design. Common failure analysis methods include fault tree analysis and failure modes, effects, and criticality analysis (FMECA).

In OOSEM, the *Mitigate Failure* use case in Figure 17.13 provides a starting point for this analysis. This use case is elaborated through further analysis of the failure and exception scenarios noted earlier in this section. The black-box specification facilitates the identification of potential failure modes and off-nominal conditions by clearly specifying the system functions and other features of the black box that can fail [59]. As the design progresses, the failure modes of the system are related to failure modes introduced by the system elements and components, as well as other external contributors to failure such as high stress environmental conditions and threat induced failures.

The identification of failures and their dependencies are input to and/or reconciled with the fault tree analysis and FMECA. The FMECA is a bottoms-up analysis that identifies failure modes associated with the components, whereas the fault tree analysis is a top-down analysis that identifies failure modes and fail events associated with the functions and performance.

The potential failures can be identified for each function by assessing the inability to perform, based on the requirements for that function. This includes the inability for the function to produce its expected outputs within its nominal performance bounds. For example, if an air conditioner is intended to maintain the steady state air temperature (T) within an acceptable temperature range between Tmin and Tmax, then the air conditioner is off-nominal when T<Tmin or T>Tmax. Off nominal performance does not necessarily imply a failure. A failure mode may be defined in terms of more extreme threshold values than the thresholds for off-nominal performance. In the air conditioner example, a **failure mode** may be defined when the temperature exceeds the minimum or maximum threshold, such as when T<Tmin-10 or when T>Tmax+10.

The failure mode for the air conditioner that occurs when the output air temperature is below the lower temperature threshold, is often a different failure mode than when the output air temperature exceeds the upper temperature threshold. For example, a room temperature below its lower threshold may be caused by a failure mode of a switch that is stuck in the cool-on position, whereas a room temperature above its upper threshold may be caused by a failure mode of the compressor, so the air conditioner is unable to cool the air. In general, for each output of each function, at least one failure mode can be identified when the output is below some minimum performance threshold and another failure mode can be identified when the output is above some maximum performance threshold.

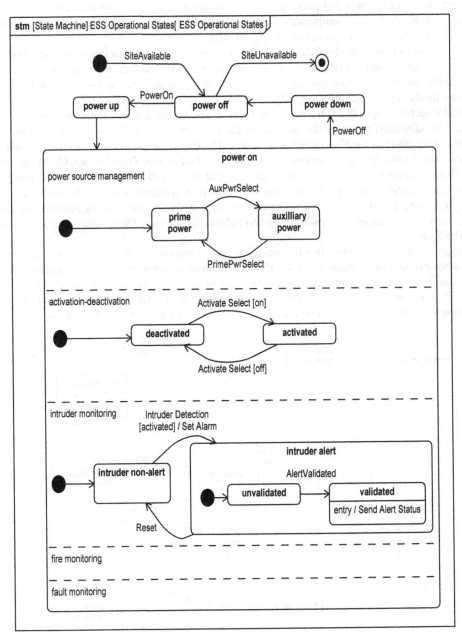

FIGURE 17.20

ESS State Machine.

The threshold for off nominal performance and failure modes may vary over time or as a function of the state of the system or component. For the air conditioner example, the temperature thresholds may be different during the night versus during the day.

Another kind of failure mode occurs when the system produces unanticipated outputs. For example, the air conditioner should not produce outputs other than conditioned air and status data for the user. If the air conditioner leaks coolant into the environment, this is considered an off-nominal condition and/or a failure mode depending on its severity.

OOSEM includes specific stereotypes to capture failure modes and their dependencies. Failure modes can be identified based on the analysis of the ESS functions in Figure 17.15. In Figure 17.21, a potential failure mode of the ESS called Alarm Signal Stuck Off is the inability for the monitor intruder to generate the Alarm Signal. A second failure mode called Alarm Signal Stuck On occurs when the Alarm Signal cannot be turned off. The Alarm Signal Stuck Off failure mode could potentially be caused by the inability for the ESS to activate system, which is required to Set Alarm based on the state machine in Figure 17.20. Other failure modes that are not shown for monitor intruder are associated with the Alert Status output, and called High Probability of Intruder False Alarm and Low Probability of Intruder Detection.

There are various contributors to a failure mode. An off-nominal input to a function can contribute to an off-nominal output of the function. The off-nominal input in turn may result from a failed output from another function, such as the impact of an Inability to Activate failure mode in Figure 17.21 causing an inability to generate an alarm signal. This may also result from a failure of the connection so that the output from one function is not received as an input to another function. The failure may also be caused

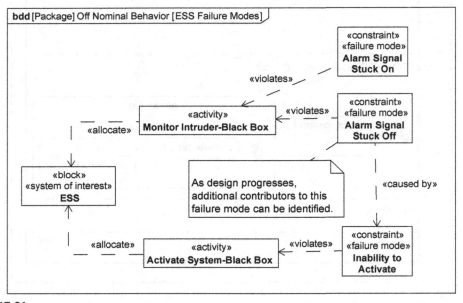

FIGURE 17.21

Failure mode identification and causal dependencies.

by a component failure that occurs from an off-nominal environmental condition, such as when a part breaks due to thermal or structural stress. The component failure can in turn impact the functions that the component performs, such as the failure of an overheated circuit card that causes the failure to perform one or more functions. As noted above, the component failures are often identified by the FMECA.

As the design progresses, lower-level functions are identified along with their failure modes. The failure modes associated with the inability of a lower-level function to meet its performance may result in the failure mode of the parent function to meet its performance. For example, the inability to flow air through a clogged air filter adversely impacts the parent function to cool the air.

An operation of the black box called manage faults imposes a requirement on the ESS to provide fault management functionality. Alternative approaches are identified to reduce the likelihood of failure and/or to detect, isolate, and recover from the failure if it does occur. The alternative fault management approaches are evaluated and selected as part of the architecture and design tradeoffs. In addition, test cases are defined to inject potential faults to verify that the mitigation performs as intended.

Analyze system requirements variation

Requirements variation analysis is intended to define the potential change in requirements that can result from different sources, such as a likely change to an external interface, a possible increase in the number of system users, or possible new functionality. A systematic approach for identifying potential requirement changes is to evaluate each feature of the system block in Figure 17.19 that correspond to the system functional, interface, and performance requirements, along with each item flow and external entity in Figure 17.17. This evaluation can identify how the system black box specification and its context are likely to change. For the ESS, some potential requirements changes can result from assessing the potential increase in the number of expected site installations shown in Figure 17.17, as indicated by the multiplicity on the *Site Installation*. Other requirements changes can result from assessing the possible additional ESS functionality, such as monitoring carbon monoxide or extinguishing fires, which can be defined as additional operations of the ESS in Figure 17.19.

Requirements variation is evaluated in terms of the probability that a requirement will change and its potential impact, which can be quantified as high, medium, or low. The results of the analysis are input to the risk analysis to assess the technical, cost, and schedule impact of the change and to develop risk-mitigation strategies. The mitigation strategy is reflected in the architecture and design approach, such as isolating the source of the changing requirement on the design. A similar approach can be applied to assess potential technology changes.

In addition to the potential variation in requirements described above, it is often the case that there are planned variant designs, each with different requirements. It is appropriate to capture the black-box specifications for each variant. This typically involves identifying the common and variant features of the black box and generating subclasses with redefinition as required. As the design evolves, each variant specification will result in a variant design. The approach to developing variant architectures is briefly described in Section 17.3.4.

Identify system design constraints

Design constraints are those constraints that are imposed on the design solution, which in this example refers to the ESS design. These constraints are typically imposed by the customer, by the development organization, or by external regulations. The constraints may be imposed on the hardware, software, data, operational procedures, interfaces, or any other part of the system. Examples may include a constraint that the system must use predefined COTS hardware or software, use of a particular algorithm, or implement a specific interface protocol. For the ESS system, the design is constrained to include the legacy central monitoring station hardware as well as the communications network between the central monitoring station and the site installations.

Design constraints can have a significant impact on the design and should be validated prior to imposing them on the solution. A straightforward approach to address design constraints is to categorize the type of constraints (e.g., hardware, software, procedure, algorithm), identify the specific constraints for each category, and capture them as system requirements in the *Requirements* package along with the corresponding rationale. The design constraints are then integrated into the physical architecture, as discussed in Section 17.3.5.

17.3.4 DEFINE LOGICAL ARCHITECTURE

The *Define Logical Architecture* activity is shown in Figure 17.22 This activity is part of the system architecture design that includes decomposing the system into **logical components** that interact to satisfy the system requirements. The logical components are abstractions of the physical components that perform the system functionality without imposing implementation constraints. An example of a logical component is a user interface that may be realized by a web browser or display console, or an entry/exit sensor that may be realized by an optical sensor or contact sensor. The logical architecture serves as an intermediate level of abstraction between the black-box system requirements and the physical architecture. It can help the design team to manage the impact of requirements and technology changes. For example, if the ESS performance requirements for detecting an intruder change, the entry/exit sensor will persist as part of the logical design but the specific technology selection may change. In addition, the logical architecture can serve as a reference architecture for a family of products that support different physical implementations to meet a range of mission requirements.

The logical architecture definition activity includes decomposing the system into logical components. Logical scenarios are created to describe how the logical components interact to realize each operation (e.g., function) of the system block. The internal block diagram of the system defines the interconnection between the logical components. The logical components identified from the initial logical decomposition may be further decomposed and refined to repartition their functionality, stores, and properties. Each logical component is then specified in a similar way as the ESS black-box specification in the previous section. A logical component may include a state machine as part of its specification if it has significant state-based behavior. The traceability between the system-level requirements and the logical components is maintained, as discussed in Section 17.3.7. The logical components are allocated to the physical components to develop the physical architecture, as described in Section 17.3.5.

Define logical decomposition

The ESS block is specified as part of the system requirements analysis described in Section 17.3.3. In OOSEM, the system block has separate logical and physical decompositions. In order to achieve this, a separate subclass of the system block is created for the logical and physical decompositions. The *ESS Logical* block is a subclass of the *ESS* block that inherits all the features of the *ESS* block, including its operations, stores, properties, and ports. The *ESS Logical* block is decomposed into logical components. An ESS Physical block is created in a similar way but is decomposed into physical components, as described in Section 17.3.5.

OOSEM includes specific techniques to decompose the *ESS Logical* block into logical components, as shown in the *ESS Logical* block definition diagram in Figure 17.23. The logical components have the «*logical*» stereotype applied. The system is decomposed into three classes of logical components:

- *External Interface Components* manage the interface to each external system or user, which includes providing the connection to the external system or user and encoding and decoding signals for transmission and processing (refer to systems and users external to ESS in Figure 17.17).

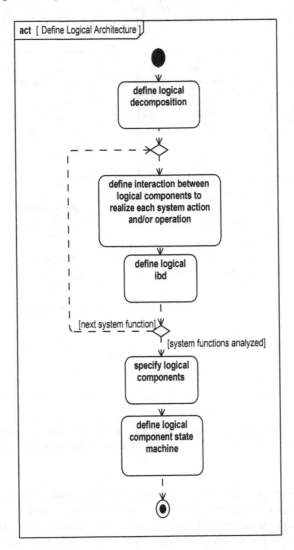

FIGURE 17.22

Define Logical Architecture activity decomposes the system into logical components and describes their interactions and interconnections needed to satisfy the system requirements.

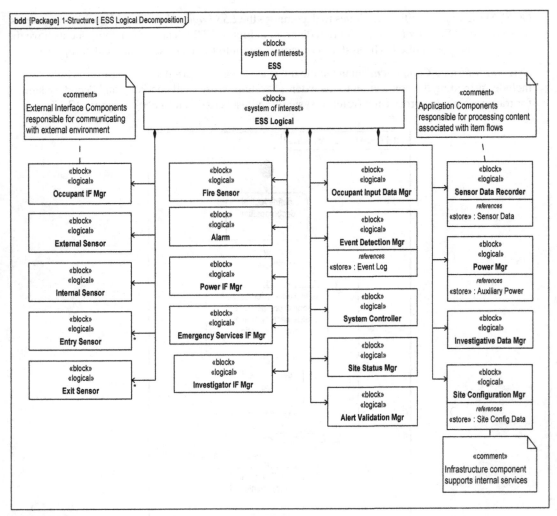

FIGURE 17.23

Block definition diagram showing the ESS Logical block as a subclass of the ESS block and its decomposition into logical components including *External Interface Components*, *Application Components*, and *Infrastructure Components*.

- *Application Components* provide the basic functionality (i.e., business logic) to process each external input and output item flow (refer to item flows in ESS context diagram in Figure 17.17).
- *Infrastructure Components* manage internal resources such as time, memory, processing, internally generated heat, and interconnection infrastructure such as wiring and plumbing. The internal resources are derived from the design and are not necessarily derivable from the external environment like the *External Interface Components* and *Application Components*.

In the ESS logical decomposition, an *Occupant IF Mgr* is an example of an *External Interface Component,* the *Site Configuration Mgr* is an example of an *Infrastructure Component,* and the *Event Detection Mgr and Alert Validation Mgr* are examples of an *Application Component.* This approach ensures that the system logical architecture includes components with the functionality to communicate and interface with external systems, process the inputs and outputs, and manage internally generated resources.

The selected ESS logical components based on the above decomposition heuristics include:

- The sensors are transducers that connect to the external environment to general signals that can be processed.
- The *Event Detection Mgr* and *System Controller* provide the business logic to process the signals from the sensors and control the actions in response to detection events. This is a typical pattern that has broad application.
- The *Auxiliary Power* managed by the *Power Manager* is introduced to support the stringent availability requirements for the ESS.
- *Occupant Input Data Mgr* validates the user when they enter the code.

Define interaction between logical components to realize each system operation or allocated activity

The operations of the *ESS Logical* block are inherited from the *ESS* block. As stated in the previous section, each operation corresponds to an action that the ESS must perform that is realized by an activity in the logical design.

Figure 17.24 shows the *Monitor Intruder-ESS Logical* activity diagram that realizes the *monitor intruder* operation of the *ESS Logical* block. The inputs and outputs of the activity match the pins from the *monitor intruder* action in the *Provide Intruder Emergency Response* scenario in Figure 17.15. The activity partitions correspond to the logical components from the *ESS Logical Block Definition Diagram* in Figure 17.23.

The *External Sensor, Entry Sensor, Exit Sensor,* and *Internal Sensor* generate *Detections.* The *Event Detection Manager* processes the *Detection* to generate an *intruder:Event* and stores the event information in the *event log.* The *System Controller* then controls the system actions in response to the *Event.* The controller actions request the *Site Status Mgr* to provide a status update. If the system has been activated, the *System Controller* sends a signal to trigger the alarm, to record the external sensor data in the *Sensor Data Recorder*, and to request validation of the alert. If the alert is validated, the alert status is communicated to *Emergency Services.* The control logic can be captured by the *System Controller* state machine or can be expressed with pre- and post-conditions on the controller action. Some of the actions in the activity diagram include streaming inputs and outputs but are not shown to simplify the diagram.

Activity diagrams are created in a similar way as above to realize each ESS black=box operation shown in Figure 17.19. For example, an activity diagram to *manage faults* defines how the logical components interact to mitigate the potential system failures identified in *Analyze System Requirements.*

Define system logical internal block diagram

The *ESS Logical* internal block diagram shown in Figure 17.25 presents the interconnection of the parts that are typed by the logical components. The enclosing frame corresponds to the *ESS Logical* block. The ports on the *ESS Logical* block are consistent with the ports defined for the *ESS* in Figure 17.17. The ports represent the external interfaces on the *ESS Logical* block and can be connected to ports on the logical parts or directly to the logical parts without ports.

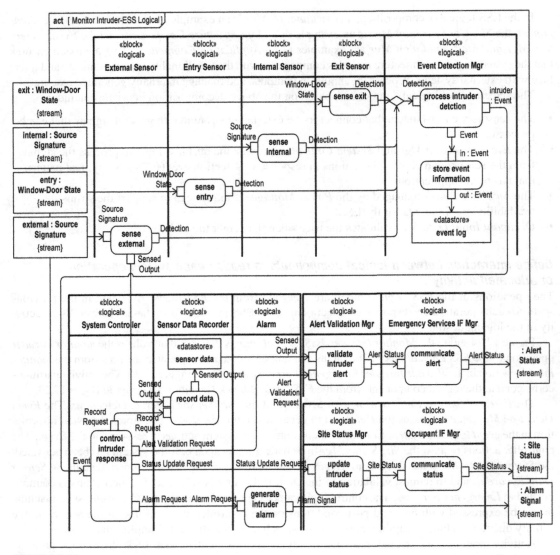

FIGURE 17.24

The *Monitor Intruder-ESS Logical activity diagram* is a thread through the ESS logical system design that realizes the *monitor intruder* operation of the *ESS Logical* block.

The parts typed by the external interface components provide the communications and interface to the ESS external environment. The parts typed by the application components provide the business logic. For example, the sensors in the figure are external interface components. The *Event Detection Mgr* and *System Controller* are application components that provide the business logic to process the detections from the sensors and control the response to the intruder detection. The connectors between the parts

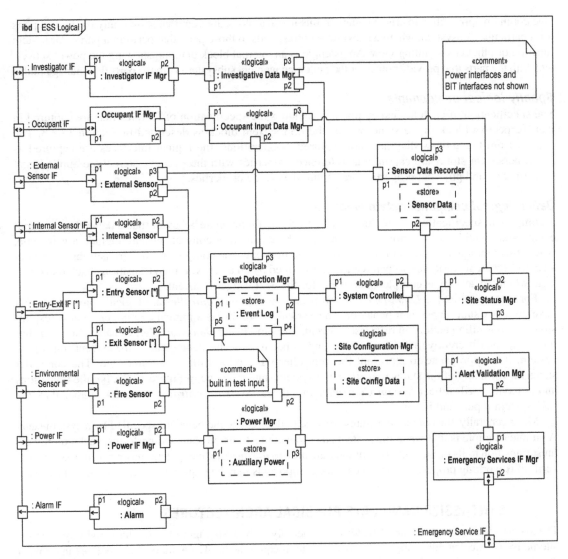

FIGURE 17.25

ESS Logical internal block diagram showing the interconnection between the logical components of the system.

enable the controller to send requests to the *Alarm, Sensor Data Recorder, Site Status Mgr,* and *Alert Validation Mgr.* In addition; the *Investigative Data Mgr* has access to the investigative data, including the *Event Log* and the *Sensor Data Recorder.* The item flows are not shown to simplify the diagrams.

When complete, the internal block diagram for the logical design contains all of the logical parts of the system. Sometimes, however, , it is desirable to view only a subset of the parts based on a particular need.

One common approach is to create a view of this internal block diagram that shows only the logical parts for a particular subsystem, where a subsystem corresponds to those parts that perform a particular system function or other cross-cutting view. An example is an internal block diagram showing the power subsystem with the parts that provide power, or the fault management subsystem with the parts that manage faults.

Specify logical components

The specification of each logical component includes the specification of features that are captured in their respective block in the same way as the *ESS* system block as described in Section 17.3.3. The actions from the activity diagrams are captured as operations; the logical interfaces are captured as ports; persistent stores are captured as reference properties with the «store» stereotype applied; and performance and physical properties are captured as value properties.

Define logical component state machine

A component specification can include a state machine if it has state behavior that is dependent on input events and conditions. A simple state-dependent behavior for a component may include a wait state, where the component waits until it receives an input event. The component then transitions to another state to execute a particular do/behavior that is defined by an activity. It then transitions back to its wait state when the activity is complete and waits for the next triggering event.

For this example, the *Event Detection Mgr* and the *System Controller* are logical components that have complex state-dependent behavior. The *System Controller* is a logical component that is responsible for controlling actions in response to events from the *Event Detection Mgr*. Because the controller must respond differently to different events and its behavior is also dependent on the current state of the system, it is appropriate to represent the controller's behavior with a state machine. The controller states mirror many of the states that are in the system state machine in Figure 17.20, but the transitions and behaviors will reflect *System Controller* inputs and *System Controller* behaviors rather than the ESS system inputs and behaviors.

More generally, the component states are specified to realize the behavior specified by a system state. A simple example is that when the system state transitions to its on state and performs, each component must transition to its on state. As part of the transition to the on state, the system may perform a self-test to verify it is working properly, in which case the components may be required to perform self-tests as well.

17.3.5 SYNTHESIZE CANDIDATE PHYSICAL ARCHITECTURES

The *Synthesize Candidate Physical Architectures* activity is shown in Figure 17.26. This activity synthesizes alternative physical architectures to satisfy the system requirements. The architecture is defined in terms of the physical components, their relationships, and their distribution across system nodes. The physical components of the system include hardware, software, persistent data, and operational procedures. The system nodes partition the components based on their physical location or other criteria such as organizational responsibility. A system that is not a distributed system is a degenerative case consisting of a single node.

The partitioning criteria are defined and used to partition the physical components and address concerns such as performance, reliability, and security. The system nodes are defined, and then the logical node architecture determines how the logical components and their associated functionality, persistent data, and control are distributed across the system nodes. A physical node architecture is then defined where each logical component in each node is allocated to one or more physical components that may include a combination of hardware, software, and persistent data components, as well as operational

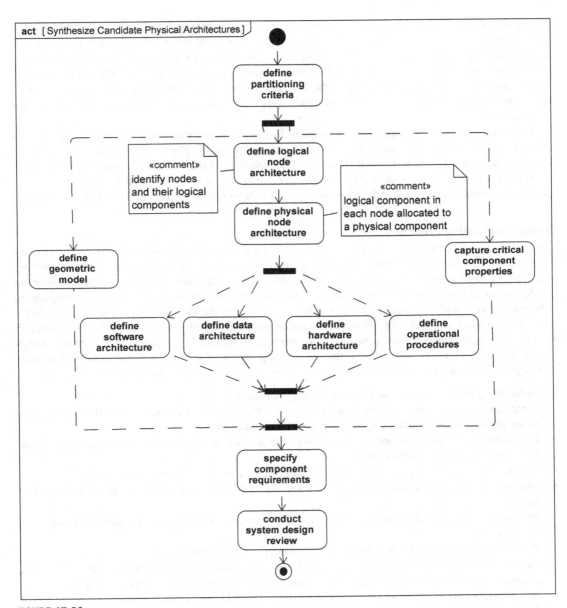

FIGURE 17.26

Synthesize Candidate Physical Architectures activity to specify the physical components of the system.

procedures performed by operators. The system design constraints that were identified in Section 17.3.3 are imposed on the physical architecture.

The software, hardware, and data architecture are specialized views of the physical architecture that only include the applicable software, hardware, and data components. For example, the software architecture focuses on the software components and their behavioral and structural relationships, whereas the hardware architecture describes the hardware components and their behavioral and structural relationships. The geometric model is developed concurrently with the system model in SysML to provide the essential geometric and spatial representation for a physical system. Defining these architectures includes additional partitioning of the components based on implementation-specific concerns. The requirements are then specified for each physical component and traced to the system requirements.

The critical component properties that are identified in this activity are input to engineering analysis and trade studies that are performed to evaluate, select, and refine the preferred physical architecture, as described in Section 17.3.6. It should be noted that trade studies and analysis are performed throughout the OOSEM process beginning with *Analyze Stakeholder Needs*. A system design review is conducted incrementally to ensure the physical architecture satisfies the system requirements and the stakeholder needs.

Define partitioning criteria

Partitioning is a fundamental aspect of systems architecting. Criteria are established to partition functionality, persistent data, and control among the logical and physical components, and to partition the components among subsystems, nodes, and layers of the architecture. Applying partitioning criteria throughout the design process can result in component designs that maximize cohesion and minimize coupling to reduce interface complexity. Applying the criteria can also reduce the impact of requirements and technology changes and more effectively address key requirements such as performance, reliability, maintainability, and security. Design practices, sometimes referred to as Design for X (e.g., design for assembly, design for maintainability), often include the definition and application of partitioning criteria as well as other design guidelines and standards. Some examples of partitioning considerations include the following:

- Refactoring common functionality into shared components;
- Partitioning components and functionality based on their update rate, such as partitioning components with high update rates versus those with low update rates;
- Partitioning software components into architecture layers based on the level of dependency of the functionality or services they provide;
- Partitioning data into separate repositories based on their security classification level;
- Physical partitioning to ease maintainability such as making low reliability components easier to access;
- Physical partitioning of components to reduce the number of moving parts for assembly and disassembly;
- Partitioning components based on the application of common patterns;
- Partitioning components to reduce the ripple impact of changes in requirements or technology (the requirements variation analysis that is performed as part of specifying the black box system requirements can be used to identify the most likely requirements changes); and
- Partitioning functionality and components based on development considerations such as whether they are part of a particular incremental delivery.

Partitioning considerations should be augmented by other design strategies, such as those indicated below, to ensure a robust and extensible design.

- Use of standard interfaces (e.g., plug and play);
- Provisions to add functionality through software upgrades;

- Use of modular and reconfigurable components;
- Strategies for fault detection, isolation, and recovery, including the ability to operate in degraded modes (e.g., safe mode); and
- Strategies for variant design.

Define geometric model

The geometric model is sometimes called the three-dimensional (3D) computer-aided design (CAD) model and is a critical representation needed to design physical systems. The geometric model is not part of the SysML model, but the two models can and should be integrated to ensure both representations of the system are consistent with each other. The general approach to integration is to ensure that the system elements in the system model have a correspondence with the components in the geometric model. The level of correspondence depends on the scope of the two models. For example, a system element may represent an assembly that is composed of multiple physical components. The geometric model is another view of the system and its components. It describes the geometric relationships that specify the spatial extent of a given component. The CAD model may also include many additional properties, such as its material properties. A typical CAD tool has the capability to compute the component mass properties and can be integrated with other engineering analysis tools to evaluate other physical characteristics such as stress and thermal profiles.

A balanced system architecture must concurrently incorporate representations of system behavior, structure, and physical layout. For example, a naval architect who is designing a new ship to achieve desired performance in terms of stability and maneuverability must account for the weight of system components and achieve an optimal spatial arrangement of components in terms of their inboard location and the resultant centroid.

The system model in SysML and the CAD model should be developed concurrently, beginning in the conceptual design phase of a system and continuing throughout the development lifecycle. The system model provides an abstract representation of the component that can specify its functionality, interface, performance, and quality characteristics, while the CAD model provides the geometric representation of the component. The system model can establish component relationships to requirements, define more generalized components, and specify the components' environment. The system model provides specification information that the geometric model can realize. At the same time, the geometric model provides essential information to the system model, including critical sizing and tolerances, other physical properties, and mechanical interconnection. The interfaces between these two models are summarized in Chapter 18 Section 18.2.2.

Define node logical architecture

Up to this point, there has been no discussion of how the functionality is distributed across system nodes. A node often represents a partitioning of components and associated functionality, control, and persistent data based on the physical location of the components. The node may include a fixed facility or a moving platform such as an aircraft. Many modern systems are distributed across multiple system nodes. Nodes may also be defined based on other criteria such as organizational responsibility (e.g., the people and resources assigned to a particular department). In OOSEM, a logical node represents an aggregation (or set) of logical components at a particular location. A physical node represents an aggregation (or set) of physical components at a particular location. The logical components at a logical node are allocated to physical components at a physical node, as described later in this section.

Functionality, control, and persistent data can be distributed in many ways. A system can be highly distributed, such that each node can autonomously handle all the functionality, control, and data. Alternatively, the distribution may be highly centralized, where most of the functionality, control, and data are associated with a central node, and the local nodes primarily provide an interface to external systems and users at a particular location. Between the extremes of highly distributed and highly centralized, functionality, control, and data can be partially distributed across regional and local nodes, where each node performs a subset of the total functionality.

A distributed system can be characterized as fully distributed, partially distributed, or centralized based on the above description. Distribution options can include any combination of a central node, multiple regional nodes, and multiple local nodes in each region. Trade studies are typically performed to optimize the distribution approach based on considerations such as performance, availability, security, and cost. Many types of systems are highly distributed, including information systems with networked communications, electrical power distribution systems, and complex system of systems such as transportation systems.

For the ESS, the nodes represent the *Central Monitoring Station* (CMS) and the *Site Installations* that are installed at a *Single-Family Residence, Multifamily Residence,* or *Small Business.* Although not included in this example, a CMS backup facility may be an additional node to provide disaster recovery to satisfy the system availability requirement.

The *ESS Node Logical* block definition diagram is shown in Figure 17.27. The *ESS Node Logical* is another subclass of the *ESS* block, which inherits all of its features, similar to the *ESS Logical* block

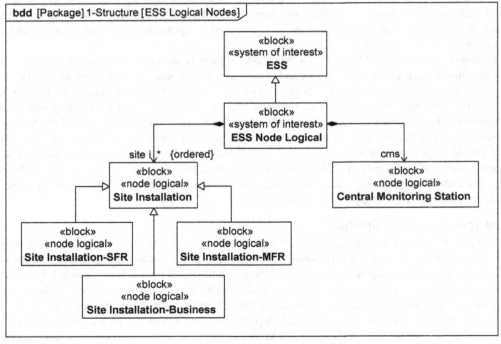

FIGURE 17.27

Block definition diagram showing the *ESS Node Logical* block as a subclass of the *ESS* block and its decomposition into the *Site Installation* and *Central Monitoring Station* logical nodes.

described in Section 17.3.4. Each subclass has its own decomposition. This block is decomposed into the *Site Installation* and *Central Monitoring Station* nodes that are stereotyped as «node logical». These nodes may include a property to define their location. For example, the site installation nodes may have a location property to specify their address.

The *Site Installation* logical node is further specialized into the *Site Installation-SFR*, *Site Installation-MFR*, and *Site Installation-Business* to represent nodes corresponding to single-family residences, multi-family residences, and small businesses respectively. Each subclass of *Site Installation* can accommodate its unique requirements and support variant design solutions.

The *Site Installation* and the *Central Monitoring Station* nodes are composed of logical components as shown in Figures 17.28 and 17.29, respectively. This decomposition includes logical components that are defined in the logical design in Section 17.3.4.

A particular logical component can be part of more than one node. However, the logical component may have different requirements for each node. An example of a logical component that is part of more than one node is the *Sensor Data Recorder* that is part of both the *Site Installation* and the *Central Monitoring Station* node. The distribution is driven by the need to record local sensor data at the site and to store sensor data from many sites at the CMS to be accessed centrally. The requirements for the CMS and site sensor data recorders are quite different in terms of the amount of data stored, backup, and access controls. In this case a subclass of the *Sensor Data Recorder* logical component is defined for both the *Site Installation* and the *Central Monitoring Station* nodes with their specialized requirements.

The *Event Log* is also part of both the *Site Installation* and the *Central Monitoring Station*, so event data from multiple sites can be accessed centrally. This imposes requirements to synchronize the data between the *Site Installations* and the *Central Monitoring Station* that the database design must address. As shown in the figure, the *Site Installation* and the *Central Monitoring Station* nodes also include components called *Site to CMS IF* and *CMS to Site IF* to support communications between the nodes. These components are derived from the distribution concept and were not part of the original logical design in Section 17.3.4.

A similar set of modeling artifacts that were used to define the *ESS Logical* architecture in the previous section can also be developed to define the *ESS Node Logical* architecture. This includes the activity diagrams and internal block diagram for the *ESS Node Logical*. An elaboration of each activity diagram that was created for the *ESS Logical* architecture is created for the *ESS Node Logical* architecture to specify how the activity is executed by the logical components that are distributed across the nodes.

The activity diagrams show the interaction of the components within each node and across nodes. The activity diagram called *Monitor Intruder-ESS Node Logical* is shown in Figure 17.30. In order to fit the page, this activity diagram only includes a portion of the overall *Monitor Intruder* behavior that is specified in the logical activity in Figure 17.24. The nodes are expressed as activity partitions, and the logical components are nested within their respective node. In this example, the *process intruder detection* and *control intruder response* actions are accomplished at the *Site Installation* node and the *validate intruder alert* is accomplished at the *Central Monitoring Station* node. The storing of event data and sensor data is performed at both nodes. The *Site to SMS IF* and the *CMS to Site IF* support the communications between the *Site Installation* and the *Central Monitoring Station* nodes. The overall behavior of this activity diagram is consistent with the behavior that was originally specified as part of the logical design in the *Monitor Intruder-ESS Logical* activity diagram in Figure 17.24. The *ESS Node Logical* internal block diagrams in Figure 17.31 and Figure 17.32 show how the logical components are

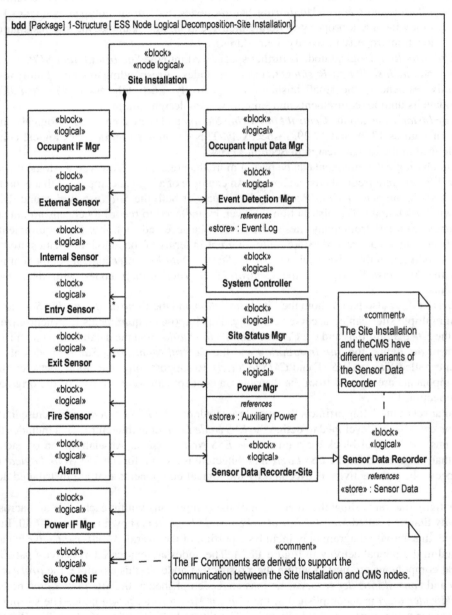

FIGURE 17.28

Decomposition of the Site Installation node into its logical components.

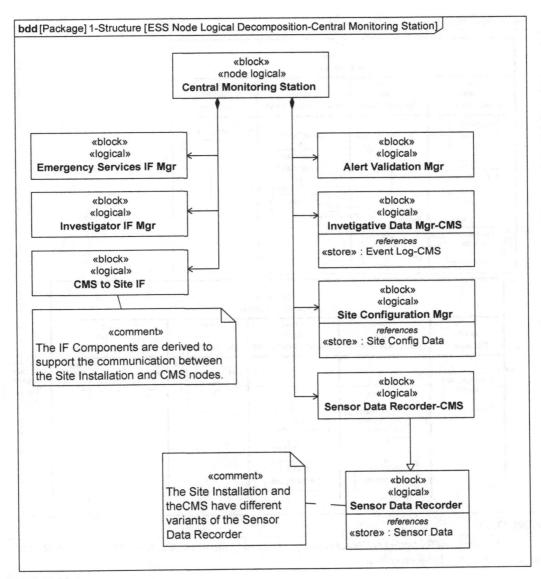

FIGURE 17.29

Decomposition of the Central Monitoring Station node into its logical components.

interconnected within each node along with the interfaces to connect across nodes. This includes the interconnection of parts that support the communication specified in the *Monitor Intruder-ESS Node Logical* activity diagram. Once again, the system external interfaces are maintained on the ports of the enclosing block, but,the nodes in this example do not have ports. Instead, the external connectors connect directly to the ports on the nested parts of the nodes.

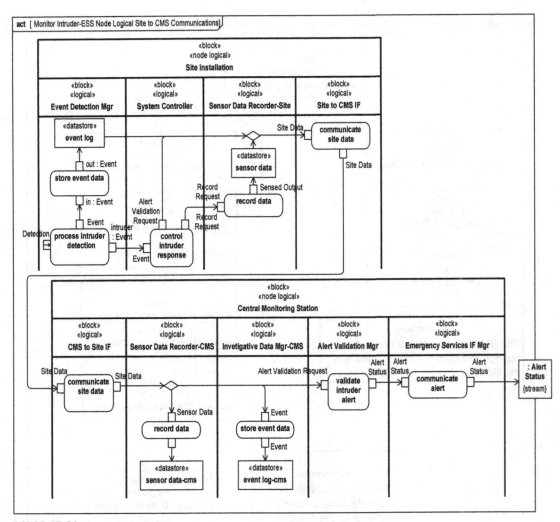

FIGURE 17.30

The *Monitor Intruder-ESS Node Logical activity diagram* showing the interaction of selected components and the communications between nodes.

Define variant designs

The approach to variant design must be integrated into all OOSEM activities. It is initiated in Section 17.3.2 by identifying variant mission requirements, moes, and enterprise use cases, and continues in Section 17.3.3 with analysis of system requirements variation. The OOSEM logical and physical architecture design activities must then identify architecture variants that can support the system requirements variation.

As noted above, there are variant designs of the *Site Installation* for single-family residences, multi-family residences, and small businesses. An example of a variant design for the *Site Installation-Business* is to provide protection against employee theft, which is applicable to a small business but not to

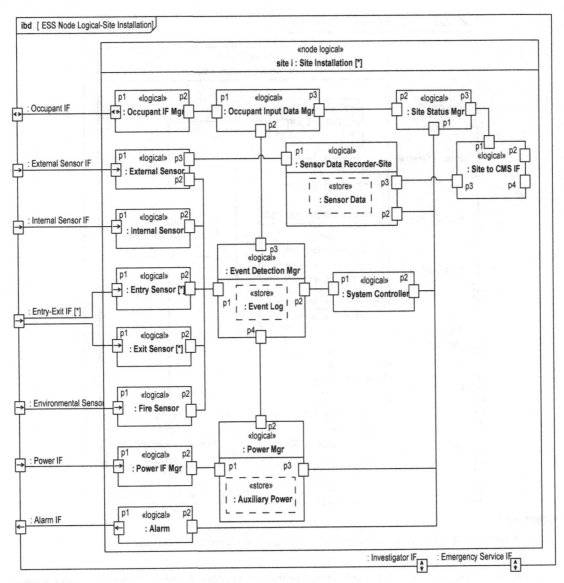

FIGURE 17.31

Site Installation internal block diagram showing the interconnection between its parts.

a residence. In this case, the *Intruder* is an employee. A variant of the *Monitor Intruder* activity diagram beginning with the logical design in the previous section is created to represent the employee theft scenarios. Similarly, variants of the internal block diagrams are created as well.

The approach to variant design leverages redefinition of features of the superclass as described in Chapter 7 Section 7.7.1. For example, a particular type of sensor may be used to monitor employee

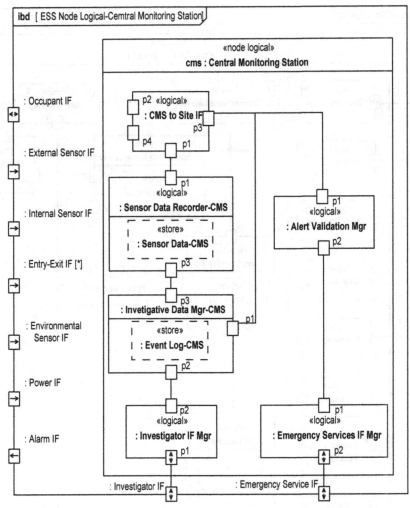

FIGURE 17.32

Central Monitoring Station internal block diagram showing the interconnection between its parts.

access to the cash register, which is used to redefine the more generic *Internal Sensor*. A design for each variant component reuses common features, while adding its unique features as needed.

An **options tree** defines all the allowable components that are available for all variants. The top level block in the option tree represents a superset of all possible variant configurations, such as a vehicle with 4-cylinder and 6-cylinder variant designs. The top-level block is decomposed at multiple levels. Each level of decomposition defines generic blocks that have optional multiplicity if they are not part of all variants. For the vehicle example, a sunroof may be part of some variants and not part of others, so its multiplicity is 0..1. Each generic block is further specialized into all its possible variants.

In this example, the generic engine includes a specialization for a 4-cylinder engine and 6-cylinder engine.

A particular variant system design is a subclass of the top-level block in the options tree. The variant redefines the generic components to represent the specific components for the variant. This may include redefining the multiplicity. For example, a variant vehicle configuration with 6-cylinder engine and a sunroof redefines the generic engine to be a 6- cylinder engine, and redefines the multiplicity of the sunroof from 0..1 to 1. Constraints define allowable combinations of components, such as a constraint that wide rim wheels are valid with the 6-cylinder engine option but not with the 4-cylinder engine option. Once the variant design is captured in a block definition diagram, it is further elaborated by generating and/or refining other OOSEM modeling artifacts to capture requirements, design, analysis, and verification artifacts for the selected variant.

Define node physical architecture

The functionality for the logical components in the ESS logical architecture is partitioned among the logical nodes and captured in the ESS node logical architecture as described in the previous section. This is accomplished by distributing the logical components to each logical node based on partitioning considerations that are somewhat independent of how the components are implemented. For example, it makes sense for the *Entry Sensor* logical component to be part of the *Site Installation* node and not part of the *Central Monitoring Station* node regardless of what technology is used to realize the *Entry Sensor*.

The logical components at each node are then allocated to **physical components** at each node to constitute the ESS node physical architecture. A partial allocation of the logical components to hardware components and logical components to software components at the *Site Installation* node and the *Central Monitoring Station* node is shown in the allocation tables in Figure 17.33 and Figure 17.34, respectively. The allocation decisions are critical design decisions, so the rationale should be captured along with the allocate relationship.

The design constraints that were identified during the system requirements analysis in Section 17.3.3 are imposed on the physical architecture as part of the logical-to-physical allocation. For example, a logical component may be allocated to a particular COTS component that has been imposed as a design constraint. A reference physical architecture may also constrain the solution space with predefined or legacy components such as a set of common services. As an example, the reference software architecture for the *Central Monitoring Station* software is a multilayered software architecture that includes specific types of components associated with each architecture layer—that is, presentation, mission application, infrastructure, and operating system layers.

The logical-to-physical component allocations may also be based on leveraging architectural patterns. The patterns may represent common solutions and their associated technologies. For example, the *Event Detection Mgr* and *System Controller* constitute a logical design pattern that can be implemented using a common software design solution.

Alternative physical architectures are often defined by allocating logical components to alternative physical components that are subject to trade-off analysis. As an example, the *Entry Sensor* includes alternative allocations to an *Optical Sensor* and a *Contact Sensor*, and the *Contact Sensor* was selected as the preferred alternative. This is a key decision, so the rationale for this decision is attached to the allocate relationship and refers to the applicable trade study that resulted in this decision.

Trade studies are performed to select the preferred physical architecture based on selection criteria that optimize the measures of effectiveness and measures of performance. In this example, the ESS

Logical to Physical Allocation (Hardware)	Auxiliary Battery	Console	Contact Sensor	Fire Detector	Hard Drive	IR Motion Detector	LAN–Site	Memory Card	Modem	Multi–Mode Alarm	Power Strip	Power Switch	Site Hardware	Site Processor	Video Camcorder	Wiring–Site	Application and?	Cabling–CMS	CMS Hardware	Disk Drive	LAN–CMS	Modem–CMS	Video Server	Video Storage D?	Workstation
Alarm										↗															
Emergency Services IF Mgr																							↗		
Entry Sensor			↗																						
Exit Sensor			↗											↗											
External Sensor													↗												
Fire Sensor				↗																					
Internal Sensor						↗																			
Investigator IF Mgr																							↗		
Occupant IF Mgr		↗																							
Power IF Mgr											↗														
Power Mgr	↗											↗													
Sensor Data Recorder																									
CMS to Site IF																							↗		
Connection Infrastructure?																	↗						↗		
Connection Inrrastructure?						↗										↗									
Invetigative Data Mgr–CMS																				↗					
Sensor Data Recorder–CMS																								↗	↗
Sensor Data Recorder–Site														↗											
Site to CMS IF						↗		↗																	

FIGURE 17.33

Allocation of logical components to hardware components in *Site Installation* and *Central Monitoring Station* nodes.

probability of intruder detection and probability of false alarm may drive the *Site Installation* performance requirements, while the number and type of *Site Installations* that are monitored and emergency response times may drive the *Central Monitoring Station* performance requirements. Performance requirements must be subject to trade-off with availability, cost, and other critical requirements to arrive at a balanced system solution.

When a logical component is allocated to software, the software component must also be allocated to a corresponding hardware component to execute it. In addition to software allocation, persistent data are allocated to hardware components that store the data, and operational procedures are allocated to operators that execute the procedures. These allocations can also be reflected in allocation tables similar to Figures 17.33 and 17.34.

A similar approach that was used to model the ESS node logical architecture can be applied to the ESS node physical architecture. The *ESS Node Physical* block is defined as a subclass of the ESS block and decomposed into physical nodes as shown in Figure 17.35. In addition to the *Site Installation* and *Central Monitoring Station* nodes, the *Communication Network* is also a node in the node physical architecture, while it was abstracted away in the node logical architecture. The *Site Installation* physical node is further specialized in to the *Site Installation-SFR*, *Site Installation-MFR*, and *Site Installation-Business*, to correspond to the single- family residences, multi-family residences, and small businesses as it was for the logical site installation nodes.

Logical to Physical Allocation (Software)	Alarm IF	Camcorder IF	Comm IF	Console IF	Contact Sensor IF	Controller	Event Mgr	Fire Detector IF	Image Processing	IR Sensor IF	Power IF	Power Manager	Site Software	Site Status Mgr	User Validation?	Admin IF	Alert Validation?	CMS Software	Comm IF-CMS	Data Access Mgr	Database Mgr	DB IF	Operator IF	Site Config Mgr
Alarm	↗																							
Alert Validation Mgr																	↗						↗	
Event Detection Mgr						↗																		
Occupant IF Mgr				↗																				
Occupant Input Data Mgr															↗									
Power Mgr											↗	↗												
Site Configuration Mgr																	↗							↗
Site Status Mgr														↗										
System Controller						↗																		
CMS to Site IF																			↗					
Invetigative Data Mgr–CMS																				↗	↗	↗		
Site to CMS IF			↗																					

FIGURE 17.34

Allocation of logical components to software components in *Site Installation* and *Central Monitoring Station* nodes.

The *ESS Node Physical* block definition diagrams for the *Site Installation* and *Central Monitoring Station* are shown in Figure 17.36 and Figure 17.37, respectively. In these block definition diagrams, the logical components from the logical nodes in Figure 17.28 and Figure 17.29 have been allocated to physical components based on the allocation tables in Figure 17.33 and 17.34. The physical components comprise the *Site Installation* and *Central Monitoring Station* physical nodes. The physical components have stereotypes applied to represent the kind of component, such as «*hardware*» or «*software*».

The *Monitor Intruder-ESS Node Physical* activity diagram for the *Site Installation* and the *Central Monitoring Station* is shown in Figure 17.38. The activity partitions correspond to the components of the ESS node physical architecture. The activity diagram captures the interaction between the hardware and the *Site Software*, as well as the operators of the system. The *Site Software* aggregates all of the software components that were allocated to the *Site Processor* and is stereotyped as a *configuration item*. This software executes on the *Site Processor*, although this is not shown as an activity partition in the activity diagram. The detailed interaction among the software components as described later in this section must preserve the interaction that was specified in the logical architecture and node logical architecture. The other activity partitions correspond to the hardware components and security operator.

The activity diagram must be consistent with the behavior from the corresponding logical and node logical activity diagrams in Figure 17.24 and Figure 17.30, respectively, and also realize the original behavior specified for the *monitor intruder* action in Figure 17.15, including its inputs, outputs, and any pre- and post-conditions. This activity diagram includes more detail to show how the physical components in each node interact.

The *ESS Node Physical* internal block diagrams for the *Site Installation* and *Central Monitoring Station* in Figure 17.39 and Figure 17.40 show how the physical parts are interconnected within

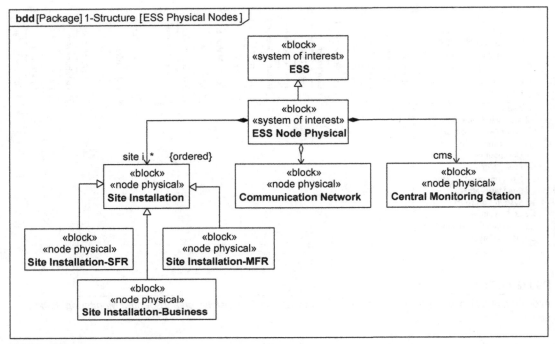

FIGURE 17.35

Block definition diagram showing the *ESS Node Physical* block as a subclass of the *ESS* block and its decomposition into the *Site Installation* and *Central Monitoring Station* physical nodes.

each node along with the interfaces to connect across nodes. The *ESS Node Physical* block is the enclosing frame.

The physical ports on each of the components are specified as physical interfaces. The external port on the *Video Camcorder* is *p2* and typed by an *Optical Interface*, which redefines the port on the *ESS* typed by *External Sensor IF* (refer to Figure 17.17). The other ports on the *Video Camcorder* include a port *p1* typed by *Video IF* and a port typed by *Power IF* (not shown). Most of the ports on the internal parts are not fully defined in this example and therefore do not show the direction of flow.

Since the *ESS Node Physical* block is a subclass of the ESS block, it inherits its features—including its ports—from the ESS block. However, the physical ports on the *ESS Node Physical* block may not share a common type with the ports on the original ESS black box, which may have been defined as logical ports. When dealing with the flow of data, the physical interface is often specified by a communications protocol, and the logical interface represents the information content. Therefore, these physical ports on the *ESS Node Physical* block need to replace the logical ports from the original ESS block. This can be accomplished by defining a multiplicity on the original ports as 0..1, such that the *ESS Node Physical* block does not have to use the original port definitions. It does this by redefining the multiplicity as 0 and then adding its own ports as required. Once this is done, the logical ports from the *ESS Node Logical* block can be allocated to the physical ports of the *ESS Node Physical* block. An alternative to replacing the port is to defer typing the port on the original ESS black box and type them on the *ESS Node Logical* and *ESS Node Physical* blocks.

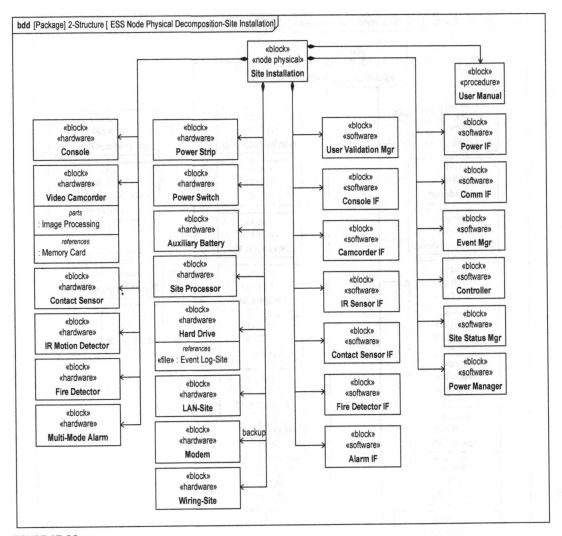

FIGURE 17.36

Site Installation physical node block definition diagram showing the hierarchy of physical components.

The item flows are defined as logical item flows in the logical architecture that are allocated to physical item flows in the physical architecture. The item flow definitions have been deferred in this example, pending the detailed interface specifications on the parts.

The ESS node physical architecture defines the physical components of the system, including hardware, software, persistent data, and other stored items (e.g., fluid, energy), and operational procedures that are performed by operators. The software components and persistent data stores are nested within the hardware component to which they are allocated. In Figure 17.39, for example, several software

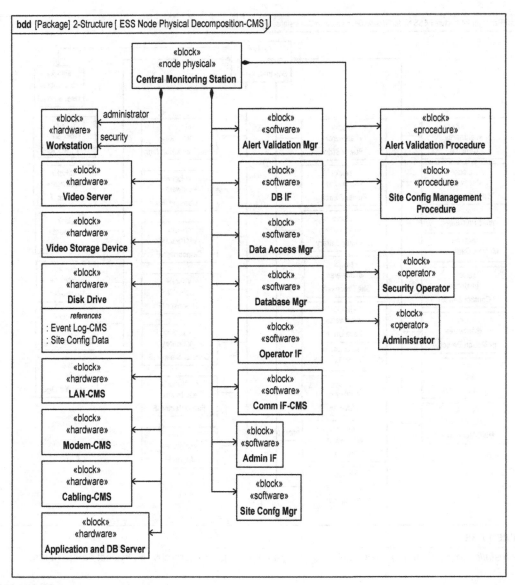

FIGURE 17.37

Central Monitoring Station physical node block definition diagram showing the hierarchy of physical components.

parts have been allocated to the *Site Processor*. The allocation of software to hardware is an abstraction of a UML deployment of a software component to a hardware processor.

The ESS node physical architecture serves to integrate the hardware and software components and operators of the system. The ESS *Node Physical Design* package in Figure 17.5 contains nested

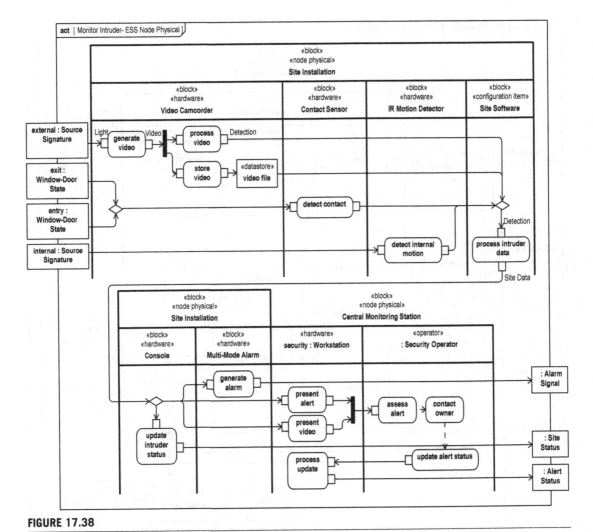

FIGURE 17.38

The *Monitor Intruder-ESS Node Physical* activity diagram showing the interaction of the physical components.

packages for *Structure* and *Behavior* of the node physical architecture. In addition, the *Node Physical Design* package also contains packages for the *Site Installation* and the *Central Monitoring Station*, which each contain additional nested packages for the hardware, software, persistent data, and operational procedures. The physical components of the system that are part of the ESS node physical architecture are contained in these nested packages. The following subsections describe the activities to architect and specify the software, data, and hardware architecture. In addition, the subsections describe how to define specialty views of the architecture, such as security, and specify the operational procedures needed to operate the system.

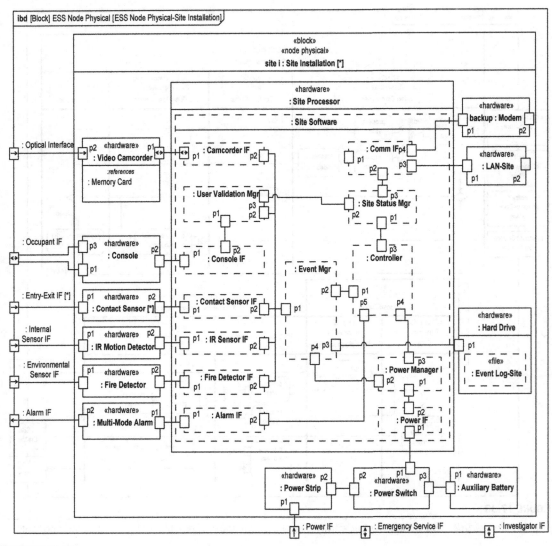

FIGURE 17.39

Site Installation physical node internal block diagram.

Define software architecture

The software architecture is a view of the overall system architecture that includes the software components and their interrelationships. Software architecting is critical to effectively specifying software components that support the system requirements.

The *ESS Software* block definition diagram is shown in Figure 17.41. The *Site Software* and the *CMS Software* blocks aggregate the software components that were defined in the ESS node physical

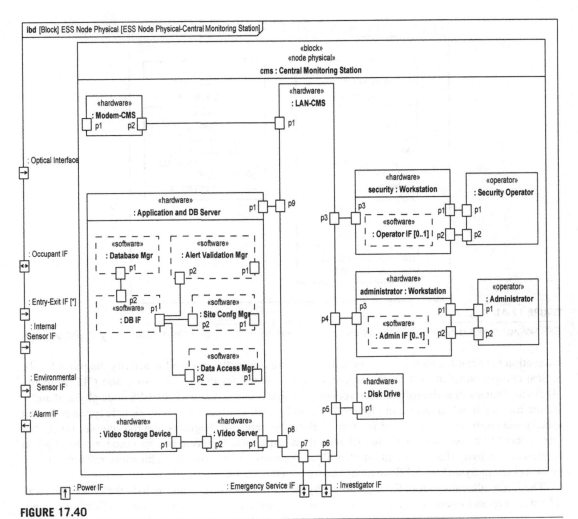

FIGURE 17.40

Central Monitoring Station physical node internal block diagram.

decompositions for the *Site Installation* and *Central Monitoring Station* in Figures 17.36 and 17.37, respectively. The *Site Software* and *CMS Software* blocks provide a means to aggregate the software into a «configuration item». The software components are contained in software packages, which in turn are contained in the applicable *Site Installation* and *Central Monitoring Station* packages.

The modeling artifacts for the system-level software architecture include modeling artifacts similar to those described previously. The software behavior can be specified to conform to the activity diagrams specified as part of the logical, node logical, and node physical activity diagrams. The behavior may be specified as activity diagrams, sequence diagrams, and/or state machine diagrams. This may include defining activity diagrams, sequence diagrams, and/or state machine diagrams to refine the

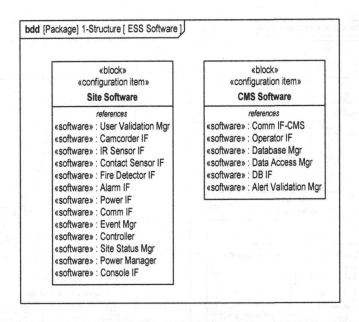

FIGURE 17.41

ESS Software block definition diagram shows the *Site Installation* software and *Central Monitoring Station* software.

interaction between the software components that were originally specified in activity diagrams for the logical components. Internal block diagrams can be created for the *Site Software* and *CMS Software* blocks to further refine the software interconnection that is consistent with the ESS node physical architecture internal block diagrams in Figures 17.39 and 17.40. The interfaces may include typed ports that specify the required and provided interfaces. Both the behavior diagrams and the internal block diagrams should be consistent with the behavioral and structural requirements specified by the physical architecture activity diagrams and internal block diagrams. The software architecture refinement may be expressed in SysML or UML as described later in this section.

The initial allocation from the logical-to-physical components may not include the allocation to all infrastructure and operating system components that are required to support the application components, so this must be addressed as part of defining the software architecture. In addition, the software components may require additional refinement to address the software-specific concerns and fully specify the software requirements. Some of the software architecture concerns depend on the application domain. For information systems, the software architecture is often a layered architecture, where each layer includes software components that may depend on a lower layer for the services it provides. This may include a presentation layer, mission application layer, infrastructure layer, operating system layer, and data layer, as shown in the package diagram for the CMS software in Figure 17.42. The software components from the physical architecture are further elaborated and partitioned into these different layers. A reference architecture can be imposed as a design constraint that includes reusable components that define the infrastructure layer, such as messaging, access control services, and database interfaces. For embedded real-time software design, the architecture must also address concerns related to scheduling algorithms and how to address concurrency, prioritization, and contention for bus,

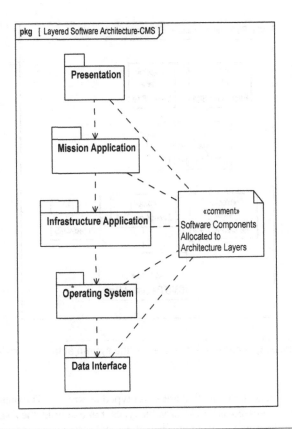

FIGURE 17.42

Package diagram showing dependencies between software layers.

memory, and processor resources. These and other concerns must be addressed to define the software architecture fully.

Define data architecture

The data architecture is a view of the physical architecture that represents the persistent data, how the data are used, and where the data are stored. The physical architecture provides the integration framework to ensure that the data architecture is consistent with the overall system design. The persistent data requirements can be derived from the scenario analysis. Persistent data are stored by a component (logical or physical) and expressed as a reference property of the component with the «store» stereotype applied. As part of the logical design, the persistent data are encapsulated in the logical component that operates on them. The logical components are allocated to physical components of the physical architecture, which may include data files and memory storage devices that store the data, and software applications such as relational database applications that manage the data.

The persistent data definition types for both the *Site Installation* and the *CMS* are specified on an *ESS Persistent Data* block definition diagram as shown in Figure 17.43. This includes the *Event Log, Video,* and

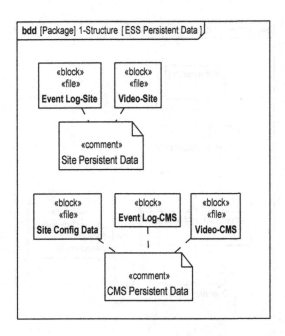

FIGURE 17.43

Block definition diagram showing persistent data stored by the system at the *Site Installation* and *Central Monitoring Station*.

Site Config Data as types of persistent data that are stereotyped as «*file*». The data definitions can be complex data structures that are expressed as blocks or value types. For example, the *Event Log* is a complex data structure that includes records of many different types of events, such as power-up events, system activation events, intruder detection events, and others, that were derived from the scenario analysis. The persistent data are contained in nested packages within the *Site Installation* and *Central Monitoring Station* packages.

The data architecture may include domain-specific artifacts to refine the data specifications. The data relationships may be specified by an entity relation attribute (ERA) diagram or directly on the block definition diagram using associations among the blocks that define the data. This description can be viewed as the conceptual data model that represents the requirements for implementing the database. The implementation of the conceptual data model is dependent on the technology employed, such as flat file, relational database, and/or an object-oriented database.

Many other domain-specific aspects of the data architecture must be considered, such as data normalization, data synchronization, data backup and recovery, and data migration strategies. One example of data synchronization is the need to synchronize the event logs from each *Site Installation* with the *Central Monitoring Station*. The selection of the data architecture and the specific technology is determined through trade studies and analyses, as described in Section 17.3.6.

Define hardware architecture

The hardware architecture is a view of the physical architecture that represents the hardware components and their interrelationships. The *ESS Hardware* block definition diagram shown in Figure 17.44

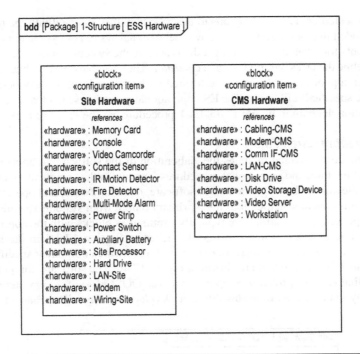

FIGURE 17.44

ESS Hardware block definition diagram shows the hardware for the *Site Installation* and *Central Monitoring Station*.

includes the *Site Hardware* and *CMS Hardware* block. These blocks aggregate the hardware components in a similar way as the *ESS Software* in Figure 17.41.

The hardware components are allocated from the logical components in Figure 17.33, as described previously. The *ESS Node Physical* internal block diagrams in Figures 17.39 and 17.40 show the interconnection of the hardware components. This can be more fully elaborated with more detailed hardware interfaces, including signal characteristics, physical connectors, and cabling. The specific selection of the hardware architecture and component technology results from the engineering analysis and trade studies, as described in Section 17.3.6. This includes the performance analysis to support sizing and other the hardware component requirements, and reliability, maintainability, and availability analysis to evaluate supportability requirements. The geometric view of the hardware components is captured in the geometric model described earlier in this section. The components in the geometric model are mapped to the hardware components in the system model as described in an earlier subsection (*Define Geometric Model*).

Define operational procedures

Operators can be external or internal to the system depending on how the system boundary is defined. For the ESS, the *Occupants* of the property are external to the system, as defined in the *Operational Domain* block definition diagram in Figure 17.12. On the other hand, the *Central Monitoring Station Security Operator* and *Administrator* in Figure 17.37 are considered internal to the ESS. Some logical components are allocated to internal operators to perform selected tasks. Both internal and external operators/users of the system are presented on activity diagrams to describe how they interact with the rest of the system. They are also included in other diagrams like any other external system or system component.

The requirements for what an operator must do to operate the system can be specified by operational procedures that define the tasks required of each *Operator*. The task analysis, timeline analyses, cognitive analysis, and other supporting analyses are performed to determine levels of task performance that are consistent with the specified skill levels. The ESS operational procedures are identified in the *ESS Procedures* block definition diagram in Figure 17.45. Each procedure has the *«procedure»* stereotype applied.

Specify component requirements

The physical architecture—which includes the elaboration of the software architecture, data architecture, hardware architecture, and operational procedures—results in the specification of the components of the system architecture to be implemented in software, data, hardware, and operational procedures, respectively. The component specifications are a primary output from systems specification and design process. The component specifications are typically captured as blocks with the appropriate black-box specification features, in a way similar to that described in Section 17.3.3 in the subsection called *Specify Black Box System Requirements*. An example of a software component specification and hardware component specification model are shown in Figure 17.46. The software component in the figure is the *Controller* that is part of the *Site Software,* with the OOSEM *«software»* stereotype applied. A stereotype property called *status* indicates this is a *Development Item*. The controller operations and

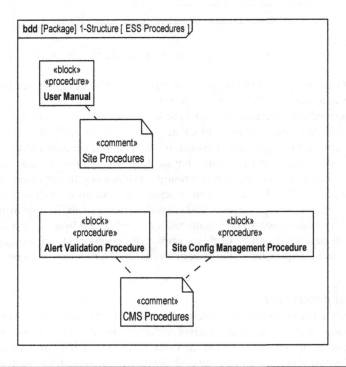

FIGURE 17.45

Block definition diagram showing operational procedures for the ESS external user and internal operators.

ports are specified. Required and provided interfaces can be reflected in the port types. Activity diagrams can be used to define the methods for the operations to specify computational and/or logic intensive algorithms. Parametric diagrams can be used to specify the algorithm performance requirements in terms of the desired input/output response. A state machine can define the main behavior for the controller in terms of the events that trigger the operations.

The *develop software* process referenced in Figure 17.1 is used to perform software requirements analysis to derive more detailed requirements, perform software design, and implement and test the software components. UML can be used to support this process. The SysML model can be referenced as a specification model by the software design team. Classes can be defined as subclasses of the SysML software component specifications or allocated from the SysML software component specification and presented on class diagrams. The UML composite structure diagram can be used to refine the SysML internal block diagram from the node physical architecture in Figures 17.39 and 17.40 to reflect

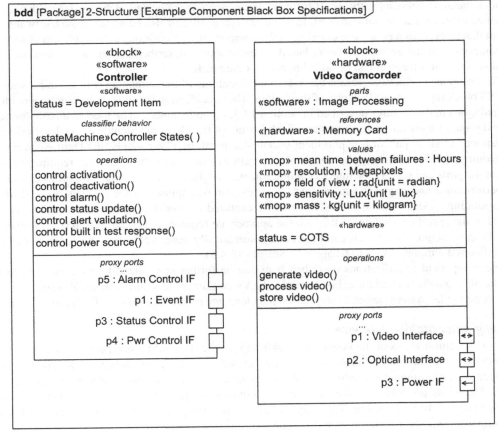

FIGURE 17.46

Example of software and hardware component specifications.

the interconnection and interfaces between the software components. The software design realizes the software component interfaces, operations, and state machine behavior specified in the SysML model by introducing more detailed structures and behaviors. The software sequence diagrams are further elaborated to show the interaction between the lower-level software design components. The UML component diagram and deployment diagram can also be used for software design to show more explicitly how the software is deployed beyond the abstract allocation of software to hardware in Figures 17.39 and 17.40.

The hardware component specification in Figure 17.46 is the *Video Camcorder* that is part of the *Site Hardware,* with the OOSEM «hardware» stereotype applied. The stereotype property called *status* indicates this is intended to be a COTS item. The black-box component specification includes functional requirements derived from the scenario analysis and performance properties with stereotype «mop» whose values are determined through engineering analysis and trade studies, as described in Section 17.3.6. The ports are used to specify the interfaces and show the direction of their flow properties. It is also apparent from the compartments that the *Video Camcorder* has a *Memory Card* and includes *Image Processing* software. If software components are allocated to the hardware, they can be presented in an allocation compartment. In addition, a property can also be added to the hardware component that references a geometric drawing of the component, or the tooling can enable direct access to the component in the geometric model based on the mapping described earlier in this section. Additional specification features can be added to address the needs.

The component blocks represent black-box specifications of the components in a similar way that the ESS block represents a black box of the system. The specification features of the component blocks are analogous to the features described in Section 17.3.3. The features can be used as a basis for defining text requirements for each component. Each feature of the block can include a text description that corresponds to all or part of a requirement's shall statement, or, alternatively, the feature can refine a text requirement. For example, the text for the operations can specify the functional requirements, the text for the ports can specify the interface requirements, and the text for the value properties can specify the performance and physical requirements. The text can be captured in the description field for the corresponding model element or the text can be captured as SysML requirements, which are then related to the specification feature through the appropriate requirements relationship (e.g., refine, satisfy). Document generation tools can be used to automatically generate the text specification based on a specification template (refer to Chapter 18 Section 18.4.5).

The component specifications described here can be further specialized to accommodate further specification and design variation. For example, the Video Camcorders may have multiple design variations. A particular system design configuration may leverage redefinition to specify a particular variant.

Defining other architecture views

Other architectural views of the system may address specific stakeholder perspectives, such as a security architecture. The security architecture can be presented as a filtered subset of the node physical architecture, which includes hardware, software, data, and procedures that address security requirements. The views provide a mechanism that can help to specify, analyze, and integrate critical cross-cutting facets of the architecture. This may include cross-cutting behavior, structure, parametrics, and requirements associated with the specific concern.

A viewpoint represents a stakeholder perspective, such as a security architect viewpoint. The viewpoint is used to specify a subset of the model that is of interest to the stakeholder and addresses their concerns. The causal analysis from Section 17.3.2 can provide inputs to identify the stakeholder concerns.

As described in Chapter 5, Section 5.6 and Chapter 15, Section 15.8, a viewpoint includes rules that specify how a particular view is constructed to reflect the stakeholder's perspective. The rules can be specified by the viewpoint method to query the model. A view presents a filtered portion of the model that conforms to the viewpoint by returning the model elements in response to the model query. A view can be presented in many different formats, such as a combination of diagrams, tables, matrixes, and trees.

The *Viewpoints* package is introduced in the discussion of model organization in Section 17.3.1 and is shown in Figure 17.5. Selected *ESS Stakeholder Viewpoints* are shown in Figure 17.47, including the *Emergency Services* viewpoint and the *System Security* viewpoint. The *System Security* viewpoint may specify query criteria to return all components needed to satisfy the system security requirements, such as the confidentiality, integrity, and availability requirements. The security view shows the information

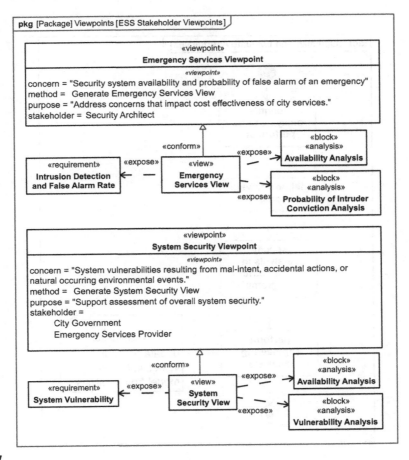

FIGURE 17.47

ESS *Viewpoints* specifies stakeholder perspectives that are reflected in views of the model.

presented to the stakeholder in response to the query and includes the model elements that satisfy the security requirements. Other stakeholder viewpoints may represent the *Company Owner,* the *Customer,* and other development team roles.

17.3.6 OPTIMIZE AND EVALUATE ALTERNATIVES

The *Optimize and Evaluate Alternatives* activity is shown in Figure 17.48. This activity is invoked throughout all other OOSEM activities to support engineering analysis and trade studies. This activity includes identifying the analysis needed, defining the analysis context, specifying the analysis in parametric diagrams, and performing the engineering analysis.

Chapter 8 describes how to model constraints with parametrics. SysML enables critical system characteristics to be captured in the model so that they can be analyzed. This provides a mechanism to integrate the system design models with the multitude of engineering analysis models, such as performance,

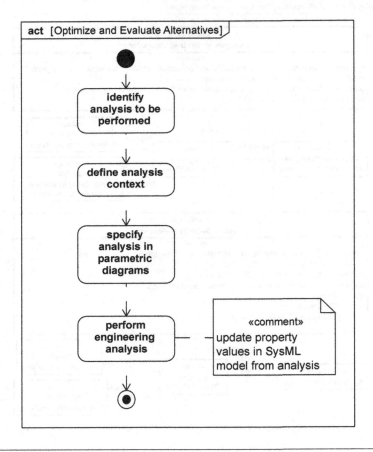

FIGURE 17.48

Optimize and Evaluate Alternatives activity to support trade studies and analysis.

reliability, and mass properties analysis. Chapter 18 includes further discussion of how engineering analysis and simulation models are integrated with SysML models in the Systems Development Environment.

Identify analyses to be performed

The analyses to be performed should support specific analysis objectives, which may include the following:

- Characterize or predict some aspect of the system, such as its performance, reliability, mass properties, or cost;
- Optimize the design through sensitivity analysis;
- Evaluate and select a preferred solution among alternative design approaches;
- Verify a design using analysis; and
- Support technical planning, such as cost estimating and risk analysis.

Different types and fidelity of engineering analyses are identified throughout the design process to meet the analysis objectives. Stereotypes can also be defined to include properties that capture additional analysis metadata, such as the analysis assumptions or information about the analysis tool or solver. (Refer to the simulation profile and model libraries in Chapter 15.)

Define the analysis context

A block definition diagram is used to define each analysis. Figure 17.49 shows a block diagram called the *ESS Analysis Context. The Analysis Context* block is composed of blocks that represent each analysis to

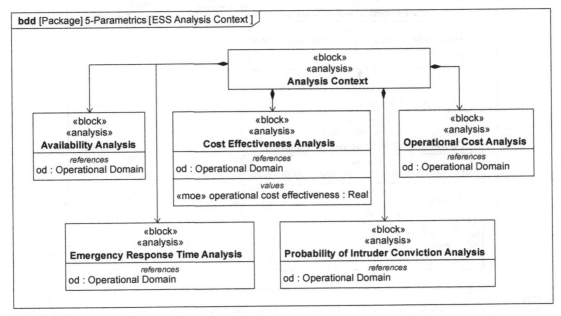

FIGURE 17.49

ESS Analysis Context defines the analysis blocks to support the analysis of the measures of effectiveness.

be performed. The «analysis» stereotype is applied to each analysis block. In this example, an analysis is identified for each of the moes listed in Section 17.3.2, including the *Availability Analysis*, *Emergency Response Time Analysis*, *Probability of Intruder Conviction Analysis*, and *Operational Cost Analysis*. In addition, the *Cost Effectiveness Analysis* block is used to analyze the overall value of the system.

Each analysis block identified in the *Analysis Context* is used to specify the analysis further. In Figure 17.50, the *Cost Effectiveness Analysis* block is composed of a constraint block called *Operational Cost Effectiveness Equation*. This constraint block has the «objectiveFunction» stereotype applied and specifies an equation that relates operational cost effectiveness to the parameters that correspond to the moes for *availability, emergency response time, probability of intruder conviction,* and *operational cost.* In this example, the equation is a weighted sum of utility functions for the parameters associated with each moe.

The *Cost Effectiveness Analysis* block also refers to the *Operational Domain* block as the subject of the analysis. In this case, the subject of the analysis is the top block in the system hierarchy. By referencing this block, a parametric diagram can be defined that relates the parameters in the analysis equations to the properties of the ESS and external systems and users. The *Operational Domain*—or more generally the subject of the analysis—can be subclassed to support trade-off analysis of variant designs. (Refer to Chapter 8, Section 8.11.)

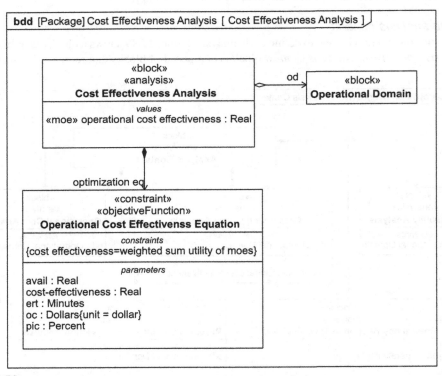

FIGURE 17.50

Cost Effectiveness Analysis block composed of an objective function that weights each parameter and references the *Operational Domain* as the subject of the analysis.

Using the same pattern as above, each analysis can be defined by decomposing the analysis block into the applicable analysis equations and referencing the subject of the analysis.

Specify analysis in parametric diagrams

The parametric diagram enables integration between the design and analysis models. It does this by binding the parameters of the analysis equations that are defined for each analysis to the properties of the subject of the analysis (e.g., the system).

The top-level parametric diagram for the ESS discussed in Section 17.3.2 is shown in Figure 17.11. This parametric diagram is derived from the *Cost Effectiveness Analysis* in the block definition diagram in Figure 17.50. The parametric diagram binds the parameters of the objective function to the moes in the *Security Enterprise* shown in Figure 17.12.

As the system design evolves, additional engineering analysis is needed to evaluate the impact of the system design properties on the moes. The *availability* property in Figure 17.11 represents a moe whose value is determined by the *Availability Analysis* identified in Figure 17,49. Figure 17.51 show the block definition diagram for the *Availability Analysis*, which includes constraint blocks for availability, reliability, and repair time. The corresponding parametric diagram that binds the parameters of the

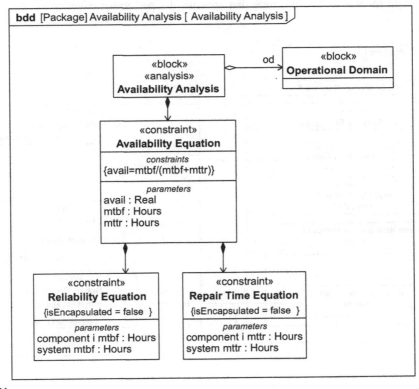

FIGURE 17.51

Availability Analysis composed of constraint block and referencing subject of the analysis.

equations to properties of the ESS, including *mean time between failures* and *mean time to repair*, is shown in Figure 17.52. The parametric diagrams provide the mechanism to maintain explicit relationships between the moes and their flow down to critical system, element, and component properties.

Parametrics can also be used to constrain inputs, outputs, and the input/output relationship associated with the behavior of a system or component. From the *Monitor Intruder-ESS Node Physical* activity diagram in Figure 17.38, a constraint block can be defined to specify the mathematical relation between the probability of detection of the signal output and the signal-to-noise ratio of the signal input to the *Video Camcorder*. The constraint block can then be used on a parametric diagram to bind to the component specific properties to analyze the detection performance.

The state of the system can also be treated as a value property that is used in parametrics. The value of this property represents the state of the system at any point in time and is determined by the ESS state machine behavior. This property can be used in parametrics by binding a state-dependent constraint to the state property. For a bouncing ball example, the constraints that apply to the forces on the ball depend on the state of the ball in terms of whether it is in contact with the ground or not. The state-dependent constraint can be conditioned on the state of the ball. In this example, the state-dependent constraint expresses one set of equations when the state of the ball is "contact with ground" and another set of equations when the state of the ball is "not in contact with the ground." For the ESS example, the *Video Camcorder* could include a state machine that specifies its performance under low-light conditions

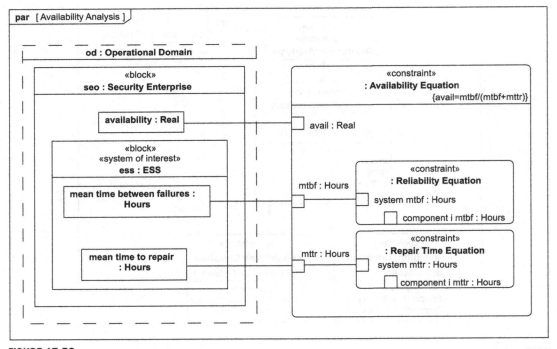

FIGURE 17.52

Availability Analysis model captured in a parametric diagram.

versus daylight conditions. The performance constraints in the parametric diagram are then dependent on the value of the camcorder state property. The property value can be set on entry to the state.

Perform engineering analysis

A computational capability is required to execute the equations in the parametric diagram. This can be done with the aid of engineering analysis tools, as described in Chapter 18. The detailed equations are often captured in the analysis model instead of in the SysML constraint blocks. The parametric diagrams specify the input and output parameters to the analysis and ensure these parameters are bound to corresponding system design properties. The analysis results determine the specific values or range of values of the system properties that satisfy the constraints. The values can be incorporated back into the system model in SysML. As an example, the mission availability resulting from executing the *Availability Analysis* in Figure 17.52 can estimate the extent to which the ESS properties for *mean time between failures* and *mean time to repair* from Figure 17.19 satisfy the availability requirement.

17.3.7 MANAGE REQUIREMENTS TRACEABILITY

The *Manage Requirements Traceability* activity is shown in Figure 17.53. This activity is invoked throughout all OOSEM activities to establish requirements traceability between the stakeholder requirements and the system specification and design model. This includes defining the specification tree; capturing the text-based requirements in the model; establishing relationships between the text-based requirements and the model elements using derive, satisfy, verify, and refine relationships; and generating the traceability reports and specification documentation. The language concepts for requirements modeling are described in Chapter 13.

Define specification tree

The *ESS Specification Tree* is shown in Figure 17.54. The specification tree shows the specifications at each level of the system hierarchy. The specification tree includes the *ESS Mission Requirements, ESS System Specification, Site Installation Specification, Central Monitoring Station Specification,* and *Site Installation* and *Central Monitoring Station Hardware* and *Software Specifications*. The trace relationship shows the traceability between the specifications at each level. The specification tree also shows traceability from the *ESS Mission Requirements* to a *Stakeholder Needs Assessment* document.

The trace relationship is used to establish coarse-grained traceability between requirements specifications that does not include the fine-grained traceability between individual requirements. The fine-grained traceability leverages other requirements relationships to relate requirements to design, analysis, and verification elements, as described in Chapter 13 and later in this section.

Capture text-based requirements in model

The stakeholder requirements are often documented in text specifications external to the modeling environment or a requirements management tool. The text-based requirements are captured in the model by creating a SysML requirement for each text requirement. Many of the SysML modeling tools provide a mechanism to import text requirements from documents or requirements management tools, and maintain synchronization between the requirements in the source tool and in the SysML modeling tool. Alternatively, text requirements can be created in the SysML modeling tool, which can be exported to a requirements management tool or output as a document in text or tabular format.

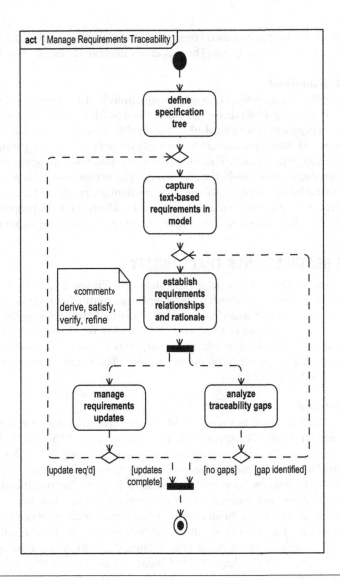

FIGURE 17.53

Manage Requirements Traceability activity, intended to maintain traceability between stakeholder requirements and the system specification and design model.

The *Requirements* package was briefly discussed in Section 17.3.1 and shown in the model organization in Figure 17.5. A nested package is created for each specification in the *ESS Specification Tree*. The requirements package contains the requirements for the specification. The requirements package for each specification is nested within the applicable level of the system hierarchy.

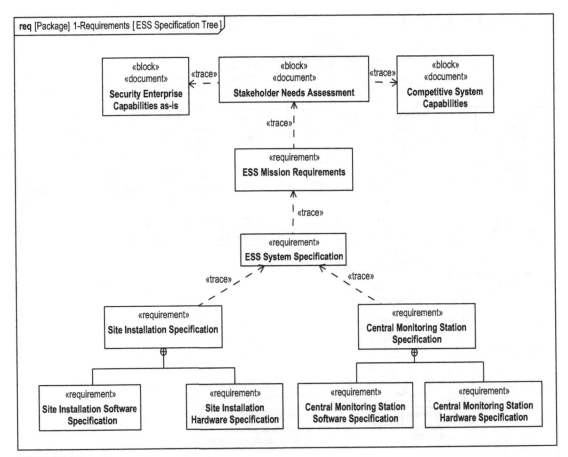

FIGURE 17.54

ESS Specification Tree on a requirement diagram showing the hierarchy of specifications.

As an example, the *ESS Requirements* are nested within the *ESS::Black Box Specification* package. The requirements are shown in the requirement diagram in Figure 17.55. The top-level requirement is the *ESS System Specification* and serves as a container for the other requirements in the specification. The containment hierarchy of requirements in each individual specification generally corresponds to the organization of the text-based specification document, as indicated by the first-tier requirements in the diagram. The requirements hierarchy includes containers for *Interface, Functional and Performance, Reliability, Maintainability,Availability*, and other typical categories of requirements. Each requirement has a name, an id, and text, and may also include additional requirement properties, such as criticality, uncertainty, probability of change, and verification method, although this information is not shown in the diagram. Tabular notations are often used as a more compact presentation of the requirements as described in Chapter 13, Section 13.7.1.

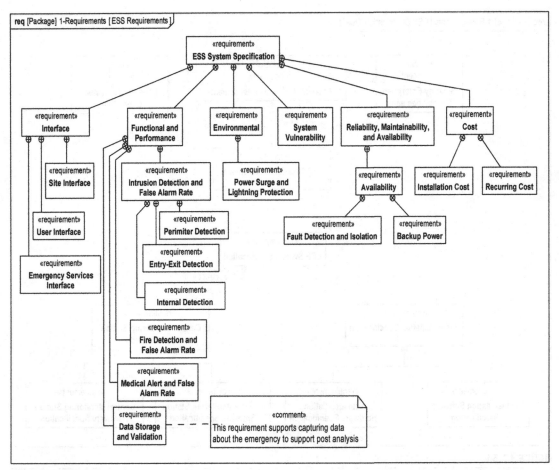

FIGURE 17.55

ESS System Specification showing the requirements contained in the system specification on a requirement diagram.

Establish requirements relationships and rationale

Requirements traceability is maintained by establishing relationships between the text-based requirements in the model and other model elements that correspond to other requirements, design elements, and test cases. The rationale for the relationship can also be captured in the model as well.

An example of requirements traceability and flow down from a mission requirement to a system requirement to a component requirement can be seen in the requirement diagram in Figure 17.56. The diagram shows traceability from the mission requirement for *Intruder Emergency Response* to the *Video Camcorder* performance requirements for *Field of View*, *Resolution*, and *Sensitivity*, and functional requirement to *Capture Video*.

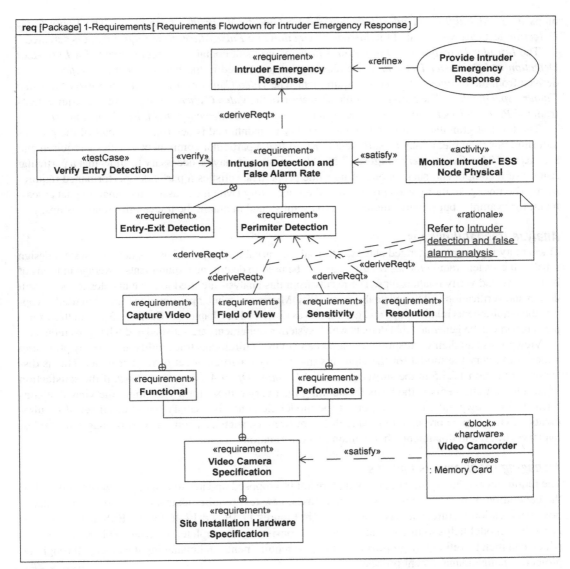

FIGURE 17.56

Requirement diagram showing traceability and flowdown from the *Intruder Emergency Response* mission requirement to *Video Camcorder* component requirements and design.

The mission requirement for *Intruder Emergency Response* is refined by the use case called *Provide Intruder Emergency Response*. The ESS system requirement for *Intruder Detection and False Alarm Rate* is derived from the mission requirement and satisfied by the *Monitor Intruder-ESS Node Physical* activity. Although not shown in the figure, the requirement may be also be refined by the ESS black box mops for *probability of intruder detection* and *probability of intruder false alarm*. The *Verify Entry Detection* test case verifies that the *Intruder Detection and False Alarm Rate* requirement is satisfied.

The *Intruder Detection and False Alarm Rate* requirement contains the requirements for *Entry-Exit Detection* and *Perimeter Detection*. The requirements contained in the *Video Camera Specification* are derived from the *Perimeter Detection* requirement. The *Video Camcorder* is asserted to satisfy the *Video Camera Specification*. The rationale for the derivation of the *Video Camcorder* performance requirements from the *Perimeter Detection* requirement refers to the *Intruder detection and false alarm analysis*.

The level of granularity at which the traceability is maintained is determined as part of the process tailoring. For example, it may be sufficient to assert that a particular component satisfies a requirement, such as the *Video Camcorder* in Figure 17.56. Alternatively, it may be necessary to show that a particular feature of a component, such as one of its value properties, satisfies a particular performance require-ment. The finer granularity adds precision to the traceability (which can assist in change impact assess-ment, for example) but requires more effort to establish and maintain the traceability relationships.

Analyze traceability gaps

Traceability reports are generated and used to analyze traceability gaps and assess how the system design satisfies the system requirements. Metrics can also be used to determine requirements coverage in terms of both satisfy and verify relationships. The results from this analysis are used to drive updates to the system design and verification and to update the traceability. Matrix and tabular presentations are often used to cap-ture the requirements relationships and gap reports as described in Chapter 13, Section 13.7.2. In this exam-ple, a report can be generated that depicts which system requirements are satisfied and what gaps remain.

Viewpoints and their corresponding views can aid in requirements traceability analysis by providing a means to query the model for the elements that satisfy a particular set of requirements. This is dis-cussed in Section 17.3.5 in the subsection called *Defining Other Architecture Views*. If the satisfaction of selected requirements is the basis for defining the query criteria for a viewpoint, the view that con-forms to the viewpoint can be a report of the model elements that satisfy the selected set of require-ments. A view can be presented in many different formats, such as a combination of diagrams, tables, matrixes, trees, and documents that contain this information.

Managing requirements updates

The requirements management activity may result in proposed updates to existing requirements and/or the generation of new requirements. In some cases, new text requirements are defined for each black-box specification feature, such as those shown in Figures 17.19 and 17.46 for the ESS and its compo-nents. The model helps to uncover ambiguous, inconsistent, incomplete, or unverifiable requirements, which can then be refined by proposing changes to requirements and managing the change through the project's change management process.

On larger projects, a requirements management tool is generally used in conjunction with the sys-tems modeling tool. Integration between the two tools is important to ensuring that the requirements and their relationships are synchronized between both tools. The change process must determine how changes to requirements are handled. One approach is to make changes to requirements text in the requirements management tool and to establish the relationships between the model elements and text requirements in the modeling tool. Chapter 18 includes additional discussion on integrating the system modeling tools with the requirements management tool. The specification document with text require-ments can also be output directly from the modeling tool using the tool's automatic document genera-tion capability and standard requirements templates.

17.3.8 OOSEM SUPPORT TO INTEGRATE AND VERIFY SYSTEM

The *Integrate and Verify System* process is part of the system development process shown in Figure 17.1 and described in Section 17.1.2. The goal of this process is to verify that the system satisfies its requirements. System, element, and component verification is typically accomplished by a combination of inspection, analysis, demonstration, and testing. The process includes developing verification plans and procedures, executing the verification procedures, analyzing verification results, and generating verification reports.

OOSEM supports this process in several ways. The system model can be used as a basis for developing test cases and associated verification procedures. The model can also be used to support other modeling artifacts that support verification planning and to support design of the verification environment. In addition, the model of the operational system can be integrated with an execution environment to support early requirements validation and design verification.

As described in Chapter 13, Section 13.12, SysML includes a test case and verify relationship, which can be used in conjunction with requirements to show how requirements can be verified at system, element, and component levels. From Figure 17.56, the *Verify Entry Detection* test case verifies the *Intrusion Detection and False Alarm Rate* requirement. This requirement can be elaborated to ensure it is verifiable by specifying the inputs, conditions, and expected outputs. The test case is expressed as an activity diagram in Figure 17.57 with the «*testCase*» key word shown in the diagram header. The *ESS Node Physical* is the *unit under test*. In this example, a *Video Source* and

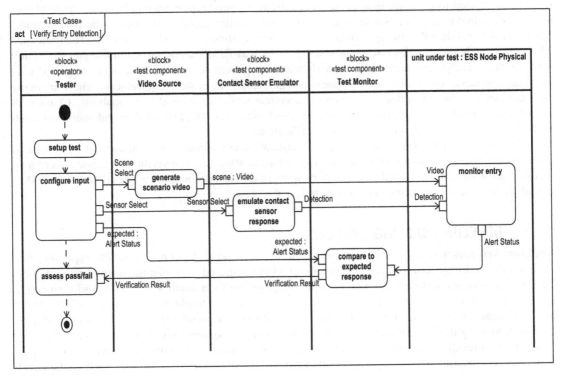

FIGURE 17.57

Verify Entry Detection test case.

the *Contact Sensor Emulator* represents the ESS external environment that generates the stimulus to the ESS, and the *Test Monitor* compares the ESS response to the expected response. A *Tester* initiates the test.

The test case specification defines the stimulus, the conditions, and the expected response. The verification result from the test case execution is compared with the expected response. The results can then be recorded to determine whether the system provideed the expected response. The result is called the verdict and may include pass, fail, undetermined, or some other set of values. The requirement verification status is updated to reflect the verification results from the test case execution.

As mentioned above, the method of verification includes inspection, analysis, demonstration, and testing. The test case definition and execution depends on the method of verification. For example, the method of verification for a system requirement that "The system shall weigh between 98 and 100 pounds" may be performed by testing or analysis. To verify the requirement by testing, a test case is defined to weigh the system on a scale and compare the measured weight against the required weight. To verify this requirement by analysis, the estimated weight of each component is summed to estimate the system weight. In the latter case, a parametric diagram may be used to verify the requirement by analysis.

To verify the requirement by analysis, an executable model can be used to represent the unit under test in place of the actual hardware or software. The results from executing the test case with the system model can be used to get early indications of requirements verification prior to building the hardware and software. In the very early stages of the system specification and design process, the system model can be used to validate that the system and component requirements satisfy the mission requirements. This may include use of a discrete event simulation such as fUML, as described in Chapter 9, Section 9.14. As the development progresses, more detailed component design models can be integrated with the system model to verify that the component designs satisfy the system requirements. There are many considerations for how to effectively leverage a system model to support this capability. Chapter 18 includes additional discussion on how SysML is used with a variety of simulation and analytical models that can be used to support requirements verification.

The execution of the test cases requires a verification environment to generate the stimulus and assess the response, and a unit under test to respond to the stimulus. The verification environment may include hardware, software, facilities, and personnel. In the next section, the application of OOSEM to model the verification environment is discussed.

17.3.9 DEVELOP ENABLING SYSTEMS

Enabling systems may need to be developed and/or modified to develop a complete capability that supports the entire system lifecycle. The enabling systems include the manufacturing system to produce the system, support systems such as support equipment to maintain the system, and verification systems to verify the system. These lifecycle considerations should be addressed early to avoid adverse impacts later. For example, if the manufacturing system capability is not considered early, the cost of producing the system may increase substantially due to imposing higher cost manufacturing methods. As a result, the enabling systems are developed concurrently with the operational system so that specific concerns, which may impact other parts of the lifecycle, are addressed early in the development process.

Figure 17.58 shows the processes for concurrent development of the ESS operational system with the ESS enabling systems for verification and installation. More generally, this process could include development of other enabling systems, such as the manufacturing system. The OOSEM method is applied to the development of the operational system in the previous sections. However, the method and associated artifacts can be tailored and applied to specify and design the enabling systems as well. For very complex enabling systems, the entire method may be applied. For simpler enabling systems, only selected aspects of the method may apply.

As an example, the verification system may be quite complex, such as when precision measurement equipment is required to verify the system. The requirements on the measurement equipment may be more stringent than the requirements on the operational system under test. If the measurement equipment is to be designed and developed, a rigorous application of OOSEM may be required, along with the application of the UML Testing Profile [50] to provide additional modeling constructs that are applicable to the test domain. In Figure 17.59, the *Verification Domain* includes the *Verification Context-Entry Detection* for the *Verify Entry Detection* test case that was shown in Figure 17.56. This supports the broader test objectives to verify intruders are detected. The test case is seen as an operation of

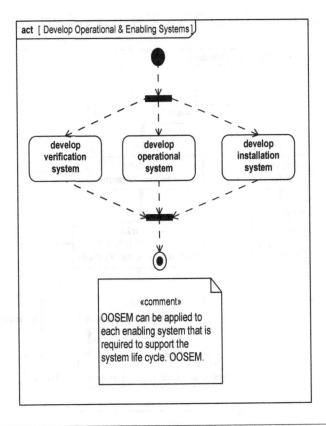

FIGURE 17.58

Concurrent development process of the operational system and enabling systems.

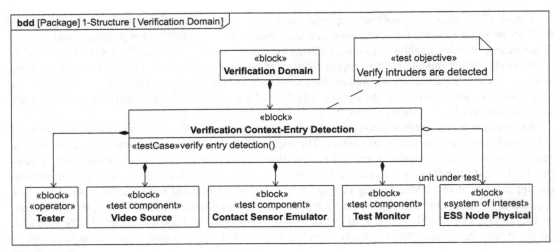

FIGURE 17.59

Block definition diagram of the *Verification Domain* to support design of the verification system.

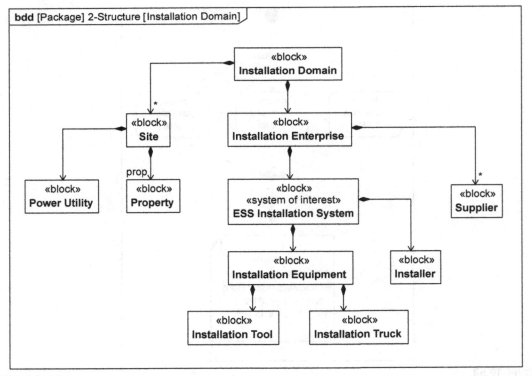

FIGURE 17.60

Installation Domain block definition diagram, a starting point for the specification and design of the *ESS Installation System.*

the *Verification Context* whose method is the activity diagram in Figure 17.57. The *Verification Context* includes the test components that are part of the verification system and references the unit under test. The *Verification Domain* block definition diagram is similar to the *Operational Domain* block definition diagram in Figure 17.12. OOSEM can be applied to develop the overall verification system using an approach similar to that applied to the specification and design of the operational system.

The *ESS Installation System* may be also complex and may warrant the application of OOSEM for its specification and design. The *Installation* package in Figure 17.5 contains the model elements that enable implementation of this part of the system lifecycle. The block definition diagram for the ESS *Installation Domain* is shown in Figure 17.60. The *Installation Enterprise* includes the *ESS Installation System* and external *Suppliers* that support the installation objectives, as defined by installation use cases. The *ESS Installation System* includes the *Installers* and their *Installation Equipment,* such as *Installation Truck*s and *Installation Tool*s. This serves as a starting point for specifying and designing the *ESS Installation System* in a similar way as the *Operational Domain* block definition diagram (in Figure 17.12), which was a starting point for the specification and design of the *ESS* operational system. The *Installation* package in Figure 17.5 has a similar structure of nested packages and contains modeling artifacts similar to those in the *Operational* package.

17.4 SUMMARY

The example described in this chapter illustrates how SysML is used as part of a model-based systems engineering method called OOSEM to solve a systems engineering problem. The top-down scenario-driven method is used to flow the requirements down from stakeholder needs to component-level specifications, which include hardware, software, persistent data, and operational procedures. The OOSEM approach includes analysis of stakeholder needs, analysis of black-box system requirements, definition of the logical architecture, synthesis of candidate physical architectures, and support of activities to optimize and evaluate alternatives and manage requirements traceability.

The method also supports the verification process in the up-side of the Vee development process and the development of other enabling systems such as the installation system. The approach illustrates how different aspects of the system are analyzed to address a multitude of concerns related to system functionality, interfaces, performance, distribution, lifecycle, and changes in requirements and technology, to develop a robust solution that satisfies the stakeholder needs.

OOSEM should be tailored to satisfy the particular project objectives and constraints by clearly defining the modeling objectives, scope, and tool and resource constraints. The tailoring involves selecting the level of rigor that is applied to each of the OOSEM activities, determining which modeling artifacts are generated and to what level of detail, and incorporating the activities and artifacts into the project schedule.

17.5 QUESTIONS

1. Develop the following artifacts for the *Provide Fire Emergency Response* use case shown in Figure 17.13.
   a. Provide Fire Emergency Response activity diagram (equivalent to Figure 17.15)
   b. Monitor Fire-ESS Logical activity diagram (equivalent to Figure 17.24)

2. The customer has introduced the following new requirement: "The ESS shall provide the ability to integrate with a fire-suppression system to extinguish fires when detected with minimal adverse impact to the property." Describe the impact of this new requirement on the system design by identifying the changes to each of the following modeling artifacts.

   a. ESS Requirements (Figure 17.55)
   b. Security Enterprise Use Cases (Figure 17.13)
   c. Provide Fire Emergency Response activity diagram (refer to response to Question 1a)
   d. System Context (Figure 17.17)
   e. ESS Black-Box Specification (Figure 17.19)
   f. *ESS Logical* Decomposition (Figure 17.23)
   g. *Monitor Fire-ESS Logical* activity diagram (refer to response to Question 1b)
   h. *ESS Logical* internal block diagram (Figure 17.25)
   i. *ESS Node Logical* block definition diagram (Figure 17.28 and Figure 17.29)
   j. *ESS Node Logical* Internal Block Diagram (Figure 17.31 and Figure 17.32)
   k. Allocation tables for logical components to hardware and logical components to software (Figure 17.33 and Figure 17.34)
   l. *Site Installation* internal block diagram (Figure 17.39)

3. How are the measures of effectiveness impacted by this requirements change?
4. How does this impact the top-level parametric diagram in Figure 17.11?
5. What additional types of analysis are required, and how can this be reflected in parametric diagrams?
6. Discuss how the preceding requirements change impacts the overall model, and how the model helps to address requirements change.

TRANSITIONING TO MODEL-BASED SYSTEMS ENGINEERING

Part IV addresses key considerations for transitioning to an MBSE approach with SysML. Chapter 18 describes how to integrate SysML into a systems development environment consisting of multi-disciplinary engineering tools. Chapter 19, the last chapter of the book, describes processes and strategies for deploying MBSE with SysML in an organization.

INTEGRATING SysML INTO A SYSTEMS DEVELOPMENT ENVIRONMENT

18

This chapter describes an approach and key considerations for integrating SysML with other models and tools in a systems development environment. This includes a discussion of the different kinds of models and their relationships, the different kinds of tools in a development environment, the logical interfaces between the system modeling tool and other tools in the development environment, configuration management concepts, approaches and applications for data exchange between tools, and criteria for selecting a SysML tool.

18.1 THE SYSTEM MODEL IN THE BROADER DEVELOPMENT CONTEXT

This section describes how the system model relates to other kinds of models, including other descriptive and analytical models and how a model relates to simulation.

18.1.1 THE SYSTEM MODEL AS AN INTEGRATING FRAMEWORK

As discussed in Chapter 2, Section 2.1.2, the system model is a primary artifact of model-based systems engineering (MBSE) and is an integral part of the technical baseline of the system. Any changes to the system requirements or design are reflected in the system model and propagated through the model artifacts, views, and other linkages to various stakeholders affected by the change. While this goal of MBSE is gaining broad acceptance across the industry [60], the specifics of how these artifacts, views, and linkages are established and maintained vary with different MBSE approaches.

The system model from Chapter 2 Figure 2.1, is depicted in Figure 18.1as an integrating framework for system development. The system model provides a consistent source of the system specification, design, analysis, and verification information, while maintaining traceability and rationale for key decisions. The information provides a context and critical input for more detailed hardware and software design and verification activities, which may also be model-based. In particular, the system model relates the text requirements to the system design, provides the system design information needed to support multi-disciplinary analysis, serves as a specification for the hardware and software design, and provides the test cases and related information needed to support verification. Each technical discipline—including mechanical, electrical, software, and test—elaborates the information contained in the system model with more detailed specification, design, analysis, and verification information. To ensure a cohesive overall representation of the system, traceability is maintained between the more detailed discipline-specific information and the information in the system model.

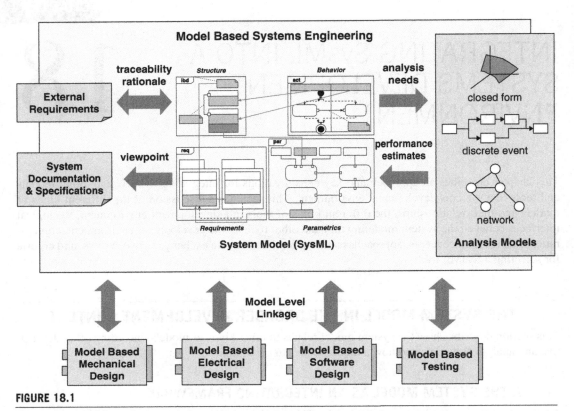

FIGURE 18.1

The system model as a framework for analysis and traceability.

18.1.2 KINDS OF MODELS IN THE SYSTEMS DEVELOPMENT ENVIRONMENT

As stated in Chapter 2, Section 2.2.1, a model is a representation of one or more concepts that may be realized in the physical world. Applying MBSE to the development of a system involves building models that represent the system and its environment. Different models are intended to describe various aspects of the system under development, and with varying degrees of fidelity. **A scale model** or **physical mockup** is a physical construction that can represent an actual system or other physical entity. A typical example is a scale model of a building, or a scale model of a vehicle that is used in a wind tunnel to determine its aerodynamic characteristics. On the other hand, **a symbolic model** is an abstraction of the system that is meant to be interpreted by humans and/or computers.

Figure 18.2 is a taxonomy of the various kinds of symbolic models that are referenced in this chapter. As described in Chapter 15, Section 15.2, these models are typically constructed using a formally defined modeling language that includes rules for abstract syntax, concrete syntax, and semantics. Some representative modeling languages are summarized in Chapter 1 Section 1.5. A further classification of symbolic models is discussed below, but it should be noted that any given model may include characteristics of more than one kind of symbolic model.

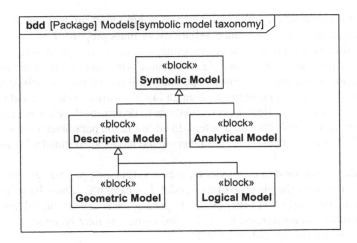

FIGURE 18.2

A taxonomy of models.

Descriptive models

A **descriptive model** describes a system or other entity and its relationship to its environment. It is generally used to help specify and/or understand what the system is, what it does, and how it does it.

A **geometric model** or **spatial model** is a descriptive model that represents geometric and/or spatial relationships. Mechanical three-dimensional computer aided design (CAD) models are geometric models that include detailed information, including dimensions, tolerances, and other descriptive data such as material characteristics. A 3D representation of land topography and other features that are often presented as maps and other visualizations is also a kind of spatial model.

A **logical model** is a descriptive model that primarily represents logical relationships and dependencies such as functional, connectivity, and traceability relationships. Examples of logical models include a circuit design model that describes electrical components and their interconnections, and a model of system composition such as a bill-of-materials.

The **system model** is a logical model that is introduced in Chapter 2 Section 2.1.2. This model captures the requirements, structure, behavior, and parametric constraints associated with a system and its environment, along with the relationships between these elements. As discussed throughout this book, SysML is a modeling language used to capture the system model. SysML supports various abstraction techniques and provides the ability to represent many different views of the system, such as a black-box view, white-box view, and a security view. The system model can also be queried and analyzed for different purposes, such as providing traceability analysis, assessing the completeness of the model, and validating model correctness.

Analytical models

An **analytical model** is primarily quantitative or computational in nature and represents the system in terms of a set of mathematical equations that specify parametric relationships and their associated parameter values as a function of time, space, and/or other system parameters. This is typically done by modeling the underlying phenomena to predict or assess how well the system performs or other system characteristics. Various kinds of analytical models are used to represent different aspects of the system and its environment, such as its performance, reliability, or mass properties.

An analytical model may represent parameter values that are a function of time, such as a model of vehicle dynamics, or parameter values that do not change with time, such as the mass properties or geometric characteristics of a static structure. The analytical model may be solved via a closed form solution such as the position of a point mass given an initial position, velocity, and constant acceleration. Other solutions require numerical analysis methods to determine the change in state of the system as a function of time, space, and other parameters. In addition, the parameter values may be deterministic or probabilistic. In the latter case, the parameters in the model are defined with an associated probability distribution.

The equations that are defined in the model must be a sufficiently precise representation of the system and environment to meet the purpose of the model. For example, it may be sufficient for a model of a spring-mass to include only first-order effects to predict the acceleration, velocity, and position of the mass, while in other circumstances, more detailed equations may be needed to provide a higher fidelity representation of some second-order affects.

The analysis results are expressed in terms of parameter values that are often functions of other parameters and time. The analysis results are presented in plots, tables, and other visualizations. Some example visualizations include response surfaces, spider charts, carpet plots, and others. Animation is a particular form of visualization that describes state changes of a system or other entity.

Relationship between model and simulation

A **simulation** of a system is a way to represent the system response as a function of time and space. A simulation can take many forms. For example, a simulation may be used to assess how well astronauts perform a particular task in a simulated weightless environment. In this example, the astronauts and the tools they use to perform their tasks are the real=world entities, but the environment is a simulated physical environment intended to represent the zero-gravity space environment.

The focus for this discussion is on computer simulations that simulate some aspect of the system and its environment. A **computer simulation** includes a **dynamic model** of the system and its environment, the initial conditions, a specification of how the external inputs to the system change over time, and an **execution environment** to execute the model. The dynamic model includes a set of equations which define how the system state changes over time, and requires numerical methods to determine the solution, rather than a **closed form solution**. A dynamic or other analytical model that is expressed sufficiently precise to be executed by an execution environment is sometimes called an **executable model**. This model is often expressed in a programming language such as Java or C++ that can be executed, or a higher-level modeling language that can be transformed to code. The execution environment applies the initial conditions to represent the initial state of the system and its environment, updates the external inputs to the system over time, and solves the equations expressed by the model to determine the change of state of the system and environment as a function of time. A model checker is usually used to validate the model and the initial conditions prior to starting the simulation.

As an example, a simulation of a robotic vacuum cleaner may be used to predict and assess the robot's cleaning performance over a wide range of trajectories and control algorithms. The simulation may include a model of the room that is being cleaned, such as a representation of the carpet, dust, and other obstacles, and a model of the robotic system that includes sensors, processors, and actuators that control the trajectory and cleaning actions. The simulation may represent how the robot cleans particular segments of the carpet given the initial conditions of the robot and the environment. A simulation may include the actual environment and/or actual hardware and software elements of the system in place of the corresponding part of the model. In other examples, the simulation may include actual or simulated operators that interact with the system.

There are many different classifications of simulation. A **system performance simulation** provides the capability for analysis of system behavior, resource consumption, and other physics-based phenomenology. The performance simulation may also include the capability to evaluate the stochastic nature of system performance (e.g., by providing a Monte Carlo capability). Data-analysis tools, sophisticated visualization tools, and animation may be used to present the results from executing the simulations.

A distributed simulation, such as the High-Level Architecture (HLA) standard [26], executes across a distributed execution environment. Simulations based on HLA require development of Federated Object Models (FOM), which represent individual simulation modules that can communicate with one another. The Run-Time Infrastructure (RTI) provides the computational environment to manage simulation time, publish/subscribe information exchange, coordinate messaging, and perform other features to coordinate the distributed simulation execution.

Other kinds of simulations are classified according to their characteristics, such as the form of the equations and/or how they are solved. For example, a discrete event simulation describes how the system responds to a sequence of events, whereas a continuous simulation solves a set of differential-algebraic equations or differential equations to describe the system response as a function of time. The simulations may be further classified in terms of whether the equations are solved using procedural or declarative (constraint-based) solvers. When the actual hardware or software is part of the simulation environment, the simulation is referred to as hardware-in-the-loop or software-in-the-loop simulations. Other references [61] elaborate the kinds of simulations and how they are used.

Further classification of models

As described earlier in this section, the different kinds of symbolic models are descriptive and analytical models. Descriptive models can be geometric or logical. The taxonomy shown in Figure 18.2 can be elaborated to include additional model classifications, such as models that represent technical, functional, and application domains. An example may be a model of an electrical design (technical domain) of a power subsystem (functional domain) of a vehicle system (application domain). A particular model can have multiple classifications, such as an electrical design model that represents a circuit layout (geometric), a circuit interconnection (logical), and/or a circuit analysis (analytical). This model taxonomy can be used to classify the diverse models in a systems development environment and assist in understanding their various roles.

18.1.3 RELATING DATA FROM DIFFERENT MODELS

The system model is generally used to represent multiple aspects of a system at a fairly abstract level. As discussed in Chapter 2, Section 2.1.2, the system model is often used to specify the system and its components down to some level of the system hierarchy. The system model is also used with other models that represent more detailed aspects of the system or may represent other aspects of the system not addressed by the system model. Since the information contained in the system model is often related to information in other models and data repositories, the consistency of the information across the different models and repositories must be maintained.

The relationship between the data contained in different models is illustrated in Figure 18.3. This figure shows a system model, a geometric design model (CAD), and an analytical model, along with a requirements repository and a configuration management repository. These models are all intended to represent various aspects of the same system. Data elements contained in the different models are indicated by the dots. The lines represent relationships between the data elements. The solid lines relate data elements contained within a single model (internal relationships), while the dashed lines relate data elements contained in different models (external relationships). An element in one model or database is said to be **equivalent** to an element in another model or data repository if the concepts they represent are intended to mean the same thing (i.e., are semantically equivalent).

These models are further highlighted with a particular *Vehicle* example in Figure 18.4. The requirements for *Vehicle Acceleration* and *Total Weight* are contained in the requirements management repository along with other requirements, such as *Engine Power* and *Engine Weight* (not shown). The requirements in the system model are equivalent to the requirements in the requirements management repository. The system model also represents the *Vehicle* and some of its properties, including *maxAcceleration* and *weight*. A satisfy relationship connects the *maxAcceleration* property and the *Vehicle Acceleration* requirement, and another satisfy relationship links the *weight* property and the *Total Weight* requirement. The system model shows the decomposition relationship of the *Vehicle* into the *Engine* and *Transmission*. The *Engine* contains a *maxPower* and *weight* property. An instance specification *veh01:Vehicle* provides a particular specification of values for these properties.

The values of *maxPower* for this instance of the *Engine* in the system model are intended to be equivalent to the values of *Est Power* in the 3D CAD model. The value of the *maxAcceleration* in this instance of the *Vehicle* in the system model is intended to be equivalent to the *Max Acceleration* property value in the analysis model. In this example, the analytical model is assumed to be the authoritative source for the maximum acceleration value, such that the value of *maxAcceleration* in the system model is updated to reflect the *Max Acceleration* parameter in the analytical model. Note that additional parameter values are required for the analytical model to calculate *Max Acceleration*, some of which may be derived from the system model—such as the initial weight of the fuel (not shown)—and from other sources. The sources may include other analytical models, such as a model that calculates the total weight of the vehicle based

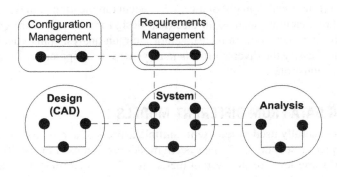

FIGURE 18.3

Relationships between data elements within and between models and repositories.

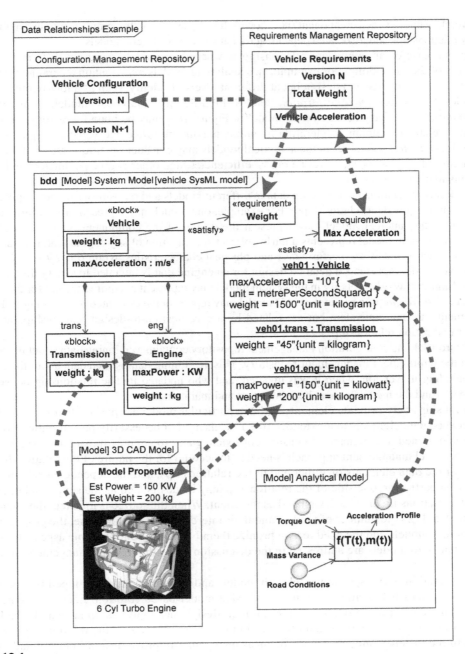

FIGURE 18.4

Equivalent relationships between system modeling and other models.

on the weight values of each component (not shown). It is evident from this simple example that there can be many relationships and associated dependencies between the different models.

A special case of an equivalent relationship is where two models represent different levels of abstraction of the same thing. For example, two analytical models may contain a parameter that represents the same property of a design but at different levels of fidelity, such as a low-fidelity analytical model to predict *maxAcceleration* and a high-fidelity analytical model. Similarly, the *maxAcceleration* property in the system model in Figure 18.4 may be bound to a very simple constraint that relates maximum acceleration to engine maximum torque and vehicle weight, where as the *Max Acceleration* parameter in the analytical models may consider the torque curve of the engine as a function of engine speed, driveline ratios, efficiencies, and other engine parameters and driving conditions that vary over time.

Other kinds of relationships between data in different models and repositories do not imply equivalence (i.e., non-equivalent relationships). For example, one model may represent the requirements for a component, and another model may represent the design of the component. In Figure 18.04, the *Engine* in the system model represents a fairly abstract specification of key engine features, such as its interfaces, functions, and key performance and physical characteristics, while *6 Cyl Turbo Engine* in the 3D CAD model represents a detailed design for an engine that is intended to satisfy this specification. The Engine's *weight* property in the system model may represent a required weight for the *Engine*, whereas the *Est Weight* property in the CAD model may represent the estimated design weight. The two data elements are not equivalent but are related by a specification-to-design relationship, such as a satisfy or realization relationship.

In Figure 18.4, the configuration management repository contains versioning data about the requirements in the requirement management repository. This versioning data is metadata about the requirement, including its version, when it was updated, and who updated it. The relationship between the requirements and the metadata must be established and maintained.

Relationships between data elements within a particular model are part of the model. Relationships between data elements that extend across models are not necessarily part of either model but must be maintained and managed to ensure consistency and to support impact assessment across models. A model management approach is needed to account for the nature of the relationships, the meaning of the data elements on either end of the relationships, and the dependencies between the elements. In particular, one side of the relationship may be designated as the source, and the other side of the relationship may be designated as the client. When the source is updated, the client must also be updated. As the number of models and their interdependencies increase, the propagation of change across models and the need to synchronize them become essential. Some aspects of managing this change to models are addressed in the discussion on configuration management in Section 18.2.3.

The integration of the system model with models and structured data developed by other engineering disciplines is essential to ensure a cohesive model-based solution. Each discipline relies on developing descriptive models to represent their design and analytical models and simulations to support performance analysis and other design decisions. Managing the relationships between the data in the different models reduce inconsistencies that improve design integrity and quality, and reduce impact analysis cycle times. The data interfaces between a system modeling tool and other system development tools must maintain these data relationships, and are discussed in Sections 18.2.2.

18.2 SPECIFYING AN INTEGRATED SYSTEMS DEVELOPMENT ENVIRONMENT

The term **systems development environment** refers to the tools and repositories used by teams to develop systems from concept through the final verification and validation of a delivered system. Typical tools may include system modeling tools; hardware and software design and development tools; simulation and analysis tools; test tools; requirements management; configuration management; and project management tools. The tools and repositories are computer-based, multi-user, networked applications supported by a computing and network infrastructure. An integrated systems development environment implies some logical connectivity between these tools and repositories to support collaborative engineering.

Establishing an integrated systems development environment requires the application of a systems engineering approach in its own right. The full lifecycle of the systems development environment should be considered, from its initial procurement, through installation and configuration, operation, and maintenance. Architecting the system's development environment should include a definition of its interfaces and the standards required to support them. This section specifies an integrated systems development environment in terms of the kinds of tools in the environment, their functionality, and the information exchange between them. The information exchange must preserve the data relationships among the different models as discussed in Section 18.1.3. Section 18.3 describes the mechanisms and approaches for exchanging this information, and Section 18.4 includes examples of integrating a system modeling tool with other standards-based tools.

18.2.1 TOOLS IN A SYSTEMS DEVELOPMENT ENVIRONMENT

A systems development environment includes a wide spectrum of modeling tools and other applications. The kinds of models can be classified by the taxonomy described in Section 18.1.2. A modeling tool is used to create, modify, store, present, exchange, and analyze a model, and check its validity. Modeling tools may support different standard and nonstandard mechanisms to exchange their modeling information.

This section defines a set of roles for tools to support system development. The tool roles describe the kind of functionality a tool provides without reference to a particular vendor implementation. A particular vendor implementation may support all or part of one or more tool roles. For example, a particular vendor implementation may support both systems modeling in SysML and some analytical modeling. For the remainder of the section, the term tool is used to reflect a tool role.

Figure 18.5 depicts an environment that integrates multiple kinds of tools that support different parts of a system development process, such as system specification and design, hardware and software development, system integration and verification, and project management activities. (Refer to the system development process in Chapter 17, Section 17.1.2.) The tools in this environment create and maintain system models, as well as mechanical, electrical, and software design models, simulation and analysis models, and verification models. Other tools provide support for requirements management, configuration and data management, project management, and document and view generation. There may be many other tools within a particular development environment that support other discipline specific activities, but this tool classification provides a representative set. These tools are summarized below.

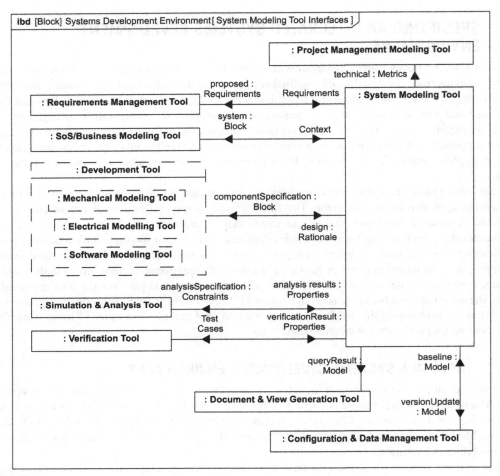

FIGURE 18.5

High level information exchange between the system modeling tool and other tools.

Project Management tools support planning, assessment, and control of the overall development effort to manage cost, schedule, and technical performance. These tools also include workflow engines to control the execution of the development process, such as orchestrating assignment of tasks and approval of deliverables.

System-of-systems modeling tools support SoS, enterprise, and business process modeling. They may include support for architecture frameworks such as DoDAF and MODAF, using modeling languages such as the Unified Profile for DoDAF/MODAF (UPDM) and the Business Process Modeling Notation (BPMN).

System modeling tools support development of the system model as described in Section 18.1.2. This is assumed to be a SysML modeling tool.

Simulation and analysis tools support trade-off analysis, sensitivity analysis, optimization, characterization, and prediction at all levels of design. These tools provide a range of execution environments and solvers to support specialized analysis (e.g., performance, reliability, safety, security, cost, mass properties analysis), and design integrity checking.

Requirements management tools generate, trace, track, and report text-based requirements and assemble them into specification documents.

Mechanical modeling tools are used to design, implement, and test the mechanical aspects of systems and components and includes two- and/or three-dimensional CAD modeling, and may include the modeling of materials, geometric dimensioning and tolerancing, and manufacturing process design. The mechanical modeling tools are supported by many different simulation and analysis tools to analyze the mechanical aspects of a design, including mass properties, stress, dynamics, and thermal characteristics.

Electrical modeling tools are used to design, implement, and test the electronic aspects of systems and components, and include circuit design/schematic capture, circuit layout, Field Programmable Gate Array (FPGA) design, and manufacturing process design. The electrical modeling tools are supported by many different simulation and analysis tools to analyze electrical designs, including power, grounding, signals, and data.

Software modeling tools are used to design, implement, and test software components and may include UML modeling tools, compilers, debuggers, and other tools that are part of an integrated software development environment. The OMG's Model Driven Architecture (MDA) approach to software development relies on capturing and maintaining the technical baseline of the software product in a model, generating code from this model, and synchronizing changes to the model with changes to the code.

A specialized class of software tools supports Real-Time Embedded (RTE) system development. Examples of RTE modeling languages include the Modeling and Analysis of Real Time and Embedded systems (MARTE) UML profile [62], and the SAE Architecture Analysis and Design Language (AADL) standard [27]. The software modeling tools are supported by many different simulation and analysis tools to analyze software designs, including scheduling, real-time performance analysis, and complexity analysis.

Software modeling can also support design of information intensive systems that include conceptual, logical, and physical database design to store, query, and synchronize data.

Verification tools are used to verify requirements are satisfied at each level of the system hierarchy, from SoS down to component level,throughout the lifecycle of system development. The verification tools address the breadth of requirements that include functional, interface, performance, physical, and environmental requirements, to name a few. The tools may support different methods of verification, including inspection, analysis, demonstration, and test. The verification environment can include tools that range from simple drivers to stimulate a component and assess its response, to complex facilities and equipment such as an environmental test facility to verify the vibration, shock, temperature, and end-of-life requirements for a system or component.

For this discussion, we assume validation tools may be a kind of verification tool. However, validation tools must support a broad range of validation methods, some of which are not typically associated with verification. For example, validation methods can include reviewing requirements with the stakeholders to ensure their needs are being addressed and conducting an operational test in an actual environment to determine how well the system addresses the user needs. The latter is an example of verification, whereas the former is not.

Document and view generation tools are used to generate documentation of the system specification and design. In a model-based environment, the documentation presents different views of the system that are generated by querying the model on demand and presenting the results in a form that is useful to the consumers of the information.

Configuration and data management tools ensure that the models and associated development artifacts—such as specifications, design, analyses, and verification artifacts—are maintained in a controlled fashion. Product data management tools encompass configuration and data management tools that manage the full lifecycle of technical data needed to specify product configurations.

18.2.2 INTERFACES BETWEEN THE SYSTEM MODELING TOOL AND OTHER TOOLS

Figure 18.5 is an internal block diagram of an integrated systems development environment emphasizing the logical connections between the system modeling tool and the other kinds of tools summarized in the previous section. Since the focus is on the interface with the system modeling tool, the connections between the other kinds of tools are not shown.

The information that is exchanged across the connections is intended to preserve the data relationships between the models as discussed in Section 18.1.3. The typical information exchanged between the system modeling tool and the other kinds of tools are also shown in Figure 18.5 and discussed below. The exchanges depicted in the figure are at a summary level but provide a starting point for defining more detailed interfaces for a specific environment. The mechanisms for how the information can be exchanged are discussed in Section 18.3.

Interface with requirements management tool

Figure 18.5 shows the data interface between the *System Modeling* tool and a *Requirements Management* tool, which includes the exchange of requirements and/or their relationships. This can be a one- or two-way exchange of information that is highly process dependent, and is a function of which tool is designated as the source of the requirements and which tool is the client.

A typical approach within a systems development environment is to capture some subset of the requirements from the *Requirements Management* tool in the *System Modeling* tool, along with a set of links that establish the equivalence relationship. The *System Modeling* tool is used to propose updates to requirements, but they are formally updated and controlled in the *Requirements Management* tool. The derive relationship (i.e., *deriveReqt*) between requirements is maintained in the *Requirements Management* tool because this relationship is only between text-based requirements. Other requirements relationships, such as satisfy, verify, and refine relationships between the requirements and the other model elements, are maintained in the *System Modeling* tool. The requirements and relationships in both tools are synchronized to maintain their equivalence.

Interface with SoS/business models and tools

Figure 18.5 shows the data interface between the *System Modeling* tool and a *SoS/Business Modeling* tool. The SoS modeling tool provides the context for the system under development and the needs of each stakeholder. The system model defines the system and how it meets the needs.

Architecture frameworks provide a structure for describing these contexts and needs. Modeling languages like UPDM [23] directly support these frameworks. UPDM also leverages SysML for its foundation, which facilitates the integration between the SysML model and the UDPM model. The integration can be achieved by using common model elements that participate in both the *SoS* and *System Model* or by maintaining separate models with equivalence relationships between them.

Interface with development models and tools

A principal reason for developing a system model is to specify the requirements and constraints on the system's components, which typically includes hardware (and equipment) and software. The interfaces between the *System Modeling* tool and hardware and software development tools are critical. In particular, the *System Modeling* tool provides the component specifications to hardware and software *Engineering Development* tools, which in turn provide design data that demonstrate how the hardware and software design models satisfy the specifications.

Figure 18.5 depicts the kinds of information that flow between a *System Modeling* tool and *Software Modeling*, *Mechanical Modeling*, and *Electrical Modeling* tools. In each case, the *System Modeling* tool provides component specifications specific to that domain, as well as the system context for the specification. The interface from the *System Modeling* tool to the development tools may be expressed as blocks that represent component black-box specifications with their ports, functions/operations, and value properties (refer to Chapter 17, Section 17.3.5, under *Specify Component Requirements*). The black-box specification can be accompanied by text-based requirements that are related through a refine relationship. In response, *Software Modeling*, *Mechanical Modeling*, and *Electrical Modeling* tools provide the relationships between their designs and their requirements with rationales, along with issues that need to be addressed.

Software development

For software development environments using UML, the interface between the *System Modeling* tool and the UML *Software Modeling* tool is dependent on the specific model-based methods employed, even though the underlying language concepts have the same roots. The software specifications from the SysML model are input to the UML modeling tool to realize the software design. The component black-box specification from the system model is mapped to corresponding elements in the software development model to maintain traceability of the design (Note: this may be an allocate or realize relationship).

As discussed in Section 18.1.2, simulation and analytical tools can be used to specify and analyze performance of systems. Some of these tools can capture both hardware processing constraints and the algorithm design implemented in software, and some can be used to automatically generate code from the model.

Mechanical hardware development

The foundation mechanical model is the geometric model from a 3D CAD tool. The interface between the *System Modeling* tool and the 3D CAD tool is generally accomplished indirectly through the product data management (PDM) application. In particular, the PDM application manages the configuration in terms of a parts breakdown or a bill-of-materials (BOM). The PDM tool maintains relationships between the parts and their corresponding CAD files. The system elements from the system breakdown in SysML can be mapped to corresponding parts in the bill-of-materials. The black-box specifications can then specify requirements for the mechanical design, including functionality, mechanical interface, key properties, and environmental requirements. Physical constraints expressed in the *System Modeling* tool can be analyzed with mechanical simulation and analysis tools that include mass properties, stress, dynamics, and thermal analysis.

Virtual mock-up capability that includes 3D animations has become increasingly important for validating manufacturing process and usability requirements. Maintaining linkage between the system model and the corresponding mechanical parts that are animated in the virtual mockup can help bridge user-to-product-to-process requirements traceability.

Electrical hardware development

Elements in the *System Modeling* tool that are associated with the electrical design, such as sensors, actuators, processors, busses, controllers, and networks, are mapped to the corresponding elements in the *Electrical Modeling* tools (e.g., Electrical Computer Aided Design [ECAD] or Computer Aided Engineering [CAE]) using a approach similar to that described for mechanical hardware development. The black-box specifications in the system model can specify electrical interfaces and behaviors, including off-nominal behaviors. Electrical performance and power constraints expressed in the *System Modeling* tool can be analyzed with electrical simulation and analysis tools.

Interface with simulations and analysis tools

As discussed in 18.1.2, the system model is a descriptive model that describes logical relationships among the system, such as whole–part, connectivity, and information flow. Analyzing the system to ensure it satisfies its requirements requires suitably detailed and accurate analytical models and simulations. The system modeling tool can be integrated with simulation and analysis tools by providing critical system specification and design information needed by the analytical models. The nature of the integration can vary significantly depending on the kind of information being exchanged as summarized below.

Although system models expressed in SysML are descriptive, the semantics for a subset of SysML models can be executed when supported by an execution environment. One example is the execution semantics of activities described in Chapter 7, Section 7.9. When the model is executed, the sequencing of actions, input/output, message flow, and state changes can be animated. The simulation can be executed using pre-scripted scenarios, or it can react to specific user interaction (e.g., "toggle this input and see what happens"). In this way, system behavior expressed in SysML can provide significant information to help validate functional and interface requirements, perform what-if behavior analysis, and explore user interaction concepts.

The behavior of the system or component may need to be further specified in terms of differential equations to analyze performance and other critical aspects of the design. A system model in SysML can be integrated with other analytical models using SysML parametrics to capture constraints and their parameters. For these cases, a portion of the system model in SysML must be expressed precisely enough for analysis to be performed. This is often done with extensions specified as profiles and/or by using opaque constructs that encapsulate statements in other languages.

The system model is often intended to represent a higher level of abstraction without capturing the detailed properties and equations. Although the system model captures critical performance and physical properties, it is generally not the intent, for example, to capture all the detailed thermal properties and equations needed to perform a high fidelity thermal analysis. There are tools much better suited for this that have the appropriate constructs to express the details of this analysis domain. In this case, the portion of the system model that represents the abstract information relevant to the analysis can be extracted, transformed, and augmented with the necessary details in the analytical model before the analysis is performed in the analytical tool. In some cases, the relevant part of the system model is a specification of the input and output parameters of the analysis. For this case, the input and output parameters of the analysis are bound to the properties of the design using SysML parametrics.

Some SysML tools include equation solvers that can operate on parametric models directly, thus integrating the system model and analytical model in the same tool. Third-party plug-ins are also available to enable a SysML parametric model to interface with external math solvers and other analytical tools.

If the system structure is modified, the analytical model must be correspondingly modified to reflect this change in structure. A simple example is a system model that represents a system with two assemblies. The weight analysis model can roll up the weights of the two assemblies by simply adding the weight of assembly one to the weight of assembly two. If the weight of one assembly changes in the system model, the weight analysis model can roll up the change in the total weight of the system. If a third assembly is added to the system model, however, the analytical model does not automatically account for the weight of the third assembly in the total weight calculation unless the analytical model is updated to reflect this new structure. The analytical model must be maintained consistent with the structure captured in the system model. A transformation can be performed to update the models each time one of the models change. An example is the SysML to Modelica Transformation that transforms the system model in SysML to a Modelica model that can be executed by a Modelica execution environment (refer to Section 18.4.1).

In all the above approaches for integrating SysML models with other analytical models, the analysis results may be returned to the system model to reflect the updated property values.

The SysML concept of viewpoint described in Chapter 15, Section 15.8, can be used to describe the purpose, stakeholders, and concerns that a particular analytical model should address. The viewpoint can also expose the relevant portion of the system model that is used to support the analysis problem. It can further specify which modeling language and tool is intended to be used to perform the analysis, and specify which view artifacts are needed to conform to the viewpoint.

Interface with verification tools

As shown in Figure 18.5, the *System Modeling* tool can provide to the *Verification* tool the context, test cases, and associated requirements to be verified for the specific system configuration under test. The system model can also provide related information to specify the verification environment and verification plans, as discussed in Chapter 17, Sections 17.3.8 and 17.3.9. Verification results can be provided to update the *System Modeling* tool with verification status.

Interface with project management tools

Effective program and technical management of a complex project may require information from all models and tools used in the systems development environment. Project management can leverage information from the system model to assist in planning and controlling the technical effort. The model-based metrics described in Chapter 2, Section 2.2.5, are examples of metrics that can be extracted from the system model to assess design quality, help track status, and support estimates of cost, schedule, and technical performance. The metrics can be automatically reported from the model, typically by using the scripting capability of a given tool.

Extensions to SysML can be specified to provide further support to project management. This may include capturing process information in terms of activities being performed and their associated deliverables, milestones, organizational roles, and work packages. The addition of a work package stereotype can facilitate traceability between the work performed and the system specification and design. Some project management extensions are already included in UPDM and other profiles, such as project, organization, milestone, and others. An executable model of the development process can be integrated with workflow engines to help automate the development process.

Interface with documentation and view generation tools

Document and View Generation tools are used to prepare and manage documentation of the system. Documents and tabular data are a traditionally effective means for organizing and communicating system specification and design information to the stakeholder community (e.g., customers, managers, design engineers, test engineers).

Figure 18.5 shows the information exchanged between the *System Modeling* tool and a *Document Generation* tool. SysML View and Viewpoint mechanisms are used to query the system model for the desired information and then pass this information to a rendering tool to present the information in the desired format. This may include a combination of textual, tabular, and graphical formats in a variety of different media (e.g., HTML). In addition to reporting the information from the model, additional capabilities can enable comments and updates of the model information from an external application—such as a web client—to facilitate broader use of the modeling information.

Many SysML tools include some inherent document-generation capability, including web publishing of the model in HTML format. Additional document and view generation capability is required to effectively span multiple models and sources of information, providing more complete and extensive views of the system design information. An approach to document and view generation that integrates with a typical system modeling tool is described in Section 18.4.5.

Interface with configuration and data management tools

The *Configuration and Data Management Tools* manage changes to the baseline technical data generated by the systems development environment throughout the system development lifecycle. This requires that the data be versioned at some level of granularity. Updates and access to the data are controlled by these tools. Figure 18.5 shows the typical information exchanged between a *System Modeling* tool and the *Configuration and Data Management* tool. The Configuration and Data Management tools provide baseline technical data to the system model, and the system model provides model updates to these tools. The concepts for configuration management as it applies to a model-based environment are discussed in Section 18.2.3.

18.2.3 USING CONFIGURATION MANAGEMENT TOOLS TO MANAGE MODEL VERSIONS

Configuration Management (CM) tools ensure that models and other development artifacts (e.g., specifications, plans, analyses, test results) are maintained in a controlled fashion, such that the latest version can always be identified. CM tools also enable the impact of each update to be considered. The content of the model is managed, along with related artifacts that may be produced from the model and the tool configuration that is used to create the model.

The focus for this section is on managing changes to the system model, where one or more modelers are making changes to the model at any given time. The complexity increases with the number of modelers and the frequency of changes, along with the number and kind of relationships between the parts of the model that are being modified. Managing updates establishes a common baseline of the system model and enables the impact of changes to be properly considered as the design evolves.

The more general scope of model management deals with updates and synchronization of different kinds of models and tools across a distributed development environment to ensure consistency of information. This broader challenge must account for the propagation of changes across different models based on the data relationships that are described in Section 18.1.2. Data exchange between models is a prerequisite to enabling effective model management. Data exchange mechanisms and applications are discussed in Sections 18.3 and 18.4.

Functions and tools for managing configurations

A configuration management environment typically fulfills three functions as part of a systems development environment:

- Manage the artifacts (often called configuration items) being developed, including controlling access to the current working set of artifacts (often called a configuration), and archiving versions of the working set (called baselines). Tools that fulfill this function are typically called **configuration management tools.**
- Manage changes to the working set, including enforcing a consistent change control process (e.g., one based on change requests) and analyzing the impact of changes to configuration items. Tools that fulfill this function are typically called **change management tools** and often incorporate configuration management functions.
- Ensure that products built from a project baseline are complete and consistent, including the identification of different variants of system components and the compatibility between them. This supports the identification of valid variant configurations and the associated bills-of-materials that are maintained throughout the product lifecycle. Tools that fulfill this function are typically called **Product Data Management tools.** They often incorporate both change management and configuration management functions.

Each of these tools stores additional data (often called metadata) about configuration items, such as their dependencies and compatibility with each other. Product data may also contain metadata, such as a part in a bill-of-materials that contains its version, requiring that the product data and configuration metadata be kept consistent.

The CM environment establishes a valid configuration by identifying a consistent set of versions of configuration items that are maintained by the different tools in the development environment. Any given tool operates on a version of configuration items that is identified by the CM environment. In practice, some tools perform both roles by identifying the version and operating on the version of configuration items.

Maintaining a model configuration

A configuration management challenge that models introduce over more traditional non-model-based artifacts is the need to maintain the fine-grain data relationships between model elements in different models as described in Section 18.1.3. This can impact the level of resolution at which configuration items are identified to be versioned and controlled. For a system model in SysML, two obvious candidates are the various kinds of packages—including models, model libraries, and profiles—and the various kinds of definitions—such as blocks and activities.

When considering packages as configuration items, a project needs a policy covering how to handle package hierarchies. The simplest approach is to treat only the top level of packages in a model as configuration items. This has the advantage of having none of the configuration items contain other configuration items. On a large project, however, this results in a flat model structure with a large number of packages at the top level of the model, making it more difficult to understand, navigate, and control. It can also lead to configuration items that become very large, making it difficult to partition work among engineers. As a result, hierarchical configuration items with a combination of packages and other model elements are often required on larger projects.

An OMG standard called MOF Versioning [63] offers a framework for configuration management of models to address the challenges posed above. Figure 18.6 shows the concept of a *Workspace*, which is used by a team or individual to manage their model data. A *Workspace* contains a collection of *configurations* and *versionedExtents*. A *VersionedExtent* is equivalent to a configuration item in traditional configuration management and refers to a set of model elements. (Note: it provides a query that returns the collection of elements.) The *VersionedExtent* can have different levels of granularity. For example, it can refer to a package and all the model elements contained in the package, or it can refer to a block and all the model elements contained in the block.

A *Configuration* identifies a set of compatible *VersionedExtents* that together comprise some significant set of model elements. The *Configuration* does not refer to the model elements directly but only identifies the set of *VersionedExtents*.

A *VersionedExtent* can also be a *Configuration* that identifies one or more of its elements as a *VersionedExtent*. In this way, configurations can be hierarchical. An example is a parent *VersionedExtent* that refers to a package and its contents, and a child *VersionedExtent* that refers to a nested package and its contents. Both the parent and child are also configurations.

The previous contents of *VersionedExtents* are stored as *Versions*, and the previous contents of *Configurations* are stored as *Baselines*. These versioning concepts define operations to manage the history

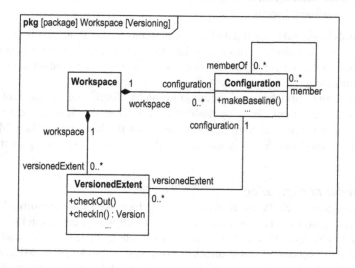

FIGURE 18.6

A workspace in the MOF Versioning specification.

of *VersionedExtent*s and Configurations. The *checkOut* operation on *VersionedExtent* makes it editable; the *checkIn* operation creates a new *Version* by taking a snapshot of its current state. The *makeBaseline* operation on *Configuration* creates a new *Baseline* from all the current *Versions* of all the *VersionedExtents* in the *Configuration*.

Figure 18.7 shows versioning of both *VersionedExtents* and *Configurations*. A *VersionHistory* contains a collection of *versions* for a *VersionedExtent*, one of which is the initial version called the *rootVersion*. Any *Version* may have any number of *previousVersions* to support branches due to long-term variants or short-term parallel development. The *baseVersion* of the *VersionedExtent* is the *Version* that holds the most recent copy of its contents. Just as a *Configuration* identifies a set of *VersionedExtents*, a *Baseline* of a *Configuration* identifies a set of versions of those *VersionedExtents* that are claimed to represent a complete and consistent set for the *Configuration*. The current source of a *Configuration* in its *Baseline* collection is called its *baseline*. As can be seen, the pattern for a *Baseline* is similar to that for a *Version,* allowing *Baselines* to also have a history to represent all of the important states of a *Configuration*. *Baselines* can have branches to represent variants and parallel development. *Baselines* can also be *members* of other *Baselines* which supports the archival of hierarchical *Configurations*.

The organization of the system model is discussed in Chapter 6. Typical model organizations are also included in the examples in Chapter 16, Section 16.3, and Chapter 17, Section 17.3.1. As noted above, packages are often used to partition the model and serve as a unit of configuration control. For large projects, the development team accesses and updates a dedicated part of the model that it controls. The *Configuration Management* tool controls changes to the model by controlling access to the model elements through check-out/check-in or read-only access. The configuration management tool also ensures that each package is appropriately versioned as model elements are updated. It typically retains these versions in a *Repository*.

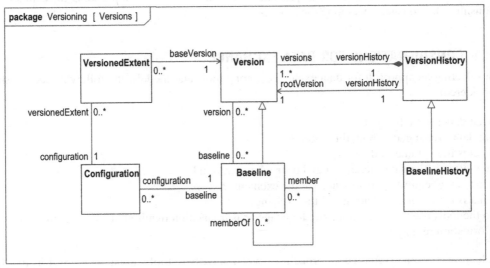

FIGURE 18.7

How versions and baselines work in the MOF Versioning specification.

Successful systems engineering on large projects requires disciplined management of technical baselines. The development and ongoing update of the technical baseline spans all the information in the systems development environment and requires configuration management environments to control this information.

Updates to the technical baseline must be reviewed and assessed to understand the impact of proposed changes on the rest of the baseline. The *System Modeling* tool can be used to assess change impacts and to query the model and generate reports of the impact. For example, if a requirement changes, the internal relationships within the system model can be navigated to identify the impacted elements. External relationships to data in other models and repositories can be navigated through external links to assess the impact on the other models and tools. Approaches for integrating the system modeling tool with other modeling tools is discussed in Sections 18.3 and 18.4.

18.3 DATA EXCHANGE MECHANISMS

Section 18.2 discussed the kinds of tools in a systems development environment and the information that is typically exchanged among them. When a model is updated—and the model has data relationships with other models—a **data exchange** may be required to maintain the consistency of the information among the different models. This exchange can be manual, automated, or a combination of the two.

A simple example of related information contained in different models is described in Section 18.1.2 and Figures 18.3 and 18.4. One set of the relationships is between the weight properties in the system model and the corresponding parameters in an analytical model or CAD model. The system model from the system modeling tool contains a weight property for the system and for each component, and an analytical tool computes the weight of the system based on the weights of each component. This section discusses standards and approaches for data exchange between tools to maintain these relationships and consistency among the models.

18.3.1 CONSIDERATIONS FOR DATA EXCHANGE

When selecting an approach for data exchange among tools and models, the following factors should be considered:

- What data are exchanged?
- Are data exchanged in both directions?
- What is the volume of data?
- How often is the data exchanged and over what duration?
- What is the required performance for the exchange?
- What is the required reliability of the exchange?
- Do the tools use the same modeling language or is translation required? If so, is additional information required?

Selecting a data exchange approach between any two tools must account for the long-term value of the tool integration in terms of efficiencies and quality versus the cost of implementation.

The data exchange mechanism

Exchange of data between tools in a systems development environment may be accomplished using the following exchange mechanisms:

- Manual exchange involving re-entering the data from one tool into another tool;
- File-based exchange using a proprietary file format or standard exchange format (e.g., XMI); or
- Interaction-based exchange using APIs.

In a file-based approach, a mapping from the domain language to a file format is defined, and tools declare their ability to write and/or read files in that format. In an API-based approach, the domain language is mapped to a set of API calls that the tool exposes to read and/or write to the model.

Direction of exchange

Data exchange may be either unidirectional or bidirectional. The exchange may be unidirectional when one side of the exchange is designated as the supplier of the data and the other side is designated as the client. This may be driven by process or by the assumption that the supplier side is the more accurate source of the data. For this case, the client side is updated to be consistent with the supplier side. Generator tools, such as code generators or document generators, are typically unidirectional from the model to the code or document. Data exchange between modeling tools—such as between a system modeling tool and an analytical modeling tool—may be bidirectional based on relationships between model elements. This provides the ability for the system modeling tool to provide input parameter values to support the analysis, and for the analytical tool to return analysis results back to the system modeling tool. The term **round-tripping** is used to describe bidirectional exchange between two tools that both modify the same data via their equivalence relationships.

Transformations

A transformation is necessary to support data exchange when the languages on the two sides of the exchange are different. The transformation involves mapping concepts between the two languages, which may be applied in one or both directions. The two languages may have similar concepts, in which case something close to a one-to-one mapping may be possible. In such a case, a transformation simply needs to translate from one modeling language to the other. Bidirectional exchange is relatively straightforward in this case.

Alternatively, one language may be more abstract than the other. When the language of the data source is more abstract, a source concept might map to a set of target concepts to establish the equivalence. For example, a state transition in state machine may map to many lines of code that may correspond to classes in a language like C++. When the data source is more concrete than the target, additional data are required to determine what the corresponding target concept should be. A common example is when the source is a programming language and the target is a modeling language. For example, the transformation may require the addition of comments in the code to support the mapping from some C++ classes to UML classes.

In round-tripping scenarios (transformations from model to code and from code back to the model), the model may need to include comments that are added to the code. For example, the transformation of an entry action on a state machine may need to include a comment to be added to the code. The comment contains information that can be used when transforming from the code back to the state machine.

Data exchange architecture

Exchange of model data may be achieved either by a point-to-point connection between two tools or through a shared repository. Point-to-point exchange between two tools is easiest when both tools conform to the same standard for data exchange (e.g., a common file format or API). When the two tools do not share a common standard, the exchange may be accomplished using a **bridge** or other interface software application.

Another approach is to use some intermediate shared repository of information. Such a **repository** is often a configuration-managed database, accessible to two or more tools, which holds data that the tools share. Repositories generally support multiple file or API standards to enable integration with many different tools. Maintaining systems engineering data in a repository enables the use of consistency checkers on the entire repository data rather than relying on consistency checkers in the individual tools. Repositories that maintain this kind of systems engineering data can publish a metadata catalog, allowing other tools access to both the data and their meaning.

18.3.2 FILE-BASED EXCHANGE

The exchange of data between modeling tools has traditionally been accomplished by creating a bridge between individual tools using the mechanisms described earlier. This can be costly, because each tool pairing requires its own interface mechanism. Implementing point-to-point interfaces can require the development of n^2 interfaces for n tools. In addition, the interface mechanism must be updated as each tool changes. The emphasis for an integrated systems development environment is on the use of data exchange and other modeling standards to support tool and model interoperability. Some of the relevant standards related to SysML are discussed next.

XML metadata interchange

XMI is short for eXtensible Markup Language (XML) Metadata Interchange [29], a standard format for exchanging UML and SysML models between tools. The XMI for SysML is based on three industry standards: XML, the Meta Object Facility (MOF) [24], and UML [52]. UML and MOF are modeling and metadata repository standards from the Object Management Group (OMG). XML is a text-based language from the World Wide Web Consortium (W3C) that supports the use of tags to describe structured data. XMI is in essence a set of rules for converting a metamodel expressed using MOF, UML, and UML profiles into a set of custom tags in XML. Hence SysML, which is a UML profile, also has implicit data exchange standards using XMI. This in turn enables a SysML model to be exchanged as an XMI file. The OMG's Model Interchange Working Group [64] established test cases to demonstrate and enhance the quality of XMI-based data exchange among UML, SysML, and UPDM tool vendors.

Figure 18.8 shows a simple SysML diagram, where *Block1* is composed of *Block2,* both of which have properties. Figure 18.9 is the equivalent XMI representation generated from the model. The XMI fragment identifies each model element in terms of its UML metaclass type, unique id, and other information depending on its metaclass.

Note that the ids in Figure 18.9 have been simplified because globally unique ids are cumbersome to include in the figure. The diagram frame denotes a package with the name *Parent* that is also captured in the XMI as the owner of both *Block1* and *Block2*. However, the diagram kind, user-defined diagram name, and other diagram information (e.g., symbol positions) are not included in the exchange.

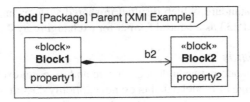

FIGURE 18.8

Simple SysML diagram for illustrating XMI.

```
-<ownedMember xmi:type="uml:Package" xmi:id="ID0" name="Parent" visibility="public">
    -<ownedMember xmi:type="uml:Class" xmi:id="ID1" name="Block1" visibility="public">
        <ownedAttribute xmi:type="uml:Property" xmi:id="ID2" name="Property1" visibility="private" />
        <ownedAttribute xmi:type="uml:Property" xmi:id="ID3" name="b2" visibility="private"
        aggregation="composite" type="ID=" association="ID4" />
    </ownedMember>
    -<ownedMember xmi:type="uml:Class" xmi:id="ID=" name="Block2" visibility="public">
        <ownedAttribute xmi:type="uml:Property" xmi:id="ID6" name="Property2" visibility="private" />
    </ownedMember>
    -<ownedMember xmi:type="uml:Association" xmi:id="ID4" visibility="public">
        <memberEnd xmi:idref="ID3" />
        <memberEnd xmi:idref="ID7" />
        <ownedEnd xmi:type="uml:Property" xmi:id="ID7" visibility="private" type="ID1" association="ID4" />
    </ownedMember>
</ownedMember>
...
<SysML:Block xmi:id="ID8" base_Class="ID1" />
<SysML:Block xmi:id="ID9" base_Class="ID5" />
<SysML:BlockProperty xmi:id="ID10" base_Property="ID2" />
<SysML:BlockProperty xmi:id="ID11" base_Property="ID3" />
<SysML:BlockProperty xmi:id="ID12" base_Property="ID6" />
```

FIGURE 18.9

Equivalent XMI (fragment) for Figure 18.12.

If the model elements represent SysML concepts, they are expressed as instances of SysML stereotypes, as described in Chapter 15, Sections 15.4 and 15.7. In this case, instances of the stereotypes reference the UML element they extend.

Application protocol 233

STEP, the Standard for the Exchange of Product Model Data (more formally known as ISO 10303 [30]), is an international standard for the computer-interpretable representation and exchange of product data. The objective is to provide a mechanism that is capable of describing product data throughout the lifecycle of a product, independent of any particular system. The nature of this description makes it suitable not only for neutral file exchange but also as a basis for implementing and sharing product databases and archiving.

Application Protocol 233 (AP233) is a STEP-based data exchange standard targeted to support the needs of the systems engineering community. It is consistent with standards in CAD; structural, electrical, and engineering analysis; and support domains. SysML was developed in coordination with the development of the AP233 standard, which resulted in shared systems engineering domain concepts. SysML tools can leverage AP233 as a neutral format for exchanging SysML models.

Diagram exchange standards

An important distinction is made between data exchange and diagram exchange. The preceding standards can support the exchange of model data but do not explicitly document how to exchange diagram layout information, including symbol definitions and where they appear on a diagram. If the model information is exchanged, some tools provide a capability to auto-generate the diagram from the model repository. However, the diagram does not reflect the original diagram layout because this information is not part of the exchange.

The OMG Diagram Definition standard [65] provides a file-based exchange of diagram information. It has two components, the **Diagram Interchange** specification (DI) and the **Diagram Graphics** specification (DG). The Diagram Interchange specification specifies a file format expressed in XML that allows two tools to exchange information about the topology of a diagram, such as whether a model element is represented by a node or arc, whether a node has any nested symbols, and its position relative to the diagram origin. The Diagram Graphics specification supports the description of the geometry and content of a diagram, such as the shape of a node and the text that appears in that node. Each graphical language defines a specific version of the Diagram Interchange specification, and a transformation from the combination of the language specification and Diagram Interchange specification into the Diagram Graphics specification.

An overview of the approach for defining diagram exchange for the SysML language is shown in Figure 18.10. *SysML DI* extends *UML DI*, which itself is a specialization of *DI*. The *SysML Mapping*

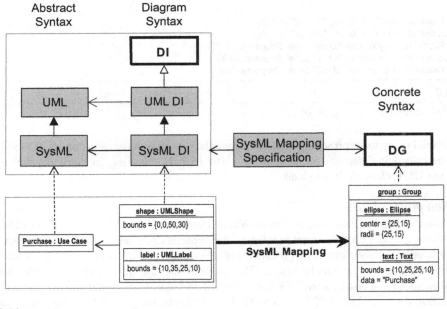

FIGURE 18.10

Diagram interchange in SysML.

Specification, which is expected to be part of a future version of the SysML specification, explains how to map from diagram elements expressed in *SysML DI* to *DG*. The bottom of the figure shows an example of a use case, *Purchase*, where *Purchase* is an element in a user model that is an instance of the metaclass *Use Case*. The diagram element is expressed as a shape containing a label using DI classes inherited from *UML DI*. The DI classes and the *SysML Mapping Specification* contain all the information necessary to map the use case diagram element into a symbol on a diagram that is specified by *DG* elements.

The SysML tools that support a standard transformation from SysML DI to Diagram Graphics and support the Diagram Graphics standard can exchange the model Diagram Interchange information along with the model data (the bottom left boxes in Figure 18.10). It is expected that standard mappings can be defined between the Diagram Graphics specification and standard graphics languages such as SVG [66] to provide additional exchange capability.

18.3.3 API-BASED EXCHANGE

An exchange of data between tools may also occur without a file exchange by direct interaction between the tools. This is facilitated by the use of a tool's **application programming interface** (API). Typically one tool will perform the exchange by using the API of the other to access the data it requires and perform any transformation, before updating its own internal model. This method can be very rapid, repeatable, and reliable, but it is important to understand how the development process anticipates using each tool, the data dependencies between tools, and how often these interactions occur.

Several standards exist for file-based exchange of modeling data, but there is no such standard for API-based exchange. Each tool has its own API, and point-to-point applications are used to facilitate exchange. MOF-based modeling tools, such as UML and SysML, may offer similar but not standard APIs. Tool vendors generally try to keep their API stable across tool versions, even when there is no standard for the API.

18.3.4 PERFORMING TRANSFORMATIONS

As described in Section 18.2.1, many different modeling tools are used on a typical development project for systems, hardware, and software development, as well as domain-specific languages for business process modeling, real-time analysis, and other functions. In Section 18.1.3, the overlap that exists between the data in different models is described. For tools to exchange model information that are expressed in different modeling languages, a model transformation is used to translate data from one modeling language to another. This involves mapping the concepts in one language to concepts in another language.

The standard for specifying transformations based on the OMG Meta Object Facility (MOF) [24] is called the **Queries, Views, and Transformations** standard (QVT) [35], which provides a foundation for transformations if the metamodel for both languages is expressed in MOF. There are many other approaches to model transformation. This area is increasingly important as standard model-based approaches and domain-specific languages become more prevalent.

A common transformation scenario is the translation from an abstract model to one that is more specific. This scenario is the basis of the OMGs **Model Driven Architecture** (MDA) approach [33, 34]. In MDA terms, a **Platform Independent Model** (PIM) is transformed into a **Platform Specific Model** (PSM) by adding data about the platform. For example, a PIM might contain details of the algorithm used for processing a radar signal, and the maximum allowable latency between a signal arriving and it becoming available. A corresponding PSM might include details of how the algorithm is distributed across processing nodes, allowing a better estimation of the actual latency.

The basis of a transformation is a description of the languages used on each side of the transformation that shows how concepts in one language map to concepts in the other. This mapping can either be defined in one direction—from source to target—or it can be defined in both directions (refer to discussion in Section 18.3.1). Models (or model fragments) defined in one language are then used as input to a translator based on the transformation, which produces transformed models or model fragments in the other language.

18.4 DATA EXCHANGE EXAMPLES BASED ON CURRENT AND EMERGING STANDARDS

Standards-based approaches to data exchange among models are expected to continue to evolve and proliferate. The following sections include five examples of data exchange from a SysML model to another standard-based model or data representation.

18.4.1 PERFORMING TRANSFORMATIONS BETWEEN SysML AND MODELICA MODELS

The transformation between SysML and Modelica demonstrates how two modeling languages can be integrated using a model transformation approach. Modelica is an analytical modeling language standardized by the Modelica Association [25]. It supports differential-algebraic equations for physics-based modeling and other analytical modeling that spans multiple engineering domains. The OMG SysML–Modelica Transformation Specification [67] defines a standard mapping between these two modeling languages. The goal is to leverage the strengths of both languages to provide a robust system design and analytical modeling capability.

Modelica is an object-oriented language that specifies acausal declarative equations. An important aspect of the Modelica modeling approach is the use of declarative equations to model the component dynamics and the interface between components using conservation laws such as Kirchhoff's laws. As an example, the interface between two electrical components, such as a resistor and capacitor, is defined using equations that assert the voltages at the two connected ends are equal and the currents at their interface sum to zero. The voltage is called an across variable and the current is designated a through variable. A similar approach can be used to specify the interfaces of many different types of physical components that are subject to similar conservation laws, such as mechanical mating surfaces and hydraulic and electromagnetic interfaces. Additional equations define the component behavior, thus enabling the analysis of interconnected components in a system.

As shown in Figure 18.11, the **SysML–Modelica Transformation Specification** includes the *SysML4Modelica profile*, the abstract syntax defining the *Modelica metamodel*, and the *SysML–Modelica Transformation* between the *SysML4Modelica profile* and the *Modelica metamodel*. The *SysML4Modelica profile* simplifies the transformation by defining SysML stereotypes that correspond directly to constructs in the *Modelica metamodel*. This mapping includes both a tabular mapping and a formal mapping using QVT.

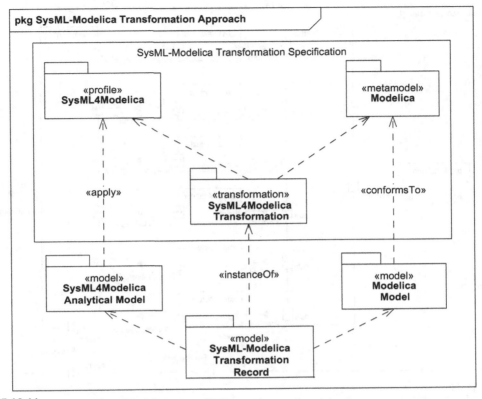

pkg SysML-Modelica Transformation Approach

SysML-Modelica Transformation Specification

«profile»
SysML4Modelica

«metamodel»
Modelica

«apply»

«transformation»
**SysML4Modelica
Transformation**

«conformsTo»

«model»
**SysML4Modelica
Analytical Model**

«instanceOf»

«model»
**Modelica
Model**

«model»
**SysML-Modelica
Transformation
Record**

FIGURE 18.11

The *SysML–Modelica Transformation Specification* is used to transform a *SysML4Modelica Analytical Model* to a *Modelica Model*.

Once the transformation is specified, a transformation engine can execute the *SysML–Modelica Transformation* for a particular model. For example, a *SysML4Modelica* model of a particular system can be input to the transformation engine, and the corresponding *Modelica model* is the output from the transformation. The input *SysML4Modelica Analytical Model* is provided in XMI format, and the output *Modelica Model* is represented in a data format that can be interpreted by a Modelica tool. The transformation is bidirectional, such that the *Modelica Model* can be input to the transformation engine, and the corresponding *SysML4Modelica Analytical Model* is the output of the transformation.

An example of applying the transformation specification to a simplified robot model is described in the SysML–Modelica Transformation Specification. Figure 18.12 shows the robot internal structure represented as a SysML internal block diagram. Figure 18.13 shows the use of allocation to define the *SysML4Modelica Analytical Model* from the SysML model. This model is then transformed into an equivalent *Modelica Model* that can be executed by a Modelica tool. The results of the execution can be passed back to the SysML model through the reverse transformation.

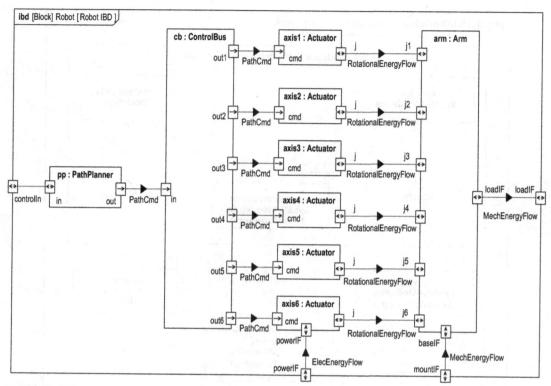

FIGURE 18.12

Example of internal structure of a Robot consistent with the SysML–Modelica Transformation specification.

18.4.2 USING OSLC AND LINKED DATA TO SUPPORT DATA EXCHANGE AND TOOL INTEGRATION

The **Open Services for Lifecycle Collaboration** (OSLC) [31] initiative is driven by an open community to develop tool integration standards based on web technology. Specifically, the focus is on using linked data concepts to create a family of web services and specifications to link data between different tools. Each OSLC compliant tool can define what data it chooses to expose through these services, similar to an API.

The term **linked data** refers to the use of the web technology to create links between related data elements as described in Section 18.1.3. Each data element that is linked is called a **resource** and is uniquely identified by its Uniform Resource Identifier (URI) [68]. A URI is used similar to the way a Uniform Resource Locator (URL) is used to access web pages.

Linked data can be expressed in a format called the Resource Description Framework (RDF) [69], which encodes data in triples composed of a subject, predicate, and object. A triple represents a statement about something, such as "a vehicle satisfies the weight requirement," where the *vehicle* is the subject, *satisfies* is the predicate, and *weight requirement* is the object. The predicate specifies how the subject and object are related. The subject and predicate of a triple are both identified with a URI. The object can be either a literal value, such as a string, or a resource identified by its URI.

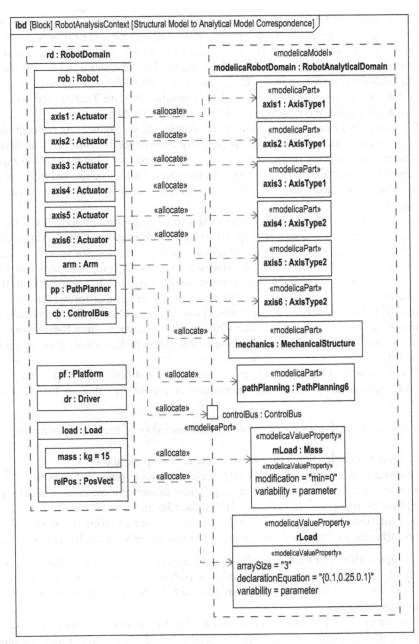

FIGURE 18.13

Defining the SysML4Modelica Model for the Robot example, using allocation to enable transformation to a Modelica model.

Linked data is accessed through HTTP, the basic protocol used for accessing web pages on the internet. HTTP is used to create, read, update, and delete linked data. HTTP provides verbs such as GET, PUT, POST, and DELETE, which allow web clients to invoke web services to manipulate linked data. Web services which can be invoked only by using HTTP—in contrast to SOAP-based web services requiring additional information in XML—are called RESTful web services or RESTful web APIs, as they conform to the principles of the Representational State Transfer (REST) architecture. Linked data are made available on the web through RESTful web APIs.

An OSLC resource is a linked data resource corresponding to an engineering concept like a requirement or a change request. An OSLC resource is typically constrained to conform to an OSLC resource shape, which is similar to a MOF metaclass or SysML stereotype (see Chapter 15, Sections 15.2.1 and 15.4). A resource shape defines the set of properties that the resource is expected to have including its type, allowed values, and cardinality. An OSLC specification defines a set of resource shapes for a particular domain.

Interoperability between OSLC tools is supported through conformance to OSLC specifications. A tool that supports OSLC can request or respond to queries from other OSLC compliant tools. For example, the OSLC Requirements Management specification defines domain-specific concepts such as a requirement and a derived requirement relationship. An OSLC-compliant tool can respond to a request from another tool for a particular requirement based on its URI and return it in RDF, according to the OSLC Requirements Management specification, as well as in other formats such as HTML.

The list of OSLC resources (i.e., data elements) and services of an OSLC-compliant tool can be discovered through its OSLC Service Provider Catalog. The storage medium for resources is not constrained by OSLC, and can be a relational database, a flat-file on disk, a source code control system, or some other medium.

An OSLC-compliant tool offers a core set of capabilities, defined in the OSLC core specification [70]. The OSLC core specification defines a number of capabilities that an OSLC service offers, including:

- Query capabilities to enable query of resources and discovery of the resources managed by the service;
- Resource paging to enable clients to retrieve resources one page at a time;
- Resource management operations via HTTP (create, retrieve, update, and delete);
- Delegation user interfaces that allow a service provider to embed a creation or selection UI into another application using a combination of HTML and JavaScript code; and
- Preview user interfaces that can be used to show a user in-context information when displaying a link to a resource and to show more information when the user's mouse hovers over the link.

Different groups within the OSLC organization are responsible for defining domain-specific specifications. Each of the domain-specific specifications is built upon the core specification described above. The OSLC specifications are managed through the OASIS standards body, which is responsible for many other web standards.

There are a number of OSLC specifications that are relevant to systems modeling, such as requirements and change management, but currently no specification covers system modeling more broadly. The OSLC4MBSE Working Group [71] was initiated as a collaborative effort between members of the OMG systems engineering and OSLC communities to develop an OSLC approach to support MBSE. An initial step is the development of an RDF representation of SysML that can be integrated with existing OSLC specifications. A standard OSLC specification for SysML provides a standard API to enable OSLC-compliant tools to request SysML data, and for SysML tools to request OSLC data from OSLC-compliant tools.

18.4.3 EXCHANGING DATA TO ENABLE CO-SIMULATION

The **Functional Mock-up Interface** (FMI) is a standard to support both model exchange and co-simulation of models expressed as ordinary differential equations (ODEs). FMI uses a combination of XML files and compiled C code. Although initially developed as part of the Modelisar project [72], the maintenance and further development of FMI is now performed by the Modelica Association Project, FMI [32]. The aim of the FMI standard is to support use cases such as:

- Simulating heterogeneous systems authored in multiple modeling tools;
- Partitioning and parallelizing large system simulations to improve simulation performance; and
- Easing the integration of hardware-in-the-loop into a simulation.

A component which implements FMI is called a **Functional Mockup Unit** (FMU). A FMU is a zipped file (*.fmu) containing an XML description file and an implementation in source or binary form that executes the equations that represent the component behavior. The XML file contains the definition of all variables of the FMU that are exposed to the environment in which the FMU will be used, including inputs, outputs, parameters, and other model information, such as units. The component implementation consists of a set of C functions, which can either be provided in source or binary form. Binary forms for different platforms can be included in the same model zip file.

FMI supports two categories of execution:

- Co-simulation, where the intention is to couple two or more FMUs in a co-simulation environment. The data exchange between these FMUs is restricted to discrete communication points. In the time between two communication points, the FMUs are solved independently from each other by their own individual solver. Master algorithms in the co-simulation environment control the data exchange between FMUs and the synchronization of all slave simulation solvers.
- Model exchange, where the intention is that the FMUs are all executed under a solver provided by an integrating simulation environment. This approach makes it possible to use the same FMU in a variety of simulation environments, including those using variable-step solver solutions. FMUs (without internal solvers) implement differential, algebraic, and discrete equations with time-, state- and step-events that are raised by a common solver.

There have also been some experiments that export SysML blocks as FMUs [73]. Future efforts are needed to map the SysML definition of a block interface to an FMI XML file. It should also be noted that FMI is designed to support the simulation of systems based on ODEs and so does not cover all of the other behavioral semantics that can be expressed by SysML models.

18.4.4 INTERCHANGING SysML MODELS AND ONTOLOGIES

An ontology represents some area of knowledge as a set of concepts within a domain and the relationships between those concepts. Ontologies are increasingly being used as part of MBSE approaches to capture knowledge about the domains involved in the development of a system, including both general domains applicable across a wide range of systems and application-specific domains.

The **Web Ontology Language** (OWL) [28] is a family of knowledge representation languages for authoring ontologies. An OWL class represents an ontological concept and can have properties and relationships to other classes. A particular ontology defines a set of OWL classes. A specific project creates instances of these classes to describe entities in their domain. A variety of tools are available to reason about these instances.

SysML on the other hand is used to describe the structure and behavior of the system being developed and to support the development of its components. There is increased interest in leveraging the expressive capability of SysML models with the formalisms and associated reasoning capability provided by OWL models.

Some organizations are taking the approach of mapping their ontologies to SysML profiles. This approach establishes a domain specific language expressed in SysML. Classes in OWL ontologies are mapped onto stereotypes in one or more SysML profiles. A SysML model with the ontology stereotypes applied can then be transformed into OWL so that OWL-based tools can reason about the model. Both file-based and API-based exchange can be used to exchange the data between the SysML modeling tool and the OWL reasoning tools.

One such example is the effort by NASA's Jet Propulsion Laboratory (JPL) to establish a mapping between SysML and OWL to support flight project development [74]. The basis of the transformation is a mapping from the concepts and properties in the JPL ontologies to SysML modeling concepts. For example, the JPL concept of Component is mapped to a SysML block, and the JPL concept of Work Package is mapped to a SysML package.

18.4.5 DOCUMENT AND VIEW GENERATION FROM MODELS

A key factor in the successful transition of MBSE from a document-based systems engineering approach is the ability to automatically generate documents and other traditional artifacts from models. Most MBSE modeling tools have document generators that can be used to generate documents in formats such as Office Open XML, Portable Document Format (**PDF**), **DocBook**, or HTML. A model-based document generator implements a unidirectional transformation from a model to a language that understands nothing of the model's meaning but is able to present the model information in a form that eases understanding for a broad range of stakeholders.

A document generator can adopt a default mapping from a model to a document (e.g., mapping each package to a chapter). Different SysML tool vendors use different document generation tools with various formatting mechanisms.

One approach, implemented as part of the European Southern Observatory Active Phasing Experiment (APE) [75], is to use a SysML profile to define the document layout and formatting. The APE DocBook profile contains stereotypes that correspond to elements in the DocBook documentation language. These include stereotypes such as `chapter`, `section`, `appendix` and `glossary`, which extend package. The profile is then used to author a model of a DocBook document, and elements in this document model reference elements in the system model. A document generator that is based on the profile can therefore understand the mapping between the structure of the system model and the structure of the generated document. Other stereotypes include a figure stereotype that can be used to dictate presentation options such as scaling and cropping for figures. A different document model can be authored for each document that needs to be generated from the model. In terms of the considerations discussed in Section 18.4.1, this application performs a unidirectional transformation from an abstract to a more concrete language, with exchange being mediated through files.

Practices continue to evolve to facilitate the generation of many different views of the information contained in the model. The views can also integrate information contained in the model with other information that is generated external to the model. These approaches leverage the SysML view and viewpoint capability as described in Chapter 15, Section 15.8, to query the model using standard libraries of query methods and then present this information in a variety of formats using standard rendering applications (refer to Section 18.2.2 under *Interface With Document and View Generation Tools*).

18.5 SELECTING A SYSTEM MODELING TOOL

This section provides guidance on the selection of a SysML modeling tool that is integrated into the systems development environment. A system modeling tool may support SysML and MBSE to a greater or lesser extent based on its conformance to the modeling standards and other strengths and weaknesses.

18.5.1 TOOL SELECTION CRITERIA

The following **criteria** form the basis for evaluating and selecting a SysML modeling tool:

- Conformance to SysML specification (latest version)
- Usability
- Document, view, and report generation capability
- Metrics support
- Model execution capability including both integration with fUML and parametric solvers
- Conformance to XMI and other exchange standards
- Access to model repository through its API
- Integration with other engineering tools (including legacy tools within the existing systems development environment)
  - Requirements management
  - Configuration and data management (including product data management)
  - Engineering analytical tools
  - Performance simulation tools
  - Software development tools
  - Electrical design tools
  - Mechanical CAD tool
  - Testing and verification tools
  - Project management tools
- Performance (maximum number of users, model size)
- Model checking to verify model conformance with well-formedness rules
- Training, online help, and support
- Availability of model libraries (e.g., units)
- Lifecycle cost (acquisition, training, support)

- Other tool lifecycle considerations (e.g., acquisition, configuration, installation, operation, support, upgrade)
- Vendor viability
- Acquirer's previous experience with the tool
- Support for selected model-based method (e.g., scripts that automate certain parts of the method, standard reports, etc.)
- Further customization support through profiles and notational enhancements (i.e., iconic representations)

18.5.2 SysML CONFORMANCE

One of the important evaluation criteria identified in the previous section is **tool conformance** to the SysML specification. Significant benefits can result from using a conforming tool, including improved model exchange capability, mitigation of tool vendor lock-in, increased opportunity to leverage future revisions to the language, and improved ability to leverage industry available training, practices, and other resources.

According to the SysML specification, "an implementation of SysML must comply with both the subset of UML4SysML and the SysML extensions," both of which are summarized in Chapter 15, Section 15.2. This includes conformance with the abstract syntax that specify the underlying language constructs, like metaclasses, stereotypes, and constraints; conformance with concrete syntax (e.g., graphical notation); and conformance with the XMI specification to support data exchange. Standard test cases are available to assess model interchange conformance among UML, SysML, and UPDM modeling tools [64]. It is anticipated that these test cases will continue to be updated over time to reflect evolving versions of the specification. However, they can also be used as examples to develop customized test cases that are unique to an organization's or project's needs.

18.6 SUMMARY

Integrating SysML into a systems development environment includes some of the following considerations.

- The system model is a descriptive model captured in SysML. It is an integral part of the overall system development effort and establishes the technical baseline used to relate text requirements to the design, provide design information needed to support analysis, serve as a specification for subsystem and component design models, and provide test case and related information needed to support verification.
- There are many different kinds of models in a development environment including descriptive and analytical. Descriptive models include geometric and logical models. Models can be further classified by their application, functional, and technical domain. A simulation consists of an executable model and an execution environment along with initial conditions.
- The relationships among the data contained in different models must be managed in order to ensure consistency of information across models and to support impact analysis.
- System modeling tools do not stand alone but must be integrated into a systems development environment that includes many other kinds of tools that support requirements management, engineering analysis, hardware and software development, verification, project management, configuration management, and document generation.

- A systems engineering approach should be applied to specify the requirements and interfaces for the integrated systems development environment.
- Data exchange between tools can be accomplished by manual, file-based, and interaction-based (i.e., APIs) mechanisms. Portions of models may be transformed between languages and tools to facilitate this data exchange. The connections may be point-to-point or through shared repositories.
- A standards-based approach to data and model exchange is the preferred approach to reduce the cost and improve the quality of the data exchange. XMI is a data exchange standard for the model content, and diagram definition is an exchange standard for the diagram layout. Other emerging standards such as OSLC provide a linked data approach to data exchange using web technologies.
- SysML tool selection should be based on an evaluation against a defined set of criteria that includes both review of vendor information and hands-on use of the tool in the expected environment. Tool compliance to the SysML standard is a critical criterion.

18.7 QUESTIONS

1. How does SysML facilitate establishing a model-based systems development environment?
2. What is the difference between a descriptive model and an analytical model?
3. What is a simulation? How does it relate to descriptive models and analytical models?
4. How can a SysML model be used with a set of analytical models? What information in the SysML model should be used in the analytical model and vice versa?
5. List three functions necessary for managing the configuration of an MBSE project.
6. What information does a SysML model provide to a component developer?
7. Describe how XMI and AP233 are used with SysML.
8. Describe the difference between file-based exchange and interaction-based exchange using APIs.
9. Why is a model transformation used?
10. List five criteria for selecting a SysML tool.
11. What can be done to limit the impact of future tool changes or upgrades on the cost of your systems development environment?

DISCUSSION TOPICS

Describe the role of the system model in the systems development environment.

Describe the meaning of the term "executable model" and the purpose for developing executable models.

Describe how the use of a system model can potentially increase the effectiveness of a systems development environment.

Build a matrix listing eight types of tools that can benefit from sharing data with a system modeling tool. In one column, list beneficial information that can flow from the system modeling tool, and in another column, list information that can flow to the system modeling tool.

Describe different ways of exchanging data between tools in a systems development environment, and when it might be most appropriate.

DEPLOYING SysML IN AN ORGANIZATION

This chapter describes how to deploy SysML and a model-based systems engineering (MBSE) approach across an organization. The first section describes an improvement process to deploy MBSE, and the second section describes key elements of a deployment strategy.

In the context of this chapter, an **organization** is a group of people with responsibilities, authorities, and a supporting infrastructure for on-going development and delivery of a range of systems and services, whereas a **project** is an organization whose scope is limited to developing and delivering particular systems and services over a specified duration. Organizations often include multiple projects.

19.1 IMPROVEMENT PROCESS

Introducing any significant change into an organization requires a strategy, a plan, and disciplined implementation to be successful. Deploying a MBSE approach with SysML should leverage the organization's **improvement process**. Clear responsibility for the improvement initiative should be established, and the expected cost and benefits of the change should be understood and accepted by the stakeholders.

A typical improvement process is shown in Figure 19.1. The includes monitoring and assessing projects to determine the issues to be addressed and the improvement goals; developing the improvement plan; defining proposed changes to the process, methods, tools, and training; piloting the approach; and incrementally deploying the capability to the project(s). The improvement process to deploy an MBSE approach is described next.

19.1.1 MONITOR AND ASSESS

To introduce a change to improve the organization's capability, a baseline for measuring the improvement should be established. In particular, the organization should assess how systems engineering is currently practiced and identify the issues, improvement goals, and costs expected from transitioning to MBSE with SysML. The MBSE benefits described in Chapter 2, Section 2.1.2 are possible motivations for the change. The issues to be addressed and the improvement goals can be used to derive metrics that can be monitored over time. These metrics can be used to assess the cost and effectiveness of the change, provide a basis for building the business case, and provide an input for follow-up improvement planning.

The maturity of MBSE will vary from project to project in a large organization. It may range from a document-based systems engineering approach on some projects with no concept of a system model to projects where the system model is developed but not maintained as part of the technical baseline, to other projects with advanced systems modeling where the system model is an integral part of the

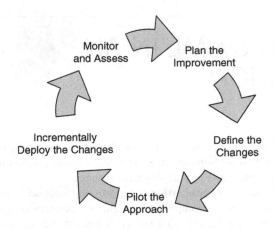

FIGURE 19.1

Improvement process for deploying SysML.

project technical baseline and is maintained along with other engineering models by the project's systems development environment (refer to Chapter 18, Section 18.2). An organization can conduct a state-of-practice assessment of the maturity of MBSE and how well MBSE is working on its projects. The assessment results can be used to identify preferred practices to be shared across projects and the issues to be addressed by the improvement plan. The results can also be used to identify and select candidate pilot projects and potential target projects for deployment.

A questionnaire can be prepared to support the assessment. It should include questions regarding the purpose and scope of MBSE on projects; the methods, tools, and training that are being used; how well they are working; and issues and lessons learned. The OMG issued a survey as part of the Systems Modeling Language Request for Information (RFI) [76] that can be adapted for use to support an organizational MBSE assessment. This questionnaire can be administered to organizational and project representatives remotely or through face-to-face meetings. Representation from multiple projects and disciplines should be sufficiently diverse to provide a comprehensive assessment.

Metrics can be defined to assess the organization's MBSE capability. The metrics reflect the maturity and capability of the organizational infrastructure to support MBSE, the level of MBSE adoption by projects, and the resulting value of MBSE to the projects. The maturity metrics reflect the readiness of the organizations' model-based tools, methods, training, and expertise to support project adoption of MBSE. Potential deployment metrics include the number and percentage of people trained in SysML and MBSE, and the number and type of projects that are applying MBSE. The value of MBSE to the projects is measured in terms of incremental improvements in productivity and quality, such as the reduction in time to assess a requirements or design change impact, or the reduction in the number of requirements changes or discrepancies that are identified during integration and test. This information provides indicators of the impact of MBSE on project cost, schedule, technical performance, and risk in terms of the benefits identified in Chapter 2, Section 2.1.2. The overall effectiveness of the improvement program is measured in terms of progress against improvement goals, how well the identified issues are being addressed, and the impact on business objectives.

19.1.2 PLAN THE IMPROVEMENT

The **improvement plan** describes how to accomplish the improvement goals and to develop and deploy change across the organization. The plan includes the activities from the improvement process in Figure 19.1 and the responsibilities, resources, and schedule for implementing these activities.

As with any plan, stakeholder participation is essential in both its formulation and its execution. It is important to get representation from the key stakeholders early in the process to ensure that their concerns are being addressed and obtain their support. The stakeholders for deploying MBSE with SysML include members of the improvement team responsible for defining the change, as well as the project stakeholders who are expected to implement the change. The stakeholder representation includes project management, systems engineering, and the development teams for software, hardware, and test, and may include customers and subcontractors.

19.1.3 DEFINE CHANGES TO PROCESS, METHODS, TOOLS, AND TRAINING

The transition to MBSE with SysML requires changes to the organization's process, methods, tools, and training. The changes should be defined, documented, reviewed, and approved by the affected stakeholders to ensure the changes are implementable and can achieve the desired results.

Process changes

It is assumed that the baseline systems engineering process for the organization and/or project is defined. If not, establishing a baseline that reflects the current process is an important first step. The process standards referred to in Chapter 1, Section 1.5 provides a starting point for defining the systems engineering process. Sometimes, a significant difference exists between the documented processes for an organization and the way those processes are implemented on projects. This issue should be addressed, but it is not the focus for this discussion. The systems engineering processes should be evaluated to determine how transitioning to MBSE with SysML impacts the current processes. This includes the impact on both the technical processes and the management processes, such as project planning, configuration management, review processes, and measurement.

Method changes

An MBSE method is selected to support the systems engineering process. The method may be adapted from existing systems engineering methods. Alternatively, the method may be adapted from MBSE methods that are available from industry sources. A simplified MBSE method is described in Chapter 3, Section 3.4, and two other methods are described in Chapters 16 and 17. Additional methods are identified in a Survey of MBSE Methodologies [6].

The criteria for selecting a method includes how well it addresses the concerns of the project, the level of tool support, and the training requirements. The method is documented, along with an example problem and the associated modeling artifacts, to show how the method is applied. The method also includes general modeling conventions (refer to Chapter 17, Section 17.3.1 for an example) and the recommended model organization (refer to Chapter 6, Section 6.4 and the examples in Chapters 16 and 17).

Tool changes

The MBSE tools also are evaluated and selected. Criteria for selecting a SysML modeling tool are included in Chapter 18, Section 18.5. The evaluation also includes trial use of the tool to see how well it addresses the evaluation criteria. Documentation is developed to describe how the tools are acquired, installed, configured, used, and maintained, as well as how the tools are integrated into the systems development environment as described in Chapter 18, Section 18.2. Documentation is also developed to describe how the method is adapted for use with the tool and how to create the modeling artifacts in the tool.

Training Changes

Training is needed to develop the skill level in the use of the language, method, and tools. SysML training should focus on the language concepts described in Part II. The method training should include examples of how the method is applied to a relevant domain such as the examples in Part III. The introductory tool training may be provided by the tool vendor to show how the tool is used. Additional training may be required on how the tool is used as part of the specific systems development environment (refer to Chapter 18) with the selected method.

19.1.4 PILOT THE APPROACH

As with any significant change, the recommendation is to walk before you run. This involves piloting the changes to validate and refine the MBSE approach, and to build expertise in the modeling language, method, and tools. Undoubtedly, modifications will be made to the initial MBSE approach based on the results of the pilot project.

A **pilot project** also requires careful planning, willing participants, necessary resources, and management support. A typical pilot plan includes the following:

- Pilot objectives and metrics
- Pilot scope
- Pilot deliverables
- Pilot schedule
- Responsibilities and staffing
- Process and method guidance
  - High-level process flow
  - Model artifact checklist
  - Tool-specific guidance
- Tool support
- Training

The pilot's objectives often include validating that the proposed MBSE method, tools, and training meet the needs of the organization and projects. A small team is identified to work on the pilot with a team lead. The continuity among the core team members must be maintained through the pilot.

The selected tools must be acquired, installed, and configured. The pilot team receives training in the language, method, and tools. The pilot team should include a member who is skilled in the language, method, and tools to provide guidance to other team members. Alternately, external support with the necessary expertise can be provided.

The pilot project adequately exercises the method and tools by selecting a thread through the system and generating at least one example of each artifact from the method. The pilot schedule includes milestones to create each modeling artifact, and the team conducts a peer-review process to review each modeling artifact and refine the MBSE approach as needed.

The pilot results are captured in a report on how well the pilot achieves its objectives, the modifications made to the MBSE approach, and lessons learned, including quantitative data and metrics where practical. The pilot report from an early application of the OOSEM method that is described in Chapter 17, is an example of how to conduct a pilot [55].

Based on a pilot's results, the process, methods, tools, metrics, and training are updated to reflect the new baseline MBSE approach. The results serve as training material for the broader MBSE rollout. The pilot participants can also become advocates to help deploy MBSE with SysML to projects.

19.1.5 DEPLOY CHANGES INCREMENTALLY

The pilot results help determine the requirements and approach for deploying MBSE to projects. The pilot provides a basis for assessing the type of training required, the time it takes to reach a level of proficiency, how to adapt the organizational MBSE method and tools to the needs of a project, and realistic expectations of the results from the modeling effort.

Criteria are established to select a project or projects for MBSE deployment. The criteria include the project's phase, longevity, size, level of internal and customer support, and the extent to which MBSE benefits can provide recognized value to the project both incrementally and over the longer term. In addition, the state-of-practice assessment referenced in Section 19.1.1 can help identify potential project opportunities to introduce MBSE based on business need and other considerations.

Different projects introduce different scopes for MBSE depending on their current state of practice, their experience level in modeling, and their particular needs. Ideally, MBSE with SysML is introduced during the start-up phase of a project or at a point in its lifecycle that is appropriate to introduce change, for example, at the start of a new development increment. It is important for the project's leadership and customers to be willing advocates for the change.

The MBSE approach is integrated into the project plan. The plan reflects realistic expectations in terms of the time, effort, deliverables, and expected results from the modeling effort. The outline for the modeling plan is similar to the pilot plan outline in Section 19.1.4. The purpose and scope of the effort is defined and balanced with project resources, as described in Chapter 2, Sections 2.2.2 and 2.2.5. The initial set up of the modeling environment, including the tools, staffing, and training is reflected in the plan and schedule, along with the MBSE activities, modeling artifacts, and related project deliverables. Typical project start-up activities are discussed in Chapter 17, Section 17.2.2.

The selected MBSE method is tailored to satisfy the modeling objectives, scope, and project constraints. The tailoring may include adding or deleting certain activities, tailoring the sequencing of activities, and customizing the modeling artifacts to satisfy the requirements for the project deliverables. Some considerations for tailoring depend on whether the system development is constrained by a legacy system design versus the development of a new system, the phase of development, and the modeling expertise available to the development team.

The model can be leveraged to provide information for the project deliverables. Auto-generation of the project documentation from the model, as described in Chapter 18, Section 18.4.5, can provide efficiencies and quality improvements.

The project organization should include roles with responsibilities for the modeling activities. A small core modeling team can be established, with a modeling lead and representatives from the other engineering teams on the project. The modeling team works closely with the rest of the project to build the model by obtaining on-going inputs to the model from the project team representatives. The modeling lead schedules regular peer reviews of the model to ensure that the model reflects the design intent of the project teams and that the MBSE method and modeling guidelines are followed. The model is a fundamental part of the technical baseline and is controlled like other primary engineering artifacts using the project's technical review process. The MBSE method and modeling guidelines are periodically reviewed and updated based on lessons learned from the project.

MBSE metrics, such as those in Chapter 2, Sections 2.2.5–6, are identified to support project objectives. The model can be an excellent source of information to assist in assessing technical, cost, and schedule performance and risk. The approach for metrics data collection is also defined, including how the data is captured from the tools. The reporting of metrics is included in the project plan, including which metrics, how often the data are collected, and how the data are used.

The selected tools are acquired, installed, and configured for use. On a larger project, the tools are configured for a multi-user environment. Additional levels of tool integration may be required, as described in Chapter 18. The configuration management approach and model organization for controlling the model baseline are defined.

The MBSE deployment includes start-up training in SysML and the selected MBSE method and tool. The training material leverages the pilot project documentation and results. Different levels of training are appropriate for different stakeholders. For example, some of the systems engineering team, which is designated as the core modeling team, require detailed training in SysML, MBSE methods, and the modeling tools, whereas other systems engineers and some hardware and software developers may only require limited SysML training sufficient to interpret the SysML models. The discipline-specific training addresses how the model impacts their particular tasks or methods. For example, testers need to understand how to derive detailed test cases from the model, and the individual responsible for requirements management needs to understand how the SysML modeling tool is used with the requirements management tool.

A successful deployment also requires ongoing support and mentoring from individuals who have expertise in the methods and tools. The improvement metrics are monitored to assess the MBSE effort, and lessons learned are captured to further refine the process, methods, and tools, and drive the improvement process.

19.2 ELEMENTS OF A DEPLOYMENT STRATEGY

The previous section describes how to deploy MBSE with SysML as part of an organizational improvement process. This section describes elements of a **deployment strategy** from both organizational and project perspectives that include:

- Stakeholder identification
- Value proposition
- Relationship to other initiatives
- Approach:
  - Method selection

- Tool selection and integration
- Skill acquisition and development
- Measurement
- Organization and roles

19.2.1 ORGANIZATIONAL DEPLOYMENT STRATEGIES

Stakeholder identification

Developing and evolving an organizational strategy to introduce an improvement involves funda-mental tenets of organizational change management. This clearly requires a champion who is will-ing and able to initiate and lead the change. The particular strategy and the primary stakeholders depend on the stage of adoption of the organization. For example, during the very early stage of adoption, it may be appropriate to initiate the change at a grassroots level with practitioners who are willing to take on the challenges and risks of being an early adopter. The early adopters have the ability to demonstrate early success and motivate others to participate, and to begin to build the knowledge of how MBSE with SysML is practiced. At later stages of adoption, it becomes critical to engage senior management who see the potential value of the change and are willing to sponsor the initiative with funding and resources. The engagement broadens to include other stakeholders to mature the practices, to build the skills, and to establish clear ownership across the organization to institutionalize the change.

Value proposition

The **value proposition** for MBSE must be adapted to the organization and to the specific stakeholders. The value proposition ultimately must be defined in terms that are meaningful to the stakeholders. For example, the practitioner must see value in terms of improving his or her job. At the same time, the value proposition for senior management must be tied to organizational and business objectives. An example may be to demonstrate how MBSE with SysML provide a discriminator to help win new busi-ness or address systemic issues that result in improvements in quality, productivity, and/or schedule reduction. Typical systemic issues are associated with integration across disciplines and/or across life-cycle phases. These issues must be stated in ways that are relevant to the organization, and the case for how MBSE with SysML address the issues and provide the value must be compelling.

As a caution, the sponsors and others may be asking for the return on investment from the onset. It is often quite challenging to get this data, particularly in the early stages of adoption. One can look for external data, but many companies do not share this data, even if they have it. Furthermore, it is often difficult to measure the return due to any specific change unless the change is performed in a controlled environment. It is often more feasible to provide a business case that is based on demonstrated mini-successes.

Relationship to other initiatives

Introducing a change into an organization can be perceived as just another initiative. Organizations may have many initiatives underway, and another initiative can be viewed by many as a burden that just requires more for them to do. It may be more effective to integrate MBSE with SysML into an on-going initiative, preferably one that is well funded with clear sponsorship and support.

Approach

An organizational strategy should address two key elements: 1) building the organizational infrastructure in terms of the methods, tools, training, and skilled practitioners needed to implement MBSE with SysML; and 2) deploying MBSE with SysML to the projects. Some of the specific considerations for both elements are discussed in Section 19.1 and further elaborated below.

Building the organizational infrastructure for MBSE

An important aspect related to the **MBSE infrastructure** is establishing a **community of practice** (COP) to share the knowledge and lessons learned across the organization. The community of practice should have a credible leader with the skills needed to engage the community. Funding the leadership role is important to the success of the COP. The lead may hold regularly scheduled telecons and webinars to provide an opportunity for practitioners to share their experiences and for tool vendors and other outside experts to introduce new capabilities.

The lead may also develop and maintain a website to host the modeling practices, guidelines, and resources, and may include identification of subject matter experts, training opportunities, and other information. The COP lead or other members may also provide direct project support beginning at project start-up by assisting in the planning of the MBSE effort. The COP should document incremental successes and lessons learned and share them more broadly. This also presents an opportunity to share models for reuse across the organization, which helps to build the business case and value proposition for MBSE with SysML.

An important aspect of transitioning MBSE to an organization is to demystify MBSE and relate it to current practice. It can be helpful to map the MBSE method to the current practices and to demonstrate how more traditional systems engineering artifacts such as concept of operations, specifications, architecture descriptions, test documentation, and others can be generated using a model-based approach. This activity can be performed by the COP.

The organization may also identify a tool lead to manage the modeling tool environment for the organization. This lead may be responsible for the selection of a standard modeling tool for use across projects and for integrating the modeling tool with other tools in the systems development environment. The tool lead is also responsible for assisting projects in setting up their modeling tool environment and providing full-lifecycle support that includes acquiring the tool, installing and configuring the tool, and managing new tool versions.

The organization may also provide a combination of in-house and vendor-provided training to projects in the modeling language, methods, and tools. In particular, this training may begin at project start-up and continue as needed throughout the lifecycle of the project. A training plan is developed that identifies training needs and defines how to provide training solutions for the organization.

The organization may also fund specific pilot projects to validate the use of MBSE with SysML. It is beneficial to pilot MBSE for specific projects so the results of the pilot can provide direct benefit to the project and so the pilot is focused on real needs. Preferably, the pilot is conducted prior to the start of the project with individuals who are going to support the project directly.

Deploying MBSE to projects

The organizational strategy must include criteria for selecting the right projects and the right time to deploy MBSE with SysML as discussed in Section 19.1. The strategy must also address on-going needs of the projects and what changes to the MBSE infrastructure are needed to provide the most effective support.

Organizational roles

The organizational roles described in this section each contribute to maintaining and improving the overall organizational MBSE capability. The strategy should include considerations for how to manage and coordinate the MBSE effort across the organization to ensure overall success.

19.2.2 PROJECT DEPLOYMENT STRATEGIES

A project that deploys MBSE with SysML may or may not be able to leverage the organizational infrastructure described above. If it is early in the adoption stage, the infrastructure may not exist or resources may not be available to leverage the infrastructure. Whether the organizational infrastructure is available or not, a project should develop a deployment strategy that addresses its unique needs.

Stakeholder identification

The primary project stakeholders for the MBSE approach generally include the chief engineer on the project, the systems engineering team, the hardware and software developers, the testers, and other members of the development team who contribute to and consume the modeling information. The stakeholders also include customers, subcontractors, and program management, all of whom may be impacted by changes to project processes and/or deliverables.

Value proposition

This begins with the value proposition for the modeling effort in terms how MBSE with SysML can support the project objectives. Typical purposes for applying MBSE are identified in Chapter 2, Section 2.2.2, and some of the potential benefits are identified in Chapter 2, Section 2.1.2. As noted in Chapter 2, Section 2.2.2, the modeling purpose depends in part on the lifecycle phase of the project, such as the conceptual design, detailed design, integration and test, production, or operation and support phase. As one shifts further down the lifecycle, the emphasis for the modeling effort shifts from exploring broad system design alternatives to managing changes to the technical baseline.

It is important to set expectations for the modeling effort to understand what it does and does not provide, and also to understand that this effort requires a steady commitment from both the modeling team and other members of the project that contribute to and/or use the model.

Modeling approach

Defining the scope of the model to support its purpose is a critical part of the project's deployment strategy and plan. An approach to establishing model scope is described in Chapter 2, Section 2.2.4, and focuses on determining the appropriate level of model breadth, depth, and fidelity. The scope must be consistent with other project constraints, such as the project schedule and funding.

As noted in Section 19.2.1, the model should initially be leveraged to create traditional systems engineering artifacts that are familiar to the project and systems engineering team. In addition, the initial scope should be small and focused, and then expanded over time. For example, the initial modeling effort may focus on developing the system block diagram and establishing traceability to the top level requirements. This can provide near-term value while the project gains familiarity with the model and begins to see its value. A well-defined system block diagram provides a shared understanding of the system that helps to integrate the subsystems and other disciplines. The level and detail of the block diagram can be incrementally increased over time, such as the addition of ports with more detailed interface information. In addition, the model can be used to identify and manage critical properties needed to support engineering analysis related to performance, physical, and other quality characteristics. Capturing key mission, system, and subsystem requirements and tracing these requirements to the system design can be part of the initial modeling effort. These modeling artifacts can be used to generate traditional systems engineering documentation such as specifications, traceability reports, and system architecture and interface descriptions.

The model can be leveraged for many different purposes. Some of these purposes are predefined while others are discovered as the model evolves. New content may be identified based on on-going reviews of the model and the need to create new kinds of reports that had not previously been available. Some content and/or certain modeling artifacts may turn out to be less useful, and a determination may be made to discontinue that part of the modeling effort. It is important to always drive the model based on purpose and intent but recognize that the purpose will evolve.

The MBSE approach must support the project objectives, and integrate with the overall project plan as described in Section 19.1.5. This includes identifying and tailoring the modeling method and artifacts, tool environment, staffing needs, training, metrics, and roles needed to support the modeling effort. The modeling milestones should provide the needed visibility to track progress of the modeling effort that is meaningful to the project and should be updated as needed.

Organizing the modeling effort

Organizing the modeling effort is an important part of the MBSE approach. The modeling team generally starts with a few modelers who have developed sufficient modeling expertise, perhaps through supporting a pilot or a previous modeling effort. The lead for the modeling effort must have technical credibility on the project and strong leadership skills. This individual needs to manage or oversee the model development and promote its adoption on the project. The lead will maintain a disciplined approach to model development and manage the scope of the effort to ensure incremental success.

The model development is divided up among members of the modeling team. For example, some members of the modeling team may be responsible for capturing the requirements and others may be responsible for selected use cases. The modeling lead should ensure that consistent guidelines are applied and that the model is subject to on-going quality reviews.

Stakeholder participation in the modeling effort

Many of the contributors to the modeling effort may not be directly involved in building the model but will contribute to the model content. Of particular importance is the establishment of ownership of the model data. For example, the subsystem leads may be responsible for the model content associated with their subsystem. They will identify the domain content for their subsystem that is to be captured in the model and review the resulting model to validate that the model reflects their intent. In the end, the model can only be as good as the quality of the source data. Clear ownership adds credibility to the model and ensures the project stakeholders have a real stake in the model.

It is also important for new design information to attain a level of stability before entering it into the model to limit unnecessary rework of the model. Teams may use other informal drawing tools for initial concepts and only capture information in the model after the concept has reached an appropriate level of stability. Additional design issues may surface as this information is captured more formally in the model and integrated with other parts of the system.

One of the key challenges facing the acceptance of the model may be the presentation of the information in a model versus more conventional document-based formats.. The model can be very precise and rich in content, but the project stakeholders that consume the modeling information must be comfortable with how the modeling information is presented. In many cases, the stakeholders may prefer to see the data presented in a way that is more familiar to them, such as tabular data, textual reports, or graphical representations with domain specific icons. This can be accomplished by extracting the data from the model and presenting the information in the desired form using the concepts of view and viewpoint that are described in Chapter 15, Section 15.8 and Chapter 18, Sections18.2.2 and 18.4.5.

The modeling information is often presented as part of technical reviews. It may be presented in traditional artifacts as described in the previous paragraph. For some audiences, it can be advantageous to conduct the review using a predefined storyboard to walk through selected parts of the model directly. Presenting the system specification, design, analysis, and verification information in this way leverages the model navigation capability to weave together important threads of an overall story.

Maintaining the model

Managing change to the model to ensure consistent and up-to-date information is critical to the success of the model. During the early phases of design, simple version control is sufficient to manage the model. As the design progresses and matures, managing change becomes more complex and more rigorous. A change to the model must be supported by change impact analysis to understand what other parts of the system model are impacted. Techniques such as branch and merge are introduced to ensure multiple independent changes are properly synchronized in a new version of the model. Other engineering models and artifacts may be impacted as well, which must be managed through the project change management process. In addition, new versions of the modeling tool may be introduced. This also must be taken into account as part of the overall configuration management approach as described in Chapter 18 Section 18.2.3.

It is important to maintain the model as part of the technical baseline. An on-going challenge is to ensure that the model is recognized as a primary source of information. The modeling team can partially measure its success in terms of the extent to which other members of the project treat the model as the source of information they use to do their job. This requires a disciplined approach to ensure overall value of the model is maintained in terms of the quality, credibility, value, and currency of the content, and the effectiveness of its presentation.

19.3 SUMMARY

SysML is deployed as part of an MBSE approach using the organization's improvement process. A successful deployment must be planned, piloted, and incrementally deployed. Success of the modeling effort on one project is a key ingredient in motivating other projects to follow. The result of the modeling effort, including its benefits and lessons learned, are quantified, where practical, and used as a basis for future deployments and improvements.

There are many elements to a MBSE deployment strategy. The deployment strategy for an organization depends on the stage of adoption of MBSE. The strategy includes a clear definition of the MBSE value proposition, a focus on building the infrastructure to enable use of MBSE on projects, the selection of the right projects at the right time for deployment, and the support needed to help make projects successful.

The deployment strategy for a project focuses on incrementally building and maintaining a model in a disciplined manner to bring value to the project, and on the means to engage the project stakeholders so they become contributors and consumers of the model content.

19.4 QUESTIONS

1. When SysML is being deployed, which other aspects of MBSE should be considered?
2. What are the activities in the improvement process?
3. Who are some of the stakeholders in the improvement process?
4. What is the purpose of the monitor and assessment activity?
5. What is the purpose of piloting the MBSE approach?
6. What are some of the up-front project activities that must be planned when deploying SysML to a project?
7. What are key elements that a deployment strategy should address?

DISCUSSION TOPICS

How might one organize an improvement effort to deploy MBSE across a large organization? Describe sample content for a modeling plan from startup of a new modeling effort through the initial design review.

SysML Reference Guide

Appendix A provides a reference guide to the graphical notation for SysML as a set of notation tables which are organized by diagram kind.

A.1 OVERVIEW

This appendix provides a reference guide to the graphical notation for SysML as a set of notation tables. It is organized by diagram kind in the following order, consistent with their introduction in Part II:

- Package Diagram
- Block Definition Diagram
- Internal Block Diagram
- Parametric Diagram
- Activity Diagram
- Sequence Diagram
- State Machine Diagram
- Use Case Diagram
- Requirement Diagram

There are also notation tables for the use of allocations and stereotypes, which are used across a number of different diagrams.

It is recommended that you read Section 4.3 in Chapter 4 for an overview of SysML diagrams and their contents before reading this appendix.

A.2 NOTATIONAL CONVENTIONS

This section describes how to interpret the notation tables in the rest of the appendix. This includes identifying those notational elements that are in the OCSMP basic features set.

NOTATION TABLES

Each diagram is described by at least one notation table. For diagrams with many symbols, there are separate tables for nodes and paths, where node symbols are typically rectangles and ovals, and path symbols are lines. Package diagrams and block definition diagrams have several subsections to describe different uses of the diagram with corresponding notation tables. The rows in each table are ordered to correspond with the order in which they are introduced in the relevant chapter or chapters.

The notation tables have four columns:

- Diagram Element—the name of the diagram element represented in this row, generally identified as a node or path. The term symbol is used when it is neither a node nor a path, such as a text expression in brackets.
- Notation—the graphical notation for the diagram element.
- Description—a description of the SysML concept represented by the diagram element.
- Section—a reference to the section(s) in Part II that contains further explanation of the relevant SysML concept.
   The following conventions are used in the tables:
- < Name>—the name of the model element represented by the symbol.
- < Element>—the name of some model element.
- < Type>—the name of some type (Block, ValueType, etc.).
- < String>—a text string.
- < Expression>, <ValueSpecification>—a text string intended to represent some kind of mathematical expression.
- < ElementKind>—the keyword representing some kind of model element.
- < Multiplicity>—a representation of multiplicity, thus: <LowerBound>… <UpperBound>, where LowerBound is any natural number and UpperBound is any natural number or "*."

The names inside the angled brackets are intended to be self-explanatory references to SysML model elements, but occasionally extra explanation is provided in the Description column of a symbol.

It should be noted that various parts of the graphical and textual notation may be elided by a modeler, and the tables do not provide guidance on what can be elided and when. In addition, certain model elements have additional keywords and properties that are listed in the Description column of the relevant symbol.

OCSMP AND SysML 1.3

The tables are shaded to identify those SysML elements which are in the OCSMP basic feature set. The shading is added as follows:
- Node and note symbols are shaded to indicate that they are in the basic feature set. If a node symbol has multiple compartments, only compartments covered by the basic feature set are shaded.
- Path symbols covered by the basic feature set are enclosed in a shaded area.
- Those parts of the description column that describe basic features have a shaded background.
   SysML 1.3 added some new features and deprecated others. Table A.7 lists the symbols for deprecated features. Tables A.4 and A.6 contain symbols for concepts that were added in SysML 1.3. SysML 1.3 notation is indicated in the description column of the affected tables.

A.3 PACKAGE DIAGRAM

Package diagrams are used principally to describe model organization. They are also used to define SysML language extensions called profiles.

Table A.1   Package Diagram Nodes and Paths

Diagram Element	Notation	Description	Section
Comment Note	`<String>`	Comments are free format descriptions of model elements.	5.5.1
Element Group	«elementGroup» {name = <String>} size = <Integer>} <String>	An element group provides a light weight mechanism for grouping model elements. The purpose of the grouping is user-defined.	5.5.2
Package Node	<Name> {uri=<String>} <Name> {uri=<String>}	A package is a container for other model elements. Any model element is contained in exactly one container, and when that container is deleted or copied, the contained model element is deleted or copied along with it.	6.3
Model Node	<Name> {uri=<String>} <Name> {uri=<String>}	A model in SysML is a top-level package in a nested package hierarchy. In a package hierarchy, models may contain other models, packages, and views.	6.3
Packageable Element Node	«<ElementKind>» <Name>	Model elements that can be contained in packages are called packageable elements and include blocks, activities, and value types among others.	6.5
Containment Path		The containment relationship relates parents to children within a package hierarchy.	6.4
Import Path	«import» <Name> «access» <Name>	An import relationship is used to bring an element or collection of elements into a namespace. Private import is marked by the keyword «access».	6.7
Dependency Path	«<DependencyType>»	A dependency relationship indicates that a change to the supplier (arrow) end of the dependency may result in a change to the other end of the dependency.	6.8

Table A.2 Notation for Describing SysML Extensions on Package Diagrams

Diagram Element	Notation	Description	Section
Metamodel Node	«metamodel» <Name {uri=<String>} «metamodel» <Name> {uri=<String>}	A metamodel describes the concepts in a modeling language, their characteristics and interrelationships.	15.2.1
Metaclass Node	«metaclass» <Name>	The individual concepts in a metamodel are described by metaclasses.	15.2.1, 15.4
Model Library Node	«modelLibrary» <Name> {uri=<String>} «modelLibrary» <Name> {uri=<String>}	A model library is a special type of package that is intended to contain a set of reusable model elements for a given domain.	15.3
Stereotype Node	«stereotype» <Name> constraints {<Constraint>} properties ^<Property>:<Type>=<Expression>	Stereotypes are used to add new language concepts, typically in support of a specific system engineering domain.	15.4
Profile Node	«profile» <Name> {uri=<String>} «profile» <Name {uri=<String>}>	A profile is a kind of package used as the container for set of stereotypes and supporting definitions.	15.5
Generalization Path	<GeneralizationSet> <GeneralizationSet>	A stereotype can be defined by specializing an existing stereotype or stereotypes, using the generalization mechanism.	15.4
Extension Path	<Multiplicity> {required} <Multiplicity>	The relationship between the metaclass and the stereotype is called an extension, and is a kind of association.	15.4
Association Path	<End> <Name> <End> <Multiplicity> <Multiplicity>	Stereotype properties can be defined using associations.	15.4.1
Reference Path	«reference»	A reference is special type of import relationship, used to import the metaclasses required by a profile.	15.5.1
Profile Application Path	«apply» {strict}	A profile is applied to a model or package using a profile application relationship.	15.6

A.4 BLOCK DEFINITION DIAGRAM

The block definition diagram is used to define the characteristics of blocks in terms of structural and behavioral features, and the relationships between the blocks, such as their hierarchical relationship. Extensions to the block definition diagram are used to define parametric constraints and to show a hierarchical view of activities.

Table A.3   Block Definition Diagram Nodes for Representing Block Structure and Values

Diagram Element	Notation	Description	Section
Block Node	**«block»** **<Name>** *properties* ^<Property>:<Type>[<Multiplicity>] *parts* ^<Part>:<Block>[<Multiplicity>] *references* ^<Reference>:<Block>[<Multiplicity>] *boundReferences* ^{/bindingPath=<Property>,...} <Reference>:<Block>[<Multiplicity>] *values* ^<ValueProperty>:<ValueType>=<ValueExpression> *classifierBehavior* <Behavior> *ownedBehaviors* <Behavior>(<Parameter>,...):<Type>	The block is the fundamental modular unit for describing system structure in SysML. Compartments are used to show structural features and behavioral features of the block. See the following tables in this section for more block compartments. Additional properties on blocks are {encapsulated, abstract}. Abstract may also be indicated by italicizing the <Name>. Additional properties on structural features include: {ordered, unordered, unique, nonunique, subsets <Property>, redefines <Property>, readOnly}. A forward slash (/) before a property name indicates that it is derived. Static properties are underlined	7.2, 7.3, 7.5, 7.7.4
Value Type Node	**«valueType»** **<Name>** *values* ^<ValueProperty>:<ValueType>=<ValueExpression> *operations* ^<Operation>(<Parameter>,...):<Type> **«valueType»** unit=<Unit> quantityKind=<QuantityKind>	A value type is used to provide a uniform definition of a quantity with units that can be shared by many value properties.	7.3.4
Enumeration Node	**«enumeration»** **<Name>** *literals* <EnumerationLiteral>	An enumeration defines a set of named values called literals.	7.3.4
Actor Node	**«actor»** **<Name>** <Name>	An actor is used to represent the role of a human, an organization, or any external system that participates in the use of some system being investigated.	12.3

Blocks have two additional compartments:

Structure, which has the same symbols as an internal block diagram.
Namespace, which has the same symbols as a block definition diagram.

Table A.4 Block Definition Diagram Nodes for Representing Interfaces

Diagram Element	Notation	Description	Section
Interface Block Node	«interfaceBlock» <Name> *flow properties* ^<Direction> <FlowProperty>:<Item> *references* ^<Direction><Reference>:<Block>[<Multiplicity>] *values* ^<ValueProperty>:<ValueType>=<ValueExpression> *operations* ^<Direction> <Operation>(<Parameter>,...):<Type> ^<Direction> «signal»<Signal>(<Parameter>,...) *proxy ports* ^<Direction> <Port>:~<InterfaceBlock>	**Note that Interface Blocks were introduced in SysML 1.3** Proxy ports are defined by interface blocks, a specialized form of block that does not contain any internal structure or behavior. <Direction> for flow properties and ports may be one of: in, out, or inout. <Direction> for operations and references may be one of prov, reqd or provreqd. values may also have a <Direction> but it is not shown Proxy ports indicate their conjugation using a tilda (~)	7.6.2
Interface Node	«interface» <Name> *operations* ^<Operation>(<Parameter>,...):<Type> ^«signal»<Signal>(<Parameter>,...)	An interface is used to specify the set of behavioral features either required or provided by a standard (service-based) port.	7.6.5
Signal Node	«signal» <Name> ^<Attribute>:<Type>	A signal defines a message that can sent and received by a block. It has a set of attributes that specify the content of the message.	7.5.2
Interface Compartments for Block Node	«block» <Name> *ports* ^<Direction> <Port>:<Block> *full ports* ^<Direction> <Port>:<Block> *proxy ports* ^<Direction> <Port>:~<InterfaceBlock> *operations* ^<Direction> <Operation>(<Parameter>,...):<Type> ^<Direction> «signal»<Signal>(<Parameter>,...)	Ports can be shown in separate compartments of a block symbol labeled full ports and proxyports. <Direction> may be one of: in, out, or inout. Proxy ports indicate their conjugation using a tilda (~). <Direction> for operations may be one of prov, reqd or provreqd. **Note that full and proxy ports and <Direction> on operations were introduced in SysML 1.3**	7.5.2, 7.6.1 ,7.6.2

Table A.5   Block Definition Diagram Paths

Diagram Element	Notation	Description	Section
Composite Association Path		A composite association relates a whole to its parts showing the relative multiplicity at both whole and part ends. A composite association always defines a part property in the whole (indicated by <Part>). Where there is no arrow on the nondiamond end of the association it also specifies a reference property to the whole in the part (indicated by <Reference>). Otherwise when there is an arrow, the name at the whole end simply gives a name to the association end (indicated by <End>).	7.3.1
Reference Association Path		A reference association can be used to specify a relationship between two blocks. A reference association can specify a reference property on the blocks at one or both ends. The white diamond is the same as no diamond, but profiles can be used to differentiate them by specifying additional constraints.	7.3.2
Association Block Path and Node		An association block, as the name implies, is a combination of an association and a block, so it can relate two blocks together but can also have internal structure and other features of its own. Participants are placeholders that represent the blocks at each end of the association block, and are used when it is desired to decompose a connector.	7.3.3
Generalization Path		A generalization describes the relationship between the general classifier and specialized classifier. A set of generalizations may either be {disjoint} or {overlapping}. They may also be {complete} or {incomplete}.	7.7

Table A.6 Nodes for Representing Ports

Diagram Element	Notation	Description	Section
Full Port Node	«full»<Name>: <Block> [<Multiplicity>] «full»<Name>: <Block> [<Multiplicity>] «full»<Name>: <Block> [<Multiplicity>] «proxy»<Name>: ~<InterfaceBlock> [<Multiplicity>]	Full ports are similar to parts, in that they are included in the parts tree of their owning block. However, unlike parts, they are shown graphically on the boundary of their parent. A port symbol can contain compartments to describe the port's features. **Note that full ports were introduced in SysML 1.3**	7.6.1
Proxy Port Node	«proxy»<Name>:~<InterfaceBlock> [<Multiplicity>] «proxy»<Name>: ~<InterfaceBlock> [<Multiplicity>] «proxy»<Name>:~<InterfaceBlock> [<Multiplicity>] «proxy» <Name>: <Block> [<Multiplicity>]	A proxy port differs from a full port in that it does not represent a distinct part of the system, but is a modeling construct that exposes features of either its owning block or parts of that block. **Note that proxy ports were introduced in SysML 1.3**	7.6.2
Proxy Port Node With Interfaces	<Interface> ○—□ «proxy»<Name>[<Multiplicity>] <Interface> ⊃—□ «proxy»<Name>[<Multiplicity>]	An interface is represented by either a ball or socket symbol with the name of the interface floating near it. The ball depicts a provided interface, and the socket depicts a required interface. A proxy port can be a behavior port that provides access to the features of its owning block.	7.6.5

Table A.7 Symbols That Are Deprecated in SysML 1.3

Diagram Element	Notation	Description	Section
Flow Specification Node	«flowSpecification» <Name> *flow properties* <Direction> <FlowProperty>:<Item>	A flow specification defines the set of input and/or output flows for a noncomposite flow port. <Direction> may be one of: in, out, or inout.	7.10.1
Port Compartments for Block Node	«block» <Name> *standard ports* <Port>:<Interface> *flow ports* <Direction> <Port>:<Type>	Ports can be shown in separate compartments labeled flow ports and standard ports. <Direction> may be one of: in, out, or inout. Non-atomic flow ports do not have a direction. Non-atomic flow ports may have the keyword {conjugated}.	7.10.1
Nonatomic Flow Port Node	<Name>:<FlowSpecification>[<Multiplicity>] <Name>:<FlowSpecification>[<Multiplicity>]	A nonatomic flow port describes an interaction point where multiple different items may flow into or out of a block. A shaded symbol implies a conjugate port.	7.10.1
Atomic Flow Port Node	<Name>:<Item>[<Multiplicity>] <Name>:<Item>[<Multiplicity>] <Name>:<Item>[<Multiplicity>]	An atomic flow port describes an interaction point where an item can flow into or out of a block, or both, as indicated by the direction of the arrow in the Atomic Flow Port Node.	7.10.1

Table A.8 Additional Notation to Define Parametric Models on Block Definition Diagrams

Diagram Element	Notation	Description	Section
Block Node with Constraint Compartment	«block» <Name> / constraints / {{<Language>}<Constraint>} ^<ConstraintProperty>:<ConstraintBlock>[<Multiplicity>]	The constraints on a block can be shown in a special compartment labeled constraints. <Constraint> contains an expression preceded by an indication of the language used to express the constraint.	8.2
Constraint Block Node	«constraint» <Name> / parameters / ^<Parameter>:<Type>[<Multiplicity>]=<ValueExpression> / constraints / {{<Language>}<Constraint>} ^<ConstraintProperty>:<ConstraintBlock>[<Multiplicity>]	A constraint block encapsulates a constraint to enable it to be defined once and then used in different contexts.	8.3

Table A.9 Additional Notation to Define Activity Models on Block Definition Diagrams

Diagram Element	Notation	Description	Section
Activity Node	«activity» <Name> / parts / ^<Part>:<Block>[<Multiplicity>] / references / ^<Reference>:<Block>[<Multiplicity>] / values / ^<ValueProperty>:<ValueType>=<ValueExpression> / constraints / {{<Language>}<Constraint>} ^<ConstraintProperty>:<ConstraintBlock>[<Multiplicity>]	On a block definition diagram, activities are shown using a block symbol with the keyword "activity."	9.12.1
Activity Composition Path	<End> <Name> «adjunct»<Action> <Multiplicity> <Multiplicity> / <End> <Multiplicity> «adjunct»<Action> <Multiplicity>	Invocation of activities via call behavior actions is modeled using the standard composition association where the calling activity is shown at the black diamond end and the called activity is at the other end of the association. Properties are related to activity elements using the adjunct property stereotype	9.12.1
Object Node Composition Path	<End> <Name> <ObjectNode> <Multiplicity> <Multiplicity> / <End> <Name> <ObjectNode> <Multiplicity> <Multiplicity> / <End> <Multiplicity> «adjunct» <ObjectNode> <Multiplicity>	Parameters and other object nodes can also be represented on the block definition diagram. By convention, the relationship from activities to object nodes is represented with a reference association.	9.12.2

Table A.10 Additional Notation to Define Instance Specifications and Physical Quantities on Block Definition Diagrams

Diagram Element	Notation	Description	Section
Instance Specification Node	<InstanceSpecification>/<Property>:<Type> <ValueSpecification> <InstanceSpecification>/<Property>:<Type> <Property>=<ValueSpecification> ...	An instance specification describes a specific instance of a block or value type. The symbol may contain a single value, or a separate compartment with values for several properties. Where the instance specification is the value for a property of an enclosing block symbol, the name of the property is part of the name string for the symbol	7.8
Association Instance Specification (Link) Path	<InstanceSpecification> <Property>	Instance specifications can be connected by links , which represent instances of associations between blocks. The ends and name string of the symbol are the same as those of the association of which it is an instance.	7.8
Quantity Kind Node	<Name>:<QuantityKind> definitionUri=<String> symbol=<String>	A quantity kind identifies a physical quantity such as length, whose value may be stated in terms of defined units, such as meters or feet.	7.3.4
Unit Node	<Name>:<Unit> definitionUri=<String> quantityKind=<QuantityKind> symbol=<String>	A unit defines a measurement unit for a physcial quantity.	7.3.4

A.5 INTERNAL BLOCK DIAGRAM

The internal block diagram is used to describe the internal structure of a block in terms of how its parts are interconnected. Please note that the symbols for ports described in are also used on the internal block diagram.

Table A.11   Internal Block Diagram Nodes

Diagram Element	Notation	Description	Section
Part Node	<Multiplicity> ^<Name>:[<Block>] *initialValues* <Property>=<ValueExpression>	A part is a property of an owning block that is defined (typed) by another block. The part represents a usage of the defined block in the context of the owning block. Note that a Part Node may have the same compartments as a Block Node, with the compartment label prefixed by a colon. [<Block>] represents a property-specific type.	7.3.1, 7.7.5
Actor Part Node	^<Name>:<Actor>[<Multiplicity>]	An actor part is a property of a owning block that is defined (typed) by an actor.	12.5
Reference Node	<Multiplicity> ^<Name>:[<Block>] *initialValues* <Property>=<ValueExpression>	A reference property of a block is a reference to another block. Note that a Reference Property Node may have the same compartments as a Block Node with the compartment label prefixed by a colon. [<Block>] represents a property-specific type.	7.3.2
Participant Property Node	«participant» {end=<Reference>} ^<Participant>:<Block>	A participant property represents one end of an association block. Using a participant property, a modeler can show the relationship between the internal structure of the association block and the internal structure of its related ends.	7.3.3
Bound Reference Node	«boundReference» ^<Reference>:<Block>	A bound reference provides a means to specify points of variation in a block that can be varied in its subclasses.	7.7.4
Value Property Node	<Multiplicity> ^<Name>:[<ValueType>]=<Expression> *initialValues* <Property>=<ValueExpression>	A value property describes the quantitative characteristics of a block. Note that a Value Property Node may have the same compartments as a Value Type Node. [<ValueType>] represents a property-specific type.	7.3.4

Table A.12 Internal Block Diagram Paths

Diagram Element	Notation	Description	Section
Connector Path	<End> <Name> <End> <Multiplicity> <Multiplicity>	A connector is used to bind two parts (or ports) and provides the opportunity for those parts to interact.	7.3.1, 7.3.3
	<End> <Name>:<Association> <End> <Multiplicity> <Multiplicity>	The symbol's name string may show the type of the connector if it has one.	
Connector Property Path and Node	<End> <End> <Multiplicity> <Multiplicity> <Name>:<Association>	More detail can be specified for connectors by typing them with association blocks. When a connector is typed by an association block it can have an associate connector property.	7.3.3
Item Flow Node	<Name>:<Item>, ... ▶◀ <Name>:<Item>, ...	An item flow is used to specify the items that flow across a connector in a particular context. An item flow specifies the type of the item that is flowing and the direction of flow. It may also be associated to a property, called an item property, of the enclosing block to identify a specific usage of an item in the context of the enclosing block.	7.4.3

A.6 PARAMETRIC DIAGRAM

Parametric diagrams are used to create systems of equations that can be used to constrain the properties of blocks.

Table A.13   Parametric Diagram Notation

Diagram Element	Notation	Description	Section
Constraint Note	{<Constraint>}	A constraint expresses a rule that the constrained model element must satisfy. The definition of a constraint may include the definition language.	8.2
Constraint Parameter Node	<Name>: <Type>[<Multiplicity>]	A constraint parameter is a special kind of property that is used in the constraint expression of a constraint block. Constraint parameters do not have direction.	8.3
Constraint Property Node	<Name>:<ConstraintBlock> {<Constraint>} «constraint» <Name>:<ConstraintBlock> {<Constraint>}	Constraint properties are defined by constraint blocks and used to bind (i.e., connect) parameters. This enables complex systems of equations to be composed from more primitive equations, and for the parameters of the equations to explicilty constrain properties of blocks. The rake symbol indicates that the constraint property refers to another parametric diagram.	8.4
Value Binding Path	<Multiplicity> <Multiplicity> <Multiplicity> «equal» <Multiplicity>	Binding connectors connect constraint parameters to each other and to value properties. They express an equality relationship between their bound elements.	7.3.1, 8.5

A.7 ACTIVITY DIAGRAM

The activity diagram is used to model behavior in terms of the flow of inputs, outputs, and control. An activity diagram is similar to a traditional functional flow diagram.

Table A.14 Activity Diagram Structural Nodes

Diagram Element	Notation	Description	Section
Activity Parameter Node	act <Activity> <Parameter>:<Type>:<Multiplicity> <Parameter>:<Type>:<Multiplicity>	Activity parameter node symbols are rectangles that straddle the boundary of the activity frame. Other annotations include: «noBuffer», «optional», «overwrite», «continuous», «discrete», {rate=<Expression>}. Parameters can be organized into parameter sets, indicated by a bounding box around the parameters in the set. Parameter sets may overlap, and may have an annotation: {probability=<Expression>}.	9.4.1
Interruptible Region Node	<InterrruptibleRegion>	An interruptible region groups a subset of the actions within an activity and includes a mechanism for stopping their execution. Stopping the execution of these actions does not effect other actions in the activity.	9.8.1
Activity Partition Node	<Partition> <Partition>	A set of activity nodes can be grouped into an activity partition (also known as a swimlane) that is used to indicate responsibility for execution of those nodes. <Partition> may be the name of a block or name and type of a part/reference. Partitions may overlap in a grid pattern.	9.11.1
Activity Partition in Action Node	(<Partition>,..) <Name>:<Behavior>	An alternative representation for an activity partition for call actions is to include the name of the partition or partitions in parentheses inside the node above the action name. This can make the activity easier to layout than when using the swimlane notation.	9.11.1
Structured Activity Node	«structured» <StructuredActivityNode>	A structured activity node executes its nested actions as a single group. A structured activity node can have a set of pins through which tokens flow to and from its internal actions.	9.8.2

Table A.15   Activity Diagram Control Nodes

Diagram Element	Notation	Description	Section
Merge Node		A merge node has one output flow and multiple input flows—it routes each input token received on any input flow to its output flow. Unlike a join node, a merge node does not require tokens on all its input flows before offering them on its output flow. Rather it offers tokens on its output flow as soon as it receives them.	9.5.1, 9.6.1
Decision Node	[<Expression>] [<Expression>] [<Expression>]	A decision node has one input flow and multiple output flows—an input token can only traverse one output flow. The output flow is typically established by placing mutually exclusive guards on all outgoing flows and offering the token to the flow whose guard expression is satisfied.	9.5.1, 9.6.1
Join Node	{join-spec= <Expression>}	A join node has one output flow and multiple input flows, so will synchronize the flow of tokens from many sources. Its default behavior can be overridden by providing a join specification, which specifies additional control logic.	9.5.1, 9.6.1
Fork Node		A fork node has one input flow and multiple output flows—it replicates every input token it receives onto each of its output flows. The tokens on each output flow may be handled independently and concurrently.	9.5.1, 9.6.1
Initial Node		When an activity starts executing a control token is placed on each initial node in the activity. The token can then trigger the execution of an action via an outgoing control flow.	9.6.1
Activity Final Node		When a control or object token reaches an activity final node during the execution of an activity, the execution terminates.	9.6.1
Flow Final Node		Control or object tokens received at a flow final node are consumed but have no effect on the execution of the enclosing activity. Typically they are used to terminate a particular sequence of actions without terminating an activity.	9.6.1
Decision Input Behavior Note	«decisionInput» <Behavior>	A decision node can have an accompanying decision input behavior, which is used to evaluate each incoming object token and whose result can be used in guard expressions.	9.5.1, 9.6.1

Table A.16 Activity Diagram Object and Action Nodes

Diagram Element	Notation	Description	Section
Call Action Node	<Name>:<Type> <Name>:<Behavior> <Name>:<Type>[<State>,...] <Name>:<Operation> via <Port> ,... target «localPrecondition» <Constraint> «localPostcondition» <Constraint>	Call actions can invoke other behaviors either directly or through an operation, and are referred to as call behavior actions and call operation actions, respectively. A call action must own a set of pins that match in number and type of the parameters of the invoked behavior/operation. A called operation requires a target. Streaming pins may be marked as {stream} or filled (as shown). Where the parameters of the called entity are grouped into sets, the corresponding pins are as well. Pre- and postconditions can be specified that constrain the action such that it cannot begin to execute unless the precondition is satisfied, and must satisfy the postcondition to successfully complete execution.	9.1, 9.3, 9.4.2
Central Buffer Node	«centralBufferNode» <Name>:<Type> [<State>,...]	A central buffer node provides a store for object tokens outside of pins and parameter nodes. Tokens flow into a central buffer node and are stored there until they flow out again.	9.5.3
Datastore Node	«dataStore» <Name>:<Type> [<State>,...]	A datastore node provides a copy of a stored token rather than the original. When an input token represents an object that is already in the store, it overwrites the previous token.	9.5.3
Control Operator Action Node	{control} «controlOperator» <Name>:<ControlOperator>	A control operator produces control values on an output parameter, and is able to accept a control value on an input parameter (treated as an object token). It is used to specify logic for enabling and disabling other actions.	9.6.2
Accept Event Action Node	<Event> «from» (<Port> ,...)	An activity can accept events using an accept event action. The action has (sometimes hidden) output pins for received data.	9.7
Accept Time Event Node	<TimeExpression>	A time event corresponds to an expiration of an (implicit) timer. In this case the action has a single (typically hidden) output pin that outputs a token containing the time of the accepted event occurrence.	9.7
Send Signal Action	signal <Signal> via <Port> ,... target	An activity can send signals using a send signal action. It typically has pins corresponding to the signal data to be sent and the target for the signal.	9.7
Primitive Action Node	«<ActionType>» <Expression>	Primitive actions include: object access/update/manipulation actions, which involve properties and variables, and value actions, which allow the specification of values. The <Expression> will depend on the nature of the action.	9.14.3

Table A.17   Activity Diagram Paths

Diagram Element	Notation	Description	Section
Object Flow Path	[<Expression>] ⟶	Object flows connect inputs and outputs. Additional annotations include «continuous», «discrete», {rate=<Expression>}, {probability=<Expression>}.	9.1, 9.5
Control Flow Path	[<Expression>] ⇢ [<Expression>] ⟶	Control flows provide constraints on when, and in what order, the actions within an activity will execute. A control flow can be represented using a solid line, or using a dashed line to more clearly distinguish it from object flow.	9.1, 9.6
Object Flow Node	<Name>:<Type> [<State>,...]	When an object flow is between two pins that have the same characteristics, an alternative notation can be used where the pin symbols are elided and replaced by a single rectangular symbol called an object node symbol.	9.5
Interrupting Edge Path	[<Expression>] [<Expression>]	An interrupting edge interrupts the execution of the actions in an interruptible region. Its source is a node inside the region and its destination is a node outside it.	9.8.1

A.8 SEQUENCE DIAGRAM

The sequence diagram is used to represent the interaction between structural elements of a block as a sequence of message exchanges.

Table A.18   Sequence Diagram Structural Nodes

Diagram Element	Notation	Description	Section
Lifeline Node	<Name>:<Type> [<ValueSpecification>] ref <Interaction>	A lifeline represents the relevant lifetime of an instance that is part of the interaction's owning block, which will either be represented by a part property or a reference property. A lifeline may reference another interaction that describes the behavior of the lifeline's children.	10.4
Single-compartment Fragment Node	<UnaryOp> [<Constraint>]	A combined fragment can be used to model complex sequences of messages. A number of combined fragments have operators with only a single compartment for all operands, shown as <UnaryOp>. These are: seq, opt, break, strict, loop, neg, assert, critical.	10.7.1, 10.7.2
Multi-compartment Fragment Node	<N-aryOp> [<Constraint>] [<Constraint>]	Two combined fragments have operators with a compartment per operand, shown as <N-aryOp>. These are par and alt. The lifelines that participate in the fragment overlay on top of the fragment (i.e., are visible) and lifelines that don't particiapte are obscured behind the fragment. (Note: This is also true of Single-Compartment Fragment Nodes.)	10.7.1
Filtering Fragment Node	<FilterOp> {<Message>,...}	There are two combined fragments with filter operators: consider and ignore, shown as <FilterOp>. Inside such a construct, messages that have been explicitly ignored (or not considered) may be interleaved with valid traces.	10.7.2
State Invariant Symbol	<State> {<Constraint>}	A state invariant on a lifeline is used to add a constraint on the required state of a lifeline at a given point in a sequence of event occurrences. The invariant constraint can include the values of properties or parameters, or the state of a state machine.	10.7.3
Interaction Use Node	ref <Attribute>=<Interaction> (<Attribute>=<Argument>,...) :<Argument>	An interaction use allows one interaction to reference another as part of its definition. The lifelines that participate in the interaction are obscured behind the fragment, and lifelines that don't participate overlay on top of the fragment (i.e., are visible). Interaction uses can include arguments corresponding to interaction parameters. A rake indicates a child diagram.	10.8

Table A.19   Sequence Diagram Paths and Activation Nodes

Diagram Element	Notation	Description	Section
Synchronous Message	\<Name\>(\<Argument\>,...)	A synchronous message corresponds to the synchronous invocation of an operation, and is generally accompanied by a reply message.	10.5.1
Asynchronous Message	\<Name\>(\<Argument\>,...)	Asynchronous messages correspond to either the sending of a signal or to an asynchronous invocation (or call) of an operation, and do not require a reply message.	10.5.1
Reply Message	\<Attribute\>=\<Name\> (\<Attribute\>=\<Argument\>,...) :\<Argument\>	A reply message shows a reply to a synchronous operation call, together with any return arguments.	10.5.1
Found Message Path	\<Name\>(\<Argument\>,...)	A lost message describes the case where there is sending event for the message but no receiving event.	10.5.2
Lost Message Path	\<Name\>(\<Argument\>,...)	A found message describes the case where there is receiving event for the message but no sending event.	10.5.2
Activation Node	\<Name\>	Activations are overlaid on lifelines and correspond to executions; they begin at the execution's start event, and end at the execution's end event. When executions are nested, the activations are stacked from left to right. An alternate notation for activations is a box symbol overlaid on the lifeline with the name of the behavior or action inside.	10.5.4
Create Message Path	\<Name\>(\<Argument\>,...)	The creation of an instance is indicated by the receipt of a create message.	10.5.5
Destroy Event Node		An instance's destruction is indicated by the ocurrence of a destroy event.	10.5.5
Coregion Symbol		Within a coregion, there is no implied order between any messages sent or received by the lifeline.	10.7.1

Table A.20 Sequence Diagram Temporal Observation and Constraint Nodes

Diagram Element	Notation	Description	Section
Duration Observation Symbol	<Name>=<DurationExpression> <Name>=<DurationExpression>	A duration observation can be used to note the time taken between two instants that represent the occurrence of events during the execution of an interaction.	10.6
Duration Constraint Symbol	{<DurationConstraint>} {<DurationConstraint>} {<DurationConstraint>}	A duration constraint identifies two events, called the start and end events, and expresses a constraint on the duration between them. A duration constraint can use a duration observation in its definition.	10.6
Time Observation Symbol	<Name>=<TimeExpression>	A time observation is used to note the time at some instant during the execution of an interaction.	10.6
Time Constraint Symbol	{<TimeConstraint>}	A time constraint identifies a constraint that applies to the time of occurrence of a single event in the interaction execution. A time constraint can use a time observation in its definition.	10.6

A.9 STATE MACHINE DIAGRAM

A state machine diagram is used in SysML to describe the state-dependent behavior of a block throughout its lifecycle in terms of its states and the transitions between them.

Table A.21   State Machine Diagram State Nodes

Diagram Element	Notation	Description	Section
State Machine with Entry- and Exit-Point Pseudostate Nodes		A state machine may have entry- and exit-point pseudostates, which are similar to junctions. On state machines, entry-point pseudostates can only have outgoing transitions and exit-point pseudostates can only have incoming transitions.	11.6.5
Atomic State Node		A state represents some significant condition in the life of a block. Each state may have entry and exit behaviors, and a do behavior. An atomic state node may also show transitions that are local to the state and events that are deferred while the state machine is in this state.	11.3
Composite State with Entry- and Exit-Point Pseudostate Nodes		A composite state is a state with nested regions; the most common case is a single region. A composite state may have entry- and exit-point pseudostates that act like junction pseudostates. Entry points have incoming transitions from outside the state and exit points have the opposite.	11.6.1
Composite State Node with Multiple Regions		A composite state may have many regions, which may each contain substates. These regions are orthogonal to each other and so a composite state with more than one region is sometimes called an orthogonal composite state.	11.6.2
Sub–State Machine Node with Connection Points		A state machine may be reused using a kind of state called a submachine state. A transition ending on a submachine state will start its referenced state machine. Transitions may also be connected to connection points on the boundary of the state. The symbol in the lower right refers to a lower level statemachine diagram. This can also be represented by a rake symbol.	11.6.5

Table A.22 State Machine Diagram Pseudostate and Transition Nodes

Diagram Element	Notation	Description	Section
Terminate Pseudostate Node		If a terminate pseudostate is reached, then the behavior of the state machine terminates.	11.3
Initial Pseudostate Node		An initial pseudostate specifies the initial state of a region.	11.3
Final State Node		The final state indicates that a region has completed execution.	11.3
Choice Pseudostate Node		The outgoing transitions of a choice pseudostate are evaluated once it has been reached.	11.4.2
Junction Pseudostate Node		A junction pseudostate is used to construct a compound transition path between states.	11.4.2
Trigger Node	<Event>,... [<Constraint>]	This node represents all the transition's triggers, with the descriptions of the triggering events and the transition guard inside the symbol.	11.4.3
Action Node	<EffectExpression>	<EffectExpression> describes the effect of the transition, either the name of a behavior or the body of an opaque behavior.	11.4.3
Send Signal Node	<Signal>(<Argument>,...)	This node represents a send signal action. The signal's name, together with any arguments that are being sent, are shown within the symbol.	11.4.3
Join Pseudostate Node		A join pseudostate has a single outgoing transition and many incoming transitions. When all of the incoming transitions can be taken, and the join's outgoing transition is valid, then all the transitions happen.	11.6.2
Fork Pseudostate Node		A fork pseudostate has a single incoming transition and many outgoing transitions. When an incoming transition is taken to the fork pseudostate, all of the outgoing transitions are taken.	11.6.2
History Pseudostate Node	H H*	A history pseudostate represents the last state of its owning region, and a transition ending on a history pseudostate has the effect of returning the region to the state it was last in.	11.6.4

Table A.23   State Machine Diagram Paths

Diagram Element	Notation	Description	Section
Time Event Transition Path	after <TimeExpression>[<Constraint>]/<Behavior> $\longrightarrow$ at <TimeExpression>[<Constraint>]/<Behavior> $\longrightarrow$	Time events indicate either that a given time interval has passed since the current state was entered (after), or that a given instant of time has been reached (at). The transition can also include a guard and effect.	11.4.1
Signal Event Transition Path	<Signal>(<Attribute>, …)[<Constraint>]/<Behavior> $\longrightarrow$	Signal events indicate that a new asynchronous message has arrived. A signal event may be accompanied by a number of arguments, which may be assigned to attributes. The transition can also include a guard and effect.	11.4.1
Call Event Transition Path	<Operation>(<Attribute>, …)[<Constraint>]/<Behavior> $\longrightarrow$	Call events indicate that an operation on the state machine's owning block has been requested. A call event may also be accompanied by a number of arguments, which may be assigned to attributes. The transition can also include a guard and effect.	11.5
Change Event Transition Path	when <Expression>[<Constraint>]/<Behavior> $\longrightarrow$	Change events indicate that some condition has been satisfied (normally that some specific set of attribute values hold). The transition can also include a guard and behavior/effect.	11.7

A.10 USE CASE DIAGRAM

The use case diagram is used to model the relationships between the system under consideration or subject, its actors, and use cases.

Table A.24 Use Case Diagram Notation

Diagram Element	Notation	Description	Section
Actor Node	«actor» <Name> <Name>	The users and other external participants in an interaction with a subject are described by actors. An actor represents the role of a human, an organization, or any external system that participates in the use of some subject. Actors may interact directly with the suject or indirectly with the system through other actors.	12.1, 12.3
Use Case Node	<Name> extension points <ExtensionPoint>,...	Use cases describe the functionality of some system in terms of how its users use that system to achieve their goals. A use case may define a set of extension points, that represent places where it can be extended. The rake symbol indicates the presence of a child use case diagram.	12.1, 12.4
Subject Node	<Name> <Use Case>	The entity that provides functionality in support of the use cases is called the system under consideration, or subject, and is represented by a rectangle. It often represents a system that is being developed.	12.4
Association Path	<End> <Name> <End> <Multiplicity> <Multiplicity>	Actors are related to use cases by associations. The multiplicity at the actor end describes the number of actors involved, and the multiplicity at the use case end describes the number of instances in which the actor or actors can be involved.	12.4
Extension Path	Condition: {<Constraint>} extension points: <ExtensionPoint>,... «extend»	The extending use case is a fragment of functionality that extends the base use case and is not considered part of the normal base use case functionality. It often describes some exceptional behavior in the interaction between subject and actors, such as error handling, which does not contribute directly to the goal of the base use case. The arrow end of the extension relationship points to the base use case that is extended.	12.4.1
Inclusion Path	«include»	The inclusion relationship allows a base use case to include the functionality of an included use case as part of its functionality. The included use case is always performed when the base use case is performed. The arrow end of the include relationship points to the included use case.	12.4.1
Generalization Path	<GeneralizationSet> <GeneralizationSet>	Use cases and actors can be classified using the generalization relationships. Scenarios and actor associations from the general use case are inherited by the specialized use case.	12.4.1

A.11 REQUIREMENT DIAGRAM

The requirement diagram is used to graphically depict hierarchies of requirements or to depict an individual requirement and its relationship to other model elements.

Table A.25 Requirement Diagram Nodes

Diagram Element	Notation	Description	Section
Requirement Node	«requirement» <Name> text = "<String>" id = "<String>" *satsifiedBy* «<ElementType>»<Element> *derived* «requirement»<Requirement> *derivedFrom* «requirement»<Requirement> *refinedBy* «ElementType»<Element> *master* «requirement»<Requirement> *verifiedBy* «<ElementType>»<TestCase>	A requirement specifies a capability or condition that must (or should) be satisfied, a function that a system must perform, or a performance condition a system must achieve. Each requirement includes predefined properties for its identification and textual description. SysML includes specific relationships to relate requirements to other requirements as well as to other model elements. The compartment notation is one method for displaying a requirement relationship between a requirement and another model element.	13.1, 13.3, 13.4, 13.5.2
Requirement Related–Type Node	«<ElementType>» <Name> *refines* «requirement»<Requirement> *satisfies* «requirement»<Requirement> *verifies* «requirement»<Requirement>	Requirements can be related to model elements that may appear in different hierarchies or on different diagrams. These relationships can be shown using the compartment notation when the requirements and related model elements do not appear on the same diagram.	13.5, 13.11, 13.12, 13.13
Trace Compartment	*tracedTo* «ElementType»<Element> *tracedFrom* «ElementType»<Element>	The trace relationship can be shown using compartment notation when the requirements and related model elements do not appear on the same diagram.	13.5, 13.14
Package Node	<Name> <Name>	Requirements can be organized into a package structure. Each package within this package structure may correspond to a different specification, each containing the text-based requirements for that specification.	13.8
Test Case Node	«testCase» <Name> *verifies* «requirement»<Requirement>	A test case can represent any method for performing the verification, including the standard verification methods of inspection, analysis, demonstration, and testing.	13.12

Table A.26 Requirement Diagram Paths

Diagram Element	Notation	Description	Section
Containment Path	⊕ ⊕	The containment relationship is used to represent how requirements are contained in specifications (packages), or how a complex requirement can be partitioned into a set of simpler requirements without adding or changing their meaning.	13.9
Derivation Path	«deriveReqt» - - - - - - ->	A derive relationship occurs between a source requirement and a derived requirement, based on analysis of the source requirement.	13.10
Satisfaction Path	«satisfy» - - - - - - ->	A satisfy relationship is used to assert that a model element corresponding to the design or implementation satisfies a particular requirement.	13.11
Verification Path	«verify» - - - - - - ->	A verify relationship is used between a requirement and a test case or other named element to indicate how to verify that the requirement is satisfied.	13.12
Refinement Path	«refine» - - - - - - ->	The refine relationship is used to reduce ambiguity in a requirement by relating it to another model element that clarifies the requirement.	13.13
Trace Path	«trace» - - - - - - ->	A trace relationship is a general-purpose way to relate a requirement and any other model element, useful for relating requirements to documents, etc.	13.14
Copy Path	«copy» - - - - - - ->	The copy relationship relates a copy of a requirement to the original requirement, to support reuse of requirements.	13.15

Table A.27   Requirement Diagram Callouts

Diagram Element	Notation	Description	Section
Trace Callout	tracedFrom «<ElementType>»<Element> / tracedTo «<ElementType>»<Element>	This callout notation is an alternative notation for depicting trace relationships. It is the least restrictive notation in that it can be used to represent a relationship between any requirement and any other model element on any diagram type.	13.5.3, 13.14
Derivation Callout	derived «requirement»<Requirement> / derivedFrom «requirement»<Requirement>	This callout notation is an alternative notation for depicting derive relationships.	13.5.3, 13.10
Verification Callout	verifies «requirement»<Requirement> / verifiedBy «testCase»<TestCase>	This callout notation is an alternative notation for depicting verify relationships.	13.5.3, 13.12
Satisfaction Callout	satisfiedBy «<ElementType>»<Element> / satisfies «requirement»<Requirement>	This callout notation is an alternative notation for depicting satisfy relationships.	13.5.3, 13.11
Refinement Callout	refines «requirement»<Requirement> / refinedBy «<ElementType>»<Element>	This callout notation is an alternative notation for depicting refine relationships.	13.5.3, 13.13
Master Requirement Callout	master «requirement»<Requirement>	This callout notation is an alternative notation for depicting copy relationships.	13.5.3, 13.15
Rationale Callout	«rationale» <Text>	A rationale is typically associated with either a requirement, or a relationship between requirements. It can also be applied throughout the model to capture the reason for any type of decision.	13.6
Problem Callout	«problem» <Text>	A problem is a particular kind of comment used to identify or flag design issues in the model.	13.6

A.12 ALLOCATION

SysML includes several notational options to provide flexibility for representing allocations of model elements across the system model. The graphical representations are similar to those used for relating requirements to other model elements.

Table A.28   Notation for Allocations

Diagram Element	Notation	Description	Section
Allocated To Callout	allocatedTo «<ElementType>»<Element>	The callout notation can be used to represent the opposite end of the allocation relationship for any model element. In this case the callout is anchored to an element that is allocated to the element name in the callout.	14.3
Allocated From Callout	allocatedFrom «<ElementType>»<Element>	The callout notation can be used to represent the opposite end of the allocation relationship for any model element. In this case the callout box is anchored to an element that is allocated from the element name in the callout .	14.3
Block Node with Allocation Compartments	«block» <Name> allocatedFrom «<ElementType>»<Element> allocatedTo «<ElementType>»<Element>	The compartment notation identifies the element at the opposite end of the allocation relationship in a compartment of the model element. When used on a block, it explicitly indicates allocation of definition to/from the block.	14.3
Part Node with Allocation Compartments	<Name>:<Block>[<Multiplicity>] allocatedFrom «<ElementType>»<Element> allocatedTo «<ElementType>»<Element>	The compartment notation identifies the element at the opposite end of the allocation relationship in a compartment of the model element. When used on a part, it explicitly indicates allocation of usage to/from the part. An inferred allocation (part typed by a block, which in turn has an activity allocated to it) should not be depicted by a compartment on the part.	14.3
Call Action Node with Allocated To Compartment	<Name>:<Behavior> allocatedTo «<ElementType>»<Element> allocatedFrom «<ElementType>»<Element>	When an allocation compartment is used on an action, it explicitly indicates allocation of usage to/from the action. An inferred allocation (action typed by an activity, which in turn is allocated to a block) should not be depicted by a compartment on the action.	14.3
Allocation Path	- - - - - «allocate» - - - - ->	This allocation relationship can be depicted directly when both ends of the allocation relationship are shown on the same diagram. The arrowhead represents the "allocatedTo" end.	14.3
Allocate Activity Partition Node	«allocate» <Partition>	The presence of an allocate activity partition on an activity diagram implies an allocate relationship between any action node within the partition and the part represented by the partition. This provides allocation of usage (action to part), but not allocation of definition (activity to block). The alternative activity partition notation (Activity Partition in Action Node in Table A.11) can also be used.	14.6.3

A.13 STEREOTYPES AND VIEWPOINTS

Stereotypes are used to introduce new concepts or augment existing concepts into SysML to customize the language for specific domains. Stereotypes may be applied to elements on any diagram using a common notation across all diagrams. Information about applied stereotypes can be shown either inside node symbols, as part of name strings, or using callout notation.

Viewpoints and views allow modelers to generate custom visualizations of their SysML models.

Table A.29   Notation for Stereotyped Element

Diagram Element	Notation	Description	Section
Name Compartment with Keywords and Properties	«\<Stereotype>» {\<Property>=\<Value>,...} \<Name>	A stereotyped model element is shown with the name of the stereotype in guillemets, followed by any values for the stereotypes properties and then the name of the model element. Multiple stereotypes and their properties may be shown before the model element name.	15.6
Name Compartment with Keywords	«\<Stereotype>,...» \<Name>	If no stereotype properties are shown in the name compartment, then multiple stereotype names can appear in a comma-separated list within one set of guillemets.	15.6
Name String with Keywords and Properties	«\<Stereotype>»{\<Property>=\<Value>,...}\<Name> *label* \<Stereotype>»{\<Property>=\<Value>,...}\<Name> ...	If the model element is represented by path symbol (e.g., a line), the stereotype name and properties are shown in a label next to the line and before the name of the element. Stereotype keywords and properties can also be shown for elements in compartments, when they are shown before the element name.	15.6
Stereotype Callout	«\<Stereotype>» \<Property>=\<Value> ...	Irrespective of the symbol representing a model element, the values for applied stereotypes properties can always be shown using callout notation. Property values from multiple stereotypes can be shown in a single note symbol.	15.6
Node with Stereotype Compartment	«\<Stereotype>,...» \<Name> «\<Stereotype>» \<Property>=\<Value> ...	Where a symbol supports compartments, the values for the properties of an applied stereotype can be shown in a compartment specific to that stereotype.	15.6

Table A.30   Nodes for Representing Views and Viewpoints

Diagram Element	Notation	Description	Section
View Node	«view» <Name> ———— «view» stakeholders=<Stakeholder>,... viewpoint=<Viewpoint>	A view conforms to a viewpoint. The view exposes a set of model elements according to the viewpoint methods and is expressed in the viewpoint languages to present the relevant information to its stakeholders.	15.8
Viewpoint Node	«viewpoint» <Name> ———— «viewpoint» stakeholders=<Stakeholder>,... purpose=<String> languages=<String>,... method=<Behavior> concerns=<String>,... ———— operations «create»View()	A viewpoint describes a perspective of interest to a set of stakeholders that is used to specify a view of a model.	15.8
Stakeholder Node	«Stakeholder» <Stakeholder> concerns=<String>,... «Stakeholder» <Stakeholder> ———— «stakeholder» concerns=<String>,...	A stakeholder is a role, group or individual that has concerns that need to be addressed	15.8
Conform Path	———— «conform» ———▷	Used to assert that a view conforms to a viewpoint.	15.8
Expose Path	- - - - «expose» - - - -▷	Used to specify a model element that is exposed by a view	15.8

References

[1] Object Management Group. OMG Systems Modeling Language (OMG SysML™). V1.4. Available at: http://www.omg.org/spec/SysML/.

[2] BKCASE Editorial Board. The Guide to the Systems Engineering Body of Knowledge (SEBoK), V1.3. R. D. Adcock (EIC). Hoboken, NJ: The Trustees of the Stevens Institute of Technology; 2014. Available at: http://www.sebokwiki.org/. BKCASE is managed and maintained by the Stevens Institute of Technology Systems Engineering Research Center, the International Council on Systems Engineering, and the Institute of Electrical and Electronics Engineers Computer Society.

[3] ANSI/EIA 632. Processes for Engineering a System. Am Natl Stand Inst/Electronic Industries Alliance 1999.

[4] IEEE Standard 1220-1998. IEEE Standard for Application and Management of the Systems Engineering Process. Inst Electrical and Electronic Eng December 8, 1998.

[5] ISO/IEC. Systems and Software Engineering—System Life Cycle Processes. Int Organ Standardization/Int Electrotechnical Comm March 18, 2008;15288:2008.

[6] Estefan Jeff A. Survey of Model-Based Systems Engineering (MBSE) Methodologies. Rev B INCOSE Technical Publication, Document No. INCOSE-TD-2007-003-01. San Diego, CA: International Council on Systems Engineering; June 10, 2008.

[7] Douglass Bruce P. The Harmony Process. I-Logix Inc March 25, 2005. white paper.

[8] Hoffmann Hans-Peter. Harmony-SE/SysML Deskbook: Model-Based Systems Engineering with Rhapsody Rev. 1.51, Telelogic/I-Logix white paper, Telelogic AB. May 24, 2006.

[9] Lykins, Friedenthal, Meilich. Adapting UML for an Object-Oriented Systems Engineering Method (OOSEM). Proc INCOSE Int Symp July 15–20, 2000. Minneapolis.

[10] Murray Cantor. RUP SE: The Rational Unified Process for Systems Engineering, The Rational Edge. Rational Software November 2001.

[11] Murray Cantor. Rational Unified Process® for Systems Engineering. RUP SE Version 2.0, IBM Rational Software white paper. IBM Corporation May 8, 2003.

[12] Ingham Michel D, Rasmussen Robert D, Bennett Matthew B, Moncada Alex C. Generating Requirements for Complex Embedded Systems Using State Analysis. Acta Astronautica June 2006;58(12):648–61.

[13] Long James E. Systems Engineering (SE) 101, CORE®: Product & Process Engineering Solutions. Vienna, VA: Vitech training materials, Vitech Corporation; 2000.

[14] Dov Dori. Object-Process Methodology: A Holistics System Paradigm. New York: Springer Verlag; 2002.

[15] Zachman John A. A Framework for Information Systems Architecture. IBM Sys J 1987;26(3):276–92.

[16] C4I Architecture Working Group. C4ISR Architecture Framework Version 2.0, December 18, 1997.

[17] US Department of Defense. DoD Architecture Framework (DoDAF). Version 2.02, August 2010. Available at: http://cio-nii.defense.gov/sites/dodaf20/index.html.

[18] Ministry of Defence. Architecture Framework (MODAF), Version 1.2.004, May, 2010.

[19] ANSI/IEEE Std. IEEE Recommended Practice for Architectural Description of Software-Intensive Systems. Am Natl Stand Inst/Inst Electrical and Electronic Eng September 21, 2000:1471–2000.

[20] ISO/IEC 42010:2007. Systems and Software Engineering—Recommended Practice for Architectural Description of Software-intensive Systems. Int Organ Stand/Int comm Comm September 12, 2007.

[21] The Open Group. The Open Group Architecture Framework (TOGAF), Version 8.1.1, Enterprise Edition. New York: VanHaren; 2007. Available at: http://www.opengroup.org/bookstore/catalog/g063v.htm.

[22] Standard for Integration Definition for Function Modeling (IDEF0). Draft Federal Information Processing Standards. Publication December 21, 1993:183.

[23] Object Management Group Unified Profile for DoDAF and MODAF (UPDM). Available at: http://www.omg.org/spec/UPDM/.

[24] Object Management Group. Meta Object Facility Core Specification. Available at: http://www.omg.org/spec/MOF/.

[25] Modelica Association. Modelica Specification. Available at: https://www.modelica.org/documents/.

[26] IEEE Standard 1516. IEEE Standard for High Level Architecture. Inst Electrical and Electronic Eng.

[27] Society of Automotive Engineering (SAE). Architecture Analysis & Design Language (AADL). Available at: http://standards.sae.org/as5506a/; January 2009.

[28] World Wide Web Consortium (W3C). Web Ontology Language (OWL). Available at: http://www.w3.org/2004/OWL/.

[29] Object Management Group. XML Metadata Interchange (XMI) Specification. Available at: http://www.omg.org/spec/XMI/.

[30] ISO TC-184 (Technical Committee on Industrial Automation Systems and Integration). SC4 (Subcommittee on Industrial Data Standards). ISO 10303–233 STEP AP233; Available at: http://www.ap233.org/ap233-public-information/.

[31] Open Services for Lifecycle Collaboration. Available at: http://open-services.net/.

[32] Modelica Association Project. Functional mock-up interface (FMI). Available at: https://www.modelica.org/projects/.

[33] Object Management Group. Model-Driven Architecture (MDA) Guide. Available at: http://www.omg.org/mda/presentations.htm.

[34] Object Management Group. The MDA Foundation Model, Draft. OMG document number ormsc/2010-09-06 September 2010.

[35] Object Management Group. Query/View/Transformation. Available at: http://www.omg.org/spec/QVT/.

[36] Wymore W. Model-Based Systems Engineering. Boca Raton, FL: CRC Press; 1993.

[37] International Council on Systems Engineering (INCOSE). Systems Engineering Vision 2020. Version 2.03, TP-2004-004-02 September 2007.

[38] Object Management Group. Object Constraint Language (OCL). Available at: http://www.omg.org/spec/OCL/.

[39] Object Management Group. OMG Certified Systems Modeling Professional (OCSMP). Available at: http://www.omg.org/ocsmp.

[40] Cecilia Haskins, editor. INCOSE Systems Engineering Handbook: A Guide for System Life Cycle Processes and Activities. v. 3.2.1, INCOSE-TP-2003-002-03.2.1 Int Council Syst Eng January 2011.

[41] Object Management Group. Semantics of a Foundational Subset for Executable UML Models (FUML). Available at: http://www.omg.org/spec/FUML/.

[42] ISO TC-184 (Technical Committee on Industrial Automation Systems and Integration), *ISO 18629* Process specification language (PSL).

[43] Object Management Group. Precise Semantics of UML Composite Structures. Available at: http://www.omg.org/spec/PSCS/.

[44] Object Management Group. Action Language for Foundational UML (ALF). Available at: http://www.omg.org/spec/ALF/.

[45] Peak R, et al. Georgia Tech response to "UML for Systems Engineering RFI". May 2002. Available at: http://eislab.gatech.edu/pubs/misc/2002-omg-se-dsig-rfi-1-response-peak/.

[46] Reisig, Wolfgang. A Primer in Petri Net Design. New York: Springer-Verlag; 1992. Available at: http://link.springer.com/book/10.1007%2F978-3-642-75329-9

[47] Haider Wagenhals, Synthesizing Levis. Executable Models of Object Oriented Architectures. J Int Council Sys Eng 2003;6(4):266–300.

[48] Conrad Bock. SysML and UML 2.0 Support for Activity Modeling. J Int Council Sys Eng 2006;9(2):160–86.

[49] Alistair Cockburn. Writing Effective Use Cases. Boston: Addison-Wesley; 2000.

[50] Object Management Group. UML Testing Profile. Available at: http://www.omg.org/spec/UTP/.

[51] Object Management Group. UML for Systems Engineering RFP OMG document number ad/03-03-41. March 28, 2003.

[52] Object Management Group. Unified Modeling Language (OMG UML). Available at: http://www.omg.org/spec/UML/.

[53] Sanford Friedenthal. Object Oriented Systems Engineering. In: Process Integration for 2000 and Beyond: Systems Engineering and Software Symposium. New Orleans: Lockheed Martin Corporation; May 1998.

[54] Meilich Abe, Rickels Michael. An Application of Object-Oriented Systems Engineering to an Army Command and Control System. In: A New Approach to Integration of Systems and Software Requirements and Design. Brighton, England: Proceedings of the INCOSE International Symposium; June 6–11, 1999.

[55] Steiner Rick, Friedenthal Sanford, Oesterheld Jerry, Thaker Guatam. Pilot Application of the OOSEM Using Rational Rose Real Time to the Navy CC & D Program. Melbourne: Proceedings of the INCOSE International Symposium; July 1–4, 2001.

[56] Rose Susan, Finneran Lisa, Friedenthal Sanford, Lykins Howard, Scott Peter. Integrated Systems and Software Engineering Process. Herndon, VA: Software Productivity Consortium; 1996.

[57] Forsberg Kevin, Mooz Harold. Application of the "Vee" to Incremental and Evolutionary Development. St. Louis: Proceedings of the Fifth Annual International Symposium of the National Council on Systems Engineering; July 1995.

[58] Izumi L, Friedenthal S, Meilich A. Object-Oriented Systems Engineering Method (OOSEM) Applied to Joint Force Projection (JPF), a Lockheed Martin Integrating Concept (LMIC). Proceedings of the INCOSE International Symposium; June 2007.

[59] Pearce P, Friedenthal S. A Practical Approach for Modeling Submarine Subsystem Architecture in SysML, Proceedings from the 2nd Submarine Institute of Australia (SIA) Submarine Science. Technology and Engineering Conference; October 2013. pp. 347–360. Available at: http://www.omgsysml.org/A_Practical_Approach_for_Modelling_Submarine_Sub-system_Architecture_in_SysML-Pearce_Friedenthal.pdf.

[60] National Defense Industrial Association (NDIA) Systems Engineering Division. Modeling & Simulation Committee Model Based Engineering (MBE) Final Report. February 2011.

[61] Law A. Simulation Modeling and Analysis. 4th ed, New York, NY: McGraw Hill; 2007.

[62] Object Management Group. UML Profile for Modeling and Analysis of Real-Time and Embedded Systems (MARTE). Available at: http://www.omg.org/spec/MARTE/.

[63] Object Management Group MOF Versioning and Development Lifecycle. Available at: http://www.omg.org/spec/MOFVD/2.0/.

[64] Object Management Group (OMG). Model Interchange Working Group (MIWG). at http://www.omgwiki.org/model-interchange/doku.php.

[65] Object Management Group. Diagram Definition. Available at: http://www.omg.org/spec/DD/.

[66] World Wide Web Consortium (W3C). Scalable Vector Graphics (SVG). Available at: http://www.w3.org/Graphics/SVG/.

[67] Object Management Group. SysML Modelica Transformation Specification. Available at: http://www.omg.org/spec/SyM/.

[68] World Wide Web Consortium (W3C). Uniform Resource Identifiers (URI). Available at: http://www.w3.org/Addressing/.

[69] World Wide Web Consortium (W3C). Resource Description Framework (RDF). Available at: http://www.w3.org/RDF/.

[70] OSLC Core Specification. Available at: http://open-services.net/bin/view/Main/OslcCoreSpecification./.

[71] OSLC4MBSE Working Group. Available at: http://www.omgwiki.org/OMGSysML/doku.php?id=sysml-oslc:oslc4mbse_working_group.

[72] Modelisar Project. Available at: https://itea3.org/project/modelisar.html.

[73] Yishai A. Feldman, Lev Greenberg, Eldad Palachi. Simulating Rhapsody SysML Blocks in Hybrid Models with FMI. Lund, Sweden: Proceedings of the 10th International Modelica Conference; March 10–12, 2014. Available at: http://www.ep.liu.se/ecp/096/004/ecp14096004.pdf

[74] Jenkins Stephen, Rouquette Nicolas. OWL Ontologies and SysML Profiles: Knowledge Representation and Modeling. NASA-ESA PDE Workshop May 2010. Available at: http://www.congrex.nl/10m05post/presentations/pde2010-Jenkins.pdf.

[75] International Council on Systems Engineering (INCOSE) Telescope Modeling Challenge Team Active Phasing Experiment (APE). http://www.omgwiki.org/MBSE/doku.php?id=mbse:telescope.

[76] Object Management Group (OMG). SysML Request for Information (RFI). OMG document number syseng/2009-06-01 June 2009. Available at: http://www.omg.org/cgi-bin/doc?syseng/2009-06-01.

Index

Note: Page numbers followed by "f" and "t" indicate figures and tables respectively.

Printed in the United States
by Baker & Taylor Publisher Services

Printed in the United States
By Bookmasters